Innovation Management and New Product Development

Visit the *Innovation Management and New Product Development*, Fifth Edition, Companion Website at **www.pearsoned.co.uk/trott** to find valuable **student** learning material including:

- Self-test multiple choice questions, arranged by chapter, to test your understanding
- Annotated links for each chapter to relevant sites on the web
- Answers to all *Pause for thought* questions to allow you to check your progress

Innovation Management and New Product Development

Fifth Edition

Paul Trott

Portsmouth Business School

Financial Times Prentice Hall is an imprint of

Harlow, England • London • New York • Boston • San Francisco • Toronto • Sydney • Singapore • Hong Kong
Tokyo • Seoul • Taipei • New Delhi • Cape Town • Madrid • Mexico City • Amsterdam • Munich • Paris • Milan

Pearson Education Limited
Edinburgh Gate
Harlow
Essex CM20 2JE
England

and Associated Companies throughout the world

Visit us on the World Wide Web at:
www.pearson.com/uk

First published 1998
Second edition published 2002
Third edition published 2005
Fourth edition 2008
Fifth edition published 2012

ISBN: 978-0-273-73656-1

British Library Cataloguing-in-Publication Data
A catalogue record for this book is available from the British Library

Library of Congress Cataloging-in-Publication Data
Trott, Paul.
Innovation management and new product development / Paul Trott. -- 5th ed.
p. cm.
ISBN 978-0-273-73656-1 (pbk.)
1. Technological innovations--Management. 2. Industrial management. 3. Product management. I. Title.
HD45.T76 2011
658.5′75--dc23

2011027628

10 9 8 7 6 5 4 3 2 1
15 14 13 12 11

Typeset in 10/12pt Sabon by 35
Printed and bound in Great Britain by Ashford Colour Press Ltd, Gosport, Hampshire

To Alison, Katherine and Thomas

Supporting resources

Visit **www.pearsoned.co.uk/trott** to find valuable online resources

Companion Website for students

- Self-test multiple choice questions, arranged by chapter, to test your understanding
- Annotated links for each chapter to relevant sites on the web
- Answers to all *Pause for thought* questions to allow you to check your progress

For instructors

- PowerPoint slides that can be downloaded and used for presentations
- Complete, downloadable Instructor's Manual

For more information please contact your local Pearson Education sales representative or visit **www.pearsoned.co.uk/trott**

Contents

13 Packaging and product development 456

14 New service innovation 486

Preface

Firms care about their ability to innovate, on which their future allegedly depends (Christensen and Raynor, 2003), and many management consultants are busy persuading companies about how they can help them improve their innovation performance. But what can firms do to improve the way they encourage and manage innovation? And can firms manage innovation? The answer is certainly yes as Bill Gates confirmed:

> *'The share price is not something we control. We control innovation, sales and profits.'*
>
> Bill Gates (2008)
>
> *Source*: Rushe and Waples (2008)

We are all well aware that good technology can help companies achieve competitive advantage and long-term financial success; just look at Apple. But there is an abundance of exciting new technology in the world and it is the transformation of this technology into products that is of particular concern to organisations. There are numerous factors to be considered by the organisation, but what are these factors and how do they affect the process of innovation? This book will explain how and why most of the most significant inventions of the past two centuries have not come from flashes of inspiration, but from communal, multilayered endeavour – one idea being built on another until a breakthrough is reached (Johnson, 2010).

In this book we see that many of the old traditional approaches to management need to change and new approaches need to be adopted. Increasingly, managers and those who work for them are no longer in the same location. Often complex management relationships need to be developed because organisations are trying to produce complex products and services and do so across geographic boundaries. Cross-functional and cross-border task forces often need to be created.

Objective of the book

It is designed to be accessible and readable. The book emphasises the need to view innovation as a management process. We need to recognise that change is at the heart of it. And that change is caused by decisions that people make. The framework (Figure 1.9) at the end of Chapter 1 attempts to capture the iterative nature of the network processes in innovation and represents this in the form of an endless innovation circle with interconnected cycles. This circular concept helps to show how the firm gathers information over time, how it uses technical *and* societal knowledge, and how it develops an attractive proposition. This is achieved through developing linkages and partnerships with those having the necessary capabilities.

Target audience

This book is written for people who want to understand how firms can improve the way they manage their innovation processes to develop new products and services.

It can be used as a text book for undergraduate or graduate courses in innovation management and new product development. A second audience is the manager who wishes to keep abreast of the most recent developments in the innovation field.

Special features

The book is designed with one overriding aim: to make this exciting and highly relevant subject as clear to understand as possible. To this end, the book has a number of important features.

- A clear and straightforward writing style enhances learning comprehension.
- Extensive up-to-date references and relevant literature help you find out more and explore concepts in detail.
- *'Innovation in action boxes'* that illustrate how real companies are managing innovation today.
- Clear chapter openers set the scene for each chapter and provide a chapter contents list which offers page references to all the sections within the chapter.
- Learning objectives at the beginning of each chapter explicitly highlight the key areas that will be explored in the chapter.
- Topical articles from the *Financial Times* illustrate how the subject is being discussed in the context of the wider business world.
- Summaries at the end of each chapter provide a useful means of revising and checking understanding.
- *Pause for thought* questions integrated within the text. These are designed to help you reflect on what you have just read and to check your understanding. Answers to all *Pause for thought* questions are given on the book's website (www.pearsoned.co.uk/trott).
- Comprehensive diagrams throughout the book illustrate some of the more complex concepts.
- Plentiful up-to-date examples within the text drive home arguments. This helps to enliven the subject and places it in context.
- A comprehensive index, including references to all defined terms, enables you to look up a definition within its context. See also the 'Key words and phrases' boxes at chapter ends. Key words are presented emboldened in colour within the main text.
- A substantial case study at the end of each chapter shows the subject in action within actual firms. These have been trialled on classes at several universities and have formed the basis of lively one-hour class seminar discussions.

What's new in the 5th edition

- *Innovation in action boxes* in every chapter. These bring the subject to life by providing a real life illustration of how firms are managing innovation today.
- All chapters have been reviewed and updated with relevant references to the literature. Illustrations within chapters have been renewed. All case studies have been updated and modified where appropriate.
- Chapter 1 – the entrepreneurship concept is expanded. The section on models of innovation is expanded to include architectural innovation and discontinuous

innovation. A new framework is presented at the end of the chapter to help better understand how to manage innovation.

- Chapter 2 – a new major case study at the end of the chapter tells the story of how three university students tried to change world trade with the development of a folding shipping container.
- Chapter 3 – new section on management tools for innovation, which reviews how well-established management tools can help the leaders of an organisation sustain innovativeness and even recover from a period of stagnation, if applied correctly and vigorously.
- Chapter 5 – a new section discusses alternative strategies to patents that have been developed by companies, where they felt other forms of IP protection were better suited to their needs.
- Chapter 6 – a new section explains how the competitive environment, process innovation, product innovation and organisational structure all interact and are closely linked together.
- Chapter 7 – a new major case study at the end of the chapter tells the story of how Sony's Blu-ray battled with Toshiba's HD-DVD. Plus a new section that discusses the practicalities of negotiating a license deal.
- Chapter 9 – a major new case study at the end of the chapter explains how the extraordinary growth in the business of DNA fingerprinting has been matched only by the mass appeal of the CSI television shows. In just a few years the industry has grown into a 20 billion dollar technology intensive colossus.
- Chapter 11 – a major new case study at the end of the chapter tells the story of how a firm developed a radical new technology for whitening teeth and then set about trying to develop a commercial product.
- Chapter 12 – a new section explores the concept of time-to-market and how agile New Product Development (NPD) can help reduce this.
- Chapter 16 – a new section explores the concept of the Valley of Death. The Valley of Death is used as a metaphor to describe a relative lack of resources and expertise in the front end of product innovation.

Web products

Log on to www.pearsoned.co.uk/trott to access learning resources which include:

For students:

- Study materials designed to help you improve your results.
- Self-test multiple choice questions, organised by chapter.
- Answers to all *Pause for thought* questions, to allow you to check understanding as you progress.
- Annotated links for each chapter to relevant companies and internet sites.

For tutors (password protected):

- Lecture notes and PowerPoint slides.
- Figures and tables from the book in PowerPoint colour slides.
- Key models as full-colour animated PowerPoint slide shows.
- Teaching/learning case studies.
- Answers to all end-of-chapter discussion questions.
- Multiple choice questions, organised by chapter for use in assessments.

References

Johnson, S. (2010) *Where Good Ideas Come From: The Natural History of Innovation*, Riverhead Books, New Jersey, USA.

Rushe, D. and Waples, J. (2008) Interview, Business, *Sunday Times*, February, p. 5.

Foreword to the Fifth edition

The purpose of innovation is to create new business. In industry, methods and tools are developed on how to organise and manage innovation processes with the objective to better control added-value, cost and risk. Employees, suppliers and customers are principal actors in the process. In academia, information from observations and case studies is transformed into scientific knowledge with the objective to better understand the successes and failures in innovation and, ultimately, to improve the chance of success.

Innovation requires a change, i.e. change in the way we think and change in the way we act. These changes may be small or big. In life cycle management, the ambition is to make continuous improvements on existing products and services. In this way the life cycle can be extended for many extra years. In innovation management, the ambition is to come up with new concepts. This means moving away from existing solutions. As a consequence, innovation shortens the life cycle of existing products and services. Schumpeter calls this property 'creative destruction': life cycle management and innovation management are in competition with each other. This may cause major dilemma's in business development. This is explored in this new edition.

Innovation processes are of a complex nature and often poorly understood. Therefore, good textbooks that provide a clear explanation of the concepts involved, also illustrating those concepts with real cases, are invaluable to further improve current innovation systems. For professionals and students who want to improve their understanding on innovation, Professor Paul Trott's book is a must.

This new edition builds on the strengths of the fourth edition. In particular the book remains very accessible and easy for students to read. The new edition has been updated with several new sections to reflect changes and developments within the literature. The introduction of several major new cases at the end of the chapters has enhanced the book and made it more interesting for students. For example, the Blu-ray case, CSI case and the case study examining the development of new teeth whitening products are particularly insightful and will be enjoyed by students. I am sure students will benefit from using this book to enhance their understanding of innovation management and new product development. Above all I am sure they will enjoy reading this book.

Professor dr.ir.Guus Berkhout

Professor Guus Berkhout started his career with Shell in 1964, where he held several international positions in R&D and technology transfer. Professor Berkhout is co-founder of the European Centre for Innovation (ECI). He is a member of the Royal Netherlands Academy of Arts and Sciences (KNAW), and the Netherlands Academy of Technology and Innovation (AcTI). He also holds chairs in Geophysics and Innovation Management at Delft University of Technology. He has written several hundred scientific papers, and a number of books in the field of acoustics, geophysics and innovation.

Acknowledgements

Author's acknowledgements

I am indebted to many for their ideas and assistance. My primary thanks go to the many academics who have advanced our knowledge of innovation and new product development and on whose shoulders I have been able to stand. The following reviewers provided feedback for this new edition: Susan Hart, Strathclyde University; Jon Sundbo, Roskilde University, Denmark; Guus Berkhout, TUDelft; Helen Perks, UMIST; Fiona Lettice, Cranfield University; Niki Hynes, Napier University Business School; Mark Godson, Sheffield Hallam Univerity; Paul Oakley, University of Birmingham; David Smith, Nottingham Business School, Nottingham Trent University; Fritz Sheimer, FH Furtwagen; Claus J. Varnes, Copenhagen Business School; Roy Woodhead, Oxford Brookes University.

It has been a pleasure to work with my editor Rachel Gear who provided encouragement, help and valuable suggestions. The task of writing has been made much easier by the support I have had from many people. Firstly, all my students who have both wittingly and unwittingly provided constant feedback to me on ideas. Also, a big thank you to the team at Pearson Education. Any errors or omissions in the book are entirely mine.

Publisher's acknowledgements

We are grateful to the following for permission to reproduce copyright material:

Figures

Figure 3.2 from *Managing Innovation: an uncertainty reduction process in Managing Innovation,* J. Henry and D. Walker (eds), Sage/OU (A.W. Pearson 1991); Figure 3.3 from Architectural Innovation: The Reconfiguration of Existing Product Technologies and the Failure of Established Firms, *Administrative Science Quarterly*, Vol. 35, No. 1 (Henderson, R. and Clark, K. 1990), Reproduced with permission of Johnson at Cornell University; Figure 3.5 from Relationships between innovation stimulus, innovation capacity and innovation performance, *R&D Management*, Vol. 36 (5), 499–515 (Prajogo, D.I. and Ahmed, P.K. 2006), Reproduced by permission of John Wiley & Sons; Figure 3.6 from Success and failure of innovation: a review of the literature, *International Journal of Innovation Management*, Vol. 7 (3), 309–338 (van der Panne, G., van Beers, C. and Kleinknecht, A. 2003); Figure 3.7 from Sectoral patterns of technological change: towards a taxonomy and theory, *Research Policy*, Vol. 13, 343–73 (Pavitt, K. 1994); Figure 4.1 adapted from *Operations Management*, 4th Ed., Pearson Education Ltd (Slack, N. *et al.* 2004); Figures 4.4, 4.5 adapted from *Operations Management*, 4th Ed., Pearson Education (Slack, N. *et al.* 2004); Figure 6.3 from *Innovation Management: Strategies, Implementation and Profit*, Oxford University Press (Afuah, A. 2003) p. 53, Fig. 3.5, By permission of Oxford University Press, Inc.; Figure 6.8 from Patterns of industrial innovation, *Technology Review*, Vol. 80, No. 7, 40–7 (Abernathy, W.J. and Utterback, J. 1978),

© 1978 by Technology Review. All rights reserved. Distributed by Tribune Media Services; Figure 6.9 from Organizational Determinants of Technological Change: Towards a Sociology of Technological Evaluation, *Research in Organizational Behavior*, 14, pp. 311–347 (Tushman, M.L. and Rosenkopf, L. 1992), © Elsevier, 1992; Figure 9.6 adapted from *Managing Engineering and Technology: An Introduction to Management for Engineers*, 2nd Ed., Prentice Hall Inc. (Morse, D. and Babcock, D.L. 1996), © 1996. Adapted by permission of Pearson Education, Inc., Upper Saddle River, NJ; Figure 10.3 adapted from *Architect or Bee? The Human Price of Technology*, Chatto & Windus (Cooley, M. 1987), Reprinted by permission of The Random House Group Ltd.; Figure 11.4 from Brand first management, *Journal of Marketing Management*, Vol. 12, 269–80 (Rubinstein, H. 1996); Figure 12.4 from How to organise for new products, *Harvard Business Review*, Vol. 35 (Johnson, S.C. and Jones, C. 1957), Reproduced with permission of Harvard Business Publishing; Figure 12.6 adapted from PDMA research on new product development practices: updating trends and benchmarking best practices, *Journal of Product Innovation Management*, Vol. 14, 429 (Griffin, A. 1997), Reproduced with permission of John Wiley & Sons; Figure 12.7 from Brand franchise extension: new product benefits from existing brand names, *Business Horizons*, Vol. 24, No. 2, 36–41 (Tauber, E.M. 1981), With permission from Elsevier; Figure 12.8 from Product replacement: strategies for simultaneous product deletion and launch, *Journal of Product Innovation Management*, Vol. 11, No. 5, 433–50 (Saunders, J. and Jobber, D. 1994), Reproduced with permission of John Wiley & Sons; Figure 12.12 from *The Design Dimension*, Blackwell Publishing Ltd (Lorenz, C. 1990); Figure 12.13 from *New Products Management*, 5th Ed., McGraw-Hill (Crawford, C.M. 1997); Figure 14.1 from *Service Operations Management*, 2nd Ed., Pearson Education (Johnston, R. and Clark, G. 2005); Figure 15.2 adapted from *Proceedings of the Annual Conference of the European Marketing Academy, Maastricht* (Saren, M.A.J. and Tzokas, N. 1994); Figure 15.3 from Competing for the future, *Harvard Business Review*, Vol. 72 (4), 122–8 (Hamel, S. and Prahalad, C.K.), Reproduced with permission of Harvard Business Publishing.

Tables

Table 1.2 from *Business Week, 25 February 2010*; Table 2.1 from *Global Shift: Transforming the World Economy*, Paul Chapman (a SAGE Publications company) (Dicken, P. 1998), Reproduced by permission of SAGE Publications, London, Los Angeles, New Delhi and Singapore; Table 3.1 from Innovation managment measurement: a review, *International Journal of Management Reviews*, Vol. 8 (1), 21–47 (Adams, R., Bessant, J. and Phelps, R. 2006), Reproduced with permission of John Wiley & Sons; Table 3.3 from Juggling entrepreneurial style and organizational structure: how to get your act together, *Sloan Management Review* (Slevin, D.P. and Covin, J.G. 1990), © 1990 from MIT Sloan Management Review/Massachusetts Institute of Technology. All rights reserved. Distributed by Tribune Media Services; Table 4.2 adapted from *Operations Management*, 5th Ed., Pearson Education (Slack, N. *et al.* 2007); Table 4.6 from www.scholastic.com/harrypotter/author/index.htm, Reproduced with permission of Scholastic Inc.; Table 5.2 from *Patents: their effectiveness and role*, Carnegie Mellon University & National Bureau of Economic Research (Cohen, W.M. 2002), With permission from Wesley Cohen; Table 5.4 from UNAIDS (2000), www.unaids.org, Reproduced by kind permission of UNAIDS, www.unaids.org; Table 6.1 from Patterns of industrial innovation, *Technology Review*, Vol. 80, No. 7, 40–7 (Abernathy, W.J. and Utterback, J. 1978), © 1978 by Technology Review. All rights reserved. Distributed by Tribune Media Services; Table 8.1 from http://iri.jrc.ed.europa.eu/research/scoreboard_2010.htm, Source: The 2010 EU Industrial R&D Investment SCOREBOARD, © European Union, 2010; Table 8.2 from www.innovation.gov.uk/rd_scoreboard (2010), Crown Copyright material is reproduced with permission under the terms of the Click-Use License; Table 8.4 from www.innovation.gov.uk/projects/rdrscoreboard (2006), Crown Copyright material is reproduced with permission under the terms of the Click-Use License; Table 9.3 adapted from *Improving the effectiveness of research and development: special report to management*, McGraw-Hill (Seiler, R.E. 1965); Table 10.3 from Strategy Analytics; Table 11.3 from *Product Strategy and Management*, Pearson Education (Baker, M. and Hart, S. 1989); Table 11.5 from Nielsen, With permission from Nielsen; Table 11.7 adapted from *Do Some Business Models Perform Better than Others? A Study of the 1000 Largest US Firms (Working Paper No.226)*, Sloan School of Management (Weill, P., Malone, T.W., D'Urso, V.T., Herman, G. and Woerner, S. 2005), © 2005 from MIT Sloan Management Review/Massachusetts Institute of Technology. All rights reserved. Distributed by Tribune Media Services; Table 12.1 from The role of marketing specialists in product development, *Proceedings of the 21st Annual Conference of the Marketing Education Group, Huddersfield*, Vol. 3, 176–91 (Johne, F.A. and Snelson, P.A. 1988); Table 12.3 from Product development: past research, present findings and future directions, *Academy of Management Review*, Vol. 20, No. 2, 343–78 (Brown, S.L. and Eisenhardt, K.M. 1995), Academy of Management; Table 12.6 from Mintel Group (2008). Smoothies, UK, 2008, Market Share; Table 14.2 from *Service Operations Management*, 2nd Ed., Pearson Education (Johnston, R. and Clark, G. 2005); Table 14.4 from *An Analysis of Internet Banking Adoption in Turkey: Consumer, Innovation and Service Developer Dimensions*, PhD Thesis, University of Portsmouth (Ozdemir, S. 2007); Table 15.1 from A dirty business, *The Guardian*, 16/03/1999, Copyright Guardian News & Media Ltd 2010.

Text

Box 1.6 from The Other Demographic Dividend, *The Economist*, 07/10/2010 (Schumpeter), © The Economist Newspaper Limited, London 2010; Box 1.6 from *The Young World Rising*, John Wiley and Sons, Inc (Salkowitz, R. 2010), © 2010, John Wiley and Sons, Inc. Reproduced with permission of John Wiley & Sons, Inc.; Boxs on page 100, page 129, page 164, page 208, page 238, page 290, page 313, page 359, page 381, page 418, page 470, page 504, page 542, page 560 from 100 thoughts, HSBC (2010) http://www.100thoughts.hsbc.co.uk; Box 4.1 from *Operations Management*, 5th Ed., Pearson Education Ltd (Slack, N. *et al.* 2007); Boxs 4.2, 4.4 adapted from *Operations Management*, 5th Ed., Pearson Education (Slack, N. *et al.* 2007); Box 5.5 from Generic drug makers get FDA clearance for versions of Prozac, *Wall Street Journal* (Carroll, J.), Reproduced by permission of Dow Jones & Company, Inc.; Box 7.3 from Delbridge, R. and Mariotti, F. (2009) Racing for radical innovation: How motorsport companies harness network diversity for discontinuous innovation, Advanced Institute of Management Research, London; Case Study on page 334 from The rise of DNA analysis in crime solving, *The Guardian*, 10/04/2010, p. 24 (Jones, T.), Copyright Guardian News & Media Ltd 2010; Box 9.3 from A little miracle, *The Sunday Times Magazine*, 16/10/1997 (Dobson, M.), Roger Dobson / The Sunday Times / NI Syndication; Box 11.5 from Biz360 (2006); Quotes on page 444, page 447 from www.innocentdrinks.co.uk, 2007; Box 13.3 from EPSRC, November 2006, www.epsrc.ac.uk/PressReleases/ChildproofPackagingNewDesignscouldsavelives.htm; Box 13.8 from *Building, Measuring and Managing Brand Equity*, 2nd Ed., Prentice Hall (Keller, K.L. 2003), Reprinted by permission of Pearson Education, Inc., Upper Saddle River, N.J.

The Financial Times

Box 1.1 from Waters R. and Menn J. (2010) Jobs unveils 'revolutionary' Apple iPad, www.ft.com, January 27; Box 2.1 from *Financial Times*, 02/03/2007 (Tobias Buck); Box 3.1

from Milne, R. (2008) The nuts and bolts of growth, March 5, www.ft.com; Box 4.5 from *The Financial Times*, 21/06/2006 (Jonathan Guthrie); Box 5.1 from Ebay claims victory in luxury fakes dispute, Murphy, M. (May 13, 2009), www.ft.com; Box 5.2 from Theft of intellectual property 'should be a crime', Greenhalgh, H. (September 24th, 2010), www.ft.com; Box 5.3 from www.ft.com (2010), October 2; Box 5.6 from www.ft.com; Box 5.7 from Plimmer, G. (2010) Dating site runs foul of easy lawyers, September 24, www.ft.com; Box 5.8 from Watkins, M. (2010) Android eats into Nokia's smartphone lead, November 10, www.ft.com; Box 6.1 from Stern, S. (2010) A little knowledge is deadly dangerous, January 11, www.ft.com; Box 7.1 from Reed, J. and schafer, D. (2010) Renault and Nissan in pact with Daimler, April 7, www.ft.com; Figure 7.1 from Reed, J. (2010) Carmaker alliances: a tangled web, May 4, www.ft.com; Box 7.5 from Setback for Disney as Pixar alliance ends, *The Financial Times*, 29/01/2004 (Waters, R. and Larsen, P.T.); Box 7.6 from Moules, J. (2010) How to keep your best people happy in the saddle, October 25, www.ft.com; Box 8.5 from www.ft.com (February 18, 2009); Box 9.1 from Quick-hit chemistry becomes more elusive, *The Financial Times*, 12/09/2001 (Michaels, A.); Box 10.2 from Moules, J. (2010) Cult carmaker defies the gloom, August 22, www.ft.com; Box 11.2 from Telecoms, September 16, 2010, www.ft.com; Box 11.3 from The importance of 'brand value', Overall, S. 19 May 2003, www.ft.com; Box 11.6 from How to avoid making a drama out of a crisis, Stern, S. April 28, 2010, www.ft.com; Box 12.1 from New products crucial to success, Marsh, P. 21 May, 2010, www.ft.com; Box 14.1 from *The Financial Times*, 13/03/2007; Box 14.2 from *The Financial Times*, 26/01/2007 (Amy Yee); Box 15.1 from *The Financial Times*, 28/10/1994; Box 15.3 from Marketing industry turns to mind reading, Kuchler, H. (April 11, 2010), www.ft.com; Box 16.2 from Year-old Bing searches for share, Nuttall, C. (24 May, 2010), www.ft.com; Box 16.3 from Coke cans plans for Dasani in France, *The Financial Times*, 25/03/2004 (Johnson, J. and Jones, A.).

Picture Credits

(Key: b-bottom; c-centre; l-left; r-right; t-top)

Alamy Images: David J. Green – technology 368bl, Len Holsborg 425tr, Chloe Johnson 87, Oliver Leedham 261cr, Pixellover RM 9 385tr, Rufus Stone 126tr; **Arla Foods:** 460t; **Corbis:** Kristi J. Black 570tr, Condé Nast Archive 183tr, George Hall 514tr, Lindsey Hebberd 491bl, John Lamm / TRANSTOCK 404tr, Anthony Redpath 111bl, Schlegelmilch 245t, Duncan Smith 284tr, Larry Williams / Larry Williams and Associates 418cr; **Mary Evans Picture Library:** 196cr; **Getty Images:** Bloomberg 4br, Mark Elias / Bloomberg 382tr, Robert Galbraith / Pool via Bloomberg 290c, Stock Illustration Source 214br; **Steve Haslip:** 460b; **Innocent Ltd:** 443br; **Mini UK:** 426br; **Morgan Motor Company:** 354tr; **Pearson Education Ltd:** A. Harrison 33br, 63tl, 219br, 259tc, 543, 581; **Pearson Education Ltd:** 334tr, Gareth Boden 504br, Burke Triolo Productions / Brand X Pictures 524br, Digital Stock 242tr, Digital Vision 489tr, Image Source Ltd. www.imagesource.com 351cr, Keith Brofsky / Photodisc 565br, Kent Knudson / Photodisc 138tl, Naki Kouyioumtzis 471tr, Michael Matisse / Photodisc 532tr, Tracy Montana / Photodisc 467tr, Kevin Peterson / Photodisc 407tr, Photodisc 34tl, 71br, 76tr, 145br, 158tr, 176tr, 303tr, 327br, Photolink / Photodisc 325tr, 81A Productions / Photolibrary 580cr, Nick Rowe / Photodisc 281tr, F. Schussler / Photodisc 97cr, Studio 8 477br, Westend 61 12br; **UK Intellectual Property Office (UKIP):** 161t; **WineSide / www.wineside.fr:** 359c.

Every effort has been made to trace the copyright holders and we apologise in advance for any unintentional omissions. We would be pleased to insert the appropriate acknowledgement in any subsequent edition of this publication.

Plan of the book

Part One Innovation management

- **Chapter 1** Innovation management: an introduction
- **Chapter 2** Economics and market adoption
- **Chapter 3** Managing innovation within firms
- **Chapter 4** Innovation and operations management
- **Chapter 5** Managing intellectual property

Part Two Turning technology into business

- **Chapter 6** Managing organisational knowledge
- **Chapter 7** Strategic alliances and networks
- **Chapter 8** Management of research and development
- **Chapter 9** Managing R&D projects
- **Chapter 10** Open innovation and technology transfer

Part Three New product development

- **Chapter 11** Product and brand strategy
- **Chapter 12** New product development
- **Chapter 13** Packaging and product development
- **Chapter 14** New service innovation
- **Chapter 15** Market research and its influence on new product development
- **Chapter 16** Managing the new product development process

Part One
Innovation management

The purpose of this part of the book is to introduce and explore the concept of innovation management. Particular emphasis is placed on the need to view innovation as a management process. A cyclic model of innovation is introduced which emphasises the importance of internal processes and external linkages. This raises the issue of the context of innovation and Chapter 2 demonstrates that innovation cannot be separated from the wider social and market processes. The United States is often cited as a good example of a system that enables innovation to flourish: hence it is necessary to explore the economic, social and market factors that facilitate innovation.

Chapter 3 explores the issue of the organisational context and it is from this vantage point that the subject of managing innovation within firms is addressed. Virtually all major technological innovations occur within organisations; hence it is necessary to look at organisations and explore how they manage innovation.

Given that many new product ideas are based on existing products and may be developed from within the production or service operations function, Chapter 4 considers the role of operations within innovation. Many new product ideas may be modest and incremental rather than radical but the combined effect of many, small, innovative ideas may be substantial.

A major part of the process of innovation is the management of a firm's intellectual effort and this is the focus of Chapter 5. Patents, trademarks, copyright and registered designs are all discussed.

The principal message of this part is this: innovation is a management process that is heavily influenced by the organisational context and the wider macro system in which the organisation exists.

Chapter 1
Innovation management: an introduction

Introduction

Innovation is one of those words that suddenly seem to be all around us. Firms care about their ability to innovate, on which their future allegedly depends (Christensen and Raynor, 2003), and many management consultants are busy persuading companies about how they can help them improve their innovation performance. Politicians care about innovation too, how to design policies that stimulate innovation has become a hot topic at various levels of government. The European Commission, for instance, has made innovation policy a central element in its attempt to invigorate the European economy (see Chapter 2). A large literature has emerged, particularly in recent years, on various aspect of innovation and many new research units focusing on innovation have been formed (Fagerberg and Verspagen, 2009).

There is extensive scope for examining the way innovation is managed within organisations. Most of us are well aware that good technology can help companies achieve competitive advantage and long-term financial success. But there is an abundance of exciting new technology in the world and it is the transformation of this technology into products that is of particular concern to organisations. There are numerous factors to be considered by the organisation, but what are these factors and how do they affect the process of innovation? This book will explain how and why most of the most significant inventions of the past two centuries have not come from flashes of for-profit inspiration, but from communal, multilayered endeavour – one idea being built on another until a breakthrough is reached (Johnson, 2010). The Apple case study at the end of this chapter helps illustrates Apple's rise and fall over the past twenty years.

Chapter contents

Learning objectives

When you have completed this chapter you will be able to:

- recognise the importance of innovation;
- explain the meaning and nature of innovation management;
- provide an introduction to a management approach to innovation;
- appreciate the complex nature of the management of innovation within organisations;
- describe the changing views of innovation over time;
- recognise the role of key individuals within the process; and
- recognise the need to view innovation as a management process.

The importance of innovation

Corporations must be able to adapt and evolve if they wish to survive. Businesses operate with the knowledge that their competitors will inevitably come to the market with a product that changes the basis of competition. The ability to change and adapt is essential to survival. But can firms manage innovation? The answer is certainly yes as Bill Gates confirmed in 2008:

> *The share price is not something we control. We control innovation, sales and profits.*
> (Rushe and Waples, 2008)

Today, the idea of innovation is widely accepted. It has become part of our culture – so much so that it verges on becoming a cliché. But even though the term is now embedded in our language, to what extent do we fully understand the concept? Moreover, to what extent is this understanding shared? A scientist's view of innovation may be very different from that of an accountant in the same organisation.

The Apple Inc. story in Illustration 1.1 puts into context the subject of innovation and new product development. In this case Apple's launch of a new product in the mobile phone market will help Apple generate increases in revenue and grow the firm. Innovation is at the heart of many companies' activities. But to what extent is this true of all businesses? And why are some businesses more innovative than others?

Illustration 1.1

Apple launches iPad

FT

With his customary flourish, Steve Jobs unveiled Apple's widely anticipated touch-screen tablet computer, dubbed the iPad, on Wednesday. Arriving with few new content deals despite months of heavy hype, the half-inch thick gadget, which looks like a giant iPhone, met with mixed reviews. But Apple's co-founder and chief executive called it a 'revolutionary product' that would fill the gap between smartphones and laptop computers. Mr Jobs said the iPad would have a wide range of uses, from e-mailing and internet browsing to viewing videos and reading e-books.

'If there's going to be a third category it has to be better at these tasks, otherwise it has no reason for being', said Mr Jobs. The Apple chief is still looking thin after a fight with cancer.

Challenging the big mobile technology companies, Mr Jobs said Apple's total revenues from mobile gear – including its iPod and iPhone lines – now exceeded those of Nokia. 'We're a mobile company. That's what we do', he said.

Source: Getty Images/Bloomberg

The new iBooks store and electronic reading functions 'stand on the shoulders' of Amazon's Kindle, Mr Jobs said, offering titles from a handful of publishers to start, including HarperCollins and Penguin.

Source: Waters, R. and Menn, J. (2010) Jobs unveils 'revolutionary' Apple iPad, Ft.com, 27 January. Reprinted with permission.

What is meant by innovation? And can it be managed? These are questions that will be addressed in this book.

'. . . not to innovate is to die', wrote Christopher Freeman (1982) in his famous study of the economics of innovation. Certainly companies that have established themselves as technical and market leaders have shown an ability to develop successful new products. In virtually every industry, from aerospace to pharmaceuticals and from motor cars to computers, the dominant companies have demonstrated an ability to innovate (*see* Table 1.1). Furthermore, in *Business Week*'s 2006 survey of the world's most innovative companies these same firms are delivering impressive growth and/or return to their shareholders (*see* Table 1.2).

Table 1.1 Market leaders in 2011

Industry	Market leaders	Innovative new products and services
Cell phones	Nokia	Design and new features
Internet-related industries	eBay; Google	New services
Pharmaceuticals	Pfizer; GlaxoSmithKline	Impotence; ulcer treatment drug
Motor cars	Toyota; BMW	Car design and associated product developments
Computers and software development	Intel; IBM and Microsoft; SAP	Computer chip technology, computer hardware improvements and software development

Table 1.2 World's most innovative companies

2009 Rank	Company	Revenue growth 2006–09 %	Margin growth 2006–09 %
1	Apple	30	29
2	Google	31	2
3	Microsoft	10	–4
4	IBM	2	11
5	Toyota	–11	n/a
6	Amazon	29	6
7	LG	16	707
8	BYD	42	–1
9	General Electric	–1	–25
10	Sony	–5	n/a
11	Samsung	17	–9
12	Intel	0	12
13	Ford	–12	n/a
14	Research in Motion	75	–6
15	Volkswagen	0	14
16	Hewlett-Packard	8	9
17	Tata	Private	Private
18	BMW	0	n/a
19	Coca-Cola	9	1
20	Nintendo	22	3

Source: *Business Week*, 25 February 2010.

Table 1.3 Nineteenth-century economic development fuelled by technological innovations

Innovation	Innovator	Date
Steam engine	James Watt	1770–80
Iron boat	Isambard Kingdom Brunel	1820–45
Locomotive	George Stephenson	1829
Electromagnetic induction dynamo	Michael Faraday	1830–40
Electric light bulb	Thomas Edison and Joseph Swan	1879–90

A brief analysis of economic history, especially in the United Kingdom, will show that industrial technological innovation has led to substantial economic benefits for the innovating *company* and the innovating *country*. Indeed, the industrial revolution of the nineteenth century was fuelled by technological innovations (*see* Table 1.3). Technological innovations have also been an important component in the progress of human societies. Anyone who has visited the towns of Bath, Leamington and Colchester will be very aware of how the Romans contributed to the advancement of human societies. The introduction over 2,000 years ago of sewers, roads and elementary heating systems is credited to these early invaders of Britain.

Pause for thought

Not all firms develop innovative new products, but they still seem to survive. Do they thrive?

The study of innovation

Innovation has long been argued to be the engine of growth. It is important to note that it can also provide growth almost regardless of the condition of the larger economy. Innovation has been a topic for discussion and debate for hundreds of years. Nineteenth-century economic historians observed that the acceleration in economic growth was the result of technological progress. However, little effort was directed towards understanding *how* changes in technology contributed to this growth.

Schumpeter (1934, 1939, 1942) was among the first economists to emphasise the importance of *new products* as stimuli to economic growth. He argued that the competition posed by new products was far more important than marginal changes in the *prices* of existing products. For example, economies are more likely to experience growth due to the development of products such as new computer software or new pharmaceutical drugs than to reductions in prices of existing products such as telephones or motor cars. Indeed, early observations suggested that economic development does not occur in any regular manner, but seemed to occur in 'bursts' or waves of activity, thereby indicating the important influence of external factors on economic development.

This macro view of innovation as cyclical can be traced back to the mid-nineteenth century. It was Marx who first suggested that innovations could be associated with waves of economic growth. Since then others such as Schumpeter (1934, 1939), Kondratieff (1935/51), and Abernathy and Utterback (1978) have argued the long-wave theory of innovation. Kondratieff was unfortunately imprisoned by Stalin for his views on economic growth theories, because they conflicted with those of Marx. Marx suggested that capitalist economies would eventually decline, whereas Kondratieff argued that they would experience waves of growth and decline. Abernathy and Utterback (1978) contended that at the birth of any industrial sector there is radical product innovation which is then followed by radical innovation in production processes, followed, in turn, by widespread incremental innovation. This view was once popular and seemed to reflect the life cycles of many industries. It has, however, failed to offer any understanding of *how* to achieve innovative success.

After the Second World War economists began to take an even greater interest in the causes of economic growth (Harrod, 1949; Domar, 1946). One of the most important influences on innovation seemed to be industrial research and development. After all, during the war, military research and development (R&D) had produced significant technological advances and innovations, including radar, aerospace and new weapons. A period of rapid growth in expenditure by countries on R&D was to follow, exemplified by US President Kennedy's 1960 speech outlining his vision of getting a man on the moon before the end of the decade. But economists soon found

Illustration 1.2

A review of the history of economic growth

The classical economists of the eighteenth and nineteenth centuries believed that technological change and capital accumulation were the engines of growth. This belief was based on the conclusion that productivity growth causes population growth, which in turn causes productivity to fall. Today's theory of population growth is very different from these early attempts at understanding economic growth. It argues that rising incomes slow the population growth because they increase the rate of opportunity cost of having children. Hence, as technology advances, productivity and incomes grow.

The Austrian economist, Joseph Schumpeter, was the founder of modern growth theory and is regarded as one of the world's greatest economists. In the 1930s he was the first to realise that the development and diffusion of new technologies by profit-seeking entrepreneurs formed the source of economic progress. One important insight arising from Schumpeter's ideas is that innovation can be seen as *'creative destruction'* waves that restructure the whole market in favour of those who grasp discontinuities faster. In his own words *'the problem that is usually visualized is how capitalism administers existing structures, whereas the relevant problem is how it creates and destroy them'*.

Robert Solow, who was a student of Schumpeter, advanced his professor's theories in the 1950s and won the Nobel Prize for economic science. Paul Romer has developed these theories further and is responsible for the modern theory of economic growth, sometimes called neo-Schumpeterian economic growth theory, which argues that sustained economic growth arises from competition among firms. Firms try to increase their profits by devoting resources to creating new products and developing new ways of making existing products. It is this economic theory that underpins most innovation management and new product development theories.

Source: Adapted from M. Parkin *et al.* (2008) *Economics*, 7th edn, Addison-Wesley, Harlow.

that there was no *direct* correlation between R&D spending and national rates of economic growth. It was clear that the linkages were more complex than first thought (this issue is explored more fully in Chapter 8).

There was a need to understand *how* science and technology affected the economic system. The neo-classical economics approach had not offered any explanations. A series of studies of innovation were undertaken in the 1950s which concentrated on the internal characteristics of the innovation process within the economy. A feature of these studies was that they adopted a cross-discipline approach, incorporating economics, organisational behaviour and business and management. The studies looked at:

- the generation of new knowledge;
- the application of this knowledge in the development of products and processes;
- the commercial exploitation of these products and services in terms of financial income generation.

In particular, these studies revealed that firms behaved differently (*see* Simon, 1957; Woodward, 1965; Carter and Williams, 1957). This led to the development of a new theoretical framework that attempted to understand how firms managed the above, and why some firms appeared to be more successful than others. Later studies in the 1960s were to confirm these initial findings and uncover significant differences in organisational characteristics (Myers and Marquis, 1969; Burns and Stalker, 1961; Cyert and March, 1963). Hence, the new framework placed more emphasis on the firm and its internal activities than had previously been the case. The firm and how it used its resources was now seen as the key influence on innovation.

Neo-classical economics is a theory of economic growth that explains how savings, investments and growth respond to population growth and technological change. The rate of technological change influences the rate of economic growth, but economic growth does not influence technological change. Rather, technological change is determined by chance. Thus population growth and technological change are exogenous. Also, neo-classical economic theory tends to concentrate on industry or economy-wide performance. It tends to ignore differences among firms in the same line of business. Any differences are assumed to reflect differences in the market environments that the organisations face. That is, differences are not achieved through choice but reflect differences in the situations in which firms operate. In contrast, research within business management and strategy focuses on these differences and the decisions that have led to them. Furthermore, the activities that take place within the firm that enable one firm seemingly to perform better than another, given the same economic and market conditions, has been the focus of much research effort since the 1960s.

The Schumpeterian view sees firms as different – it is the way a firm manages its resources over time and develops capabilities that influences its innovation performance. The varying emphasis placed by different disciplines on explaining how innovation occurs is brought together in the framework in Figure 1.1. This overview of the innovation process includes an economic perspective, a business management strategy perspective and organisational behaviour which attempts to look at the internal activities. It also recognises that firms form relationships with other firms and trade, compete and cooperate with each other. It further recognises that the activities of individuals within the firm also affect the process of innovation.

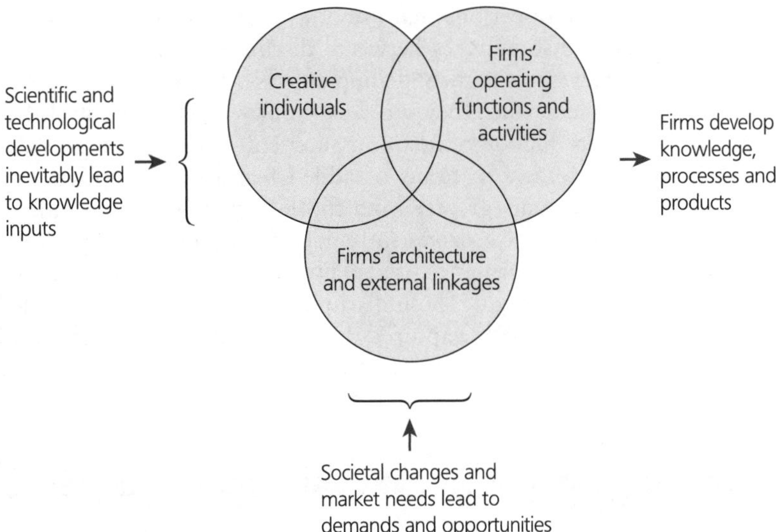

Figure 1.1 Overview of the innovation process

Each firm's unique **organisational architecture** represents the way it has constructed itself over time. This comprises its internal design, including its functions and the relationships it has built up with suppliers, competitors, customers, etc. This framework recognises that these will have a considerable impact on a firm's innovative performance. So too will the way it manages its individual functions and its employees or individuals. These are separately identified within the framework as being influential in the innovation process.

Recent and contemporary studies

As the twentieth century drew to a close there was probably as much debate and argument concerning innovation and what contributes to innovative performance as a hundred years ago. This debate has, nonetheless, progressed our understanding of the area of innovation management. It was Schumpeter who argued that modern firms equipped with R&D laboratories have become the central innovative actors. Since his work others have contributed to the debate (Chandler, 1962; Nelson and Winter, 1982; Cohen and Levinthal, 1990; Prahalad and Hamel, 1990; Pavitt, 1990; Patel and Pavitt, 2000). This emerging Schumpeterian or evolutionary theory of dynamic firm capabilities is having a significant impact on the study of business and management today. Success in the future, as in the past, will surely lie in the ability to acquire and utilise knowledge and apply this to the development of new products. Uncovering how to do this remains one of today's most pressing management problems.

The importance of uncovering and satisfying the needs of customers is the important role played by marketing and these activities feed into the new product development process. Recent studies by Hamel and Prahalad (1994) and Christensen (2003) suggest that listening to your customer may actually stifle technological innovation and be detrimental to long-term business success. Ironically, to be successful in industries characterised by technological change, firms may be required to pursue innovations that are not demanded by their current customers. Christensen (2003) distinguishes between 'disruptive innovations' and 'sustaining innovations' (radical or incremental innovations). Sustaining innovations appealed to existing customers, since they provided improvements to established products. For example, the introduction of new computer software usually provides improvements for existing customers in terms of added features. Disruptive innovations tend to provide improvements greater than those demanded. For example, while the introduction of 3.5-inch disk drives to replace 5.25-inch drives provided an enormous improvement in performance, it also created problems for users who were familiar with the previous format. These disruptive innovations also tended to create new markets, which eventually captured the existing market (*see* Discontinuous innovations, later in this chapter for more on this).

The need to view innovation in an organisational context

During the early part of the nineteenth century manufacturing firms were largely family oriented and concentrated their resources on one activity. For example, one firm would produce steel from iron ore, another would roll this into sheet steel for use by, say, a manufacturer of cooking utensils. These would then be delivered to shops for sale. Towards the latter part of the century these small enterprises were gradually replaced by large firms that would perform a much wider variety of activities. The expansion in manufacturing activities was simultaneously matched by an expansion in administrative activities. This represented the beginnings of the development of the diversified functional enterprise. The world expansion in trade during the early part of the twentieth century saw the quest for new markets by developing a wide range of new products (Chandler, 1962).

Unfortunately, many of the studies of innovation have treated it as an artefact that is somehow detached from knowledge and skills and not embedded in know-how. This inevitably leads to a simplified understanding, if not a misunderstanding, of what constitutes innovation. This section shows why innovation needs to be viewed in the context of organisations and as a process within organisations.

The diagram in Figure 1.1 shows how a number of different disciplines contribute to our understanding of the innovation process. It is important to note that firms do not operate in a vacuum. They trade with each other, they work together in some areas and compete in others. Hence, the role of other firms is a major factor in understanding innovation. As discussed earlier, economics clearly has an important role to play. So too does organisational behaviour as we try to understand what activities are necessary to ensure success. Studies of management will also make a significant contribution to specific areas such as marketing, R&D, manufacturing operations and competition.

As has been suggested, in previous centuries it was easier in many ways to mobilise the resources necessary to develop and commercialise a product, largely because the resources required were, in comparison, minimal. Today, however, the resources required, in terms of knowledge, skills, money and market experience, mean that significant innovations are synonymous with organisations. Indeed, it is worthy of note that more recent innovations and scientific developments, such as significant discoveries like mobile phones or computer software and hardware developments,

Table 1.4 Twentieth-century technological innovations

Date	New product	Responsible organisation
1930s	Polythene	ICI
1945	Ballpoint pen	Reynolds International Pen Company
1950s	Manufacturing process: float glass	Pilkington
1970/80s	Ulcer treatment drug: Zantac	GlaxoSmithKline
1970/80s	Photocopying	Xerox
1980s	Personal computer	Apple Computer
1980/90s	Computer operating system: Windows 95	Microsoft
1995	Impotence drug: Viagra	Pfizer
2000s	Cell phones	Motorola/Nokia
2005	MP3 players	Creative; Apple

are associated with organisations rather than individuals (*see* Table 1.4). Moreover, the increasing depth of our understanding of science inhibits the breadth of scientific study. In the early part of the twentieth century, for example, the German chemical company Bayer was regarded as a world leader in chemistry. Now it is almost impossible for a single chemical companies to be scientific leaders in all areas of chemistry. The large companies have specialised in particular areas. This is true of many other industries. Even university departments are having to concentrate their resources on particular areas of science. They are no longer able to offer teaching and research in all fields. In addition, the creation, development and commercial success of new ideas require a great deal of input from a variety of specialist sources and often vast amounts of money. Hence, today's innovations are associated with groups of people or companies. Innovation is invariably a team game. This will be explored more fully in Chapters 3, 6 and 15.

Pause for thought

If two different firms, similar in size, operating in the same industry spend the same on R&D, will their level of innovation be the same?

Individuals in the innovation process

Figure 1.1 identifies individuals as a key component of the innovation process. Within organisations it is individuals who define problems, have ideas and perform creative linkages and associations that lead to inventions. Moreover, within organisations it is individuals in the role of managers who decide what activities should be undertaken, the amount of resources to be deployed and how they should be carried out. This has led to the development of so-called key individuals in the innovation process such as inventor, entrepreneur, business sponsor, etc. These are discussed in detail in Chapter 3.

Problems of definition and vocabulary

While there are many arguments and debates in virtually all fields of management, it seems that this is particularly the case in innovation management. Very often these centre on semantics. This is especially so when innovation is viewed as a single event. When viewed as a *process*, however, the differences are less substantive. At the heart of this book is the thesis that innovation needs to be viewed as a process. If one accepts that inventions are new discoveries, new ways of doing things, and that products are the eventual outputs from the inventions, that process from new discovery to eventual product is the innovation process. A useful analogy would be education, where qualifications are the formal outputs of the education process. Education, like innovation, is not and cannot be viewed as an event (Linton, 2009).

Arguments become stale when we attempt to define terms such as new, creativity or discovery. It often results in a game of semantics. First, what is new to one company may be 'old hat' to another. Second, how does one judge success in terms of commercial gain or scientific achievement? Are they both not valid and justified goals in themselves? Third, it is context dependent – what is viewed as a success today may be viewed as a failure in the future. We need to try to understand how to encourage innovation in order that we may help to develop more successful new products (this point is explored in Chapters 11 and 12).

Entrepreneurship

Illustration 1.3 shows the remarkable entrepreneurial skills of an eight-year-old boy. This has been the traditional view of **entrepreneurship**; that entrepreneurs often seem

Illustration 1.3

Penny apples – selling them thrice over

In his autobiography the Irish entrepreneur Billy Cullen (2003) tells the story of how, as an eight-year-old boy, he demonstrated sharp entrepreneurial skills. In a poverty stricken area of Dublin young Billy would buy wooden crates of apples for a shilling and then sell the apples on a Saturday afternoon to the hundreds of local people who would flock to watch their local football team play. This provided Billy with a healthy profit of a shilling if he could sell all the apples. But, his entrepreneurial skills did not stop there. He would then take the wooden apple boxes to the football ground and sell them for a penny to people at the back of the crowds so that they could stand on the box for a better view. And finally, when the match had finished Billy would collect up the wooden boxes, break them up and sell them in bundles for firewood.

Source: Pearson Education Ltd/Westend 61

Illustration 1.4

Paypal entrepreneur nets $1.3 billion in sale to eBay

Elon Musk (born 28 June 1971) is a South African-American engineer, entrepreneur and philanthropist. He is best known for co-founding PayPal. He is currently the CEO and Product Architect of Tesla Motors, and has degrees in business and physics from the University of Pennsylvania. In March 1999, Musk co-founded X.com, an online financial services and email payment company. One year later, X.com merged with Confinity, originally a company formed to transfer money between Palm Pilots. The new combined entity focused on email payments through the PayPal domain, acquired as part of Confinity. In February 2001, X.com changed its legal name to PayPal. In October 2002, PayPal was acquired by eBay for US$1.5 billion in stock.

Musk decided to invest some of his fortune in Tesla Motors, of which he is a co-founder, chairman of the board and the sole product architect. First investing in April 2004, he led several rounds of financing, and became CEO in October 2008. Tesla Motors built an electric sports car, the Tesla Roadster, and plans to produce a more economical four-door electric vehicle. Musk is responsible for a business strategy that aims to deliver affordable electric vehicles to mass-market consumers.

to have innate talents. In the United States the subject of innovation management is often covered in terms of 'entrepreneurship'. Indeed, it has been taught for many years and there are many courses available for students in US business schools on this topic. In a study of past and future research on the subject of entrepreneurship, Howard Stevenson, who did so much to establish entrepreneurship as a discipline at Harvard Business School and was Director of the Arthur Rock Centre for entrepreneurship there, defines entrepreneurship as:

> *the pursuit of opportunity beyond the resources you currently control.*
>
> (Stevenson and Amabile, 1999)

It is the analysis of the role of the individual entrepreneur that distinguishes the study of entrepreneurship from that of innovation management. Furthermore, it is starting small businesses and growing them into large and successful businesses that was the traditional focus of attention of those studying entrepreneurship. This has been changing over the past ten years especially across Europe. Where there is now considerable emphasis especially within the technical universities on trying to understand how entrepreneurship and innovation can help create the new technology intensive businesses of tomorrow. Moreover it is the recognition of the entrepreneur's desire to change things that is so important within innovation. We will see later that the role of an entrepreneur is central to innovation management. Illustration 1.4 shows how a serial entrepreneur has driven innovation and new product development in several industries.

Design

The definition of design with regard to business seems to be widening ever further and encompassing almost all aspects of business (*see* the Design Council, www.Designcouncil.com). For many people design is about developing or creating something; hence we are into semantics regarding how this differs from innovation. Hargadon and Douglas (2001: 476) suggest design is concerned with the emergent arrangement of concrete details that embody a new idea. A key question, however, is how design relates to research and development. Indeed, it seems that in most cases the word *design* and the word *development* mean the same thing. Traditionally design referred to the development of drawings, plans and sketches. Indeed, most dictionary definitions continue with this view today and refer to a designer as a 'draughtsman who makes plans for manufacturers or prepares drawings for clothing or stage productions' (*Oxford English Dictionary*, 2005). In the aerospace industry engineers and designers would have previously worked closely together for many years, developing drawings for an aircraft. Today the process is dominated by computer software programmes that facilitate all aspects of the activity; hence the product development activities and the environments in which design occurs have changed considerably. Figure 1.2 shows, along the horizontal axis, the wide spectrum of activities that design encompasses from clothing design to design within electronics. The vertical axis shows how the areas of design feed into outputs from choice of colour to cost effectiveness; all of which are considered in the development of a product. The position taken by this book is to view design as an applied activity within research and development, and to recognise that in certain industries, like clothing for example, design is the main component in product development. In other industries, however, such as pharmaceuticals, design forms only a small part of the product development activity.

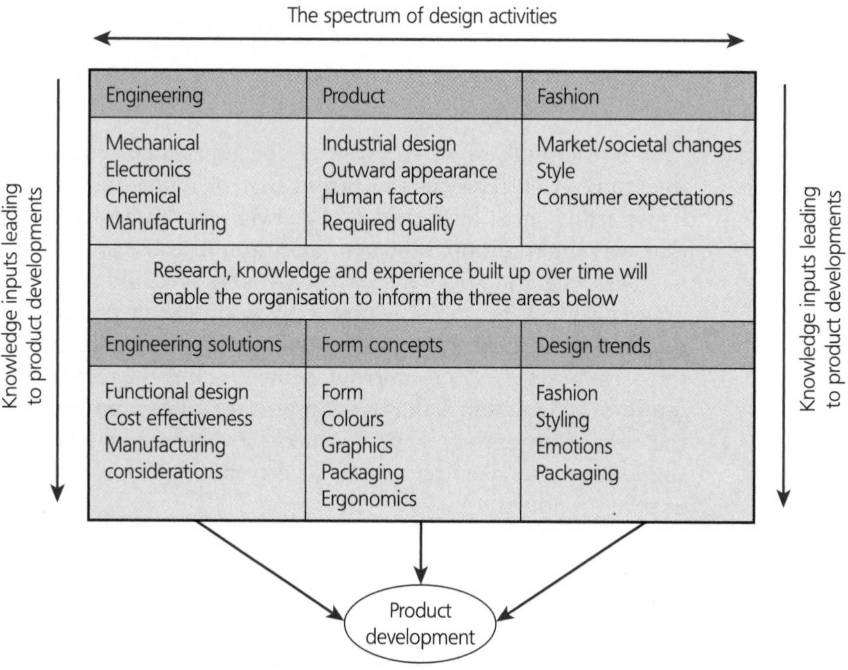

Figure 1.2 The interaction between development activities and design environment

Innovation and invention

Many people confuse these terms. Indeed, if you were to ask people for an explanation you would collect a diverse range of definitions. It is true that innovation is the first cousin of invention, but they are not identical twins that can be interchanged. Hence, it is important to establish clear meanings for them.

Innovation itself is a very broad concept that can be understood in a variety of ways. One of the more comprehensive definitions is offered by Myers and Marquis (1969):

> *Innovation is not a single action but a total process of interrelated sub processes. It is not just the conception of a new idea, nor the invention of a new device, nor the development of a new market. The process is all these things acting in an integrated fashion.*

It is important to clarify the use of the term 'new' in the context of innovation. Rogers and Shoemaker (1972) do this eloquently:

> *It matters little, as far as human behaviour is concerned, whether or not an idea is 'objectively' new as measured by the lapse of time since its first use or discovery. . . . If the idea seems new and different to the individual, it is an innovation.*
>
> [emphasis added]

Most writers, including those above, distinguish innovation from invention by suggesting that innovation is concerned with the *commercial and practical application* of ideas or inventions. Invention, then, is the conception of the idea, whereas innovation is the subsequent translation of the invention into the economy. The following simple equation helps to show the relationship between the two terms:

Innovation = theoretical conception + technical invention + commercial exploitation

However, all the terms in this equation will need explanation in order to avoid confusion. The *conception* of new ideas is the starting point for innovation. A new idea by itself, while interesting, is neither an invention nor an innovation; it is merely a concept or a thought or collection of thoughts. The process of converting intellectual thoughts into a tangible new artefact (usually a product or process) is an **invention**. This is where science and technology usually play a significant role. At this stage inventions need to be combined with hard work by many different people to convert them into products that will improve company performance. These later activities represent *exploitation*. However, it is the *complete* process that represents *innovation*. This introduces the notion that innovation is a process with a number of distinctive features that have to be managed. This is the view taken by this book. To summarise, then, innovation depends on inventions but inventions need to be harnessed to commercial activities before they can contribute to the growth of an organisation. Thus:

> *Innovation is the management of all the activities involved in the process of idea generation, technology development, manufacturing and marketing of a new (or improved) product or manufacturing process or equipment.*

This definition of **innovation as a management process** also offers a distinction between an innovation and a product, the latter being the output of innovation. Illustration 1.5 should help to clarify the differences.

Illustration 1.5

An example of an invention

Scientists and development engineers at a household cleaning products company had been working for many months on developing a new lavatory cleaning product. They had developed a liquid that when sprayed into the toilet pan, on contact with water, would fizz and sparkle. The effect was to give the impression of a tough, active cleaning product. The company applied for a patent and further developments and market research were planned.

However, initial results both from technical and market specialists led to the abandonment of the project. The preliminary market feedback suggested a fear of such a product on the part of consumers. This was because the fizz and sparkle looked too dramatic and frightening. Furthermore, additional technical research revealed a short shelf-life for the mixture. This is a clear example of an invention that did not progress beyond the organisation to a commercial product.

It is necessary at this point to cross-reference these discussions with the practical realities of managing a business today. The senior vice-president for research and development at 3M, one of the most highly respected and innovative organisations, recently defined innovation as:

> *Creativity: the thinking of novel and appropriate ideas. Innovation: the successful implementation of those ideas within an organisation.*

Successful and unsuccessful innovations

There is often a great deal of confusion surrounding innovations that are not commercially successful. A famous example would be the Kodak Disc Camera or the Sinclair C5. This was a small, electrically driven tricycle or car. Unfortunately for Clive Sinclair, the individual behind the development of the product, it was not commercially successful. Commercial failure, however, does not relegate an innovation to an invention. Using the definition established above, the fact that the product progressed from the drawing board into the marketplace makes it an innovation – albeit an unsuccessful one.

Pause for thought

Apple's iPhone looks set to be as successful as the iPod, but Apple has experienced similar success before with its Apple Mac computer and eventually lost out to Microsoft. Will history repeat itself?

Different types of innovation

Industrial innovation not only includes major (radical) innovations but also minor (incremental) technological advances. Indeed, the definition offered above suggests that successful commercialisation of the innovation may involve considerably wider organisational changes. For example, the introduction of a radical, technological innovation, such as digital cameras by Kodak and Fuji, invariably results in substantial internal organisational changes. In this case substantial changes occurred with the manufacturing, marketing and sales functions. Both of these firms decided to concentrate on the rapidly developing digital photography market. Yet both Fuji and Kodak were the market leaders in supplying traditional 35mm film cartridges. Their market share of the actual camera market was less significant. Such strategic decisions forced changes on all areas of the business. For example, in Kodak's case the manufacturing function underwent substantial changes as it began to substantially cut production of 35mm film cartridges. Opportunities existed for manufacturing in producing digital cameras and their associated equipment. Similarly, the marketing function had to employ extra sales staff to educate and reassure retail outlets that the new technology would not cannibalise their film-processing business. While many people would begin to print photographs from their PCs at home, many others would continue to want their digital camera film processed into physical photographs. For both Fuji and Kodak the new technology has completely changed the photographic industry. Both firms have seen their revenues fall from film cartridge sales, but Kodak and Fuji are now market leaders in digital cameras whereas before they were not.

Hence, technological innovation can be accompanied by additional managerial and organisational changes, often referred to as innovations. This presents a far more blurred picture and begins to widen the definition of innovation to include virtually any organisational or managerial change. Table 1.5 shows a typology of innovations.

Innovation was defined earlier in this section as the application of knowledge. It is this notion that lies at the heart of all types of innovation, be they product, process or service. It is also worthy of note that many studies have suggested that product innovations are soon followed by process innovations in what they describe as an industry innovation cycle (*see* Chapter 6). Furthermore, it is common to associate innovation with physical change, but many changes introduced within organisations involve very little physical change. Rather, it is the activities performed

Table 1.5 A typology of innovations

Type of innovation	Example
Product innovation	The development of a new or improved product
Process innovation	The development of a new manufacturing process such as Pilkington's float glass process
Organisational innovation	A new venture division; a new internal communication system; introduction of a new accounting procedure
Management innovation	TQM (total quality management) systems; BPR (business process re-engineering); introduction of SAPR3*
Production innovation	Quality circles; just-in-time (JIT) manufacturing system; new production planning software, e.g. MRP II; new inspection system
Commercial/marketing innovation	New financing arrangements; new sales approach, e.g. direct marketing
Service innovation	Internet-based financial services

*Note: SAP is a German software firm and R3 is an enterprise resource planning (ERP) product.

by individuals that change. A good example of this is the adoption of so-called Japanese management techniques by automobile manufacturers in Europe and the United States.

It is necessary to stress at the outset that this book concentrates on the management of product innovation. This does not imply that the list of innovations above are less significant; this focus has been chosen to ensure clarity and to facilitate the study of innovation.

Technology and science

We also need to consider the role played by *science and technology* in innovation. The continual fascination with science and technology at the end of the nineteenth century and subsequent growth in university teaching and research have led to the development of many new strands of science. The proliferation of scientific journals over the past 30 years demonstrates the rapidly evolving nature of science and technology. The scientific literature seems to double in quantity every five years (Rothwell and Zegveld, 1985).

Science can be defined as systematic and formulated knowledge. There are clearly significant differences between science and technology. Technology is often seen as being the application of science and has been defined in many ways (Lefever, 1992).

Illustration 1.6

The young world rising

Three forces are shaping the twenty-first century: youth, entrepreneurship and ICT. Young entrepreneurs around the world are blending new technologies and next-generation thinking, building radically new kinds of organisations adapted to a flat and crowded world. Rob Salkowitz *illustrates* the new centres of entrepreneurial innovation on five continents. He identifies an exciting new trend in global business and introduces us to a fresh young cast of entrepreneurs whose ideas are literally changing the world.

The Boston Consulting Group (BCG) confirms that the information-technology revolution continues apace. It calculates that there are already about 610 million internet users in the BRICI countries (Brazil, Russia, India, China and Indonesia). BCG predicts that this number will nearly double by 2015. And in one respect many consumers in emerging markets are leapfrogging over their western peers. They are much more likely to access the internet via mobile devices (which are ubiquitous in the emerging world) rather than PCs. That gives local entrepreneurs an advantage, says Rob Salkowitz, the author of *The Young World Rising*. Whereas western companies are hampered by legacy systems and legacy mindsets, they can build their companies around the coming technology. One of the most popular films in America at the moment is *The Social Network*, about a group of young Harvard students who founded one of the world's fastest-growing companies, Facebook. The next Facebook is increasingly likely to be founded in India or Indonesia rather than middle-aged America or doddery old Europe.

Sources: *The Economist* (2010) Schumpeter: The other demographic dividend, 7 October © The Economist Newspaper Limited London 2010; Salkowitz, R. (2010) *The Young World Rising*, John Wiley and Sons, New Jersey.

It is important to remember that technology is not an accident of nature. It is the product of deliberate action by human beings. The following definition is suggested:

Technology is knowledge applied to products or production processes.

No definition is perfect and the above is no exception. It does, however, provide a good starting point from which to view technology with respect to innovation. It is important to note that technology, like education, cannot be purchased off the shelf like a can of tomatoes. It is embedded in knowledge and skills.

In a lecture given to the Royal Society in 1992 the former chairman of Sony, Akio Morita, suggested that, unlike engineers, scientists are held in high esteem. This, he suggested, is because science provides us with information which was previously unknown. Yet technology comes from employing and *manipulating science* into concepts, processes and devices. These, in turn, can be used to make our life or work more efficient, convenient and powerful. Hence, it is technology, as an *outgrowth of science*, that fuels the industrial engine. And it is *engineers* and not scientists who make technology happen. In Japan, he argued, you will notice that almost every major manufacturer is run by an engineer or technologist. However, in the United Kingdom, some manufacturing companies are led by chief executive officers (CEOs) who do not understand the technology that goes into their own products. Indeed, many UK corporations are headed by chartered accountants. With the greatest respect to accountants, their central concerns are statistics and figures of *past* performance. How can an accountant reach out and grab the future if he or she is always looking at *last* quarter's results (Morita, 1992)?

The above represents the personal views of an influential senior figure within industry. There are many leading industrialists, economists and politicians who would concur (Hutton, 1995). But there are equally many who would profoundly disagree. The debate on improving economic innovative performance is one of the most important in the field of political economics. This debate should also include '*The young world rising*' (*see* Illustration 1.6).

Innovation in action

Put your waste to work

Ahmed Khan was so concerned about the amount of plastic waste his company was producing he decided to do something about it.

Discarded plastic bottles and bags are a major problem in India. Discarded bags have even clogged underground drainage systems which means that roads are more prone to cracking and washing away in monsoon rains. Khan and his brother decided to turn the problem into the solution – roads made with recycled plastic.

Their company, Bangalore-based KK Plastic Waste Management, mixes waste plastic with asphalt into a product they call 'polymerised bitumen'. This is used to build roads that last longer than traditional ones. The surface also offers less resistance to tyres and so improves fuel efficiency.

So far the Khans have helped build 1,600 kilometres of 'plastic' roads around Bangalore and shown how, with a bit of ingenuity, environmental benefits can mean economic gains.

Source: 100 Thoughts (2010) HSBC, London.

Popular views of innovation

Science, technology and innovation have received a great deal of popular media coverage over the years, from Hollywood and Disney movies to best-selling novels (*see* Figure 1.3). This is probably because science and technology can help turn vivid imaginings into a possibility. The end result, however, is a simplified image of scientific discoveries and innovations. It usually consists of a lone professor, with a mass of white hair, working away in his garage and stumbling, by accident, on a major new discovery. Through extensive trial and error, usually accompanied by dramatic experiments, this is eventually developed into an amazing invention. This is best demonstrated in the blockbuster movie *Back to the Future*. Christopher Lloyd plays the eccentric scientist and Michael J. Fox his young, willing accomplice. Together they are involved in an exciting journey that enables Fox to travel back in time and influence the future.

Cartoons have also contributed to a misleading image of the innovation process. Here, the inventor, usually an eccentric scientist, is portrayed with a glowing lightbulb above his head, as a flash of inspiration results in a new scientific discovery. We have all seen and laughed at these funny cartoons.

This humorous and popular view of inventions and innovations has been reinforced over the years and continues to occur in the popular press. Many industrialists and academics have argued that this simple view of a complex phenomenon has caused immense harm to the understanding of science and technology.

Figure 1.3 The popular view of science

Models of innovation

Traditional arguments about innovation have centred on two schools of thought. On the one hand, the social deterministic school argued that innovations were the result of a combination of external social factors and influences, such as demographic changes, economic influences and cultural changes. The argument was that *when* the conditions were 'right' innovations would occur. On the other hand, the individualistic school argued that innovations were the result of unique individual talents and such innovators are born. Closely linked to the individualistic theory is the important role played by serendipity; more on this later.

Over the past ten years the literature on what 'drives' innovation has tended to divide into two schools of thought: the market-based view and the resource-based view. The market-based view argues that market conditions provide the context which facilitate or constrain the extent of firm innovation activity (Slater and Narver, 1994; Porter, 1980, 1985). The key issue here, of course, is the ability of firms to recognise opportunities in the marketplace. Cohen and Levinthal (1990) and Trott (1998) would argue that few firms have the ability to scan and search their environments effectively.

The resource-based view of innovation considers that a market-driven orientation does not provide a secure foundation for formulating innovation strategies for markets which are dynamic and volatile; rather a firm's own resources provide a much more stable context in which to develop its innovation activity and shape its markets in accordance to its own view (Penrose, 1959; Wernerfelt, 1984; Wernerfelt, 1995; Grant, 1996; Prahalad and Hamel, 1990; Conner and Prahalad, 1996; Eisenhardt and Martin, 2000). The resource-based view of innovation focuses on the firm and its resources, capabilities and skills. It argues that when firms have resources that are valuable, rare and not easily copied they can achieve a sustainable competitive advantage – frequently in the form of innovative new products. Chapter 6 offers a more detailed overview of the resource-based theory of the firm.

Serendipity

Many studies of historical cases of innovation have highlighted the importance of the unexpected discovery. The role of serendipity or luck is offered as an explanation. As we have seen, this view is also reinforced in the popular media. It is, after all, everyone's dream that they will accidentally uncover a major new invention leading to fame and fortune.

On closer inspection of these historical cases, serendipity is rare indeed. After all, in order to recognise the significance of an advance one would need to have some prior knowledge in that area. Most discoveries are the result of people who have had a fascination with a particular area of science or technology and it is following extended efforts on their part that advances are made. Discoveries may not be expected, but in the words of Louis Pasteur, 'chance favours the prepared mind'.

Linear models

It was US economists after the Second World War who championed the linear model of science and innovation. Since then, largely because of its simplicity, this model has taken a firm grip on people's views on how innovation occurs. Indeed, it dominated science and industrial policy for 40 years. It was only in the 1980s that management schools around the world began seriously to challenge the sequential linear process. The recognition that innovation occurs through the interaction of the

Figure 1.4 Conceptual framework of innovation

science base (dominated by universities and industry), technological development (dominated by industry) and the needs of the market was a significant step forward (*see* Figure 1.4). The explanation of the interaction of these activities forms the basis of models of innovation today. Students may also wish to note that there is even a British Standard (BS7000), which sets out a design-centred model of the process (BSI, 2008).

There is, of course, a great deal of debate and disagreement about precisely what activities influence innovation and, more importantly, the internal processes that affect a company's ability to innovate. Nonetheless, there is broad agreement that it is the linkages between these key components that will produce successful innovation. Importantly, the devil is in the detail. From a European perspective an area that requires particular attention is the linkage between the science base and technological development. The European Union (EU) believes that European universities have not established effective links with industry, whereas in the United States universities have been working closely with industry for many years.

As explained above, the innovation process has traditionally been viewed as a sequence of separable stages or activities. There are two basic variations of this model for product innovation. First, and most crudely, there is the technology-driven model (often referred to as 'technology push') where it is assumed that scientists make unexpected discoveries, technologists apply them to develop product ideas and engineers and designers turn them into prototypes for testing. It is left to manufacturing to devise ways of producing the products efficiently. Finally, marketing and sales will promote the product to the potential consumer. In this model the marketplace was a passive recipient for the fruits of R&D. This technology-push model dominated industrial policy after the Second World War (*see* Figure 1.5). While this model of innovation can be applied to a few cases, most notably the

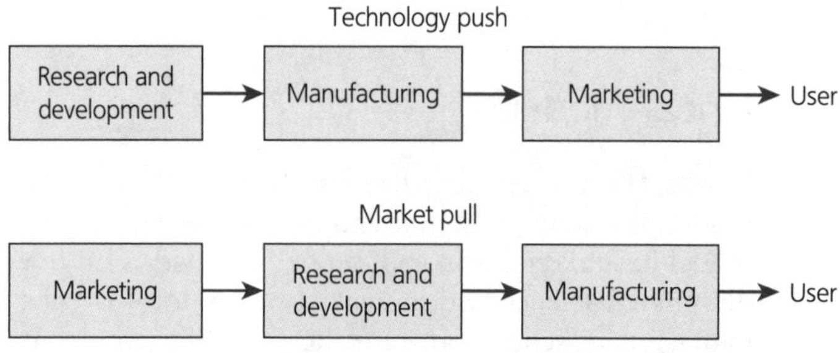

Figure 1.5 Linear models of innovation

pharmaceutical industry, it is not applicable in many other instances; in particular where the innovation process follows a different route.

It was not until the 1970s that new studies of actual innovations suggested that the role of the marketplace was influential in the innovation process (von Hippel, 1978). This led to the second linear model, the 'market-pull' model of innovation. The customer need-driven model emphasises the role of marketing as an initiator of new ideas resulting from close interactions with customers. These, in turn, are conveyed to R&D for design and engineering and then to manufacturing for production. In fast-moving consumer goods industries the role of the market and the customer remains powerful and very influential. The managing director of McCain Foods argues that knowing your customer is crucial to turning innovation into profits:

> *It's only by understanding what the customer wants that we can identify the innovative opportunities. Then we see if there's technology that we can bring to bear on the opportunities that exist. Being innovative is relatively easy – the hard part is ensuring your ideas become commercially viable.* (Murray, 2003)

Simultaneous coupling model

Whether innovations are stimulated by technology, customer need, manufacturing or a host of other factors, including competition, misses the point. The models above concentrate on what is driving the downstream efforts rather than on *how* innovations occur (Galbraith, 1982). The linear model is only able to offer an explanation of *where* the initial stimulus for innovation was born, that is, where the trigger for the idea or need was initiated. The simultaneous coupling model shown in Figure 1.6 suggests that it is the result of the simultaneous coupling of the knowledge within all three functions that will foster innovation. Furthermore, the point of commencement for innovation is not known in advance.

Architectural innovation

Henderson and Clark (1990) divide technological knowledge along two new dimensions: *knowledge of the components* and knowledge of the linkage between them, which they called *architectural knowledge*. The result is four possible types of innovation: incremental, modular, radical and architectural innovation. Essentially they distinguish between the components of a product and the ways they are integrated

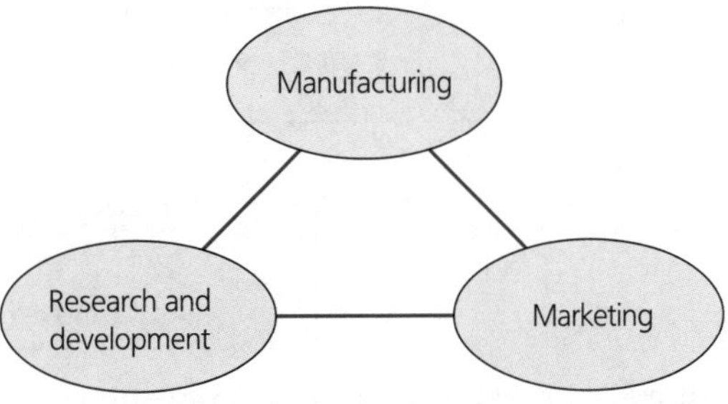

Figure 1.6 The simultaneous coupling model

into the system, that is, the product 'architecture', which they define as innovations that change the architecture of a product without changing its components. Prior to the Henderson and Clark model the radical/incremental dimension suggests that incumbents will be in a better position if the innovation is incremental since they can use existing knowledge and resources to leverage the whole process. New entrants, on the other hand, will have a large advantage if the innovation is radical because they will not need to change their knowledge background. Furthermore incumbents struggle to deal with radical innovation both because they operate under a 'managerial mindset' constraint and because strategically they have less of an incentive to invest in the innovation if it will cannibalise their existing products.

Kodak illustrates this well. The company dominated the photography market over many years, and throughout this extended period all the incremental innovations solidified its leadership. As soon as the market experienced a radical innovation – the entrance of digital technology – Kodak struggled to defend its position against the new entrants. The new technology required different knowledge, resources and mindsets. This pattern of innovation is typical in mature industries. This concept is explored further in Chapter 6.

Interactive model

The interactive model develops this idea further (*see* Figure 1.7) and links together the technology-push and market-pull models. It emphasises that innovations occur as the result of the interaction of the marketplace, the science base and the organisation's capabilities. Like the coupling model, there is no explicit starting point. The use of information flows is used to explain how innovations transpire and that they can arise from a wide variety of points.

While still oversimplified, this is a more comprehensive representation of the innovation process. It can be regarded as a logically sequential, though not necessarily continuous, process that can be divided into a series of functionally distinct but interacting and interdependent stages (Rothwell and Zegveld, 1985). The overall innovation process can be thought of as a complex set of communication paths over which knowledge is transferred. These paths include internal and external linkages. The

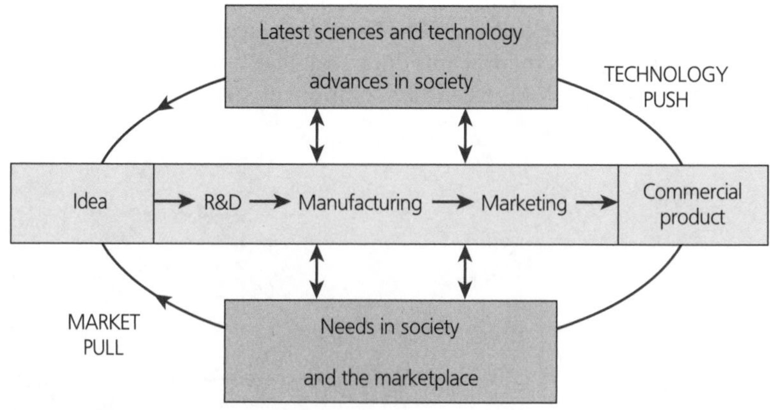

Figure 1.7 Interactive model of innovation

Source: Adapted from R. Rothwell and W. Zegveld (1985) *Reindustrialisation and Technology*, Longman, London.

innovation process outlined in Figure 1.7 represents the organisation's capabilities and its linkages with both the marketplace and the science base. Organisations that are able to manage this process effectively will be successful at innovation.

At the centre of the model are the organisational functions of R&D, engineering and design, manufacturing and marketing and sales. While at first this may appear to be a linear model, the flow of communication is not necessarily linear. There is provision for feedback. Also, linkages with the science base and the marketplace occur between all functions, not just with R&D or marketing. For example, as often happens, it may be the manufacturing function which initiates a design improvement that leads to the introduction of either a different material or the eventual development by R&D of a new material. Finally, the generation of ideas is shown to be dependent on inputs from three basic components (as outlined in Figure 1.4): organisation capabilities; the needs of the marketplace; the science and technology base.

Innovation life cycle and dominant designs

The launch of an innovative new product into the market is usually only the beginning of technology progress. At the industry level, the introduction of a new technology will cause a reaction: competitors will respond to this new product, hence technological progress depends on factors other than those internal to the firm. We need to consider the role of the competition. Product innovation, process innovation, competitive environment and organisational structure all interact and are closely linked together. Abernathy and Utterback (1978) argued there were three different phases in an innovation's life cycle: fluid, transitional and specific. This concept will be discussed in detail in Chapter 6, but at this stage we need only to recognise that one can consider innovation in the form of a life cycle that begins with a major technological change and product innovation. This is followed by the emergence of competition and process innovations (manufacturing improvements). As the life cycle proceeds a dominant design usually emerges prior to standardisation and an emphasis on lowering cost. This model can be applied to many consumer product innovations over the past 20–30 years, such as VCRs, CD players and mobile phones.

Open innovation and the need to share and exchange knowledge (network models)

Innovation has been described as an information–creation process that arises out of social interaction. Chesbrough (2003), adopting a business strategy perspective, presents a persuasive argument that the process of innovation has shifted from one of closed systems, internal to the firm, to a new mode of open systems involving a range of players distributed up and down the supply chain. Significantly, it is Chesbrough's emphasis on the new knowledge-based economy that informs the concept **open innovation**. In particular it is the use of cheap and instant information flows which places even more emphasis on the linkages and relationships of firms. It is from these linkages and the supply chain in particular that firms have to ensure that they have the capability to fully capture and utilise ideas.

Furthermore, the product innovation literature, in applying the open innovation paradigm, has been debating the strengths and limitations of so-called 'user toolkits' which seem to ratchet up further this drive to externalise the firm's capabilities to capture innovation opportunities (von Hippel, 2005).

Authors such as Thomke (2003), Schrange (2000) and Dodgson *et al.* (2005) have emphasised the importance of learning through experimentation. This is similar to Nonaka's work in the early 1990s which emphasised the importance of learning by doing in the 'knowledge creating company' (Nonaka, 1991). However, Dodgson *et al.* argue that there are significant changes occurring at all levels of the innovation process, forcing us to reconceptualise the process with emphasis placed on the three areas that have experienced most significant change through the introduction and use of new technologies. These are: technologies that facilitate creativity, technologies that facilitate communication and technologies that facilitate manufacturing. For example, they argue that information and communication technologies have changed the way individuals, groups and communities interact. Mobile phones, email and websites are obvious examples of how people interact and information flows in a huge osmosis process through the boundaries of the firm. When this is coupled with changes in manufacturing and operations technologies, enabling rapid prototyping and flexible manufacturing at low costs, the process of innovation seems to be undergoing considerable change (Dodgson *et al.*, 2005; Chesbrough, 2003; Schrange, 2000). Models of innovation need to take account of these new technologies which allow immediate and extensive interaction with many collaborators throughout the process from conception to commercialisation.

Table 1.6 summarises the historical development of the dominant models of the industrial innovation process.

Table 1.6 The chronological development of models of innovation

Date	Model	Characteristics
1950/60s	Technology-push	Simple linear sequential process; emphasis on R&D; the market is a recipient of the fruits of R&D
1970s	Market-pull	Simple linear sequential process; emphasis on marketing; the market is the source for directing R&D; R&D has a reactive role
1970s	Dominant design	Abbernathy and Utterback (1978) illustrate that an innovation system goes through three stages before a dominant design emerges
1980s	Coupling model	Emphasis on integrating R&D and marketing
1980/90s	Interactive model	Combinations of push and pull
1990	Architectural innovation	Recognition of the role of firm embedded knowledge in influencing innovation
1990s	Network model	Emphasis on knowledge accumulation and external linkages
2000s	Open innovation	Chesbrough's (2003) emphasis on further externalisation of the innovation process in terms of linkages with knowledge inputs and collaboration to exploit knowledge outputs

Discontinuous innovation – step changes

Occasionally something happens in an industry which causes a disruption – the rules of the game change. This has happened in many different industries: for example, telephone banking and internet banking have caused huge changes for the banking industry. Likewise, the switch from photographic film to digital film changed the landscape in that industry. And the music industry is still grappling with the impact of downloading as the dominant way to consume music. These changes are seen as not continuous, that is **discontinuous**: the change is very significant (see Figure 1.8). Sometimes this is referred to as disruptive innovation. Schumpeter referred to this concept as creative destruction.

The term disruptive innovation as we know it today first appeared in *The Innovator's Dilemma*. In this book, Clayton Christensen investigated why some innovations that were radical in nature reinforced the incumbent's position in a certain industry, contrary to what previous models (for instance the Henderson–Clark model) would predict. More specifically he analysed extensively the disk drive industry because it represented the most dynamic, technologically discontinuous and complex industry one could find in the economy. Figure 1.8 shows how a disruptive innovation creates a step change in performance.

This very same pattern of disruption can be observed with video rental services, department stores and newspapers. The appearance of online news services, web portals and other media platforms such as blogs and wikis clearly represent a disruptive innovation for the traditional newspaper industry. Will the likes of *The Times*, the *Guardian* and the *New York Times* be able to survive such disruption? For many years newspapers embraced the web and provided content online, but sales of newspapers continued to decline. A key question for the industry is: *What indispensable roles can we play in the lives of the consumers we want to serve?*

Other examples of disruptive innovations are:

- steamships (which disrupted sailing ships);
- music downloads (which disrupted CDs); and
- internet shopping (which disrupted high street retailing).

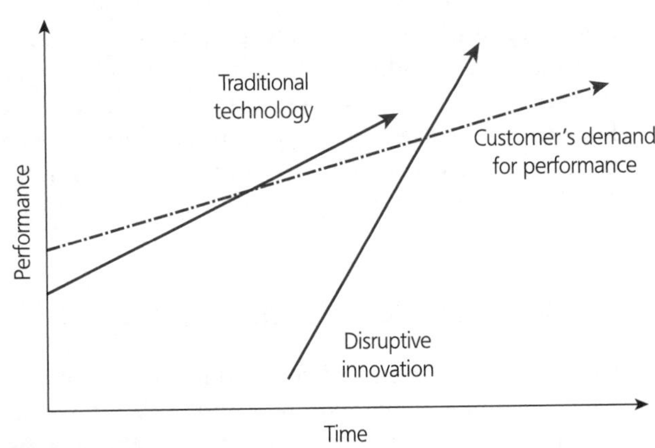

Figure 1.8 Disruptive innovations

Discontinuity can also come about by reframing the way we think about an industry. Table 14.3 shows a wide range of new services that also created new business models. This includes online gambling and low cost airlines. What these examples – and many others – have in common is that they represent the challenge of discontinuous innovation. How do incumbent firms cope with these dramatic shifts in technology, service and/or the business model.

What many firms would also like to know is how they can become the disruptor or radical innovator. In a study of radical innovation in the highly innovative motorsport industry Delbridge and Mariotti (2009) found that successful innovators:

- engage in wide exploratory innovation search activities, looking beyond their own knowledge base and domain of expertise;
- identify the advantages offered by new combinations of existing knowledge, through the application of technologies and materials initially developed elsewhere;
- often partner with 'unusual' firms, beyond the usual sphere of collaboration;
- engage with partner companies to establish a close working relationship;
- promote lateral thinking within an existing web of partners.

Innovation as a management process

The fact is coming up with an idea is the least important part of creating something great. The execution and delivery are what's key.

(Sergey Brin, Co-founder of Google, quoted in the *Guardian* (2009)).

The statement by Sergey Brin, Co-founder of Google, confirms that we need to view innovation as a management process. The preceding sections have revealed that innovation is not a singular event, but a series of activities that are linked in some way to the others. This may be described as a process and involves:

1 a response to either a need or an opportunity that is context dependent;
2 a creative effort that if successful results in the introduction of novelty;
3 the need for further changes.

Usually, in trying to capture this complex process, the simplification has led to misunderstandings. The simple linear model of innovation can be applied to only a few innovations and is more applicable to certain industries than others. The pharmaceutical industry characterises much of the technology-push model. Other industries, like the food industry, are better represented by the market-pull model. For most industries and organisations innovations are the result of a mixture of the two. Managers working within these organisations have the difficult task of trying to manage this complex process.

A framework for the management of innovation

Industrial innovation and new product development have evolved considerably from their early beginnings outlined above. We have seen that innovation is extremely complex and involves the effective management of a variety of different activities. It is precisely how the process is managed that needs to be examined. Over the past

Table 1.7 Explanations for innovative capability

Innovative firm	Explanation for innovative capability
Apple	Innovative chief executive
Google	Scientific freedom for employees
Samsung	Speed of product development
Procter & Gamble	Utilisation of external sources of technology
IBM	Share patents with collaborators
BMW	Design
Starbucks	In-depth understanding of customers and their cultures
Toyota	Close cooperation with suppliers

Table 1.8 Studies of innovation management

	Study	Date	Focus
1	Carter and Williams	1957	Industry and technical progress
2	Project Hindsight – TRACES (Isenson)	1968	Historical reviews of US government-funded defence industry
3	Wealth from knowledge (Langrish *et al.*)	1972	Queens Awards for technical innovation
4	Project SAPPHO (Rothwell *et al.*)	1974	Success and failure factors in chemical industry
5	Minnesota Studies (Van de Ven)	1989	14 case studies of innovations
6	Rothwell	1992	25-year review of studies
7	Sources of innovation (Wheelwright and Clark)	1992	Different levels of user involvement
8	MIT studies (Utterback)	1994	5 major industry-level cases
9	Project NEWPROD (Cooper)	1994	Longitudinal survey of success and failure in new products
10	Radical innovation (Leifer *et al.*)	2000	Review of mature businesses
11	TU Delft study (van der Panne *et al.*)	2003	Literature review of success and failure factors

50 years there have been numerous studies of innovation attempting to understand not only the ingredients necessary for it to occur but also what levels of ingredients are required and in what order. Furthermore, a study by the Boston Consulting Group reported in *Business Week* (2006) of over 1,000 senior managers revealed further explanations as to what makes some firms more innovative than others. The key findings from this survey are captured in Table 1.7. While these headline-grabbing bullet points are interesting, they do not show us what firms have to do to become excellent in design (BMW) or to improve cooperation with suppliers (Toyota). Table 1.8 captures some of the key studies that have influenced our understanding.

This chapter so far has helped to illustrate the complex nature of innovation management and also identified some of the limitations of the various models and schools of thought. Specifically, these are:

- Variations on linear thinking continue to dominate models of innovation. Actually, most innovation models show innovation paths, representing a stage-gate type of activity, controlling the progress from idea to market introduction, rather than giving insight into the dynamics of actual innovation processes.
- Science is viewed primarily as technology orientated (physical sciences) and R&D is closely linked to manufacturing, causing insufficient attention to be paid to the behavioural sciences. As a consequence, service innovation is hardly addressed.
- The complex interactions between new technological capabilities and emerging societal needs are a vital part of the innovation process, but they are underexposed in current models.
- The role of the entrepreneur (individual or team) is not captured.
- Current innovation models are not embedded within the strategic thinking of the firm; they remain isolated entities.

Innovation needs to be viewed as a management process. We need to recognise that change is at the heart of it. And that change is caused by decisions that people make. The framework in Figure 1.9 attempts to capture the iterative nature of the network processes in innovation and represents this in the form of an endless innovation circle with interconnected cycles. This circular concept helps to show how the firm gathers information over time, how it uses technical *and* societal knowledge, and how it develops an attractive proposition. This is achieved through developing linkages and partnerships with those having the necessary capabilities ('open innovation'). In addition, the entrepreneur is positioned at the centre.

The framework in Figure 1.9 is referred to as the the 'cyclic innovation model' (CIM) (Berkhout *et al.*, 2010); a cross-disciplinary view of change processes (and their interactions) as they take place in an open innovation arena. Behavioural sciences and

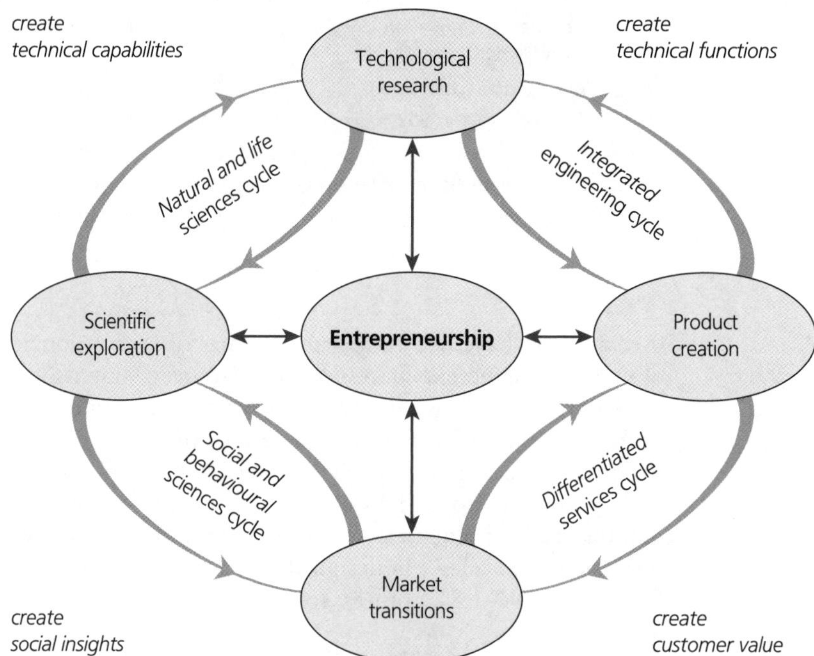

Figure 1.9 The innovation circle with interconnected cycles

Source: Berkhout *et al.* (2010).

engineering as well as natural sciences and markets are brought together in a coherent system of processes with four principal nodes that function as roundabouts. The combination of the involved changes leads to a wealth of business opportunities. Here, entrepreneurship plays a central role by making use of those opportunities. The message is that without the drive of entrepreneurs there is no innovation, and without innovation there is no new business. Figure 1.9 shows that the combination of change and entrepreneurship is the basis of new business.

Adopting this approach to the management of innovation should help firms as processes should not be forced into simple one-way pipelines, but rather be organised by interconnected cycles with feedforward and feedback connections: from linear to non-linear thinking. In that way, a dynamic network environment is created in which the social and behavioural sciences are linked to engineering, and where the natural and life sciences connect with market goals (Berkhout, 2000). This is what is captured in the proposed innovation framework. Supported by today's powerful communication technology, serial process management along a linear path is replaced by parallel networking along a largely self-organising circle. Vital decisions in innovation do not occur in the gates of a staged project management pipeline, but do occur on the innovation shop floor itself; or in the nodes of the cyclic networks. In my experience young people like to work in such an environment. Moreover, according to Salkowitz (2010), young entrepreneurs around the world are blending new technologies and next-generation thinking, building radically new kinds of organisations adapted to a flat and crowded world (*see* Illustration 1.6).

The cyclic innovation model is the result of a combination of analysis of theory and practical evidence, based on many years of experience within industries that work with scientists to develop valuable new products and services. Furthermore, evidence has been gathered from Delphi, a science-industry consortium which consists of a large number of international companies within the field of geo-energy (Berkhout *et al.*, 2010).

The most important feature of Figure 1.9 is that the model architecture is not a chain but a *circle*: innovations build on innovations. Ideas create new concepts, successes create new challenges, and failures create new insights. Note that new ideas may start anywhere in the circle, causing a wave that propagates clockwise and anti-clockwise through the circle. In an innovative society businesses are transparent and the speed of propagation along the circle is high, resulting in minimum travel time along the innovation path. Today, time is a crucial factor in innovation. Indeed, when it comes to managing the process within the firm the stage-gate approach dominates practice. This is because the project management advantages tend to outweigh the limitations it poses to the innovation process. This can be illustrated within Figure 1.9; here the central position in the innovation circle is frequently occupied by a manager, who adopts a stage-gate approach and culture, rather than an entrepreneur; having an entrepreneur in the centre enhances the innovation process.

New skills

The framework in Figure 1.9 underpins the way managers need to view the management of innovation. Many of the old traditional approaches to management need to change and new approaches need to be adopted. Increasingly, managers and those who work for them are no longer in the same location. Gone are the days when managers could supervise the hour-to-hour work of individuals. Often complex management relationships need to be developed because organisations are trying to produce complex products and services and do so across geographic boundaries. Cross-functional and cross-border task forces often need to be created. And managers have to manage without authority. In these circumstances, individual managers need to work with and influence people who are not their subordinates and over whom they have no formal authority. Frequently this means leadership must be shared across the team members. An important part of getting work done without authority is having an extensive network of relationships. In today's complex and virtual organisations, managers need information and support from a wide range of individuals. To summarise then, new skills are required in the following areas:

- virtual management;
- managing without authority;
- shared leadership;
- building extensive networks.

Pause for thought 

Surely all innovations start with an idea and end with a product; so does that not make it a linear process?

Innovation and new product development

Such thinking is similarly captured in the framework outlined in Figure 1.9. It stresses the importance of interaction and communication within and between functions and with the external environment. This networking structure allows lateral communication, helping managers and their staff unleash creativity. This framework emphasises the importance of informal and formal networking across all functions (Pittaway *et al.*, 2004).

This introduces a tension between the need for diversity, on the one hand, in order to generate novel linkages and associations, and the need for commonality, on the other, to facilitate effective internal communication.

The purpose of this book is to illustrate the interconnections of the subjects of innovation management and new product development. Indeed, some may argue they are two sides of the same coin. By directly linking together these two significant areas of management the clear connections and overlaps between the subjects can be more fully explored and understood.

It is hoped that this framework will help to provide readers with a visual reminder of how one can view the innovation process that needs to be managed by firms. The industry and products and services will determine the precise requirements necessary. It is a dynamic process and the framework tries to emphasise this. It is also a complex process and this helps to simplify it to enable further study. Very often product innovation is viewed from a purely marketing perspective with little, if any, consideration of the R&D function and the difficulties of managing science and technology. Likewise, many manufacturing and technology approaches to product innovation have previously not taken sufficient notice of the needs of the customer. Into this mix we must not forget the role played by the entrepreneur in visioning the future.

Case study

The success of the iPod and iPhone raises the licensing question for Apple . . . again

Introduction

This case study explores the rise of the Apple Corporation. The Apple iPod is one of the most successful new product launches of recent years, transforming the way the public listens to music, with huge ramifications for major record labels. More than 100 million iPod's have been sold since its launch in November 2001. Mobile phones have long been regarded as the most credible challenger to MP3 players and iPods. The launch of digital download services via mobile phones illustrates the dramatic speed of convergence between the telecoms and media industries, which has ushered in a new era of growth for smart phones. Users are willing to pay more for additional services and many analysts predict that mobile phone handsets will eventually emerge as the dominant technology of the age, combining personal organisers, digital music players and games consoles in a single device. Indeed, Microsoft founder Bill Gates predicted that mobile phones would supersede the iPod as the favoured way of listening to digital music. Apple has responded to this challenge by launching the iPhone, but will this be enough. Apple faces tough competition from not only Microsoft, but also Blackberry, Google and Nokia.

Apple and the iPod

For those not yet fully plugged into digital music listening, MP3 is an acronym for MPEG layer 3, which is a compressed audio format. A compression ratio of up to 12 to 1 compression is possible, which produces high sound quality. Layer 3 is one of three coding schemes (layer 1, layer 2 and layer 3) for the compression of audio signals. It reduces the amount of data required to represent audio, yet still sound like a faithful reproduction of the original uncompressed audio to most listeners. It was invented by a team of German engineers of the Fraunhofer Society, and it became an ISO/IEC standard in 1991. This format of compression facilitates the transfer of audio files via the internet and storage in portable players, such as the iPod, and digital audio servers.

The remarkable success of the iPod music player has propelled Apple back into the FT100 ranking of global companies. This marks a return of the technology company to the ranks of the world's top companies after falling out of the list in 2001. Its shares have risen dramatically in the past two years, valuing the company at $220 billion (£150 billion), finally surpassing its great rival Microsoft in 2010. Apple, founded (in 1975) 35 years ago by Steven Jobs, who is now chief executive, has seen its fortunes ebb and flow. Mr Jobs has achieved a transformation since his return to the company in 1997 after leaving some 10 years earlier following a dispute with John Sculley, who was then chief executive (Coggan, 2005).

Historically Apple is a computer company and its core customer base today is only about 10 million active users; in a world of 400 million Windows users. Apple has always understood that its core franchise was very closely connected to the core computer franchise. Consumer electronics products, for example, are sold through different channels and they have different product life cycles. Making the transition has been extremely hard. What made the iPod transition easier is that the iPod began as a PC peripheral, even though it is ultimately a consumer electronics product. Eventually, Apple recognised that the iPod could not be limited to the Mac and it

Source: A. Harrison/Pearson Education Ltd

Source: Pearson Education Ltd/Photodisc

had to become a PC peripheral as well. The move into the PC market enabled Apple to access a much broader market than its core customer base. Indeed sales of the iPod started sluggishly as sales were directed initially towards a relatively small audience of Macintosh users, and even when a PC version of the iPod was released, its FireWire-only design limited its appeal to mainstream PC users.

Apple's iTune Music Store website

Apple's success with its iPod is helped by its iTune Music Store website (www.Apple.com/itunes), which offers consumers the ability to digitise all their CDs as well as download new music at 79p per song. This site has sold over 6 billion songs since its launch in April 2003, bringing considerable revenue to Apple (Schonfeld, 2009). However, downloads from the iTunes Music Store will only play on Apple's iPods (Webb, 2007). The site is universally regarded as being simple and fun; it also offers a legal way to add music to your library. To import songs into iTunes, you simply insert a CD into your computer and click 'Import CD'. iTunes also compresses and stores music in AAC – a format that builds upon state-of-the-art audio technology from Dolby Labs. It also offers users the ability to select different audio formats. iTunes lets you convert music to MP3 at high bit-rate at no extra charge. Using AAC or MP3, you can store more than 100 songs in the same amount of space as a single CD. iTunes also supports the Apple Lossless format, which gives you CD-quality audio in about half the storage space.

The rise and fall and rise of Apple

Apple computers began in 1977 when Steven Wozniak and Steven Jobs designed and offered the Apple I to the personal computer field. It was designed over a period of years, and was only built in printed circuit-board form. It debuted in April 1976 at the Homebrew Computer Club in Palo Alto, but few took it seriously. Continual product improvements and wider technological developments including microprocessor improvements led to the launch of the Apple Macintosh personal computer in 1984.

The Macintosh computer was different because it used a mouse driven operating system; all other PCs used the keyboard driven system known as MS DOS (Microsoft disc operating system). Early in the 1980s Microsoft licensed its operating system to all PC manufacturers, but Apple decided against this approach, opting instead to stay in control of its system. The 1980s was a period of dramatic growth for personal computers as virtually every office and home began to buy into the PC world. Slowly Microsoft became the market leader, not because its technology was better, but largely because its system became the dominant standard. As people bought PCs, so with it they would buy the operating system: MS Windows; hence it became the de-facto dominant standard. The Apple operating system was only available if you bought an Apple PC. Consequently Apple's market share plummeted. This was also the time when Steven Jobs quit Apple after disagreements with other members of the board. Interestingly in 1986 Steven Jobs became involved in another new venture, Pixar Animation Studios (see Illustration 1.7). By the mid-1990s Apple had grown to a $12 billion company, twice the size of Microsoft; but Microsoft was powering ahead on the back of the launch of Windows and it would soon become the colossus firm it is today (Schofield, 2005; 2009).

In 1993 Apple launched the Newton, its first completely new product in many years. Indeed, it represented Apple's entry into (and perhaps creation of) an entirely new market: personal digital assistants (PDAs). The PDA market was barely present when the Newton was released, but other companies were working on similar devices. The Newton Message Pad featured a variety of personal-organisation applications, such as an address book, a calendar and notes, along with communications capabilities such as faxing and email. It featured a pen-based

Illustration 1.7

Pixar Animation Studios

Pixar Animation Studios eventually became the Academy Award winning computer animation pioneer. The northern California studio has created six of the most successful and beloved animated films of all time: *Toy Story* (1995); *A Bug's Life* (1998); *Toy Story 2* (1999); *Monsters, Inc.* (2001); *Finding Nemo* (2003); and *The Incredibles* (2004). Pixar's six films have earned more than $3 billion at the worldwide box office to date. *Toy Story 3* is launched in 2010.

interface, which used a word-based, trainable handwriting recognition engine. Unfortunately this engine had been developed by a third party, and was notoriously difficult to use and was partly responsible for the product's failure.

In the mid-1990s Apple's future in the computer technology industry looked bleak, with a diversified product portfolio and a low market share within the PC market of only 3 per cent. It was also building a portfolio of product failures including the Apple Pipin (a games consol). Many were therefore surprised when Steven Jobs returned to the company as chief executive in 1997. He quickly set about culling many product lines and much of its operations and decided to focus on only a few products including the new looking iMac. This coincided with the economic boom in the late 1990s and allowed Apple to generate cash very quickly. This provided revenue for the development of the iPod, which was launched in 2003 (*see* Figure 1.10).

iPod dominates MP3 market, but competition is fierce

Since 2003 the spectacular growth of Apple's iconic digital music player sent the company's share price soaring. The challenge for Apple, however, is how to maintain the success of the iPod, especially with its indirect impact on sales of its PCs: most notably the iMac and its Notebook range of portable PCs, including the Mac Air laptop. Apple could continue to cut prices, but this would mean smaller margins. The launch of the iPhone, to capitalise on the convergence

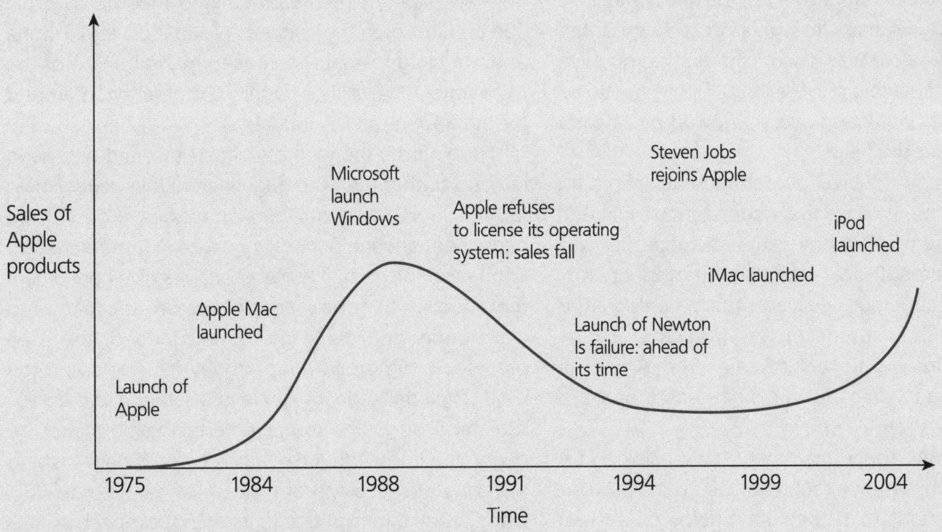

Figure 1.10 The rise and fall and rise of Apple

of technologies between mobibe phones and media, has helped boost growth of the firm. In actual fact Apple began fighting the competition in the MP3 market by cutting prices and improving the product. In 2005 it launched lower-priced versions of its best selling iPod digital music player, the Shuffle, with significantly improved battery performance, plus an ultra thin iPod Nano. Later came the iPod Touch with its impressive touch screen interface (the precursor to the iPhone). However, at the same time a potential big threat in the form of Sony Electronics announced a new, low-price, high-performance digital music player under its Walkman brand. Since October 2001, when Apple first launched its iPod, it has slowly reduced the price and improved the performance of the product. The design and styling have significantly contributed to Apple's success with its 50 per cent market share for MP3 players. Competitors including Dell, Creative Technologies and Rio have launched many rival players, most cheaper and offering better battery performance. Yet it seems the iPod has an iconic status that is proving difficult to attack.

iPod patent battles

Despite the success of the iPod and iPhone Apple continues to fend off challenges to the propriety of its technology. In August 2005 Creative Technology, the Singapore maker of the Zen digital music player, suggested it was considering a legal battle with several digital music manufactures including Apple Computer, alleging that the US company's popular iPod and iPod mini music players use Creative's recently patented technology. Creative was one of the first companies to market digital music players in 2000, but the company's devices have been overshadowed by Apple's popular iPod product line.

Apple has extensive experience of fighting patent infringement cases and understands that such legal battles can take many years to settle. Its own battle with Microsoft over infringement of its operating system technology was eventually settled after eight years without a satisfactory outcome. It may be better for Creative to seek royalties from Apple, as patent cases can drag out for many years and are highly unpredictable.

More recently Apple has been fighting Nokia in a battle over mobile phone technologies. Nokia is suing Apple for violations of 10 patents it holds on several wireless technologies. The patents in question, Nokia says, are fundamental to making devices like the iPhone compatible with certain wireless network standards on which the iPhone operates around the world, as well as wireless LAN technologies, which means Wi-Fi and UMTS. Apple countersued Nokia in January 2010, claiming that Nokia phones infringe on 13 Apple patents. Nokia responed by asking that the countersuit be dismissed. Experts have suggested Nokia is probably seeking royalty payments from iPhone (and now iPad) sales, rather than a full injunction. This would afford Nokia a 1–2 per cent cut from each sale.

The rise of Apple as a lifestyle brand

'iMac', 'iPod', 'iPhone', 'iPad' have all been very successful products for Apple. The impact has been more than simply sales and profits. At the centre of Apple's recent success is the emergence of Apple as a lifestyle brand rather than as a technology company. Apple is very keen, for instance, to reinforce its California heritage (the person credited with designing the iPod is Johnathan Ive, a graduate from Newcastle Polytechnic and now Apple's vice president for design). Every iPod comes with the words 'Designed in California'. Also, it may have been a subtle move, but remaining friendly – not just user-friendly but friendly, as opposed to the unfriendly giant Microsoft – may be helping to increase the brand's appeal. It may be that people at last have become tired of Microsoft and efficiency and effectiveness and now are searching for something different. If Apple can capitalise on the success of the iPod and iPhone and translate this into increased market share of the PC market, this will truly signify a dramatic turnaround for the firm in the PC industry.

To reinforce the idea of a lifestyle brand one need look no further than the huge increase in accessories for the iPod. It seems cool-conscious iPod buyers cannot get enough of carrying cases, adaptors, microphones or software; these accessories give consumers the edge as they take their iPods on the road, into classrooms and on to the street. Indeed, the road provides a big growth opportunity for Apple and the iPod. The challenge for Apple is whether it can establish the iPod in the in-car entertainment market by becoming the product of choice for those wishing to move effortlessly from *'home-to-car-to-sidewalk'* without any interruptions to listening, simply by plugging and unplugging your digital music player.

Apps

App is short for application software. iPhone apps are applications for the Apple iPhone. Most iPhone apps are meant for the newer iPhone 3G model and will also work on the most recent versions of the iPod Touch. Free or purchased Apps can be downloaded from the iTunes music store to an iPhone or iPod Touch. When the new app is downloaded, it will place an icon on the screen of an iPhone or iPod Touch, so you can access the app directly by touching the icon on the screen. Accessing applications this way eliminates the step of having to use the web browser. There are thousands of apps for the iPhone and iPod Touch. Categories of apps include Business, Games, Entertainment, Sports, Education, Medical, Fitness, News, Travel, Photography, etc. There are both paid and free app categories.

In March 2010 Apple launched its iPad. This is essentially a combination of a smartphone and a laptop. Many analysts and commentators argued that the product offered nothing new and that it was too big as a phone and too small as a laptop. Yet, two months after its launch Apple announced that sales of its iPad had reached 2 million units. The touchscreen tablet has been more successful than experts predicted. This may partly reflect the power of the Apple brand and its successful new product launch strategy.

The licensing question returns to haunt Apple

Since Apple launched the iPod in 2001 and the iPhone in 2007, doubters have said it was only a matter of time before Microsoft, Nokia or Google developed a cheaper industry-standard music player that would relegate Apple to the fringes of the market; just like Microsoft did with Windows. Few forget how Apple's refusal to license its technology contributed to its demise in the personal computer market and critics say the company appears determined to make the same mistake again. A key issue for Apple is whether it can sustain the huge premiums that it earns with the iPod and iPhone when Dell, Google, Nokia and others begin entering the market with much lower priced product offerings. Also, Apple is running into the same challenge as it experienced with the Mac of selling a proprietary solution. That is, music on the iPod cannot play on non-Apple devices.

Essentially, just like the mid-1980s, there is a standards war; just as there was between VHS and Betamax. There is a proprietary standard with iTunes, and there will be alternative standards pushed by Microsoft, Real Networks, and others. One can still detect an Apple orientated approach to growth rather than one driven by absolute growth. For example, iTunes, was initially available only on the Mac. This was meant to drive Macintosh sales, and then six or nine months later Apple would bring out a Windows version. The problem is that it gave competitors six to nine months to bring out Window's products, which creates a more competitive environment. Some analysts argue that if Apple had really been thinking in terms of breaking away from Apple users and its heritage, it would have started out on Windows and come to Macintosh later like everybody else in the world. But, critics argue that is not the way Apple thinks.

There are clearly advantages when developing a new product to target the 400 million market and then target the total Apple user and ex-user market of 25 million. But there are also advantages of doing it the Apple way.

If Apple does not open itself up and make sure that it becomes the dominant standard, it could end up becoming again the niche product, which makes it a little bit less attractive for users. Apple may be able to learn from Sony's experiences, for although Sony lost the VCR industry standards battle it did win huge market shares with its Walkman. Sony drove the Walkman into a mass audience by drastically bringing down the price. Apple may be able to do this successfully with the iPod, but it has never been very good at very high volume manufacturing at very low costs. However, it may be that the iPod is becoming the dominant platform in MP3 players just as Microsoft managed with its Windows operating system. It is less clear though that the iPhone is equally becoming the dominant standard in the smartphone market.

The key issue here is whether Apple can do what Microsoft did in the 1980s and 1990s and get people to pay it large amounts of cash via licensing. Apple could license its technology to other manufacturers as Microsoft did with its DOS and later Windows operating systems. Every mobile phone or MP3 player that is sold would potentially result in a licensing fee to Apple, in the same way as Microsoft receives a royalty for every PC, laptop, notebook and netbook that is sold with Windows installed. This could be a

→

serious windfall. Apple would have to change strategy and decide to license its iPod/iPhone technology to the 'masses' and undo its hardware exclusivity. If Apple adopted this approach it is likely that it would make up the money in its walled garden of iTunes and applications and Apple would really become the Microsoft of the next decade. However, this looks unlikely.

More significantly, new smart phones are emerging based on the Google open source Android operating system. Worryingly for Apple, in terms of technical performance, these look superior. Moreover, some of these products are much cheaper than the iPhone. For example, Blackberry and its RIM technology are gaining market share from Apple, and Blackberries are three times cheaper! If one peers into the future, and recognising what we know from past experience, creativity is likely to emerge from the open source Android operating system, particularly as its use becomes more widespread. For Apple it may be that in seeking control it may be stifling creativity and innovation.

Troubles ahead?

The inexorable shift from separate devices to a single handheld device appears to be gathering momentum (see Figure 1.11). In particular third-generation (3G) smartphones offer the capability to download high-speed data over the airwaves including television pictures. Not surprisingly, Google, Blackberry, Nokia and others are entering the market with smartphones. Apple's iPod sales have grown every year since its 2001 launch. But during 2009 Apple sold fewer iPods than the previous year. This marks the first time that iPod sales have dropped year-over-year. Sales of the iPod have been replaced by sales of the iPhone and iPod touch, which look as if they may be the future of the iPod product line. Apple expects sales of its traditional MP3 players to decline over time as it cannibalises sales for the iPod touch and the iPhone. Nonetheless, the products still perform a useful function as an introduction to the iPod line for first-time buyers.

An area of criticism levelled against Apple Inc. that has also received considerable media coverage is the issue of excessive secrecy and obsessive control exerted by Apple on its suppliers. One of these suppliers is Foxconn, the world's biggest contract maker of IT goods including the iPhone. It is far less well known than the brands it assembles, but it is one of Taiwan's largest companies. Reuters news agency reported in 2010 that Apple goes to 'extreme lengths' to protect even the smallest details of its new products under development (Pomfret and Soh, 2010). At Foxconn's assembly plant in Longhua, South China, workers swipe security cards at the gate and guards check the occupants of each vehicle with fingerprint recognition scanners. It resembles a fortress – so much for open innovation! Many of Apple's finished gadgets, from iPods to iPads, are assembled at industrial compounds like the one in Longhua. Some of Apples's tactics seem like they have emerged from a James Bond film: information is assiduously

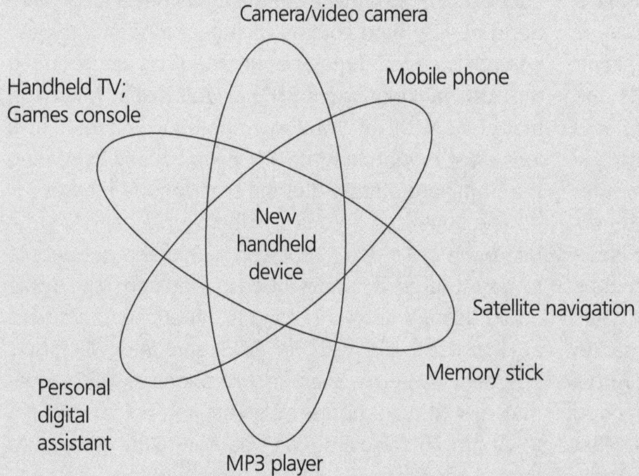

Figure 1.11 The future handheld device will probably incorporate many separate devices

guarded and handed out only on a need-to-know basis; employees suspected of leaks may be investigated by the contractor; and the company makes it clear that it will not hesitate to sue if secrets are spilled. To try to control information, Apple will give contract manufacturers different products, just to try them out. That way, the source of any leaks becomes immediately obvious.

Apple's obsession with secrecy is the stuff of legend in Silicon Valley. Over the years, it has fired executives over leaks and sued bloggers to stop trade secrets from being exposed. Apple also helps keep its components out of the mainstream by insisting on custom designs rather than off-the-shelf parts – a practice that leaves many suppliers frustrated. Not surprisingly, landing a contract with Apple will always include a confidentiality clause. And they usually come with stiff penalties in the event that a breach is discovered. Such agreements often come on top of unannounced checks by Apple officials to maintain standards. However, the difficulty lies in proving the source of a leak. In the absence of solid evidence, the most Apple can do is to switch suppliers once the contract runs out. At times all of this secrecy seems to run out of control. In a case that made global headlines, a Foxconn employee in China was believed to have jumped to his death after being interrogated by his employer. According to local press reports, he was under suspicion of taking an iPhone prototype – to which he had access – out of the factory (Watts, 2010).

Conclusions

The success of the Apple iPod, and to a lesser extent the iPhone, has been remarkable by any measure. It has surprised Apple's competitors but, moreover, it has surprised market analysts and investors, who had largely believed Apple was a niche player in the computer world. To be successful in the mainstream mass market is unusual for Apple. Many people recognise the Apple brand, but far fewer buy its products. Profit margins are small for its range of PCs and laptops; this is why it is difficult for Apple to produce any revenue from the iMac despite its success. Indeed, it is the iPod that has delivered the cash for Apple.

Apple has been here before, 20 years ago in fact. The success of the Apple Mac in 1984 delivered piles of cash for Apple and a rising market share of the growing PC market, yet it was Microsoft that emerged the winner largely because it licensed its operating system to all PC manufacturers, whereas Apple decided against this approach, opting instead to stay in control of its system. Microsoft has gone on to be the dominant software company in the world.

In 2010 Apple's iPod/iPod Touch is the leading digital music player, but should it license its successful technology? There are certainly lots of mobile phone handset manufacturers that would like to incorporate iPod/iPhone technology into their products. And there are many electronic companies such as Sony, Sharp, Cannon and others that would be able to develop digital music players using iPod technology. It may be that Apple feels the technology, in this case the software, is an integral part of the physical product and that to separate the aesthetics of the music player/phone from the software would damage the brand, leading to a commoditisation of the digital music player market and an overall decline in the iPod and iPhone. Furthermore, margins are relatively good for Apple and licensing the technology would surely mean increased competition and reduced margins.

Apple, once best known for its Macintosh computers, and now known for its iPod, iPhone and its iTune online Music Store is as last making up for its lack of market gains in the highly competitive PC market. It is necessary to remind students of business that ultimately this is about money and Apple was twice the size of Microsoft in 1992 and since then has largely failed to deliver growth for its shareholders. It is only in the past few years that Apple has started to repay investors, reaching an equivalent market value of Microsoft in 2010. Fortunes change quickly in technology intensive industries, but they change even quicker in the world of fashion.

Sources: Coggan, P. (2005) iPod's popularity fires Apple back into FT500 ranks, *Financial Times*, 11 June; Durman, P. (2005) A second bite of Apple, *Sunday Times*, Business, 25 September, p. 5; Inman, P. (2005) Fraudsters use iPods to steal company information, *Guardian*, 14 June; Morrison, S. (2005) Wall St wants Apple to raise iPod volume, FT.com, 12 July; Schofield, J. (2005) Microsoft gets creative to stave off its midlife crisis, *Technology Guardian*, 29 September, p. 9; Webb, A. (2007) The end of the road for DRM, *Technology Guardian*, 8 February, p. 10; Pomfret, J. and Soh, K. (2010) For Apple suppliers loose lips can sink contracts, Reuters, 17 February; Watts, J. (2010) iPhone factory offers pay rises and suicide nets as fears grow over spate of deaths, *Guardian*, 29 May, p. 30; Schonfeld, E. (2009) iTunes Sells 6 Billion Songs, And Other Fun Stats, from The Philnote, Techcrunch, http://techcrunch.com, 6 January.

→

Questions

1. Explain how the iPod is helping Apple achieve increased sales of its range of Mac personal computers.
2. What are the potential benefits and limitations of licensing the iPod software to other MP3 manufacturers?
3. With sales of the iPod falling and Apple facing fierce competition from all quarters such as Sony, Dell and other electronics firms as well as mobile phone makers who are incorporating MP3 players into their devices, can the iPod survive?
4. If Open Innovation has been so successful for Procter & Gamble and others, why is Apple not adopting this model of innovation?
5. Can Apple continue to be successful in the long term by adopting a 'BMW strategy' (BMW strategy is to target high-premium segments) for its iPod, iPhone and iPad?
6. What are the advantages and disadvantages of the Apple approach to launching a new product at Apple users first and then the larger Microsoft Windows user audience second?
7. Discuss whether Apple's demands for secrecy from its suppliers may have gone too far.

Chapter summary

This initial chapter has sought to introduce the subject of innovation management and place it in context with the theory of economic growth. One can quickly become ensnarled in stale academic debates of semantics if innovation is viewed as a single event, hence the importance of viewing it as a process. The chapter has also stressed the importance of understanding how firms manage innovation and how this can be better achieved by adopting a management perspective.

The level of understanding of the subject of innovation has improved significantly over the past half century and during that time a variety of models of innovation have emerged. The strengths and weaknesses of these were examined and a conceptual framework was presented that stressed the linkages and overlaps between internal departments and external organisations.

Discussion questions

1. Explain why it is necessary to view innovation as a management process.
2. What is wrong with the popular view of innovation in which eccentric scientists develop new products?
3. How does an 'Open Innovation' approach help firms?
4. What is the difference between an unsuccessful innovation and an invention?
5. To what extent do you agree with the controversial view presented by the chairman of Sony?

6 Show how the three forces shaping the twenty-first century, according to Salkowitz (2010) – youth, entrepreneurship and ICT – are captured in the cyclical model of innovation.

7 Explain Sergey Brin's (co-founder of Google) comment that coming up with an idea is easy, but innovation is difficult.

Key words and phrases

Economic growth *6*
Organisational architecture *9*
Entrepreneurship *9*
Invention *15*
Innovation as a management process *15*
Models of innovation *20*
Resource-based theory of the firm *21*
Open innovation *25*
Discontinuous innovation *27*

References

Abernathy, W.J. and Utterback, J. (1978) 'Patterns of industrial innovation', in Tushman, M.L. and Moore, W.L. *Readings in the Management of Innovation*, HarperCollins, New York, 97–108.

Berkhout, A.J. (2000) *The Dynamic Role of Knowledge in Innovation. An Integrated Framework of Cyclic Networks for the Assessment of Technological Change and Sustainable Growth*, Delft University Press, Delft, The Netherlands, 2000.

Berkhout, A.J., Hartmann, D. and Trott, P. (2010) Connecting technological capabilities with market needs using a cyclic innovation model, *R&D Management*, Vol. 40, No. 5, 474–90.

BSI (2008) *Design Management Systems*, Guides to Managing Innovation, British Standards Institute, London.

Burns, T. and Stalker, G.M. (1961) *The Management of Innovation*, Tavistock, London.

Business Week (2006) The world's most innovative firms, 24 April.

Carter, C.F. and Williams, B.R. (1957) The characteristics of technically progressive firms, *Journal of Industrial Economics*, March, 87–104.

Chandler, A.D. (1962) *Strategy and Structure: Chapters in the History of American Industrial Enterprise*, MIT Press, Cambridge, MA.

Chesbrough, H. (2003) *Open Innovation: The new imperative for creating and profiting from technology*, Harvard Business School Press, Boston, MA.

Christensen, C.M. (2003) *The Innovator's Dilemma: When New Technologies Cause Great Firms to Fail*, 3rd edn, HBS Press, Cambridge, MA.

Christensen, C. M. and Raynor, M.E. (2003) *Six Keys to Creating New-Growth Businesses*, Harvard Business School Press, Boston, MA.

Cohen, W.M. and Levinthal, D.A. (1990) A new perspective on learning and innovation, *Administrative Science Quarterly*, Vol. 35, No. 1, 128–52.

Conner, K.R. and Prahalad, C.K. (1996) A resource-based theory of the firm: knowledge versus opportunism, *Organisation Science*, Vol. 7, No. 5, 477–501.

Cooper, R. (1994) Third generation new product processes, *Journal of Product Innovation Management*, Vol. 11, No. 1, 3–14.

Cullen, B. (2003) *It's a long way from penny apples*, Coronet, London.

Cyert, R.M. and March, J.G. (1963) *A Behavioural Theory of the Firm*, Prentice-Hall, Englewood Cliffs, NJ.

Delbridge, R. and Mariotti, F. (2009) *Reaching for radical innovation: How motorsport companies harness network diversity for discontinuous innovation*, Advanced Institute of Management Research (AIM), London.

Dodgson, M., Gann, D. and Salter, A. (2005) *Think, Play, Do*, Oxford University Press, Oxford.

Domar, D. (1946) Capital expansion, rate of growth and employment, *Econometra*, Vol. 14, 137–47.

Eisenhardt, K.M. and Martin, J.A. (2000) 'The knowledge-based economy: from the economics of knowledge to the learning economy', in Foray, D. and Lundvall, B.-A. (eds) *Employment and Growth in the Knowledge-Based Economy*, OECD, Paris.

Fagerberg, J. and Verspagen, B. (2009) Innovation studies – The emerging structure of a new scientific field, *Research Policy*, Vol. 38, No. 2, 218–33.

Freeman, C. (1982) *The Economics of Industrial Innovation*, 2nd edn, Frances Pinter, London.

Galbraith, J.R. (1982) Designing the innovative organisation, *Organisational Dynamics*, Winter, 3–24.

Grant, R.M. (1996) Towards a knowledge-based theory of the firm, *Strategic Management Journal*, Summer Special Issue, Vol. 17, 109–22.

Guardian (2009) Interview with Technology Guardian, 18 June, p. 1.

Hamel, G. and Prahalad, C.K. (1994) Competing for the future, *Harvard Business Review*, Vol. 72, No. 4, 122–8.

Hargadon, A. and Douglas, Y. (2001) When innovations meet institutions: Edison and the design of the electric light, *Administrative Science Quarterly*, Vol. 46, 476–501.

Harrod, R.F. (1949) An essay in dynamic theory, *Economic Journal*, Vol. 49, No. 1, 277–93.

Henderson, R. and Clark, K. (1990) Architectural innovation: the reconfiguration of existing product and the failure of established firms, *Administrative Science Quarterly*, Vol. 35, 9–30.

Hutton, W. (1995) *The State We're In*, Jonathan Cape, London.

Isenson, R. (1968) 'Technology in retrospect and critical events in science' (Project Traces), Illinois Institute of Technology/National Science Foundation, Chicago, IL.

Kondratieff, N.D. (1935/51) 'The long waves in economic life', *Review of Economic Statistics*, Vol. 17, 6–105 (1935), reprinted in Haberler, G. (ed.) *Readings in Business Cycle Theory*, Richard D. Irwin, Homewood, IL (1951).

Langrish, J., Gibbons, M., Evans, W.G. and Jevons, F.R. (1972) *Wealth from Knowledge*, Macmillan, London.

Lefever, D.B. (1992) 'Technology transfer and the role of intermediaries', PhD thesis, INTA, Cranfield Institute of Technology.

Leifer, R., Colarelli O'Connor, G. and Peters, L.S. (2000) *Radical Innovation*, Harvard Business School Press, Boston, MA.

Linton, J. (2009) De-babelizing the language of innovation, *Technovation*, Vol. 29, No. 11, 729–37.

Morita, A. (1992) 'S' does not equal 'T' and 'T' does not equal 'I', paper presented at the Royal Society, February 1992.

Murray, S. (2003) 'Innovation: A British talent for ingenuity and application', www.ft.com, 22 April.

Myers, S. and Marquis, D.G. (1969) 'Successful industrial innovation: a study of factors underlying innovation in selected firms', National Science Foundation, NSF 69–17, Washington, DC.

Nelson, R.R. and Winter, S. (1982) *An Evolutionary Theory of Economic Change*, Harvard University Press, Boston, MA.

Nonaka, I. (1991) The knowledge creating company, *Harvard Business Review*, November–December, 96–104.

Oxford English Dictionary (2005) Oxford University Press, London.

Patel, P. and Pavitt, K. (2000) 'How technological competencies help define the core (not the boundaries) of the firm', in Dosi, G., Nelson, R. and Winter, S.G. (eds) *The Nature and Dynamics of Organisational Capabilities*, Oxford University Press, Oxford, 313–33.

Pavitt, K. (1990) What we know about the strategic management of technology, *California Management Review*, Vol. 32, No. 3, 17–26.

Penrose, E.T. (1959) *The Theory of the Growth of the Firm*, Wiley, New York.

Pittaway, L., Robertson, M., Munir, K., Denyer, D. and Neely, A. (2004) Networking and innovation: a systematic review of the evidence, *International Journal of Management Reviews*, Vol. 5/6, Nos 3 and 4, 137–68.

Porter, M.E. (1980) *Competitive Strategy*, The Free Press, New York.

Porter, M.E. (1985) *Competitive Strategy*, Harvard University Press, Boston, MA.

Prahalad, C.K. and Hamel, G. (1990) The core competence of the corporation, *Harvard Business Review*, Vol. 68, No. 3, 79–91.

Rogers, E. and Shoemaker, R. (1972) *Communications of Innovations*, Free Press, New York.

Rothwell, R. (1992) Successful industrial innovation: critical factors for the 1990s, *R&D Management*, Vol. 22, No. 3, 221–39.

Rothwell, R. and Zegveld, W. (1985) *Reindustrialisation and Technology*, Longman, London.

Rothwell, R., Freeman, C., Horlsey, A., Jervis, V.T.P., Robertson, A.B. and Townsend, J. (1974) SAPPHO updated: Project SAPPHO phase II, *Research Policy*, Vol. 3, 258–91.

Salkowitz, R. (2010) *Young World Rising: How youth technology and entrepreneurship are changing the world from the bottom up*, John Wiley & Sons, NJ.

Schrange, M. (2000) *Serious Play – How the world's best companies stimulate to innovate*, Harvard Business School Press, Boston, MA.

Schumpeter, J.A. (1934) *The Theory of Economic Development*, Harvard University Press, Boston, MA.

Schumpeter, J.A. (1939) *Business Cycles*, McGraw-Hill, New York.

Schumpeter, J.A. (1942) *Capitalism, Socialism and Democracy*, Allen & Unwin, London.

Simon, H. (1957) *Administrative Behaviour*, Free Press, New York.

Slater, S.F. and Narver, J. (1994) Does competitive environment moderate the market orientation performance relationship? *Journal of Marketing*, Vol. 58 (January), 46–55.

Stevenson, H.H. and Amabile, T.M. (1999) 'Entrepreneurial Management: In Pursuit of Opportunity', in McCraw, T.K. and Cruikshank, J.L. (eds) *The Intellectual Venture Capitalist: John H. McArthur and the Work of the Harvard Business School, 1980–1995*, Harvard Business School Press, Boston, MA.

Thomke, S.H. (2003) *Experimentation Matters: Unlocking the potential of new technologies for innovation*, Harvard Business School Press, Boston, MA.

Trott, P. (1998) Growing businesses by generating genuine business opportunities, *Journal of Applied Management Studies*, Vol. 7, No. 4, 211–22.

Utterback, J. (1994) *Mastering the Dynamics of Innovation*, Harvard Business School Press, Boston, MA.

Van de Ven, A.H. (1989) *The Innovation Journey*, Oxford University Press, New York.

van der Panne, G. van Beers, C. and Kleinknecht, A. (2003) Success and failure of innovation: A review of the literature, *International Journal of Innovation Management*, Vol. 7, No. 3, 309–38.

von Hippel, E. (1978) Users as innovators, *Technology Review*, Vol. 80, No. 3, 30–4.

von Hippel, E. (2005) *Democratizing Innovation*, MIT Press, Cambridge, MA.

Wernerfelt, B. (1984) A resource based view of the firm, *Strategic Management Journal*, Vol. 5, No. 2, 171–80.

Wernerfelt, B. (1995) The resource-based view of the firm: ten years after, *Strategic Management Journal*, Vol. 16, No. 3, 171–4.

Wheelwright, S. and Clark, K. (1992) *Revolutionising Product Development*, The Free Press, New York.

Woodward, J. (1965) *Industrial Organisation: Theory and Practice*, 2nd edn, Oxford University Press, Oxford.

Further reading

For a more detailed review of the innovation management literature, the following develop many of the issues raised in this chapter:

Adams, R., Bessant, J. and Phelps, R. (2006) Innovation management measurement: A review, *International Journal of Management Reviews*, Vol. 8, No. 1, 21–47.

Berkhout, A.J., Hartmann, D. and Trott, P. (2010) Connecting technological capabilities with market needs using a cyclic innovation model, *R&D Management*, Vol. 40, No. 5, 474–90.

Evans, H. (2005) The Eureka Myth, *Harvard Business Review*, 83, June, 18–20.

Linton, J. (2009) De-babelizing the language of innovation, *Technovation*, Vol. 29, No. 11, 729–37.

Salkowitz, R. *Young World Rising: How youth technology and entrepreneurship are changing the world from the bottom up*, John Wiley & Sons, NJ.

Shavinina, L.V. (ed.) (2003) *The International Handbook on Innovation*, Elsevier, Oxford.

Tidd, J., Bessant, J. and Pavitt, K. (2009) *Managing Innovation*, 4th edn, John Wiley & Sons, Chichester.

Chapter 2
Economics and market adoption

Introduction

This chapter explores the wider context in which the process of innovation occurs and also explores how national governments can help firms. The national systems of innovation have for many years been exploring what factors influence a nation's ability to undertake innovation. The United States, in particular, is frequently cited as a good example of a nation where the necessary conditions for innovation to flourish are in place. This includes both tangible and intangible features, including, on the one hand, economic, social and political institutions and, on the other, the way in which knowledge evolves over time through developing interactions and networks. This chapter examines how these influence innovation.

The role of the market within the wider context of innovation is ever-present; hence this chapter explores this key challenge within innovation. The relationship between new technology and the market is examined within the diffusion of innovations and market adoption.

The case study at the end of this chapter tells the story of how three university students had an idea for a folding shipping container and went about building a business. One of the key problems they faced was how to get the industry to adopt a new container.

Chapter contents

Learning objectives

When you have completed this chapter you will be able to:

- understand the wider context of innovation and the key influences;
- recognise that innovation cannot be separated from its local and national context and from political and social processes;
- understand that the role of national states considerably influences innovation;
- identify the structures and activities that the state uses to facilitate innovation;
- recognise the role marketing plays in the early stages of product innovation;
- explain how market vision helps the innovation process; and
- understand how the pattern of consumption influences the likely success or failure of a new product.

Innovation in its wider context

According to many, the process of innovation is the main engine of (continued) economic growth. As far back as 1943 Joseph Schumpeter (in what is known as Schumpeterian theory) emphasised that:

> *the fundamental impulse that sets and keeps the capitalist engine in motion comes from the new consumers' goods, the new methods of production or transportation, the new markets, the new forces of industrial organisation that capitalist enterprise creates.*
> (1943: 10)

However, such potential to create new products, processes, markets or organisations are path-dependent in the sense that there are certain nations and locations which seem to have acquired that capability over time, for innovation relies upon the accumulation and development of a wide variety of relevant knowledge (Dicken, 1998).

The view that much needs to be in place for innovation to occur and that there is a significant role for the state is confirmed by Alfred Marshall, whose ideas were responsible for the rebuilding of Europe after the Second World War. He commented on both the tangible and intangible aspects of the Industrial Revolution and suggested that 'the secrets of Industry are in the air'. Marshall (cited in Dicken, 1998: 20) recognised a number of characteristics that influenced innovation:

- the institutional set-up;
- the relationship between the entrepreneurs and financiers;
- society's perception of new developments;
- the openness to science and technology;
- networks between scientific and academic communities and business circles;
- the productive forces and financial institutions;
- the growing liberal–individualist economic paradigm;
- the role played by the state in accommodating and promoting capitalistic changes and preparing the framework for the development of capitalism.

The process of innovation has so far been treated as an organisational issue. We have seen, and will continue to see over the course of the book, that within the organisation, management of the innovation process is an extremely demanding discipline, for converting a basic discovery into a commercial product, process or service is a long-term, high-risk, complex, interactive and non-linear sequence. However, the capability of organisations in initiating and sustaining innovation is to a great extent determined by the wider local and national context within which they operate. This is essentially why 'innovation within' requires a favourable 'context outside'. That is, economic and social conditions will play a major role in whether the organisations or corporate actors will take the risk and establish the longer-term vision that innovation is key to competitiveness, survival and sustained growth. To get a better understanding of this, it is necessary to 'look out of the window' at the business environment in which economic actors strive to get an upper hand in the marketplace in a mix of competition and cooperation through network, market and hierarchical relations. This notion is reinforced by the interactions between the organisation and the external environment, which is emphasised in Figure 1.7.

Much can be learned from glancing at recent history. The development of science and technology in the West opened a wide gap between the so-called industrialised nations and their followers, 'late-industrialisers'. Late-industrialisers refer to countries with no or limited indigenous technology development capacity. Some states, including Japan and some east Asian countries, have managed to close that gap with strategies that focus mainly on industrialisation. In these countries, economic growth was achieved through imitation by diffusion of technology, development of new technology and efforts to develop their own capacities. So the cycle that began with imitation was later turned into a creative and broader basis upon which economic transformation could be achieved. This transformation required continual efforts by entrepreneurs and businesses and a collaborative framework promoted by the state. However, to reach maturity in today's economy, i.e. to be able to create high-value-added and knowledge-based products and services, would appear to be a gigantic task for the states and societies of the latecomers. Apart from its regulatory and redistribution functions, the state must play a significant role through strategic intervention into infrastructure development and technological capacity formation as well as into human capital formation.

This wider view of the economic environment is referred to as *integral economics*, where the economic processes are viewed in their social and political entirety. As pointed out by Dicken (1998: 50), 'technology is a social process which is socially and institutionally embedded'. In this context, it would be useful to remind ourselves that innovation cannot be separated from its local and national (as well as global) contexts and from political and social processes, let alone main economic trends.

Given the nature of 'the game', however, there is always the risk that entrepreneurs and businesses may only focus on high-return opportunities in the short term, marginalise strategic and innovative perspective and ignore the long-term implications of such behaviour (as will be seen in Chapter 14). Economies dominated by this type of philosophy will have serious difficulties in moving beyond commercial activities (that is, in current popular business discourse, 'moving boxes'). This so called 'short-termism' has characterised the economy of Turkey which, despite its strategic geographic position, has failed to develop significantly. In this context, we find that the businesses themselves and the business philosophy were progressively created by the Republican state within a modernist approach only to observe that the so-called entrepreneurs opted to become rich rather than entrepreneurs. So, the act of 'business-making' was only undertaken on the surface; and policy changes such as liberalisation only led the entrepreneurs and businesses to seek their ends in the short run with no calculated risk-taking in business. Thus, business in Turkey developed its own weakness by becoming dependent on the weaknesses of the Turkish state, e.g. using high and growing budget deficits as a money-making opportunity. In this chapter, we will try to highlight why the situation for economies such as the Turkish economy remain unchanged, while some societies and economies enjoyed sustained growth over several decades and have become powerful players in the global economy.

Pause for thought 

For Schumpeter, the idea of being entrepreneurial was not simply buying something cheap and selling it for a quick profit. It was bound up with new products and new methods of production; by implication it was long term rather than short term in nature. Is our understanding of **entrepreneurship** different now?

The role of the state and national 'systems' of innovation

To support our understanding of the process of innovation within the capitalist enterprise we must also grasp a basic understanding of the way the economy interrelates with global and regional economies on local and national levels. Not only do national economies tend to be dominated by a form of economic organisation (e.g. the *Chaebol* in South Korea or *Keiretsu* in Japan), it is also the case that the relationship between state and business differs radically from one national space to the other. Such interrelationships in society generate a business environment with a unique business value system, attitude and ethic. Historically, this difference created advantages and disadvantages for business organisation across a range of activities, the most important of which may be perceived as the process of innovation. This would seem to be the case given the crucial role played by innovation in the history of capitalism.

The answer to the question of whether there is a role for the state in the process of innovation has been addressed in different contexts (e.g. Porter, 1990; Afuah, 2003). The literature on the subject has attracted attention to the following points, where state action may be necessary:

1 *The 'public' nature of knowledge that underpins innovation.* This refers to the role that can be played by the government in the process of idea generation and its subsidisation and distribution. This way, economic actors may be stimulated to work on new ideas, alongside state organisations, and may endeavour to convert such ideas into marketable goods or services. For instance, by granting intellectual property rights to producers of knowledge and by establishing the necessary legal infrastructure to support those rights, the state may promote knowledge generation.

2 *The uncertainty that often hinders the process of innovation.* Macroeconomic, technological or market uncertainties may hinder innovation. When the companies are risk-averse in investing funds in innovation projects, then the state may promote such activities through subsidising, providing tax advantages and supporting firms to join R&D projects. Forming a stable economic environment, where funds could be extended by the banking system to productive firms, also creates a favourable long-term perspective, for one of the first preconditions of strategy making is economic stability. Thus, expectations of low inflation, low interest rates and stable growth will encourage firms to invest in entrepreneurial activity (particularly given that other areas, e.g. portfolio investments, are less profitable to invest in).

3 *The need for certain kinds of complementary assets.* Provision of electricity, roads and water has historically assisted industrial development; recently, the establishment of communication systems (e.g. communication superhighways), legal infrastructure and the formation of industrial districts have been issues where state action has led to favourable outcomes with tangible and intangible conditions created for enterprises.

4 *The need for cooperation and governance, resulting from the nature of certain technologies.* For the development of possible networks, which will enhance and promote the diffusion of new technologies and innovations, the state may set the vision and enhance the possibilities for better communication and joint decision making. In the United Kingdom the government is providing funds (through

education and promotion) to encourage households to switch from analogue television signal to a digital television signal. Such action helps countries/society to upgrade from one old established technology to a newer improved technology.

5 *Politics*. Lastly, in terms of politics, national states still have a key role in foreseeing and contributing to international and regional standards of business making within the system of 'national states' and in creating consent and cohesion in the national arena among domestic forces. Such standards are increasingly becoming environmental, safety and human rights standards in industrial or business activities. The German government has an impressive record of being at the forefront of introducing legislation in automobile safety and environmental recycling which has contributed to Germany becoming a world leader in these two industries.

How national states can facilitate innovation

Figure 2.1 highlights the possible roles that can be played by national states. It takes Porter's industry attractiveness framework and develops the role the state can play in relation to innovation. It underlines a firm's relationship with the buyers, factor conditions (e.g. labour, capital, raw materials), related and supporting industries (e.g. technology providers, input providers, etc.) and other institutions that help facilitate strategic orientation and innovative capabilities. These will determine to a great extent the firm's opportunities – notwithstanding the fact that its inner strengths, i.e. its strategy-making capabilities and structural features, will clearly affect this potential.

As a financier of R&D and major purchaser, the state has a significant impact on strategic direction towards critical industries and encouraging entrepreneurial spirit. For instance, in 1995, the United States committed to a budget for R&D spending of $71.4 billion, which was spent on defence, health, space, general science, energy,

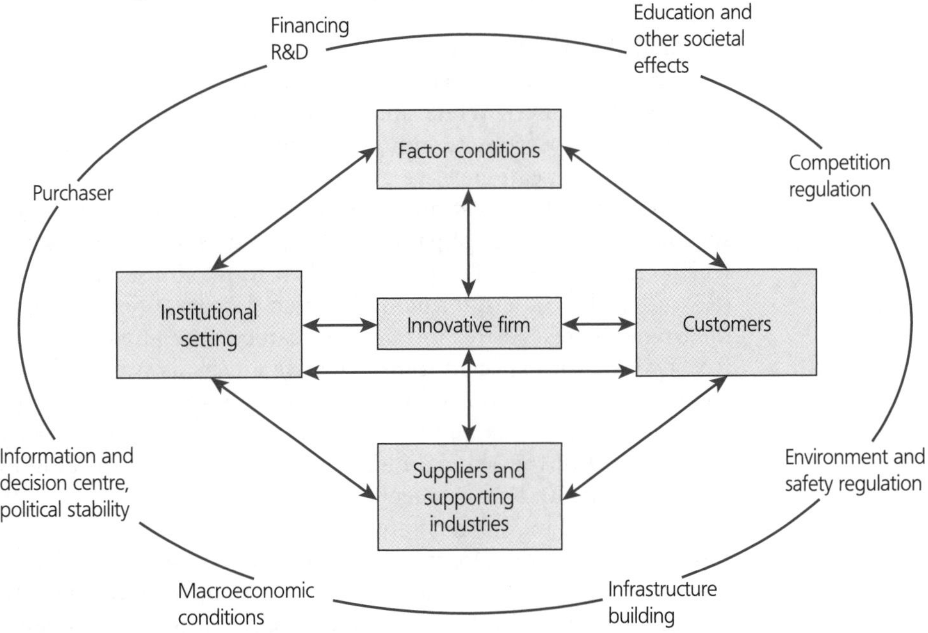

Figure 2.1 The role of the state in innovation

transportation, environment and agriculture. Most of the funds went to industrial research laboratories, universities, non-profit laboratories and federally funded research R&D centres. There are also indirect ways of financing R&D, such as tax exemptions, subsidies, loan guarantees, export credits and forms of protection. For example, Boeing paid no taxes between 1970 and 1984, and also received a tax refund amounting to $285 million (Afuah, 2003). As a major purchaser, the state will also reduce uncertainty and create favourable cash flows for firms by its willingness to pay higher (monopolistic) prices for early models.

Through education, information dissemination, governance and other societal actions, the state can impact upon the way the society perceives discoveries and adapts new technologies at the same time as creating cohesion in the society and making strategic interventions to promote, for instance, the formation of a highly qualified workforce. Interdependency between state and society may create a favourable national culture which welcomes scientific development, and removes the potential for conflict between leading sectors and traditional sectors, economic interests and social forces and cultural traditions and new trends. By incubating a form of unity between state and society, the state may set in motion an overall vision and dynamic in the society and for the industry.

Regulation of competition is another critical area for the reproduction/expansion of the capitalist system, as the state can promote the system by preventing monopolies that can result in under-innovation and by protecting the society against possible abuse by companies. Microsoft's very high profile antitrust case with the European Union (EU) is a good illustration (*see* Illustration 2.1). A summary of the complex way in which the state can impact upon the behaviour of capitalist firms and how they manage their economic and social relationships is shown in Figure 2.1.

Fostering innovation in the United States and Japan

Although local characteristics also play a very significant role in the innovation process, the overall tendencies of nations and nation states are linked to success on a very local level. While some states, such as Japan, provided extensive support and subsidies to promote industrial innovation, others, such as the United States, have aimed to create positive effects in the economy by letting the market achieve the most efficient allocation of resources with minimal possible intervention. The so-called Chicago School paradigm for promoting competitiveness and innovation, which created a belief in the free market to maximise innovation and productivity (Rosenthal, 1993), has, for more than two decades, been the dominant perspective in the United States. At this instance, we can cite the impact on the industry of public R&D with such expected transformative effects as provided by the internet's later commercial application, initially a military project initiated by the state. In fact, the United States is leading the way in performing half of the world's basic research, making most of the seminal discoveries, thanks to the trillion-dollar investment in US universities and government laboratories.

In the case of more interventionist states, incentives were provided either as direct support (e.g. subsidies, location provision, etc.) or in the form of 'governance', assuming a coordinating and leading role in the management of innovation projects. In this instance governance refers to the efforts at creating cohesion and complementarity, which are directed to the realisation of a joint objective that is deemed to be mutually beneficial to the various parties involved. A good example of the latter was the role played by the Japanese state in bringing universities, state organisations (primarily the Ministry of International Trade and Industry (MITI)), sector organisations and business enterprises together for research on the development of the Trinitron television (a technology that dominated home electronics for more than two decades) with financial support attached. Although the Japanese model has come under severe criticism, particularly by Porter *et al.* (2000), as a result of the recent economic slowdown, the weaknesses mainly attributed to the lack of concern for strategy in Japanese companies and being stuck in between two competitive strategies of cost and quality, as well as low profitability, the success of the model has been long acknowledged (*see*, for instance, Johnson, 1982; Hart, 1992; Castells, 1992). In the case of innovation, governance requires the establishment of a proper framework for the smooth flow of knowledge between universities, state institutions, private sector organisations and corporations until the end result takes some form of a marketable commodity. In this framework, while some economies are better placed with innovation capabilities, some are at a disadvantage because of their characteristics.

Illustration 2.1

Brussels threatens Microsoft with further antitrust fines

Microsoft was yesterday dealt a serious setback in its long-running antitrust battle with the European Commission, when Brussels threatened to impose yet another massive fine on the US software group for failing to comply with a landmark competition ruling handed down almost three years ago.

Europe's top antitrust regulator yesterday issued a new set of charges against Microsoft, a step that is likely to result in another ruling and a new fine against the group. Since the Commission opened its probe against the world's largest software maker more than eight years ago, Microsoft has been fined close to €780 million (£526 million) for abusing its dominant market position and failing to respect the regulator's ruling.

The Commission refused to comment on the size of any new fine that could arise from yesterday's charges. However, Brussels could – in the worst-case scenario for Microsoft – hit the group with a penalty in excess of €800 million. The Commission accused Microsoft of demanding excessive royalties from companies wishing to license technical information about its Windows operating system. The order to make such information available to rivals formed a key plank of the Commission's March 2004 ruling against the group. The Commission stressed that Microsoft was the first group to be accused of ignoring a European Union antitrust ruling. 'This is a company which apparently does not like to have to conform with antitrust decisions', said the spokesman for Neelie Kroes, the EU competition commissioner. Brad Smith, Microsoft's general counsel, rejected the Commission's allegations. He said Microsoft's proposed pricing scheme would be 30 per cent cheaper than comparable licensing fees.

Under the terms of the 2004 ruling, Microsoft has to make available 'interoperability' information to other software makers so that rivals can design server software that functions smoothly with Windows-driven computers and servers. The Commission said yesterday it had found 'no significant innovation in the interoperability information'. It also claimed that companies were being asked to give Microsoft 35 per cent of the net operating profits they made by selling products designed with the help of the licence.

The original 2004 ruling is under appeal in front of an EU court, which is expected to issue its ruling in the next six months.

Source: Tobias Buck, *Financial Times*, 2 March 2007. Reprinted with permission.

The concept of 'developmental states' is used to show the way in which some states achieved a major transformation of the economy and society. At the other end of the spectrum there are the 'predatory states', which capture most of the funds in the economy and reallocate them in the form of rents to a small group of the population, thus impeding the growth potential in the state (Evans, 1989). This development was found in particular to be a major characteristic of some east Asian states, especially the so-called Tigers of Korea, Taiwan, Singapore and Hong Kong (Castells, 1992). Although such states were not immune to corruption, fraud and other forms of inefficiency, they brought about major changes in the economy, particularly in upgrading the potential of the industry from imitation towards innovation and technology development, which is by no means an easy task.

Pause for thought 

Is it true that in a developed market economy the role of the state is a minor one? Why is it *not* surprising that many consumer products such as in-car satellite navigational guidance, mobile telephones and computers have their origins in defence research?

The right business environment is key to innovation

Schumpeter preached technology as the engine of growth but also noted that to invest in technology there had to be spare resources and long time-horizons. So the business environment must give the 'right' signals to the business units for them to invest in such operations. In this regard, not only does macroeconomic stability play a significant role but also the availability of quick (short-term) returns and opportunistic trends needs to be suppressed so that the money can flow into basic research and R&D. Likewise, the approach of business would differ if it faced strong (external or internal) competition. A protected domestic market more often than not amounts to signalling to business units that they should seek monopolistic or oligopolistic returns by not making enough investment into new product development or even product improvement.

The next chapter explores the organisational characteristics that need to be in place for innovation to occur. From the preceding discussion one can already begin to see what these characteristics might be.

Waves of innovation and growth: historical overview

When we investigate the history of capitalist development, there is a pattern of economic growth. The work of Kondratieff and Schumpeter has been influential in identifying the major stages of this development. The five waves, or growth cycles, are identified in Figure 2.2. This highlights that technological developments and innovations have a strong spatial dimension; however, leadership in one wave is not necessarily maintained in the succeeding waves. So one can observe shifts in the

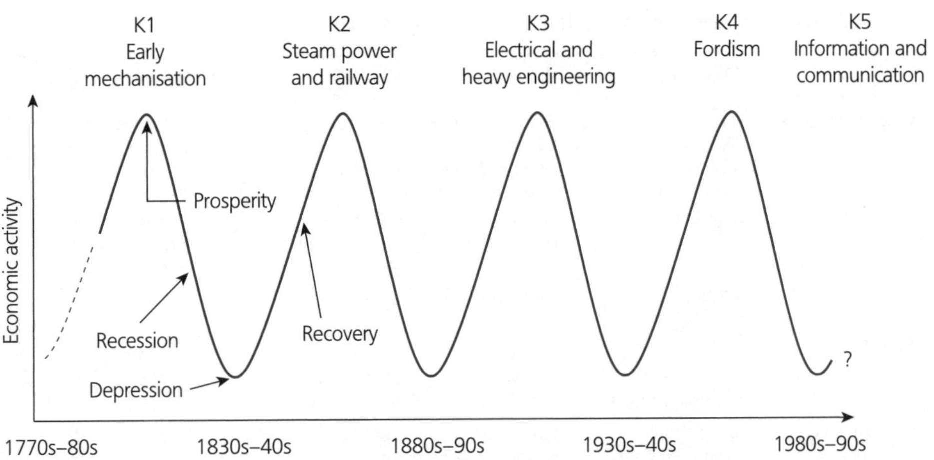

Figure 2.2 Kondratieff waves of growth and their main features

geography of innovation through time. The leaders of the first wave were Britain, France and Belgium. The second wave brought new players into the game, namely the United States and Germany. Wave three saw the strengthening of the positions of the United States and Germany. In wave four, Japan and Sweden joined the technology and innovation race. More recently, in wave five, Taiwan and South Korea are becoming key players in the global economy.

In these Kondratieff waves, the capitalist economy grew on the basis of major innovations in product, process and organisation with accompanying shifts in the social arena. Kuhn's theory on the nature of scientific revolutions has been justified: each wave comes to an end due to its major shortcomings and the successive wave fundamentally restructures and improves those weaknesses. Each major phase of innovation produced a 'star' industry or industry branch, which seemed to affect the way the economy was organised. The leap forward provided by such industry(ies) resulted in a major transformation of the economy and economic relations – given that other factors such as demand, finance, industrial and social conditions were favourable. Products, processes and organisations created by technological development became universal and cheaply available to a vast population, which, in turn, created the economic shift. These Kondratieff waves took place in the order of early mechanisation, steam power and railways, electrical and heavy engineering, 'Fordism' (i.e. use of mass-production methods), and information and communication. The last of these waves is currently underway with what is now termed the information revolution. Almost every day we are presented with a number of 'new' ways in which we can do business, search for information, communicate and socialise with other people or carry out our bank operations. This means that the new developments deeply affect not only economic relations but also our private (home and relations) and work (public) spheres.

In the very first Kondratieff wave, the rise of the factory and mechanisation in textiles was only part of the story. The need to produce in greater quantities to start serving the growing overseas markets with the improved transport methods now available was complemented by the abundance of finance with the money flowing in from the colonies, particularly the United States. Universally and cheaply available input (i.e. cotton), improving nationwide transport infrastructure (with rising

Table 2.1 Characteristics of the five waves of growth

	Wave 1	Wave 2	Wave 3	Wave 4	Wave 5
Main branches	Textiles Textile machinery Iron working Water power Pottery	Steam engines Steamships Machine tools Iron and steel Railway equipment	Electrical engineering Electrical machinery Cable and wire Heavy engineering Steel ships Heavy chemicals	Automobiles Trucks/tractors/ planes Consumer durables Process plant Synthetic materials Petrochemicals	Computers Electronic capital goods Telecommunications Robotics Information services
Universal and cheap key factors	Cotton	Coal, iron	Steel; electricity	Oil; plastics	Gas; oil; microelectronics
Infrastructure	Trunk canals Turnpike roads	Railways Shipping	Electricity supply and distribution	Highways; airports/ airlines	Digital networks; satellites
Limitations of previous technoeconomic paradigm; solutions	Limitations of scale, process control and mechanisation in 'putting out' system; solutions offered through mechanisation and factory organisation towards productivity and profitability	Limitations of water power: inflexibility of location, scale of production, reliability; solutions offered through steam engine and transport system	Limitations of iron as an engineering material (strength, durability, precision, etc.) overcome by steel and alloys; limitations of steam engine overcome by unit and group electrical machinery, power tools, permitting layout improvement and capital saving; standardisation	Limitations of batch production overcome by flow processes and assembly line; full standardisation and replaceability of components and materials; universal availability and cheapening of mass consumption goods	Inflexibility of dedicated assembly line and process plant overcome by flexible manufacturing systems, networking and economies of scope; electronic control systems and networking provide for necessitated flexibility
Organisation of firms	Individual entrepreneurs and small firms (<100 employees); partnership between technical innovators and financial circles	Small firms dominate but large firms and large markets emerge; limited liability and joint stock companies emerge	Emergence of giant firms, cartels, trusts, mergers; regulation of or state ownership of natural monopolies; concentration of finance and banking capital; emergence of middle management	Oligopolistic competition; TNCs; 'arm's-length' subcontracting or vertical integration; bureaucratic control and bureaucratisation	Networks of large and small firms based increasingly on computers; trust-based networks with close cooperation in technology, quality control, training and production planning (e.g. JIT)
Geographical focus	Britain, France, Belgium	Britain, France, Belgium, Germany, United States	Germany, United States, Britain, France, Belgium, The Netherlands, Switzerland	United States, Germany, other EU, Japan, Switzerland, other EFTA, Canada, Australia	Japan, United States, Canada, Germany, Sweden, other EU and EFTA, Taiwan, Korea

Note: EFTA, European Free Trade Association; JIT, just-in-time; TNC, transnational corporation.

Source: Reproduced and adapted from P. Dicken (1998) *Global Shift: Transforming the World Economy*, Paul Chapman, London (a Sage Publications company); C. Freeman and L. Soete (1997) *The Economics of Industrial Innovation*, 3rd edn, Pinter, London (Cengage Learning Services Ltd).

investment in canals and roads by landlords), the advent of the so-called adventurers (now widely recognised as entrepreneurs), pools of labour available for employment in some local markets, the growing education infrastructure, the role played by academic and scientific societies and the attitude of the state towards manufacturing interests were the other complementary factors affecting change (Freeman and Soete, 1997).

With the decline of the previous techno-economic paradigm, the next one starts to take shape with features that offer solutions to the weaknesses of the earlier phase. As Marx foresaw, capitalism has always found a way of reproducing itself with changes in the way factors of production were organised. For instance, the organisational characteristics have changed from the first through to the fifth wave, and the early emphasis on individual entrepreneurs has given way to small firms, then to the monopolists, oligopolists and cartels of the third wave, centralised TNCs (transnational corporations) of the fourth wave and, finally, to the so-called 'network' type, flexible organisations of the information age (*see* Table 2.1 for an overview of the waves of growth).

Pause for thought

The Kondratieff theory suggests that networks constitute a key organisational attribute to the current wave of economic growth. Does this mean it is not possible for a firm to be innovative on its own?

Fostering innovation in 'late-industrialising' countries

We have already noted that there is no guarantee for continued technological leadership. The geography of innovation has shown regional, national or local variations in time. One proof in this regard has been the case of south-east Asia. Although the late developers followed more or less similar paths towards industrialisation, some managed significant achievements, particularly in the attitude of the private sector to innovation and technology development (for example, Taiwan, Malaysia and Korea). Almost all latecomers started with the exports of basic commodities, and through the application of a mix of policies in different periods, they aimed for industrialisation. When innovation is considered, the focus of entrepreneurs and businesses was initially on imitative production (so-called 'reverse engineering') in relatively unsophisticated industries. More recently Hobday *et al.* (2004) have illustrated that Korean firms have adopted a policy of 'copy and develop', which has taken them to the technological frontier in industries from automotive to telecommunications. When the business environment became conducive to business activity, after initial capital accumulation in key industries, then an upward move was observed along the ladder of industrialisation. In many countries such a transformation required an envisioning state, actively interfering with the functioning of the private enterprise system. In some cases, it set 'the prices wrong' deliberately (Amsden, 1989) to protect and promote infant industries; in others, it created enterprises itself in order to compensate for the lack of private initiative in the economy (Toprak, 1995).

Although there are significant differences between the cases of Latin American countries and their south Asian counterparts, their paths of industrialisation also bear similarities. Initially, all were exporters of raw materials and importers of higher-technology products. In achieving the transformation, the move from simple technology sectors towards higher-value-added and heavy industries seems to be the key to their successes. This was achieved with the complementary use of (inward-looking) import-substituting industrialisation (ISI) and (outward-looking) export-oriented (EOI) economic policies. The main difference in south Asian economies, which, in retrospect, seems to be their main advantage, was that after the initial phase of ISI, they opened up to international competition through an EOI regime in contrast particularly to Latin American countries and Turkey. Turkey had a set of problems that were established over a long period of time, which led to a weak business system. This was partly due to the nation building and 'Turkification' of the economy during the twentieth century. This resulted in the Turkish business system becoming state dependent. Thus trying to create a business class from scratch during the 1970s and 80s had its costs: entrepreneurs and businesses, which are expected to invest their accumulation into business activities along the value chain were after easy and quick returns ('petty entrepreneurship') or invested their accumulation into luxury goods. In a favourable environment, such accumulation could have meant the deepening of the economy. However, the case of Turkey proved that without a proper legal and institutional framework, and a social code, established business values and ethic, the outcome turned out to be a sluggish business system.

Pause for thought 

In order to compete much emphasis is placed on the need to cut costs and improve efficiency. Why would an emphasis on efficiency alone be bad for businesses and economic growth in general?

Innovation within the 25 EU states

In a response to increased competition and globalisation the European Council argued for increased and enhanced efforts to improve the EU's performance in innovation. In March 2000 in the picturesque city of Lisbon the EU set itself the goal of becoming the most competitive and dynamic knowledge-based economy in the world within the next decade. Fine words one may say, but precisely how does one set about achieving this laudable goal? A strategy was developed and presented in Stockholm in March 2001. The strategy was to build on the economic convergence that had been developed over the past 10 years within the EU single market and to coordinate an 'open method' of developing policies for creating new skills, knowledge and innovation. To support this approach the European Commission stated that there was a need for an assessment of how member countries were performing in the area of innovation. The idea of a 'Scoreboard' was launched to indicate the performance of member states. This would be conducted every year as a way of assessing the performance of member countries. It is essentially a benchmarking exercise where the European Union can assess its performance against other countries, most notably Japan and the United States. The Scoreboard also analyses Bulgaria, Romania, Turkey, Iceland and Switzerland.

This is an extremely ambitious project to try to assess innovative ability. There have been many studies over the past two decades that have tried to identify the factors necessary for innovation to occur (*see* Table 1.8), and while many factors have been identified several of these are necessary but not sufficient in themselves. Moreover, some governments have attempted to develop 'innovation toolkits' and 'scorecards' to try to help firms in their own countries to become more innovative (for example, the UK Department of Trade and Industry). Most of these have not been successful. This ambitious project by the European Union is full of limitations and is generally regarded as oversimplistic. This is largely because the economic conditions of the member countries are so very different and all have a wide variety of strengths and weaknesses. Nonetheless, in order to assess where the European Union should target help and the precise type of help required by each member it is necessary to analyse the innovative performance of countries. The latest European Innovation Survey was conducted in 2009 (EIS, 2010). Figure 2.3, shows a map of

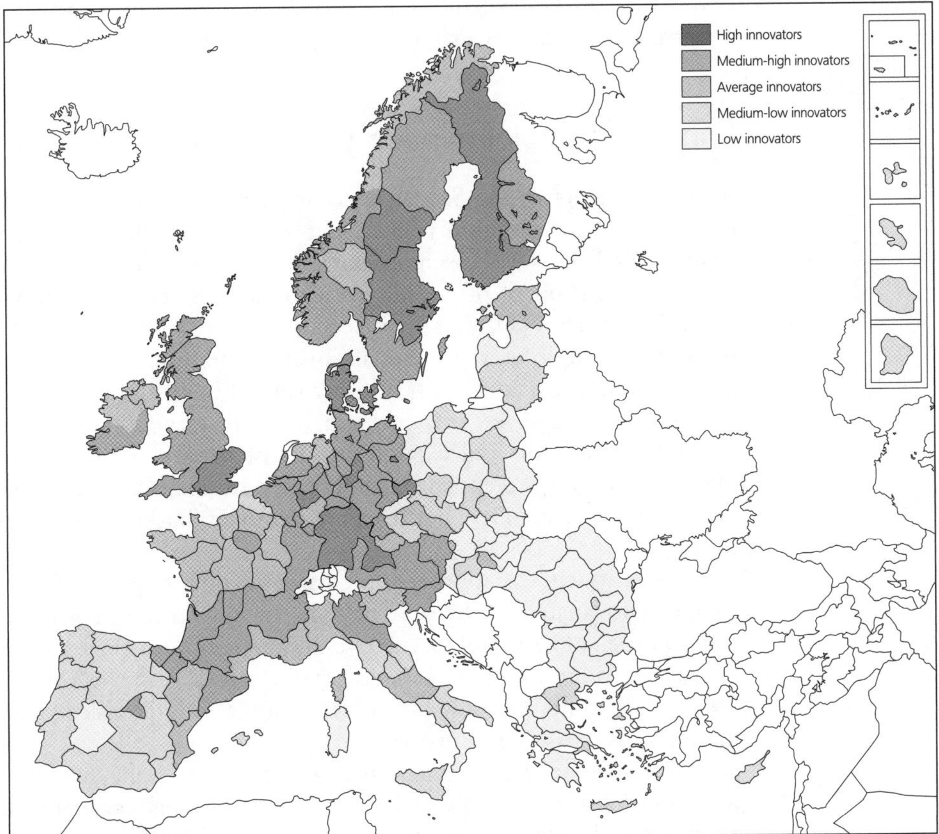

Figure 2.3 The EU showing five performance groups, ranging from the highest to lowest overall performers

Table 2.2 Four different groups

Group	Growth rate (%)	Growth leaders	Moderate growers	Slow growers
Innovation leaders	1.5	Switzerland (CH)	Finland (FI), Germany (DE)	Denmark (DK), Sweden (SE), United Kingdom (UK)
Innovation followers	2.7	Cyprus (CY), Estonia (EE)	Iceland (IS), Slovenia (SI)	Austria (AT), Belgium (BE), France (FR), Ireland (IE), Luxembourg (LU), Netherlands (NL)
Moderate innovators	3.3	Czech Republic (CZ), Greece (GR), Malta (MT), Portugal (PT)	Hungary (HU), Lithuania (LT), Poland (PL), Slovakia (SK)	Italy (IT), Norway (NO), Spain (ES)
Catching-up countries	5.5	Bulgaria (BG), Romania (RO)	Latvia (LV)	Turkey (TR), Croatia (HR)

the European Union indicating five performance groups, ranging from the highest to the lowest overall performers. Table 2.2 illustrates how the EIS (2010) divides the countries into four key groups.

Improving the innovation performance of the EU

All the elements in the Scoreboard are necessary but not sufficient in themselves to ensure that innovation occurs. For example, in this chapter we have seen the example of Turkey, a late-industrialising country on the edge of Europe, a country with a population of 60 million, already a member of the North Atlantic Treaty Organisation (NATO) and a prospective member of the European Union. Turkey is a good example of a late-industrialising economy. Sitting on the edge of Europe and bestriding two continents, Turkey should be in a position to develop a successful economy. However, in Turkey there seems to be a missing link in terms of the innovative intention and capabilities of enterprises. Turkey needs to put in place many of the things detailed in the Scoreboard. This would surely help to develop enterprise in the country, but it will not convert Turkey into a Germany or Finland overnight.

By identifying, comparing and disseminating best practices in financing and technology transfer, Europe can improve its innovation performance. One area that needs particular attention is the overall perception of the entrepreneur. The image of the entrepreneur needs to have greater value, as in the United States where the drive to try to market new products, with the in-built risk of failure, is seen much more positively than in Europe.

The Scoreboard may be helpful to governmental policymakers in deciding where to invest substantial sums of money. However, this chapter and Chapter 1 have emphasised that firms behave differently given similar circumstances and that some firms appeared to be more successful than others. Given this, the Scoreboard's practical help is likely to be extremely limited.

The times they are a changing: how frugal innovation is providing a future path for firms in emerging markets

The emerging world, long a source of cheap labour, now rivals the rich countries for business innovation. Developing countries are becoming hotbeds of business innovation in much the same way as Japan did from the 1950s onwards. They are coming up with new products and services that are dramatically cheaper than their western equivalents: $3,000 cars, $300 computers and $30 mobile phones that provide nationwide services for just 2 cents a minute. They are reinventing systems of production and distribution, and they are experimenting with entirely new business models.

The United Nations World Investment Report calculates that there are now around 21,500 multinationals based in the emerging world. The best of these, such as India's Bharat Forge (forging), China's BYD (batteries) and Brazil's Embraer (jet aircraft), are as good as anybody in the world. The number of companies from Brazil, India, China or Russia on the Financial Times 500 list more than quadrupled in 2006–08.

Furthermore, the world's biggest multinationals are becoming increasingly happy to do their research and development in emerging markets. Companies in the Fortune 500 list have 98 R&D facilities in China and 63 in India. And the opportunities are equally impressive. The potential market is huge. Populations are already much higher than in the developed world and growing much faster.

This combination is producing an exciting cocktail of creativity. Because so many consumers are poor, companies have to go for volume. And because piracy is so commonplace, they also have to keep upgrading their products. Again the similarities with Japan in the 1950s are striking.

The very nature of innovation is having to be rethought. Most people in the West equate it with technological breakthroughs, embodied in revolutionary new products that are taken up by the elites and eventually trickle down to the masses. But many of the most important innovations consist of incremental improvements to products and processes aimed at the middle or bottom of the income pyramid. The emerging world has already surpassed the West in areas such as mobile money (using mobile phones to make payments).

In Chennai, India, Tata Consultancy Services (TCS) has developed a low-tech water filter. It uses rice husks (which is one of the country's most common waste products) to purify water. It can provide a family with an abundant supply of bacteria free water for about $24. Tata is planning to produce 1 million of the devices over the next year. Frugal innovation is more than simply cutting costs. Nokia's cheapest handsets come equipped with flashlights (because of frequent power cuts), multiple phone books (because they often have different users), rubberised key pads and menus in several languages.

Finally, the developing world's most innovative business model may be the application of mass-production techniques to sophisticated services. Extending Henry Ford's manufacturing revolution to heart and eye surgery is truly innovative.

Innovation and the market

We have explored the reasons why some state contexts are more conducive to deeper levels of entrepreneurial activity and innovation, while some others promote 'petty entrepreneurialism' with short-term, accumulation-ridden intentions. This chapter has also tried to explain how some nations achieved a strong transformation from basic industries and joined the vanguard of technology development. In that respect, it was suggested that although knowledge accumulation is a socially and spatially focused process, geographical shifts have occurred throughout history when 'state–societal arrangements' were conducive and there may be possible openings for late-developing nations in the future. This, however, is by no means a simple process.

Chapter 1 emphasised the inclusion of commercialisation within the process of innovation. It is this part of the innovation process that proves so extremely difficult for many firms. There have been many exciting scientific advances such as Alexander Flemming's discovery of penicillin (1928) and Crick and Watson's discovery of DNA (1953), but in both cases it was over 20 years later that commercial products emerged from the science and technology: antibiotics in the first case and numerous genetic advances including genetic fingerprinting in the second. Commercialising technology and new products in particular, then, is one of the key challenges within innovation. We now turn our attention to this process and in particular the diffusion of innovations and market adoption.

Innovation and market vision

We all respond differently to different types of innovations and in different ways. It is because of this that the role of marketing is so valuable to firms developing new products and services. For example, in the context of disruptive innovations which require a greater change in existing patterns of behaviour and thinking, consumers would perceive a higher level of risk and uncertainty in their adoption decisions relative to continuous innovations that depend on established behavioural patterns and perceptions. Take internet banking as an example: this is a type of service that necessitates changes in perceptions and the established patterns of behaviour and requires the formation of new consumption practices. Indeed, the underlying internet technology itself is a disruptive innovation. Yet herein lies the problem: highly innovative products have an inherent high degree of uncertainty about exactly how an emerging technology may be formulated into a usable product and what the final product application will be. Market vision, or the ability to look into the future and picture products and services that will be successful is a fundamental requirement for those firms wishing to engage in innovation. It involves assessing ones own technological capability and present or future market needs and visioning a market offering that people will want to buy. While this may sound simple it lies at the heart of the innovation process and focuses our attention on the need to examine not only the market but the way the new product offering is used or consumed.

Innovative new products and consumption patterns

Consumption pattern refers to the degree of change required in the thinking and behaviour of the consumer in using the product. Products involving consumption pattern changes such as internet banking or MP3 players can require customers to alter their thinking and habits and this may affect their willingness to embrace a new product. A product can be familiar or novel in the way it requires users to interact

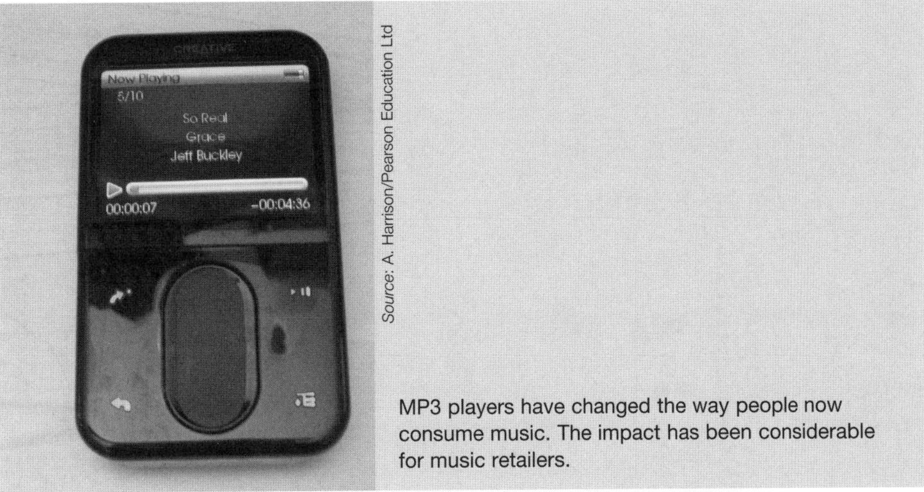

Source: A. Harrison/Pearson Education Ltd

MP3 players have changed the way people now consume music. The impact has been considerable for music retailers.

with it. The nature of the change involved with respect to this aspect of a new product can play a significant role in product evaluation and adoption (Veryzer, 2003). It is this dimension that Apple Inc. has so successfully addressed in its MP3 player, the iPod. Apple was not the first to develop an MP3 player. Indeed, five years after launch its capabilities are still fewer than its rivals (for example, in 2006 it did not have an FM radio). Yet, in terms of ease of use it is considerably ahead of its nearest rival. In considering highly innovative products it is crucial to take the customer's view and experience of the product into account. A technology focused approach to innovation that does not consider the customer's perspective would surely result in a product that is at odds with the market's perception of it. Even though technology is the means for enabling an innovation, new products are more than simply bundles of technology. As Apple has demonstrated with its iPod. Innovative new products must deliver benefits and be used by people who can enjoy them and the advantages that they can bring about.

This introduces another variable that needs to be considered by the firm developing innovative products. In addition to new technology within the product and product capabilities the firm must also consider how these will affect consumption of the product. Figure 2.4 illustrates the relationship between these three key variables

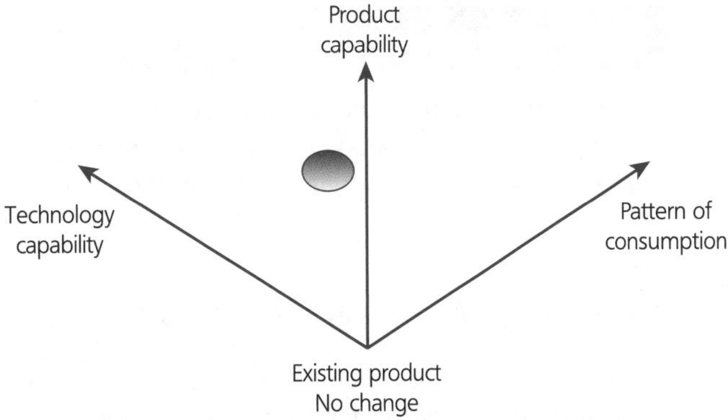

Figure 2.4 Three critical dimensions of change-of-technology intensive products

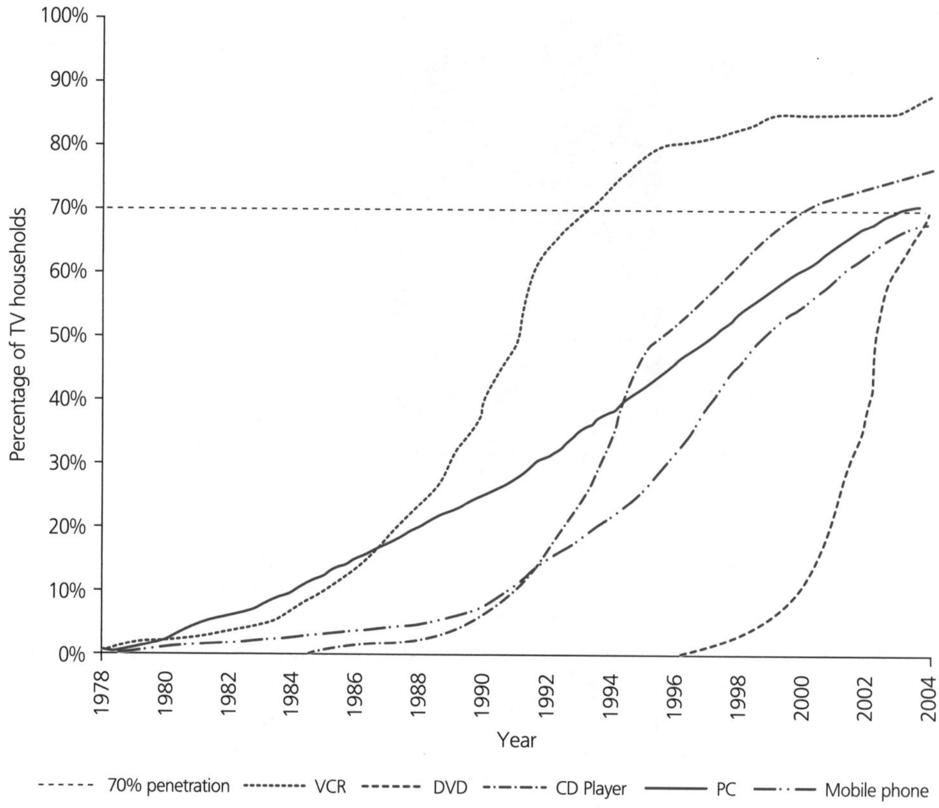

Figure 2.5 Penetration of consumer electronics, 1978–2004

that the firm needs to consider as it develops new product ideas. Sometimes, while the technology has been proven and the capabilities of the product demonstrated to be superior to existing products, if the extent of change in the pattern of consumption by the consumer is too great, the product may yet fail or take a long time to succeed. A good example of this would be the failed Apple Newton (personal digital assistant) or even the personal computer which, as Figure 2.5 illustrates, took over 20 years to achieve a 70 per cent market penetration rate.

Pause for thought

If consumers are unwilling to embrace new products that impose a high degree of change in the consumption pattern for consumers, does this mean that firms should only introduce products that are similar to existing products?

Marketing insights to facilitate innovation

Marketing can provide the necessary information and knowledge required by the firm to ensure the successful development of innovative new products and the successful acceptance and diffusion of new products. In both cases it is usually the insights with respect to understanding potential customers that marketing supplies. Uncovering and understanding these insights is where effective marketing is extremely valuable. The Viagra case in Chapter 8 illustrates this very clearly. The deep insights necessary for truly innovative products requires great skill as much of the information gained from customers for such products needs to be ignored (Veryzer, 2003). Research within marketing has shown for many years that gaining valuable insight from consumers about innovative new market offerings, especially discontinuous new products, is extremely difficult and can sometimes lead to misleading information (Veryzer, 2003; King, 1985; Tauber, 1974; Martin, 1995; Hamel and Prahalad, 1994). Indeed, frequent responses from consumers are along the lines of 'I want the same product, only cheaper and better'. Von Hippel has suggested that consumers have difficulty in understanding and articulating their needs and has described this phenomenon as 'sticky information'. That is, information which is difficult to transfer (similar to the notion of tacit knowledge). Recently 'user toolkits' have been shown to facilitate the transfer of so-called 'sticky information' and have enabled firms to understand better the precise needs and desires of customers (Franke and Piller, 2004). The greater uncertainties involved with discontinuous innovations demands both insight and foresight from firms. Advanced technology presents significant technical and market uncertainty, especially when the technology is emerging and industry standards have yet to be established. Appreciating and understanding the potential new technology and uncovering what the market will and will not embrace is a key challenge for marketing. Indeed, bridging the technology uncertainty and the market need is critical for a commercially viable new product. Figure 2.5 illustrates the penetration over time of a range of consumer electronic products from DVD players to mobile phones. The penetration rates differ considerably with some achieving a 70 per cent market penetration within a few years, such as DVD players, whereas PCs took over 20 years.

Highly innovative or discontinuous new products are particularly demanding in terms of early timely information if they are to avoid being harshly judged later by the market. Whether this information and knowledge is provided by marketing personnel or by R&D scientists and engineers does not matter, but its input into the new product development process is essential. The product development team need to determine (Leifer *et al.*, 2000: 81):

- What are the potential applications of a technology as a product?
- Which application(s) should be pursued first?
- What benefits can the proposed product offer to potential customers?
- What is the potential market size and is this sufficient?

Beyond consumer concerns that are relevant to the development and marketing of innovative products are more 'macro' influences that can affect adoption and thus need to be considered. The substitution of one technology for another is an obvious concern (the case study in Chapter 6 discusses this in more detail with regard to screw-caps replacing cork). Along with this, the issue of product complementarity, or when there is a positive interrelationship between products (e.g. a computer printer and a computer), can also be important with respect to product adoption. Thus, in addition to displacing products, new technological innovations often modify or complement existing products that may still be diffusing throughout a given market. This has significant implications for market planning decisions for both products since their diffusion processes are interlinked (Norton and Bass, 1987, 1992; Dekimpe *et al.*, 2000). In such cases, e.g. new electric motor vehicles, the following need to be carefully considered:

- whether there is a positive interdependence between a new product and existing products;
- whether the old technology will be fully replaced by a newer product;
- how the size of the old technology's installed base will affect the speed of diffusion of the new product or product generation.

Innovation in action

A $900 shop

Looking to build a new office or shop? How about adopting the ultimate in recycling – a building made out of stacked shipping containers?

It's generally too expensive to ship an empty container back to its point of origin so there are thousands of them sitting in docks around the world. They are strong, stackable and cost as little as $900.

The Dordoy Bazaar in Bishkek, Kyrgyzstan is one of Asia's largest markets. It stretches for more than a kilometre and is almost entirely constructed from empty shipping containers stacked two high.

(See the case study at the end of this chapter for further details on shipping containers.)

Source: 100 Thoughts (2010) HSBC, London.

Lead users

When it comes to technology-intensive products it is so-called 'lead users' that form the basis for much insight into products and also help with the diffusion process. Lead users are those who demand requirements ahead of the market and indeed are often involved themselves in developing product ideas because there is nothing in the market at present to meet their needs. For example, Stephan Wozniak co-founded Apple Computer with Steve Jobs in 1976 and created the Apple I and Apple II computers in the mid-1970s. He was a lead user computer engineer, ahead of the general population. Such lead users can help to co-develop innovations, and are therefore often early adopters of such innovations. The initial research by Eric von Hippel in the 1970s suggested that lead users adopt an average of seven years before typical users. In a recent study Morrison *et al.* (2004) identified a number of characteristics of lead users:

- recognise requirements early;
- expect high level of benefits from the product;
- develop their own innovations and applications;
- perceived to be pioneering and innovative.

Lead users are particularly significant for products that are using technology at the frontiers of development and those within technology-intensive industries such as software, engineering and science.

Innovation diffusion theories

Innovation diffusion theories try to explain how an innovation is diffused in a social system over time; the adoption of an innovation is therefore a part of the wider diffusion process. Such theories tend to be more comprehensive relative to their **adoption theory** cousins. This is because they investigate the reasons for adoption at the aggregate level. Perceived innovation characteristics theory, which is a part of the innovation **diffusion theory** of Rogers (1962), is similar to adoption theories such as the theory of reasoned action (TRA), the theory of planned behaviour (TPB) and the technology acceptance model (TAM) as it includes analysis down to the individual level. Yet, diffusion of innovations theories in general includes many more factors such as the influences of psychological or personal features, technology perceptions, communication behaviour and socio-demographic attributes on diffusion or adoption process. It is worth saying at this point that the study of how and why consumers purchase goods and services falls within the arena of consumer buyer behaviour and there are lots of very good textbooks that explore this subject in great detail. The purpose of introducing some of these concepts here is to ensure the reader is aware of the important influence of this body of research on explaining how and why some new product innovations are successful and why others are not.

Everett Rogers is usually credited with introducing the concept of diffusion theory to the business community. Rogers' work was initially undertaken in developing countries where he studied the diffusion of new ideas among communities (Rogers, 1962). He later developed his work and applied it to new product innovations in the market and was able to illustrate different consumer categories on the basis of its relative time of adoption. Rogers (1983) stated that the adopter categorisation in relation to adoption time requires the determination of the number of adopter categories, the percentage of adopters in each category, and a method to define these categories. Rogers' (1962) adopter categorisation is based on a normal distribution curve that shows the adoption of an innovation over time on a frequency basis which takes the form of an 'S' when plotted on a cumulative basis (*see* Figure 2.6). Indeed, the diffusion curve is much related to the concept of the product life cycle, which shows the level of total sales

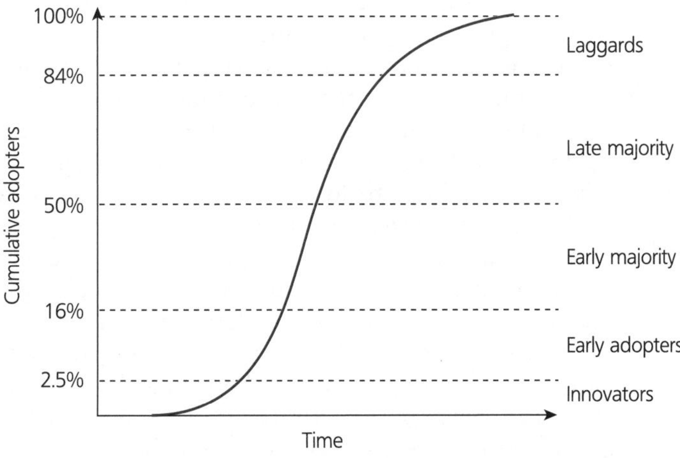

Figure 2.6 S-curve of cumulative adopters

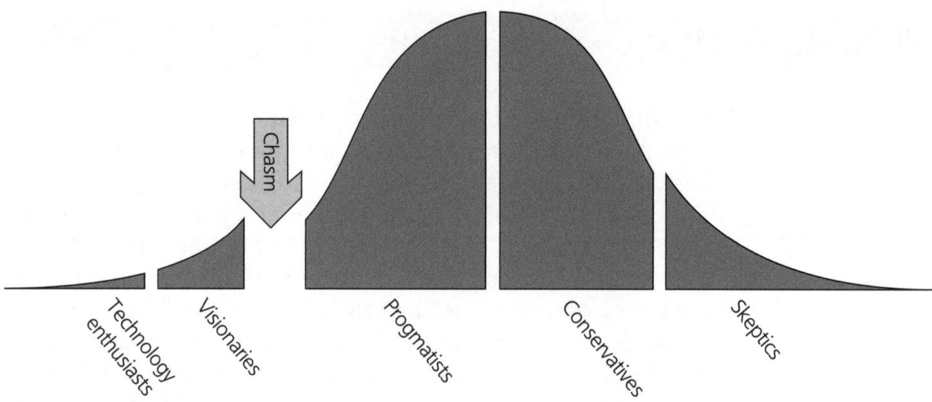

Figure 2.7 Adopter categorisation on the basis of innovativeness
Source: Adapted from Moore, G.A. (1991) *Crossing the Chasm*, Harper Business.

over time. The close relationship between these two concepts would be expected to the extent that sales are proportional to cumulative adoption.

In this model, Rogers (1962) classified different adopter segments in terms of their standard deviation positions from the mean time of adoption of the innovation for the entire market. In this way, he utilised the average and a normal distribution of adopters in order to group them into five categories and obtain the percentage of individuals to be included in each of these categories (*see* Figure 2.7). Rogers stated that innovators comprise the adopter segment which adopts an innovation earlier than the other adopter groups. Innovators are followed by early adopters, early majority, late majority and laggards. In this context, Rogers assumed that these five diverse adopter segments differ on the basis of their demographical features, personality-related characteristics, communication behaviour and social relationships.

Rogers classifies stages in the technology life cycle by the relative percentage of customers who adopt it at each stage (Rogers, 1995). Early on are the innovators and early adopters (who are concerned with the underlying technology and its performance). Then come in succession the early majority pragmatists, the late majority conservatives and lastly the laggards (all of whom are more interested in solutions and convenience). In a contribution to this debate Geoffrey Moore depicts the transition between the early adopters and early majority pragmatists as a chasm that many high-technology companies never successfully cross (*see* Figure 2.7) (Moore, 2004). Moore's contribution to the diffusion debate helped create new approaches for marketing in high-tech industries. His successful book *Crossing the Chasm* has proved popular for helping firms bring cutting-edge products to progressively larger markets. Clayton Christensen prefers to look at the phenomenon of technology take-up from the perspective of the level of performance required by average users (those in the early and late majority categories in Figure 2.7) (Christensen, 1997). He argues that once a technology product meets customers' basic needs they regard it as 'good enough' and no longer care about the underlying technology.

In terms of demographical characteristics, earlier adopters such as innovators and early adopters are presumed to be younger, wealthier and better educated people. When personality-related characteristics are considered, the most distinguishing features of earlier adopters are that they are more eager to take risks and they hold more positive perceptions towards technology in general. Communication behaviours of earlier adopters are assumed to differ on the basis of their media usage behaviour and interpersonal communications with the rest of the consumer segments. Therefore these people are supposed to be opinion leaders in their social relationships throughout the diffusion process.

Diffusion may also be examined from an even more macroperspective, and in some instances it can be particularly important to do so. For example, researchers like Dekimpe *et al.* (2000) have investigated the global diffusion of technological innovations. In their work they focus on issues concerning the two-stage (implementation stage and confirmation stage) nature of the global diffusion process as defined by Rogers (1983), the irregularity of a diffusion pattern due to network externalities and/or central decision makers, and the role of the installed base of older-generation technologies that an innovation replaces (Dekimpe *et al.*, 2000: 51). As they point out, 'for most innovations, the adoption process of each country starts with the implementation stage, which is followed by the confirmation stage'. However, they point out that for technological innovations within-country diffusion might be instantaneous – due to network externalities (e.g. established standards) or central decision makers – and, as such, the confirmation stage for certain countries may have a zero duration. A good example of this is the introduction of digital television within the UK. The UK government, through the BBC, has invested considerable sums of money to educate and inform the population about the advantages of digital television over analogue and to explain that the country will eventually stop transmitting television over analogue signals.

Pause for thought 

Given that internet banking has been available for over 10 years, do you think internet banking has crossed the 'chasm'? Is it always just a matter of time and, so long as you are patient, products will always eventually succeed?

Adopting new products and embracing change

Diffusion is essentially consumer willingness to embrace change. But change can be simple and complex. These range from a change in perception to a significant change in required behaviour in order to use the product. For example, dishwasher appliances require a significant shift in the way people behave in the kitchen and their approach to using cutlery and crockery; similarly for MP3 players with regard to storing and collecting music. Consumers' reactions to innovative new products and their willingness to embrace them are also, of course, driven by the benefit they expect to derive from the products. For discontinuous innovations such products, which often involve new technologies, frequently require changes in thinking and behaviour and hence require more from the consumer. Unsurprisingly these products carry a high risk of market failure. When it comes to technology, consumers have a love–hate relationship with it and this is because of the paradoxes of technological products. For example, products such as appliances that are purchased in order to save time often end up wasting time. In their codification of the various paradoxes discussed across the technology literature, Mick and Fournier (1998) present a

Table 2.3 Paradoxes of technological products

Paradox	Description	Illustration
Control–chaos	Technology can facilitate order and it can lead to disorder	Telephone answering machine can help record messages but leads to disorder due to uncertainty about whether the message has been received
Freedom–enslavement	Technology can provide independence and it can lead to dependence	The motor car clearly gives independence to the driver but many drivers feel lost without it
New–obsolete	The user is provided with the latest scientific knowledge but this is soon outmoded	Computer games industry
Efficiency–inefficiency	Technology can help reduce effort and time but it can also lead to more effort and time	Increased complexity in VCRs has led to many wasting time in setting recordings
Fulfils needs–creates needs	Technology can help fulfil needs and it can lead to more desires	The internet has satisfied the curiosity of many but has also stimulated many desires
Assimilation–isolation	Technology can facilitate human togetherness and can lead to human separation	Email and chat rooms help communication but in some cases heavy users can become isolated
Engaging–disengaging	Technology can facilitate involvement but it can also lead to disconnection	Advances in mobile phone memory means that many people no longer need or have the skills to discover the telephone number from a telephone directory

Source: Adapted from Mick and Fournier (1998).

typology of paradoxes of technological products. These are captured in Table 2.3. These paradoxes play an important role in shaping consumers' perceptions of innovations as well as determining their willingness to adopt new products.

In addition to the various trade-offs or paradoxes that affect consumers' willingness to embrace innovative products – an aspect of a new product offering that should be considered in the design stage as well as the later product launch stage – consumers develop their own ways of coping with innovations and these can impact diffusion as well. Potential customers may ignore a new technology altogether, delay obtaining the new product, attempt to try an innovative new product without the risk of outright purchase, embrace the product and master it, and so on (Carver *et al.*, 1989; Mick and Fournier, 1998). Furthermore, in evaluating discontinuous new products, there are certain factors that are likely to come into play more than they do for less innovative products. Lack of familiarity, 'irrationality', user-product interaction problems, uncertainty and risk, and accordance or compatibility issues may play a decisive role in customers' evaluations of products in either the development and testing stages or once the product is introduced into a market (Veryzer, 1998a: 144). For example, during the course of one radical innovation development project, managers were struck by how 'irrational' customers were in that they often focused on things that the product development team thought to be unimportant, and test customers ignored aspects of a prototype product that the team had expounded a great deal of effort and money on. Even though this type of 'irrationality' may frustrate product development teams, in the domain of highly innovative products, assumptions must be checked against those who will be the final arbitrators of success (Veryzer, 1998b).

Generally, radical innovations are not easily adopted in the market. Potential adopters experience difficulties to comprehend and evaluate radical innovations due to their newness in terms of technology and benefits offered. Consequently, adoption intentions may remain low. A study by Reinders *et al.* (2010) shows that product bundling enhances the new product's evaluation and adoption intention, although it does not increase comprehension of the radical innovation. Thus offering a radical innovation in a product bundle could be a fruitful strategy for companies that target customers with little or no prior knowledge of the product domain.

Market adoption theories

There is a considerable amount of confusion with regard to adoption and diffusion. This is largely due to differences in definition. Most researchers in the field, however, view adoption of innovations as a process though which individuals pass from awareness to the final decision to adopt or not adopt; whereas diffusion concerns the communication over time within a wider social system. The adoption research is derived mainly from social psychology and focuses on the individual. This includes such models as the theory of reasoned action (TRA), the theory of planned behaviour (TPB) and the technology acceptance model (TAM). The diffusion of innovations theory combines both adoption and the wider societal issues derived from sociology (*see* Yu and Tao, 2009). As previously mentioned, the study of how and why consumers purchase goods and services falls within the arena of consumer buyer behaviour and is beyond the scope of this book.

Case study

How three students built a business that could affect world trade

This case study tells the story of how three MSc students at the Technical University of Delft in The Netherlands had an idea for a folding shipping container and went about building a business. There are many examples of university students starting businesses, but few of these have the potential to revolutionise world trade.

Source: Pearson Education Ltd/Photodisc

Almost all containers today that you see on ships, trains or on trucks are 20 ft or 40 ft in length. The reason for the massive change in both transportation and the global economy is because of this simplicity of size – a small set of standard sizes that allowed ships, trucks, receiving bays, and all of the related logistical systems to easily adapt to an industry-wide standard. Prior to standardisation there were major inefficiencies in commercial shipping: packaging and crating was inconsistent. But, what about empty containers? Are there ships travelling the world with containers that are empty? If so is this a business opportunity?

Introduction

Jan, Mark and Stephan were studying for their MSc in mechanical engineering at the Technical University of Delft in The Netherlands. They had arrived late for their lecture and had been forced to sit at the front. They had cycled the short distance from their house on the other side of town and would have arrived on time if it had not been for the lifting bridge over the canal, which had to be raised for a large boat carrying steel shipping containers. This incident was to prove significant. For it was during the lecture by a professor of mechanics that the students hit upon the idea of a folding steel container. The professor was explaining that springs can, in theory, be used to lift very heavy weights providing the springs are large enough. We are all aware of the Anglepoise lamp that uses springs to enable the movement of its steel arm and lamp. The same principle can be used to move much larger objects providing one has much larger springs. Initially, the students thought about springs to raise and lower a bridge, but this was soon dismissed. A steel container that could be folded into a small space had many more attractions. The three students went away to experiment with their idea and conduct calculations on weight, force, stress and strain measurements. Eventually they developed a prototype and modelled it on a computer simulation program. It worked. After much dancing around the computer lab the three then looked at each other as if to say 'now what?' It was a good question. Should they run and get a patent on their idea before someone else steals it? What are the benefits of a folding container? Maybe a folding container already exists? A working computer simulation is a long way from a folding 40 ft steel container. (By way of illustration you can drive a large car into one of these containers.) Would anyone be interested? And how can we make any money out of the idea? Having interesting technology is a long way from a profitable money-making business.

The first thing Jan did was to contact the Port of Rotterdam, which is only 15 km from Delft and is one of the world's busiest container ports (see Table 2.4). Eventually he was able to speak to the Commercial Director of the Port. He explained to Jan that folding and collapsible containers have been around for many years, but they have never really worked. This is primarily because they are expensive to manufacture (usually 10 per cent more than the standard container) and bits get lost, for example the roof from one container sometimes does not fit another container, and the additional equipment required to assemble the containers all adds to the cost. The list of criticisms seemed to be very long. At the end Jan asked what about folding containers that are all

Table 2.4 Busiest container ports

	Port	Country	TEUs* (000s)	% change from 2004
1	Singapore	Singapore	23,192	8.7
2	Hong Kong	China	22,427	2.0
3	Shanghai	China	18,084	24.2
4	Shenzhen	China	16,197	19.0
5	Busan	South Korea	11,843	3.6
6	Kaohsiung	Taiwan (Republic of China)	9,471	0.0
7	**Rotterdam**	**Netherlands**	**9,287**	**12.2**
8	Hamburg	Germany	8,088	15.5
9	Dubai	United Arab Emirates	7,619	18.5
10	Los Angeles	USA	7,485	2.2

*Twenty-foot equivalent units.

in one piece, where the sides can be folded down by hand? The Director laughed and said: 'Yeah, right, like on the Disney channel!' Jan reported back to his friends that potential customers may not believe that they could deliver such a product.

The friends faced a number of difficulties and many uncertainties. They needed advice, after all they were engineers, very clever engineers, but not experts in developing businesses. Fortunately, the university had a business incubator that helped students develop their ideas and create businesses. It would be able to help them with their patent application, but Jan, Mark and Stephan soon realised they did not know simple answers to questions such as: Who would buy it? Who are the customers? How many containers are there in the Netherlands/Europe/world? How much does it cost to make a container? How much does it cost to buy one? It was soon clear that many days of research lay ahead. This would have to be squeezed in between lectures and coursework.

A brief history of shipping containers

The students' research uncovered the following. During the 1960s, 1970s and 1980s the standardisation of shipping containers revolutionised global trade and has dramatically reduced the cost of transporting goods around the world. According to Marc Levinson (2006), author of *The Box: How the Shipping Container Made the World Smaller and the World Economy Bigger*, much of this revolution was down to one man – Malcolm McLean – who challenged the norm and introduced standardised, packaged shipping. More than 50 years ago, Malcom McLean, a North Carolina trucking entrepreneur, originally hatched the idea of using containers to carry cargo. He loaded 58 containers onto his ship, *Ideal X*, in Newark, New Jersey, and once the vessel reached Houston, Texas the uncrated containers were moved directly onto trucks – and reusable rectangular boxes soon became the industry standard. What was new in the USA about McLean's innovation was the idea of using large containers that were never opened in transit between shipper and consignee and that were transferable on an intermodal basis, among trucks, ships and railroad cars.

Now, most students of business will immediately recognise the benefits that can flow from the introduction of a uniform standard. And history is littered with examples of industries struggling to grow until a single uniform standard is adopted, thereby signalling the end of uncertainty and the start of the adoption of the standard technology. Prior to a standard width gauge, the UK railway industry had two competing gauges and the computer industry has battled for many years over operating systems. The shipping industry was in a similar position with many different types of containers. Packaging and crating products was inconsistent and inefficient. Large numbers of people were employed in ports around the world to break bulk cargo. Frequently separate items had to be handled individually, such as bags of sugar or flour packed next to copper tube. Today, approximately 90 per cent of non-bulk cargo worldwide moves by containers stacked on transport ships. Some 18 million containers make over 200 million trips per year. For the past 10 years, demand for cargo capacity has been growing almost 10 per cent a year.

This background research on the industry proved to be more interesting than the students had first thought and it delivered some exciting findings. Most importantly, that this was a growing industry, it had international firms with large budgets. And they had uncovered the fact that the storage of containers poses a significant problem for the shipping lines that are always on the look out for ways to reduce this cost.

Background: containers

The students now needed to explore in detail the shipping container and how it is used. More research was required and soon they uncovered more useful information. The history of the use of purpose-built containers for trade can be traced back to the 1830s; railroads on several continents were carrying containers that could be transferred to trucks or ships, but these containers were small by today's standards. Originally used for shipping coal on and off barges, 'loose boxes' were used to containerise coal from the late 1780s. By the 1840s, iron boxes were in use as well as wooden ones. The early 1900s saw the adoption of closed container boxes designed for movement between road and rail. Towards the end of the Second World War, the US Army began using specialised containers to speed up the loading and unloading of transport ships. After the US Department of Defense standardised an 8 ft × 8 ft cross-section container in multiples of 10 ft lengths for military use it was rapidly adopted for shipping purposes. These standards were adopted in the United Kingdom for containers and rapidly displaced the older wooden containers in the 1950s.

→

Table 2.5 Specifications of the three most common types of container

		20′ container		40′ container		45′ high-cube container	
		Imperial	Metric	Imperial	Metric	Imperial	Metric
External dimensions	Length	20′ 0″	6.096 m	40′ 0″	12.192 m	45′ 0″	13.716 m
	Width	8′ 0″	2.438 m	8′ 0″	2.438 m	8′ 0″	2.438 m
	Height	8′ 6″	2.591 m	8′ 6″	2.591 m	9′ 6″	2.896 m
Volume		1,169 ft^3	33.1 m^3	2,385 ft^3	67.5 m^3	3,040 ft^3	86.1 m^3
Maximum gross mass		66,139 lb	30,400 kg	66,139 lb	30,400 kg	66,139 lb	30,400 kg
Empty weight		4,850 lb	2,200 kg	8,380 lb	3,800 kg	10,580 lb	4,800 kg
Net load		61,289 lb	28,200 kg	57,759 lb	26,600 kg	55,559 lb	25,600 kg

Containers, also known as intermodal containers or as ISO containers because the dimensions have been defined by the ISO, are the main type of equipment used in intermodal transport, particularly when one of the modes of transportation is by ship. Containers are 8 ft wide by 8 ft high. Since their introduction, there have been moves to adopt other heights. The most common lengths are 20 ft and 40 ft although other lengths exist. They are made out of steel and can be stacked on top of each other.

Container capacity is often expressed in *twenty-foot equivalent units* (TEU, or sometimes teu). An equivalent unit is a measure of containerised cargo capacity equal to one standard 20 ft (length) × 8 ft (width) container. The use of Imperial measurements to describe container size reflects the fact that the US Department of Defense played a major part in the development of containers. The overwhelming need to have a standard size for containers, in order that they fit all ships, cranes, and trucks, and the length of time that the current container sizes have been in use, makes changing to an even metric size impractical. Table 2.5 shows the weights and dimensions of the three most common types of container worldwide. The weights and dimensions quoted above are averages, different manufactured series of the same type of container may vary slightly in actual size and weight.

Handling containers

On ships, containers are typically stacked up to seven units high. When carried by rail, containers can be loaded on flatcars or in container well cars. When the container ship arrives at the container terminal (port) specialist equipment is required. The transfer from ship to land may be between ships and land vehicles, for example trains or trucks. Maritime container terminals tend to be part of a larger port, whereas inland container terminals tend to be located in or near major cities, with good rail connections to maritime container terminals.

A container crane or gantry crane, is used at container terminals for loading and unloading shipping containers from container ships. Cranes normally transport a single container at once, however some newer cranes have the capability to pick up up to four 20 ft containers at once. Handling equipment is designed with intermodality in mind, assisting with transferring containers between rail, road and sea. These can include:

- Transtainer for transferring containers from sea-going vessels onto either trucks or rail wagons. A transtainer is mounted on rails with a large boom spanning the distance between the ship's cargo hold and the quay, moving parallel to the ship's side.
- Gantry cranes, also known as straddle carriers, are able to straddle rail and road vehicles allowing for quick transfer of containers. A spreader beam moves in several directions allowing accurate positioning of the cargo.
- Reach stackers are fitted with lifting arms as well as spreader beams and lift containers to swap bodies or stack containers on top of each other.

Container shipping companies

Informally known as 'box boats' these vessels carry the majority of the world's manufactured goods. Cargoes like metal ores, coal or wheat are carried in bulk carriers. There are large mainline vessels that ply the deep-sea routes, and then many small 'feeder' ships that supply the large ships at centralised hub ports. Most container ships are propelled by diesel engines, and have crews of between 20 and 40. Container ships now carry up to 15,000 TEU. The world's largest container ship, the M/V *Emma Mærsk* has a capacity of 15,200 containers.

The capacity of a container ship is measured in TEUs, which is the number of standard 20-foot containers a vessel can carry. This not withstanding, most containers used today measure 40 ft (12 m) in length. Above a certain size, container ships do not carry their own loading gear, so loading and unloading can only be done at ports with the necessary cranes. However, smaller ships with capacities of up to 2,900 TEU are often equipped with their own cranes.

The world's oceans can be a scary places in bad weather, hence the transit of containers around the world inevitably carries a considerable risk. And yet, the well-known challenging routes, such as round the Cape Horn, are not where most containers are lost. Most risks are linked to the loading and unloading of containers. The risks involved in these operations affect both the cargo being moved on to or off the ship, as well as the ship itself. Containers, due to their fairly nondescript nature and the sheer number handled in major ports, require complex organisation to ensure they are not lost, stolen or misrouted. In addition, as the containers and the cargo they contain make up the vast majority of the total weight of a cargo ship, the loading and unloading is a delicate balancing act, as it directly affects the whole ships centre of mass. There have been some instances of poorly loaded ships capsizing at port.

It has been estimated that container ships lose over 10,000 containers at sea each year. Most go overboard on the open sea during storms but there are some examples of whole ships being lost with their cargo. When containers are dropped, they immediately become an environmental threat – termed 'marine debris'.

It is not surprising that when the three students visited Rotterdam Container Port to discuss their idea with senior managers from the port, the managers were very enthusiastic about containers and the benefits they deliver. They explained that container cargo could be moved nearly 20 times faster than pre-container break bulk cargo. They also argued that while there were increased fuel costs, due to the extra weight of the containers, labour efficiencies more than compensate. Nonetheless, for certain bulk products this makes containerisation unattractive. On railways the capacity of the container is far from its maximum weight capacity. In some areas (mostly the USA and Canada) containers are double-stacked, but this not usually possible in other countries.

At the end of the meeting the Commercial Director explained to the students that, for their idea to succeed, they would need to receive the necessary certification from agencies such as Lloyds Register or Bureau Veritas. Their approval is required regarding the seaworthiness of any marine equipment. Without such certification no shipping company would be interested in their ideas. There seemed to be many obstacles to their business idea.

Table 2.6 Biggest shipping container companies

Top 10 container shipping companies in order of TEU capacity			
Company	**TEU capacity**	**Market share (%)**	**Number of ships**
A.P. Moller-Maersk Group	1,665,272	18.2	549
Mediterranean Shipping Company S.A.	865,890	11.7	376
CMA CGM	507,954	5.6	256
Evergreen Marine Corporation	477,911	5.2	153
Hapag-Lloyd	412,344	4.5	140
China Shipping Container Lines	346,493	3.8	111
American President Lines	331,437	3.6	99
Hanjin-Senator	328,794	3.6	145
COSCO	322,326	3.5	118
NYK Line	302,213	3.3	105

→

Business opportunity: moving empty containers

Containers are intended to be used constantly, being loaded with a new cargo for a new destination soon after being emptied of the previous cargo. This is not always possible, and in some cases the cost of transporting an empty container to a place where it can be used is considered to be higher than the worth of the used container. This can result in large areas in ports and warehouses being occupied by empty containers left abandoned. The shipping industry spends a great deal of time and money in repositioning empty containers. If trade was balanced, there would be no empty containers. But trade imbalance, especially between Europe and North America with Asia, has resulted in approximately 2.5 million TEUs of empty containers stored in yards around the world with empties comprising 20–23 per cent of the movement of containers around the world. According to research conducted by International Asset Systems, the average container is idle or undergoing repositioning for over 50 per cent of its life span. The research also determined that shipping companies spend $16 billion in repositioning empties. To compensate for these costs, carriers add surcharges, ranging from $100 to $1,000 per TEU, to freight rates.

Folding containers would provide further advantages: for example, they would relieve congestion at ports. Storing empty containers takes up prime real estate. For example, the storage yards around the Port of Jersey, UK, are cluttered with an estimated 100,000 empty containers belonging to leasing companies and an additional 50,000 belonging to ocean carriers. Folding containers would be quicker to load (four at a time), resulting in faster turnaround time for ships. Energy costs would drop as well, as one trailer rather than four would transport empties. Finally, there is also a security feature to the folded container built to ISO standards. Nothing can be smuggled in a collapsed empty. It is estimated that if 75 per cent of empty containers were folded by 2010, the result would be a yearly saving in shipping of 25 million TEUs or 50 per cent of the total volume of empty containers shipped.

Concept to product

The background research had been done. There was genuine interest from potential customers. The students now needed money to build a working scale model of the folding container. They had to

Source: Pearson Education Ltd/Photodisc

prove to everyone that it would work. Moreover, the concept also had to be compatible with existing equipment for intermodal transport. That is, it would need to be exactly the same size/shape/weight, etc. It would also have to have proper sealing and locking devices, and should interlock with other containers. Computer models were fine to a point, but a physical model was now required, especially if they were going to convince people to invest. With the help of the university and the Incubator the students set about constructing a full working steel model. It was to be a 1/10th scale. So it would be 2 ft long 0.8 ft high. Real working springs would have to be in place. The friends realised immediately that a patent drawing is theory and it did not resemble reality. Numerous fabrication and manufacturing problems had to be overcome. Eventually, after two months of experimenting with steel springs and welding equipment in the workshop a fully working model emerged that required two people to manoeuvre the steel box. More importantly it had taken a considerable amount of time and investment in materials and equipment. When the model was demonstrated to senior figures at the Port of Rotterdam they were very impressed and immediately wanted to see a full size version – a prototype. But, who would pay for a full size prototype? It would be enormous and probably cost thousands of euros to produce.

The three students had made some significant steps forward with their business idea, but they still did not have an order, let alone any sales or cash. Was this to be just a hobby, something they enjoyed but did not generate any cash? Would anyone pay for one of these things? The students needed money to finance the next stage, but as well as being impoverished they were not manufacturers!

Decision time

All three students were excited about the possibilities and the huge potential that existed. They would love to start their own business, rather than work for someone else. There were many uncertainties: money, career, what happens if they fail? As if to underline their concerns an open page of the *Financial Times* glared at them and gave them further worries:

> ***Credit crunch hits shipping as trade falls***
>
> *2009 has seen a considerable slowdown in global trade. It has left the Indian shipping industry high and dry, with the country's idle capacity set to rise from 150,000 TEUs in October 2008 to 750,000. Not surprisingly freight rates for container ships from India have also fallen by almost 80 per cent since summer 2008. The freight rates on the India–UK sector was $1,100 for a 20 ft container and this has come down to $280 to $300, And to ferry a 20 ft container unit to the Gulf is just $90 against $550 in 2007. Globally, things are similar elsewhere. In Singapore, one of the world's busiest ports, some vessels are now being used to store empty containers to save on port rentals. Port-related businesses, such as inland container ports and container freight stations, are also suffering.*

The global downturn raised further worries for the friends – maybe this was the wrong time to start a business?

Source: Levinson, M. (2006) *The Box: How the Shipping Container Made the World Smaller and the World Economy Bigger*, Princeton University Press, Princeton.

Questions

1 Would you advise the students to start this business?
2 Who are their customers going to be?
3 Who can they license the technology to?
4 Can they form any partnerships or alliances?
5 How would you enter this market?
6 What aspects of product diffusion will they need to address?
7 Use the CIM (Figure 1.9) to illustrate the innovation process in this case.
8 Is patent protection essential here? If not why not?
9 How can the students help customers adopt the product?
10 Standardisation led to growth in container usage: what will be the effect of this non-standard folding container?

Note: This case has been written as a basis for class discussion rather than to illustrate effective or ineffective managerial or administrative behaviour. It has been prepared from a variety of sources and from observations.

Chapter summary

This chapter has explored the wider context of innovation, in particular the role of the state and the role of the market. It has shown that innovation cannot be separated from political and social processes. This includes both tangible and intangible features, including economic, social and political institutions, and processes and mechanisms that facilitate the flow of knowledge between industries and firms. It has also shown the powerful influence of the market on innovation; in particular the need to consider long time frames when developing technology and innovative new products. Finally, this chapter discussed an aspect of innovation that is frequently overlooked – the pattern of consumption of the new product or new service. It is changes to the way the new product or service is consumed that all too often determines whether it will be a success or not.

Discussion questions

1 Discuss the tangible features that it is necessary for the state to put in place to foster innovation.

2 How can the state encourage entrepreneurs and businesses to invest in longer time horizons?

3 Explain Schumpeter's view of entrepreneurial behaviour and economic growth.

4 Discuss the evidence for the fifth Kondratieff wave of growth.

5 What is meant by a 'weak business system'?

6 How does diffusion differ from adoption?

7 What role should marketing play in the early stages of product innovation?

8 List some of the additional factors that affect the adoption of highly innovative products.

9 Explain how market vision can help the innovation process.

10 How does the pattern of consumption influence the likely success or failure of a new product?

Key words and phrases

Schumpeterian theory *48*
Short-termism *49*
Entrepreneurship *49*
National systems of innovation *50*
Corruption *54*
Kondratieff waves of growth *55*
Business system *58*
Market vision *62*
Lead-user theory *66*
Adoption theory *67*
Diffusion theory *67*

References

Afuah, A. (2003) *Innovation Management: Strategies, Implementation and Profits*, 2nd edn, Oxford University Press, Oxford.

Amsden, A. (1989) *Asia's Next Giant: South Korea and Late Industrialisation*, Oxford University Press, Oxford.

Carver, C.S., Scheier, M.F. and Weintraub, J.K. (1989) Assessing coping strategies: A theoretically based approach, *Journal of Personality and Social Psychology*, Vol. 56, 267–83.

Castells, M. (1992) 'Four Asian Tigers with a dragon head: a comparative analysis of the state, economy, and society in the Asian Pacific Rim', in Appelbaum, R.P. and Henderson, J. (eds) *States and Development: The Asian Pacific Rim*, Oxford University Press, Oxford, 33–70.

Christensen, C.M. (1997) *The Innovator's Dilemma: When new technologies cause great firms to fail*, HBS Press, Cambridge.

Dekimpe, M.G., Parker, P.M. and Sarvary, M. (2000) 'Multimarket and global diffusion', in Mahajan, V., Muller, E. and Wind, Y. (eds) *New-product diffusion models*, Kluwer Academic, Dordrecht, The Netherlands, 49–73.

Dicken, P. (1998) *Global Shift: Transforming the World Economy*, Paul Chapman, London.

European Innovation Scoreboard (EIS) (2010) Pro Inno Europe Paper No. 15, http://www.proinno-europe.eu/metrics.

Evans, P.B. (1989) Predatory, developmental, and other apparatuses: a comparative political economy perspective on the Third World state, *Sociological Forum*, Vol. 4, No. 4, 561–87.

Franke, N. and Piller, F. (2004) Value creation by toolkits for user innovation and design: The case of the watch market, *Journal of Product Innovation Management*, Vol. 21, No. 6, 401–16.

Freeman, C. and Soete, L. (1997) *The Economics of Industrial Innovation*, 3rd edn, Pinter, London.

Hamel, G. and Prahalad, C.K. (1994) Competing for the future, *Harvard Business Review*, Vol. 72, No. 4, 122–8.

Hart, J.A. (1992) *Rival Capitalists: International Competitiveness in the United States, Japan, and Western Europe*, Cornell University Press, London.

Hobday, M., Rush, H. and Bessant, J. (2004) Approaching the innovation frontier in Korea: the transition phase to leadership, *Research Policy*, Vol. 33, No. 10, 1433–57.

Johnson, C. (1982) *MITI and the Japanese Miracle: The Growth of Industrial Policy 1925–75*, Stanford University Press, Stanford, CA.

King, S. (1985) Has marketing failed or was it never really tried?, *Journal of Marketing Management*, Vol. 1, No. 1, 1–19.

Leifer, R., Colarelli O'Connor, G., Peters, L.S., Rice, M. Veryzer, R.W. and McDermott, C.M. (2000) *Radical Innovation*, HBS Press, Boston, MA.

Martin, J. (1995) Ignore your customer, *Fortune*, Vol. 1, No. 8, 121–5.

Mick, D.G. and Fournier, S. (1998) Paradoxes of Technology: Consumer Cognizance, Emotions, and Coping Strategies, *Journal of Consumer Research*, Vol. 25, No. 9, 123–47.

Moore, G.A. (2004) *Crossing the chasm: Marketing and selling technology products to mainstream customers*, 2nd edn, Capstone, Oxford.

Morrison, P.J., Roberts, J. and Midgley, D. (2004) The nature of lead users and measurement of leading edge status, *Research Policy*, Vol. 33, 351–62.

Norton, J.A. and Bass, F.M. (1987) A diffusion theory model of adoption and substitution for successive generations of high technology products, *Management Science*, Vol. 33, No. 9, 1069–86.

Norton, J.A. and Bass, F.M. (1992) Evolution of technological change: The law of capture, *Sloan Management Review*, Vol. 33, No. 2, 66–77.

Porter, M. (1990) *The Competitive Advantage of Nations*, Macmillan, London.

Porter, M., Takeuchi, H. and Sakakıbara, M. (2000) *Can Japan Compete?*, Perseus Pub., Cambridge, MA.

Reinders, M.J., Frambach, R.T. and Schoormans, J.P.L. (2010) Using Product Bundling to Facilitate the Adoption Process of Radical Innovations, *Journal of Product Innovation Management*, Vol. 27, 1127–40.

Rogers, E.M. (1962) *Diffusion of innovations*, Free Press, New York.

Rogers, E.M. (1983) *Diffusion of innovations*, 3rd edn, The Free Press, New York.

Rogers, E.M. (1995) *Diffusion of innovations*, 4th edn, The Free Press, New York.

Rosenthal, D.E. (1993) Reevaluating the Chicago School paradigm for promoting innovation and competitiveness, *Canada–United States Law Journal*, Vol. 19, 97–104.

Schumpeter, J. (1943) *Capitalism, Socialism and Democracy*, Allen & Unwin, London.

Tauber, E.M. (1974) Predictive validity in consumer research, *Journal of Advertising Research*, Vol. 15, No. 5, 59–64.

Toprak, Z. (1995) National Economics-National Bourgeoisie: Economy and Society in Turkey 1908–1950 (in Turkish: Milli Iktisat-Milli Burjuvazi: Türkiye'de Ekonomi ve Toplum 1908–1950), Türkiye Toplumsal ve Ekonomik Tarih Vakfı, Istanbul.

van der Panne, G., van Beers, C. and Kleinknecht, A. (2003) Success and failure of innovation: a review of the literature, *International Journal of Innovation Management*, Vol. 7, No. 3, 309–38.

Veryzer, R.W. (1998a) Key factors affecting customer evaluation of discontinuous products, *Journal of Product Innovation Management*, Vol. 15, No. 2, 136–50.

Veryzer, R.W. (1998b) Discontinuous innovation and the new product development process, *Journal of Product Innovation Management*, Vol. 15, No. 4, 304–21.

Veryzer, R. (2003) 'Marketing and the development of innovative products', in Shavinina, L. (ed.) *International Handbook on Innovation*, Pergamon Press, Canada, 43–54.

Yu, C. and Tao, Y. (2009) Understanding business-level innovation technology adoption, *Technovation*, Vol. 29, No. 2, 92–109.

Further reading

For a more detailed review of the role of the state in innovation management, the following develop many of the issues raised in this chapter:

Afuah, A. (2003) *Innovation Management: Strategies, Implementation and Profits*, 2nd edn, Oxford University Press, Oxford.

Freeman, C. and Soete, L. (2009) Developing science, technology and innovation indicators: What we can learn from the past, *Research Policy*, Vol. 38, No. 4, 583–9.

HSBC (2010) 100 thoughts, HSBC, London.

Hobday, M., Rush, H. and Bessant, J. (2004) Approaching the innovation frontier in Korea: The transition phase to leadership, *Research Policy*, Vol. 33, No. 10, 1433–57.

Moore, G.A. (2004) *Crossing the Chasm: Marketing and selling technology products to mainstream customers*, 2nd edn, Capstone, Oxford.

Rogers, E.M. (2003) *Diffusion of Innovations*, 5th edn, Free Press, New York.

Veryzer, R. (2003) 'Marketing and the development of innovative products', in Shavinina, L. (ed.) *The International Handbook on Innovation*, Pergamon Press, Canada.

Chapter 3
Managing innovation within firms

Introduction

Virtually all innovations, certainly major technological innovations such as pharmaceutical and automobile products, occur within organisations. The management of innovation within organisations forms the focus for this chapter. The study of organisations and their management is a very broad subject and no single approach provides all the answers. The identification of those factors and issues that affect the management of innovation within organisations is addressed here. The W.L. Gore case study at the end of this chapter shows how this firm has developed an organisation culture that supports innovation and creativity. Also, Gore is a regular winner of the *Sunday Times* 'best organisation to work for' award.

Chapter contents

Learning objectives

When you have completed this chapter you will be able to:

- identify the factors organisations have to manage to achieve success in innovation;
- explain the dilemma facing all organisations concerning the need for creativity and stability;
- recognise the difficulties of managing uncertainty;
- identify the activities performed by key individuals in the management of innovation; and
- recognise the relationship between the activities performed and the organisational environment in promoting innovation.

Organisations and innovation

Chapter 1 outlined some of the difficulties in studying the field of innovation. In particular, it emphasised the need to view innovation as a management process within the context of the organisation. This was shown to be the case especially in a modern industrialised society where innovation is increasingly viewed as an *organisational activity*. Chapter 2 offered an overview of the wider issues of innovation, in particular the economic and market factors, which ultimately will be the judge of any product or service that is launched. This chapter tackles the difficult issue of managing innovation within organisations. To do this, it is necessary to understand the patterns of interaction and behaviour which represent the organisation.

The dilemma of innovation management

Within virtually all organisations there is a fundamental tension between the need for stability and the need for creativity. On the one hand, companies require stability and static routines to accomplish daily tasks efficiently and quickly. This enables the organisation to compete today. For example, the processing of millions of cheques by banks every day, or the delivery of food by multiples to their retail outlets all over the country, demands high levels of efficiency and control. On the other hand, companies also need to develop new ideas and new products to be competitive in the future. Hence they need to nurture a creative environment where ideas can be tested and developed. This poses one of the most fundamental problems for management today (*see* Figure 3.1).

Take any medium to large company and examine its operations and activities. From Mars to Ford, and from P&G to Sony, these companies have to ensure that their products are carefully manufactured to precise specifications and that they are delivered for customers on time day after day. In this hectic, repetitive and highly organised environment the need to squeeze out any slack or inefficiencies is crucial to ensure a firm's costs are lower than their competitors'. Without this emphasis on cost reductions a firm's costs would simply spiral upwards and the firm's products and services would become uncompetitive. But we have already seen in the previous chapter that long-term economic growth is dependent on the ability of firms to make improvements to products and manufacturing processes.

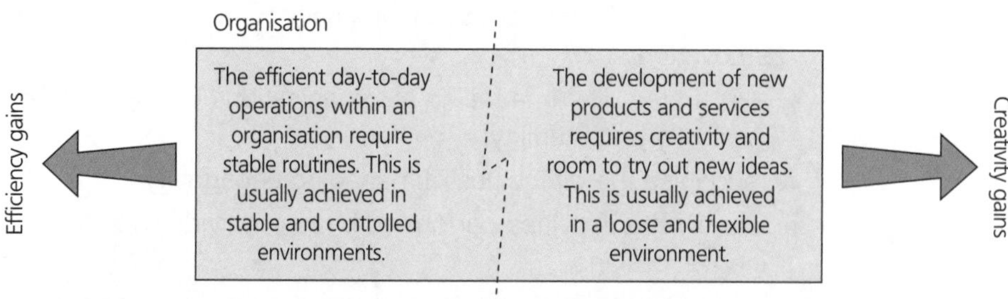

Figure 3.1 Managing the tension between the need for creativity and efficiency

This means that firms need to somehow make room for creativity and innovation, that is, allow slack in the system.

Here then is the dilemma: how do firms try to reduce costs and slack to improve competitiveness on the one hand and then try to provide slack for innovation on the other? As usual with dilemmas the answer is difficult and has to do with balancing activities. The firm needs to ensure there is a constant pressure to drive down costs and improve efficiency in its operations. At the same time, it needs to provide room for new product development and improvements to be made. The most obvious way forward is to separate production from research and development (R&D) but while this is usually done there are many improvements and innovations that arise out of the operations of the firm, as will be seen in the next chapter. Indeed, the operations of the firm provide enormous scope for innovation.

This is the fundamental tension at the heart of an enterprise's long-run survival. The basic problem confronting an organisation is to engage in sufficient exploitation to ensure its future viability. Exploitation is about efficiency, increasing productivity, control, certainty and variance reduction. Exploration is about search, discovery, autonomy, innovation and embracing variation. Ambidexterity is about doing both. O'Reilly and Tushman (2008) argue that efficiency and innovation need not be strategic tradeoffs and highlight the substantive role of senior teams in building dynamic capabilities. In organisational terms, dynamic capabilities are at the heart of the ability of a business to be ambidextrous – to compete simultaneously in both mature and emerging markets – to explore and exploit. Ambidexterity entails not only separate structure subunits for exploration and exploitation but also different competencies, systems, incentives, processes and cultures – each internally aligned (O'Reilly and Tushman, 2008; Smith and Tushman, 2005).

Pause for thought

To resolve the innovation dilemma, why do not firms simply separate the creative side of their business from the operational side?

Managing uncertainty

While management in general involves coping with uncertainty, sometimes trying to reduce uncertainty, the *raison d'être* of managers involved in innovation is to develop something different, maybe something new. The management of the innovation process involves trying to develop the creative potential of the organisation. It involves trying to foster new ideas and generate creativity. Managing uncertainty is a central feature of managing the innovation process. This has been recognised for over 40 years within the innovation and R&D management literature (Pearson, 1983). Nonetheless, it continues to be a cause for concern for firms. At the very least there is the uncertainty of output (including market uncertainty) – i.e. what is required – and also uncertainty of process – i.e. how to produce it. Pearson offered a helpful uncertainty matrix for managers to help them deal with different levels of uncertainty. This recognised that different environments required different management styles (*see* Figure 3.2).

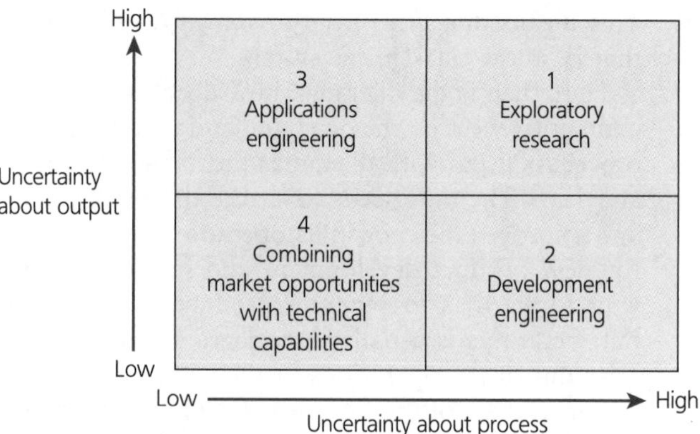

Figure 3.2 Pearson's uncertainty map

Source: A.W. Pearson (1991) 'Managing innovation: an uncertainty reduction process', in *Managing Innovation*, J. Henry and D. Walker (eds), Sage/OU.

Pearson's uncertainty map

Pearson's uncertainty map (Pearson, 1991) provides a framework for analysing and understanding uncertainty and the innovation process. The map was developed following extensive analysis of case studies of major technological innovations, including Pilkington's float glass process, 3M's Post-It Notes and Sony's Walkman (Henry and Walker, 1991). In these and other case studies a great deal of uncertainty surrounded the project. If it involves newly developed technology this may be uncertainty about the type of product envisaged. For example, Spencer Silver's unusual adhesive remained unexploited within 3M for five years before an application was found. Similarly, if a market opportunity has been identified the final product idea may be fairly well established, but much uncertainty may remain about how exactly the company is to develop such a product.

So Pearson's framework divides uncertainty into two separate dimensions:

- uncertainty about ends (what is the eventual target of the activity or project); and
- uncertainty about means (how to achieve this target).

The development of Guinness's 'In-can system' clearly highlights the problems of managing uncertainty about means. Here, several projects were unsuccessful and there were probably several occasions where decisions had to be taken regarding future funding. Decisions had to be made such as whether to cancel, continue or increase funding. In these situations, because the degree of uncertainty is high, senior managers responsible for million-dollar budgets have to listen carefully to those most closely involved and those with the most information and knowledge. Further information and knowledge are usually available with the passage of time, so time is another element that needs to be considered. Indeed, it is because time is limited that decisions are required. It is clear, however, that many decisions are made with imperfect knowledge, thus there is usually an element of judgement involved in most decisions.

Pearson's framework, shown in Figure 3.2, addresses the nature of the uncertainty and the way it changes over time. The framework is based on the two dimensions discussed above, with uncertainty about ends on the vertical axis and uncertainty about means on the horizontal axis. These axes are then divided, giving four quadrants.

Quadrant 1

Quadrant 1 represents activities involving a high degree of uncertainty about means and ends. The ultimate target is not clearly defined and how to achieve this target is also not clear. This has been labelled '**exploratory research**' or 'blue sky' research, because the work sometimes seems so far removed from reality that people liken it to working in the clouds! These activities often involve working with technology that is not fully understood and where potential products or markets have also not been identified. This is largely the domain of university research laboratories, which are usually removed from the financial and time pressures associated with industry. Some science-based organisations also support these activities, but increasingly it is only large organisations that have the necessary resources to fund such exploratory studies. For example, Microsoft conducts the majority of its research in Seattle, United States. Interestingly it calls this centre a 'campus'.

Quadrant 2

In this area the end or target is clear. For example, a commercial opportunity may have been identified but as yet the means of fulfilling this has yet to be established. Companies may initiate several different projects centred on different technologies or different approaches to try to achieve the desired product. Also, additional approaches may be uncovered along the way. Hence, there is considerable uncertainty about precisely how the company will achieve its target. This type of activity is often referred to as development engineering and is an ongoing activity within manufacturing companies which are continually examining their production processes, looking for efficiencies and ways to reduce costs. A good example of a successful development in this area is the Guinness 'In-can system'. The company was clear about its target – trying to make the taste of Guinness from a can taste the same as draught Guinness. Precisely how this was to be achieved was very uncertain and many different research projects were established.

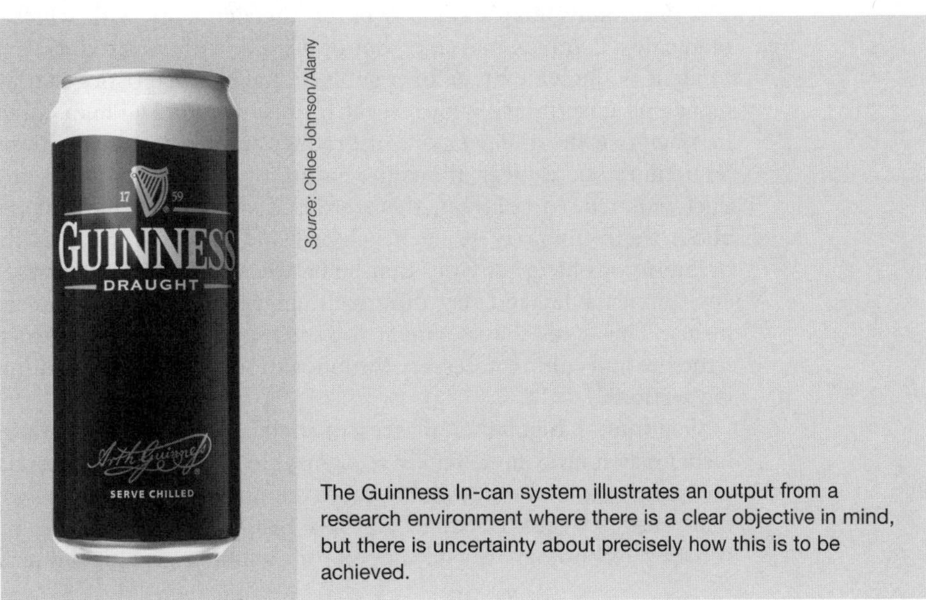

Source: Chloe Johnson/Alamy

The Guinness In-can system illustrates an output from a research environment where there is a clear objective in mind, but there is uncertainty about precisely how this is to be achieved.

Quadrants 3 and 4 deal with situations where there is more certainty associated with how the business will achieve the target. This usually means that the business is working with technology it has used before.

Quadrant 3

In this area there is uncertainty regarding ends. This is usually associated with attempting to discover how the technology can be most effectively used. Applications engineering is the title given to this area of activity. Arguably many new materials fall into this area. For example, the material kevlar (used in the manufacture of bullet-proof clothing) is currently being applied to a wide range of different possible product areas. Many of these may prove to be ineffective due to costs or performance, but some new and improved products will emerge from this effort.

Quadrant 4

This area covers innovative activities where there is most certainty. In these situations activities may be dominated by improving existing products or creating new products through the combination of a market opportunity and technical capability. With so much certainty, similar activities are likely to be being undertaken by the competition. Hence, speed of development is often the key to success here. New product designs that use minimal new technology but improve, sometimes with dramatic effect, the appearance or performance of an existing product are examples of product innovations in this area. A good exponent of this is Nokia. It has demonstrated an ability to introduce new mobile phones incorporating new designs rapidly into the market, thereby maintaing its position as market leader.

Applying the uncertainty map in practice

The uncertainty map's value is partly the simplicity with which it is able to communicate a complex message, that of dealing with uncertainty, and partly its ability to identify the wide range of organisational characteristics that are associated with managing uncertainty with respect to innovation. The map conveys the important message that the management of product and process innovations is very different. Sometimes one is clear about the nature of the target market and the type of product required. In contrast, there are occasions when little, if anything, is known about the technology being developed and how it could possibly be used. Most organisations have activities that lie between these two extremes, but such differing environments demand very different management skills and organisational environments. This leads the argument towards the vexed question of the organisational structure and culture necessary for innovation, which will be addressed in the following sections.

Quadrant 1 highlights an area of innovative activity where ideas and developments may not be immediately recognisable as possible commercial products. There are many examples of technological developments that occurred within organisations that were not recognised. In Xerox's Palo Alto laboratories, the early computer software technology was developed for computer graphical interface as far back as the early 1970s. Xerox did not recognise the possible future benefits of this research and decided not to develop the technology further. It was later exploited by Apple Computer and Microsoft in the 1980s. This raises the question of how to evaluate research in this area. Technical managers may be better able to understand the technology, but a commercial manager may be able to see a wide range of commercial opportunities. Continual informal and formal discussions are usually the best way to explore all possibilities fully, in the hope that the company will make the correct decision regarding which projects to support and which to drop. This is a problem that will be returned to in Chapter 9.

At the other extreme is Quadrant 4, where scientists often view this type of activity as merely tinkering with existing technology. However, commercial managers often get very excited because the project is in a 'close-to-market' form with minimal technical newness.

Between these two extremes lie Quadrants 2 and 3. In the applications engineering quadrant, where the business is exploring the potential uses of known technology, management efforts centre on which markets to enter; whereas in the development engineering quadrant special project-management skills are required to ensure that projects either deliver or are cancelled before costs escalate.

In all of the above, particular organisational environments and specialist management skills are required depending on the type of activity being undertaken. These will be determined by the extent of uncertainty involved.

Pause for thought 

If most new products are minor modifications of existing products, why do firms continue with high-risk, high-cost projects?

Managing innovation projects

We now need to examine innovation projects. Henderson and Clark examined product innovations and demonstrate that product innovations are complex entities embedded in organisational capabilities, which are difficult to create and costly to adjust (Nelson and Winter, 1982; Hannan and Freeman, 1984). Henderson and Clark (1990) divide technological knowledge along two dimensions: *knowledge of the components* and knowledge of the linkage between them, which they called *architectural knowledge* (*see* Figure 3.3). In this framework, technology development could be a radical innovation only if it revolutionises both component and architectural knowledge. Similarly an incremental innovation will build upon existing component and architectural knowledge. Modular innovations will require new knowledge for one or more components, but the architectural knowledge remains unchanged. Whereas architectural innovation will have a great impact upon the linkage of components, the knowledge of single components will remain the same.

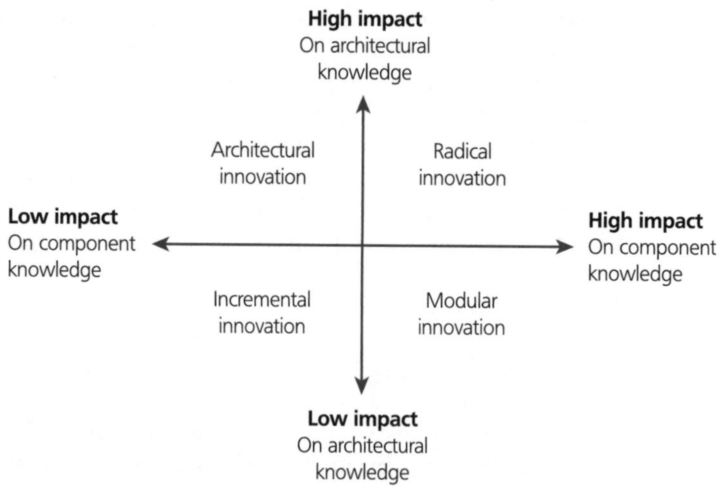

Figure 3.3 Matrix of complexity of architectural/component knowledge

Source: Architectural Innovation: The Reconfiguration of Existing Product Technologies and the Failure of Established Firms, *Administrative Science Quarterly*, Vol. 35, No. 1 (Henderson, R. and Clark, K. 1990). Reproduced with permission of Johnson at Cornell University.

It is against the backcloth of the above discussions that theoretical indications for having more than one model for project management are clear. We need also to recognise that to develop an existing product further is not generally viewed by R&D managers as a high-risk activity. Indeed, these types of low-uncertainty projects are so very different from high-uncertainty R&D projects that it is evidently clear why a classification of project types is necessary. Figure 3.4 uses a two-dimensional typology of innovation projects to illustrate the range of innovation projects required to be managed. The vertical axis classifies project style and uses Coombs *et al.*'s (1998) classification of R&D project. The horizontal axis captures technological uncertainty. The traditional distinction within innovation management between research projects and development projects, however outmoded and inappropriate, may nonetheless

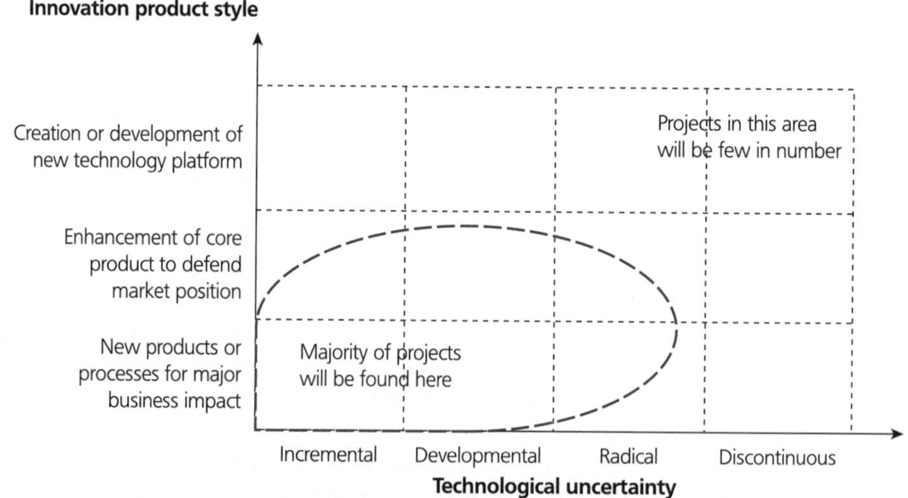

Figure 3.4 A two-dimensional typology of innovation projects

still retain usefulness in the practical realities of the laboratory. In particular it distinguishes between the management of projects which deliver mainly knowledge, and those which deliver a physical product. There is also an emphasis (not surprisingly within the new product development (NPD) literature) on project management models that explicitly focus on the new product development process (for example, see Cooper, 1986). This emphasis may have overlooked the need for subtly different approaches to project management for innovation management and R&D in particular that does not necessarily lead directly to the launch of a new product.

Organisational characteristics that facilitate the innovation process

The innovation process, outlined at the end of Chapter 1, identified the complex nature of innovation. It also emphasised the need to view innovation within the context of the organisation. In a recent study examining the relationship between innovation stimulus, innovation capacity and innovation performance Prajogo and Ahmed (2006) found that there was a strong relationship between innovation stimulus and innovation capacity and a strong relationship between innovation capacity and innovation performance. Figure 3.5 illustrates this diagrammatically. The findings did not find any direct relationship between innovation stimulus and innovation performance. The implications of this for firms are clear: if firms wish to improve innovation performance they first need to put in place and then develop factors that stimulate innovation, such as appropriate leadership, R&D and creativity. Within such an environment the nurturing and building of innovation capacity can then occur. Prajogo and Ahmed (2006) argue that innovation capacity is the combination of technological and human factors. In other words, having good science and laboratories is necessary but insufficient. In addition, effective intangible skills are required such as project management, innovative experience and risk management.

Armed with this information the challenge for firms remains immense. Putting in place the necessary stimulus and then nurturing capacity may sound straightforward, but what does this mean? A recent review of the innovation management literature by van der Panne *et al.* (2003) provides us with some of the answers. This research examined factors that contribute to success and failure of innovative projects within firms (*see* Figure 3.6). This major review identified a wide range of factors but this is classified into four major groups:

1 Firm-related factors.
2 Project-related factors.
3 Product-related factors.
4 Market-related factors.

Figure 3.5 Innovation stimulus, capacity and performance

Source: D.I. Prajogo and P.K. Ahmed (2006).

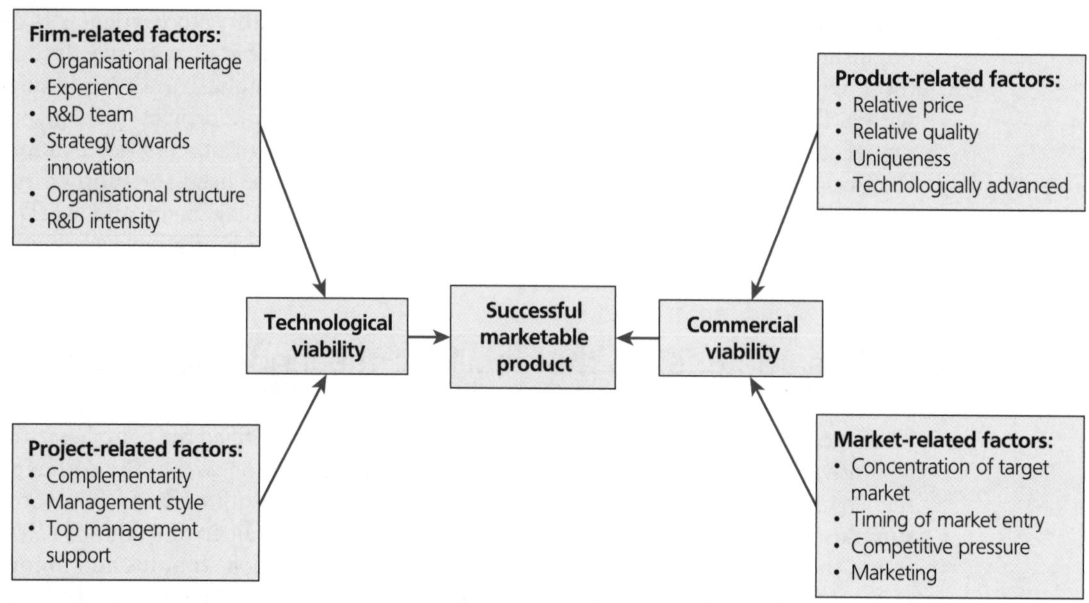

Figure 3.6 Critical factors for innovation success

Source: van der Panne *et al.* (2003).

In this chapter we will concentrate on firm-related factors that affect innovative success for the firm. Other chapters in this book address the three other areas. For example, project-related factors are discussed in Chapters 9 and 16. Product-related factors are addressed in Chapters 10, 11, 12, 13 and 14. And finally market-related factors are addressed in Chapters 2, 5, 11 and 15.

Over the past 50 years a considerable literature has accumulated on the subject of innovation and how best to manage the process within the firm (Porter and Ketels, 2003). Within this literature there is evidence that competitive success is dependent upon a firm's management of the innovation process (Adams *et al.*, 2006). Yet, attempting to measure the process of innovation is a major challenge because for practitioners and academics it is characterised by diversity of approaches and practices. Nonetheless, for those of us attempting to understand better how innovation management can be improved, we need to know 'ingredients' and possibly 'recipes' that at least give us some indication of what is required and if and when we are to turn ideas into marketable products. Adams *et al.* (2006) developed a framework of the innovation management process with illustrative measures to map the territory. This framework is shown in Table 3.1.

This framework enables managers within firms to evaluate their own innovation activities. This enables them to explore the extent to which innovation is embedded within their organisation and identify areas for improvement. Hopefully, readers of this book now recognise that innovation is not a linear process where resources are fed in at one end and at the other emerges a new product or process. Innovation requires a variety of competencies at key stages in the innovation cycle. Each of these requires its own space and time but along with specialised skills comes the need for coordination and management. The framework in Table 3.1 shows the wide variety of elements that need to be in place and can be measured. There are still big questions

Table 3.1 Innovation management measurement areas

Framework category	Measurement area
Inputs	People Physical and financial resources Tools
Knowledge management	Idea generation Knowledge repository Information flows
Innovation strategy	Strategic orientation Strategic leadership
Organisation and culture	Culture Structure
Portfolio management	Risk/return balance Optimisation tool use
Project management	Project efficiency Tools Communications Collaborations
Commercialisation	Market research Market testing Marketing and sales

Source: Adams *et al.* (2006).

that remain regarding precisely how one measures these elements and which metric is used but, nonetheless, it provides a starting point.

The above discussions present an overview of how innovation is successfully managed within organisations. Figures 3.5 and 3.6 together with Table 3.1 provide us with a solid base of evidence from which we can develop a list of organisational characteristics that influence the innovation process. If we add to this the major findings from the studies detailed in Table 1.8 we have a useful checklist of factors that firms need to consider. Table 3.2 then is a summary of the organisational characteristics that facilitate the innovation process. The W.L. Gore case at the end of this chapter provides an illustration of these internal organisational attributes, which contribute to innovative success, in action.

Growth orientation

It is sometimes surprising to learn that not all companies' first and foremost objective is growth. Some companies are established merely to exploit a short-term opportunity. Other companies, particularly family-run ones, would like to maintain the company at its existing size. At that size the family can manage the operation without having to employ outside help. Companies that are seeking growth are more likely to be interested in innovation than those that are not. For those companies whose objective is to grow the business, innovation provides a means to achieving growth. This does not imply that they make large profits one year then huge losses the next, but they actively plan for the long term. There are many companies that make this explicit in their annual reports, for example Nokia, Siemens, Google and Microsoft (see Dobini, 2010).

Table 3.2 Summary of the organisational characteristics that facilitate the innovation process

Organisational requirement	Characterised by
1 Growth orientation	A commitment to long-term growth rather than short-term profit
2 Organisational heritage and innovation experience	Widespread recognition of the value of innovation
3 Vigilance and external links	The ability of the organisation to be aware of its threats and opportunities
4 Commitment to technology and R&D intensity	The willingness to invest in the long-term development of technology
5 Acceptance of risks	The willingness to include risky opportunities in a balanced portfolio
6 Cross-functional cooperation and coordination within organisational structure	Mutual respect among individuals and a willingness to work together across functions
7 **Receptivity**	The ability to be aware of, to identify and to take effective advantage of externally developed technology
8 Space for creativity	An ability to manage the innovation dilemma and provide room for creativity
9 Strategy towards innovation	Strategic planning and selection of technologies and markets
10 Coordination of a diverse range of skills	Developing a marketable product requires combining a wide range of specialised knowledge

Pause for thought

If we know what organisational characteristics are required for innovation, why are not all firms innovative?

Organisational heritage and innovation experience

A firm's heritage and culture is undisputedly considered crucial to the firm's technological capabilities as it fosters and encourages widespread recognition of the need to innovate. This is clearly illustrated in the extent to which groups and departments are willing to cooperate. Numerous problems arise when individuals and groups are either unwilling or reluctant to work together and share ideas. At the very least it slows down communication and decision making and at worse leads to projects being abandoned due to lack of progress. Frequently, the difference between a firm succeeding or not lies not in their scientific ability or commercial knowledge but simply in the firm's internal ability to share information and knowledge. The pharmaceutical firm Pfizer is frequently cited as delivering exceptional new products yet its R&D is not more highly regarded than other firms. In other words, it is the ability of the firm to convert technology into products that sets it apart from its competitors.

Previous experience with innovative projects is clearly conducive to the firm's technology and R&D management capabilities as these enhance the skills that are necessary to turn technology into marketable products. Numerous advantages also flow from learning by doing and learning from failure effects.

Vigilance and external links

Vigilance requires continual external scanning, not just by senior management but also by all other members of the organisation. Part of this activity may be formalised. For example, within the marketing function the activity would form part of market research and competitor analysis. Within the research and development department scientists and engineers will spend a large amount of their time reading the scientific literature in order to keep up to date with the latest developments in their field. In other functions it may not be as formalised but it still needs to occur. Collecting valuable information is one thing, but relaying it to the necessary individuals and acting on it are two necessary associated requirements. An open communication system will help to facilitate this. Extensive external linkages with the market, competitors, customers, suppliers and others will all contribute to the flow of information into the firm (see Kang and Kang, 2009; also *see* Chapter 10).

Commitment to technology and R&D intensity

Most innovative firms exhibit patience in permitting ideas to germinate and develop over time. This also needs to be accompanied by a commitment to resources in terms of intellectual input from science, technology and engineering. Those ideas that look most promising will require further investment. Without this long-term approach it would be extremely difficult for the company to attract good scientists. Similarly, a climate that invests in technology development one year then decides to cut investment the next will alienate the same people in which the company encourages creativity. Such a disruptive environment does not foster creativity and will probably cause many creative people to search for a more suitable company with a stronger commitment to technology.

In addition, it seems almost obvious to state that a firm that invests more in R&D will increase its total innovative output. But the relationship between R&D expenditures as a percentage of sales and commercial success is less clear-cut. This will be examined in more detail in Chapter 8.

Acceptance of risks

Accepting risks does not mean a willingness to gamble. It means the willingness to consider carefully risky opportunities. It also includes the ability to make risk-assessment decisions, to take calculated risks and to include them in a balanced portfolio of projects, some of which will have a low element of risk and some a high degree of risk.

Cross-functional cooperation and coordination within organisational structure

Interdepartmental conflict is a well-documented barrier to innovation. The relationship between the marketing and R&D functions has received a great deal of attention in the research literature. This will be explored further in Chapter 16, but generally this is because the two groups often have very different interests. Scientists and technologists can be fascinated by new technology and may sometimes lose sight of the business objective. Similarly, the marketing function often fails to understand the technology involved in the development of a new product. Research has shown that the presence of some conflict is desirable, probably acting as a motivational force (Souder, 1987). It is the ability to confront and resolve frustration and conflict that is required. In addition, a supportive organisational structure underpinned by a robust information and communication technology system all contribute to facilitating the organisation to coordinate cross-functional cooperation (see later sections in this chapter).

Receptivity

The capability of the organisation to be aware of, identify and take effective advantage of externally developed technology is key. Most technology-based innovations involve a combination of several different technologies. It would be unusual for all the technology to be developed in-house. Indeed, businesses are witnessing an increasing number of joint ventures and alliances (*see* Chapter 7), often with former competitors. For example, Sony and Ericsson have formed a joint venture to work on the development of mobile phone handsets (*see* the case study on Sony-Ericsson in Chapter 10 for more details). Previously these two companies fought ferociously in the battle for market share in the mobile phone handset market.

Space for creativity

While organisations place great emphasis on the need for efficiency, there is also a need for a certain amount of 'slack' to allow individuals room to think, experiment, discuss ideas and be creative (Dobini, 2010). In many R&D functions this issue is directly addressed by allowing scientists to spend 10–15 per cent of their time on the projects they choose. This is not always supported in other functional areas. (*See also* ambidexterity page 85.)

Strategy towards innovation

An explicit strategic approach towards innovation can come in many forms, as is shown in Chapter 6. For the firm and those within it, however, it means that the firm has developed plans for the future regarding selection of markets to enter and which technologies may be appropriate for the firm. Recognising that the organisation possesses skills, technology and knowledge and that there are appropriate markets that suit these requires careful planning, probably utilising a project portfolio approach. This will involve further long-term planning, establishing a range a projects some of which will subsequently provide opportunities that the firm will be able to exploit. This long-term planning and investment with regard to technology and markets distinguishes such firms from their 'short-termism' counterparts (*see* Dobini, 2010).

Diverse range of skills

Organisations require a combination of specialist skills and knowledge in the form of experts in, say, science, advertising or accountancy and generalist skills that facilitate cross-fertilisation of the specialist knowledge. In addition they require individuals of a hybrid nature who are able to understand a variety of technical subjects and facilitate the transfer of knowledge within the company. Similarly, hybrid managers who have technical and commercial training are particularly useful in the area of product development (Wheelwright and Clark, 1992). It is the ability to manage this diversity of knowledge and skills effectively that lies at the heart of the innovation process. This is wonderfully illustrated below in the analysis of conducting or managing an orchestra. On the one hand, great individual musical talent is required and yet, at the same time, individuals must play as part of the team. The parallel between an orchestra and a business is portrayed in Illustration 3.1.

Illustration 3.1

The nuts and bolts of growth

Reinhold Würth likes setting targets. For more than five decades one of Germany's best-known entrepreneurs has driven growth at Würth – the world's largest seller of screws, nuts, bolts and other fasteners – by setting seemingly daunting 10-year goals for workers.

In 1987, Würth made DM1.4bn (€700m) in revenues and Mr Würth came up with a bold prediction: by 2000 the German group would make DM10bn. 'Workers looked at me like I was mad', he says. But when the accounts closed in early 2000 Würth had hit the number.

Mr Würth, 72, has sustained an entrepreneurial spirit in the company, despite it being based in one of the most basic industries in the world: selling fasteners and other products to workshops around the world. His formula has been a simple business model, the early pursuit of internationalisation and a focus on innovation to repel the threat of low-cost competitors.

Würth has enjoyed a compound annual growth rate of 25 per cent since he took over from his father in 1954. This year it is on target to make €9.4bn ($14.3bn). 'When you think we don't sell anything high-tech – just screws, dowel pins and machine tools – it is a little astounding', says Mr Würth, who still owns the company despite stepping back from day-to-day management.

Source: Pearson Education Ltd/F. Schussler/Photodisc

Mr Würth's business story began at the age of 14, when he left school to start an apprenticeship at the company his father had just founded. Five years later, on his father's death, he found himself in charge of two other workers. In his first full year the business grew by 20 per cent and has never looked back. The company now employs 63,000 people worldwide; Mr Würth, meanwhile, became a professor of entrepreneurship at the University of Karlsruhe and a prominent business figure in Germany, with a penchant for Harley-Davidsons and collecting modern art.

Würth's innovative business model was based on outsourcing – before the word was coined. Instead of making its own products, it would get

➔

suppliers to do it for them and then market them under the Würth brand. The key, he says, is a focus on being the best. 'Quality beats price is our motto', says Mr Würth, in an office adorned with modern art at the company's headquarters in the rural southern German town of Künzelsau. 'We never went into low-cost, as our customers would never have understood it.'

His earliest obstacle was simply finding the products. Germany was in its post-Second World War boom and it was difficult to keep up with demand. 'It was sometimes harder to buy the products than to sell them', he says.

Mr Würth relied from the beginning on an army of salesmen – now with more than 30,000, the largest full-time employed salesforce in the world – to create relationships with professional customers such as mechanics and small workshops. To this day the average sale at Würth is for just five articles with a value of about €200 – but there are 20,000 such orders daily.

Mr Würth spotted an opportunity to expand the business abroad, opening a subsidiary in the Netherlands in 1962. Würth today has 400 subsidiaries in 86 countries from Costa Rica to Indonesia. 'We went international before the word "globalisation" even existed', he says. Würth operates in what he calls a 'polypoly' (in contrast to an oligopoly) in that his main competitors are the hundreds of thousands of local companies supplying workshops with material. 'In this scenario it is not so difficult to win market share. We don't need any market studies from McKinsey or the like to help us', he says.

Würth's market share is 5 per cent in Germany and less abroad; Mr Würth believes it can always be improved and woe betide any manager who disputes his targets: 'In a recession demand on screws goes down by maybe 2 per cent, but we can gain market share. Nobody in this company is allowed to talk about the economy or recession as excuses.'

In his view, low-cost competitors, such as those in China, cannot compete with Würth because they fail to provide the quality the small workshops need. Even if they could, he adds, they would not enjoy the close relationship a Würth salesman cultivates with his customers. And the internet has yet to damage the model; mechanics still prefer to see a human face than order their products over the web.

Mr Würth says he learned his entrepreneurial skills on the job – 'my university was life' – but says he devoured management and economics books from an early age. One of his favourites is von Clausewitz's *On War*:

'Von Clausewitz writes that if you have to defend a fortress of the empire and you are surrounded by enemies you should send out a minor part of your troops to engage the enemy as far away as possible to enable the rest of your troops time to prepare.'

He put this into practice to defend his business of selling to professional customers – a highly profitable market. Mr Würth started by selling bulk industry products to large manufacturers, a lower margin business and one he didn't care much about. 'But it kept our competitors very busy so that they didn't even entertain the idea of going to our main customers', he recounts with glee.

Not everything has been plain sailing. In the early 1970s he had to close Würth Bau, the construction subsidiary he had built up, with a loss of DM10m and 250 workers. But despite not being directly involved, he went to see the workers himself and afterwards found new jobs for nearly all of them. 'Even though I wasn't involved I took political responsibility for it. People knew that when Mr Würth says he has to close [a plant] he has looked at all other options', he says.

He espouses a broader belief that innovation and efficiency can only thrive when employees are given their head. Divisions at Würth operate with an unusual degree of latitude, a decision he says has paid off: 'The more successful the worker is, the more freedom he or she receives. It is one of the strengths of this company that we can run it in a decentralised manner but if something goes wrong we switch to centralised mode immediately – be it helping an individual or a country.' When trouble looms, task forces are sent out straightaway to assess the problem. This happened recently when dozens of employees in Canada left the company for no apparent reason.

Mr Würth's longer-term aim is a desire to give all workers a vision they can share. But it comes with strings attached, in this case an eye-watering target of €22.5bn in revenues by 2017: 'If the management doesn't think that a company can grow by 15–20 per cent then it won't happen', he says.

'The balance sheet is just a mirror of how management thinks. I happen to believe any company that doesn't grow by 10 per cent annually is sick.'

Cash bonuses, flights and art galleries keep workers inspired

Worker motivation is a pet topic of Reinhold Würth. He says that when there are rumours of workers being unmotivated, in 95 per cent of cases it is because 'they have nothing to do'.

He adds: 'It is like children in a sandbox. They are angry because they have nothing to do until you bring along a Lego box and then they are happy. It is the same for people of 30, 40 or 50. People need to have challenges.'

He believes in rewarding managers when they have worked hard. This ranges from the commonplace – every worker at Würth's logistics centre in Künzelsau received a €65 bonus in January as revenues in Germany rose by 8 per cent to €94m – to the extravagant: every two years the top workers and their spouses are flown to a different location – the next is South Africa – for conferences and sightseeing.

Motivational initiatives extend beyond work to art galleries in various national headquarters filled with work bought by Mr Würth, who has amassed one of the largest modern art collections in Germany with 11,000 works.

Source: Milne, R. (2008) The nuts and bolts of growth, ft.com, 5 March. Reprinted with permission.

Pause for thought

The uncertainty map tries to explain that varying levels of uncertainty create very different working environments and, hence, different management skills are necessary for each quadrant. Is it possible for firms to operate across all four quadrants?

Industrial firms are different: a classification

A brief look at companies operating in your town or area will soon inform you that industrial firms are very different. You may say that this is axiomatic. The point is, however, that in terms of innovation and product development it is possible to argue that some firms are users of technology and others are providers. For example, at the simplest level most towns will have a range of housebuilding firms, agricultural firms, retail firms and many others offering services to local people. Such firms tend to be small in size, with little R&D or manufacturing capability of their own. They are classified by Pavitt (1994) as *supplier-dominated firms*. Many of them are very successful because they offer a product with a reliable service. Indeed, their strength is that they purchase technologies in the form of products and match these to customer needs. Such firms usually have limited, if any, product or process technology capabilities. Pavitt offers a useful classification of the different types of firms with regard to technology usage; this is shown in Figure 3.7.

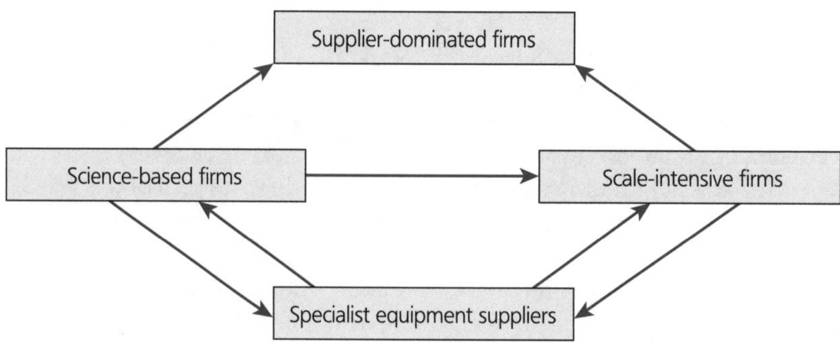

Figure 3.7 Technological linkages among different types of firms

Source: K. Pavitt (1994) Sectoral patterns of technological change: towards a taxonomy and theory, *Research Policy*, Vol. 13, 343–73.

At the other end of the scale are science-based firms or technology-intensive firms. These are found in the high-growth industries of the twentieth century: chemicals, pharmaceuticals, electronics, computing, etc. It is the manipulation of science and technology usually by their own R&D departments that has provided the foundation for the firms' growth and success. Unlike the previous classification, these firms tend to be large and would include corporations such as Bayer, Hoechst, Nokia, GlaxoSmithKline, Sony and Siemens.

The third classification Pavitt refers to as scale-intensive firms, which dominate the manufacturing sector. At the heart of these firms are process technologies. It is their ability to produce high volumes at low cost that is usually their strength. They tend to have capabilities in engineering, design and manufacturing. Many science-based firms are also scale-intensive firms, so it is possible for firms to belong to more than one category. Indeed, the big chemical companies in Europe are a case in point.

Innovation in action

Set up a date

The dating business model is highly profitable – but most companies have been slow to spot its potential for other industries.

Spanish company Busuu.com, however, spotted an opportunity and started an online language school with a difference – there are no teachers. 'Every user is not only a student of a foreign language but also a tutor of his own mother-tongue', says co-founder Bernhard Niesner.

Busuu directly connects native speakers in different countries who want to learn a language – so a Spaniard seeking to learn English can connect with an English speaker wishing to learn Spanish. Lessons take place in online video chats, with guidance notes provided for structure. Users correct each other's written work.

It's popular, and people stick with it. Bernhard puts this down to the peer-to-peer model: 'Normally when you start a new language you are quite insecure. But if you see others also making mistakes and you can help them, it motivates you to continue.'

Source: 100 Thoughts (2010), HSBC, London.

The final classification is specialist equipment suppliers. This group of firms is an important source of technology for scale-intensive and science-based firms. For example, instrumentation manufacturers supply specialist measuring instruments to the chemical industry and the aerospace industry to enable these firms to measure their products and manufacturing activities accurately.

This useful classification highlights the flows of technology between the various firms. This is an important concept and is referred to in later chapters to help explain the industry life cycle in Chapter 12, the acquisition of technology in Chapter 9, the transfer of technology in Chapter 10 and strategic alliances in Chapter 7.

Organisational structures and innovation

The structure of an organisation is defined by Mintzberg (1978) as the sum total of the ways in which it divides its labour into distinct tasks and then achieves coordination among them. One of the problems when analysing organisational structure is recognising that different groups within an organisation behave differently and interact with different parts of the wider external environment. Hence, there is a tendency to label structure at the level of the organisation with little recognition of differences at group or department level. Nonetheless, there have been numerous useful studies exploring the link between organisational structure and innovative performance.

The seminal work by Burns and Stalker (1961) on Scottish electronic organisations looked at the impact of technical change on organisational structures and on systems of social relationships. It suggests that 'organic', flexible structures, characterised by the absence of formality and hierarchy, support innovation more effectively than do 'mechanistic' structures. The latter are characterised by long chains of command, rigid work methods, strict task differentiation, extensive procedures and a well-defined hierarchy. Many objections have been raised against this argument, most notably by Child (1973). Nevertheless, flexible rather than mechanistic organisational structures are still seen, especially within the business management literature, as necessary for successful industrial innovation. In general, an organic organisation is more adaptable, more openly communicating, more consensual and more loosely controlled. As Table 3.3 indicates, the mechanistic organisation tends to offer a less suitable environment for managing creativity and the innovation process. The subject of organisation structures is also discussed in Chapter 16 in the context of managing new product development teams.

Formalisation

Following Burns and Stalker, there have been a variety of studies examining the relationship between formalisation and innovation. There is some evidence of an inverse relationship between formalisation and innovation. That is, an increase in formalisation of procedures will result in a decrease in innovative activity. It is unclear, however, whether a decrease in procedures and rules would lead to an increase in innovation. Moreover, as was argued above, organisational planning and routines are necessary for achieving efficiencies.

Table 3.3 Organic versus mechanistic organisational structures

Organic	Mechanistic
1 **Channels of communication** Open with free information flow throughout the organisation	1 **Channels of communication** Highly structured, restricted information flow
2 **Operating styles** Allowed to vary freely	2 **Operating styles** Must be uniform and restricted
3 **Authority for decisions** Based on the expertise of the individual	3 **Authority for decisions** Based on formal line management position
4 **Free adaptation** By the organisation to changing circumstances	4 **Reluctant adaptation** With insistence on holding fast to tried and true management principles despite changes in business conditions
5 **Emphasis on getting things done** Unconstrained by formally laid out procedures	5 **Emphasis on formally laid down procedures** Reliance on tried and true management principles
6 **Loose, informal control** With emphasis on norm of cooperation	6 **Tight control** Through sophisticated control systems
7 **Flexible on-job behaviour** Permitted to be shaped by the requirements of the situation and personality of the individual doing the job	7 **Constrained on-job behaviour** Required to conform to job descriptions
8 **Decision making** Participation and group consensus used frequently	8 **Decision making** Superiors make decisions with minimum consultation and involvement of subordinates

Source: D.P. Slevin and J.G. Covin (1990) Juggling entrepreneurial style and organizational structure: how to get your act together, *Sloan Management Review*, Winter, 43–53.

Complexity

The term complexity here refers to the complexity of the organisation. In particular, it refers to the number of professional groups or diversity of specialists within the organisation. For example, a university, hospital or science-based manufacturing company would represent a complex organisation. This is because within these organisations there would be several professional groups. In the case of a hospital, nurses, doctors and a wide range of specialists represent the different areas of medicine. This contrasts sharply with an equally large organisation that is, for example, in the distribution industry. The management of supplying goods all over the country will be complex indeed; but it will not involve the management of a wide range of highly qualified professional groups.

Centralisation

Centralisation refers to the decision-making activity and the location of power within an organisation. The more decentralised an organisation, the fewer levels of hierarchy are usually required. This tends to lead to more responsive decision making closer to the action.

Organisational size

Size is a proxy variable for more meaningful dimensions such as economic and organisational resources, including number of employees and scale of operation. Below a certain size, however, there is a major qualitative difference. A small business with fewer than 20 employees differs significantly in terms of resources from an organisation with 200 or 2,000 employees.

The role of the individual in the innovation process

The innovation literature has consistently acknowledged the importance of the role of the individual within the industrial technological innovation process (Rothwell *et al.*, 1974; Langrish *et al.*, 1972; Utterback, 1975; van de Ven, 1986; Wolfe, 1994; Martins and Terblanche, 2003). Furthermore, a variety of *key roles* have developed from the literature stressing particular qualities (*see* Table 3.4).

Rubenstein (1976) went further, arguing that the innovation process is essentially a *people process* and that organisational structure, formal decision-making processes, delegation of authority and other formal aspects of a so-called well-run company are not necessary conditions for successful technological innovation. His studies revealed that certain individuals had fulfilled a variety of roles (often informal) that had contributed to successful technological innovation.

Table 3.4 Key individual roles within the innovation process

Key individual	Role
Technical innovator	Expert in one or two fields. Generates new ideas and sees new and different ways of doing things. Also referred to as the 'mad scientist'.
Technical/commercial scanner	Acquires vast amounts of information from outside the organisation, often through networking. This may include market and technical information.
Gatekeeper	Keeps informed of related developments that occur outside the organisation through journals, conferences, colleagues and other companies. Passes information on to others, finds it easy to talk to colleagues. Serves as an information resource for others in the organisation.
Product champion	Sells new ideas to others in the organisation. Acquires resources. Aggressive in championing his or her cause. Takes risks.
Project leader	Provides the team with leadership and motivation. Plans and organises the project. Ensures that administrative requirements are met. Provides necessary coordination among team members. Sees that the project moves forward effectively. Balances project goals with organisational needs.
Sponsor	Provides access to a power base within the organisation: a senior person. Buffers the project team from unnecessary organisational constraints. Helps the project team to get what it needs from other parts of the organisation. Provides legitimacy and organisational confidence in the project.

Source: Based on E.B. Roberts and A.R. Fushfield (1981) Staffing the innovative technology-based organisation, *Sloan Management Review*, Spring, 19–34.

In a study of biotechnology firms, Sheene (1991) explains that it is part of a scientist's professional obligation to keep up to date with the literature. This is achieved by extensive scanning of the literature. However, she identified feelings of guilt associated with browsing in the library by some scientists. This was apparently due to a fear that some senior managers might not see this as a constructive use of their time. Many other studies have also shown that the role of the individual is critical in the innovation process (Allen and Cohen, 1969; Allen, 1977; Wheelwright and Clark, 1992; Hauschildt, 2003).

IT systems and their impact on innovation

The impact of large IT systems on firms and the way they operate has been one of the most noticeable changes within organisations of the late 1990s and early twenty-first century. Enterprise resource planning (ERP) business software has become one of the most successful products in the world. For many firms such as Microsoft, Owens–Corning, ICI, UBS and Procter & Gamble, it has changed the way they work (Gartner, 2002). Indeed, substantial claims are made about the software's capabilities. A complete system could take several years and several hundred million dollars to deploy. The market leaders in this highly lucrative business-to-business market are SAP, Oracle, Baan and PeopleSoft. SAP has over 20,000 R/3 products installed worldwide and Oracle has installed databases in nearly every one of the world's top 500 companies. However, the impact of these systems on a firm's innovative capability is now under scrutiny. In some creative working environments, where previously autonomous and creative minds were free to explore, they are now being restricted to what's on offer via 'pull-down' menus.

ERP systems have been adopted by the majority of large private sector firms and many public sector organisations in the United Kingdom, Europe and the industrialised world in general. This growing trend towards ERP systems would not materialise unless significant advantages were to be expected from its introduction. Although there may be some isomorphic effects at work that facilitate the spread of perceived best practice and help the marketing efforts of key players in the industry to succeed, these factors on their own would not be able to explain the widespread adoption of ERP systems in the absence of real benefits.

The principal benefits that can arise from ERP systems are linked to expected gains in the efficiency and effectiveness of business processes that come about with the availability of more accurate and timely information. ERP offers integration of business functions and can reduce data collection and processing duplication efforts.

In summary some of the potential benefits of implementing ERP systems are:

- more efficient business processes;
- reduction of costs to several business procedures;
- better coordination and cooperation between functions and different company departments;
- better management monitoring and controlling functions;
- modification and adaptation abilities accordingly to company and market requirements;

- more competitive and efficient entrance to electronic markets and electronic commerce;
- possible redesigning of ineffective business functions;
- access to globalisation and integration to the global economy;
- inventory visibility and better decision support;
- active technology for market research and media environment; and
- improving communication between partners of the channel.

Business managers of organisations with significant ERP experience suggest that ERP system introduction into an organisation amounts to a near reinvention of the organisation. ERP systems do not easily fit any organisation. ERP systems offer significant advantages, but, in order to work efficiently and effectively, they require that organisational processes be made to fit their system demands. As we will discuss below, the price to be paid for efficiency and effectiveness comes with a prescribed rigidity that may hinder innovation and creativity.

There is also a problem with the impact of ERP on the innovative climate in organisations and on the existent company operations (Johannessen *et al.*, 2001). In short, ERP systems very often require a reconfiguration of work processes and routines. Many people, however, feel unhappy when they are asked to change established 'ways of doing things' and they may rightly feel that new standardised work processes may undermine their autonomy enjoyed in current non-standardised operations. ERP systems, however, can only deliver the promised efficiency gains with a standard information set and leave no alternatives to a standardised approach. But it is not only that information processing and work routines have to be standardised; with an integrated system everyone's performance and achievements become much more visible. Information sharing can easily be perceived as serving the purpose of tightening management control if the organisational climate has deteriorated in the ERP implementation process. If employees feel that they are losing their autonomy and that they are subjected to a culture of instant accountability, then this may have dramatic effects on their productivity and creativity and may nullify some of the potential ERP gains.

There are several ways in which ERP systems operations may have a negative impact on individual creativity. First of all, ERP systems may reduce the richness of information content when informal communication processes get increasingly replaced by standardised data exchanges made available through ERP systems. The previous section noted the role of tacit knowledge with respect to innovation and that it is embedded in social processes. If ERP becomes the key communication medium and information has to be made palatable to its data requirements, then tacit knowledge outside the system may be sidelined (Johannessen *et al.*, 2001; Nonaka, 1991). As a consequence, explicit knowledge may get preference over tacit knowledge. But individual and group creativity is not only dependent on rich information. There are motivational factors at work as well. If ERP leads to a culture of instant control and accountability, then this may undermine the intrinsic motivation of employees and may lead to a culture where risk taking and experimentation becomes increasingly less desirable. It will always be safer to use the available ERP data than to look elsewhere for inspiration. Diligent users of the ERP system are more difficult to blame for their mistakes or lack of achievement. ERP can become a very useful legitimating tool.

More significantly, firms must recognise that ERP systems (like any database) are driven from master data such as customer records, bill of material records (BoM), and, like other databases, are unforgiving. Get a field entry wrong and it can cause serious problems. Most likely the internal logic of ERP systems will require large amounts of time being devoted to ensuring the correct entry is made. This is yet another example of how the IT infrastructure impacts on people's working practices. A simple example may be useful here. Consider the activities of an architect working for a major property developer in Europe. The architect develops a variety of homes for consideration and specifies the building design and materials required. While in the past the architect may have flicked through some trade catalogues or contacted suppliers for what might be available, now all possible options available are prescribed via a pull-down menu. The advantages are clear to see: reduced time searching, order processing at the press of a few keys. But what about the impact on the creativity of the design of the building?

Unlike other IT management information systems, ERP has a dramatic impact on the way people work. Indeed, such business intelligence systems force change on an organisational structure, working practices, policies and procedures. The interdependence of the organisational components is never more clearly illuminated. Indeed, it is the knock-on effects of ERP in other aspects of the organisation such as staff skills, budgets, performance measurement procedures and so on that frequently cause most angst.

The level of personal autonomy individuals have and perceived to hold is frequently cited as one of the key people issues during the implementation of ERP systems (Sauer, 1993). There is much more emphasis on correct routines and prescribed ways of working; indeed, individual peculiar working practices have to be removed for ERP to be effective. Staff may find their daily activities dominated by highly prescriptive procedures on their computer screens. The overall perception is often one of the enterprise moving towards a more autocratic, centralised management style. There are a significant number of conflicts between the demands on the organisation of an ERP system and the necessary characteristics that have been identified within the literature for innovation to occur. For example, ERP requires discipline and aids managerial control, whereas freedom and creativity in the form of professional autonomy is continually cited as necessary for innovation to occur. Figure 3.8 provides an overview over some of the key fundamental clashes of organising principles between ERP systems requirement and the success factors of innovative organisations (Trott and Hoecht, 2004).

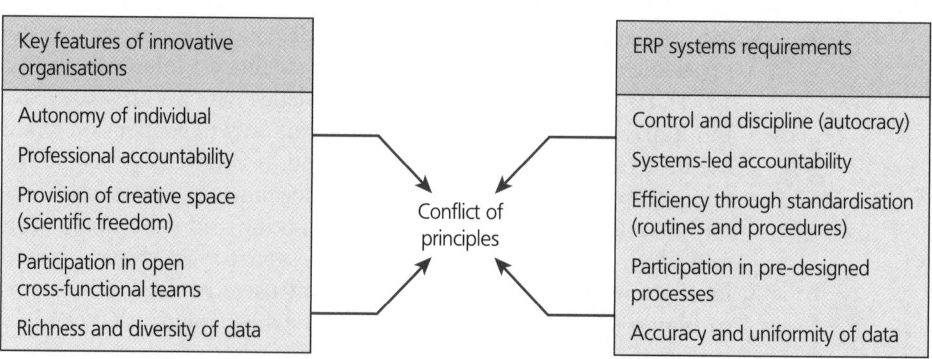

Figure 3.8 Paradox of ERP systems and innovation organisational requirements

Management tools for innovation

Many science and technology related organisations innovate for a time, successfully exploit their innovations to gain status in their industry or field of research, then stagnate. Well-established management principles can help the leaders of an organisation sustain innovation and even recover from a period of stagnation, if they are applied correctly and vigorously. This section explores some of these principles and the relevant tools and techniques that may help leaders of firms ensure they remain leaders in their industry.

We do not have to look very far to draw up a lists of successful firms that later became less successful. Indeed, Peters and Waterman's (1982) famous study of successful firms in the 1980s that were less than successful in the 1990s in a useful reminder. Firms such as Disney, IBM, Ford, General Motors, AT&T and Philips can all be found here. If we focus on technology-intensive industries where firms are innovative for a period and then stagnate the list may take slightly longer to compile, but it too provides us with a timely reminder of the need for good management and the impact that poor management can have. Firms like 3M have an impressive record of innovation. It frequently received accolades as the most innovative firm in the 1980s and 1990s, but struggled to deliver a return for its shareholders in 2000 and beyond. Pilkington Glass, similarly heralded as a world leader in glass technology as a result of its float glass process in the 1960s and 1970s, failed to follow up this technology development. It was sold in 2006 to Nipon Glass. Even Apple Inc., while extremely successful at present with its iPod and iPhone, struggled in the late 1980s with a series of product failures including the Pippin (a games consul) and Newton (a personal digital assistant).

Innovation management tools and techniques

Developing successful innovative products does not always mean using the latest patented technology. Being successful at managing innovation is rather a way of thinking and finding creative solutions within the company. With this in mind, innovation management can benefit from well-established management principles to help the leaders of an organisation sustain innovativeness and even recover from a period of stagnation, if applied correctly and vigorously. We need to look at the range of tools and techniques that have been shown to be helpful to firms as they manage the innovation process. Coombs *et al.* (1998) identified three major types of R&D projects and offered a template for their management. This study also identified a wide range of management tools that could be used to help facilitate the management of these projects. Ten years later in a major review of innovation management techniques and tools Hidalgo and Albors (2008) identified some of the most widely used innovation methodologies and tools. Together these studies provide a comprehensive overview of innovation management tools and techniques (*see* Table 3.5).

There is no universal project management procedure that fits all organisations. As the previous sections have outlined there are different types of projects (with varying levels of uncertainty) and different types of firms operating in different types of industries. This necessarily means a diversity of solutions is required and thankfully is available. It cannot be claimed that there is a closed set of developed and proven

Table 3.5 Innovation management tools and methodologies

Innovation management typologies	Methodologies and tools
Knowledge and technology management	Knowledge audits Knowledge mapping Technology road maps Industry foresight panels Document management IPR management
Market intelligence	Technology watch/technology search Patents analysis Business intelligence Competitor analysis Trend analysis Focus groups Customer relationship management (CRM)
Cooperation and networking	Groupware Team-building Supply chain management Industrial clustering
Human resources management	Teleworking Corporate intranets Online recruitment e-Learning Competence management
Interface management	R&D – marketing interface management Concurrent engineering
Creativity development	Brainstorming Lateral thinking TRIZ* Scamper method Mind mapping
Process improvement	Benchmarking Workflow Business process re-engineering Just in time
Innovation project management	Project management Gannt charts Project appraisal Stage-gate processes Project portfolio management
Design and product development	CAD systems Rapid prototyping Usability approaches Quality function deployment Value analysis NPD computer decision models
Business creation	Business simulation Business plan Spin-off from research to market

*This is a Russian acronym and stands for: Теория решения изобретательских задач (***T****eoriya* ***R****esheniya* ***I****zobretatelskikh* ***Z****adatch*), which is a problem-solving, analysis and forecasting tool. In the English language the name is typically rendered as the Theory of Inventive Problem Solving. It was developed by the Soviet inventor and science fiction author Genrich Altshuller in the 1940s.

Source: Hidalgo and Albors (2008) and Coombs *et al.* (1998).

innovation management tools capable of solving all challenges faced by business. There are, however, some principles of good practice and Table 3.5 illustrates a wide range of tools and techniques. Many of these are very well known and have been used for many years, hence there is no need for an explanation of each one.

The use of these tools and techniques to improve the management of innovation within the firm cannot be considered in isolation. Firms will often use combinations of tools and techniques to ensure a particular project is successful. In addition, techniques are continually trialled, adopted and/or dropped. The benefit gained by the company depends on a combination of tools and techniques and the firm itself, and the mix of these two elements is what determines an effective outcome.

Applying the tools and guidelines

Over the past 50 years numerous models, guidelines and tools have been developed to try to help firms achieve successful product innovation. While there is debate within the literature about the detailed design and content of the models, generally the literature argues that by following a common formalised model so that projects pass through a series of phases an organisation will improve its level of product development (Engwall *et al.*, 2005). What is less clear is the extent to which firms' and managers' practical actions adhere to the formalised model. Indeed, there is plenty of evidence to suggest that these models are not rigidly followed (Leonard-Barton, 1987; Sauer and Lau, 1997; Werr, 1999).

Other research has found that the models serve a variety of different purposes other than that originally intended: for example, creating legitimacy, attracting support for a project, disciplining the project team and providing an illusion of a sense of control (Sapolsky, 1972; Brunson, 1980; Huczynski, 1993; Hodgson, 2002). It seems there is a lack of studies on the actual use of models in practice. In their study of project managers Engwall *et al.* (2005) found:

- that structured development models contributed to NPD;
- they were seen as guides for action but not followed rigidly;
- that models need to be applied pragmatically; and
- they provided a common language.

Analysing the range of well-established management principles that can help the leaders of an organisation sustain innovativeness and even recover from a period of stagnation is clearly necessary, but we also need to recognise that the decision to implement or use one or more of these techniques may be down to the leaders themselves. Innovation leadership is discussed either by innovation management researchers in the context of top management support or by leadership scholars under the heading of 'leadership and organisational change'. Nonetheless the key challenges in innovation for any manager or leader are (Deschamps, 2003):

- the urge to do new things;
- the obsession to redefine customer value;
- the courage to take risks;
- an ability to manage risk;
- speed in spotting opportunities and project execution;
- a shift in focus and mindset from business optimisation to business creation.

These drivers of change could equally be used to characterise entrepreneurship (long recognised as a key factor in firm innovation) and indeed, it is the role of the entrepreneur that is often missing from many models of innovation. Even within extremely successful companies that have had many years of innovation success, top managers have to be reminded of their responsibility to support and champion innovation leaders: those people who exercise their initiative and create change. Such people will make mistakes, but many of the tools and techniques discussed in this chapter can help firms manage risks and reduce the level of mistakes.

Case study

Gore-Tex® and W.L. Gore & Associates: An innovative company and a contemporary culture

This case study explores the role of organisational management and culture within a very innovative firm, which is responsible for some very well known products such as the famous Gore-Tex fabric, and yet few people know very much about this remarkable organisation. It is operated in a similar way to that of a cooperative such as the John Lewis Partnership in the United Kingdom, where the employees are also owners. In addition, the organisation seeks to minimise management with the emphasis on action and creativity. Today this enigmatic firm employs approximately 7,000 people in more than 45 plants and sales locations world-wide. Manufacturing operations are clustered in the United States, Germany, Scotland, Japan and China. Proprietary technologies with the versatile polymer polytetrafluoroethylene (PTFE) have resulted in numerous products for electronic signal transmission; fabrics laminates; medical implants; as well as membrane, filtration, sealant and fibre technologies for a range of different industries. Today the organisation divides its products into four main groupings: medical products; fabric products; electronic products; and industrial products. Gore has approximately 650 US patents and thousands worldwide. Further details of these can be found by visiting the US Patent & Trademark office website at www.uspto.gov.

Introduction

W.L. Gore & Associates is probably best known in Europe for its Gore-Tex product (that piece of material in your coat that keeps you dry yet allows your body to breathe), yet few people know very much about this privately owned and relatively secret company. Fewer still realise the very innovative and contemporary way the organisation is run – it seeks to have an 'unmanagement style'. Annual revenues top $1 billion. W.L. Gore is a privately held company ranking in the top 200 of the Forbes top 500 privately held companies for 2002. Indeed, W.L. Gore would rank in the Fortune 500 companies in terms of profits, market value and equity value. Given that the firm is a privately held corporation many details of the company's operations and strategies are not widely known. Unlike publicly listed firms it does not need to share information on such topics as marketing strategies, manufacturing processes or technology development. The company is owned primarily by its employees (known as associates) and the Gore family. W.L. Gore enterprises has more than 7,000 associates at over 45 locations around the world.

W.L. Gore & Associates was founded in 1958 in Newark, Delaware, when Bill and Vieve Gore set out to explore market opportunities for fluorocarbon polymers, especially polytetrafluoroethylene (PTFE). First developed by Bill Gore when he worked as a scientist for the Dupont Corporation. Gore could not get anyone at Dupont to invest in his new idea, so he bought the patent and went into business on his own. Within the first decade alone, W.L. Gore wire and cables landed on the moon (the firm supplied cables for the 1969 lunar missions); the company opened divisions in Scotland and Germany; and a venture partnership took root in Japan.

W.L. Gore has introduced its unique technical capabilities into hundreds of diverse products. It has defined new standards for comfort and protection for workwear and activewear (Gore-Tex); advanced the science of regenerating tissues destroyed by disease or traumatic injuries; developed next-generation materials for printed circuit boards and fibre optics; and pioneered new methods to detect and control environmental pollution.

Gore-Tex®, a breathable fabric

In 1969, Bob Gore discovered that rapidly stretching PTFE created a very strong, microporous material (this became known as expanded PTFE, or ePTFE), which offered a range of new, desirable properties. To be effective a waterproof fabric needs to be able to prevent moisture getting from the outside to the inside. Furthermore, a waterproof fabric must have the ability to withstand water entry in active conditions such as walking in wind-driven rain and sitting or kneeling on a wet surface. In the case of garments for wear especially in active conditions, perspiration is a common problem. If perspiration vapour becomes trapped inside clothing, it can condense into liquid moisture that causes dampness – and wet heat loss is 23 times faster than dry heat loss. A fabric that would enable moisture to escape and at the same time prevent moisture from entering would seem unachievable, but that is precisely what the Gore-Tex fabric does. Raincoats incorporating the Gore-Tex fabric were first introduced way back in 1976, hence the patent for the breathable fabric expired in 1996. However, new patents are still active on improved methods of making Gore-Tex fabric. There are now many generic versions of breathable fabric on the market. The success of the product has largely been witnessed in the 1990s as outdoor pursuits grew rapidly in popularity during this period. This led to an explosion in sales of Gore-Tex related products, such as coats, back-packs, shoes and trousers. Indeed, clothing manufacturers who used the Gore-Tex fabric in their garments, such as Berghaus, Karrimor and North Face, became household names as this once esoteric specialised clothing market became mainstream.

Source: © Anthony Redpath/Corbis

Working within W.L. Gore Associates

The very unusual organisational structure and management sets this firm apart from its competitors. Moreover, there is some evidence to support its claim to be highly creative and innovative as Gore–US has made all six annual lists of the '100 Best Companies to Work for' in *Fortune* magazine from 1998 to 2003. Its UK firm was ranked among the '100 Best Places to Work in the UK' (McCall, 2002). Gore–Italy ranked among the '35 Best Places to Work in Italy' (2003). Gore–Germany ranked among the '50 Best Places to Work in Germany' (2003). It is often cited as a model for effective management of innovation, and the firm is proud of its heritage and how it works:

> *We encourage hands-on innovation, involving those closest to a project in decision-making. Teams organize around opportunities and leaders emerge. Our founder, Bill Gore created a flat lattice organization. There are no chains of command nor pre-determined channels of communication. Instead, we communicate directly with each other and are accountable to fellow members of our multi-disciplined teams.*
>
> *Associates are hired for general work areas. With the guidance of their sponsors (not bosses) and a growing understanding of opportunities and team objectives, associates commit to projects*

→

that match their skills. Everyone can quickly earn the credibility to define and drive projects. Sponsors help associates chart a course in the organization that will offer personal fulfilment while maximizing their contribution to the enterprise. Leaders may be appointed, but are defined by 'followership.' More often, leaders emerge naturally by demonstrating special knowledge, skill, or experience that advances a business objective.

Associates are committed to four basic guiding principles articulated by Bill Gore:

> *freedom to encourage, help, and allow other associates to grow in knowledge, skill, and scope of fairness to each other and everyone with whom we come in contact; responsibility; the ability to make one's own commitments and keep them; and consultation with other associates before undertaking actions that could impact the reputation of the company by hitting it below the waterline.* (Gore, 2003)

Non-hierarchical corporate culture

The firm's unique structure was born out of Bill Gore's frustration with a large corporate bureaucracy; the W.L. Gore culture seeks to avoid taxing creativity with conventional hierarchy. The company encourages hands-on innovation, involving those closest to a project in decision making; hence decision making is based on knowledge rather than seniority. Teams organise around opportunities and leaders emerge based on the needs and priorities of a particular business unit. To avoid the traditional pyramid of bosses and managers, Bill created a flat lattice organisational structure in which there are no chains of command and no predetermined channels of communication. Instead, employees communicate directly with each other and are accountable to fellow members of multidisciplinary teams. The company bases its business philosophy on the belief that given the right environment, there is no limit to what people can accomplish.

The formula seems to have worked. In 40 years of business, W.L. Gore & Associates has developed hundreds of unique products that reflect an underlying commitment to fluoropolymer technologies. The company is passionate about innovation and has built a unique work environment to support it based on a corporate culture that encourages creativity, initiative and discovery. According to Gore:

> *you won't find the trappings of a traditional corporate structure here: no rigid hierarchy, no bosses, and no predictable career ladder. Instead, you'll find direct communication, a team oriented atmosphere, and one title – associate – that's shared by everyone. It's an unusual corporate culture that contributes directly to the business' success by encouraging creativity and opportunity.*
>
> (Gore, 2003)

The last principle is meant to protect the company from inappropriate risk. While employees are given wide latitude to pursue entrepreneurial opportunities, no one can initiate projects involving significant corporate financial commitments without thorough review and participation by qualified associates.

An individual starting at W.L. Gore is assigned three sponsors. A starting sponsor helps get the associate acquainted with W.L. Gore. An advocate sponsor makes sure the associate receives credit and recognition for their work and a compensation sponsor makes sure the associate is paid fairly. One person can fill all three sponsor roles. Compensation is determined by committees and relies heavily on evaluations by other associates as well as the compensation sponsor.

Employee ownership structure

The goal of Gore's highly flexible and competitive programme is to maximise freedom and fairness for each associate. The benefit plans consist of core benefits and flexible benefits. Core benefits are basic plans and services provided by Gore to all eligible associates. They include an Associate Stock Ownership Plan, vacation, holidays, profit sharing, sick pay, basic life insurance, travel accident insurance and adoption aid.

The Associate Stock Ownership Plan (ASOP) is the most valuable financial benefit. Its purpose is to provide equity ownership, and through this ownership, to provide financial security for retirement. All associates have an opportunity to participate in the growth of the company by acquiring ownership in it. Every year W.L. Gore contributes up to 15 per cent of pay to an account that purchases W.L. Gore stock for each participating associate. W.L. Gore contributes the same percentage of pay for each associate active in the plan. An associate is eligible for this benefit after one full year of employment and qualifies for full ownership of their accounts after five years of service, when they are fully vested. Valued quarterly, W.L. Gore stock is privately held and is not traded on public markets. The ASOP, although it does not own all of the W.L. Gore shares, does own a majority of them, with the remainder owned by the Gore family.

Associates also qualify for cash profit-sharing distributions when corporate profit goals have been reached. Profit-sharing distributions typically occur an average of twice a year. In addition, each pay period associates are provided with pre-tax benefits, called flex dollars, to use for the purchase of 'flexible benefits'. These include medical plans, dental plans, long-term disability insurance, personal days, supplemental individual life insurance, family life insurance and health care or dependent care spending accounts.

Unique characteristics of ownership culture

W.L. Gore believes that given the right environment, there is no limit to what people can accomplish. That is where the W.L. Gore lattice system comes in to play. It gives the associates the opportunity to use their own judgement, select their own projects and directly access the resources they need to be successful. Another unique aspect of the lattice system is the company's insistence that no single operating division become larger than 200 people in order to preserve the intimacy and ease of communications among smaller work groups. As divisions grow, they are separated into constituent parts to preserve that culture.

Discussion

This case illustrates some of the organisational characteristics that are necessary for innovation to occur. The unique organisational model seems to work for W.L. Gore. It is certainly contemporary and does seem to help to unleash creativity and to foster teamwork in an entrepreneurial environment that seeks to provide maximum freedom and support for its employees (associates). Many of the organisational characteristics are not, however, unique to W.L. Gore and there are many other firms where these characteristics can be found, such as 3M, Hewlett-Packard, Corning, Dyson, BP and Shell. It does reinforce the need for firms wishing to be innovative to adopt these characteristics (*see* Table 3.2).

There are several key characteristics that help make the W.L. Gore company successful, both financially and as a place to work. First, the high-quality technology and heritage of the firm that encourages an emphasis on developing superior products. Second, the use of small teams encourages direct one-on-one communication; this contributes to the ability to make timely, informed decisions and get products to market very quickly. Third, the channels of communications are very open, the lattice structure allowing all employees the freedom to meet and discuss projects, situations, concerns and share congratulations with everyone. Fourth, W.L. Gore believes that providing equity compensation to its employees establishes a sense of ownership and increased commitment among its employees. The ASOP program at W.L. Gore is the majority owner of the company. Fifth, W.L. Gore provides a comprehensive set of employee benefits and is continually looking for ways to improve upon what is currently available. Sometimes that just means re-evaluating what the employees want and need. Finally, making sure that the individual work groups do not get too large to be effective is a key element of 'right-sizing' for the company culture. This way W.L. Gore maintains a sense of intimacy and ease of communications among its work groups.

While the employee share ownership sounds attractive, any decrease in performance and fall in value of the shares can cause enormous resentment within the firm as they see the value of their savings decrease. And unlike publicly listed firms these shareholders cannot remove the managers. W.L. Gore's competitors are varied and diverse: there is no single company which competes with Gore in every product area. Firms such as Bayer, Hoecht, Corning, Dow and Du-Pont all compete in Gore's product fields: medical, fabric, industrial and electronic applications.

The business strategy pursued by W.L. Gore Associates has been very successful to date. However, in some of its markets competition is beginning to emerge. Gore must decide whether it wants to become involved in and attempt to win a price war in these markets or to try to offer superior name-brand products. Alternatively it could decide to rely on its traditional approach of utilising its R&D to develop new product applications that will enable it to enter new markets, often as the sole business offering certain product types. Gore may need to reassess its

→

R&D activities to focus on specific and marketable new technology if it wishes to keep its position as the technological leader in many of its industries. Rather than allowing individual associates to organise and conduct their own projects, more emphasis could be placed on strategic R&D programmes where the business sees opportunities for growth to enable it to create new ventures.

Sources: Anfuso, D. (1999) Core values shape W.L. Gore's innovative culture, *Workforce* magazine (US), March, 48–53; Gore (2003) Extract from the W.L. Gore Associates website; Harrison, L. (2002) We're all the boss, *Time*, Inside Business edition, 8 April; McCall, A. (ed.) (2002) The firm that lets staff breathe, *Sunday Times* (London), 24 March, '100 Best Companies to Work For', special section; Milford, M. (1996) A company philosophy in bricks and mortar, *New York Times*, 1 September, Sec. R, p. 5. *The Sunday Times* (2007) '100 Best Companies to Work For' supplement, 11 March.

Questions

1 Explain what happened to the Gore-Tex brand after the patent expired. What activity can firms use to try to maintain any advantage developed during the patent protection phase?

2 List some of the wide range of products where the Gore-Tex fabric has been applied.

3 It seems that Gore Associates is heavily oriented towards technology; what are some of the dangers of being too heavily focused on technology?

4 Cooperatives and share-ownership schemes provide many attractions and benefits, but there are also limitations; discuss these.

5 What has been the Gore strategy to achieving success in its markets? How is this strategy now being challenged?

6 Using CIM (Figure 1.9) illustrate the innovation processes within W.L. Gore.

Note: This case has been written as a basis for class discussion rather than to illustrate effective or ineffective managerial or administrative behaviour. It has been prepared from a variety of published sources, as indicated, and from observations.

Chapter summary

This chapter has helped to explain how firms can manage innovation. In particular, it explored the organisational environment and the activities performed within it that are necessary for innovation to occur. Emphasis was placed on the issue of uncertainty and how different types of projects require different types of skills.

Another key component of successful innovation management is the extent to which an organisation recognises the need for and encourages innovation. This is often easy for firms to say but it seems much more difficult for firms to do.

This chapter also examined the range of well-established management tools and methodologies that may be helpful to firms to manage innovation. In addition, several roles were identified as necessary for innovation to occur and it was stressed that these are often performed by key individuals.

Discussion questions

1 Can organisations operate across the entire spectrum of innovation activities?

2 Explain the fundamental dilemma facing organisations and the tensions it creates.

3 Discuss the impact to the firm of changes in architectural knowledge and component knowledge.

4 Explain how management tools for innovation may help a firm regain its innovative performance.

5 Explain how organisational characteristics can facilitate the innovation process.

6 Explain the key individual roles within the innovation process and the activities they perform.

Key words and phrases

Dilemma of innovation *84*
Slack *84*
Ambidexterity *85*
Managing uncertainty *85*
Exploratory research *87*
Architechtual knowledge *90*
Receptivity *94*
Gatekeeper *103*
Product champion *103*

References

Adams, R., Bessant, J. and Phelps, R. (2006) Innovation management measurement: a review, *International Journal of Management Reviews*, Vol. 8, No. 1, 21–47.

Allen, T.J. (1977) *Managing the Flow of Technology*, MIT Press, Cambridge, MA.

Allen, T.J. and Cohen, W.M. (1969) Information flow in research and development laboratories, *Administrative Science Quarterly*, Vol. 14, No. 1, 12–19.

Brunsson, N. (1980) The functions of project management, *The Journal of Management Studies*, Vol. 10, No. 2, 61–71.

Burns, T. and Stalker, G.M. (1961) *The Management of Innovation*, Tavistock, London.

Child, J. (1973) Predicting and understanding organisational structure, *Administrative Science Quarterly*, Vol. 18, 168–85.

Coombs, R., McMeekin, A. and Pybus, R. (1998) Toward the Development of Benchmarking Tools for R&D Project Management, *R&D Management*, Vol. 28, No. 3, 175–86.

Cooper, R.G. (1986) *Winning at New Products*, Addison-Wesley, Reading, MA.

Deschamps, J.-P. (2003) 'Innovation and Leadership', in L. Shavina (ed.) *International Handbook on Innovation*, Elsevier, Amsterdam.

Dobini, C. (2010) The relationship between an innovation orientation and competitive strategy, *International Journal of Innovation Management*, Vol. 14, No. 2, 331–57.

Engwall, M., Kling, R. and Werr, A. (2005) Models in Action: How Management Models are Interpreted in New Product Development, *R&D Management*, Vol. 35, No. 4, 427–39.

Gartner (2002) How Proctor & Gamble runs its global business on SAP, CS-15-3473, Research Note, 25 February 2000.

Hannan, M. and Freeman, J. (1984) Structural inertia and organizational change, *American Sociological Review*, Vol. 49, 149–64.

Hauschildt, J. (2003) 'Promoters and champions in innovations: development of a research paradigm', in Shavinina, L. (ed.) *The International Handbook on Innovation*, Elsevier, Oxford.

Henderson, R. and Clark, K. (1990) Architectural innovation: the reconfiguration of existing product and the failure of established firms, *Administrative Science Quarterly*, Vol. 35, 9–30.

Henry, J. and Walker, D. (eds) (1991) *Managing Innovation*, Sage/Oxford University Press, London.

Hidalgo, A. and Albors, J. (2008) Innovation Management Techniques and Tools: A Review from Theory and Practice, *R&D Management*, Vol. 38, No. 2, 113–127.

Hodgson, D. (2002) Disciplining the professional: The case of project management. *The Journal of Management Studies*, Vol. 39, No. 6, 803.

Huczynski, A. (1993) *Management Gurus*, Routledge, London.

Johannessen, J., Olaisen, J. and Olsen, B. (2001) Management of tacit knowledge: the importance of tacit knowledge, the danger of information technology, and what to do about it, *Journal of Information Management*, Vol. 21, No. 1, 3–20.

Kang, K. and Kang, J. (2009) How do firms source external knowledge for innovation? Analysing effects of different knowledge sourcing methods, *International Journal of Innovation Management*, Vol. 13, No. 1, 1–17.

Langrish, J., Gibbons, M., Evans, W.G. and Jevons, F.R. (1972) *Wealth from Knowledge*, Macmillan, London.

Leonard-Barton, D. (1987) Implementing Structured Software Methodologies: A Case of Innovation in Process Technology, *Interfaces,* Vol. 17, No. 3, 6–17.

Martins, E.C. and Terblanche, F. (2003) Building organizational culture that stimulates creativity and innovation, *European Journal of Innovation Management*, Vol. 6, No. 1, 64–74.

Mintzberg, H. (1978) Patterns in strategy formulation, *Management Science*, Vol. 24, 934–48.

Nelson, R.R. and Winter, S.G. (1982) *An Evolutionary Theory of Economic Change*, Harvard University Press, Cambridge, MA.

Nonaka, I. (1991) The knowledge-creating company, *Harvard Business Review*, November–December, 96–104.

O'Reilly, C.A. and Tushman, M.L. (2008) Ambidexterity as a dynamic capability: Resolving the innovators' dilemma, *Research in Organization Behavior*, Vol. 28, 185–206.

Pavitt, K. (1994) Sectoral patterns of technological change: towards a taxonomy and theory, *Research Policy*, 13, 343–73.

Pearson, A.W. (1983) Planning and Monitoring in Research and Development: A 12 Year Review of Papers in *R&D Management, R&D Management*, Vol. 13, No. 2, 107–16.

Pearson, A. (1991) 'Managing innovation: an uncertainty reduction process', in Henry, J. and Walker, D. (eds) *Managing Innovation*, Sage/Oxford University Press, London, 18–27.

Peters, T.J. and Waterman, R.H. (1982) *In Search of Excellence*, Harper and Row, New York.

Porter, M.E. and Ketels, C.H.M. (2003) *UK Competitiveness: Moving to the next stage*, Department of Trade and Industry, London.

Prajogo, D.I. and Ahmed, P.K. (2006) Relationships between innovation stimulus, innovation capacity and innovation performance, *R&D Management*, Vol. 36, No. 5, 499–515.

Rothwell, R., Freeman, C., Horlsey, A., Jervis, V.T.P., Robertson, A.B. and Townsend, J. (1974) SAPPHO updated: Project SAPPHO phase II, *Research Policy*, Vol. 3, 258–91.

Rubenstein, A.H. (1976) Factors influencing success at the project level, *Research Management*, Vol. 19, No. 3, 15–20.

Sapolsky, H. (1972) *The Polaris System Development*, Harvard University Press, Cambridge, MA.

Sauer, C. (1993) *Why Information Systems Fail: A Case Study Approach*, Alfred Waller, Henley-on-Thames.

Sauer, C. and Lau, C. (1997) Trying to Adopt Systems Development Methodologies – a case-based exploration of business users' interests, *Information Systems Journal*, Vol. 7, 255–75.

Sheene, M.R. (1991) The boundness of technical knowledge within a company: barriers to external knowledge acquisition, paper presented at R&D Management Conference on *The Acquisition of External Knowledge*, Kiel, Germany.

Smith, W.K. and Tushman, M.L. (2005) Managing strategic contradictions: A top management model for managing innovation streams, *Organization Science*, Vol. 16, No. 5, 522–36.

Souder, W.E. (1987) *Managing New Product Innovations*, Lexington Books, Lexington, MA.

Trott, P. and Hoecht, A. (2004) Enterprise resource planning (ERP) and its impact on innovation, *International Journal of Innovation Management*, Vol. 8, No. 3, 381–98.

Utterback, J.M. (1975) The process of technological innovation within the firm, *Academy of Management Review*, Vol. 12, 75–88.

van der Panne, G., van Beers, C. and Kleinknecht, A. (2003) Success and failure of innovation: a review of the literature, *International Journal of Innovation Management*, Vol. 7, No. 3, 309–38.

van de Ven, A.H. (1986) Central problems: the management of innovation, *Management Science*, Vol. 32, No. 5, 590–607.

Werr, A. (1999) *The Language of Change – the roles of methods in the work of management consultants*, The Economic Research Institute, Stockholm School of Economics, Stockholm.

Wheelwright, S.C. and Clark, K.B. (1992) *Revolutionising product development*, The Free Press, New York.

Wolfe, R.A. (1994) Organisational innovation: review and critique and suggested research directions, *Journal of Management Studies*, Vol. 31, No. 3, 405–31.

Further reading

For a more detailed review of the innovation management literature, the following develop many of the issues raised in this chapter:

Adams, R., Bessant, J. and Phelps, R. (2006) Innovation management measurement: a review, *International Journal of Management Reviews*, Vol. 8, No. 1, 21–47.

Berkhout, A.J., Hartmann, D. and Trott, P. (2010) Connecting technological capabilities with market needs using a cyclic innovation model, *R&D Management*, Vol. 40, No. 5, 474–90.

Dobini, C. (2010) The relationship between an innovation orientation and competitive strategy, *International Journal of Innovation Management*, Vol. 14, No. 2, 331–57.

HSBC (2010) 100 Thoughts, HSBC, London.

Prajogo, D.I. and Ahmed, P.K. (2006) Relationships between innovation stimulus, innovation capacity and innovation performance, *R&D Management*, Vol. 36, No. 5, 499–515.

van der Panne, G., van Beers, C. and Kleinknecht, A. (2003) Success and failure of innovation: a review of the literature, *International Journal of Innovation Management*, Vol. 7, No. 3, 309–38.

Chapter 4
Innovation and operations management

Richard Noble
University of Portsmouth

Introduction

Effective research and development (R&D) requires close links with the part of the organisation that produces the product (or service) – that is, operations. Many new product ideas are based on existing products and may be developed from within the production or service operations function and it is necessary, therefore, to examine the role of operations and its management when studying innovation. These innovative ideas are likely to be ideas for improvement in the process of manufacture or delivery of the product or service. A large number of these ideas may be modest and incremental rather than radical, but the combined effect of many small innovative ideas may be substantial. The case study at the end of this chapter on the publishing industry shows how the operational activities of publishing support the creativity and innovation of the author.

Chapter contents

Learning objectives

When you have completed this chapter you will be able to:

- recognise the importance of innovation in operations management;
- recognise the importance of sales volume in product design;
- recognise the importance of design in the process of making and delivering a product or service;
- appreciate that the nature of design is context dependent;
- recognise that much innovation is not patentable; and
- provide an understanding of a number of approaches to design and process management.

Operations management

Most organisations provide items that are a combination of product and service elements – for example, a restaurant provides a product (the food) and a service (delivery to your table). The term operations management was coined to bring together the skills and techniques developed in the manufacturing and service sectors in order to help encourage the transfer of the best practices. In an age of global mass production and competition, it is often the service element of any purchase that gives the supplying operation its crucial competitive advantage. The case study at the end of this chapter shows how the production of a book is only part of the operation involved in publishing a book and getting it to the customer. Innovation within the operations function is therefore crucial in achieving the organisation's strategic objectives.

Operations management is about the control of a conversion process from an *input* to an *output* (*see* Table 4.1).

This chapter considers the design and management of the conversion processes given in Table 4.1. A large percentage of the asset base of the organisation normally lies within these boundaries, and it is essential that the assets be used to effect, to gain an advantage in this increasingly competitive world. In particular, the degree of innovation involving these expensive assets is crucial if the organisation is to prosper. Figure 4.1 illustrates the operation function and includes the elements of design, planning and control and improvement.

To this process (Figure 4.1) need to be added three other very important dimensions:

1 the customer who becomes part of the process as in self-service supermarkets or in the education process taking place in tutorials;
2 information from customers (complaints or compliments), market research or government agencies (standards, laws, EU directives, etc.); and
3 the physical and business environment in which the organisation operates.

Table 4.1 Operations inputs and outputs

Organisation	Input	Processes include	By-products	Output
A car producer	Material (steel, rubber, glass) People Skills Energy	Welding Painting Assembly	Material waste Heat waste	Cars Salaries
A university	Students Teachers Information Knowledge	Lectures Seminars Research Learning	Waste paper	Graduates Academic papers
A hospital	Doctors Patients Medicines Knowledge	Medical operations Radiotherapy	Clinical waste	Healthy patients
A publishing company	Paper Ink Author's work	Editing Binding Printing	Paper pulp Chemical waste	Books Royalties

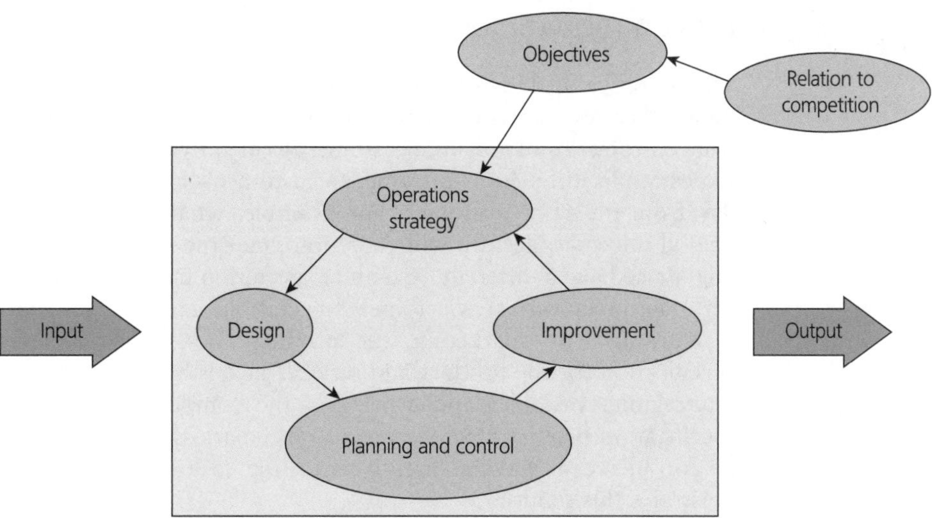

Figure 4.1 The operations manager's role

Source: Adapted from *Operations Management*, 4th edn (Slack, N. *et al.*, 2004), © Pearson Education Limited.

The nature of design and innovation in the context of operations

Some innovations are described as 'leading edge' and are based upon work from within the R&D laboratories and may involve patent applications. Innovation (as we saw in Chapter 1) may also be a new application of an existing technique to a different situation. Something that is new and innovative to one company may be a tried and tested procedure or product to another. Also, every innovative idea may not be suitable to patent but, to those concerned, the novelty, the ingenuity, the problems associated with its introduction and the cost–benefit to the organisation may be just the same.

Although in many companies designers quite frequently make inventions, designing and inventing are different in kind. Design is usually more concerned with the process of *applying* scientific principles and inventions (Roy and Weild, 1993). Design is a compromise between the different elements that constitute the design. For example, increasing the wall thickness of a product made from steel may increase the product's strength, reliability and durability but only with the consequential increase in product weight and cost.

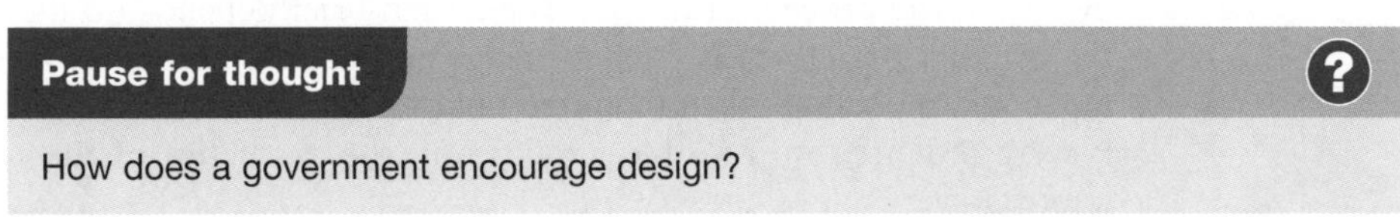

Design requirements

The objective of design is to meet the needs and expectations of customers. Good design therefore starts and ends with the customer. Marketing gathers information from customers and *potential* customers to identify customer needs and expectations. Expectations differ from customer to customer – indeed, they may vary from day to day from the same customer. For example, what would constitute the design of a good university lecture will vary from one student to another. The same student might also have a different need and expectation from the lecturer after a long lunch break in the union bar. Customer expectations vary.

Working with marketing, the product and service designer then designs a specification for the product and service. This is a complex task involving complex interrelating variables and aspects of the company's objectives. To help in the specification process Slack *et al.* (2007) remark that all products and services can be considered as having three aspects (the case study at the end of this chapter illustrates this point):

- a *concept* – the expected benefits the customer is buying;
- a *package* of component products that provides those benefits defined in the concepts, i.e. what the customer actually purchases and constitutes the ingredients of the design; and
- the *process*, which defines the relationship between the component product and services by which the design fulfils its concept.

A meal in a restaurant consists of products (the food and drink) and services such as the style of waitress service and background music. Some products or service elements are core to the operation and could not be removed without destroying the nature of the package. Other parts of the package serve to enhance the core. In a fast-food restaurant the food and the speed of delivery are essential core elements of the package while the ambience and layout of the restaurant supports the core (*see* Illustration 4.1).

By changing the core, or adding or subtracting supporting services, organisations can provide different packages and therefore design very different products and services. In a fast-food restaurant the customer may order the food at the counter (and possibly pay the bill) and stand for a moment or two until the choice is delivered in disposable containers. The service is substantially different from that purchased in an exclusive restaurant.

Another example of product design comes from Braun, a leading European manufacturer of small domestic appliances. Braun has over 60 per cent of its sales from products with less than five years from product launch. Given the design brief to combine together, and perform as least as well as, three specialist kitchen appliances, the designers applied 10 industrial design principles to the Braun Multimix product (*see* Illustration 4.2). For a similar list of design principles in the service sector, *see* Van Looy *et al.* (2003), Chapter 14.

The different examples of the design parameters considered illustrate the complexity of the process of design. The design brief depends on the market for which the product or service is created. For example, the aesthetics of a domestic water tap is not important when mounted out of sight under the kitchen sink. If, however, it were mounted in a visible application, the aesthetics of the tap would be very important.

Illustration 4.1

A fast-food restaurant

The success of fast-food restaurants like McDonald's could be due to a number of factors but among the most important would be the design of its operating system that ensures consistency and uniformity of its *products* and *service* in all their premises. In London, New York, Vancouver and Hong Kong, the customer will be familiar with the layout and decor and will know the food to expect. This recipe for success has been duplicated and copied by competitive organisations the world over.

The original key innovation was to have a very simple menu of just three foods and six drinks. This simplicity allowed straightforward cooking and preparation procedures that ensured consistent product quality. McDonald's were able to influence and manage their supply chain to ensure uniformity of raw material, again helping the consistency of product produced.

Simple menu, simple procedures, standard facilities and good operations management combine to give a cost-effective operation.

Fast-food restaurants often have other operational characteristics that contribute to their success. If there is a counter to queue at it will be well away from the door – a *fast*-food restaurant would *not* want to advertise a queue. You pay for the food in advance, avoiding the need to revisit the counter. Furthermore, they do not encourage you to linger – filling the place with customers who have paid and been served is not to their advantage. The seats, if they exist, tend to be uncomfortable.

Source: From *Operations Management*, 5th edn (Slack, N. *et al.*, 2007), © Pearson Education Limited.

Roy and Weild (1993) suggest a design spectrum, which ranges from the concept designer whose primary concern is ensuring technical excellence to the focus of the industrial designer on 'manufacturability' and the ease of use of the product.

For example, the design team involved in the manufacture of a hi-fi set would include:

- an electronics engineer concerned with the ability of the electrical circuits to faithfully produce sound from the CD – i.e. the function of the product;
- the marketing department members who would be concerned about the look of the product, i.e. the aesthetics, the ease of use, the market price and so on;
- an industrial engineer who will be concerned with the sales volume required; how the product is to be made and assembled, i.e. the operations tasks involved in creating the product;
- consideration of the packaging requirements for items on display for protection during transport (see Chapter 13 on packaging).

In this illustration the knowledge required by a designer in the design spectrum ranges from acoustics, electronics, mechanics, plastic processing technology and industrial engineering to ergonomics and is therefore so broad and complex that no one person can be professionally competent in the whole range of disciplines required. In addition to their own specific competence the designer also needs an appreciation of the problems of other elements of the design spectrum. Managing such a diverse range of disciplines is a complex matter.

Illustration 4.2

Design principles at Braun AG

1 *Usefulness*. The product was designed with the electric motor aligned vertically with the attachments (competitive products have horizontal motors and vertical attachments requiring a more complex gearbox).

2 *Quality*. Braun designers emphasised four aspects of quality:

(a) Versatility – the design included the full range of expected tasks required in cooking: mixing, blending, kneading and chopping.

(b) High mechanical efficiency providing high performance across the range of required tasks.

(c) Safety features to prevent contact with moving parts.

(d) Integrating injection moulding of the main housings into a single manufacturing tool.

3 *Ease of use*. Great emphasis was placed on the human engineering of the product to ensure ease of use and cleaning.

4 *Simplicity*. What was relevant was stressed, what was superfluous was omitted.

5 *Clarity*. The need for complex instructions was avoided. For example, inserting attachments automatically set the required motor speed.

6 *Order*. All the details of the product had a logical and meaningful place.

7 *Naturalness*. The designers avoided any contrived or artificially decorative elements.

8 *Aesthetics*. Although not a primary objective it was achieved by simplicity, attention to detail and the quest for order and naturalness.

9 *Innovation*. Braun was committed to achieving long-lasting appeal for its design so the innovations involved were carefully developed and managed.

10 *Truthfulness*. The principle that 'only honest design can be good design' was applied, avoiding any attempt to play on people's emotions and weaknesses.

This approach has been successful in producing many new products and the aesthetics of Braun's products have been recognised, with samples on display in the Museum of Modern Art in New York.

Source: Adapted from N. Slack *et al.* (2007) *Operations Management*, 5th edn, Pearson, London.

Design and volumes

All the operations management functions involve making decisions – some are tactical or structured and have short-term consequences while others are more strategic with longer-term implications for both the operations function and the organisation as a whole. One such major decision relates to the implications of the production volume required.

The highly skilled eighteenth-century craftsman making furniture at the rate of a few per year is a different type of person from the individual on a twenty-first-century assembly line making furniture at a production rate of hundreds per day. As well as a different type of person, the machinery, the processing techniques used, the materials and the design will also be very different. Choosing the most appropriate and cost-effective method of manufacture is critical to the continued success of the organisation.

When a designer first has an innovative idea for a product, he may have made (possibly make himself) a model to look at and to handle in order to help develop the idea. He may want to show this model to his colleagues or potential customers. Even with all the modern technology available (CAD/CAM, etc.) the 'one-off' models are frequently produced to refine the design or to help gauge customer interest in the product (as witnessed by the concept cars seen at motor shows). At this stage in the innovation process, detailed drawings may not be required or appropriate and highly skilled and expensive personnel therefore make the product. At this stage of a product life cycle the term used to describe the manufacturing process is the *project method of manufacture*. Projects are unique or 'one-off' and the required disciplines and techniques involved can be found in projects of all scales, from an academic dissertation to that of building the Channel Tunnel.

To illustrate this point, consider the development of a simple product such as a toolbox. The design engineer (or innovator), after preliminary meetings with the marketing people and/or potential customers, makes a scale model of the product. In the earliest stage of this product it is best made by the personnel, machinery and techniques involved in a *project* style of production process. The innovator or designer listens to the observations and is able to reflect on these points in the development of the design (*see* Figure 4.2).

The design is well received and after minor modifications the design team decides to have a sample batch made (using common fasteners) by the operations function to help evaluate the market. The toolbox is shown to a range of customers who are each keen to buy a large batch at a competitive price. The industrial design team recognises that by changing the design by avoiding the need for fasteners, investing in tools to shape the individual elements of the box and welding the components together, the assembly time will be reduced and substantial costs saved. *As the required volume increases, the most appropriate method of manufacture changes.*

Another key point is that assembly skills required to produce the product have become *embedded in the process machinery* and the workers involved have become machine minders (*see* Illustration 4.3 on the production of blocks on HMS *Victory*). If the volume required increases even more, by having robots on the assembly line the direct labour involved is further reduced. If the product demand rises even further it may be appropriate that the product is redesigned again and made out of a plastic material (lighter and stronger) requiring investment in a very different processing technology.

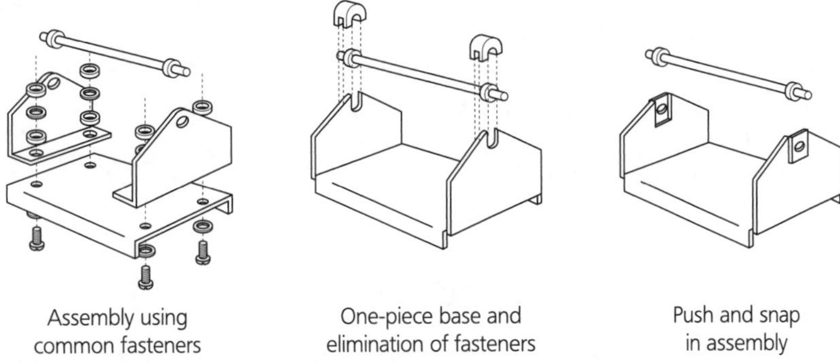

Figure 4.2 Design simplification

Illustration 4.3

Innovation and design in the manufacturing process

The first use of machine tools in mass production was during the Napoleonic wars in the early 1800s. The British Navy, based in Portsmouth, had a need for 100,000 blocks (blocks house the sail ropes) per annum to both equip new ships and to provide spares. For example, HMS *Victory* alone required 900 blocks and each of these was individually carved by skilled craftsmen. Because the blocks were subject to storm, sea water, wind, ice and sun, each ship would sensibly set sail with a full set of replacements and the many suppliers just could not cope with such a high demand.

HMS *Victory*

Source: Rufus Stone/Alamy Images

Marc Brunel (born in France in 1769) was in 1798 dining with the British aide-de-camp in Washington, DC, a Major General Hamilton, when the conversation turned to ships and navies and to the particular problems with the manufacture of these wooden blocks. This was an opportunity to innovate in the process of manufacture and Brunel seized it. His idea was to simplify the manufacturing process into many more stages and to design specialist machines for each part of the operation of manufacture, thus enabling the large volume production of blocks.

In 1799 and with the help of an introduction from General Hamilton to Earl Spencer of Althorp, Brunel persuaded the British Navy to install the 43 Brunel-designed machine tools in a factory in the naval dockyards in Portsmouth. By 1807 the facility was providing all the needs of the navy with only 10 unskilled men. Moreover, as the human element had been much removed from the process, the resulting blocks were far more likely to be consistent in dimensions and therefore of 'better' quality. The machines were still in use over 100 years later and seven are on display in the Portsmouth Naval Museum.

Brunel also applied the same innovative process design logic to other manufacturing problems. In 1809 he was shocked to see the damaged feet of returning war veterans that had been caused by their poorly made and fitted footwear. He therefore designed a set of machines that produced boots and shoes in nine different sizes with 24 disabled soldiers manning the machines. The boots and shoes were very successful and in 1812 the production volume was expanded to meet the army's *total* requirements.

Marc's son, Isambard Kingdom Brunel, designed and built steam ships, railways and many bridges for which he is correctly revered as one of most influential engineers in British history. However, most of what we consume and take for granted is based on the innovation in the processes of manufacture of 200 years ago by men such as Marc Brunel who introduced the concepts of mass production.

Source: www.brunelenginehouse.org.uk/people, 5 April 2007; and the Portsmouth Naval Museum, United Kingdom.

Craft-based products

Some products are craft based and will only ever be made in small volumes – for example, products from the *haute couture* fashion houses. Unique gowns are handmade by very skilled personnel and paraded at the fashion show (a new product launch). The designs are 'copied' by other organisations and there is a rush to get copies made and supplied to the high street retailers. These copies may look similar but are usually made from different materials using different techniques and are consequently less costly to make and to purchase. The operations management of the supplier to the high street has to be able to respond very quickly to get the goods to the market before the fashion changes. The flexibility and speed of response of the operation is therefore critical to the success of the organisation. In this illustration, good marketing is also vital to avoid the end-of-season excess stocks that ambitious and unrealised sales can cause.

Pause for thought 

Is the illustration concerning block manufacture for HMS *Victory* the first example of a mass production system?

Design simplification

The purpose of design is to develop things that satisfy needs and meet expectations. By making the design such that the product is easy to produce, the designer enables the operation to *consistently* deliver these features.

If the product is simple to make, the required quality management procedures will be less complex, easy to understand and, therefore, likely to be more effective. If a design is easy to make, there will be fewer rejects during the manufacturing process and less chance that a substandard product reaches the customer. Referring to the toolbox illustration (Figure 4.2), the reduction in the number of components from over thirty to less than five, makes material control simpler. This in turn leads to simpler purchasing of components and less complex facility layouts. The same logic applies equally well in service sector applications (Brown *et al.*, 2001; Johnston and Clark, 2001).

The application of technology and the technique of 'concurrent engineering' (where research, design and development work closely or in parallel rather than in sequence) have made important contributions to this area of management (Waller, 1999). Innovation within the manufacturing function involves searching for new ways of saving costs and is a continual process, and the closer designers work with operations and marketing personnel, the more likely the organisation is to succeed. This point is developed in the quality function deployment (QFD) section below.

It can take several years and cost millions of pounds to plan and build a major assembly facility such as a car plant. With such a huge investment it is essential that the design of the product is 'correct' at an early stage, as errors detected later can be prohibitively expensive to rectify.

The 4 Vs of operations

As well as the volume of output required, process designers have to consider the **visibility** of the product to the customers. For example, a pile of rejects in a television manufacturing plant may be tolerated but a pile of rejects in a supermarket, with the customers being present, is a different matter. To these considerations process designers also have to consider variation – the number of items on a restaurant menu – and variability – how many meals are required at any one time, i.e. the capacity of the process. Each of these 4 Vs is important in the design activity of manufacturing and service applications.

Process design and innovation

The process design is based on the technology being used within the process. The metal-forming processes, the chemical processing industry, the plastic material processing and electronic assembly are all sophisticated subjects with their own literature.

In order to illustrate a feature of innovation within process design, consider one of the important elements of operations – that of the design of the layout of the facility providing the goods or service. In service-type operations, the customer may be inside and will have visibility of the company's operations function and the significance of layout is even more important.

If an employee spends his working day assembling automotive car seats on an assembly line he quickly becomes expert in that area of manufacture and design. Most people spend the bulk of their 'awake' time involved with work and enjoy talking about their job if the opportunity arises. In all organisations it is the intellect of the employees that is the source of innovation and it is the role of senior managers to create an atmosphere to encourage appropriate intellectual activity if the organisation is to prosper. We go to art galleries or concerts to be entertained and inspired and so it should be in our place of work, in order that the elusive spark of innovation is encouraged.

The importance of the working environment is also recognised in the consideration given to the planning and layout of whole business areas (Wallis, 1995) and university campuses. The case study at the end of this chapter illustrates the importance of bookshop layout in influencing sales. The Chinese have Feng Shui, which is devoted to the impact of these factors on our working and personal environment. The design of the process is linked with the technology involved in the process and is fundamentally linked both to the organisation and job design.

Figure 4.3 models the relationship between the elements of process design and this is as applicable to the service sector as it is to the manufacturing sector. The flow of product within a factory operation may correspond to the flow of the customer (as with an airport design) or of information (as in the headquarters of a bank). The impact on the people involved in delivering the service is clear.

The product design engineer considers the ergonomics of the product, such as a car seat (a key feature in a car purchase decision), while the process design engineer considers the ergonomics of a workstation on an assembly line.

In the service sector the process design parameters of minimising the flow of information are even more critical as the customer is often within the organisation itself. Customers may be made part of the process, as in carrying their own luggage at airports or serving themselves in what is essentially the organisation's stock room at the supermarket. Clear signs and directions, easy-to-understand routes through the operation, understandable forms and approachable staff are all features of a well-designed service system. These are examples of *keeping things simple* – if the customer

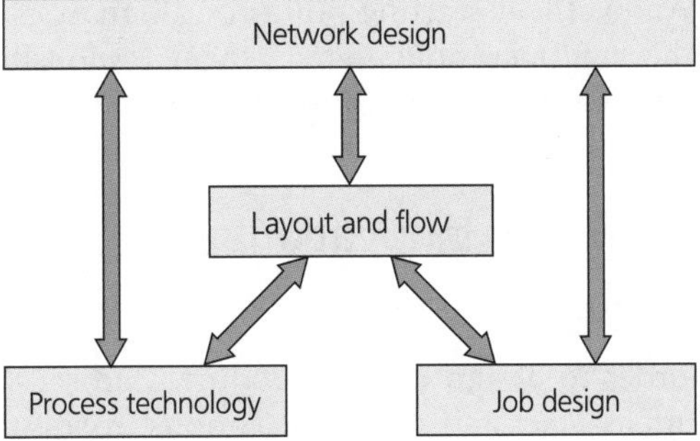

Figure 4.3 The design of processes

does not have to communicate with an employee to obtain the service there is less chance for communication and quality problems. Think of and compare the children's party game of 'Chinese whispers' with the processing of paperwork or messages through several different departments in a large organisation. At every point of information transfer there is an opportunity for the quality of the information to be degraded.

Innovation in action

Be creative about distribution

'Our consumers tell us the number one reason why they don't buy Jones Soda is because they can't find it', says Jonathan Ricci, CEO of Jones Soda.

When Jones Soda tried to launch their range of drinks in Seattle, they found it difficult to get products into the established retail outlets such as supermarkets and convenience stores as these were dominated by the big soft drink brands.

Rather than give up, they looked at the other types of stores that their target customers liked to go to – snowboarding shops, tattoo parlours and music retailers – and provided them with chillers and a supply of drinks. In these retailers there was no competition, and the brand quickly built-up enough sales and customer loyalty that the main distributors then wanted to get in on the action.

Source: 100 Thoughts (2010) HSBC, London.

Innovation in the management of the operations process

The task of all managers is to improve their operation – otherwise they are supervisors and do not justify their job title. New, innovative ways of working within the operations process (including packaging – *see* Chapter 13 on packaging) to gain competitive advantage is therefore part of every operations manager's duties. The question is often how to start? How to trigger off an investigation resulting in an improvement? One approach is first to identify techniques or triggers to help this improvement process and a number of these triggers are discussed in the following sections.

An excellent starting point for all analysis is the customer. Quality performance is the key operations management responsibility and innovation to help improve quality performance is critical to all organisations.

Triggers for innovation

Gap analysis

In order to design quality products and services it is necessary to fully understand your customer and their expectations. Assessing expectations is difficult as customers are different from each other and change with time. Twenty-five years ago teachers used acetates and overhead projectors in the classroom. Today's students expect a computer-generated image (for example, PowerPoint) presentation with the occasional video/CD clip to illustrate the lecture, i.e. the student expectations and requirements have increased with time.

A technique used extensively to aid understanding of the differences (or gaps) between the customer and producer view or experience of a product or service is called 'gap analysis'. Consider the example given by Figure 4.4 about a service product – a university lecture, where the same lecture is experienced by the teacher and the student. However, viewing the lecture from the student's (customer's) viewpoint is different from that of the producer (the lecturer or university).

The student's expectations are based upon the university's and the lecturer's image, experience and word of mouth exchanges. These combine and may lead to the student having a 'specification' of what he/she expects from the lecture. The university, through its management, has a concept of what should be in the lecture (the syllabus). The lecturer takes this concept and produces his slides, handouts (hopefully simple and easy to understand) and delivers the lecture. These differences or gaps are shown in the figure and each is a source of dissatisfaction with the lecture from the student's or university's perspective.

These identified gaps help to show those corrective actions required in the design of the lecture or its delivery process. Table 4.2 illustrates these points.

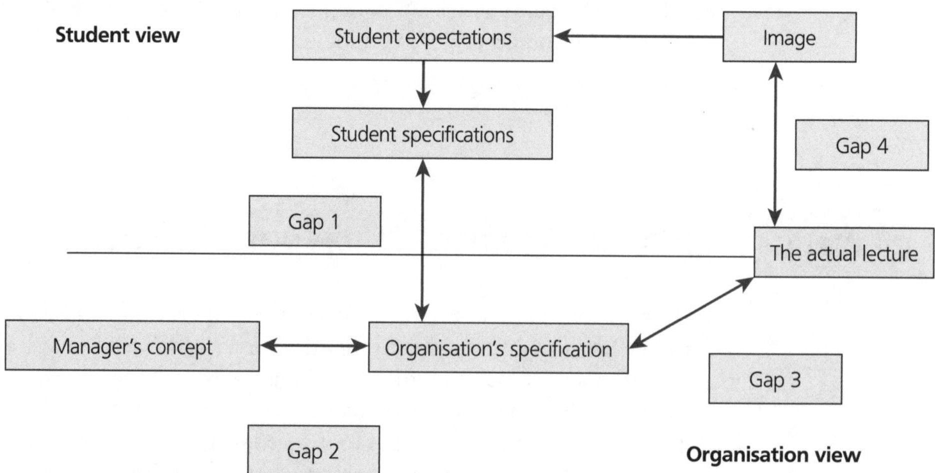

Figure 4.4 Innovation gap analysis

Source: Adapted from *Operations Management*, 4th edn (Slack, N. *et al*., 2004), © Pearson Education Limited.

Table 4.2 Gap analysis

Gap	Action required to ensure high perceived quality	Action by
Gap 1	Ensure consistency between internal quality specifications and the expectations of the students	Marketing Course development and management
Gap 2	Ensure internal specification meets the intended design of the course	Marketing Course development
Gap 3	Ensure actual lecture conforms to its internally specified quality level	The lecturing team Course management
Gap 4	Ensure that promises made to the students concerning the teaching can really be delivered	Marketing

Source: Adapted from *Operations Management*, 5th edn (Slack, N. *et al*. 2007), © Pearson Education Limited.

Quality circles and process improvement teams

A quality circle is a small group of voluntary workers who meet regularly to discuss problems (not necessarily restricted to quality matters) and determine possible solutions. The quality circle concept was developed from the ideas of Deming, Juran and Ishikawa in the 1960s. Most people are expert in their job and appreciate this being acknowledged. Members of quality circles are given training in quality control and evaluation techniques. An idea coming from a member of the quality circle is far more likely to be adopted than an idea imposed from above. Quality circles therefore reflect and exploit the advantages of the human resource theories embedded in employee participation and empowerment approaches. Furthermore, the recognition by senior managers that the employees are worth listening to helps to improve the total quality ethos of the company with beneficial effects on the company and its customers.

Since their introduction it is estimated that over 10 million Japanese workers have been part of a quality circle with an average saving of several thousand US dollars (Russel and Taylor, 2003). The later term 'process improvement team' was used (among others) to reflect the need to look at the whole business process being considered. There has been adoption of the quality circle approach by organisations in Europe and the United States but some argue that the cultural and adversarial differences between management and unions have inhibited the success of the approach in certain situations. However, quality circles can be a rich source of innovative solutions to problems and cost savings and patent applications may follow.

Total quality management (TQM)

Most business texts have chapters on quality from their marketing, human resources or operations perspectives. It is the concept of total quality management that has been among the most significant in its effect. First introduced by Arm and Feigenbaum in the 1950s and then developed and refined by others (including Crosby, Deming, Ishikawa and Juran), TQM became defined as:

> *An effective system for integrating the quality development, quality maintenance and quality improvement efforts of the various groups in an organisation so to enable production and service at the most economical levels which allows for full customer satisfaction.*
> (Feigenbaum, 1986: 96)

Illustration 4.4

Different approaches to quality

IBM of Canada ordered a batch of components from a Japanese supplier and specified that the delivery should have an acceptable quality level of three defective parts per thousand. When the parts arrived they were accompanied by a letter which expressed the supplier's bewilderment at being asked to supply defective parts as well as good ones. The letter also explained that they had found it difficult to make parts that were defective but had done so and were included and wrapped separately with the delivery.

Source: Adapted from *Operations Management*, 5th edn (Slack, N. *et al.*, 2007), © Pearson Education Limited.

The TQM philosophy stresses the following points:

- meeting the needs and expectations of customers;
- covering all the parts of the organisation;
- everyone in the organisation is included;
- investigating all costs related to quality (internal and external);
- getting things right by designing in quality;
- developing systems and procedures which support quality improvements; and
- developing a continuous process of improvement.

Meeting expectations is difficult: as the quality level of products improves this in turn increases customer expectations. For example, in 1970 it was accepted that family-size cars required servicing every 3,000–6,000 miles and lasted for 60,000–70,000 miles. The automotive technical improvements now mean that a service interval of 15,000 miles and cars that last for over 100,000 miles are now the norm and are *expected*. Innovation in the ways to achieve what the customer expects in the combination of product and service provided is one way to gain sustainable advantage over your competition. The humorous and much quoted example in Illustration 4.4 shows the different approaches to quality management.

For a TQM approach to be successful all the staff in all departments have to be involved. Quality is the responsibility of everyone and not some other manager or department. Quality and employee improvements are therefore inextricably linked and should be part of a continuous cycle. If a modest innovative and improvement cycle continues, by embedding the approach in the culture of the organisation, the long-term and total result may exceed that of a radical solution. The 'knowledge' of the organisation has thereby increased. No organisation has the ability to recruit and retain all the very best brains and operation managers need to recognise that they need to exploit the skills and enthusiasm of all their people. The impact of small, relatively easy to achieve, improvements can be very positive. Much of the improvement in the reliability of cars over the past 20 years has been attributed to a very large number of incremental improvements initiated by thousands of employees in all the car manufacturing companies and their suppliers.

TQM, with its continuous improvement, employee involvement and process ownership, has shown itself to be an effective policy in managing organisations not least because of the enthusiastic implementation (team building). TQM is not a substitute for real leadership or a passing fad. However, if an idea generated meant that an element of the process was no longer needed and jobs were lost, what then of employee involvement? Many, if not most, employees would be unwilling to suggest losing jobs. Even in circumstances when alternative work was available to those displaced, many would be reluctant to vigorously pursue the idea. The very feeling of process ownership by the employees may *obstruct* all radical change, i.e. TQM may not support major innovation (Giaever, 1998). This problem is where management and leadership are required.

Quality function deployment (QFD)

Making design decisions concurrently rather than sequentially requires superior coordination among the parties involved – marketing, engineering, operations and, most importantly, the customer. Quality function deployment (QFD) is a structured approach to this problem that relates the *voice* of the customer to every stage of the design and the delivering process. In particular QFD:

- promotes better understanding of customer demands;
- promotes better understanding of design interactions;
- involves operations in the process at the earliest possible moment;
- removes the traditional barriers between the departments; and
- focuses the design effort.

Also known as the 'House of Quality', the technique is regarded by some as a highly complex technique only suitable for projects in large organisations. Others see QFD as a solution to the complex problems faced by designers and deserving of the perseverance necessary. This was the case in the Japanese car component firm, Kayaba, which attempted to use the QFD systems of Toyota and initially suffered almost total failure. Kayaba went on to develop its own successful version, which it called 'Anticipatory Development' and won the company a Deming Prize for its quality achievements (Lowe and Ridgway, 2000).

The ISO 9000 approach

Many countries developed their own quality systems and standards and in 1994 these were 'combined' to become the International Standards Organisation ISO 9000 – a set of standards governing documentation of a quality programme. A qualified external examiner checks that the company complies with all the requirements specified and certifies the company. Once certified, companies are listed in a directory and this information is made available to potential customers. As many large organisations *insist* on all suppliers having the ISO quality standards, much time and effort was spent in new, innovative ways of controlling and developing processes to maintain the agreed and certified standards. Completing the certification process can be long and expensive (Krajewski and Ritzman, 2001: 267); however, compliance with ISO 9000 says nothing about the *actual quality* of the product.

In part to reflect this point, the ISO 9000 (2000) developed to include four additional principles:

- quality management should be customer focused;
- quality performance should be measured;
- quality management should be improvement driven;

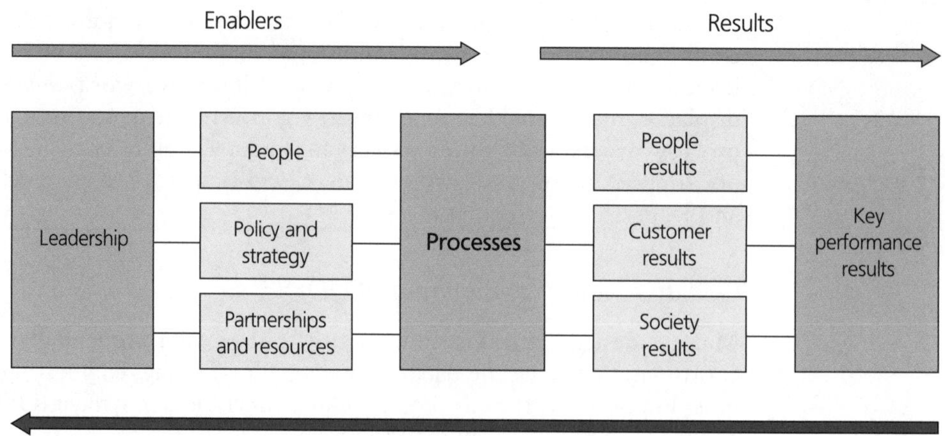

Figure 4.5 The EFQM excellence model

Source: Adapted from *Operations Management*, 4th edn (Slack, N. *et al.*, 2004), © Pearson Education Limited.

- top management must demonstrate their commitment to maintaining and continually improving management systems.

Despite these revisions, the ISO approach is not seen as beneficial by all parties (Slack *et al.*, 2007: 667).

The EFQM excellence model

In 1988, 14 leading Western European companies formed the European Foundation for Quality Management and gave an award for the most successful application of TQM in Europe. In 1999 this idea and model was refined and developed into the *EFQM Excellence Model* that reflected the increased understanding and emphasis on customer (and market) focus and is results oriented. The underlying idea is that *results* (people, customer, society and key performance) are achieved through a number of *enablers* (Figure 4.5) in managing and controlling the input/output transformation *processes* involved.

Performance measurement is by self-assessment, which EFQM defines as 'a comprehensive, systematic, and regular review of an organisation's activities and results referenced against a model of business excellence'. It may be easier to understand *and apply* this approach than is the case with some of the more philosophical concepts within TMQ. Furthermore, the EFQM excellence model also embeds *innovation and learning* in the performance of the organisation (Slack *et al.*, 2007; Van Looy *et al.*, 2003).

Pause for thought 

How well does the EFQM business excellence model apply to service sector situations?

Design of the organisation and its suppliers – supply chain management

Figure 4.3 shows the relationships between network, process and job design while Figure 4.6 extends this network to include suppliers and customers.

Delivering prompt, reliable products and services cost-effectively form part of most organisations' strategic plan. The term **supply chain management** describes the system of managing all the activities across company boundaries in order to drive the whole chain network towards the shared objective of satisfying the customers. Material (or information) flows through a series of operations in both directions and the principles of operations management apply.

Increasingly organisations concentrate on their core activities and subcontract more of their support activities to their suppliers (Hoecht and Trott, 2006). In many situations these suppliers are global and supply chain management has become a key strategic issue for many organisations.

Inclusion of suppliers in design activities is, therefore, essential. Much of the improvement in car design has been at the initiative of their suppliers. Developments such as automatic braking and engine management systems have come with the extensive involvement from the industrial suppliers to the automotive industry. With the involvement of suppliers in the new product development process it has also been found that more cost-effective designs have been created (Christopher, 2004).

For a company to achieve its own quality goals it must consider the quality of the product from its suppliers and the suppliers' own quality control procedures. For example, large organisations may help its smaller suppliers with training in quality circles. Successful supply chain management is, therefore, very dependent on good network coordination mechanisms, business relationships and information technology.

McDonald's built a restaurant in Moscow. To achieve its required and expected level of quality and service, the company set up an entire supply chain for growing, processing and distributing the food to its stores. McDonald's made sure that all parties along the whole chain understood its expectations of performance and closely monitored performance (Upton, 1998).

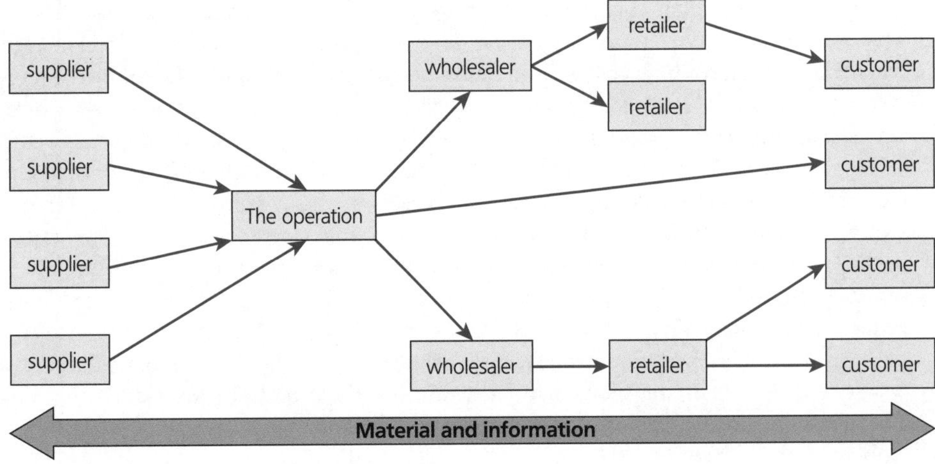

Figure 4.6 Supply chain management

Waste is a by-product of many processes (Table 4.1) and by definition costs money. Waste can take many forms – material, rejects, wasted movements, waiting time, over production, i.e. any activity that does not add value. Waste avoidance and process efficiency combine in the management principle termed 'just in time' (JIT), a definition of which is:

> *JIT aims to meet demand instantaneously, with perfect quality and no waste.*
>
> (Slack *et al.*, 2007)

Japan has limited natural resources. Consequently the Japanese were champions of waste avoidance in their processes and were among the first to introduce the 'just in time' techniques and processes to their large-scale manufacturing plants in the early 1970s. Quality circles, process improvement teams, QFD and quality assurance systems were all used as triggers for many small incremental *innovative improvements*. Working in teams, continuous improvement, simplifying operations, keeping things simple, doing them well and eliminating waste in all its forms helped JIT to be extended to develop what has become known as the 'lean' philosophy (Slack *et al.*, 2007: 469).

Illustration 4.5

Here's to health and Toyota

The hospital trolley in front is a Toyota, or soon could be. The production philosophy of the vehicles group is gaining a surprising toehold in the NHS. Several hospitals are deploying a manufacturing methodology dreamt up in Japan half a century ago to help them cure sick Britons. Sooner or later some Smart Alec will suggest going the whole hog and turning over the health service to Toyota. It might as well be me.

Ever shoulder-charged a door only to find it unlocked, and tumbled coccyx over humorous? That was the undignified trajectory I began tracing when I attended a conference where metal bashers declared their love of lean manufacturing, the zero-waste, demand-driven factory system pioneered by Toyota engineer Taiichi Ohno in the 1950s. Lean has become so entrenched an orthodoxy across swathes of manufacturing that it can appear cultish to outsiders. At its heart is a selective devolution of power to the shop floor, where workers redesign processes to raise quality and cut waste. Converts view production as a continuous flow rather than a sequence. Teams matter more than individuals. The managing director wears the same logo-bearing clobber as the cleaner.

At the conference, Anglo-Saxon manufacturers for whom Skegness represented the Far East explained how lean concepts such as kaizen (continuous improvement) and jidoka (automation with a human touch) had saved their businesses. Why the hell didn't the NHS give it a whirl too, I wondered. Lean methods have made Toyota one of the world's top three carmakers and highly profitable. This year Japanese-owned plants, applying their varying versions of lean, will produce more than half the cars made in the UK. Meanwhile, the NHS has floundered in spite of record investment. Overspending has doubled to £536m. Financial crises have hit admissions. A new records system has been a costly embarrassment.

These unflattering comparisons made me feel cross, a welcome feeling for a columnist since angry articles are easier to write than approving ones. The trick was not going to work for me this time, though. When I visited Toyota's car factory near Derby, I found NHS executives had beaten me to it. Toyota officials said a succession of them had already ridden the dinky electric train that transports managerial rubber neckers around the plant.

Riding the train myself, I could imagine the happy daydream the trip might trigger in a hospital chief executive. He would envisage beds gliding along a conveyor as smoothly as Corolla or Avensis car shells, while robotic trolleys plied patients with grapes and Lucozade. Doctors and nurses would install new organs and artificial hips with the calm purposefulness of Toyota workers fitting engines or constant velocity joints. A stream of buses would ferry grateful convalescents away from the dispatch area.

NHS bureaucrats have, in fairness, adapted lean thinking rather more sensibly than this. For example, the Royal Bolton Hospital has staged a series of 'rapid improvement events' in which employees have brainstormed process improvements. As a result, the death rate for patients undergoing hip operations has fallen by a third. The time taken to process some important categories of blood samples has been cut from more than a day to about three hours. The Royal Devon & Exeter Hospital Trust has, for its part, used lean techniques to cut fat from its back office, helping it meet financial targets.

According to Paul Walley of Warwick Business School, a scattering of other hospitals are dabbling in lean thinking. WBS has just produced a report, commissioned by the Scottish Executive, urging other public bodies to do likewise. Last week, the NHS Confederation, which represents health authorities and trusts, published a paper that was equally enthusiastic about the philosophy.

However, Mr Walley warns: 'The NHS could be one of the most difficult places to implement lean thinking because of the duality of control.' In other words, reformers could expect a scrap with senior medics, whose formidable power base within hospitals inspires a professional hauteur equalled only by QCs and the smarter variety of French waiter.

Those NHS managers who have scrambled from their silos to learn from manufacturing are to be congratulated. But their disparate efforts may not be enough to raise health service efficiency. The simplest fix would be for the government to contract the management of hospitals to Toyota, just as it plans to outsource the purchasing of patient care to insurers. Public service unions could be relied on to scream blue murder. Toyota might also take some persuading. At present all it has to do is produce reliable, affordable cars in the teeth of remorseless international competition. Rather more taxingly, the NHS is expected to banish sickness from a nation of lardy gym dodgers.

The objections of those involved must be balanced against an immense upside. I am not just talking about higher quality care and lower costs. As importantly, the Toyota ethos would require high-falutin' hospital consultants to shed their bespoke tailoring and don the same corporate wear polo shirts and baseball caps as the porters. A few post-operative patients might burst their stitches laughing. But overall, the resulting improvement in patient morale would be incalculable.

Source: Jonathan Guthrie, *Financial Times*, 21 June 2006.

The application and relevance of the 'lean' philosophy to service-type operations is the subject of debate (Young *et al.*, 2004).

Identifying the causes of uncertainty, determining how this affects other activities in the supply chain and formulating ways of reducing or eliminating the uncertainty is essential to the management of all the processes involved. Web technology with its ability to communicate easily, cheaply and quickly has had a major impact on reducing uncertainty in the supply chain.

Recent development within supply chain management focuses on the ability of suppliers to respond quickly to changes in demand, i.e. they are *agile* in their approach (Christopher, 2004).

The JIT system has a likely outcome of smaller and more frequent deliveries. The agile supplier, who is quick to respond to an order change, may also increase the number of deliveries. The result of these factors is to increase the volume of traffic on our roads. A quarter of all road freight in the UK (by vehicle miles) is double

Source: Pearson Education Ltd/ Kent Knudson/Photodisc

The JIT system has an unintended outcome of smaller and more frequent deliveries, increasing the volume of traffic on our roads.

that of 1974 (www.eta.co.uk) and is a significant contributor to traffic congestion, accidents and pollution.

The TQM team-based philosophy requires trust between all the parties involved for it to be effective. The same trust level needs to be present with suppliers for successful supply chain management. This aspect is made more complicated in the globalised business world as different cultures and systems need to work together.

Furthermore, as the supplying network expands across the world, so does that of competitive organisations. The competition then becomes essentially the *efficiency of one supply chain versus another*. Only by working together and *innovating* within the organisation's supply chain, in terms of product and service, will the organisation survive.

Business process re-engineering (BPR)

A contrast to the incremental ideas of process improvement is that of the radical breakthrough approach of **business process re-engineering (BPR)**. First attributed to Hammer (1990), the technique is a blend of a number of ideas found within operations (process flow-charting, network management) and the need for customer focus. These were bought together to define BPR as:

> *The fundamental rethinking and radical redesign of business processes to achieve dramatic improvements in critical, contemporary measures of performance, such as cost, quality, service and speed.* (Slack *et al.*, 2007)

An existing organisation and its procedures reflect the way that business was conducted and may not support the core business in the future. For example, in the 1980s BPR techniques were used extensively in the IT industry when the cheap and progressively more powerful networked PC began to replace mainframes.

The approach is not without critics and certainly was used as one of the major 'downsizing' tools common in the 1980s and 1990s. The combination of radical downsizing and redesign can mean the loss of core experience from the operation. If taken too far (for example, if the short-term profit improvement was achieved at the expense of support for R&D expenditure) the resulting organisation could became 'hollow' and die. Also, the core business has to be sound otherwise BPR is akin to 'flogging a dead horse'.

The BPR approach is similar to the ideas put forward by Peters (1997), who makes the case for the total destruction of company systems, hierarchy and procedures and replacing them with a multitude of single-person business units working as professionals. He argues that the small modest improvement enshrined in TQM detracts effort from the real need to reinvent the business, i.e. 'Incrementalism is an enemy of innovation'. Tom Peters argues that a radical approach is the only way organisations can be sufficiently innovative to survive in the twenty-first century.

Making the resources available to continuously innovate and improve the service to customers and developing new markets for products is a difficult and complex task. The emphasis on the need to understand and be close to customers has helped to improve organisations across the world. However, commercial history is littered with successful oganisations that failed to recognise the emergence of new technologies. Christensen (1999) develops the philosophy of *disruptive innovations* that introduce a very different package of attributes to the marketplace from the ones that mainstream customers have historically valued. Christensen argues that leading companies failed to maintain their position at the top of their sector when the technology or markets changed because they ignored the emerging disruptive technology. Chapter 15 discusses this issue in more detail.

Thus we have the radical breakthrough approach of Hammer, Christensen and Peters versus the diametrically opposite incremental methodologies enshrined in the philosophies of TQM. It may be possible, even necessary, to follow both at different times. Large and significant improvements can be followed by incremental and less spectacular innovations and improvements but senior managers and company directors must be aware of the strengths and weaknesses of both.

Operations and technology

The most significant technological advance that has impacted on operations has been the application of computers. Among the many applications was the work in the 1970s and 1980s with the transfer of information (later funds) electronically between elements of the secure private networks along the organisation's supply chains. For example, electronic data interchange (EDI) facilitated the application of the just-in-time (JIT) approach in manufacturing operations (*see* Table 4.3 and Illustration 4.5). The technology (the agreement on network protocols and software) and the innovative techniques they made possible were an integral part of the drive to generate business value across the supply chains. The phrase electronic commerce or e-commerce was coined to bring together a range of activities involved in the different industries and business sectors. E-commerce is defined as a transaction by which the order is placed

Table 4.3 The development of e-commerce and the impact on operations

Phase	Operations activities
Phase 1	Electronic data interchange (EDI) supporting innovations such as JIT
Phase 2	Establishing a web presence – sales information-based
Phase 3	Conducting e-commerce – progressive application across different sectors
Phase 4	Automation – customer-based

– not the payment delivery channels (www.statistics.gov.uk/themes/economy, 2004). The growth of e-commerce has been very rapid as companies and governments recognised the vast potential of this global technology that can integrate customers and content in highly innovative and previously impossible ways.

The second phase (Table 4.3) was the very rapid publication of product information on the web and by the end of the 1990s most organisations in the United States and the United Kingdom had websites. Many were very extensive; for example, in 1999 General Motors Corporation offered 18,000 pages of information that included 98,000 links to the company's products and services (Turban *et al.*, 2000).

The effect on some organisations has been dramatic. In the early 1990s, the *Encyclopaedia Britannica* was leather-bound and found on most library shelves. By the mid-1990s the same content was in CD form at less than 10 per cent of the bound volume price. In October 1999 the information was available free on the web at Britannia.com, the required revenue coming from advertising alongside the data. Later, by 2001, the organisation withdrew the advertising and introduced a fee to access the internet version. The products, the technology of the processes producing the product and the business strategy have all been changed in less than a decade. The organisation has clearly introduced change and innovation.

The web technology allows you 'into' the supply chain and you are able to design and monitor the progress of your own product through the producing operating system. Dell Computers is a very good illustrative example (*see* Illustration 4.6).

Dell successfully adapted its processes to take advantage of the technology while remaining close to the fundamental of understanding the needs of its customers.

Illustration 4.6

How Dell has successfully adapted

Michael Dell founded the Dell Corporation in Texas, USA, in 1984 and was the pioneer in the direct selling of custom-built computers by mail order. By 1998 Dell had over 25 per cent of sales from the internet and had become the largest manufacturer of business PCs in the world.

Dell's story is very impressive and analysts have searched for reasons for their success.

- Mass customisation
- SCM good links with flexible vendors
- Background in telemarketing
- Customer knowledge leading to 'premier pages' that have saved Ford $2m
- High reliability: Dell has received 174 awards for performance
- Delivery support 24/7
- Adaptive business strategy by moving up the value chain
- Concentrating on what customers wanted

Source: Adapted from E. Turban *et al.* (2004) *Electronic Commerce – A Managerial Perspective*, Prentice-Hall, Englewood Cliffs.

What is less obvious is the power of the internet to unlock value by separating different types of systems, business processes and companies, and give organisations the ability to use their resources most effectively. Illustration 4.7 shows how companies are able to decouple their back-office operations from customer-facing activities so that common services can be centralised while customer-facing activities can be moved closer to clients. And by decoupling different activities in industry value chains, the internet enables companies to concentrate on their core skills while broadening their network of partners.

Illustration 4.7

Use the internet's power to divide and rule

When we think about how the internet creates value, we naturally think about its power to connect systems, processes and companies to each other. That is how we define a network such as the internet: computer systems linked together in a way that makes it easier to share information.

What is less obvious is the power of the internet to unlock value by separating different types of systems, business processes and companies, and give organisations the ability to use their resources most effectively. The internet has ushered in an era of connectivity based on open standards where people, devices and applications can communicate regardless of their location.

This flexibility in location allows different types of functionality and expertise to be decoupled – separated from each other and relocated to make the most of specialisation.

Just as water finds its own level when disparate sources are connected with pipes, functionality and expertise can flow to their ideal locations when systems, business processes and companies are connected over a ubiquitous network.

Decoupling allows organisations to benefit from scale as well as specialisation, differentiation as well as vertical integration and centralisation as well as decentralisation. In the design of IT systems, the internet allows IT infrastructure to be decoupled from end-user applications, so systems can be agile and responsive at the level of applications, yet robust and scalable in their infrastructure.

It lets companies decouple their back-office operations from customer-facing activities so that common services can be centralised while customer-facing activities can be moved closer to clients. And by decoupling different activities in industry value chains, the internet enables companies to concentrate on their core skills while broadening their network of partners.

To understand how decoupling overcomes design compromises in IT systems, consider a simple example – designing a personal computer that is powerful yet user-friendly. In the absence of a network such as the internet, all functionality, applications and data need to be located on the same personal computer. This involves a hidden compromise.

On the one hand, you want your computer to be small, flexible and user-friendly – in a word, personal. On the other hand, you want it to be powerful, have lots of memory and be highly reliable – more like a mainframe computer. What you end up with is a computer that is neither user-friendly as an appliance, nor as powerful as a mainframe.

If we introduce a network such as the internet into the picture, the situation changes dramatically. Now you can move the mainframe-like functions of the computer, such as storage and processing, to a central server that is powerful, reliable and scalable. At the same time, you can allow the PC-like functions, such as displaying information and taking user input, to stay close to the user.

By separating the back-end infrastructure functions that belong on a large server from the front-end functions that are best housed on the client device, the internet breaks the design compromise inherent in co-location.

In fact, infrastructure-like functions can be delivered over a pipe, just like water, electricity and natural gas. This is the essence of the 'utility computing' idea that is currently animating International Business Machines and other computer vendors. But utility computing presents a paradox: infrastructure will become more centralised, while devices and user applications will become more decentralised.

I foresee the emergence of a few large information utility companies that will supply IT infrastructure. At the same time, though, I predict the creation of billions of highly focused information appliances for end-users.

The decoupling logic also applies to the design of business processes in a company. For decades, companies have struggled to find the right balance

→

between centralisation and decentralisation of their operations. On the one hand, centralisation allows for better economies of scale and improved coordination of activities across a company. On the other, it makes companies less responsive to their customers and local markets.

To see how decoupling can help resolve this dilemma, think about how a company's activities can be classified into 'front-office' activities (those that directly involve customers, such as sales, solution design and customer relationship management), and 'back-office' activities (those that provide support, such as administration, human resource management and accounting).

Front-office activities are most effective when they are tailored to the needs of specific customer segments. Conversely, back-office activities are most effective when they are standardised and centralised. The internet allows companies to decentralise front-end activities and move them closer to customers, while allowing back-end activities to be centralised into set of shared services.

Consider how General Electric is taking advantage of decoupling as it redesigns its global processes. GE's India-based GE Capital International Services provides 15 of the top GE businesses with services that include accounting, business analysis and software development. GECIS allows GE companies to manage their front-end activities closer to their markets while benefiting from improved scale and lower labour costs at the India-based back-end operations. The growth of IT-enabled business services in India is being fuelled by the realisation that companies can benefit by decoupling and relocating their back-office operations to lower-cost locations.

Decoupling is also reshaping the way companies decide the scope of their activities within the industry value chain.

In the days of Alfred Sloan, companies believed that competitive advantage was gained through vertical integration. However, it is difficult to be good at all activities in the value chain. Therefore, it makes sense for companies to focus on what they do best and to outsource the rest.

However, if you cannot communicate effectively with partners and suppliers, the benefits of specialisation are diluted because of the cost of coordinating activities across companies.

With the internet, companies no longer need to compromise between specialisation and integration. By reducing the cost of interaction between companies and their partners, the internet allows companies to limit their operations to what they do best, and to outsource non-core activities. The result: a disaggregation of industry value chains into networks of specialised companies called 'business webs' or 'value networks'.

Consider the value network that Cisco Systems, the networking company, has created to offer e-learning services to its enterprise customers. Cisco starts with a family of products and augments it with specialised products and services from a network of partners. The internet allows Cisco to benefit from the specialisation of its partners, while delivering an integrated solution to its customers.

The internet allows companies to resolve age-old debates between specialisation and generalisation, centralisation and decentralisation and scale versus focus through its ability to decouple systems, processes and companies. If you understand the power of decoupling, you can go beyond these seemingly irreconcilable conflicts and unlock new value for your company.

Source: Mohanbir Sawhney, 'Use the power of the net to divide and rule FT Summer School', www.FT.com, 18 August 2003. Reprinted with permission.

Pause for thought

How much of the success of Dell can be attributed to patents?

The final phase 4 (Table 4.3) includes auctions where companies publish their requirements on the internet and organisations across the globe are invited to quote. Traditional competitors are coming together, forming trading exchanges for their supplies. For example Ford, DaimlerChrysler, Renault, Peugeot Citroën and GM amalgamated elements of their supply chain in the *Covisint* exchange. The potential membership of the exchange is 30,000 suppliers (Turban *et al.*, 2004).

The impact of the internet is present in all business areas. In education there is an increasing wealth of good quality information freely available on the internet and there are increased opportunities for changing the processes involved in education (for example, distance learning). Consequently governments take e-commerce very seriously. At the EU summit in February 2000 the creation of 20 million new jobs were forecast (*Independent*, 2000). Twenty million *different* jobs was a much more likely outcome as companies develop their systems and procedures to reflect the technology.

A common feature of global business forecasts is that the business-to-business e-commerce (B2B) is predicted to be substantially larger than business-to-consumer e-commerce (B2C) (see emarketer.com and forrester.com). The EDI links between organisations in the 1980s were relatively easy to adapt to the web-based trading relationships possible in the 1990s. Within B2B e-commerce substantial savings in purchase and administration costs are reported (Turban *et al.*, 2004) in many, if not all, business sectors. The performance of this high-technology sector has been difficult and many 'dot-com' companies have failed to achieve the initial promise of the late 1990s. Being innovative always carries a risk. Being first to market has not been much of an advantage to many 'dot-com' companies (Leadbeater, 2001). Some car manufacturers limit their involvement with the web-trading Covisint exchange to simple products (screws, nuts and bolts, etc.), as perhaps they feel that the emphasis on price, which is implicit in an auction, would have a negative impact on quality and the working relationships between the participants (Cope, 2001; McMcracken, 2001). Business pragmatism has been applied to the over-hyped 'dot-com' revolution with focus being on the basics (Skapinker, 2001).

However, beyond an early cost saving achieved by internet-enabled technology, perhaps the longer lasting and more sustainable additional value of the internet is when it facilitates a purchase *that would not otherwise have happened.*

Highly innovative strategic alliances have been taking place – for example, the collaboration of Amazon.com and Wal-Mart, i.e. the traditional high street retailer and cyber shopping combining (Rushe, 2001; Fiorina and London, 2001). With the impact of technology on the supply chains and the creation of trading exchanges, the *re-design of business sectors* is taking place. A good illustration is the internet auction house eBay, which has a community of almost 100 million users, providing a living for thousands of people and transacting over $3.3 billion in sales in 2004. Some individuals have amassed a fortune in a marketplace that did not exist in 1995 (Turban *et al.*, 2004: 432). Innovatively, eBay has continued to introduce new products and pursued the classic business development of taking existing products to new markets.

Pause for thought 

What do you think has happened to the UK antique market following the growth of eBay?

Innovation as an operations process itself

A necessary starting point for a business analyst (researcher or consultant) beginning a new assignment is to understand the subject organisation. A useful approach is to appreciate that managers control *processes* which may be viewed as having inputs, processes of conversion and outputs from these processes. These processes include that of the innovation process itself, i.e. the subject of this whole book. Referring back to Table 4.1 and Figure 4.1 yields Figure 4.7.

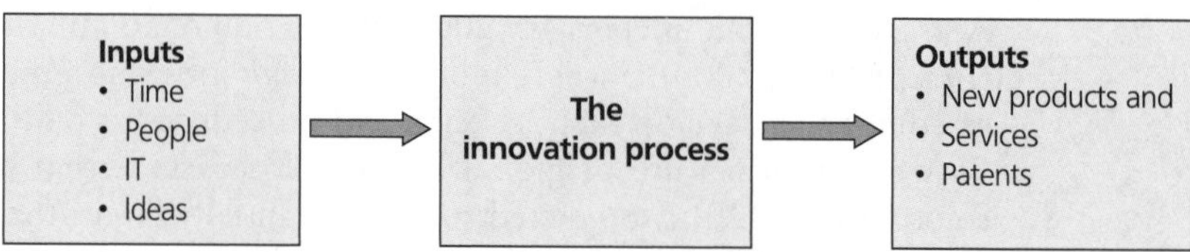

Figure 4.7 Innovation as an operations process itself

To be effective and efficient all management activities must include some form of measure or measurement. Applying this principle to the *innovation process*, we have Table 4.4.

Table 4.4 Innovation measures

Input measures	Process measures (*Efficiency* of process)	Output measures (*Effectiveness* of process)
Number of new ideas	Percentage of ideas screened out	Percentage of sales from new products
Number of personnel involved in innovation	Time to market	Number of patents granted
Information technology	Effectiveness of teams	Number of product launches
Percentage of sales on process innovation	Loss associated with project abandonment	Market share
Percentage of sales on R&D spend	Personnel morale	Research papers and media coverage of new ideas

The appropriate and relevant performance measures depend on the organisation and business environment in which it operates. Similar to the EFQM model (page 134), the organisation chooses its priorities and how best to focus its attention. In many ways performance measures have to be designed with much of the same thought processes followed as in product and process design. Therefore, the most appropriate measures will change over time as the business develops and matures or priorities change. To help in this process Goffin and Mitchell (2005: 315) remark that performance measures are often too much or complex and suggest that only a few measures should be used. 'Performance Measurement Design' can therefore be added to the design activities, extending even further the range of knowledge and skills required by managers. The range of the various design competencies required within an organisation is therefore huge and may be represented by a spectrum of knowledge (*see* Figure 4.8).

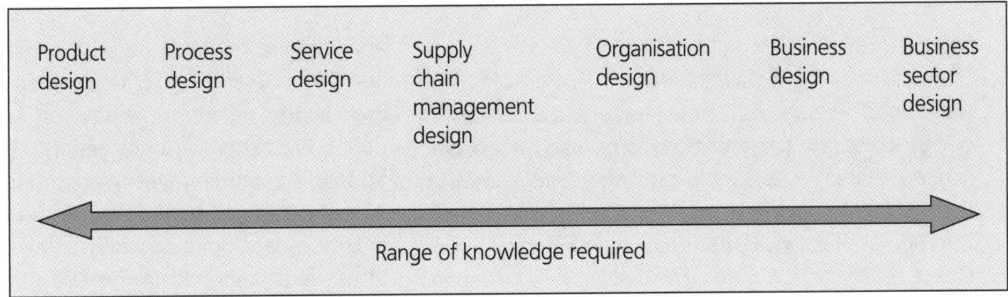

Figure 4.8 The design spectrum

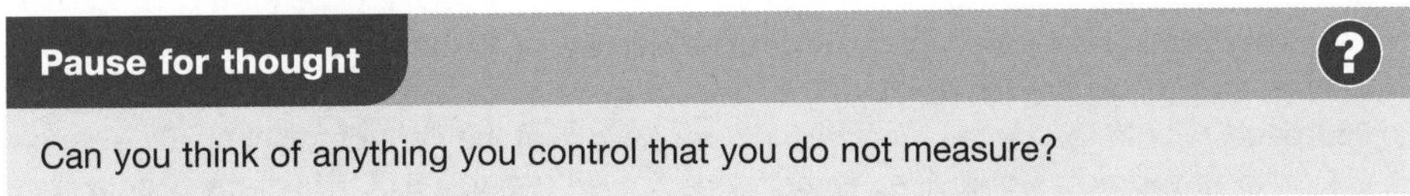

Pause for thought

Can you think of anything you control that you do not measure?

There can be few individuals who fully understand the complexity of this range of expertise but a competent CEO or general manager must manage the diverse disciplines involved. They must at the very least understand how these disciplines overlap and relate.

Case study

Novels, new products and Harry Potter

This case study explores the world of publishing and examines how a new product in this industry reaches the customer. While many publishers spend enormous sums of money promoting their bestsellers (Bloomsbury and Harry Potter is an obvious example), sometimes little money, if any, is spent investing in the new publishing products and talents of tomorrow, that is, new authors. In effect, some publishers are simply printing books without the necessary promotion. This case illustrates that in this relatively straight-forward new product there are many factors, some very surprising, that influence the success or not of a new book. The role of the publisher, the role of the agent, the role of the retailer, the role of the buyer, the role of the critic – all influence success in this industry. While all publishers would like to have the next Harry Potter, this case illustrates that this is unlikely to happen if they do not invest in new product development today.

Source: Pearson Education Ltd/Photodisc

→

Introduction

Record-breaking sales of *Harry Potter and the Half-Blood Prince* sent retailers worldwide calling on Bloomsbury (United Kingdom) and Scholastic (United States), the book's publishers, to speed up their orders to save leaving their shelves bare. It sold 2 million copies on its first day (www.FT.com, 2005). Copies of *Harry Potter and The Order of The Pheonix*, the fifth in J.K. Rowling's seven-part series about the boy wizard sold faster than any other book in history: 5 million copies sold in the United States on the first day. Scholastic's first print run was 6.8 million, with a second of 1.7 million. Amazon.com, the online retailer, said it had delivered 420,000 copies of the 768-page book in the United Kingdom and received 1.3 million pre-orders worldwide, almost three times more than the previous record holder, *Harry Potter and the Goblet of Fire*, the fourth book in the series. Tesco, Britain's biggest retailer, originally ordered 500,000 copies and sold 317,400 books in the first 24 hours. In comparison, the group sold only 42,000 copies of the last Potter book over the whole of its first week. But, the sales phenomenon does not necessarily translate to big profits. Tesco and other groups slashed the prices of the book to drive sales and snatch market share from specialist retailers. Asda, the Leeds-based chain owned by Wal-Mart, sold 120,000 copies in the first 24 hours at one of the lowest prices £8.96 ($15). Waterstones, the specialist chain owned by HMV Group, said the scale of the launch was unprecedented. At its flagship store in Piccadilly, central London, the group saw more than 2,000 people queueing, many for hours, to buy a copy (www.FT.com, 2003).

When it comes to considering the development of a new product, one of the most identifiable and simple to imagine is a book. Compared to a new product in the aircraft or motor industries a new novel is simple and straightforward. Moreover, books have been produced for thousands of years, it is a mature industry and, surely when it comes to publishing, everything is thoroughly understood? In reality the industry continues to develop and continues to surprise even the most experienced publisher.

A book is published in the hope and expectation that it will sell thousands, maybe even millions, of copies for the author and publisher. Yet, despite the best efforts of many publishers, some books defy expectations and flop. Consider Anthea Turner's auto-biography. Despite all the media hype, it sold just 451 copies in its first week and was soon piled high in the discount 'remainder' bookshops (Kean, 2001). Publishers are not eager to discuss such disappointing stories, yet Waterstones suggests that 15 per cent of all books are returned to the publisher. In fact, most books do not sell. In 2001, 116,000 new titles were launched in the UK, that is, about 2,000 new titles a week! As we have seen, even celebrity status is no guarantee of success, although it is usually a substantial help.

Success depends on many things including whether or not your publisher is willing to pay up to £10,000 to book retailers in order to have a book displayed at the front of the shop. Or even paying a retail chain up to £6,000 to have a book selected as 'read of the week'. This may all sound unfair and devious – welcome to the modern world of publishing, where the looks of the author count almost as much as the writing. Daunta Kean (Kean, 2001) argued that most books in the bestseller lists were there due to at least some money changing hands between retailers and publishers and by authors working hard to promote themselves. It should come as no surprise to the student of business that the role of the retailer is as important in books as it is in other consumer products. In many ways a novel is just another consumer product, a combination of product and service.

A growing and profitable industry, but only for the few

The world of publishing continues to be an exciting and profitable business. Sales continue to grow and more and more books are published each year. Table 4.5 shows the historical context and the rapid growth in the number of titles published in the last

Table 4.5 Book titles published

Year	Book titles published
1850	2,200
1900	7,500
1960	20,000
1991	67,704
1995	95,064
2000	116,415

Source: E.J. Hobsbawm (1990) *Industry and Empire*, Penguin, London; C. O'Grady, A book's life, *Guardian*, 18 August, 9.

ten years. Yet few books make any significant amount of money for the author or the publisher. So why are so many more books being published? The answer, of course, is that you only need one J.K. Rowling out of a hundred or even a thousand new authors to justify the publisher's speculation, especially when the publisher, in this case Bloomsbury, only paid £2,500 for her first book (Burkeman, 2001). The film rights for Harry Potter were sold to Warner Brothers for over £50 million and J.K. Rowling has earned more than £40 million from the Harry Potter series. AOL–Time Warner settled on a single sponsor, Coca-Cola, which paid $150 million for exclusive marketing rights. The film will also help to increase sales still further, in the lucrative US market, from the current 19 million (Bloomsbury sold the US publishing rights to Scholastic Inc.). Mattel and Hasbro have recently bought the licence to merchandise products from the film, all of which will be future profits for Bloomsbury and Rowling (*see* Illustration 4.8). The worldwide sales of Harry Potter books are now in excess of 115 million copies.

Illustration 4.8

J.K. Rowling

Like that of her own character, Harry Potter, J.K. Rowling's life has the lustre of a fairy tale. Divorced, living on public assistance in a tiny Edinburgh flat with her infant daughter, Rowling wrote *Harry Potter and the Philosopher's Stone* at a table in a café during her daughter's naps – and it was Harry Potter that rescued her. First, the Scottish Arts Council gave her a grant to finish the book. Upon the enthusiastic response of Bryony Evans, a reader who had been asked to review the book's first three chapters, the London-based Christopher Little Literary Agents agreed to represent Rowling in her quest for a publisher. The book was handed to twelve publishing houses, all of which rejected it. A year later she was finally given a £2,500 advance by editor Barry Cunningham from the small publisher Bloomsbury. The following spring, an auction was held in the United States for the rights to publish the novel, and was won by Scholastic Inc., which paid Rowling more than $100,000. Rowling has said she 'nearly died' when she heard the news. In October 1998, Scholastic published *Philosopher's Stone* in the US under the title of *Harry Potter and the Sorcerer's Stone*, a change Rowling claims she now regrets and would have fought if she had been in a better position at the time.

After its sale to Bloomsbury (UK), the accolades began to pile up. Harry Potter won the British Book Awards, Children's Book of the Year, and the Smarties Prize, and rave reviews on both sides of the Atlantic. Book rights have been sold to England, France, Germany, Italy, Holland, Greece, Finland, Denmark, Spain and Sweden.

Table 4.6 Harry Potter books

Book 1	1997	*Harry Potter and the Philosopher's Stone*
Book 2	1998	*Harry Potter and the Chamber of Secrets*
Book 3	1999	*Harry Potter and the Prisoner of Azkaban*
Book 4	2000	*Harry Potter and the Goblet of Fire*
Book 5	2003	*Harry Potter and the Order of the Phoenix*
Book 6	2005	*Harry Potter and the Half-Blood Prince*
Book 7	2007	*Harry Potter and the Deathly Hallows*

→

To date, six of the seven volumes of the Harry Potter series, have already been published and all have broken sales records. The last three volumes in the series have been the fastest-selling books in history, grossing more in their opening 24 hours than blockbuster films. Book six of her series earned The Guinness World Records Award for being the fastest-selling book ever. The sixth book of the series sold more copies in 24 hours than *The Da Vinci Code* sold in a year. (*The Da Vinci Code* was the best-selling book of the previous year.)

Rowling has completed the seventh and final book of the series. Its title was revealed on 21 December 2006 to be *Harry Potter and the Deathly Hallows*. On 1 Febuary 2007, Rowling announced on her website that its release date was to be 21 July 2007.

The journey from manuscript to published book

Once the author, especially a new or unknown author, has completed a manuscript, the key task is to get it published. This is extremely difficult, as many prospective writers will tell you. Thousands of manuscripts land on the desks of publishers and agents every week. Most are 'binned' or returned to the author. Agents and publishers reject manuscripts that later turn out to be best-selling novels, but they will argue that this is the nature of the business. This, of course, is of little help to the author whose novel has been rejected for the fifth time. 'Don't give up', the agent will say, 'Harry Potter was rejected by several publishers.'

Most publishers will only work through agents and will not communicate directly with authors. This is because the agents understand the business and sometimes know the individual commissioning editors. The publishers view the agents as helpful in weeding out the 'rubbish', leaving the editors with the better manuscripts to consider.

The author–agent relationship is a business partnership. The specifics of the partnership will vary depending on the nature of the work in question, the author's needs, and the agent's policies and practices. In general, though, an agent will review his client's work and advise on quality and potential marketability and the possible strategy for securing its publication. For that work, the agent receives a commission (usually 15 per cent) against the author's advance and all subsequent income relevant to the sold product.

But even the best agent cannot sell inferior work. The commissioning editor is the buyer, and, as a rule, an author gets only one chance per editor. After an editor reads whatever is put before him or her, some deep, perhaps indelible impression is formed. This corresponds to quality management issues in other industries. If the author has written a second-rate book, and if the agent has not vetted it beforehand, the editor is likely not only to reject the work but also to refuse to see anything else from that author in future.

T. Colgan, senior editor, Berkley Publishing, offers some frank advice on the role of a commissioning editor (www.authorlink.com/index.html). There are many reasons why commissioning editors reject a manuscript and here are the most common ones:

- *The editor*. All people have likes and dislikes, and editors are no different. Most editors have deep-seated ideas about what their readers are looking for that go far beyond what the actual numbers show. That is why many editors insist on staying with an author after several bad outings or why they push to take on a talented new author in a category that is on the wane.
- *The market*. This is the trickiest consideration to gauge. It is not as simple as looking at the numbers. It is true, this will give you a pretty good idea of the market today, but when an editor buys a book he or she needs to be thinking about the market up to two years from now. After all, it is going to take the author six months to a year to finish his or her work. Once he or she delivers, it is going to be about a year before you can get the book in the schedule.
- *The house*. 'Thank you for submitting your material, but, unfortunately, this is not right for our list.' List in this instance refers to a publisher's portfolio of products. Anyone who's ever received a rejection letter is familiar with that sentence or something similar. Sure, a lot of times, it's just code for: 'Your manuscript stinks!' But there are plenty of times when it means just what it says. They may already have a mystery series that is similar to yours, or you may be writing in an area that is not one of their fortes. Each publishing house has its own strengths and

weaknesses. Some publishing houses do well with true crime while others will not touch it. Some have great success with cosy mysteries, and others find them utter failures.

- *The author*. You should write because you want to, and you should write what you want to. Let the market take care of itself. Attempting to pattern yourself after a successful author is an almost certain way to strangle your own voice and collect an impressive number of rejection slips.

The publisher and the contract

At the initial stage of acceptance the publisher is as much interested with the looks of the author as with the writing. This may sound surprising but good looks can help with sales, especially if the author is young (O'Grady, 2001). Once another commissioning editor has read the manuscript, the original commissioning editor tries to convince other departments that they should make an offer to the agent. The agent will discuss this offer with the author, but royalties for first books are usually standard at between 7–15 per cent of the net price of the book. Any advance, which is taken out of future royalties, is also negotiated. Most first-time authors are simply relieved to get their work published. J.K. Rowling agreed an advance of £2,500 for the first Harry Potter book. The negotiations do not end here. For there are foreign and film rights to be discussed. If applicable, and they are usually not, these will produce more revenue than UK sales. Clearly the agent will want to retain these rights but frequently these are signed over to the publisher. An interesting footnote here is that J.K. Rowling's agent and not the publisher signed the film rights to Harry Potter, while the publisher signed the foreign publishing rights.

Drafts, revisions and presentation

The editor assigned to any book will work closely with the author once the contract has been signed. The original manuscript may need months or even years of reworking. This is a good example of the iterative process of new product development. Also the new word-processing software facilitates this process. Other editors may also make suggestions for changes to the plot or scenes or how the story could be improved. A copy-editor will also be involved checking the details, facts and consistency. Eventually it will be typeset and checked again for correctness, grammar, etc. Advanced proofs may even be sent to reviewers or trade buyers, in the hope of an advance order. This brings us to the next stage: the book jacket. The designers are briefed – they may even go so far as to read a chapter! Within a few weeks, several cover ideas are submitted before a design is chosen, usually by a combination of the editor and the marketing department. The author has little if any input.

The size of the final book is almost as important as the design of the jacket cover. For in the publishing industry size really does matter. First, there is the question of whether to publish in hardback and paperback or just paperback. Some critics argue that to be taken seriously a book needs to be published in hardback. This may sound slightly snobbish, but in some sections this view is taken seriously and it is certainly taken seriously by authors, all of whom it seems want to be seen in hardback. There are three main size formats: A, B and C. The A format measures 110mm × 178mm and is the typical size of most best-selling paperbacks. Format B is slightly larger at 130mm × 198mm and is considered to be slightly more upmarket and associated with more prestigious authors. Format C is 135mm × 216mm and is the size of many hardbacks. Industry insiders suggest that the format of the book is an indication to retailers and consumers about the type of book on the shelf. Few consumers may be aware of this but as a way of illustration almost all books being considered for the prestigious Booker prize are published in hardback first. To be fair, many years ago there was a significant difference in production costs but with the introduction of computer software into printing and design the difference in production costs are not as significant as they once were.

Retailers

The number of book retailers has decreased over the past 20 years, yet the number of sales of books has increased. The market is now dominated by a few very large retailers; WH Smith and Waterstones handle 25 per cent of all book sales; book clubs account for a further 16 per cent (Amazon.com, an internet bookseller, has had a significant impact on this industry). In addition, the multiples are now stocking and selling a narrow range of the best-selling books at discounted prices. The big retailers, like any other retailer, have to concentrate on books that will sell, whereas the specialist bookshops, frequently owned and operated by people for interest rather than profit, would be willing to stock a wider variety but cannot compete with the multiples who stock only best-selling titles.

→

To become a bestseller a book needs to be available in the large retail outlets, and it needs to be visible in these outlets. Publishers will go to great lengths to secure shelf space for a book they wish to promote. This includes entertaining the retail buyers with extravagant 'business trips', for example to the Wimbledon tennis championships or to a Formula One motor race, to try to influence the buyer's decision. According to Oliver Burkeman (2001) one year Collins bought all the available space in WH Smith for back-to-school dictionaries and sales of Oxford University Press dictionaries plummeted. High sales depend on shelf space: some publishers have argued that a bestseller is 70 per cent the book and 30 per cent the marketing.

The other major influence on the success of a book is the role played by 'critics' in the media. If a book receives the praise of one of the mainstream newspaper book critics, this will have an enormous positive influence on sales, similarly from a radio book critic or even better a television book critic. The key issue here is getting the book in front of the critic and getting them to read it. Once again publishers will use some of the tactics used with buyers to try to further their cause.

Conclusions

The truth is sometimes painful and difficult to accept, but most authors do not earn very much money from their writing. A Society of Authors report stated that half of all writers earn less than the minimum wage (Kean, 2001). This may simply be due to the fact that what is written is not very good or not wanted, but the evidence seems to suggest that publishers are contributing to the problem. What is of concern is that increasingly publishers are selecting fewer books to promote, for without promotion a book is only being printed. Promotion is an integral part of publishing. Indeed, most dictionaries define publishing as 'to make widely known'. Printing a book and leaving it piled high in a warehouse is not making it widely known. Printing is only part of the activity of publishing. It is understandable that all publishers have limited promotional budgets, but to decide not to invest any promotion at all in a book is deceiving the author. If authors were aware that little, if any, effort was being targeted at his or her book they would surely be better advised to move to another publisher or to get it printed themselves.

The future of publishing depends on new authors. To be innovative, publishers need to nurture and find new talent. This is effectively the research and development (R&D) of publishing. Without this activity publishers will soon find they have no new products to sell. Supporting a best-selling author is fine and necessary but so is uncovering tomorrow's J.K. Rowling. The case highlights that the big retailers who, understandably, adopt a short-term market-pull approach increasingly dominate the market. This leads to fewer titles being promoted and made available (despite an increasing number of titles being printed) and stifles innovation. Consumers are not always able to communicate their needs; frequently consumers do not know whether they are going to enjoy a story about a child and his wizard-like powers until they have read it.

Source: www.FT.com (2003) Harry Potter storms the bookstores, 23 June; www.FT.com (2005) The year in pictures, 7 December; O'Grady, C. (2001) A book's life, *Guardian*, 18 August, 9; Burkeman, O. (2001) Price wars, *Guardian*, 18 August, 9; Kean, D. (2001) How to be a bestseller, *Guardian*, 4 August, 8.

Questions

1. Explain why you think the Harry Potter series of books have been so successful.
2. Explain how a new book has three aspects of a product (concept, package and process).
3. How can publishers exploit writers?
4. When it comes to developing new products for tomorrow, compare how football clubs try to invest in developing new products/players and how publishers try to invest in new products/authors.
5. Using the CIM (Figure 1.9) identify the key actors and processes in the publishing industry.
6. What influence have supermarkets had on book publishing and retailing?
7. How can small independent publishers compete with the large internationals?
8. What has been the rationale of publishing in hardback one year prior to paperback?
9. Explain the modern publishing dilemma.

Note: This case has been written as a basis for class discussion rather than to illustrate effective or ineffective managerial or administrative behaviour. It has been prepared from a variety of published sources, as indicated, and from observations.

Chapter summary

The quality of design and management within operations is thus seen as an essential part of innovation management. Indeed, the process of innovatation can be judged as an operations process with inputs and outputs. Often by understanding the basics of good design by perhaps 'keeping things simple' and looking at your products and services as your customers receive them will help to deliver a continual stream of new product and service improvements. Continuous redesign of the company (e.g. Dell) and its products and service, listening to your customers, watching your competitors, keeping aware of inventions and emerging technologies is a daunting task. We are not just talking about *fitting* the various departments and functions together as a team, but creating a *resonance* across all the constituents of the design spectrum.

Discussion questions

1. What do you understand by *innovation* within the education sector?
2. Apply Braun's principles to your university or college.
3. Which elements of the TQM philosophy could you apply to your university or college? What might be the benefits?
4. Do you think the EFQM model of excellence could apply to your university? What might be the benefits?
5. Consider the innovation activities of the design spectrum. How much of the range would involve patents?
6. Can you think of any circumstances in which the philosophy of 'keeping things simple' would not apply?
7. 'Technology changes. The laws of economics do not.' Discuss the implications and validity of this statement.

Key words and phrases

References

Brown, S., Blackmon, K., Cousins, P. and Maylor, H. (2001) *Operations Management*, Butterworth-Heinemann, Oxford.

Christenson, C.M. (1999) *Innovation and the General Manager*, McGraw-Hill, London.

Chistopher, M. (2004) *Logistics and Supply Chain Management*, Prentice Hall, London.

Cope, N. (2001) B2B hubs in reverse spin, *Independent*, 22 February.

Feigenbaum, A.V. (1986) *Total Quality Control*, McGraw-Hill, New York.

Fiorina, C. and London, S. (2001) Corporate restructuring, *Financial Times*, 22 August.

Giaever, H. (1998) Does Total Quality Management Restrain Innovation?, DNV report no. 99–2036.

Goffin, K. and Mitchell, R. (2005) *Innovation Management: Strategy and implementation using the pentathlon framework*, Palgrave Macmillan, London.

Hammer, M. (1990) Re-engineering work: don't automate, obliterate, *Harvard Business Review*, July/August, 104–12.

Hoecht, A. and Trott, P. (2006) Innovation risks of outsourcing, *Technovation*, Vol. 26, No. 4, 672–81.

Independent (2000) Internet reforms will help case for euro, 25 March.

Johnston, R. and Clark, G. (2001) *Service Operations Management*, Prentice Hall, London.

Krajewski, L.J. and Ritzman, L.P. (2001) *Operations Management*, Prentice Hall, London.

Leadbeater, C. (2001) Fallacies and first movers, *Financial Times*, 1 February.

Lowe, A. and Ridgway, K. (2000) UK user's guide to quality function deployment, *Engineering Management Journal*, June.

McMcracken, J. (2001) Southfield, Mich.-based online automotive exchange, *Detroit Free Press*, 11 August.

Peters, T. (1997) *The Circle of Innovation*, Hodder & Stoughton, London.

Roy, R. and Weild, D. (1993) *Product Design and Technological Innovation*, Open University Press, Milton Keynes.

Rushe, D. (2001) Amazon and Wal-Mart in alliance talks, *Sunday Times*, 3 March.

Russel, R. and Taylor, B. (2003) *Operations Management*, Prentice-Hall, Englewood Cliffs, NJ.

Skapinker, M. (2001) Death of the net threat, *Financial Times*, 12 March.

Slack, N., Chambers, S., Harland, C., Harrison, A. and Johnson, R. (2007) *Operations Management*, 5th edn, Pearson Education Limited, London.

Turban, E., Lee, U., King, D. and Chung, H.M. (2000) *Electronic Commerce – A Managerial Perspective*, Prentice-Hall, Englewood Cliffs, NJ.

Upton, D.M. (1998) *Designing, Managing and Improving Operations*, Prentice-Hall, Englewood Cliffs, NJ.

Van Looy, B., Gemmel, P. and Van Dierdonck, R. (2003) *Services Management*, Prentice Hall, London.

Waller, D.L. (1999) *Operations Management – A Supply Chain Approach*, International Thomson Publishing, London.

Wallis, Z. (1995) The good the bad and the ugly – what does your office say about your company?, *Facilities*, Vol. 13, No. 2, 26–7.

Young, T., Brailsford, S., Connel, C., Davies, R., Harper, P. and Kelin, J. (2004) Using industrial processes to improve patient care, *BMJ*, 328, 162–5.

Further reading

Barney, J.B. and Clark, D.N. (2007) *Resource-based Theory: Creating and Sustaining Competitive Advantage*, Oxford University Press, Oxford.

Chang, H. and Luo, C. (2010) Analyze innovation strategy of technical-intensive industries: Scenario analysis viewpoint, *Business Strategy Series*, Vol. 11, No. 5, 302–7.

Christensen, C.M. (2003) *The Innovator's Dilemma: When New Technologies Cause Great Firms to Fail*, 3rd edn, HBS Press, Cambridge, MA.

Drucker, P.F. (2002) *Managing in the Next Society*, Butterworth-Heinemann, Oxford.

HSBC (2010) 100 Thoughts, HSBC, London.

Reichstein, T. and Salter, A. (2006) Investigating the sources of process innovation among UK manufacturing firms, *Industrial and Corporate Change*, Vol. 15, 653–82.

Chapter 5
Managing intellectual property

Introduction

Intellectual property concerns the legal rights associated with creative effort or commercial reputation. The subject matter is very wide indeed. The aim of this chapter is to introduce the area of intellectual property to the manager of business and to ensure that they are aware of the variety of ways that it can affect the management of innovation and the development of new products. The rapid advance of the internet and e-commerce has created a whole new set of problems concerning intellectual property rights. All these issues will be discussed in this chapter. Finally, the case study at the end of this chapter explains how the pharmaceutical industry uses the patent system to ensure it reaps rewards from the drugs that it develops.

Chapter contents

Learning objectives

When you have completed this chapter you will be able to:

- examine the different forms of protection available for a firm's intellectual property;
- identify the limitations of the patent system;
- explain why other firms' patents can be a valuable resource;
- identify the link between brand name and trademark;
- identify when and where the areas of copyright and registered design may be useful; and
- explain how the patent system is supposed to balance the interests of the individual and society.

Intellectual property

The world of intellectual property (IP) changes at an alarming rate. The law, it seems, is always trying to keep up with technology changes that suddenly allow firms to operate in ways previously not considered. Illustration 5.1 shows how legal events over the past few years have fundamentally affected the activities of so-called grey marketers and the subsequent powers granted to the owners of a range of branded marks including famous lucrative names such as L'Oréal, Levi's, Nike and Calvin Klein. The pronouncements from the French Court, together with other national court decisions, have created a degree of confusion. The decision has proved immensely controversial with regard to the operation of trademark law throughout the European Union. The decision seems to allow people in the EU to continue to buy grey market goods online via eBay against the wishes of the brand owner.

Illustration 5.1

Victory for eBay in court battle with L'Oréal over bid to block sale of bargain beauty products

Shoppers can continue to buy cheap 'grey market' goods on eBay after the auction site saw off a legal challenge by beauty giant L'Oréal yesterday. The French manufacturer had attempted to block the sale of any of its products via the website unless eBay could guarantee they came from approved sources. If it had been successful, eBay could have found it impossible to allow its users to trade global brands at knock-down prices.

Cheap L'Oréal cream is being auctioned on eBay after the beauty giant failed in a legal bid that would have made it impossible for traders to sell its products online.

Many eBay traders buy genuine designer merchandise at cheap prices from outside the EU, most commonly the Far East, and then resell it to UK customers. These 'grey market' bargains may be illegal under trademark laws, but a High Court judge ruled yesterday that eBay was not jointly liable for any trademark infringements committed by traders using its website. This means that L'Oréal itself will have to track and take action against any traders it suspects of selling its merchandise without approval.

At the hearing, eBay insisted that it was merely a trading platform and could not be held responsible for any trademark infringements. After the ruling, eBay's head of trust and safety, Richard Ambrose, said: 'This is an important judgment because it ensures that consumers can continue to buy genuine products at competitive prices on eBay. 'It is a victory for consumers and the thousands of entrepreneurs who sell legitimate goods on eBay every day.' L'Oréal said one of the main reasons it brought the case was because it is concerned that consumers are being sold counterfeit goods. However, eBay said that last year it hosted 2.7 billion listings globally and only 0.15 per cent were identified as potentially counterfeit.

A grey market also known as parallel market is the trade of a commodity through distribution channels which, while legal, are unofficial, unauthorized, or unintended by the original manufacturer. A grey market good is a foreign manufactured good, carrying a valid trademark, imported into a country without the consent of the trademark holder. As grey market goods illegally enter the market, these goods compete with goods of the same brand which the trademark holder lawfully imported into the country.

Source: Murphy, M. (2009) eBay claims victory in luxury fakes dispute, FT.com, 13 May. Reprinted with permission.

This chapter will explore this dynamic area of the law and illustrate why firms need to be aware of this increasingly important aspect of innovation.

If you just happen to come up with a novel idea, the simplest and cheapest course of action is to do nothing about legal protection, just keep it a secret (as with the recipe for Coca-Cola). While this in theory may be true, in reality many chemists and most ingredients and fragrance firms would argue that science can now detect a droplet of blood in an entire swimming pool, and to suggest that science cannot analyse a bottle of cola and uncover its ingredients is stretching the bounds of reason. The keep-it-secret approach prevents anyone else seeing it or finding it. Indeed, the owner can take their intellectual property to their grave, safe in the knowledge that no one will inherit it. This approach is fine unless you are seeking some form of commercial exploitation and ultimately a financial reward, usually in the form of royalties.

One of the dangers, of course, with trying to keep your idea a secret is that someone else might develop a similar idea to yours and apply for legal protection and seek commercial exploitation. Independent discovery of ideas is not as surprising as one might first think. This is because research scientists working at the forefront of science and technology are often working towards the same goal. This was the case with Thomas Edison and Joseph Swan, who independently invented the light bulb simultaneously either side of the Atlantic. Indeed, they formed a company called Ediswan to manufacture light bulbs at the end of the nineteenth century.

Table 5.1 shows an overview of the different forms of intellectual property and rights available for different areas of creativity.

The issues of intellectual property are continually with us and touch us probably more than we realise. Most students will have already confronted the issue of intellectual property, either with recording pre-recorded music or copying computer software. The author is always the owner of his or her work and the writing of an academic paper entitles the student to claim the copyright on that essay. Indeed, the submission of an academic paper to a scientific journal for publication requires the author to sign a licence for the publisher to use the intellectual property. Patenting is probably the most commonly recognised form of intellectual property, but it is only one of several ways to protect creative efforts. Registered designs, trademarks and copyright are other forms of intellectual property. These will be addressed in the following sections. However, before you get into the details of intellectual property have a read of Illustration 5.2. Trevor Baylis the inventor of the wind-up radio argues that intellectual property theft should be regarded as a criminal offence. This illustration also discusses the long-standing issue about whether intellectual property is merely a smokescreen.

Table 5.1 An overview of the main types of intellectual property

Type of intellectual property	Key features of this type of protection
1 Patents	Offers a 20-year monopoly
2 Copyright	Provides exclusive rights to creative individuals for the protection of their literary or artistic productions
3 Registered designs	As protected by registration, is for the outward appearance of an article and provides exclusive rights for up to 15 years
4 Registered trademarks	Is a distinctive name, mark or symbol that is identified with a company's products

Illustration 5.2

Theft of intellectual property 'should be a crime'

FT

Source: Pearson Education Ltd/Photodisc

Trevor Baylis is angry. The inventor of the clockwork radio believes inventors and entrepreneurs are having their intellectual property (IP) stolen, while the government and the courts fail to offer adequate protection.

'The theft of intellectual property should become a white-collar crime', Baylis says.

'If I stole from you, then I would probably go to jail. But if I were to steal your intellectual property, which potentially could be worth billions of pounds, it would only be a civil case – and, even then, most of us can't afford to pay £350 an hour for a lawyer.'

For Baylis, it is the inventor who underpins society. 'Art is pleasure, but invention is treasure. What is more important to society: a sheep in formaldehyde or a paperclip?'

It's a good question, and while Damien Hirst, along with other artists, musicians and writers, is protected by automatic copyright laws, the inventor – at the pre-patent application stage – has no legal recourse should someone decide to patent their idea first. Even with a patent, copyright or trademark (around a business name or brand) in place, IP theft is still extremely common. Gill Grassie, head of IP and technology at Maclay Murray & Spens, a Scottish firm of solicitors, points out that recent studies have shown the impact of counterfeiters on all industry sectors in the UK is as much as £11bn a year. Adam Morallee, a partner in the IP Group at Mishcon de Reya, a commercial law firm based in London, says his firm recovered more than £100m in the last five years alone for its clients who have had their IP rights infringed.

In 2006, Japan and the US established the Anti-Counterfeiting Trade Agreement (Acta) to fight the growing tide of counterfeiting and piracy. Preliminary talks started that year, and it is hoped some sort of global agreement – now that the two founders have been joined by 35 other nations – can be reached later this year. However, at the UK level, patent infringement is currently a civil offence, which for some remains the best way to deal with it.

Grassie says: 'In the area of patents, it is more debatable whether infringement should be a criminal offence as often there may be arguments regarding the validity of the patent or indeed whether there truly has been infringement in the first place.'

As it is a civil matter, one benefit is that you can claim for damages, notes Clive Halperin, a partner at GSC Solicitors. In addition, those seeking to protect their rights only have to prove the matter on the *balance of probabilities, rather than beyond all reasonable doubt* as in a criminal case.

Yet part of the problem faced by entrepreneurs and inventors is the sheer cost of registering a patent in the first place.

'The patent process is slow, expensive and time-consuming', says Stephen Streater, chief executive of Forbidden Technologies and the founder of Eidos, a video games company.

Mark Redgrave, chief executive of OpenAmplify, an online text analysis service, notes that his business has secured 14 patents over the past eight years, but this has cost his company hundreds of thousands of pounds. Registering a patent in eight European countries alone for 10 years can cost up to £40,000. Even if an entrepreneur can afford these costs, protecting a patent against possible infringement can simply be prohibitive.

Mark England, chief executive of Sentec, a metering technology specialist, says: 'If you go to court in a patent case, then effectively you need to have £1m in your back pocket to be able to finance the case, which of course most small companies cannot afford to do.'

This is why many entrepreneurs consider the whole issue of intellectual property as nothing more than a smokescreen.

'Intellectual property has become the genie in the lamp of the 21st-century business landscape; an overblown smokescreen that entrepreneurs and businesses are afraid to release for fear of idea theft', says René Carayol, a writer and broadcaster on business and entrepreneurship.

'Yes, IP is important and, yes, people must be wary about others stealing a march on a good initiative, but this is more about trust than it is about employing high-cost IP lawyers . . . This obsession with intellectual property is stifling progress. Those that make the biggest waves are those that have the confidence to fire first, aim, then get ready.'

A simple way to overcome a lack of trust is to make sure potential colleagues or financial backers agree to sign a non-disclosure agreement. 'You've got to make sure you have one so that you have protection', says Halperin at GSC. 'Once the idea is out there, you've lost your chance.'

Indeed, when John Barrington-Carver, now director at PRAM, a Leeds-based public relations and marketing consultancy, worked with Baylis on the invention of the clockwork radio, he says his job was to keep it out of the media in general to prevent large south-east Asian electronics companies from taking the idea and throwing money at developing a successful production prototype before Baylis could protect the patent.

According to the Intellectual Property Office, the UK patents authority, there are no plans to make patent infringement into a criminal offence. Without this, Baylis believes the inventor or entrepreneur will not gain true recognition: 'We have to make society realise that the most important thing the nation has is knowledge and creativity.'

Source: Greenhalgh, H. (2010) Theft of intellectual property 'should be a crime', FT.com, 24 September. Reprinted with permission.

Pause for thought

Given the impressive advances made in science over the past 50 years, especially in the area of detecting substances and ingredients, scientists now claim to be able to detect one drop of blood in a swimming pool full of water. Does anyone still believe that the ingredients in Coca-Cola, for example, are secret and unknown?

Trade secrets

There are certain business activities and processes that are not patented, copyrighted or trademarked. Many businesses regard these as trade secrets. It could be special ways of working, price costings or business strategies. The most famous example is the recipe for Coca-Cola, which is not patented. This is because Coca-Cola did not want to reveal the recipe to their competitors. Unfortunately, the law covering intellectual property is less clear about the term *trade secret*. Indeed, Bainbridge (1996) argues there is no satisfactory legal definition of the term.

An introduction to patents

Foreign applications for Chinese patents have been growing by over 30 per cent a year. With foreign companies more deeply engaged with the Chinese economy, returns from protecting their intellectual property in China have increased. This has been driven by domestic Chinese firms' ability to imitate foreign technology, and competition between foreign firms in the Chinese market: such competitive threats create an urgency for protecting intellectual property (Hu, 2010). Illustration 5.3 dramatically illustrates the importance of patents to the business world. A patent is a contract between an individual or organisation and the state. The rationale behind the granting of a temporary monopoly by the state is to encourage creativity and innovation within an economy. By the individual or organisation disclosing in the patent sufficient detail of the invention, the state will confer the legal right to stop others benefiting from the invention (Derwent, 1998). The state, however, has no obligation to prevent others benefiting from it. This is the responsibility of the individual or organisation who is granted the patent. And herein lies a major criticism of the patent system. The costs of defending a patent against infringement can be high indeed. This point is explored later.

Illustration 5.3

Microsoft sues Motorola over Android

Microsoft, the world's largest software company, alleged that former ally Motorola infringed nine of its patents in the Android-based smartphones, which run on software built by Google Inc. Microsoft makes its own Windows phone software, which it charges handset makers to use in their phones. Motorola, like some rivals, has shifted toward Google's free Android as a more attractive option, straining the relationship between the two companies. The suits come before Microsoft launches the new version of its mobile software, which it hopes will win back market share from Apple Inc's iPhone and Google.

The patents in question relate to synchronising e-mail, calendars and contacts, scheduling meetings and notifying applications of changes in signal strength and battery power, Microsoft said in a statement. A Motorola spokeswoman said the company has not yet received a copy of the suit, but based on its strong intellectual property portfolio, plans to 'vigorously defend itself'.

Google said it was disappointed in Microsoft's move, which it claimed would threaten innovation in the sector. 'While we are not a party to this lawsuit, we stand behind the Android platform and the partners who have helped us to develop it', the company said in an e-mailed statement.

The suit is the latest in a complicated series of legal actions between various phone makers and software firms over who owns patents to the technology used in smartphones, kicked off by Nokia suing Apple last year, and Apple subsequently suing handset maker HTC Corp. Oracle Corp has also sued Google over Android software.

Source: FT.com (2010) 2 October.

The UK Intellectual Property Office is an operating name of the Patent Office

Source: UK Intellectual Property Office (UKIP).

The UK Patent Office was set up in 1852 to act as the United Kingdom's sole office for the granting of patents of invention. From 2 April 2007 the UK Patent Office changed its name to the UK Intellectual Property Office. This is to reflect that patents now represent only part of its activities along with Registered Designs and Trademarks. The origins of the patent system stretch back a further 400 years. The word patent comes from the practice of monarchs in the Middle Ages (500–1500) conferring rights and privileges by means of 'open letters', that is, documents on which the royal seal was not broken when they were opened. This is distinct from 'closed letters' that were not intended for public view. Open letters were intended for display and inspection by any interested party. The language of government in medieval England was Latin and the Latin for open letters is 'litterae patentes'. As English slowly took over from Latin as the official language the documents became known as 'letters patent' and later just 'patents'.

- *Monopoly for 20 years*. Patents are granted to individuals and organisations that can lay claim to a new product or manufacturing process, or to an improvement of an existing product or process, which was not previously known. The granting of a patent gives the 'patentee' a monopoly to make, use or sell the invention for a fixed period of time, which in Europe and the United States is 20 years from the date the patent application was first filed. In return for this monopoly, the patentee pays a fee to cover the costs of processing the patent, and, more importantly, publicly discloses details of the invention.
- *Annual fees required*. The idea must be new and not an obvious extension of what is already known. A patent lasts up to 20 years in the United Kingdom and Europe, but heavy annual renewal fees have to be paid to keep it in force.
- *Patent agents*. The role of a patent agent combines scientific or engineering knowledge with legal knowledge and expertise and it is a specialised field of work. Many large companies have in-house patent agents who prepare patents for the company's scientists. They may also search patent databases around the world on behalf of the company's scientists.

The earliest known English patent of invention was granted to John of Utynam in 1449. The patent gave Mr Utynam a 20-year monopoly for a method of making stained glass that had not previously been known in England. For a patent to benefit from legal protection it must meet strict criteria:

- novelty;
- inventive step; and
- industrial application.

Novelty

The Patent Act 1977, section 2(1), stipulates that 'an invention shall be taken to be new if it does not form part of the state of the art'. A state of the art is defined as all matter, in other words, publications, written or oral or even anticipation (see *Windsurfing International Inc.* v. *Tabur Marine (GB) Ltd.* below), will render a patent invalid.

Inventive step

Section 3 of the Patent Act 1977 states that 'an invention shall be taken to involve an inventive step if it is not obvious to a person skilled in the art'. In the United States the term 'non-obvious' is used as a requirement for patentability. Although the basic principle is roughly the same, the assessment of the inventive step and non-obviousness varies from one country to another. A set of rules regarding the approach taken by the United Kingdom courts was laid out by the Court of Appeal in *Windsurfing International Inc.* v. *Tabur Marine (GB) Ltd.* [1985] RPC 59, in determining the requirements for inventive step:

1 identifying the inventive concept embodied in the patent;
2 imputing to a normally skilled but unimaginative addressee what was common general knowledge in the art at the priority date;
3 identifying the differences if any between the matter cited and the alleged invention; and
4 deciding whether those differences, viewed without any knowledge of the alleged invention, constituted steps which would have been obvious to the skilled man or whether they required any degree of invention.

Industrial applications

Under the Patent Act an invention shall be taken to be capable of industrial application if it can be a machine, product or process. Penicillin was a discovery which was not patentable but the process of isolating and storing penicillin clearly had industrial applications and thus was patentable.

Pause for thought

If states and governments in particular are determined to outlaw monopolistic practices in industry and commerce, why do they offer a 20-year monopoly for a patent?

Exclusions from patents

Discoveries (as opposed to inventions), scientific theory and mathematical processes are not patentable under the Patent Act 1988. Similarly, literary artistic works and designs are covered by other forms of intellectual property such as trademarks, copyright and registered designs.

The patenting of life

The rapid scientific developments in the field of biology, medical science and biotechnology has fuelled intense debates about the morality of patenting life forms. Until very recently there was a significant difference between the US patent system, which enabled the granting of patents on certain life forms, and the European patent system, which did not. Essentially the US system adopted a far more liberal approach to the patenting of life. This difference was illustrated in the 'Harvard oncomouse' case (Patent No. 4,581,847). The Harvard Medical School had its request for a European patent refused because the mouse was a natural living life form and, hence, unpatentable. This European approach had serious implications for the European biotechnology industry. In particular, because the R&D efforts of the biotechnology industry could not be protected, there was a danger that capital in the form of intellectual and financial could flow from Europe to the United States, where protection was available. The other side of the argument is equally compelling: the granting to a company of a patent on certain genes may restrict other companies' ability to work with those genes. On 27 November 1997 the European Union agreed to Directive 95/0350(COD) and COM(97)446 which permits the granting of patents on certain life forms. This had a particular significance in the area of gene technology.

The subject of cloning a new life form from existing cells stirs the emotions of many. When Dolly, the first large mammal to be created from cells taken from other sheep, was announced it generated enormous controversy and publicity. This was especially so for the group of scientists from the Roslin Institute, a publicly funded institute, and PPL Therapeutics, a biotechnology company that developed Dolly. The debate about the ethics of the science continues and related to this is the intellectual property of the gene technology involved (*see Financial Times* (1997) and Rowan (1997) for a full discussion of this debate).

Human genetic patenting

Eight years ago this industry barely existed: today it is worth over £30 billion. Across Europe there are now 800 small and medium-sized enterprises in the business of making something new from life itself. Public institutions and private enterprises have filed claims on more than 127,000 human genes or partial human gene sequences. All are seeking wealth from DNA. These organisations are searching for tests, treatments, cures and vaccines for thousands of diseases; they are looking for new ways of delivering and new ways of making medicines.

There are many, of course, who take a more pessimistic view of this new science and argue that scientists should not play with nature and even that it is a threat to the future of mankind. A brighter view is that science is on the edge of a new frontier and the future will be one where human suffering is relieved and where incurable illnesses are treated. Whichever view you take, it is worthy of note that many of these firms are small start-ups headed by one or two scientists who have staked the future of the firm on several patent applications. Indeed, the firms' capitalisation is often based on the future predictions of patent applications. This is a very precarious situation for investors. This raises the issue of whether the patent developed all those years ago is suitable for this type of industry or the twenty-first century in general.

In 1998 the European Union harmonised patent law to give European scientists and investors the chance to make one application for one big market, rather than separate applications to member states. It also gave European entrepreneurs the right to patent genes or life. In the past few years the biotechnology firms have been making numerous patent applications for genes or partial human gene sequences. This, of course, leads to the argument that human genes are being turned into intellectual property and licensed to the highest bidders. The key question is, will this property then be made widely available to help the hungry, the sick and the desperate? Or will a few rich firms profit from many years of publicly funded science and exploit the poor and vulnerable? These are clearly difficult ethical questions that you may wish to debate among yourselves, but at the heart of this is patent law. This is illustrated in the case study at the end of this chapter. The purpose of any patent system is to strike a balance between the interests of the inventor and the wider public. At present many believe that US patent law is too heavily biased towards the needs of inventors and investors and does not take into account the poor and developing countries of the world.

Innovation in action

One for you, one for them

The boundaries between business and charity are becoming increasingly blurred. Companies are keen to be seen as ethical while charities are discovering the power of commercial thinking. The latest combination of the two is the 'Get one, give one' business model. Nicholas Negroponte, a serial entrepreneur from Massachusetts, set up 'One Laptop Per Child' with the vision of providing computers to children in the third world to improve their education. His team designed a cheap, rugged laptop that could sell for $199, but that's sometimes still too much for developing countries, making it difficult to persuade governments to purchase in large numbers. In an entrepreneurial twist he put the laptop on sale in the US with a requirement that each customer had to buy two; one for them, and one for a third-world schoolchild.

The first campaign sold 162,000 laptops, raising $35 million. It was such a success that they repeated the campaign again recently, becoming the best-selling laptop on Amazon during the campaign. Production capacity currently can't keep up with demand.

Source: HSBC (2010) 100 Thoughts, HSBC, London.

The configuration of a patent

For a patent to be granted, its contents need to be made public so that others can be given the opportunity to challenge the granting of a monopoly. There is a formal registering and indexing system to enable patents to be easily accessed by the public. For this reason patents follow a very formal specification. Details concerning country of origin, filing date, personal details of applicant, etc., are accompanied by an internationally agreed numbering system for easy identification (*see* Appendix). The two most important sources of information relating to a patent are the *patent specification* and the *patent abstract*. Both of these are classified and indexed in various ways to facilitate search.

The specification is a detailed description of the invention and must disclose enough information to enable someone else to repeat the invention. This part of the document needs to be precise and methodical. It will also usually contain references to other scientific papers. The remainder of the specification will contain claims. These are to define the breadth and scope of the invention. A patent agent will try to write the broadest claim possible as a narrow claim can restrict the patent's application and competitors will try to argue that, for example, a particular invention applies only to one particular method. Indeed, competitors will scrutinise these claims to test their validity.

The patent abstract is a short statement printed on the front page of the patent specification which identifies the technical subject of the invention and the advance that it represents (*see* Appendix). Abstracts are usually accompanied by a drawing. In addition these abstracts are published in weekly information booklets.

It is now possible to obtain a patent from the European Patent Office for the whole of Europe, and this can be granted in a particular country or several countries. The concept of a world patent, however, is a distant realisation. The next section explores some of the major differences between the two dominant world patent systems.

Patent harmonisation: first to file and first to invent

Most industrialised countries offer some form of patent protection to companies operating within their borders. However, while some countries have adequate protection, others do not. Moreover, different countries are members of different conventions and some adopt different systems. The European and the US patent systems have many similarities, for example a monopoly is granted for 20 years under both systems. There is, however, one key difference. In the United States the patent goes to the researcher who can prove they were the first to invent it, not – as in Europe – to the first to file for a patent.

The implications of this are many and varied but there are two key points that managers need to consider.

1 In Europe, a patent is invalid if the inventor has published the novel information before filing for patent protection. In the United States there are some provisions which allow inventors to talk first and file later.
2 In Europe, patent applications are published while pending. This allows the chance to see what monopoly an inventor is claiming and object to the Patent Office if there are grounds to contest validity. In the United States the situation is quite different – applications remain secret until granted.

The issue of patent harmonisation has a long history. The Paris Convention for the Protection of Industrial Property was signed in 1883, and since then it has received many amendments. At present its membership includes 114 countries. European countries have a degree of patent harmonisation provided by the European Patent Convention (EPC) administered by the European Patent Office.

The sheer size of the US market and its dominance in many technology-intensive industries means that this difference in the patent systems has received, and continues to receive, a great deal of attention from various industry and government departments in Europe and the United States.

Some famous patent cases

- *1880: Ediswan.* It is rare that identical inventions should come about at the same time. But that is what happened with the electric light bulb, which was patented almost simultaneously on either side of the Atlantic by Thomas Edison and Joseph Swan. To avoid patent litigation the two business interests combined in England to produce lamps under the name of 'Ediswan', which is still registered as a trademark.
- *1930: Whittle's jet engine.* While Frank Whittle was granted a patent for his jet engine, his employers, the RAF, were unable to get the invention to work efficiently and could not manufacture it on an industrial scale. It was left to the US firms of McDonnell Douglas and Pratt and Witney to exploit the commercial benefits from the patents.
- *1943: Penicillin.* Alexander Fleming discovered penicillin in 1928 and 13 years later, on 14 October 1941, researchers at Oxford University filed Patent No. 13242. The complete specification was accepted on 16 April 1943 (*see* Illustration 5.4).

Illustration 5.4

BTG

Penicillin was discovered in a London hospital by Alexander Fleming in 1928. It was to take another 12 years (1940) before a team working at Oxford University discovered a method of isolating and storing the drug. However, as a result of the Second World War, which drained Britain of much of its financial resources, Britain did not have the capability to develop large-scale fermentation of the bacteria. Help was sought from the United States and the success of the technology is well known.

The UK government was concerned that it gave away valuable technology. By way of a response to this, following the end of the Second World War, it established the National Research Development Corporation (NRDC) in 1948 to protect the intellectual property rights of inventors' efforts which had been funded by the public sector. For example, this included research conducted in universities, hospitals and national laboratories.

From its very beginning the NRDC soon began generating funds. Oxford University developed a second generation of antibiotics called cephalosporins. They were patented worldwide and the royalties secured the financial base of the NRDC for many years.

The NRDC changed its name to the British Technology Group (BTG) and has continued to be successful in arranging and defending patents for many university professors. In 1994 BTG became an independent public limited company.

Historically BTG was involved only in UK intellectual property issues, but its activities have expanded. It was recently involved in litigation with the US Pentagon for patent infringement on the Hovercraft as well as another case concerning Johnson and Johnson, the US healthcare group. BTG was so successful in this case that Johnson and Johnson asked BTG to manage a portfolio of nearly 100 inventions to try to generate royalties.

Patents in practice

There are many industrialists and small business managers who have little faith in the patent system. They believe, usually as a result of first-hand experience, that the patent system is designed primarily for those large multinational corporations that have the finances to defend and protect any patents granted to them. The problem is that applying and securing a patent is only the beginning of what is usually an expensive journey. For example, every time you suspect a company may be infringing your patent you will have to incur legal expenses to protect your intellectual property. Moreover, there are some examples of large corporations spending many years and millions of dollars in legal fees battling in the courts over alleged patent infringement. One of the most well-known cases was *Apple Computer Inc.* v. *Microsoft*, where Apple alleged that Microsoft had copied its Windows operating system. The case lasted for many years and cost each company many millions of dollars in legal fees.

Many smaller firms view the patent system with dread and fear. Indeed, only 10 per cent of the UK patents are granted to small firms. Yet small firms represent 99 per cent of companies (*Guardian*, 1998).

Fees to file a UK patent at the UK IPO are £30 for the examination and £100 for the initial search to be made within 12 months of applying. The substantive examination needs to be made within 18 months of filing and that fee is £70. On the fourth anniversary of the filing date the patent must be renewed and every year after that. The fees for renewing in the fifth year are £50. It then goes up every year until the 20th year which costs £400.

In theory it sounds straightforward – £225 to apply for a UK patent. In practice, however, companies should be considering £1,000–£1,500 to obtain a UK patent. Furthermore, protection in a reasonable number of countries is likely to cost more like £10,000. Illustration 5.2 highlights many of the limitations of the patent system.

In some industries it seems the rules of intellectual property may need to change. Some have argued that reforming the intellectual property law may help to stimulate more innovation and that a growing part of the economy (e.g. services, information technology) is only weakly protected under current intellectual property law. One possible way to encourage innovation is by extending coverage to these products and broadening legal protection to cover new product ideas for a short period. Small companies and individual entrepreneurs would benefit most from this broader but shorter protection (Alpert, 1993).

Expiry of a patent and patent extensions

There is much written on the subject of patent application and the benefits to be gained from such a 20-year monopoly. There is, however, much less written about the subject of the effects of patent expiry. In other words, what happens when the patent protecting your product expires? A glance at the pharmaceutical industry reveals an interesting picture. Illustration 5.5 shows the reality for a firm when its patent expires.

For any firm operating in this science-intensive industry, the whole process of developing a product is based around the ability to protect the eventual product through the use of patents. Without the prospect of a 20-year monopoly to exploit many years of research and millions of dollars of investment, companies would be less inclined to engage in new product development. On expiry of a patent competitors are able to use the technology, which hitherto had been protected, to develop their own product. Such products are referred to as generic drugs (a generic sold on its chemical composition). When a generic drug is launched, the effect on a branded drug which has just come off-patent can be considerable. For example, Takeda is expecting a drop in sales of 90 per cent when its $4 billion anti-ulcer treatment drug Prevacid comes off-patent in 2009 (*see* Figure 5.1). Remarkably, market share falls of 85 per cent are typical (*Chemistry & Industry News*, 1995; Nakamoto and Pilling, 2004). A generic drug is cheap to produce as no extensive research and development costs are incurred and pharmaceutical drugs are relatively easy to copy. It is in effect a chemical process. The principal forms of defence available to manufacturers are brand development and further research.

Illustration 5.5

FDA gives approval for generic versions of Eli Lilly's Prozac

Washington – Federal regulators approved several generic versions of Eli Lilly & Co's popular antidepressant Prozac, ushering in one of the biggest generic-drug launches in history. The Food and Drug Administration approved Barr Laboratories Inc., of Pomona, NY, to market a 20-milligram capsule, the most common dosage. The FDA also approved an oral solution made by Teva Pharmaceutical Industries Ltd., of Jerusalem; a 40 mg capsule from Dr. Reddy's Laboratories Ltd, of Hyderabad, India; a 10 mg capsule from Geneva Pharmaceutical, of Broomfield, CO; and 10 mg and 20 mg tablets from Pharmaceutical Resources Inc., of Spring Valley, NJ. Barr started shipping its version yesterday, when Prozac's patent and market protection expired. Because it was the first to file for approval with the FDA, Barr will be the only company allowed to offer the 20 mg for 180 days. Afterwards, others with FDA approval can market the drug in that form. Barr said its version will be widely available by next week, and as early as today for those who placed orders ahead of time. Barr wouldn't say precisely how much its version would cost, but said it would be between 25% and 40% less than Prozac, which runs about $2.50 a day. Two other forms of Prozac – a weekly pill and one for women – remain under patent protection. Sales of the blockbuster drug, known generically as fluoxetine hydrochloride, totaled about $2.5 billion last year, according to Lilly, of Indianapolis. 'Millions of American consumers will immediately begin to benefit from savings, and millions more who might otherwise have had to forgo this medicine because of its high cost will have access to a more affordable version of Prozac,' said Barr Chairman Bruce L. Downey. The generic approvals come one year after Barr won a court victory that cut nearly three years off Lilly's Prozac patent. At the time, Lilly predicted a significant drop in sales when generic versions hit the market.

Source: From Generic drug makers get FDA clearance for versions of Prozac, *Wall Street Journal*, 3 August 2001. (Carroll, J.), reprinted by permission of *The Wall Street Journal*,

Pause for thought

If you obtain a patent for an invention and pay all the necessary fees, what happens if one day you see your invention in a shop window? Can you call in at the local police station and report it? Who will pay to bring a case against the retailer and manufacturer?

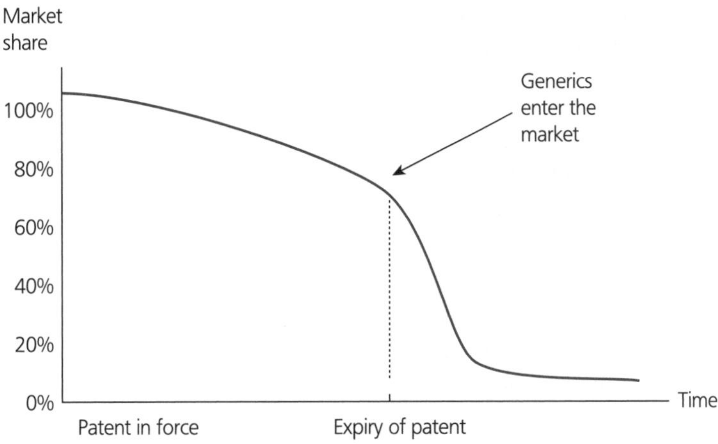

Figure 5.1 The effect on its market share of a drug coming off-patent

Developing a brand requires long-term development. Pharmaceutical companies with a product protected by patents will usually have between 10 and 20 years to develop a brand and brand loyalty, the aim being that even when the product goes off-patent customers will continue to ask for the branded drug as opposed to the generic drug. In practice, companies adopt a combination of aggressive marketing to develop the brand, and technical research on existing drugs to improve the product still further and file for additional patents to protect the new and improved versions of the product.

Patent extensions

Patent extensions are known in Europe as Supplementary Protection Certificates, usually abbreviated to 'SPC'. They were introduced in Europe in the mid-1990s to compensate patent owners for regulatory delays in approving their pharmaceuticals and agrochemicals. The approvals sometimes took so long that the patent had reached the end of its 20-year life, thus opening the invention to all comers, before the inventor had had much chance to commercialise it.

The SPC was designed to provide a level playing field for all pharmaceuticals/agrochemicals patent owners that had suffered regulatory delay exceeding five years, to restore to them an effective 15-year term of protection. The SPC takes effect at the instant of patent expiry, and then lasts for the length of time by which regulatory approval exceeded five years. Each SPC therefore has its own fixed duration, but, to protect the public, the maximum duration is five years' effect.

The United States achieves a similar result by a different route, namely by directly extending the lifetime of those individual patents where the applicant can show regulatory delay in getting the product on to the market. Japan has been considering legislation to achieve broadly similar results (BTG, 2004).

Every month of patent extension can mean hundreds of millions of dollars in additional revenues for blockbuster products. A number of companies, including Bristol Myers Squibb, AstraZeneca, GlaxoSmithKline and Schering-Plough have been accused of using such tactics to boost profits. However, a Federal Trade Commission report found only eight instances of suspect patent extensions between 1992 and 2000 (Bowe and Griffith, 2002).

The use of patents in innovation management

Patent offices for each country house millions of patents. In the United Kingdom there are over 2 million British patents and all this information is available to the public. Each publication, because of the legal requirement that details of patents be disclosed, is a valuable source of technological knowledge. Indeed, the information provision activities of the Patent Office have increased in their function. For example, scientists working in a particular field will often search patent databases to see how the problems they face have been tackled in the past. They will also use previous patents to identify how their current area of work fits in with those areas of science and technology that have been developed and patented previously. Very often patents can provide a valuable source of inspiration.

In addition, many firms also use the patent publication register to find out what their competitors are doing. For example, a search of the worldwide patent databases may reveal that your major competitor has filed a series of patents in an area of technology that you had not considered previously. Armed with prior knowledge of the industry and the technology it may be possible to uncover the research direction in which your competitor is heading, or even the type of product line that it is considering developing. All this industrial intelligence can help research teams and companies to develop and modify their own strategy or to pursue a different approach to a problem.

Do patents hinder or encourage innovation?

According to Professor William Haseltine, the rush for patents did not hamper AIDS research. In the 1980s he worked for a team that deciphered the DNA of the HIV virus, worked out the sequences of its genes, and discovered some of the proteins those genes made. His name is on more than a dozen patents on the AIDS virus, but the patents are held by the cancer institute he then worked for at the Harvard Medical School. He makes a very strong case in favour of the patent system for fostering innovation. Indeed, he thinks the patents speeded up the assault on the virus itself.

> *I would guess there may be 1000 patents filed by now (for HIV tools), each one building on the other. You would be very hard pressed to make the case that a patent on the virus, a patent on the genome sequence, a patent on individual sequences, is in any way inhibiting rather than stimulating of productive research, both in academia and in companies. I can think of no case in which a patent has ever inhibited an academic scientist.*
>
> (Professor W. Haseltine, *Guardian*, 2000)

There is, however, another school of thought: Andrew Brown (2007) argues that submarine patents – those that surface only after the technologies they protect have come into wide use – are obviously dangerous. But even ordinary, open, honest patents now function as a brake on innovation. He uses the illustration of the French company Alcatel suing Microsoft for infringing its patents on the MP3 compression scheme. This he argues is an example of firms abusing intellectual property law. The patents arising from the MP3 technology joint venture (between Bell Labs, US telephone company, and the Fraunhofer Institute, Germany), were thought by everyone to belong to the German Research Organisation, which duly licensed them, and made a reasonable amount of money from this. Microsoft, for example, paid $16 million to incorporate MP3 support into Windows Media Player. But when Alcatel bought the remains of Bell Labs, now known as Lucent Technologies, it behaved as any modern company would, and tried to squeeze maximum value from the patents it had acquired. It asserted that these covered some of the MP3 technology that everyone assumed Fraunhofer owned, and sued two PC companies – Dell and Gateway – for selling computers equipped to play MP3s. Microsoft promised to fight the suit on their behalf and so the case came eventually to court.

Table 5.2 shows the reasons why firms patent. It is clear from this that most firms use the patent system to prevent other firms copying their technology and blocking. Blocking here refers to owners of a patent preventing others from using the technology. It is this area that is a growing concern for firms and governments around the world. For the aim of the patent system is to encourage innovation and yet there is increasing evidence that it is now being used to prevent other firms developing technology.

The European Federal Trade Commission (2006) investigated the role of patents to see whether the balance between protection for the intellectual property owners and stimulating innovation had now shifted too much in favour of protection. Their investigation revealed that patents can indeed impair competition, innovation and the economy. In particular the EFTC found that there was an increasing use of patent thickets in software and internet-related industries. A patent thicket is a form of defensive patenting where firms unnecessarily increase the number of patents to increase complexity. This forces competing companies to divert resources from original R&D into paying to use the patents of other firms. Patent thickets make it

Table 5.2 Reasons why firms patent

	Products %	Processes %
Prevent copying	96	78
Patent blocking	82	64
Prevent suits	59	47
Use in negotiations	48	37
Enhance reputation	48	34
Licensing revenue	28	23
Measure performance	6	5

Source: Cohen, W.M. (2002) *Patents: Their Effectiveness and Role*, Carnegie Mellon University & National Bureau of Economic Research. With permission from Wesley Cohen.

more difficult to commercialise new products and raise uncertainty and investment risks for follow-on firms. Specifically patents deter innovation by:

- denying follow-on innovators access to necessary technologies (EULA);
- increasing entry barriers;
- the expense required to avoid patent infringement;
- the issuance of questionable patents.

This view was confirmed in March 2007 when the Commission accused Microsoft of demanding excessive royalties from companies wishing to license technical information about its Windows operating system. The EU fined Microsoft €800 million.

The case study at the end of this chapter examines whether the pharmaceutical industry is generating supra industry profits as a result of the patent system.

Alternatives to patenting

The previous discussions would seem to suggest that firms consider patenting to be a useful appropriation mechanism. Yet, when studies are compared, it seems that the value of patents as an appropriation mechanism remains questionable. For example, Cohen *et al.* (2000) found that in only 26.67 per cent of product innovations and 23.33 per cent of process innovations were patents considered an effective appropriation mechanism in the semiconductor industry. It seems that there are two other appropriation mechanisms that are considered superior by semiconductor firms, namely secrecy and lead time or first mover advantage. Research shows that there are a number of reasons why large companies in the semiconductor industry patent, and that these reasons are mostly strategic. For example, small firms in the semiconductor industry use patents in order to acquire venture capital and prefer secrecy as an appropriation mechanism over patents (Hall and Ham Ziedonis, 2001; Arundel, 2001).

Similarly the benefits of owning a patent have changed from protection of innovation to a number of strategic uses. An important benefit of a patent is the freedom-to-operate that it allows. In the semiconductor industry freedom-to-operate is an important issue, because a lot of the innovations overlap. This is why the large semiconductor firms cross-license patents, and allow competition to use each others patents (Grindley and Teece, 1997). A strong patent portfolio provides firms with a strong negotiation position. If firms do not provide the freedom to operate they can block. Patenting with the intention to block competition is quite common, and in the semiconductor industry 75 per cent of the participants declared blocking a reason to patent (Cohen, *et al.*, 2000). In a study of German firms Blind *et al.* (2009) find clear evidence that a company's patenting strategies are related to the characteristics of its patent portfolios. For example, companies using patents as bartering chips in collaborations receive fewer oppositions to their patents. Patents are sometimes also used as an indicator of value to an external party, through the promise of income, or as a signal of innovative and protected capability. In the semiconductor industry small firms have indicated that a reason to patent is to attract venture capital (Hall, 2005; Hall and Ham Ziedonis, 2001).

A number of alternative strategies to patents (*see* Table 5.3) have been developed by companies, where they felt other forms of intellectual property protection were better suited to their needs (Leiponen and Byma, 2009).

Table 5.3 Alternative strategies to patenting

Alternatives to patents	Definition
Secrecy	Relatively easy, no legal protection.
Accumulated tacit knowledge	Acquired through experience, it is an asset that is difficult to imitate.
Lead time	Market share and profits need to be secured quickly.
After-sales service	Market share acquired by the lead time advantages can be sustained through after-sales service. If a better and cheaper product is introduced, especially in business-to-business, customer loyalty can disappear very quickly.
Learning curve	Prior knowledge has made the process more efficient.
Complementary assets	Additional useful, extra products are offered to make the original product more desirable.
Product complexity	Helps avoid imitation by increasing product complexity. The semiconductor industry is a good example of this, because expensive devices are needed to reverse engineer semiconductor products.
Standards	A highly effective (but risky) way of getting large returns on the investment in R&D. Winners can take the whole market and losers get nothing.
Branding	Branding is an important way to appropriate returns from innovation; it can also create customer loyalty.

Trademarks

Trademarks have particular importance to the world of business. For many companies, especially in the less technology-intensive industries where the use of patents is limited, trademarks offer one of the few methods of differentiating a company's products. The example of Coca-Cola is a case in point. Trademarks are closely associated with business image, goodwill and reputation. Indeed, many trademarks have become synonymous with particular products: Mars and chocolate confectionery, Hoover and vacuum cleaners and Nestlé and coffee. The public rely on many trademarks as indicating quality, value for money and origin of goods. Significant changes have been made to trademark law in the United Kingdom. The Trade Marks Act 1994 replaced the Trade Marks Act 1938, which was widely recognised as being out of touch with business practices today. The United Kingdom now complies with the EC directive on the approximation of the laws of member states relating to trademarks and ratified the Madrid Convention for the international registration of trademarks. The law relating to trademarks is complex indeed. For example, what is a trademark? Bainbridge (1996) offers a comprehensive review of law surrounding intellectual property. The following section offers a brief introduction to some of the key considerations for product and business managers.

Section 1(1) of the Trade Marks Act 1994 defines a trademark as:

> *being any sign capable of being represented graphically which is capable of distinguishing goods or services of one undertaking from those of other undertakings.*

This can include, for example, Apple Computers, the Apple logo and Macintosh, all of which are registered trademarks. Some of the first trademarks were used by gold- and silversmiths to mark their own work. The first registered trademark, No. 1, was issued to Bass in 1890 for their red triangle mark for pale ale. Illustration 5.6 on the Mr Men offers an example of the effective and successful use of trademarks.

There are certain restrictions and principles with the use of trademarks. In particular, a trademark should:

- satisfy the requirements of section 1(1);
- be distinctive;
- not be deceptive; and
- not cause confusion with previous trademarks.

Illustration 5.6

Mr Hargreaves and the Mr Men

Each one of the Mr Men characters is trademarked. The Mr Men books have sold a staggering 100m copies in no fewer than 30 countries. They are nearly 40 years old. They were the invention of Roger Hargreaves, a shrewd Sussex-based advertising copywriter who saw in the books a way of quitting the rat race and enjoying the prosperity he craved. His dream paid off. His first book, Mr Tickle, became an instant success and five more quickly followed. Within three years, Roger had sold a million copies and ultimately became so wealthy he moved to Guernsey as a tax exile. But in 1988 the dream came to an abrupt end when he suffered a stroke while walking down to breakfast. He was taken to hospital but died later that day, aged just 53.

That could have been the end of the Mr Men, but Roger's eldest son, Adam, valiantly stepped into the breach. On the face of it, he wasn't the most obvious candidate. He was 25, working as a dairyman and stockman, and throughout his teens had studiously ignored his father's day job, finding the whole thing acutely embarrassing. Despite his substantial real estate, Adam, now 46, seems untainted by wealth or success. In fact, he's as unshowy as they come – affable, modest and self-effacing. Adam believes the secret of their appeal lies in the Mr Men's universal personality traits. And then there's the collectability factor, which is something children are always going to enjoy.

In 2004, Adam and his family made the decision to sell the intellectual property rights of the Mr Men to the entertainment group Chorion, for a cool £24 million. 'The sale of the likes of Thomas the Tank Engine to multi-national corporations had made us aware that there was a big market for property rights and many of our rivals were now getting a huge amount of investment that we had no hope of matching', he says. 'Our business was happily ticking along, but there were limits to what we could achieve from our small office in Sussex. We knew that a much larger company with marketing skills, investment opportunities and contacts, could open up the worldwide market much more effectively.' He had few qualms about the sale. Though it was a difficult wrench for his mother, he knew that his father would have approved. Roger Hargreaves' commercial nous was also evident in the way that he and his agent seized on the potential of licensing in the mid-Seventies, following in the footsteps of Disney. They licensed everything and anything. And the beauty of the Mr Men was that they could be associated with an enormous range of products – from Mr Messy baby bibs to Mr Grumpy slippers for Father's Day. All of which now deliver profits to Chorion.

Source: sussex.greatbritishlife.co.uk/.../interview-with-**adam**-hargreaves--**mr-men**-illustrator-and-writer-17832/.

Should satisfy the requirements of section 1(1)

The much wider definition of a trademark offered by the 1994 Act opened the possibility of all sorts of marks that would not have previously been registrable. Sounds, smells and containers could now be registered. A number of perfume manufacturers have applied to register their perfumes as trademarks. Coca-Cola and Unilever have applied to register their containers for Coca-Cola and Domestos respectively. In 2010 Lego failed to get its plastic eight-stud brick trademarked. The European Court of Justice ruled that a three-dimensional image of Lego's eight-stud bricks did not qualify for a trademark because the blocks served a functional purpose. The case centred on an EU ruling that shapes used for a technical result did not qualify for a trademark (Farrell, 2010).

Distinctive

A trademark should be distinctive in itself. In general this means that it should not describe in any way the product or service to which it relates. Usually words that are considered generic or descriptive are not trademarked. In addition, it should not use non-distinctive expressions which other traders might reasonably wish to use in the course of a trade. For example, to attempt to register the word beef as a trademark for a range of foods would not be possible since other traders would reasonably want to use the word in the course of their trade. It would, however, be acceptable to use beef in association with a range of clothing because this would be considered distinctive. Laudatory terms are not allowed, for example the word heavenly for a range of cosmetics would not be possible since it is a laudatory term. The law, however, concerning this aspect of distinctiveness looks set to change following a recent ruling in the European courts. Illustration 5.7 shows an example of a trademark infringement involving easyJet.

Non-deceptive

A trademark should also not attempt to deceive the customer. For example, to attempt to register Orlwoola, as happened in 1900, as an artificial fibre would not be possible, since the very word could persuade people to believe the material was made of wool.

Not confusing

Finally, a trade or service mark will not be registered if it could be confused with the trademark of a similar product that has already been registered. For example, 'Velva-Glo' was refused as a trademark for paints because it was judged to be too near the word 'Vel-Glo' which was already registered.

Illustration 5.7

Easydate collides with easyJet over trademark infringement

Source: Pearson Education Ltd/Photodisc

Stelios Haji-Ioannou, the founder of the easyJet empire, has threatened action against online dating group Easydate in a row over alleged trademark infringement. Easydate, which trades under brands including benaughty.com, and girlsdateforfree.com, has been using the name for the five years since it launched. Easydate is based in Edinburgh but a growing number of its members are from overseas. It has launched a range of services such as psychology-based matchmaking website LoveChemistry and niche products datingforparents.com, speeddater.com and maturedating.com. The company was set up by Bill Dobbie and his Ukrainian business partner Max Polyakov in 2005 and employs 140 staff, although the vast majority are part of an in-house technical and online marketing team based in the Ukraine.

The group has 9m members in 29 countries, but only came to Sir Stelios' attention after Easydate listed on the Aim stockmarket for small companies in June. Sir Stelios, who licenses the 'easy' name to businesses including easyJet, easyCar and easyHotel, claimed Easydate was trying to pass itself off as part of the 'easy' brand and warned it to change the company name.

'Easydate is taking unfair advantage of the strong reputation of my easy brand in order to obtain an undeserved commercial advantage. Unless Easydate stops using its brand and domain name, I will take further action to protect the easy name', Sir Stelios said.

Easydate said it had consulted lawyers but would seek to resolve the issue out of court.

The case is the latest in a long line of colourful disputes fought by Sir Stelios. The entrepreneur has registered 1,000 trademarks with the easy prefix since launching the brand 15 years ago and said on Friday he was confident he would win in court.

'I'd be delighted to talk to them provided they agree with me. It's not too difficult for them to change the name of the holding company', Sir Stelios said.

Easycurry, an Indian restaurant near Luton airport, was forced to change its name two years ago. Although Sir Stelios quit the easyJet board in May, his family still hold a combined 38 per cent stake in the low-cost operator.

Source: Plimmer, G. (2010) Dating site runs foul of easy lawyers, FT.com, 24 September. Reprinted with permission.

Brand names

Increasingly the link between the **brand name** and the **trademark** is becoming closer and stronger. The literature tends to separate the two, with brands remaining in the sphere of marketing and trademarks within the sphere of law. In terms of a property right that is exploitable, however, brand names and trademarks are cousins. They both serve to facilitate identity and origin. That origin in turn indicates a certain level of quality, as reflected in the goods. Indeed, it is worthy of note that many brands have been registered as trademarks.

Like other capital assets owned by a firm such as manufacturing equipment or land, a brand can also be considered an asset, and a valuable one at that. 'Brand equity' is the term used to describe the value of a brand name. Accountants and marketers differ in their definitions and there have been a variety of approaches to define the term (Feldwick, 1996):

- the total value of a brand as a separable asset – when it is sold, or included on a balance sheet;
- a measure of the strength of consumers' attachment to a brand; and
- a description of the associations and beliefs the consumer has about the brand.

Brand equity creates value for both customers and the firm. The customers can clearly use brand names as simplifying heuristics for processing large amounts of information. The brand can also give customers confidence in the purchasing situation. Firms benefit enormously from having strong brand names. Investment in a brand name can be leveraged through brand extensions and increased distributions. High brand equity often allows higher prices to be charged; hence it is a significant competitive advantage.

A firm may decide to purchase a brand from another company rather than to develop a brand itself. Indeed, this may be less expensive and less risky. IKEA, for example, purchased the Habitat brand. Habitat had a strong UK presence in the furniture and household products market and enabled IKEA to increase its presence in the UK furniture market.

Using brands to protect intellectual property

Product managers, product designers and R&D managers all recognise that despite their best efforts sometimes the success of a product can be dependent on the brand. In the cigarette market, for example, over 70 per cent of consumers are loyal to a particular brand (Badenhausen, 1995), and this makes entry to this market very difficult. Brands help buyers to identify specific products that they like and reduce the time required to purchase the product. Without brands, product selection would be random and maybe more rational, based on price, value and content of the product. It would certainly force consumers to select more carefully. If all the products in a store had the same plain white packaging but information was made available on ingredients, contents and details of the manufacturing process, consumers would spend an enormous amount of time shopping. Brands symbolise a certain quality level and this can be transferred to other product items. For example, Unilever extended the Timotei shampoo name to skin-care products. This clearly enabled the company to develop a new range of products and use the benefits of brand recognition of Timotei.

An area of branding that is growing rapidly is that of the licensing of trademarks. Using a licensing agreement, a company may permit approved manufacturers to use its trademark on other products for a licensing fee. Royalties may be as low as 2 per cent of wholesale revenues or as high as 10 per cent. The licensee is responsible for all manufacturing and marketing and bears the cost if the product fails. Today the licensing business is a huge growth industry. The All England Tennis and Croquet Club license their brand to a small group of companies each year. During the summer those companies use the association with Wimbledon to promote their products.

Products such as Robinson's soft drinks, Wedgwood pottery, Slazenger sports goods and Coca-Cola have all signed licence agreements with the All England Club. For an organisation like the All England Club the advantages are obvious: increased revenue and, to a lesser extent, increased promotion of the tournament. To other firms like JCB, Jaguar Cars and Harley-Davidson, all of whom license their trademarks to clothing manufacturers, it clearly provides increased revenues, but also raises opportunities for diversification. The major disadvantages are a lack of control over the products, which could harm the perception and image of the brand. The All England Club, for example, have numerous committee meetings to consider very carefully the type of organisation and product that will bear its trademark.

Exploiting new opportunities

Product and brand managers must continually be vigilant about changes in the competitive market. This will help to realise new development opportunities for the brand. Some companies have developed reputations for exploiting the latest technology developments; indeed, some of these firms are responsible for the breakthroughs. The following list of examples illustrates how pioneering firms have exploited opportunities and developed their brands:

- *New technology*. Sony and Rank Xerox are examples of firms that over the past 20 years have continually exploited new technology.
- *New positioning*. First Direct and The Body Shop uncovered and developed unique positions for themselves in the market. First Direct was one of the pioneers of telephone banking and continued to build on this position. Similarly The Body Shop was a pioneer of 'green' cosmetics and has exploited this position.
- *New distribution*. Direct Line and Argos Stores developed new channels of distribution for their products and services. Direct Line exploited the concept of telephone insurance and later expanded into other financial services, and Argos Stores developed the concept of warehouse-catalogue shopping.

Frequently, rival firms will develop generic products and services to rival the brand. Nowhere is this more apparent than in the pharmaceutical industry, as the previous section illustrated. One of the key issues for brand managers is whether the brand can sustain its strong market position in the face of such competition. It is possible to defend a brand through effective marketing communications, but this is rarely enough. Usually the brand will need to innovate in one or more of the areas listed above. Some brands have failed to innovate and have then struggled in the face of fierce competition. One example is the Kellogg's brand. Over the past 10 years Kellogg's has seen its share of the cereal market gradually decline in the face of strong competition from store brands. Critics of Kellogg's argue that its brand managers have failed to innovate and develop the brand.

Pause for thought

Intellectual property does not just lie in physical products, it can also reside in services and ways of operating. What role does the brand play in service-based industries such as airlines?

Brands, trademarks and the internet

Nowhere is the subject of trademarks and brands more closely intertwined than on the internet. Individuals and firms are linked up and identified through so-called 'domain names'. These are essentially an address, comprising four numbers, such as 131.22.45.06. The numbers indicate the network (131), an internet protocol address (22 and 45) and a local address (06). Numeric addresses, however, are difficult to remember. Internet authorities assigned and designated an alphanumeric designation and mnemonic which affords the consumer user-friendly information with regard to identity and source – the 'domain name' (for example, microsoft.com and ports.ac.uk).

It can be seen then that domain names act as internet addresses. They serve as the electronic or automated equivalent to a telephone directory, allowing web browsers to look up their intended hits directly or via a search engine such as Alta Vista. One may argue at this point that domain names act as electronic brand names. Moreover, the characteristics of a domain name and a trademark are considerable. A recent US judgment has pronounced that domain names are protectable property rights in much the same way as a trademark (www.webmarketingtoday.com).

Duration of registration, infringement and passing off

Under the Trade Marks Act 1994 the registration of a trademark is for a period of 10 years from the date of registration which may be renewed indefinitely for further 10-year periods. Once accepted and registered, trademarks are considered to be an item of personal property.

The fact that a trademark is registered does not mean that one cannot use the mark at all. In the case of *Bravado Merchandising Services Ltd* v. *Mainstream Publishing Ltd*, the respondent published a book about the pop group Wet Wet Wet under the title *A Sweet Little Mystery – Wet Wet Wet – The Inside Story*. Wet Wet Wet was a registered trademark and the proprietor brought an injunction against the use of the name. The court decided that the trademark had not been infringed because the respondent was using the mark as an indication of the main characteristic of the artefact which, in this instance, was a book about the pop group (Bainbridge, 1996).

Where a business uses a trademark that is similar to another or takes unfair advantage of or is detrimental to another trademark, infringement will have occurred. This introduces the area of passing off and is the common law form of trademark law. Passing off concerns the areas of goodwill and reputation of the trademark. In *Consorzio de Prosciutto di Parma* v. *Marks & Spencer plc* (1991) Lord Justice Norse identified the ingredients of a passing off action as being composed of:

- the goodwill of the plaintiff;
- the misrepresentation made by the defendant; and
- consequential damage.

Illustration 5.8 highlights many of the concerns expressed by businesses in what they see as unfair competition. This area of law has many similarities to trademark law and is considered to be a useful supplement to it (*see* Bainbridge, 1996, for a full explanation of the law of passing off).

Illustration 5.8

Copycats or competition: Android eats into Nokia's smartphone lead

Sales of mobile phones operating on Google's Android system are threatening Nokia's lead in the highly lucrative smartphone sector, just as the Finnish handset maker is feeling pressure at the other end of the market from low-cost Asian rivals, many of whom are copycat producers.

More than a quarter of the smartphones sold globally in the third quarter of 2010 ran on the Android operating platform compared with 3.5 per cent a year ago, according to new figures from research firm Gartner. Nokia, which runs on Symbian, saw its share of the market slip from 44.6 to 36.6 per cent over the same period.

The results highlight how the adoption of Google's open source platform by more than a dozen manufacturers including Samsung and HTC, as well as strong demand for Apple's iPhone, is making it harder for Nokia to retain its lead.

About a fifth of the handsets sold globally were high-margin smartphones, which offer a range of multimedia services.

'We've been very bullish on Android', said Carolina Milanesi, research vice-president at Gartner. 'For me, the story is about Samsung and how when you have a heavyweight supplier, you see how quickly volume grows.'

Apple, which ranks third in the smartphone market after being overtaken by Android-operated phones in the last quarter, saw a slight dip in its market share though overall unit sales rose.

All of the big players are seeing their overall global market share of the handset market eroded at the low end by a growing army of non-branded or copycat manufacturers. These 'white-box' manufacturers – which largely operate out of China and other parts of Asia – buy ready-made chipsets and then package their low-cost phones for sale to emerging markets. Some of the bigger players operate legally but many more garage-style operations shift their goods to India, Africa and Latin America without licences or proper identifying codes.

Gartner said that global sales of handsets rose 35 per cent in the third quarter to 417m units. However, a third of the devices sold were made by companies that were not among the major players – many of whom were white-box manufacturers.

Ms Milanesi said that the massive jump in shipments from non-branded and copycat phone groups was 'having a profound effect on the top five mobile handset manufacturers' combined share'.

Nokia's overall share of the global market fell from 36.7 to 28.2 per cent in the third quarter, its lowest level since 1999. Samsung's share dropped from 19.6 to 17.2 per cent, while third-ranked LG declined from 10.3 to 6.6 per cent.

On the back of growth in white-box sales, Gartner is now predicting a 30 per cent rise in overall handset sales for the year.

Source: Watkins, M. (2010) Android eats into Nokia's smartphone lead, FT.com, 10 November. Reprinted with permission.

Registered designs

A new product may be created which is not sufficiently novel or contain an inventive step so as to satisfy the exacting requirements for the granting of a patent. This was the situation faced by Britain's textile manufacturers in the early nineteenth century. They would create new textile designs but these would be later copied by foreign competitors. The Design Registry was set up in the early 1800s in response to growing demands from Britain's textile manufacturers for statutory protection for the designs of their products. Today, designs that are applied to articles may be protected by design law. There are two systems of design law in the United Kingdom.

One is similar to that used for patent law and requires registration; the other system of design protection is design right and is provided along copyright lines. There is a large area of overlap between the two systems.

The registered designs system is intended for those designs intended to have some form of aesthetic appeal. For example, electrical appliances, toys and some forms of packaging have all been registered.

A design as protected by registration is the *outward appearance of an article*. Only the appearance given by its actual shape, configuration, pattern or ornament can be protected, not any underlying idea. The registered design lasts for a maximum of 15 years. Initially the proprietor is granted the exclusive right to a design for a fixed term of five years. This can be renewed for up to five further five-year terms.

To be registered a design must first be new at the date an application for its registration is filed. In general a design is considered to be new if it has not been published in the United Kingdom (i.e. made available or disclosed to the public in any way whatsoever) and if, when compared with any other published design, the differences make a materially different appeal to the eye. For example, if a company designed a new kettle that was very different from any other kettle, the company could register the design. This would prevent other kettle manufacturers from simply copying the design. Clearly, the kettle does not offer any advantage in terms of use, hence a patent cannot be obtained, but a good design is also worth protecting.

Copyright

This area of the law on intellectual property rights has changed significantly over the past few years, mainly because it now covers computer software. Computer software manufacturers are particularly concerned about the illegal copying of their programs. The music industry has also battled with this same problem for many years. It is common knowledge that this was an exceptionally difficult area of law to enforce and new technology may at last provide copyright holders with an advantage. Up to now they have fallen prey to copying technology, but Waldmeir (2002) suggests that compact discs will begin to include technology that prevents them from being copied. The impact of this may be to hinder creativity in the long term (*see* Illustration 5.9).

For the author of creative material to obtain copyright protection it must be in a tangible form so that it can be communicated or reproduced. It must also be the author's own work and thus the product of his or her skill or judgement. Concepts, principles, processes or discoveries are not valid for copyright protection until they are put in a tangible form such as written or drawn. It is the particular way that an idea is presented that is valid for copyright. This particular point, that ideas cannot be copyrighted, often causes confusion. If someone has written an article, you cannot simply rephrase it or change some of the words and claim it as your own. You are, however, entitled to read an article, digest it, take the ideas from that article together with other sources and weave them into your own material without any copyright problems. In most instances common sense should provide the answer.

Illustration 5.9

Intellectual property laws can prevent access to knowledge and thereby hinder innovation

Let us examine the growing view that intellectual property laws may be hindering creativity and innovation. Let us take the field of copyright for example. In Shakespeare's time there was no protection for copyright at all. Today's copyright laws would have suffocated much Elizabethan creativity. The length of copyright – 50 years – seems excessive. The vast majority of income from books and music comes immediately after publication (with the exception of a tiny number of very successful artists). The key issue here of course is monopolisation. Monopolies can lead to higher prices and lower output, and the costs can be especially high when monopoly power is abused. What's more, the hoped-for benefit of enhanced innovation does not always materialise. Let us not forget the most important input into research is knowledge, and IP sometimes makes this less accessible. This is especially true when patents take what was previously in the public domain and 'privatise' it. The patents granted on Basmati rice and on the healing properties of turmeric are good examples. Furthermore, as Stiglitz argues (2006) 'conflicting patent claims make profitable innovation more difficult. Indeed, a century ago, a conflict over patents between the Wright brothers and rival aviation pioneer Glenn Curtis so stifled the development of the airplane that the US government had to step in to resolve the issue'.

Patents are not the only way of stimulating innovation. For example, the Royal Society of Arts has long advocated the use of prizes. The alternative of awarding prizes would be more efficient and more equitable. It would provide strong incentives for research, but without the inefficiencies associated with monopolisation.

Source: Trott, P. and Hoecht, A. (2010) How should firms deal with counterfeiting: A review of the success conditions of anti-counterfeiting strategies, Internal Report, University of Portsmouth Business School, No. 12. Reprinted with permission. Stiglitz, J.E. (2006) Innovation: A better way than patents, *New Scientist*, Sept., p. 20.

Copyright is recognised by the symbol © and gives legal rights to creators of certain kinds of material, so that they can control the various ways in which their work may be exploited. Copyright protection is automatic and there is no registration or other formality.

Copyright may subsist in any of nine descriptions of work and these are grouped into three categories:

1 original literary, dramatic, musical and artistic works;
2 sound recordings, films, broadcasts and cable programmes; and
3 the typographical arrangement or layout of a published edition.

Each of these categories has more detailed definitions. For example, films in category 2 include videograms; and 'artistic work' in category 1 includes photographs and computer-generated work.

The duration of copyright protection varies according to the description of the work. In the United Kingdom for literary, dramatic, musical and artistic works copyright expires 70 years after the death of the author, in other cases 50 years after the calendar year in which it was first published. The period was for 75 years in the United States (but is now 50 years for all works created after 1978), but this issue is currently causing a great deal of concern for one of the most well-known organisations in the world (*see* Illustration 5.10).

Illustration 5.10

Mickey Mouse is now past 75 and was to be out of copyright

This issue of copyright is currently causing great concern for one of the most famous organisations in the world and certainly the most famous cartoon character. In the USA copyright lasts for 75 years (for creations prior to 1978) and Mickey Mouse in 2003 was 75 years old. At this point, the first Mickey Mouse cartoon was to be publicly available for use by anyone. *Plane Crazy* was released in May 1928 and was to slip from the Disney empire in 2003. In the autumn of 1928 Disney released *Steam Boat Willie*, the world's first synchronised talking cartoon and soon after Disney copyrighted the film.

At first glimpse one may be tempted to have some sympathy for the Disney organisation. However, Walt Disney wisely registered Mickey Mouse as a trademark, recognising from an early date that Mickey Mouse had value far beyond the screen. Hence, the use by others of the character on numerous products produces large licensing revenues for the Disney Corporation.

Source: Corbis/Condé Nast Archive

The Disney Corporation managed to secure a twenty-year extension from Congress under the 1998 Copyright law.

Source: James Langton, *Sunday Telegraph*, 15 February 1998; *Financial Times*, 10 January 2002.

Remedy against infringement

There are some forms of infringement of a commercial nature such as dealing with infringing copies that carry criminal penalties. Indeed, HM Customs have powers to seize infringing printed material. Also a civil action can be brought by the plaintiff for one or more of the following:

- damages;
- injunction; and
- accounts.

Damages

The owner of the copyright can bring a civil case and ask the court for damages, which can be expected to be calculated on the basis of compensation for the actual loss suffered.

Injunction

An injunction is an order of the court which prohibits a person making infringing copies of a work of copyright.

Accounts

This is a useful alternative for the plaintiff in that it enables access to the profits made from the infringement of copyright. This is useful especially if the amount is likely to exceed that which might be expected from an award of damages.

Counterfeit goods and IP

The production and sale of counterfeit products is big business in the international economy. The value of counterfeit products marketed annually in the world is estimated to be over $1 trillion. Counterfeiters are serving a market as willing to buy their illicit wares as they are to sell them. Nowhere is this more evident than in China (Hung, 2003; Naim, 2005). The massive expansion of the Chinese economy has led to a huge increase in foreign direct investment (FDI) and international technology transfer (ITT) and has brought the issue of intellectual property to the fore. The extent of product counterfeiting operations in China is astounding; estimates range from 10 per cent to 20 per cent of all consumer goods manufactured in the country. The Quality Brands Protection Committee (QBPC), for example, an anti-piracy body under the auspices of the China Association of Enterprises with Foreign Investment, claims that government statistics show that counterfeit products outnumber genuine products in the Chinese market by 2:1. Indeed, in a review of the intellectual property system in China, Yang and Clarke (2004) concluded that the emerging IP system requires improvements in legislation, administration and enforcement, in order to create a secure IP environment in line with the international standard. Enforcement efforts are made even more futile by popular acceptance of piracy in China. Rising incomes have created an enthusiasm for foreign goods and brands, but Chinese consumers have become so accustomed to cheap, pirated goods that they are unwilling to pay full prices for the real thing. It almost seems like imitation in modern China is a way of life.

Many argue that authentic manufacturers have contributed to the problem of counterfeiting due to their unyielding self-interest of pursuing lowest possible manufacturing cost (McDonald and Roberts, 1994; Tom *et al.*, 1998). Even in the face of increased counterfeiting these firms have continued to seek production opportunities in developing countries where counterfeiting is a known problem. It may be that given the short-term gains of lower production costs, firms may be either lacking in risk management or even willing to risk the loss of intellectual property with its potential long-term damage of loss of competitive advantage for the sake of short-term gains. If this is the case then the risk of losing intellectual property is the cost of doing business in China (Naim, 2005).

Furthermore, the effectiveness of the current approaches towards counterfeiting is questionable. Indeed, in fast moving technology intensive industries legal remedies tend to be too slow and too costly for regulating complex technological developments and their associated intellectual property and ownership rights (Deakin and Wilkinson, 1998; Liebeskind and Oliver, 1998). Furthermore, Thurow has argued that the whole approach to the defence of the intellectual property rights is simplistic because it applies the same rule to all types of products in all types of industries. He argues that, for example, the 'Third World's need to get low-cost pharmaceuticals is not equivalent to its need for low-cost CDs. Any system that treats such needs equally, as our current system does, is neither a good nor a viable system' (Thurow, 1997: 99; Vaidhyanathan, 2001). This view is shared by other economists (e.g. Sachs, 1999). Moreover, we should acknowledge that society seems content with a system that only provides protection for rich owners. It was more than 25 years ago that the Advisory Council for Applied Research and Development (ACARD, 1980) in the United Kingdom noted that if society wanted to treat intellectual property like tangible property, the state would prosecute alleged offenders at public expense. Since this time little has changed and it remains that if intellectual property is stolen, responsibility generally rests with the owner to prosecute.*

Pause for thought

Who owns the copyright on your essays that you write? What can you do if you find sections of one of your essays in a newspaper or in a book?

Case study

Pricing, patents and profits in the pharmaceutical industry

This case study explains how the pharmaceutical industry uses the patent system to ensure it reaps rewards from the drugs that it develops. Increasingly, however, there is alarm at the high costs of these drugs to the underdeveloped world, especially against a backcloth of the AIDS epidemic in Southern Africa. While the pharmaceutical industry has responded with several concessions, the case against the industry is that it enjoys a privileged position partly due to the patent system.

Introduction

There is a story about a pharmaceutical executive on a tour of the US National Mint who inquired how much it cost to produce each dollar bill. On hearing the answer, the man smiled. Making pills, it seemed, was even more profitable than printing money. Whether true or not, the three most profitable businesses in the world are reputed to be narcotics, prostitution and ethical pharmaceuticals. A recent Oxfam report showing the scale of the AIDS problem in Southern Africa has brought the pharma companies into the spotlight. The allegation is that these companies exploit the poor in the developing world. With a median 35 per cent return on equity, pharmaceuticals is far and away the world's most profitable major industry. With profits of more than $6 billion, pharma companies such as Pfizer and GlaxoSmithKline dwarf the likes of Unilever, BT or

→

*UK IP law does contain some criminal provisions (e.g. S 92 TM Act 1994, and S 107 Copyright Patents and Designs Act 1988). Some European countries have criminal provisions relating to patent infringement as well, though that is less common. Nonetheless, the target of criminal law relating to IP is usually deliberate counterfeiters rather than inadvertent infringers or those who might legitimately argue they are not infringing. See the *National Intellectual Property (IP) Enforcement Report* (2005), 1–139.

Coca-Cola. Yet every year in the developing world millions of people die from diseases, such as malaria and tuberculosis, which the rich developed world has eradicated. Table 5.4 shows the scale of the problem.

In the past the pharmaceutical industry has maintained that many of the drugs that could benefit the suffering in the underdeveloped world are expensive and have taken years to research and develop. The only way the pharmaceutical industry can claw back its expenditure on research and development is by patenting their drugs, thereby providing them with a 20-year monopoly in which to generate sales and profits. The social contract underlying the patents system is based on an agreement that in return for such investment – and for publishing through patents the details of the research results – a company is entitled to an exclusive right to the sale of the resulting product for a limited period of time: 20 years.

The case against the pharmaceutical industry

Most drug prices bear no relation to the very small cost of production because the industry has a contract with society, enshrined in the patent system. For a limited period (usually 10 years not allowing for clinical trials, etc.) pharmaceutical companies charge monopoly prices for patented medicines. In return, they invest huge amounts of research dollars in pursuit of the next innovation.

At a time when the AIDS epidemic appears to have stabilised in most advanced countries, thanks largely to the use of sophisticated drugs, the disease is continuing to spread at an ever more alarming rate through developing countries (*see* Table 5.4).

Yet those countries now suffering the most from the disease are also those least able to afford the drugs necessary to control it. The issue, of course, challenges the whole patenting system.

It is not just the underdeveloped countries that are experiencing difficulties with intellectual property laws and medicine. A 30-year-old London woman contacted Bristol-Myers Squibb, a US pharmaceutical company, begging help to obtain Taxol. This drug could have controlled her breast cancer, but her National Health Service region did not prescribe it because of its exorbitant cost. There is no patent on Taxol as the US government discovered it. But Bristol-Myers Squibb, because it performed minor work calculating dosage levels, holds the intellectual property rights on dose-related data, even though the data was originally collected by the government. Ultimately, the company was shamed into offering her free medicine if she moved to the United States. However, doctors concluded that the offer was probably too late.

Table 5.4 The scale of the AIDS epidemic in Southern Africa (% of adult population infected)

Botswana	35.8
Lesotho	23.5
Malawi	15.9
Mozambique	13.2
Namibia	19.5
South Africa	9.9
Swaziland	25.2
Tanzania	8.9
Zambia	19.9
Zimbabwe	25.6

Source: UNAIDS (2000). Reproduced by kind permission of UNAIDS, www.UNAIDS.org.

> *In AIDS and breast cancer, the stricken North and South share a horrific commonality as the new landless peasantry in the apartheid of intellectual property rights.* (*Guardian*, 27 July 2000)

The developing countries are demanding changes. They argue that patent laws should be relaxed, allowing, for example, either for their own companies to produce cheaper generic versions of the expensive anti-AIDS drugs, or for the import of such generic copies from other countries. In February 2001 the Indian company Cipla offered to make a combination of AIDS drugs available at about one-third of the price being asked by companies in developing countries. This price is already less than those in the West. If ever there was a good example of profiteering here it is. Worst of all, it seems to be profiteering at the expense of the poor. The charge of unethical behaviour seems to be ringing loudly. But for how long will the legal systems and courts in the world tolerate thousands of deaths before one of them decides enough is enough? The pharmaceutical industry is aware of the strength of public opinion and the mounting pressure it is under and has made significant concessions, including cutting the price of many of its drugs to the developing world. Will this, however, be enough? The whole industry, it seems, is now under pressure to justify the prices it charges for its drugs. If it fails to convince governments, it may see the introduction of legislation and price controls.

The case for the pharmaceutical industry

The pharmaceutical industry can claim that it has been responsible for helping to rid many parts of the world of dreadful diseases. It is able to claim that the enormous sums of money that it spends each year on research and development is only possible because of the patent system. Any change in the system will put at risk the billions of dollars that are spent on research into heart disease, cancer and other killers. This is usually enough for most governments and others to back away from this very powerful industry. Not surprisingly, the drugs industry is appalled at the prospect of price controls. Sidney Taurel, chief executive of the US drugs company Eli-Lilly, has warned, 'If we kill free markets around the world, we'll kill innovation.'

The industry clearly has a unique structure and differs markedly from many others, but whether there is evidence for supra-normal profits is questionable. Professor Sachs, director of the Center for International Development at Harvard University, argues that if price controls were introduced, companies would simply scale back their investments in research. This is often seen by many as a 'threat' that the industry uses against governments. Once again there is limited evidence to suggest this would necessarily happen. Sachs suggests, 'This is an extremely sophisticated, high cost, risky business with very long lead-in times and an extremely high regulatory hurdle', he says. 'My sense is that every rich country that has said, "You're making too much money" and has tried to control prices has lost the R&D edge.'

The pharmaceutical industry has a powerful voice. It is a large employer, invests large sums of money in science and technology and is without doubt an industry that will grow in this century. Most governments would like to have a thriving pharmaceutical industry and hence try to help and not hinder their efforts. Moreover, there are thousands of people in the developed world whose lives are being saved and extended by new sophisticated drugs that are being developed every month. The industry has many advocates and supporters.

Price cuts

In June 2001 Britain's biggest drugs company, GlaxoSmithKline, reduced the cost to the developing world of drugs for treating malaria, diarrhoea and infectious diseases. Merck and Bristol-Myers Squibb, two of the world's largest drugs companies, had already announced earlier in the year that they were supplying AIDS drugs at cost price or less to all developing countries. Bristol-Myers Squibb also announced that it would not be enforcing its patent rights in Southern Africa.

The field of pricing pharmaceutical products is complicated because in most countries prices are determined by what governments, the main buyers in the industry, are prepared to pay. The same pill made by the same company may cost half in Canada of what it does in the United States. In Mexico, it may cost still less. Such differential pricing is fundamental to the pharmaceutical industry. Because consumers are not paying for raw materials, but rather for intellectual property, drug companies charge what they can get away with and governments pay what they deem affordable. The United States, however, is the exception, as here prices are determined on the open market. However, it seems things are about to change, for the US upper house, the Senate, has challenged the existing market arrangements. It argues that US citizens should not be paying substantially more for patented drugs, while citizens in other countries get the same drugs at much lower prices because their government is only willing to pay a certain price. The Senate's amendment would allow drugs to be imported from any foreign factory approved by the Food and Drug Administration. As there are plenty of those in India and China, Senators are effectively demanding that US citizens get medicine at developing world prices. Clearly, social and economic pressures are mounting on the industry. In December 2003 the National Health Service (NHS) in the United Kingdom launched a £30 million lawsuit, which accuses seven firms of price-fixing by controlling and manipulating the market in penicillin-based antibiotics (Meikle, 2003).

Conclusions

It is the unique structure of the industry and the patent system that is at the crux of the problem. Europe, the United States and Japan account for virtually all the profits of the pharmaceutical companies.

→

In most other markets profits are driven down by the power and price sensitivity of customers. But in pharmaceuticals, neither the patient who consumes the drugs nor the doctor who prescribes them is price sensitive. Customers for medicines are not price sensitive because they do not pay for them. In Europe it is the taxpayer who foots the bill.

Whereas most companies have profits capped by aggressive industry buyers, the pharmaceutical firms have to negotiate only with civil servants, and, argues Professor Doyle, 'when taxpayers' money is available, commercial disciplines frequently disappear' (Doyle, 2001). But, even in the United States where a free market exists, the pharmaceutical companies are able to charge even higher prices, hence the US Senate's proposed changes. Once again this is because the pharmaceutical companies are frequently selling to private health insurers. Many US employers offer health insurance as part of the employment package.

Competition is another key force that drives down prices in most industries. In electronics – an industry even more innovative than pharmaceuticals – excess profits from a new product soon disappear as competitors bring out copies. But, in the pharmaceutical business, it is the patent system that ensures high profits continue for an average of 10 years. The consequence of this ability to negotiate very high prices and the absence of competitive threat is that the giant pharmaceuticals have no incentive to compete on price. It also helps to explain why the pharma companies have been unwilling to sell cheap medicines to the poor in Africa and Asia. The real worry is that dropping prices to the developing world would undermine the enormous margins being received in Europe and the United States. Buyers would soon be reimporting medicines at a fraction of the official price, which may be the case soon in the United States.

The industry's justification for its high prices and patent monopolies is that it encourages innovation, but to what extent is this true? In most other industries it is intense competition and a fight to survive and win market share that drives forward innovation. Without new and better products companies such as Hewlett-Packard and Canon know they will not maintain growth and market share. As we have seen in Chapters 1, 2 and 3, innovation is dependent on a collection of factors and the patent system alone cannot stimulate innovation. It is necessary but not sufficient.

The industry's most popular argument to defend the patent system is that it has unusually high cost structures due to the enormous sums of money it has to invest in science and technology. Increasingly, however, the industry is spending more on marketing existing products than it is on developing new ones. Professor Doyle argues that marketing costs are now typically almost double the R&D spend. GlaxoSmithKline, for example, has 10,000 scientists but 40,000 salespeople! Even this well-rehearsed argument is now beginning to sound hollow.

The pharmaceutical industry has enjoyed 50 years of substantial growth and substantial profits and many people have benefited. The patent system is intended to balance the interests of the individual and society; increasing numbers of people are questioning this balance. The pharmaceutical companies need to consider every step carefully for they surely do not want to become the unacceptable face of globalisation.

Sources: Doyle, P. (2001) AIDS and the pharmaceutical industry, *Guardian*, 10 March; Meikle, J. (2003) NHS seeks £30m from drug firms in price fixing claim, *Guardian*, 23 December, 6.

Questions

1 Explain how the pricing of drugs contributes to the acquisition of supra-normal profits in the pharmaceutical industry.

2 It is because drugs are absolutely essential to life that the pharmaceutical industry is able to justify large profits. Discuss the merits of this argument. Consider also that bread and milk companies do not make huge profits.

3 Explain why drugs are not price-sensitive.

4 Explain why the patent system may not be working as originally intended.

5 Use CIM (Figure 1.9) to illustrate the innovation process in this case.

6 Nobe Prize winning economist Joseph Stiglitz argues that prizes rather than patents could stimulate scientific competition. Explain how this might work.

Chapter summary

This chapter has explored the area of intellectual property and the different forms of protection available to a firm. This is a dynamic area of business. The operation of trademark law throughout the European Union is now controversial, as is the area of patents. It seems that the pharmaceutical industry is preparing itself for significant changes. This chapter also made it clear that the patent system has fierce critics, largely due to the associated costs involved with defending a patent against infringement. The patent system, however, was also highlighted as a valuable source of technological knowledge that is used by many companies.

Discussion questions

1. Explain why many research organisations are against the patenting of life forms.
2. Explain why theft of intellectual property should be a crime.
3. Explain why discoveries are not patentable.
4. Discuss some of the limitations of the patent system.
5. Is the pharmaceutical industry the unacceptable face of globalisation (consider the anti-capitalist demonstrations of recent years)?
6. Discuss why Lego wanted to trademark its block.
7. Explain, with the use of examples, when it would be appropriate to use trademarks and copyright to protect a firm's intellectual property.

Key words and phrases

Grey market *156*
Patent *157*
Copyright *157*
Registered design *157*
Patent extension *169*
Brand name *176*
Trademark *176*
Brands as intellectual property *177*
Generic products *178*
Infringement of intellectual property *183*

References

ACARD (1980) *Exploiting Invention*, report to the Prime Minister, London, December.

Alpert, F. (1993) Breadth of coverage for intellectual property law: encouraging product innovation by broadening protection, *Journal of Product and Brand Management*, Vol. 2, No. 2, 5–17.

Arundel, A. (2001) The Relative Effectiveness of Patents and Secrecy for Appropriation, *Research Policy*, Vol. 30, 611–24.

Badenhausen, K. (1995) Brands: the management factor, *Financial World*, 1 August, 50–69.

Bainbridge, D.I. (1996) *Intellectual Property*, 3rd edn, Financial Times Pitman Publishing, London.

Blind, K., Cremers, K. and Mueller, E. (2009) The influence of strategic patenting on companies' patent portfolios, *Research Policy*, Vol. 38, No. 2, 428–36.

Bowe, C. and Griffith, V. (2002) Proposal on patents set to hit revenues, *Financial Times*, 22 October.

Brown, A. (2007) Beware the backwards-looking patents that can stifle innovation, *Guardian*, 1 March, www.guardian.co.uk/technology.

BTG (2004) About patents, www.BTGPLC/info/patents.

Chemistry & Industry News (1995) ci.mond.org/9521/952107.html.

Cohen, W.M., Nelson, R.R. and Walsh, J.P. (2000) *Protecting their Intellectual Assets: Appropriability Conditions and Why U.S. Manufacturing Firms Patent (or not)*, Working Paper 7552, Cambridge National Bureau of Economic Research (available at www.nber.org/papers/w7552).

Court of Appeal (1985) Reports of Patent, Design and Trade Mark Cases (RPC), No. 59.

Deakin, S. and Wilkinson, F. (1998) 'Contract law and the earning of inter-organisational trust', in Lane, C. and Bachmann, R. (eds) *Trust within and between organisations: Conceptual issues and empirical applications*, Oxford University Press, Oxford, 146–72.

Derwent (1998) Derwent World Patents Index, Derwent Scientific and Patent Information: www.Derwent.com.

European Federal Trade Commission (2006). See European Union (2006).

European Union (2006) *European Innovation Scoreboard: Comparative analysis of innovation performance*, Brussels, retrieved 3 February 2007 from European Union website: www.proinno-europe.eu/doc/EIS2006_final.pdf.

Farrell, S. (2010) Just another brick in the wall: Lego's bid to trademark blocks fails in court, *Daily Telegraph*, Business Section, 15 September, 2.

Feldwick, P. (1996) Do we really need brand equity?, *Journal of Brand Management*, Vol. 4, No. 1, 9–28.

Financial Times (1997) Gene is out of the bottle, 30 October, 15.

Grindley, P.C. and Teece, D.J. (1997) Managing Intellectual Capital: Licensing and Cross-Licensing in Semiconductors and Electronics, *California Management Review*, Vol. 39, No. 2, 1–34.

Guardian (1998) Keep your ideas to yourself, 17 February, 22.

Guardian (2000) Patenting life, 15 November, 4.

Hall, B.H. (2005) Exploring the Patent Explosion, *Journal of Technology Transfer*, Vol. 30, No. 1, 35–48.

Hall, B.H. and Ham Ziedonis, R. (2001) The Patent Paradox Revisited: An Emperical Study of Patenting in the U.S. Semiconductor Industry, 1979–1995, *RAND Journal of Economics*, Vol. 32, No. 1, 101–28.

Hall, B.H. and Ham Ziedonis, R. (2007) An Empirical Analysis of Patent Litigation in the Semiconductor Industry. Paper presented at the American Economic Association.

Hu, A.G. (2010) Propensity to patent, competition and China's foreign patenting surge, *Research Policy*, Vol. 39, No. 7, 985–93.

Hung, C.L. (2003) The business of product counterfeiting in China and the post-WTO membership environment, *Asia Pacific Business Review*, Vol. 10, No. 1, 58–77.

Leiponen, A. and Byma, J. (2009) If you cannot block, you better run: Small firms, cooperative innovation, and appropriation strategies, *Research Policy*, Vol. 38, No. 9, 1478–88.

Liebeskind, J. and Oliver, A. (1998) 'From handshake to contract: intellectual property, trust and the social structure of academic research', in Lane, C. and Bachmann, R. (eds) *Trust within and between organisations: Conceptual issues and empirical applications*, Oxford University Press, Oxford, 118–45.

McDonald, G.M. and Roberts, C. (1994) Product piracy: The problem will not go away, *Journal of Product & Brand Management*, Vol. 3, No. 4, 55–65.

Naim, M. (2005) *Illicit*, William Heinemann, London.

Nakamoto, M. and Pilling, D. (2004) Tough tasks ahead at Takeda, *Financial Times*, 23 August.

National Intellectual Property Enforcement Report (2005) The Patent Office, London (www.ipo.gov.uk).

Rowan, D. (1997) Signing up to a patent on life, *Guardian*, 27 November, 19.

Sachs, J. (1999) Helping the world's poorest, *The Economist*, 14 August, 16–22.

Thurow, L.C. (1997) Needed: A new system of intellectual property rights, *Harvard Business Review*, Vol. 75, 95–103.

Tom, G., Garibaldi, B., Zeng, Y. and Pilcher, J. (1998) Consumer demand for counterfeit goods, *Psychology and Marketing*, Vol. 15, No. 5, 405–21.

Vaidhyanathan, S. (2001) *Copyrights and Copywrongs*, New York University Press, New York.

Waldmeir, P. (2002) If technology switches to the side of copyright, *Financial Times*, 10 January, 15.

Yang, D. and Clarke, P. (2004) Review of the current intellectual property system in China, *International Journal of Technology Transfer and Commercialisation*, Vol. 3, No. 1, 12–37.

Further reading

For a more detailed review of the intellectual property literature, the following develop many of the issues raised in this chapter:

Borg, E.A. (2001) Knowledge, information and intellectual property: implications for marketing relationships, *Technovation*, Vol. 21, 515–24.

The Economist (2000) The knowledge monopolies: patent wars, 8 April, 95–9.

HSBC (2010) 100 Thoughts, HSBC, London.

Naim, M. (2005) *Illicit*, William Heinemann, London.

Part Two
Turning technology into business

New technologies are transforming markets, businesses and society at an ever-increasing rate. Businesses need somehow to manage their way through this new terrain. Given that virtually all firms are established to generate funds for their owners, one of the fundamental issues for them to address is how to transform technology into profits. In this second part of the book we turn our attention to this key issue in innovation: knowledge and technology. Chapter 6 looks at how firms accumulate knowledge and utilise this to develop business opportunities. It is these opportunities that are at the heart of new product ideas. To profit from these technologies, however, firms need to offer products that are a lower price or different from their competitors; for long-term success they need to ensure what they offer is not easily copied by others.

A firm's capabilities lie not just within but also outwith the linkages and networks that it has established over time – Chapter 7 examines the subject of strategic alliances. It is not only large international companies that are using alliances to develop products and technology; small innovative companies also recognise the potential benefits of working with others.

Chapter 8 examines how companies manage research and development (R&D). It details the main activities performed by R&D departments and how these can influence the development of new products. Chapter 9 explores the challenges faced by R&D managers as they wrestle with project selection and evaluation. Important questions are raised concerning when to stop pouring money into struggling research projects. The extent to which a company can acquire technology developed outside the organisation via technology transfer is studied in Chapter 10.

Chapter 6
Managing organisational knowledge

Introduction

The ability of firms to identify technological opportunities and exploit them is one of the most fundamental features that determines successful from unsuccessful firms. But technology by itself will not lead to success. Firms must be able to convert intellect, knowledge and technology into things that customers want. The ability to use its assets to perform value-creating activities can lead to the development of firm-specific competencies. These competencies provide firms with the ability to generate profits from their technology assets. This chapter examines the role of competencies and how these determine the innovative potential of firms.

The case study at the end of this chapter explores how the cork industry is responding to the challenge from synthetic plastic closures in the wine industry. It seems the cork industry had not recognised the significant changes taking place in the wine industry to which it acts as a supplier.

Chapter contents

Learning objectives

When you have completed this chapter you will be able to:

- explain the significance of technology trajectories for firms investing in technology;
- recognise the importance of firm-specific competencies in generating long-term profits;
- provide an understanding of the role of an organisation's knowledge base in determining innovative capability;
- provide an understanding of the concept of the learning organisation;
- recognise the importance of technical and commercial capabilities in innovation management; and
- recognise a variety of different innovation strategies.

The battle of Trafalgar

The battle of Trafalgar in 1805 may not seem like an appropriate place to begin the study of strategy and technological innovation. It does, however, provide an interesting historical example of how strategy (in this case military strategy) is often linked to new technological developments.

Source: Mary Evans Picture Library

The battle of Trafalger in 1805 was influenced by technology.

For those who are unable to recall their eighteenth- and nineteenth-century maritime history, Nelson defeated the French and Spanish fleets in the Battle of Trafalgar. Today Nelson's ship, HMS *Victory*, stands in a drydock in Portsmouth harbour (*see* p. 126). The battle was fought off the south-west coast of Spain and the sailing ships of the day were armed with cannons that used gunpowder to launch cannon balls at the enemy's ships, the aim being to hole the ship so that it would ultimately sink. Failure to achieve this would either result in being 'holed' oneself or being invaded by the enemy's crew if they were able to get alongside.

Nelson's fleet, while composed of fewer vessels, had a crucial strategic advantage. It possessed a simple but important piece of technology that, arguably, was instrumental in securing victory. The Spanish and French armadas were armed with cannons, but theirs were fired by lighting a short fuse that burned and then ignited the gunpowder. There were several limitations to this ignition process. First, the fuse would not always burn and, second, valuable time was being wasted while waiting for it to burn. Nelson's ships, on the other hand, had overcome this limitation through the development of a simple hammer-action ignition system that ignited the gunpowder. The firing process involved placing a cannon ball in the cannon and rolling it into position, with its nose poking through the aperture in the side of the ship. A cord would be pulled to trigger the hammer action and ignite the gunpowder, causing an explosion that would force the cannon ball out towards the target. Nelson's ships were able to load and fire several cannon balls while the enemy's fleet was waiting for fuses to burn.

Technology trajectories

The Battle of Trafalgar provides a useful illustration of the pivotal role of technology in competition. Nowhere is this more evident than in the world of business. Firms with superior technology have delivered spectacular financial rewards to their owners: Intel's microprocessors, Nokia's mobile telephones and Pfizer's Viagra to name only a few. But, as we have seen in Chapter 1, technology alone cannot deliver victory; technology, however, coupled with a market opportunity and the necessary organisational skills to deliver the product to the market will help significantly.

In Admiral Nelson's case the choice of where to deploy technological effort was far more limited than that open to firms today. Large firms and to a lesser extent small firms have a bewildering array of opportunities to exploit, especially when they have products operating in many markets across several industries. As one would expect, those given responsibility for charting the direction of the firm, the leaders, will have views on where the firm should be heading, but the technology capability of the firm frequently dictates what is possible and what can or cannot be achieved in a given time-frame. In other words, a firm's opportunities are constrained by its current position and current knowledge base, i.e. it is path-dependent. This introduces the notion of technological trajectories first put forward by Nelson and Winter (1982) and developed by Dosi (1982). For example, many firms may marvel at the huge profits generated by Pfizer from its Viagra drug, but few firms are in a position to develop a similar or superior product. Only those operating in the pharmaceutical industry will be in a position to respond and even then the possible entrants will be limited to those who have prior knowledge of the related fields of technology, determined by its range of research projects. Acquiring knowledge about technology takes time, involves people and experiments and requires learning. To exploit technological opportunities a firm needs to be on the 'technology escalator'. As we will see later in this chapter, firms cannot move easily from one path of knowledge and learning to another. According to David Teece and Gary Pisano (1994) the choices available to the firm in terms of future direction are dependent on its own capabilities, that is, the firm's level of technology, skills developed, intellectual property, managerial processes and its routines. Furthermore, they argue the choices made by any firm must take place in a changing environment, characterised by changing levels of technology, changing market conditions and changing societal demands. Teece and Pisano refer to this concept as the dynamic capabilities of firms.

Pause for thought

If technology trajectories are determined by a firm's past, how can it change trajectories and get on another one?

The acquisition of firm-specific knowledge

Arguing for knowledge and the need to acquire it is a bit like arguing for peace or education. Few can argue against such a laudable aim. But it is not any knowledge that is required, it is firm-specific knowledge; knowledge that is useful and applicable. Otherwise reading the telephone directory would constitute acquiring knowledge but this clearly has limited benefits. For example, 3M is often cited as having core competencies in coatings and adhesives, hence one would expect the firm to have a wide range of research projects related to these technologies. This then is the key: how do firms know what knowledge to acquire and when do they know when they have acquired it? This is clearly dependent on the firm's prior knowledge and introduces the notion of absorptive capacity. This refers to a firm's ability to acquire and utilise new knowledge. This notion is further explored in the chapters on R&D management and technology acquisition.

The resource-based perspective

The impact and influence of the development over the past 20 years of the resource-based perspective within strategic management has been considerable. This is not just in terms of philosophical management debate but also within the boardrooms of firms. For example, such questions as 'What are our key resources?' and 'How can we diversify using our core competencies?' are now not uncommon. This is a significant shift away from questions such as 'What is our corporate mission?' and 'What business are we in?' There has been a reorientation in the way firms consider strategic decision making from, to put it crudely, an external analysis of the environment and aligning the firm to it, to an internal analysis and aligning the firm's resources to the external environment. This later approach is referred to as a resource-based perspective (RBP). The perspective is dependent on two basic principles:

- There are differences between firms based upon the way they manage resources and how they exploit them (Nelson, 1991).
- These differences are relatively stable.

If the RBP is dependent on these two key principles then a key question arises, which is: how does one identify these differences that determine the success of a firm? It is the detail that is significant here. Here, by differences we mean strengths and it is around this concept of strengths that so much of the debate has taken place.

Strengths have been interpreted as resources, capabilities and competencies (Wernerfelt, 1984; Barney, 1991). Hamel and Prahalad (1990) developed the idea of core competence for a very specific type of resource. Indeed, they developed three tests that they argue can be used to identify core competencies, namely 'customer value', 'competitor differentiation' and 'extendibility' (Hamel and Prahalad, 1994). Yet, despite the widespread acknowledgement of the salience of core competencies for acquiring and sustaining a competitive position, the notion of core competencies has remained largely amorphous (Onyeiwu, 2003).

It is Jay Barney (1991) that is considered by many to have made a significant contribution to the debate on the RBP when he argued that there can be heterogeneity of firm level differences among firms that allow some of them to sustain competitive advantage. He therefore emphasised strategic choice, where responsibility lies with the firm's management to identify, develop and deploy resources to maximise returns. He further proposed that above industry average rents can be earned from resources when they are: valuable, rare, imperfectly imitable and non-substitutable (so called VRIN attributes).

A key issue for debate within the literature has been over what form resources take. It is now widely accepted that resources include tangible ones such as patents, properties and proprietary technologies and intangible resources such as relationships and trust built up over time (Galbreath and Galvin, 2004). It is this wider interpretation of the concept of resources and in particular the recognition that resources include information, knowledge and skills that has further developed the concept of RBP.

Significantly, the idea that firms develop firm-specific routines as they conduct their business differentiated the concept of RBP from the more static 'SWOT' framework. Teece *et al.* (1997) put forward the idea that firms develop dynamic capabilities that are difficult to replicate and it is this that makes firms different. This seems to chime well with the ideas of the founding mother of the RBP: Edith Penrose (1959), who suggested that it is resources that enable firms to create services or flows.

Dynamic competence-based theory of the firm

The *dynamic competence-based theory of the firm* sees both the external and internal environments as dynamic: the external environment is constantly changing as different players manoeuvre themselves and a company's internal environment is also evolving. The management of this internal process of change together with an understanding of the changes in the external environment offers a more realistic explanation of the challenges facing senior management. In addition, firms are seen as different (Nelson, 1991) and hence compete on the basis of competencies and capabilities (Tushman and Anderson, 1986; Nelson and Winter, 1982; Hamel and Prahalad, 1990, 1994; Pavitt, 1990; Cohen and Levinthal, 1990; Seaton and Cordey-Hayes, 1993). This literature presents a related theoretical view that centres around an organisation's ability to develop specific capabilities. These capabilities tend to be dependent on the organisation's incremental and cumulative historical activities. In other words, a company's ability to compete in the future is dependent on its past activities. This view of an organisation's heritage is developed by Cohen and Levinthal (1990) in the context of the management of research and development. In their research, they developed the notion of 'absorptive capacity'.

In their study of the US manufacturing sector Cohen and Levinthal reconceptualise the traditional role of R&D investment, which was viewed simply as a factor aimed at creating specific innovations. They see R&D expenditure as an investment in an organisation's absorptive capacity. They argue that an organisation's ability to evaluate and utilise external knowledge is related to its *prior knowledge* and expertise and that this prior knowledge is, in turn, driven by prior R&D investment. Similarly, the notion of 'receptivity', advocated by Seaton and Cordey-Hayes (1993), is defined as an organisation's overall ability to be aware of, identify and take effective advantage of technology. This is explored in Trott and Cordey-Hayes (1996), who present a process model of receptivity showing the activities necessary for innovation to occur.

The issue of an organisation's capacity to acquire knowledge was also addressed by Nelson and Winter (1982) who emphasised the importance of 'innovative routines'.

A useful example of tacit knowledge is tying a shoelace. Virtually everyone knows how to tie a shoelace. However, it is extremely difficult to explain to someone in diagrams, words or speech how to perform this task. Hence, tacit knowledge may be described as knowledge that is acquired but difficult to explain to others.

Figure 6.1 Tacit knowledge

They argue that the practised routines that are built into the organisation define a set of competencies that the organisation is capable of doing confidently. These routines are referred to as an organisation's core capabilities. It is important to note that the notion of routines here does not necessarily imply a mechanistic, bureaucratic organisational form (*see* Chapter 3). The potential for controversy is resolved by Teece (1986), who distinguishes between 'static routines', which refer to the capability to replicate previously performed tasks, and 'dynamic routines', which enable a firm to develop new competencies. Indeed, dynamic organisational routines are very often those activities that are not easily identifiable and may be dominated by tacit knowledge (*see* Figure 6.1).

The point here is that over long periods organisations build up a body of knowledge and skills through experience and learning-by-doing. In addition to these internal organisational processes, Kay (1993) suggests that the *external linkages* that a company has developed over time and the investment in this network of relationships (generated from its past activities) form a distinctive competitive capability. Moreover, this can be transformed into competitive advantage when added to additional distinctive capabilities such as technological ability and marketing knowledge (Casper and Whitley, 2003).

Developing firm-specific competencies

The ability of firms to identify technological opportunities and exploit them is one of the most fundamental features that determines successful from unsuccessful firms. Increasingly economists are using the notion that firms possess discrete sets of capabilities or competencies as a way of explaining why firms are different and how firms change over time. During the 1990s the management literature changed its emphasis from trying to understand what firms must do to position themselves in the competitive environment to exploring what capabilities are required for survival and change. The most influential analysts in this later field are Gary Hamel and C.K. Prahalad (1994). Their ideas have been readily embraced by business leaders around the world. To summarise they are: that competitive advantage resides not in a firm's products but in their competencies. These are defined as knowledge, skills, management processes and routines acquired over time that are difficult to replicate

– this may be because they are constantly changing and updating them. Furthermore, they state that few companies are likely to develop world leadership in more than five or six fundamental competencies. The case study of Gore Inc. at the end of Chapter 3 illustrates how this firm has developed unparalleled knowledge and skills on the polymer polytetrafluoroethylene (PTFE). Indeed, this knowledge base has enabled the firm to develop a range of product applications for a variety of markets over 30 years. It is, however, not just physical technologies where firms can develop competencies. Tesco stores in the United Kingdom have developed a range of skills, know-how and routines in retailing and distribution with which their competitors find it difficult to compete. Furthermore, even after years of studying the Tesco approach competitors are struggling to replicate what it does. According to Hamel and Prahalad it is because firms are not readily able to replicate Tesco's activities that this would indicate that these competencies are at the core of the organisation's abilities, and are probably based on tacit knowledge and embedded routines. They use the metaphor of the tree to show the linkages between core competencies and end products. They suggest that a firm's core competencies are comparable to the roots of a tree, with the core products representing the trunk and business units smaller branches and final end products being flowers, leaves and fruit (*see* Figure 6.2). Technology in itself does not mean success; firms must be able to convert intellect, knowledge and technology into things that customers want. This ability is referred to as a firm's competencies: *the ability to use its assets to*

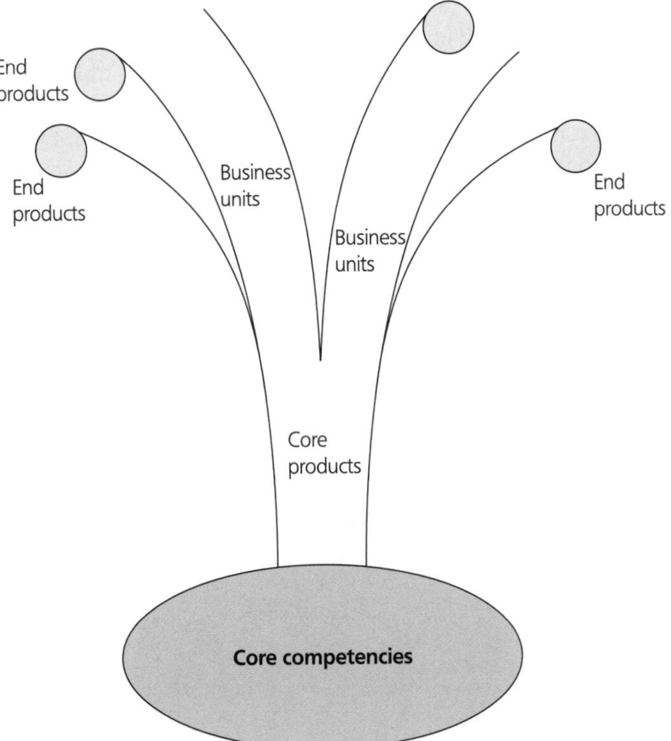

Figure 6.2 Core competencies

Source: Adapted from G. Hamel and C.K. Prahalad (1990) The core competence of the corporation, *Harvard Business Review*, May/June, 79–91.

perform value-creating activities. This frequently means integrating several assets such as: product technology and distribution; product technology and marketing effort; and distribution and marketing.

Competencies and profits

According to Hamel and Prahalad a firm's ability to generate profits from its technology assets depends on the level of protection it has over these assets and the extent to which firms are able to imitate these competencies. For example, are competencies at the periphery or the centre of a firm's long-term success? If they are at the centre and difficult for firms to imitate, then long-term profits are assured, e.g. Honda and its ability to produce performance engines. Over the past 50 years few firms have been able to imitate Honda's success in developing engines. The following are examples of other firms that have been cited as having core competencies that are difficult to replicate:

- Intel's ability to develop microprocessors that exploit its copyrighted microcode;
- Coca-Cola's ability to develop products that people are willing to pay a premium for;
- Honda's ability to produce high quality and performance engines; and
- 3M's ability to develop a wide range of products from coatings and adhesives.

These firms can be placed in the uppermost right-hand quadrant of the matrix in Figure 6.3. These firms have been able to generate long-term profits based on their core competencies and few firms have been able to imitate their activities. If a competence is non-core and imitability is high, then one may not be able to make profits from it, all else being equal. If it is non-core but imitable, the firm may be able to make some negligible profits from it. If, however, the competence is core but easily imitated, the firm can make profits, but these are likely to be temporary as competitors will soon imitate.

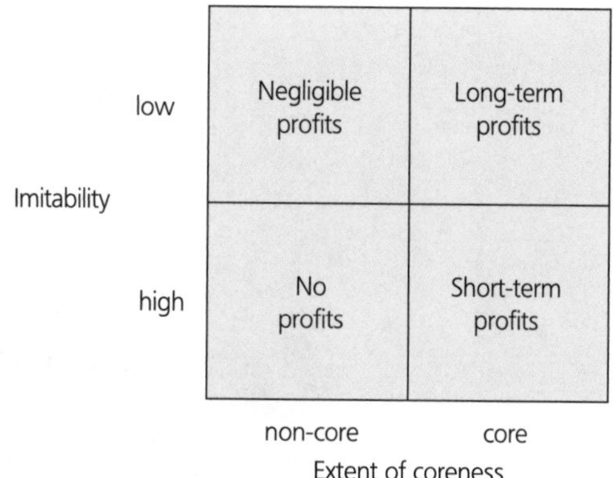

Figure 6.3 Core competencies, imitability and profits

Source: A. Afuah (2003) *Innovation Management: Strategies, Implementation and Profit*, p. 53, Fig. 3.5, Oxford University Press Inc., New York.

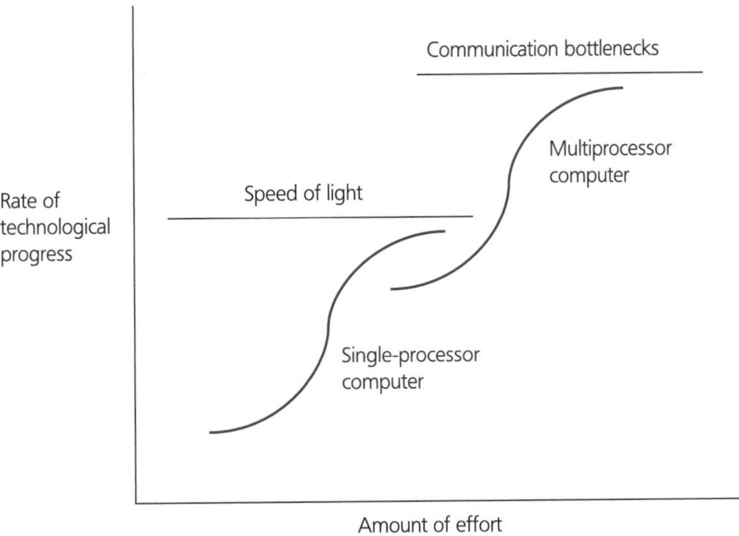

Figure 6.4 Technology life cycles and S-curves

Technology development and effort required

Foster (1986) and Abernathy and Utterback (1978) argue that the rate of technological advance is dependent on the amount of effort put into the development of the technology. As was pointed out in Chapter 1 with President Kennedy's pledge to get a man on the moon, if unlimited resources are made available, as in the Kennedy example, there may well be very few limits. Under normal circumstances, however, technological progress starts off slowly then increases rapidly and finally diminishes as the physical limits of the technology are approached. This is diagrammatically referred to as an S-curve. Slow progress at the start equates to a horizontal line, rapid progress as knowledge is acquired equates to a vertical line and slow progress towards the end equates to a horizontal line. It is usually at this point that a new technology replaces the existing one; indeed it is necessary if advances are to continue. Figure 6.4 illustrates the development of supercomputers.

Pause for thought 

Other than through the use of patents and copyright how can a firm prevent its competencies from being imitated?

The knowledge base of an organisation

Many organisations have shown sustained corporate success over many years. This does not only mean unbroken periods of growth or profit, but also combinations of growth and decline that together represent sustained development and advancement. Research by Pavitt *et al.* (1991: 82) on innovative success led them to remark:

> *Large innovating firms in the twentieth century have shown resilience and longevity, in spite of successive waves of radical innovations that have called into question their established skills and procedures . . . Such institutional continuity in the face of technological discontinuity cannot be explained simply by the rise and fall of either talented individual entrepreneurs or of groups with specific technical skills. The continuing ability to absorb and mobilise new skills and opportunities has to be explained in other terms.*

Pavitt *et al.* (1991) identifies a number of properties of innovative activities in large firms. He places a great deal of emphasis on the concept of firm-specific competencies that take time to develop and are costly to initiate. Key features of these competencies are the ability to convert technical competencies into effective innovation and the generation of effective *organisational learning*. The observations made earlier suggest a need to analyse organisational knowledge and the processes involved in realising that knowledge rather than analysing organisational structure. If we can uncover the internal processes that determine a company's response to a given technology, this may help to explain the longevity of large innovating companies.

But what is meant by organisational knowledge? One may be tempted to think that the collective talents and knowledge of all the individuals within an organisation would represent its knowledge base. It is certainly the case that one individual within an organisation, especially within a large organisation, rarely sees or fully understands how the entire organisation functions. Senior managers in many large corporations have frequently said, with some amusement, when addressing large gatherings that they do not understand how the organisation operates! The following quote is typical:

> *I am constantly being surprised as I travel around the many different parts of this organisation; while I know that we are in the car production business I am constantly amazed at the wide range of activities that we perform and how we do what we do. We regularly convert our raw materials of steel and many different component parts into fine automobiles, and then get them all over the world all within a matter of days. It's amazing and difficult to explain how we do it.*
>
> (Senior executive from a US car producer)

This statement highlights the notion that *an organisation itself can seem to have knowledge*. That is, no one individual, even those people charting the course of the company, actually fully understands how all the internal activities and processes come together and function collectively. This concept of the organisation retaining knowledge is developed by Willman (1991: 2), who argues that 'the organisation itself, rather than the individuals who pass through it, retains and generates innovative capacity, even though individuals may be identified who propagate learning'.

The whole can be more than the sum of the parts

It is important to recognise that the knowledge base of an organisation is not simply the sum of individuals' knowledge bases. If this were the case, and knowledge was only held at the individual level, then an organisation's expertise and acquired abilities would change simply by employee turnover. The wealth of experience built up by an organisation through its operations is clearly not lost when employees leave. The employment of new workers and the retirement of old workers does not equate to

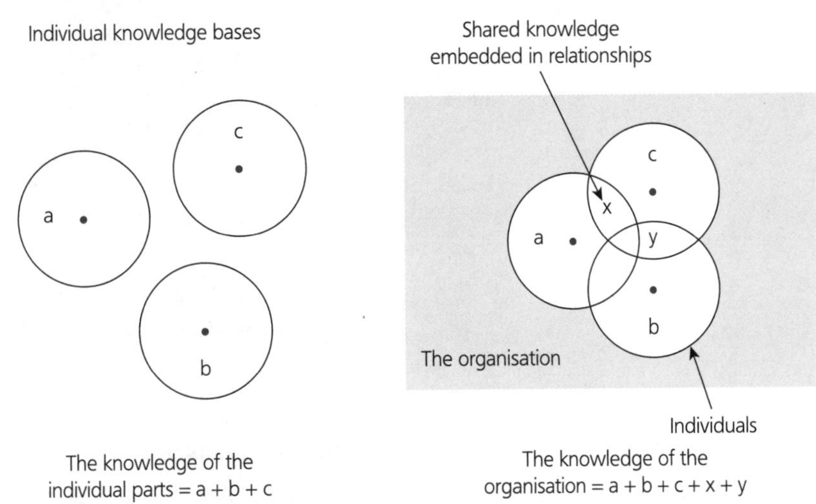

Figure 6.5 How the whole can be viewed as more than the sum of the parts

changing the skills of a firm. Figure 6.5 attempts to show how a collective knowledge base is larger than the sum of individual knowledge bases. (*See also* Illustration 6.1.)

Organisational heritage

Organisational knowledge is distinctive to the firm. That is, it is not widely available to other firms. Hence, the more descriptive term organisational heritage. It is true that technical knowledge, in the form of patents, or commercial knowledge, in the form of unique channels of distribution, although used by an organisation are available to other firms. However, organisational knowledge includes these and more. For example, a vehicle manufacturer may use a wide variety of technologies and patents. This knowledge will not necessarily be unique to the organisation, that is, other companies will be aware of this technology. But the development and manufacture of the vehicle will lead to the accumulation of skills and competencies that will be unique to the organisation. Hence, it is the individual ways in which the technology is applied that lead to organisation-specific knowledge.

To explore the above example further, groups or teams of people will develop specific skills required in the manufacture of a product. Over time, the knowledge, skills and processes will form part of the organisation's routines, which it is able to perform repeatedly. Individuals may leave the organisation and take their understanding to other organisations. But even if large groups of people leave, it is likely that understanding will have been shared with others in the organisation and it will have been recorded in designs or production planning records for use by others.

When the performance of the organisation is greater than the abilities of individuals

The notion of organisational knowledge was popularised by Kay (1993) who puts forward the idea of 'architecture' as a source of distinctive capability. This builds on

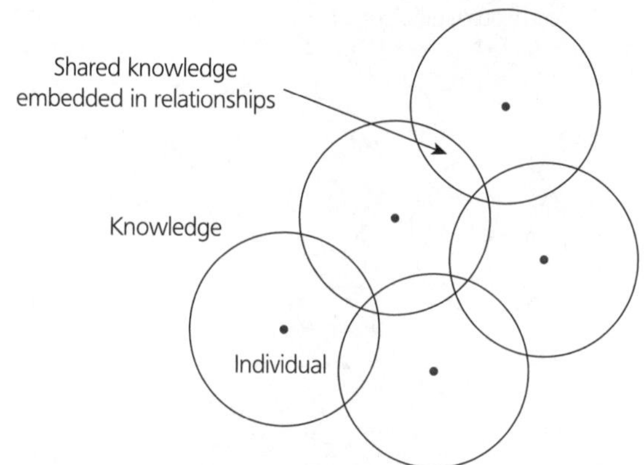

Figure 6.6 Knowledge embedded in relationships

the work of Nelson and Winter (1982), Dosi (1982), Pavitt (1990) and Hamel and Prahalad (1994) referred to earlier. The image of a football team is often used at this point to illustrate the argument that a team such as, say, Charlton Athletic in the English Premier League has recently consistently performed well, but also better than the combined abilities of its players would seem to allow. This can also be said of many industrial organisations that have been able to generate exceptional long-term success from relatively ordinary employees. This, argues Kay (1993), is the result of the organisation's architecture. Whatever label one chooses, it seems clear that a firm's organisational knowledge plays a significant role in its firm's ability to innovate and survive in the long term.

Organisational knowledge represents internal systems, routines, shared understanding and practices (*see* Figure 6.6). In the past it was loosely described as part of an organisation's culture, along with anything else that could not be fully explained. Organisational knowledge, however, represents a distinctive part of the much broader concept of organisational culture.

There are several tangible representations of this knowledge, such as minutes of meetings, research notebooks, databanks of customers, operating procedures, manufacturing quality control measures, as well as less tangible representations such as tried and tested ways of operating. Nelson and Winter (1982) argue that such learning-by-doing is captured in organisational routines. It is evident that the knowledge base of an organisation will be greater, in most cases, than the sum total of the individual knowledge bases within it. Willman (1991) argues that this is because knowledge is also embedded in social and organisational relationships (*see* Figure 6.6). At its simplest level, suggests Kay, organisational knowledge is where each employee knows one digit of the code which opens the safe; clearly, this information is only of value when combined in the correct sequence with the information held by all the others.

Japanese organisations and the role of organisational knowledge

It has been argued that Western managers fail to understand the nature and concept of organisational knowledge and consequently they are unable to manage it, let alone exploit it. This is because the traditions of Western management have become ingrained with writings and theories, from Frederick Taylor to Herbert Simon, which see the organisation as merely a machine to process information (Nonaka, 1991). According to this view, the only useful knowledge is formal and systematic: hard data and codified procedures. Similarly, the measurement of this knowledge is hard and quantifiable: increased efficiency, lower costs, improved return on investment, etc. Nonaka suggests that there is another way to consider organisational knowledge found most commonly in highly successful Japanese companies. He explains (p. 100):

> *The centre-piece of the Japanese approach is the recognition that creating knowledge is not simply a matter of processing objective information. Rather, it depends on tapping the tacit and often highly subjective insights, intuitions, and hunches of individual employees and making those insights available for testing and use by the company as a whole.*

The knowledge base of an organisation is defined in this view as 'the accumulation of the knowledge bases of all the individuals within an organisation *and* the social knowledge embedded in relationships between those individuals'. These relationships are often recognised as organisational processes and procedures (Kogut and Zander, 1992; Nonaka, 1991). The interactions and relationships between individuals may be said to represent a form of 'organisational cement' that performs two functions. First, it combines individual knowledge bases into a larger body of knowledge. Second, it enables individual knowledge bases to be accessed by the organisation, effectively via interaction with other individuals.

Characterising the knowledge base of the organisation

Discussions concerning the knowledge base of an organisation tend to focus on R&D activities and other technical activities. However, an organisation's ability to develop new products that meet current market needs, to manufacture these products using the appropriate methods and to respond promptly to technological developments, clearly involves more than technical capabilities. Nelson (1991) has argued that in industries where technological innovation is important firms need more than a set of core capabilities in R&D:

> *These capabilities will be defined and constrained by the skills, experience, and knowledge of the personnel in the R&D department, the nature of the extant teams and procedures for forming new ones, the character of the decision making processes, the links between R&D and production and marketing, etc.* (Nelson, 1991: 66)

The wide range of skills mentioned by Nelson implies that the commonly held view of an organisation's knowledge base comprising only technical matters is too narrow. This is supported by Adler and Shenhar (1990), who suggest that an organisation's knowledge base is made up of several dimensions. The following five dimensions can be considered (*see* Figure 6.7):

- *Individual assets* – the skills and knowledge of the individuals that form the organisation. It is the application of these that influences corporate success.
- *Technological assets* – the most immediately visible elements of the technological base, the set of reproducible capabilities in *product*, *process* and *support areas*. Technological assets can be more or less reliably reproduced; the other elements are, by contrast, fundamentally relational, which makes them much more difficult to replicate.

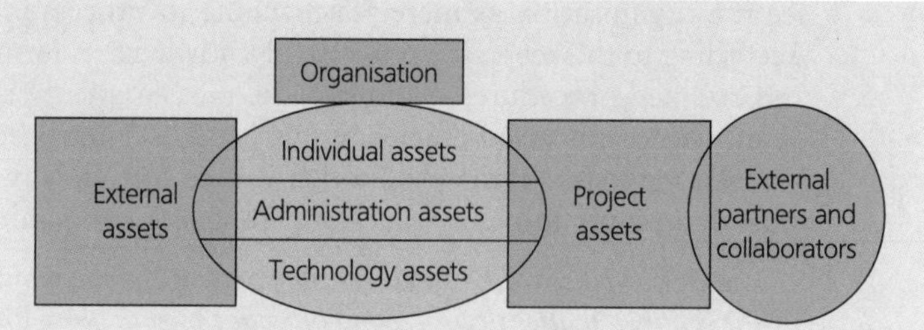

Figure 6.7 The knowledge base of an organisation

- *Administration assets* – the resources that enable the business to develop and deploy individual and technological assets. These are specifically the skill profile of employees and managers, the *routines*, *procedures* and *systems* for getting things done, the organisational structure, the strategies that guide action and the culture that shapes shared assumptions and values.
- *External assets* – the relations that the firm establishes with current and potential allies, rivals, suppliers, customers, political actors and local communities, e.g. joint ventures, distribution channels, etc.
- *Projects* – the means by which technological, organisational and external assets are both deployed and transformed. Projects should be considered as part of the knowledge base in so far as the organisation's *modus operandi* is a learned behavioural pattern that can contribute to or detract from technological and business performance.

Innovation in action

Go back to basics for boomers

Mobile phone makers seem locked in an arms-race trying to out do each other with more complex functions. But are they at risk of alienating a customer base who don't want all the bells and ring-tones – the massively lucrative baby boomer market?

'The mobile industry seemed to be losing touch with a huge number of customers', says David Inns, CEO of San Diego-based Jitterbug. 'There are people who don't want a giant chunk of functionality jammed into their mobile phones.'

Jitterbug aims to ring the changes with its new phone. It has a bigger and simpler keyboard, and industry-leading background noise reduction. When subscribers call customer service, they speak to an operator who helps them with tasks such as programming in contacts. Jitterbug also offers 24-hour roadside assistance and a Live Nurse function.

Launched in 2006 with 10 employees, Jitterbug now employs 335. 'It's a big market', Inns explains. 'You could easily say it's a little less than half of the boomers and then go from there.

Source: HSBC (2010) 100 Thoughts, HSBC, London.

This more realistic assessment of an organisation's knowledge base shows how the various components of an organisation are interrelated. The inclusion of external networks is an important point. The formal and informal links an organisation has developed, often over many years, are a valuable asset. Pennings and Harianto (1992) include history of technological networking within the organisational skills necessary for innovation. At this point one may argue that it would be more appropriate to consider an organisation's knowledge base rather than select individual parts for analysis, which may be compared to trying to establish a racing car's performance by only analysing the engine. There are clearly other factors that will also have a dramatic impact on the car's performance.

The suggestion that an organisation's knowledge base is also time-dependent, that the acquisition of knowledge takes place over many years, introduces the notion of organisational heritage, discussed above. If we accept the notion of organisational knowledge, this leads to the question of whether it is possible for organisations to learn.

The learning organisation

The concept of the learning organisation has received an unprecedented level of attention in the management literature. A special edition of *Organisational Science* was dedicated to the subject and it has received the attention of mainstream economics (Malbera, 1992). The emphasis of much of the early literature on this subject was on the history of the organisation, and the strong influence of an organisation's previous activities and learning on its future activities. That is, the future activities of an organisation are strongly influenced by its previous activities and what it has learned (Pavitt *et al.*, 1991; Dosi, 1982; Nelson and Winter, 1982; Tidd, 2000).

Unfortunately, the term organisational learning has been applied to so many different aspects of corporate management, from human resources management to technology management strategies, that it has become a particularly vague concept. At its heart, however, is the simple notion that successful companies have an ability to acquire knowledge and skills and apply these effectively, in much the same way as human beings learn. Arguably, companies that have been successful over a long period have clearly demonstrated a capacity to learn. Cynics have argued that this is just another management fad with a new label for what successful organisations have been doing for many years. However, according to Chris Argyris (1977), organisations can be extremely bad at learning. Indeed, he suggests that it is possible for organisations to lose the benefits of experience and revert to old habits. It is necessary to engage in double-loop rather than single-loop learning, argues Argyris, since the second loop reinforces understanding. At its most simple level, single-loop learning would be the adoption of a new set of rules to improve quality, productivity, etc. Double-loop learning occurs when those sets of rules are continually questioned, altered and updated in line with experience gained and the changing environment.

Innovation, competition and further innovation

Chapters 1, 2 and 3 illustrated how innovation occurs within the firm and indicated the important knowledge flows and linkages beyond the boundary of the firm. The launch of an innovative new product into the market, however, is usually only the beginning of technology progress. At the industry level, the introduction of a new technology will cause a reaction: competitors will respond to this new product, hence technological progress depends on factors other than those internal to the firm. We need to consider the role of competition. Product innovation, process innovation, competitive environment and organisational structure all interact and are closely linked together. Abernathy and Utterback (1978) argued there were three phases in an innovation's life cycle: fluid, transitional and specific (*see* Table 6.1). The first phase they call the *fluid phase*, where technological and market uncertainties prevail, and a large experimental game occurs in the marketplace. In this phase of uncertainty the manufacturing process relies on craftsmanship and highly skilled labour and general purpose equipment: there is almost no process innovation and the many, small firms competing will base their advantage on differentiated product features. Competition tends not to be as fierce as in later phases because companies have no clear idea about potential applications for the innovation, or in which direction the market might grow. There is low bargaining power from suppliers since no specialised materials are used in the production. The major threats come from the old technology itself and from new entrants if the innovation was radical and competence-destroying. Abbernathy and Utterback argued that frequently a firm will try to outmanoeuvre the competitors and establish its product as the 'dominant design' (something Apple Inc. achieved with the iPod, but failed to achieve with the Apple Mac), this strategy will involve agreements with distributors and marketing investments (such as brand development) to affect customers' perceptions. Alternatively the firm can try to take control of complementary assets and wait for the appearance of the dominate design; then once the standard becomes clear it will try to secure most of the profits basing its competitive advantage on distribution channels, supplier contracts, complementary technologies, value-added services, etc.

The passage of time sees further technological development as producers start to learn more about the technology application and about customers' needs, and

Table 6.1 Phases of innovation and technology development

Variable	Innovation phase		
	Fluid	**Battle for dominant design**	**Commoditisation**
Innovation	Product changes/radical innovations	Major process changes, architectural innovations	Incremental innovations, improvements in quality
Product	Many different designs, customisation	Less differentiation due to mass production	Heavy standardisation in product designs
Competitors	Many small firms, no direct competition	Many, but declining after the emergence of a dominant design	Few, classic oligopoly
Organisation	Entrepreneurial, organic structure	More formal structure with task groups	Traditional hierarchical organisation
Threats	Old technology, new entrants	Imitators and successful product breakthroughs	New technologies and firms bringing disrupting innovations
Process	Flexible and inefficient	More rigid, changes occur in large steps	Efficient, capital intensive and rigid

Source: Abernathy and Utterback (1978).

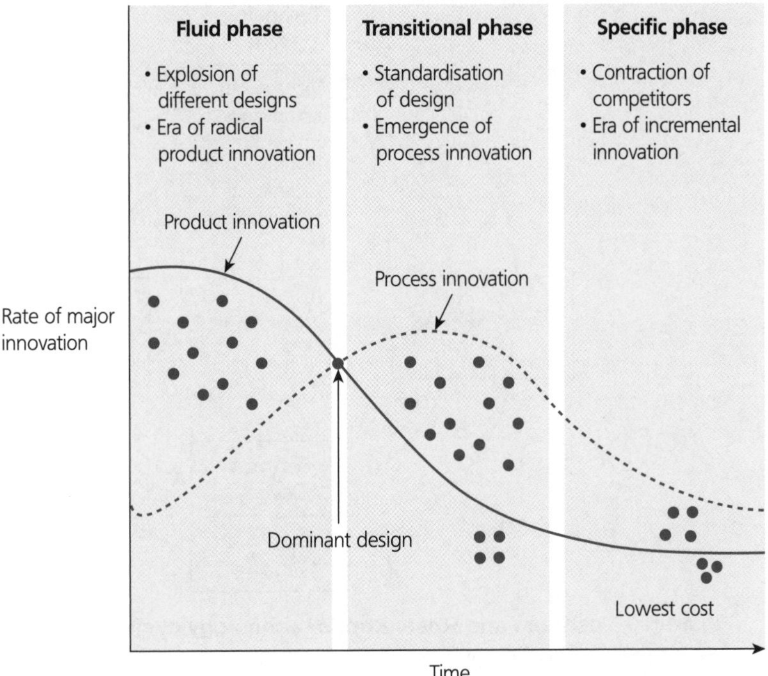

Figure 6.8 Abernathy and Utterback's three phases of innovation

Source: Utterback (1994).

some standardisation will emerge (this is when standards battles occur such as that for VCRs and computer operating systems). Usually by this time the acceptance of the innovation starts to increase and the market starts growing; these are signals that according to Abbernathy and Utterback mark the *transitional phase*. The convergence pattern in this phase will lead to the appearance of a dominant design, which 'has features to which competitors and innovators must adhere if they hope to command significant market share following' (Utterback, 1994).

Dominant design

Winning the battle for the **dominant design** is desirable because it will enable the firm to collect monopoly rents providing imitation can be limited, possibly with the use of intellectual property rights. Even if the standard is 'open' the developer can build complementary products or enhanced versions faster, possibly establishing a new standard in the future. (Samsung has achieved remarkable success in the mobile phone handset market through a combination of reverse engineering, product design and rapid manufacture.) Microsoft managed to establish 'Windows' as the dominant design for graphical operating systems largely because of its previous dominant position with the MS-DOS operating system. The threat of new entrants during the transitional phase is linked to the technology involved in the innovation: if it is proprietary then incumbents are favoured. Firms in this phase will use strategies to consolidate their product positioning and start increasing production capacity and process innovation in order to face the next phase: the *specific phase*. Competition now shifts from differentiation to product performance and costs. Companies now

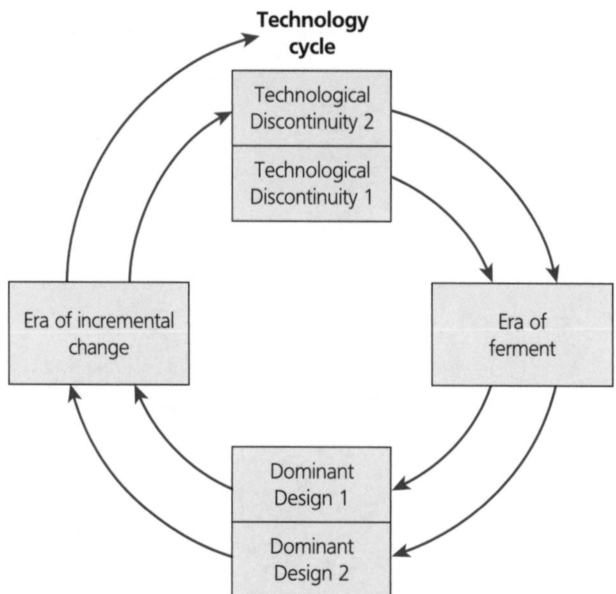

Figure 6.9 Tushman and Rosenkopf's technology cycle

Source: Tushman and Rosenkopf (1992).

have a clear picture of market segments and will therefore concentrate on serving specific customers. Manufacturing will use highly specialised equipment with the ability to produce the product on a large scale, hence highly skilled labour becomes less important. Since there is commoditisation taking place, the bargaining power of both suppliers and customers will increase. Competition becomes more intense and the market moves towards an oligopoly. As a consequence, incumbents are able to secure their position through supplier relations, distribution channels and other complementary assets that will create entry barriers to new entrants. Lastly, Tushman and Rosenkopf (1992) argued that the more complex the technology the more intrusion from sociopolitical factors during the evolution of the technology. This is clearly evidenced in the current development of electric powered automobiles where legislation and political decision making are influencing the shape and size of the future market (*see* Figure 6.9).

Table 6.1 captures and summarises the Abbernathy and Utterback model which attempts to illustrate the linkages between technology development and its impact upon products and processes, to market dynamics and competition, and to organisational structure and strategic decisions within companies.

How firms cope with radical and incremental innovation

In the analysis in Table 6.1 one of the key dimensions that requires further attention is that of the innovation itself and in particular the technology. For it is the level of newness and corresponding changes caused by this that will shape strategic decision making for the firm. Much of the debate in this area has centred on the incremental-radical product dichotomy. Radical and incremental innovations have such different competitive consequences because they require quite different organisational capabilities.

Organisational capabilities are difficult to create and costly to adjust (Nelson and Winter, 1982; Hannan and Freeman, 1984). Incremental innovation reinforces the capabilities of established organisations, while radical innovation forces them to ask a new set of questions, to draw on new technical and commercial skills, and to employ new problem-solving approaches (Burns and Stalker, 1966; Hage, 1980; Ettlie *et al.*, 1984; Tushman and Anderson, 1986). There are two dimensions that we can use to separate an incremental from a radical innovation:

- The first is an internal dimension, based on the knowledge and resources involved. An incremental innovation will build upon existing knowledge and resources within the firm leading to the enhancement of its competencies. Whereas a radical innovation will require completely new knowledge and/or resources and may, therefore, destroy many of the existing competencies.
- The second dimension is external. It differentiates the innovation based on the technological changes and the impact upon the market competitiveness. An incremental innovation will involve modest technological changes and the existing products in the market will remain competitive. A radical innovation will instead involve large technological advancements, rendering the existing products uncompetitive and eventually obsolete.

The radical-incremental conceptual framework clearly suggests that incumbents will be in a better position if the innovation is incremental since they can use existing knowledge and resources to leverage the whole process. New entrants, on the other hand, will have a large advantage if the innovation is radical because they will not need to change their knowledge background. Furthermore incumbents struggle to deal with radical innovation both because they operate under a 'managerial mindset' constraint and because strategically they have less of an incentive to invest in the innovation if it will cannibalise their existing products. Kodak illustrates this well. The company dominated the photography market over many years, and throughout this extended period all the incremental innovations solidified its leadership. As soon as the market experienced a radical innovation – the entrance of digital technology – Kodak struggled to defend its position against the new entrants. The new technology required different knowledge, resources and mindsets.

This pattern of innovation is typical in mature industries. However, in some of the newly established industries, such as software and mobile phones, there have been cases where new entrants managed to displace incumbents with incremental innovations and other cases where incumbents kept their leadership exploiting a radical innovation. An explanation for this was put forward by Henderson and Clark (1990) who argued that some innovations might appear incremental at first sight, yet this may not be the case, especially in technology-intensive industries with broad technology bases. In such circumstances it is necessary to analyse how the innovation impacts on the technological knowledge required to develop new products, and consequently to introduce innovations. Henderson and Clark (1990) divide technological knowledge along two new dimensions: *knowledge of the components* and knowledge of the linkage between them, which they called *architectural knowledge* (*see* Figure 3.3). In this framework technology development could be a radical innovation only if it revolutionises both component and architectural knowledge. Similarly an incremental innovation will build upon existing component and architectural knowledge. Modular innovations will require new knowledge for one or more components, but the architectural knowledge remains unchanged. Whereas architectural innovation will have a great impact upon the linkage of components, the knowledge of single components will remain the same. For example, the technology architecture of portable computers is significantly different from the architecture of desktop computers. The portability dimension introduces new design constraints and demands architectural innovation; in particular, the need to minimise the size of all components and also their energy consumption. These tighter design constraints posed by the new architecture illustrates the relationship and differences between component innovation and architectural innovation.

The above discussions reveal that when technology development is viewed through a wider lens it can be seen as a complex system containing elements that function interdependently. The complexity is expressed by the matrix of interdependencies between elements in complex systems called a system's architecture (*see* Figure 3.3). Companies, therefore, must be careful in distinguishing between incremental and architectural or modular innovations because the competencies and strategies required to exploit one might not suit perfectly the other, if at all. Canon was able to invade Xerox's market because it developed the right architectural knowledge required to redesign the photocopier machine with smaller dimensions. Within this wider systems view, if we also consider the role of the consumer and in particular the extent of change required in the consumption of the product we can see that some innovations cause disruption (forces consumers to alter the way they consume and use the product such as MP3 players) and others sustain because they improve the performance of existing products along the dimensions that mainstream customers value. Significantly Christensen (1997) argued that disruptive innovations will frequently have characteristics that traditional customer segments may not want, at least initially. Furthermore, they may appear as cheaper, simpler and even with inferior quality if compared to existing products, but some marginal or new segment will value them.

Illustration 6.1

A little knowledge is deadly dangerous

FT

It is the 'unknown knowns' that can kill you. But this was the category of information which Donald Rumsfeld, the former US defence secretary, left off his famous list ('known knowns', 'known unknowns') a few years ago.

A pity. One of the lessons of the September 11 2001 hijackings, as well as the recent attempt to blow up an aircraft on Christmas day, is that organisations may already possess the information they need to avoid disaster. It is just that they do not know that they know.

In criticising his security services last week, Barack Obama summed up this management dilemma well. 'This was not a failure to collect intelligence', he said. 'It was a failure to integrate and understand the intelligence that we already

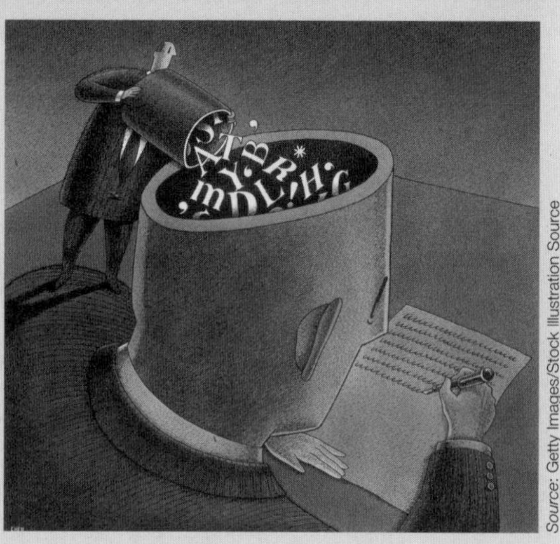

Source: Getty Images/Stock Illustration Source

had.' His colleagues had neglected to 'connect the dots', he observed.

This is a familiar story to business leaders. 'If only Unilever knew what Unilever knows', went the old lament. And you can substitute the name of almost any other company into that last sentence.

It was this lingering sense of unconnectedness, of dots not being joined up, that led to the emergence of 'knowledge management' as a business discipline two decades ago. It was based on the idea that all sorts of valuable information – about customers' preferences or what employees knew – was simply disappearing into the cracks that separated teams and business units. People within their silos could not or would not share knowledge.

Tom Stewart, chief marketing and knowledge officer for consultants Booz, moved the debate on with his 1997 book *Intellectual Capital – the New Wealth of Organizations*, which described what properly managed knowledge could do for businesses. Surely things were about to change?

Maybe knowledge management was too drab a label to hold people's attention. Perhaps it all sounded too much like hard work. But 'KM' soon fell prey to the curse of the management fad. It was talked about, popularised, then – too often – forgotten. Today too few companies can be confident that their employees share the knowledge and information that they need. Do their people know what they know?

The events over Detroit this Christmas confirmed the danger of ignoring the information that circulates, whether unprocessed or imperfectly understood, within organisations. In a blog post last week, Harvard Business School's Rosabeth Moss Kanter said that dispatching e-mails or entering comments into databases is not enough. Only 'relentless follow-up' would hold colleagues accountable for what they were supposed to be doing.

Smart knowledge management involves spotting useful patterns in the data that you have. Leaders should reward 'pattern recognisers', she said. They should also 'stress the importance of passing on items of value to others'.

But while Prof Kanter is hopeful that social networking technology will lead to a greater sharing of information, others are not so sure. Morten Hansen, professor at Berkeley and Insead and author of last year's well-regarded book, *Collaboration*, sees other factors at play. The failure of colleagues to communicate effectively 'requires a change in culture and incentive systems, not an IT fix', he says.

It is not always easy to recognise the value of the information you have. The father of the alleged Detroit bomber, a former banker from Nigeria, warned US officials about his concerns over his son. For whatever reason – fatigue, overwork – the crucial tip-off was ignored. Too casual by half. The son's name was even mis-spelled by one official, confusing his identity.

But information must be taken seriously. Managers need more than gut instinct and past experience to help them make good decisions. This means that knowledge has to be seen as an asset, something to be both respected and exploited.

This is why the collective corporate memory is so important. People forget – or just never get to learn – crucial details about the markets they are operating in. Veteran CIA officers understand this. As one former field operative, Bob Baer, told the BBC last week, it is no wonder his former colleagues seem 'clueless' about where the next threat is coming from. 'You're seeing the price the CIA is paying for getting rid of so many people in the 1990s', he said. 'We fired people or let them retire.'

If we didn't know then how unwise that approach was, we know now.

Source: Stern, S. (2010) A little knowledge is deadly dangerous, FT.com, 11 January.

Developing innovation strategies

The innovation framework outlined in Chapter 1 emphasises the interaction that any firm has with the external environment, both in terms of markets and science and technology. The developments taking place in these external environments will continue largely independent of the individual firm. Any firm's ability to survive is dependent on its capability to adapt to this changing environment. This suggests that a firm has a range of options open to it. A company will attempt to look ahead and try to ensure that it is prepared for possible forthcoming changes and in some instances a firm can modify world science and technology. But mostly the future is unknown – some firms will prosper; others will not. In virtually all areas of business it is not always clear who are the players in the innovation race. Very often contenders will emerge from the most unexpected places. Furthermore, companies often find themselves in a race without knowing where the starting and finishing lines are! Even when some of these are known, companies often start out with the aim of becoming a leader and end up being a follower (Pavitt *et al.*, 1991).

The development of new products and processes has enabled many firms to continue to grow. However, there is a wide range of alternative strategies which they may follow, depending on their resources, their heritage, their capabilities and their aspirations. Collectively these factors should contribute to the direction that the corporate strategy takes. Unfortunately, technology is rarely an explicit element of a firm's corporate strategy. This is so even in science- and technology-intensive firms. Very often, along with manufacturing, technology is the missing element in the corporate strategy. Until very recently technological competencies were not viewed as an integral part of the strategic planning process. They were seen as things to be acquired if required. As was discussed earlier, scientific knowledge cannot be bought like a can of tomatoes, off the shelf. By definition (*see* Chapter 1), technology is embedded in products and processes and, while it is possible to acquire a patent, for example, this does not necessarily mean that the company will also possess the technological capability to develop products and processes from that patent. This has been an expensive lesson learned by many international chemical companies which have acquired licences from other chemical companies to develop a chemical process, only to experience enormous difficulties in producing the product. In one particular case the company abandoned the plant, having already sunk several million pounds into the project.

The innovation policy pursued cuts a wide path across functions such as manufacturing, finance, marketing, R&D and personnel, hence the importance attached to its consideration. The four broad innovation strategies commonly found in technology-intensive firms (Freeman, 1982; Maidique and Patch, 1988) are discussed below. These are not mutually exclusive or collectively exhaustive. A wide spectrum of other strategies is logically possible; indeed, very often a firm adopts a balanced portfolio approach with a range of products. It is worth remembering, as Table 6.2 shows late entrants surpass pioneers.

Leader/offensive

The strategy here centres on the advantages to be gained from a monopoly, in this case a monopoly of the technology. The aim is to try to ensure that the product is

Table 6.2 Throughout the twentieth century 'late entrants' have been surpassing pioneers

Product	Pioneer(s)	Imitator/Later Entrant(s)	Comments
35mm Cameras	Leica (1925) Contrax (1932) Exacta (1936)	Canon (1934) Nikon (1946) Nikon SLR (1959)	The pioneer was the technology and market leader for decades until the Japanese copied German technology, improved upon it, and lowered prices. The pioneer then failed to react and ended up as an incidental player.
CAT Scanners (Computer Axial Tomography)	EMI (1972)	Pfizer (1974) Technicare (1975) GE (1976) Johnson & Johnson (1978)	The pioneer had no experience in the medical equipment industry. Copycats ignored the patents and drove the pioneer out of business with marketing distribution, and financial advantages, as well as extensive industry experience.
Ballpoint pens	Reynolds (1945) Eversharp (1946)	Parker 'Jotter' (1954) Bic (1960)	The pioneers disappeared when the fad first ended in the late 1940s. Parker entered eight years later. Bic entered last and sold pens as cheap disposables.
MRI (Magnetic Resonance Imaging)	Fonar (1978)	Johnson & Johnson's Technicare (1981) General Electric (1982)	The tiny pioneer faced the huge medical equipment suppliers, which easily expanded into MRI. The pioneer could not hope to match their tremendous market power.
Personal Computers	MITS Altair 8800 (1975) Apple II (1977) Radio Shack (1977)	IBM-PC (1981) Compaq (1982) Dell (1984) Gateway (1985)	The pioneers created computers for hobbyists, but when the market turned to business uses, IBM entered and quickly dominated, using its reputation and its marketing and distribution skills. The cloners then copied IBM's standard and sold at lower prices.
VCRs	Ampex (1956) CBS-EVR (1970) Sony U-matic (1971) Catrivision (1972) Sony Betamax (1975)	JVC-VHS (1976) RCA Selectra Vision (1977) made by Matsushita	The pioneer focused on selling to broadcasters while Sony pursued the home market for more than a decade. Financial problems killed the pioneer. Sony Betamax was the first successful home VCR but was quickly supplanted by VHS, a late follower, which recorded for twice as long.
Word-processing software	Wordstar (1979)	WordPerfect (1982) Microsoft Word (1983)	The pioneer was stuck with an obsolete standard when it failed to update. When it did update, Wordstar abandoned loyal users, offered no technical support, and fought internally. The follower took advantage.

launched into the market before the competition. This should enable the company either to adopt a price-skimming policy, or to adopt a penetration policy based on gaining a high market share. Such a strategy demands a significant R&D activity and is usually accompanied by substantial marketing resources to enable the company to promote the new product. This may also involve an element of education about the new product, for example Toyota's Prius and Apple's iPad.

Fast follower/defensive

This strategy also requires a substantial technology base in order that the company may develop improved versions of the original, improved in terms of lower cost, different design, additional features, etc. The company needs to be agile in manufacturing, design and development and marketing. This will enable it to respond quickly to those companies that are first into the market. In the mobile phone market Alcatel, Sagem and Samsung are able to get new mobile phone handsets into the market quickly. None of these firms competes with Nokia, Motorola, Apple and Sony-Ericsson in terms of innovative technology, but they have none the less delivered profits and a return for their investors (*see* Case study in Chapter 10). Without any in-house R&D their response would have been much slower, as this would have involved substantially more learning and understanding of the technology.

Very often both the first two strategies are followed by a company, especially when it is operating in fierce competition with a rival. Sometimes one is first to the market with a product development, only to find itself following its rival with the next product development. This is commonly referred to as healthy competition and is a phenomenon that governments try to propagate.

Cost minimisation/imitative

This strategy is based on being a low-cost producer and success is dependent on achieving economies of scale in manufacture. The company requires exceptional skills and capabilities in production and process engineering. This is clearly similar to the defensive strategy, in that it involves following another company, except that the technology base is not usually as well developed as for the above two strategies. Technology is often licensed from other companies. However, it is still possible to be extremely successful and even be a market leader in terms of market share. Arguably HP has achieved this position in the PC market. Originally its PCs were IBM clones but were sold at a cheaper price and are of a superior quality to many of the other competitors.

This is a strategy that has been employed very effectively by the rapidly developing Asian economies. With lower labour costs these economies have offered companies the opportunity to imitate existing products at lower prices, helping them enter and gain a foothold in a market, for example footwear or electronics. From this position it is then possible to incorporate design improvements to existing products.

Market segmentation specialist/traditional

This strategy is based on meeting the precise requirements of a particular market segment or niche. Large-scale manufacture is not usually required and the products tend to be characterised by few product changes. They are often referred to as traditional products. Indeed, some companies promote their products by stressing the absence of any change, for example Scottish whisky manufacturers.

A technology strategy provides a link between innovation strategy and business strategy

For each of the strategies discussed above there are implications in terms of the capabilities required. When it comes to operationalising the process of innovation, this invariably involves considering the technology position of the firm. Hence, the implementation of an innovation strategy is usually achieved through the management of technology.

Many decisions regarding the choice of innovation strategy will depend on the technology position of the firm with respect to its competitors. This will be largely based on the heritage of the organisation. In addition, the resource implications also need to be considered. For example, a manufacturer of electric lawn-mowers wishing to adopt an innovation leadership strategy would require a high level of competence in existing technologies such as electric motors, blade technology and injection moulding relative to the competition, as well as an awareness of the application of new technologies such as new lightweight materials and alternative power supplies. Adopting a follower strategy, in contrast, would require more emphasis on development engineering and manufacture.

In terms of resource expenditure, while the figures themselves may be very similar it is where the money is spent that will differ considerably, with the leader strategy involving more internal R&D expenditure and the follower strategy involving more emphasis on design or manufacturing. This area of technology strategy and the management of technology is explored in more detail in Chapters 8, 9 and 10.

Case study

The cork industry, the wine industry and the need for closure

Introduction

This case study explores the use of cork as a way of sealing wine in a bottle; referred to as a closure in the wine industry. This 400-year-old industry with all its associated working practices has continued largely unaffected by technology changes in almost all other industries – until, that is, the 1990s when synthetic plastic closures were used by some wine producers instead of natural cork. With a requirement of over 17 billion wine bottle closures a year, the cork industry could arguably afford a little competition, but it seems the cork industry had not recognised the significant changes taking place in the wine industry to which it acts as a supplier (Cole, 2006). The wine industry was experiencing a revolution where new producers from Australia, California and Chile had new and different requirements. In a matter of a few years the industry had changed completely.

Source: A. Harrison/Pearson Education Ltd

The cork industry

The Portuguese cork industry is facing an environmental and economic disaster as wine makers and large grocery chains defect from natural cork closures to modern synthetic closures, such as rubber or plastic. Portugal supplies more than half of the world's cork and has been experiencing a slow move away from cork since the mid-1990s. More recently the trickle

→

Table 6.3 Cork production

Country	Forest area Hectares	% of world's forest area	Production Tons (000)	% of world's production
Portugal	725,000	33	175	52
Spain	510,000	23	110	32
Italy	225,000	10	20	6
Morocco	198,000	9	15	4
Algeria	460,000	21	6	2
Tunisia	60,000	3	9	3
France	22,000	1	5	1
TOTAL	2,200,000	100	340	100

has turned into a flood as changes in the wine industry and buying behaviours contribute to the rise in demand for modern closures. The cork industry accounts for nearly 3 per cent of Portugal's GDP. Its cork forests, and workers, are under threat from innovation in one of the oldest industries in the world. For hundreds of years cork was the accepted method of closure for bottles, especially wine, but a wide range of closures for bottles have existed for many years including screw caps and resealable plastic caps.

Few in the wine industry believed that vineyards, bottlers and wine drinkers would ever wish to use anything other than natural cork. However, the wine industry has changed significantly over the past 20 years. The historical dominant producers of Europe – France, Germany, Italy and Spain – are being challenged by new wine producers such as California, Australia, New Zealand, South Africa, Chile, etc. Moreover, these new producers have developed international wine brands such as Jacobs Creek and Blossom Hill, which have fundamentally changed the wine market. This is because the international brands have demanded a consistent product that has little variation. This is in complete contrast to the traditional wine products which have always had a degree of variety dependent on the grape, the climate and production. Furthermore, the buyers of wine were changing too – the supermarket chains, such as Tesco, Sainsbury, Carrefour, Wall-Mart, had become the biggest buyers and they now have enormous power in the industry and are able to offer wine producers access to millions of consumers and correspondingly millions of sales of bottled wine.

Cork is harvested exclusively from the cork oak, found predominantly in the Mediterranean region. Though the tree can flourish in many climates, the conditions that favour commercial use are fairly narrow. The major cork-producing nations are listed above in Table 6.3. Cork is harvested in a steady cycle that promotes healthy growth to the tree over its expected lifespan of over 200 years. Typically, virgin cork is not removed from saplings until the 25th year, and reproduction cork (the first cycle) may not be extracted for another 9–12 years. Cork suitable for wine stoppers is not harvested until the following 9 to 12-year cycle, so farmers have invested over 40 years before natural wine corks are produced.

The cork forests, owing to the mutual efforts of the European Union (EU) and various environmental groups, is expected to increase due to the active efforts to protect existing forests and sponsorship of significant new plantings. Cork bark is removed from trees in spring or summer. At this time of year the cork comes away easily from the trunk because the tree is growing and the new, tender cork cells being generated break easily. Harvest difficulties occur if the process is not carried out when the tree is in full growth. To keep the trees in good productive health, there are laws which regulate the harvest of cork oaks. In Portugal, trees are harvested every nine years and on the island of Sardinia (Italy) the harvest occurs every 12 years. (Numbers are painted on to the bark to keep track of when a tree was stripped.) Therefore, harvest forecasting is based on nine or 12-year cycles, i.e. projections for the 2006 Portuguese cork harvest are based on the kilos harvested in 1997. It is in the forests where the management of cork quality begins.

Cork production has shown significant expansion in recent years – reflecting the impact of approximately 120,000 hectares of highly productive, new cork forests in Spain and Portugal (see Table 6.3).

Table 6.4 Applications of cork

Industry segment	Value in eurodollars ($000)	Value in %
Wine stoppers	1,000,000	66
Floor and wall coverings	300,000	20
Expanded agglomerated cork	100,000	7
Other products	100,000	7
Total cork products	1,500,000	100

Source: corkindustry.com, 2006.

Applications of natural cork

Cork is used in a wide variety of products – from construction materials to gaskets and, most importantly, as a stopper for wines. The cork industry employs an estimated 30,000 workers in a variety of jobs. Wine corks are the most visible and most profitable of the many products derived from cork. They account for approximately 15 per cent of total production by weight and two-thirds of cork revenues. Table 6.4 displays a comparison of the different segments of the cork industry as measured by revenue generated (Corkindustry.com, 2006). The wine industry is by far the most important customer of the cork industry, the dominant cork producer being Amorim. More than 13 billion wine bottle closures are needed each year and the market is growing.

The wine industry

Wine consumption in the UK has grown dramatically over the past five years and this has been the case in the US too. Research from the International Organisation of Vine and Wine (OIV) claims that French wine consumption dropped 2 per cent between 2004 and 2005, while British wine consumption rose 5 per cent in 2005. Britain and the United States are the world's two fastest growing wine markets. Consumption in the United States grew 3 per cent in 2005 and if this trend continues, the US will oust France from the top spot within three years. French wine exports fell 11 per cent between 2002 and 2005, while global consumption grew by 0.1 per cent to 23.56 billion litres between 2004 and 2005. The study highlights growth in the popularity of imported wine among drinkers in their 20s and heightened recognition of the health benefits of drinking wine as the primary causes of the increase (Cole, 2006).

Wine has become a fixture on the weekly grocery list of UK consumers, alongside bread and eggs. This has meant that the UK multiples (Tesco, Sainsbury's, M&S, Morrison's, ASDA) have become some of the largest buyers of wine in the world. With this buying power has come the ability to make demands on suppliers. In particular, a homogeneous product free from fault. The world of wine has changed considerably over the last couple of decades, and while many of the changes have been for the better, some are giving cause for concern. One area of considerable change is the growth in branded wines or so-called 'modern' wine by traditionalists.

According to the traditionalists wine may be divided simply into two categories: the first is a commodity; that is, grapes are grown, crushed and made into wine, which is then sold cheaply and consumed uncritically. In this case, as long as the quality is adequate and the price is right, consumers aren't too worried about the source. This first category accounts for the majority of wine across the world. This is the 'modern' approach to wine production and distribution. The second type of wine is 'traditional' wine that is purchased and consumed not because of low price, but because of interest. This interest stems from the fact that there exists a diversity of wine types that are each able to express elements of their cultural and geographical origins in the finished product. Crucial here is the importance of the starting material – the grapes. Unlike lager or whisky, where the agricultural input (wheat or barley) is minimal and the human input is dominant, this kind of winemaking is best viewed as a process of stewardship rather than one of manufacturing.

The diversity of wine is vast. Not only are hundreds of different grape varieties in relatively common use, but there are also the complex influences of soil types, climate, viticulture (the study and production of grapes) and winemaking practices. There's also a rich traditional heritage in the more established wine-producing countries, whereby cultural and viticultural influences collude to produce a variety of wine classifications (appellations in France), that is, geographical areas where grapes for certain wines were grown. According to the traditionalists it is this diversity that makes wine so interesting. They argue that, divorced from its geographical origins, wine is only marginally more interesting than fruit juice, lager or gin. And you don't get people naming either of these three beverage types as one of their interests or hobbies.

→

Table 6.5 Modern and traditional wine

Branded (modern)	Estate (traditional)
• volume of production is managed • typically made from bought-in grapes • often 'international' in style, lacking a sense of place • usually defined by winemaking style • made to a style and to fit a price point • because production is limited only by the supply of suitable purchased grapes, these wines are often widely available • heavily marketed • lack diversity	• made from grapes grown in one vineyard, or several neighbouring vineyards • vineyards supplying the grapes are usually owned by the company making the wine, or are supplied by growers on long-term contracts • limited production, subject to vintage variation • typically display regional influences or a 'sense of place' • availability is sometimes a problem because of the limited production • marketing is often minimal • hugely diverse

These two genres of wine have coexisted quite happily, and there's no reason that they can't continue to do so, sitting side-by-side on the shelf. They serve different functions, and are consumed in different situations, and often by different groups of consumers. These two genres may also be labelled 'branded' and 'estate bottled' (*see* Table 6.5).

The modern retailing environment

The traditionalists argue that estate bottled wine doesn't sit well with the modern retail environment (*see* Figure 6.10). They argue that because wine is an agricultural product, not a manufactured one in the eyes of the big retailer, this is a bad thing. The way the modern multi-outlet branded/franchised shop is configured, continuity of supply and economies of scale are hugely important. This is not something the traditional wine producers, most notably in France, have been willing to embrace. It is the diversity within wine that the traditionalists want to celebrate: vintage variation – at times a frustrating reality, but one which adds an extra level of interest – and typically the limited production of each producer means that wine is not an easy product to deal with. It usually comes

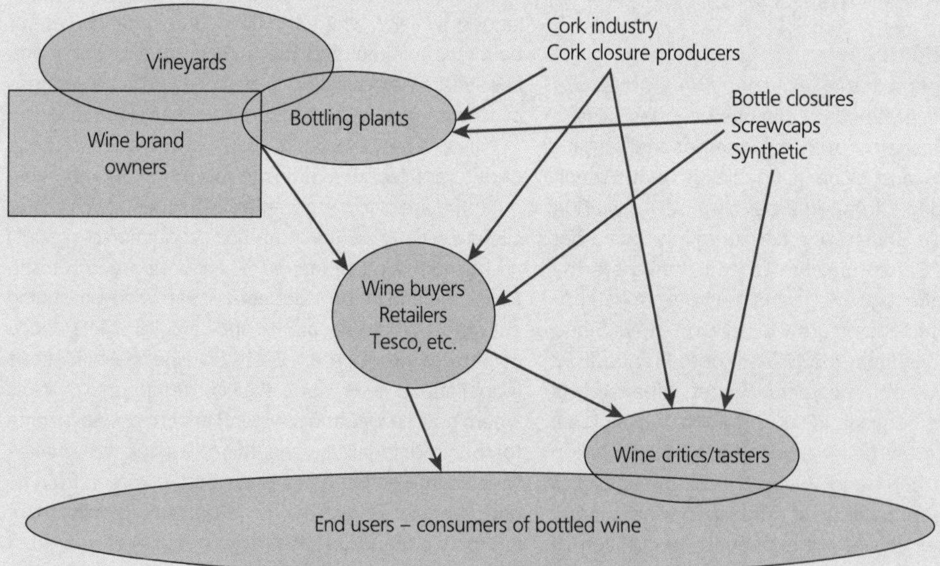

Figure 6.10 Power and influence in the supply chain of wine

in small parcels, and the production level changes each year. Modern retailing, however, is big business. To survive in the modern retailing environment you need to be big, highly visible, and with lots of outlets. Effective marketing in this modern environment is an expensive business and you can only really make use of it if you are a big player. This automatically rules out almost all estate wines, leaving the market open to the international brands. Figure 6.10 illustrates the power and influence within the supply chain of wine.

The illusion of choice

Supermarkets and other multiple outlets don't like dealing with the diversity and complexity of wine, but they are quite attached to the 'idea' of diversity. So typically they will stock hundreds of different lines, giving the consumer the impression of a broad portfolio of wines. The problem here is that this diversity is actually an illusory one. The wines are almost always industrially produced, in large quantities, and to a formula. For example, you may have in your minds the romantic notion that all wine is discovered by a dedicated wine hound who has trekked across remote parts of the world stopping at cellar after cellar searching out a wine that will give your tastebuds a treat. The truth is very different. Most wine purchased by the supermarkets today is led by financial motives, which are driven by cost sheets and market forecasts. Remember also that wines that appear on recipe cards or in magazines have been paid for. Waitrose charges suppliers a nominal fee of £300 for a mention in its *Wine List* magazine (Moore, 2007). According to the traditionalists, while customers now experience far less risk of picking a bad bottle, they also have far less chance of picking a wine that is at all interesting. Traditionalists argue that while high quality is desirable a uniformity of style is disastrous. They maintain that branded wines, with their manufactured, processed character and lack of connection with the soil hinders complete choice and diversity. Worst of all, they argue, their growing dominance of the marketplace threatens the very existence of the traditional article: estate wines.

Wine bottle closures

Cork has been used as a closure for bottles for hundreds of years. Indeed, one might reasonably ask why it has survived so long. It is partly because it is a natural product that breathes, which is a quality required for some wines. For most wine drinkers the pop of the cork from the bottle is an intrinsic part of the wine drinking experience, and they love it. Wine producers, on the other hand, view natural corks with deep suspicion, largely due to the rogue chemical 2-4-6 trichloranisole (TCA, a compound created by the interplay of a cork-borne fungus, the chlorine used to

Illustration 6.2

Breaking into the UK wine market

Consider the lot of a wine producer looking to break into the UK market. With 75 per cent of wine sales in the UK going through supermarkets, you might want to target them first. So you approach the supermarket buyers. If you are from a relatively unfashionable country like Portugal, you'll probably be talking to a 22-year-old junior buyer fresh out of college who has, perhaps, two slots to fill at a £3.99–4.99 price point. They want serious volumes, a fresh, fruity style, and the cheaper the better. If you are from Australia, you may have better luck, but the volumes required will be huge and the price points will be very keen. Even at the higher price points, the continuity of supply and volume issues favour the branders very heavily. If you are selling wine from recognised appellations such as Chablis or St Emilion, then the buyers will be looking for the best Chablis at the entry-level price point for this wine, effectively ruling out the estate wines here also. A supermarket would much rather have a vaguely palatable Chablis at £5.99 – which will fly out of the door – than a really good one at £8.99. That's life . . . its hard.

Source: Wine Anorak.com, 2006.

→

sanitise wine corks, and plant phenols), often referred to as cork taint that makes wine taste anything from slightly muted to very mouldy. Although it is harmless if swallowed by humans, TCA imparts a musty, wet cardboard smell and taste to the wine it affects. TCA is detectable in wine at concentrations as low as four parts per trillion, and although some wine drinkers are more sensitive to it than others, the taste and smell of a 'corked' wine are as unforgettable as the disappointment a sommelier (trained wine professional) or host feels upon the discovery of a tainted bottle. The wine industry argues that this had risen to an unacceptable level. Estimates of this level vary wildly, as do different people's sensitivity to and awareness of TCA. The cork industry quotes less than 2 per cent. Some wine producers claim it is as high as 15 per cent. Whatever the precise figure, wine producers are deeply worried that a significant proportion of their customers experience a substandard form of the liquid they originally put in the bottle. And they are almost more worried by a light incidence of TCA which simply flattens the aroma and fruit of their wines than by TCA at its most obvious, virtually undrinkable extreme. In the first case, the consumer will probably think, wrongly, that the fault lies with the wine rather than the cork. The cork industry has been working hard to introduce new techniques that minimise the incidence of TCA taint in their products, and to demonstrate that TCA can arise not just from corks but other sources such as wooden pallets. Because of all this uncertainty, wine producers have been seeking alternative bottle stoppers, or closures, with much lower or minimal risks of TCA taint, and closure manufacturers have identified this business opportunity that demands more than 13 billion wine bottle closures and is a growing market. But they risk alienating their customers who love cork or at least the 'pop' of the closure.

It is wider changes in the wine industry that has led to innovation in wine bottle closures, and suitable remedial activity in the natural cork industry itself, even though this problem/opportunity has been obvious to all in the wine business for at least 15 years. The first generation of alternatives to natural cork were synthetic copies of the real thing, cylinders of various oil-industry-derived materials, 'plastic corks' which, though improved, can still be difficult to get out of a bottle neck, and even more difficult to put back in. They retain natural cork's disadvantage of needing a special tool to extract them. In 1999 the synthetic cork was dealt a significant blow by the Australian Wine Research Institute (regarded by the industry as the most important impartial research project) comparing the technical performance of different closures. This showed that synthetic corks started to let in dangerous amounts of oxygen after about 18 months, which means they are really suitable only for the most basic wines for early consumption.

In terms of costs, synthetic was initially more expensive than natural cork, but fierce competition between different manufacturers and economies of scale have brought synthetic cork prices down; rising oil prices has put pressure on this but, generally, a plastic cork costs considerably less than a natural one – well under 3p each, when a good quality cork can easily cost more than 10p. Cork and synthetic require a foil capsule over the top, which costs 0.8p. Synthetic corks have several more big drawbacks such as they are non-biodegradable, unlike natural cork. Furthermore, the ecosystem of southern Portugal depends on our continuing to buy natural corks – an argument that is questionable given that the cork forests of Alentejo were planted expressly for the cork industry.

Screwcaps

Both natural and synthetic are cheaper than the next most obvious alternative, screwcaps, which are currently the favourite closure for many a wine technician (anyone who has to open a lot of bottles), although the special bottles needed for screwcaps are expected to become cheaper as screwcaps become more common – and there is no need to pay for a foil capsule over a screwcap.

Unlike synthetic corks, screwcaps are extremely good at keeping wine's enemy, oxygen, out of the bottle – almost too good in fact. It is becoming increasingly clear that screwcaps are associated with the opposite of oxidation: reduction, which can suppress wine's all-important aroma and even imbue it with a downright nasty one. This problem particularly affects Sauvignon Blanc, a grape that tends naturally to reduction, but not Riesling.

For the moment these two grapes are those most frequently found under screwcap, because their bright, aromatic, unoaked wines have so far seemed to respond best to this particular seal.

In New Zealand and Australia, an estimated 30 per cent of all wines, red and white, are already bottled under screwcaps, which are gradually spreading throughout the northern hemisphere. But the jury is still out on the effect of screwcaps on oaked whites and reds, which may actually need more oxygen during the ageing process than screwcaps allow.

But not all consumers are as thrilled by screwcaps as producers. They still carry the stigma of being associated with cheap wines and spirits – and, unlike the natural cork, they involve precious little theatre of cork screw and pop. Furthermore, screwcap application requires the installation of a completely new set of machinery from the old cork insertion kit. This has discouraged many smaller producers from adopting the screwcap, or Stelvin as it is known in many markets after the market leader. It has also made plastic corks seem a much more attractive alternative.

In Australia and New Zealand there is near total acceptance that the screwcap is the preferable closure. In the UK they are now commonplace in mass market wines; UK wine bottlers report that the proportion of all wine they stopper with a screwcap has risen to 85 per cent in the past three years. But in much of mainland Europe and certainly in the US there is still considerable consumer resistance to this innovation.

More innovative alternatives now include the Vinolok, a glass stopper reminiscent of an old-fashioned pharmacy, currently being trialled in Germany; Gardner Technologies' MetaCork, a US stopper which can be screwed off but is lined with a natural cork for resealing; and more recently from Australia the Zork, a plastic, peel-off stopper which so far seems good at keeping oxygen out and also provides the vital 'pop' when being extracted (*see* Illustration 6.3).

Zork has the disadvantage for producers of being a relatively late arrival on the scene and, initially at least, being more expensive than any other closure. But it is extremely easy to use and may well find favour with consumers because of what the manufacturers describe as 'the sex appeal of the cork'.

The cork industry fights back

The cork industry has launched its own offensive against synthetic closures. First, the cork industry via the Cork Quality Council (CQC) is sponsoring ongoing research into the relationships between TCA, cork and bottled wine. The following research has been carried out by ETS Laboratories over the

Illustration 6.3

ZORK

According to its manufacturer, Zork is a revolutionary new wine closure product that combines the benefits of cork and screwcap. They humorously suggest that Zork is Australian for cork. Similar to synthetic and screwcap closures, Zork offers the winemaker a competitively priced, quality-controlled consistent barrier to oxygen, that will not taint the wine or scalp its flavour. Unlike synthetic, however, it is made from durable, food-grade polymers, and is fully recyclable.

Zork, developed and manufactured in Adelaide, South Australia, seals like a screw cap and pops like a cork. The ZORK snaps on to a standard cork mouth wine bottle and after simple, low-cost modification can be applied at high speed using industry standard capping equipment.

The ZORK closure consists of three parts; a robust outer cap that provides a tamper evident clamp that locks on to the European CETIE band of a standard cork mouth bottle, an inner metal foil which provides an oxygen barrier similar to a screwcap, and an inner plunger which creates the 'pop' on extraction and reseals after use. The closure is easy to remove by hand and simple to reseal.

To open the bottle, peel the seal to remove the tamper-evident tab. The closure can then be pulled out like a cork, and pop! After pouring, the bottle can be resealed by pushing it back in. According to the advertising copy: ZORK delivers a superior technical seal but retains the sense of celebration associated with traditional closures.

No corkscrew, no crumbling, no cork taint, no worries.

→

past two years. It involves the use of chemical tests to quantify TCA content in individual corks and in cork harvests. The results have shown several interesting characteristics of TCA in cork soaks (cork soaking is the process prior to putting the cork in the bottle). It has also demonstrated a direct relationship between the level of TCA found in a cork soak and TCA that is transmitted to bottled wine. Testing has proven to be more quick, sensitive and accurate than previous analysis available to the industry. The procedure offers an immediate improvement in cork quality control procedures involving screening manufactured corks. Further value is seen in other research projects designed to eliminate TCA prior to the completion of cork manufacture. The chemical test is now being used by CQC member companies to supplement sensory analysis of incoming cork shipments.

Second, Cork manufacturers have invested $200 million in the past five years in new plants and supply chain integration, says APCOR (Association of Portuguese Cork Producers). The industry passed a self-regulatory code in 2000 to standardise manufacturing practices. Currently, 190 Portuguese cork makers have been certified. Cork producers have also vertically integrated their distribution channels. For example, Amorin Cork, the largest producer of natural corks, has taken over supply and distribution lines it once contracted out.

Marketing the benefits of cork

Third, in 2003 the Portuguese government and APCOR members launched a 12-month $6.5 million marketing campaign to turn consumers against synthetic closures (Almond, 2003). One of the tactics has been to stress the dangers of switching to synthetic and the environmental disasters that could result. Another has been to gain support from wildlife groups to stress their concerns to wildlife if the cork forests are lost. In 2004 WWF, the conservation group, urged wine drinkers to avoid bottles sealed with plastic 'corks' or screwtops. It said that falling demand for traditional corks was threatening the habitat of the Iberian lynx, the world's rarest big cat. The latest figures from the IUCN, the World Conservation Union, show that there are only 150 lynx left, prompting the IUCN to upgrade its status to 'critically endangered' (Houlder, 2002).

A slightly more sophisticated tactic has been to focus on the consumer. For example, surveys show that wine drinkers dislike synthetic closures, long associated with cheap wine. Yet the synthetic market share is growing, mainly from medium-end wines from 'new world' markets: Argentina, Chile and Australia. Synthetics account for 7–8 per cent of a worldwide market of an estimated 17 billion bottle stoppers, growing at a rate of 10–30 per cent a year, according to US-based Supreme Corq, the largest synthetic cork maker. The challenge for the cork industry is to try to nurture the consumers' love of natural cork.

The use by some wine brands of the flanged bottle (roll top rim) first introduced in 1999 to try to convey a premium product, is now being replaced by the standard shaped bottle. This is partly in response to consumer research which reveals that premium quality is no longer associated with the flanged bottle largely because the design became almost universal among the international wine brands. A similar argument could be made with the use of screwcaps, where there may be a consumer backlash because people may associate screwcaps with mass market wines which would result in enormous damage to the premium labels (Almond, 2003).

Conclusions

This case study has explored some of the issues surrounding changes in the wine industry and their impact on one of the world's oldest industries – cork wine closures. The issues stir strong emotions and there are powerful lobby groups at work trying to influence consumers and government officials. Environmentalists say that undercutting demand for natural cork will render cork forests less profitable, and spark an ecological and economic disaster. Such arguments, while they play well with certain consumer groups, are hard to sustain when many of the forests have been specifically planted to harvest cork.

It seems the switch to screwcap has been made for the benefit of the wine, not just the image or for reduced costs. The cork industry's response has been to invest in research to address the issue of cork taint and to increase promotional campaigns about the benefits of cork. This, however, has largely been through the use of fear, arguing that the cork forests of Portugal will be lost, along with all the associated wildlife if the move from cork as a closure continues and to suggest that consumers will reject wine from a screwcap bottle. The evidence for this last claim is not there, certainly in many parts of the world.

According to wine industry figures, faults attributable to the use of cork as a seal run between 3–7 per cent depending on who you ask; this is high and would be labelled a disaster in any other industry, especially for food and beverage. It's particularly so when there are ways the industry can directly address the issue, by looking at alternative seals, as they are now doing. The decision to change closure, however, has to include consideration of costs and consumer preference. At present a plastic cork costs considerably less than a natural one – well under 3p each, when a good quality cork can easily cost more than 10p. With regard to consumer preference, this is more difficult to gauge. In some countries, most notably Australia and New Zealand, consumers, it seems, have readily embraced the screwcap. Indeed, the corkscrew is rapidly becoming redundant in both countries. When even Kay Brothers of McLaren Vale, the dusty old winery that has hardly changed since the eponymous brothers bought it in 1890, is using screwcaps exclusively, the time for a cork revival may be too late.

According to the cork industry more than one in two wineries are considering using the screwcap. However, many in the industry will continue to use natural cork for higher-priced bottles largely, they say, because of cork's ability to facilitate the proper aging of wine and overall consumer acceptance. The new synthetic corks have succeeded in getting the natural cork producers to take quality control far more seriously, and as a result the quality of cork closures has improved. But many wine makers and retailers remain unimpressed and argue that the cork industry has not yet eliminated cork taint.

While the battle over closures rages, the so-called traditionalists argue that the wine industry is merely exploiting profits in the short term by producing large volumes of homogenised wine and that this may harm the wine industry in the long term because consumers will grow bored with the uniformity of style.

Source: Almond, M. (2003) The cork industry spins out the fear factor, FT.com, 23 March; Cole, E. (2006) Americans set to overtake French in wine consumption, *Decanter*, Vol. 8, No. 4; Houlder, V. (2002) Wildlife body takes a pop at plastic corks, *Financial Times*, 27 December; Moore, V. (2007) The great wine rip-off, *Guardian*, G2, 5 April, 4–7; Randolph, N. (2002) Cork industry fights off taint, *Financial Times*, Commodities and Agriculture, 27 August; Robinson, J. (2004) A question of closure, FT.com, 11 June.

Questions

1 To what extent is the cork industry guilty of complacency and a lack of innovation?

2 If consumers love corks, why are the producers not providing what their customers want?

3 Is it wine quality or costs that have driven producers to synthetic?

4 How could technology forecasting have helped the cork industry?

5 What level of R&D investment would be required to help the industry diversify and develop new opportunities for its materials?

6 What portfolio of R&D projects would you establish for the cork industry?

7 What role have the wine buyers (end users and others in the supply chain) played in contributing to the fall in demand for cork as a closure?

8 Use the CIM (Figure 1.9) to illustrate the innovation process in this case.

9 In terms of closures, what are the disadvantages that the cork industry needs to address and what are the advantages that it could promote?

10 Will the cork industry have to concede defeat to the Zork?

Chapter summary

This chapter examined how business strategy affects the management of innovation. In so doing it introduced the notion of an organisation's knowledge base and how this links strategy and innovation. The heritage of a business was also shown to form a significant part of its knowledge base. Moreover, a firm's knowledge base largely determines its ability to innovate and certainly has a large influence on the selection of any innovation strategy.

Discussion questions

1. Explain the role played by core competencies in a firm's strategic planning.
2. What is meant by the technology escalator in the concept of technology trajectories?
3. Explain why a business's heritage needs to be considered in planning future strategy.
4. Try to plot two firms in each of the quadrants on the profit–competency matrix (Figure 6.3).
5. Explain the difference between individual knowledge and organisational knowledge and show how an organisation's knowledge can be greater than the sum of individual knowledge bases.
6. How would you compare the knowledge bases of two organisations?
7. How can late entrants win the innovation race?

Key words and phrases

Technology trajectories *197*
Dynamic capabilities *197*
Core competency *198*
Knowledge base of an organisation *203*
Organisational heritage *205*
Learning organisation *209*
Dominant design *211*
Degree of innovativeness *216*
Technology strategy *218*

References

Abernathy, W.J. and Utterback, J. (1978) Patterns of industrial innovation, *Technology Review*, Vol. 80, No. 7, 40–7.

Adler, P.S. and Shenhar, A. (1990) Adapting your technological base: the organizational challenge, *Sloan Management Review*, Autumn, 25–37.

Argyris, C. (1977) Double loop learning in organizations, *Harvard Business Review*, September/October, 55.

Barney, J. (1991) Firm resources and sustained competitive advantage, *Journal of Management*, Vol. 17, 99–120.

Burns, T. and Stalker, G.M. (1961) *The Management of Innovation*, Tavistock, London.

Casper, S. and Whitley, R. (2003) Managing competencies in entrepreneurial technology firms: a comparative institutional analysis of Germany, Sweden and the UK, *Research Policy*, Vol. 33, 89–106.

Cohen, W.M. and Levinthal, D.A. (1990) A new perspective on learning and innovation, *Administrative Science Quarterly*, Vol. 35, No. 1, 128–52.

Christensen, C.M. (1997) *The Innovator's Dilemma: When New Technologies Cause Great Firms to Fail*, Harvard Business School Press, Boston, MA.

Dosi, G. (1982) Technical paradigms and technological trajectories: a suggested interpretation of the determinants and directions of technical change, *Research Policy*, Vol. 11, No. 3, 147–62.

Ettlie, J.E., Bridges, W.P. and O'Keefe, R.D. (1984) Organization strategy and structural differences for radical versus incremental innovation, *Management Science*, Vol. 30, 682–95.

Foster, R. (1986) *Innovation: The Attacker's Advantage*, New York: Summit Books.

Freeman, C. (1982) *The Economics of Industrial Innovation*, 2nd edn, Frances Pinter, London.

Galbreath, J. and Galvin, P. (2004) Which resources matter? A fine-grained test of the resource-based view of the firm, Academy of Management Best Paper Proceedings, p. L1–6, 6p; (AN 13863763), August, New Orleans, LA.

Hage, J. (1980) *Theories of organizations*, Wiley, New York.

Hamel, G. and Prahalad, C.K. (1990) The core competence of the corporation, *Harvard Business Review*, May/June, 79–91.

Hamel, G. and Prahalad, C.K. (1994) Competing for the future, *Harvard Business Review*, Vol. 72, No. 4, 122–8.

Hannan, M. and Freeman, J. (1984) Structural inertia and organizational change, *American Sociological Review*, Vol. 49, 149–64.

Henderson, R. and Clark, K. (1990) Architectural innovation: the reconfiguration of existing product and the failure of established firms, *Administrative Science Quarterly*, Vol. 35, 9–30.

Kay, J. (1993) *Foundations of Corporate Success*, Oxford University Press, Oxford.

Kogut, B. and Zander, U. (1992) Knowledge of the firm, combinative capabilities, and the replication of technology, *Organisation Science*, Vol. 3, No. 3, 495–7.

Maidique, M. and Patch, P. (1988) 'Corporate strategy and technology policy', in Tushman, M.L. and Moore, W.L. (eds) *Readings in the Management of Innovation*, HarperCollins, New York.

Malbera, F. (1992) Learning by firms and incremental technical change, *Economic Journal*, Vol. 102, 845–59.

Nelson, R.R. (1991) Why do firms differ, and how does it matter?, *Strategic Management Journal*, Vol. 12, No. 1, 61–74.

Nelson, R.R. and Winter, S. (1982) *An Evolutionary Theory of Economic Change*, Harvard University Press, Boston, MA.

Nonaka, I. (1991) The knowledge creating company, *Harvard Business Review*, Vol. 69, No. 6, 96–104.

Onyeiwu, S. (2003) Some determinants of core competencies: Evidence from a binary-logit analysis, *Technology Analysis and Strategic Management*, Vol. 15, No. 1, 43–63.

Pavitt, K. (1990) What we know about the strategic management of technology, *California Management Review*, Vol. 32, No. 3, 17–26.

Pavitt, K., Robson, M. and Towsend, J. (1991) Technological accumulation, diversification and organisation in UK companies, 1945–1983, *Management Science*, Vol. 35, No. 1, 81–99.

Pennings, J.M. and Harianto, F. (1992) Technological networking and innovation implementation, *Organisational Science*, Vol. 3, No. 3, 356–82.

Penrose, E.T. (1959) *The theory of the firm*, John Wiley, New York.

Seaton, R.A.F. and Cordey-Hayes, M. (1993) The development and application of interactive models of technology transfer, *Technovation*, Vol. 13, No. 1, 45–53.

Stewart, T.A. (1997) *Intellectual Capital: The new wealth of organizations*, Doubleday, New York.

Teece, D. (1986) Profiting from technological innovation: implications for integration, collaboration, licensing and public policy, *Research Policy*, Vol. 15, 285–305.

Teece, D.J. and Pisano, G. (1994) The dynamic capabilities of firms: an introduction, *Industrial and Corporate Change*, Vol. 3, No. 3, 537–56.

Teece, D.J., Pisano, G. and Shuen, A. (1997) Dynamic capabilities and strategic management, *Strategic Management Journal*, Vol. 18, No. 7, 509–33.

Tidd, J. (2000) *From Knowledge Management to Strategic Competence: Measuring Technological Market and Organisational Innovation*, Imperial College Press, London.

Trott, P. and Cordey-Hayes, M. (1996) Developing a receptive R&D environment: a case study of the chemical industry, *R&D Management*, Vol. 26, No. 1, 83–92.

Tushman, M. and Anderson, M. (1986) Technological discontinuities and organisational environments, *Administrative Science Quarterly*, Vol. 31, No. 3, 439–65.

Tushman, M.L. and Rosenkopf, L. (1992) Organizational determinants of technological change: toward a sociology of technological evolution, *Research in Organizational Behavior*, Vol. 14, 311–47.

Utterback, J.M. (1994) *Mastering the dynamics of innovation: How companies can seize opportunities in the face of technological change*, Harvard Business School Press, Boston, MA.

Wernerfelt, B. (1984) A resource based view of the firm, *Strategic Management Journal*, Vol. 5, No. 2, 171–80.

Willman, P. (1991) Bureaucracy, innovation and appropriability, paper given at ESRC Industrial Economics Study Group Conference, London Business School, November 22.

Further reading

For a more detailed review of the knowledge management literature, the following develop many of the issues raised in this chapter:

Argyris, C. (1977) Double loop learning in organizations, *Harvard Business Review*, September/October, 55.

Gibbert, M. (2006) Generalizing about uniqueness: An essay on an apparent paradox in the Resource-Based View, *Journal of Management Inquiry*, Vol. 15, No. 2, 124–34.

HSBC (2010) 100 Thoughts, HSBC, London.

Kay, J. (1996) Oh Professor Porter, whatever did you do?, *Financial Times*, 10 May, 17.

Newbert, S.L. (2007) Empirical research on the resource-based view of the firm: An assessment and suggestions for future research, *Strategic Management Journal*, 28, 121–46.

Chapter 7
Strategic alliances and networks

Introduction

In strategic alliances firms cooperate out of mutual need and share the risks to reach a common objective. Strategic alliances provide access to resources that are greater than any single firm could buy. This can greatly improve its ability to create new products, bring in new technologies, penetrate other markets and reach the scale necessary to survive in world markets.

Collaboration with other firms, however, can take many forms. Virtually all firms have networks of suppliers, and in some cases this can form part of a firm's competitive advantage.

This case study at the end of this chapter explores the development of high-definition video and the format war between Sony's Blu-ray and Toshiba's HD-DVD. The influence of strategic alliances in this war is clearly evident.

Chapter contents

Learning objectives

When you have completed this chapter you will be able to:

- recognise the reasons for the increasing use of strategic alliances;
- recognise the role of embedded technology in strategic alliances;
- provide an understanding of the risks and limitations of strategic alliances;
- explain how the role of trust is fundamental in strategic alliances;
- examine the different forms an alliance can take;
- explain how the prisoner's dilemma game can be used to analyse the behaviour of firms in strategic alliances; and
- identify the factors that affect the success of an alliance.

Defining strategic alliances

Faced with new levels of competition many companies, including competitors, are sharing their resources and expertise to develop new products, achieve economies of scale, and gain access to new technology and markets. Many have argued that these strategic alliances are the competitive weapon of the next century. A strategic alliance is a contractual agreement among organisations to combine their efforts and resources to meet a common goal. It is, however, possible to have a strategic alliance without a contractual agreement, hence a more accurate definition would be:

> *A strategic alliance is an agreement between two or more partners to share knowledge or resources, which could be beneficial to all parties involved.*

One of the major factors that prevents many firms from achieving their technical objectives and, therefore, their strategic objectives, is the lack of resources. For technology research and development (R&D), the insufficient resources are usually capital and technical 'critical mass'. The cost of building and sustaining the necessary technical expertise and specialised equipment is rising dramatically. Even for the largest corporations leadership in some market segments they have traditionally dominated cannot be maintained because they lack sufficient technical capabilities to adapt to fast-paced market dynamics.

In the past, strategic alliances were perceived as an option reserved only for large international firms. Intensified competition, shortening product life cycles and soaring R&D costs mean that strategic alliances are an attractive strategy for the future. Moreover, Slowinski *et al.* (1996) argue that strategic alliances provide an opportunity for large and small high-technology companies to expand into new markets by sharing skills and resources. They argue it is beneficial for both parties since it allows large firms to access the subset of expertise and resources that they desire in the smaller firm, while the smaller company is given access to its larger partner's massive capital and organisational resources.

For many firms the thought of sharing ideas and technology in particular with another company is precisely what they have been trying to avoid doing since their conception. It is a total lack of trust that lies at the heart of their unwillingness to engage in any form of cooperation. The element of trust is highlighted through the use of the prisoner's dilemma.

Technology partnerships between and in some cases among organisations are becoming more important and prevalent. From 1976 to 1987, the annual number of new joint ventures rose sixfold; by 1987, three-quarters of these were in high-technology industries (Faulkner, 1995; Kaufman *et al.*, 2000; Lewis, 1990). As the costs, including risk associated with R&D efforts, continue to increase, no company can remain a 'technology island' and stay competitive. Illustration 7.1 explains how three automobile firms have formed an alliance to compete across the globe.

The term strategic alliance is used to cover a wide range of cooperative arrangements. The different forms of strategic alliances will be explored later in this chapter.

Illustration 7.1

Renault and Nissan in pact with Daimler

Renault, Nissan and Daimler on Wednesday revealed a strategic partnership that will see the three carmakers swap equity stakes and develop and build small cars, engines and vans together.

The tie-up will allow the Franco-Japanese auto alliance and the German luxury group to pool efforts on new vehicles and technologies and add essential volumes to their production plants at a time of intense competition and rising production and environmental compliance costs in their industry. The companies said the partnership would yield combined benefits of €4bn ($5.3bn) over five years. 'We are creating a technological powerhouse that would benefit all partners', Renault and Nissan's chief executive Carlos Ghosn said. Dieter Zetsche, Daimler's chief executive, said that the two groups had found the 'right cultural fit' for the partnership. They also said they would explore co-operating on technologies relating to electric vehicles and their batteries. Before the deal, Nissan owned 15 per cent of Renault and Renault 44.3 per cent of Nissan.

The tie-up falls short of a full-fledged alliance such as the 11-year-old one between Renault and Nissan, which own large equity stakes in one another. However, it goes well beyond the limited short-term co-operation on individual cars and engines favoured by rival carmakers such as PSA Peugeot Citroën, BMW and Ford.

Daimler's history of difficult alliances

While Daimler has an unhappy history of partnerships with other automakers, its chief executive on Wednesday vowed not to repeat the mistakes of the past.

Dieter Zetsche said the strategic partnership with Renault-Nissan was the 'opposite' of the carmaker's merger with America's Chrysler, which was dissolved in 2008 after nine years that brought Daimler huge losses.

'The main difference is . . . that with Chrysler, we agreed on a merger but had no ideas about areas of collaboration', Mr Zetsche said. He said that Daimler and Renault/Nissan had agreed to take 'small symbolic stakes' in each other only after months of talks on concrete areas of co-operation. 'This is just the opposite of what we did with Chrysler and I am very optimistic that the outcome will be the opposite as well', Mr Zetsche said.

Daimler's boss is wary not to repeat the mistakes of his predecessor, Jürgen Schrempp, whose attempt to create a global carmaker dubbed 'World Inc' by acquiring Chrysler and minority stakes in Japan's Mitsubishi Motors and South Korea's Hyundai failed miserably. The episode caused massive cracks in Daimler's previously self-confident corporate culture.

'We have been very successful as a German carmaker for more than a century', said one senior director of the company. 'But then we got hit from two sides: by the Chrysler problems and by the economic crisis, which caught us off-guard.'

Now Daimler is returning to partnership mode in a push to renew its product range at a time of high costs and pressure to be present in a widening array of technologies, vehicle segments and overseas markets. 'What we need now is a changing culture that allows us to work with other carmakers and accept that they are doing good things as well', the senior director said.

Renault and Daimler had been discussing working together on a new model for the German carmaker's Smart sub-brand, but the talks were expanded to include Nissan and the exchange of mutual stakes.

Daimler has an unhappy history of partnerships with other carmakers, notably Chrysler, with which it avoided sharing swaths of its technology during their nine-year pairing that ended in 2007.

The German carmaker's decision to join forces with Renault and Nissan was driven largely by Europe's tightening of regulation on carbon dioxide, which is forcing premium carmakers to expand into small cars.

Under the share exchange, Daimler will take a 3.1 per cent stakes in both Renault and Nissan, and the allied French and Japanese carmakers will share a 3.1 stake in their German partner, holding 1.55 per cent each.

Source: Reed, J. and Schäfer, D. (2010) Renault and Nissan in pact with Daimler, FT.com, 7 April.

The fall of the go-it-alone strategy and the rise of the octopus strategy

Businesses are slowly beginning to broaden their view of their business environment from the traditional *go-it-alone* perspective of individual firms competing against each other. The formation of strategic alliances means that strategic power often resides in sets of firms acting together. The development of mobile phones, treatments for viruses such as AIDS, aircraft manufacture and motor cars are all dominated by global competitive battles between groups of firms. For example, the success of the European Airbus strategic alliance has been phenomenal. Formed in 1969 as a joint venture between the German firm MBB and the French firm Aerospatiale, it was later joined by CASA of Spain and British Aerospace of the United Kingdom. The Airbus A300 range of civilian aircraft achieved great success in the 1990s, securing large orders for aircraft ahead of its major rival Boeing.

The so-called octopus strategy (Vyas *et al.*, 1995) gets its name from the long tentacles of the eponymous creature. Firms often develop alliances with a wide range of companies. Car making may be one of the world's most competitive big industries, but rival producers have always been ready to cooperate on expensive new technologies and products when the cost or risk of going it alone was too high. The hunt for partners is now intensifying as automakers seek to build scale, cut costs, and pool efforts in areas like small cars, vehicle electrification, and emerging markets as Figure 7.1 shows.

It is not just large established firms that are rushing into new fields in which they are comparatively small and inexperienced. Many small and medium-sized firms are also entering strategic alliances with a variety of different firms. For example, in a survey of 137 Chinese manufacturing SMEs, Zeng *et al.* (2010) find that there are many significant positive relationships between inter-firm cooperation. Furthermore, they find that inter-firm cooperation has the most significant positive impact on the innovation performance of SMEs. They are able to offer their existing skills, knowledge and technology, which together with other areas of expertise can create 'hybrid' technologies such as bioelectronics, or by combining process and product innovations from different industries. Even competitors are collaborating. Ritala and Hurmelinna-Laukkanen (2009) found that collaborating with competitors (coopetition) has been found to be an effective way of creating both incremental and radical innovations, especially in high-tech industries. Firms are increasingly finding they need an array of complementary assets (Teece, 1998).

Pause for thought 

Many small firms are reluctant to engage in any form of sharing information and knowledge, because they believe other firms may steal their valuable information and customers. Maybe there are some firms that should not engage in alliances?

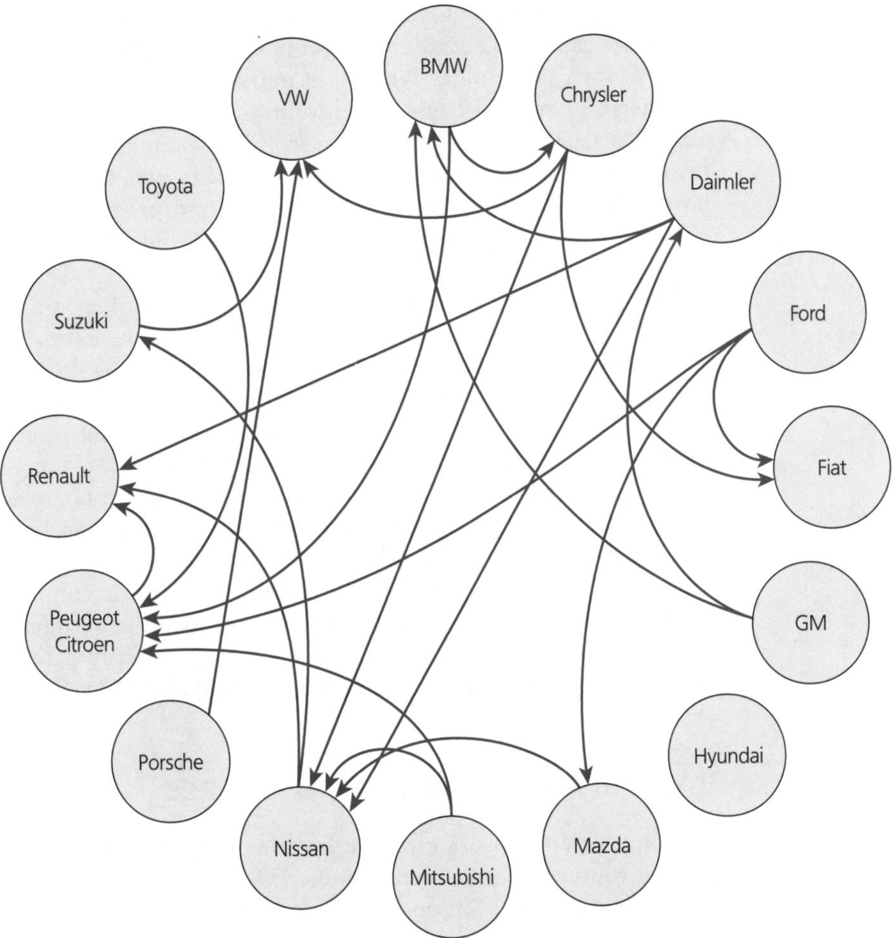

Figure 7.1 The tangled web of alliances between car manufacturers

Source: FT.com, 4 May 2010.

Complementary capabilities and embedded technologies

The example of the automotive sector above illustrates that even firms with a long and impressive heritage to defend see technology as the main determinant of competitive success. As a result they increasingly realise they need access to new technology. Moreover, they also realise they cannot develop it all themselves. Acquiring technology from outside using technology transfer (the subject of technology transfer is explored in much more detail in Chapter 10) and forming alliances with others is now regarded as the way forward.

Many large established firms such as Sony, IBM and Nokia have developed global brands and sophisticated distribution infrastructures, but these are of limited value in the computer hardware industry without a constant stream of new products and technologies. Hence, these firms have developed extensive linkages or networks around the world. Hamel (1991) argues that this is necessary because historically regions of the world have developed skills and competencies in certain areas. For example, European countries have a long history of developing science-based inventions, but suffer from a poor understanding of markets and frequently fail to capture the full commercial potential from their inventions. American firms have demonstrated an ability to generate significant profits from market innovations, but then do not make the continual improvements in cost and quality, whereas Japanese and Asian firms have extensive skills in the areas of quality and production efficiencies. Given this global spread of expertise firms have consequently developed linkages with a wide variety of firms all over the world.

The mechanisms of patents, licensing and technology transfer agreements help to create an efficient market for technology, but as we have seen in earlier chapters, technology is usually embedded with experience, know-how and tacit knowledge. Hence, alliances allow not only for exchange of technology but also for the exchange of skills and know-how often referred to as competencies. For example, General Motors used its joint venture with Toyota to learn about 'lean' manufacturing practices. Similarly Thompson, the French consumer electronics group, relied on its alliance with JVC, from Japan, to learn to mass produce the micromechanic subsystem key to successful videocassette recorder production (Doz and Hamel, 1997). The embedded nature of new technologies has forced firms to view technologies as competencies (clearly some technologies will be more embedded than others). This has resulted in an increasing number of alliances, whereas previously a technology licensing or purchase agreement may have been used (Nadler and Tushman, 1997).

Interfirm knowledge-sharing routines

The only way to ensure effective learning for both parties is to build knowledge-sharing routines (Nelson and Winter, 1982; Cohen and Levinthal, 1990; Trott and Cordey-Hayes, 1996; Day and Shoemaker, 2000). This will involve sharing information,

Innovation in action

Creativity comes in small packages

Looking at the logo designed for the London 2012 Olympics, the Australian founders of Design-Crowd.com were frustrated. It had been produced by a major agency for a large budget, but they believed they knew dozens of people who could do better, but were never given the opportunity.

It was a familiar refrain from the design community. There's a world of creativity out there, and yet large companies restrict themselves to a 'preferred suppliers' list of the largest design agencies. Spurred by this thought, Design-Crowd created a website to enable large companies and small businesses to get ideas and designs from thousands of freelance designers or smaller agencies around the world. The client specifies its requirements for the design, and the amount it will pay for the winning design. It then receives dozens or even hundreds of submissions from different designers, and can pick its favourite.

Source: HSBC (2010) 100 Thoughts, HSBC, London.

know-how and skills. Information can readily be shared via hard copy and electronic data transfer, but know-how and skills are much more difficult, as we have seen in Chapter 6. None the less, it is possible and many firms rely on individuals spending time within other firms, either on secondment for a set time or through exchanges of staff. It is the interpersonal interaction which facilitates the transfer of tacit knowledge. Design and manufacturing alliances such as those established by Nike are very effective at knowledge-sharing routines and hence become more innovative than their competitors. This then becomes a powerful competitive advantage which is extremely difficult to replicate and copy and may give a firm an advantage for many years. Moreover, it is an advantage that a firm may possess which does not require costly patent protection and avoids the risk of copycat branding.

Forms of strategic alliance

Strategic alliances can occur *intra-industry* or *inter-industry*. For example, the three major US automobile manufacturers have formed an alliance to develop technology for an electric car. This is an example of an *intra-industry alliance* and is in response to US legislation requiring a certain percentage of US cars to be gasoline-free by 2010. The UK pharmaceutical giant GlaxoSmithKline has established many *inter-industry* alliances with a wide range of firms from a variety of industries; it includes companies such as Matsushita, Canon, Fuji and Apple.

Furthermore, alliances can range from a simple handshake agreement to mergers, from licensing to equity joint ventures. Moreover, they can involve a customer, a supplier or even a competitor (Chan and Heide, 1993). Research on collaborative activity has been hindered by a wide variety of different definitions. There are eight generic types of strategic alliance (Bleeke and Ernst, 1992; Gulati, 1995; Faulkner, 1995; Conway and Stewart, 1998):

- licensing;
- supplier relations;
- outsourcing;
- joint venture;
- collaboration (non-joint ventures);
- R&D consortia;
- industry clusters; and
- innovation networks.

Licensing

Licensing is a relatively common and well-established method of acquiring technology. It may not involve extended relationships between firms but increasingly licensing another firm's technology is often the beginning of a form of collaboration. There is usually an element of learning required by the licensee and frequently the licensor will perform the role of 'teacher'. While there are clearly advantages of licensing, such as speed of entry to different technologies and reduced cost of technology development, there are also potential problems, particularly the neglect of internal technology development. In the videocassette recording (VCR) industry JVC licensed its VHS recording technology to many firms including Sharp, Sanyo and Thompson. This clearly enabled these firms to enter the new growth industry of the time. But these firms also continued to develop their own technologies in other fields. Sharp, in particular, built on JVC's technology and developed additional features for its range of videocassette recorders.

Supplier relations

Many firms have established close working relations with their suppliers, and without realising it may have formed an informal alliance. Usually these are based on cost-benefits to a supplier. For example:

- lower production costs that might be achieved if a supplier modifies a component so that it 'fits' more easily into the company's product;
- reduced R&D expenses based on information from a supplier about the use of its product in the customer's application;
- improved material flow brought about by reduced inventories due to changes in delivery frequency and lot sizes; and
- reduced administration costs through more integrated information systems.

At its simplest level one may consider a sole-trader electrician, who over time builds a relationship with his equipment supplier, usually a wholesaler. This can be regarded as simply a 'good customer' relationship, where a supplier will provide additional discounts and services for a good customer such as obtaining unusual equipment requests, making special deliveries, holding additional stock, etc. The next level may involve a closer working relationship where a supplier becomes more involved in the firm's business and they share experience, expertise, knowledge and investment, such as developing a new product. For example, the French electronics firm Thompson originally supplied radiocassette players to the car manufacturer Citroën. This relationship developed further when Citroën asked Thompson if it could help with the development of radio controls on the steering wheel. This led to an alliance in the development of new products. Many manufacturing firms are increasingly entering into long-term relationships with their component suppliers. Often such agreements are for a fixed term, say five years, with the option of renewal thereafter. British Aerospace adopt this approach when negotiating component suppliers for its aircraft. Such five-year agreements may also include details of pricing, where British Aerospace will expect the price of the component to fall over time as the supplier benefits from economies of scale and manufacturing experience.

Outsourcing

Outsourcing became popular during the 1980s and expanded during the 1990s. It often refers to the delegation of non-core operations from internal provision or production to an external entity specialising in the management of that operation. The decision to outsource is often made in the interests of lowering firm costs, redirecting or conserving energy directed at the competencies of a particular business, or to make more efficient use of worldwide labour, capital, technology and resources. A good illustration of this is the outsourcing of IT services to specialist providers and of telephone call centres by the financial services industry.

Outsourcing involves transferring or sharing management control and/or decision making of a business function to an outside supplier, which involves a degree of two-way information exchange, coordination and trust between the outsourcer and its client. Such a relationship between two economic entities is qualitatively different from traditional relationships between buyer and seller of services. This is because the two parties involved in an 'outsourcing' relationship dynamically integrate and share management control of the labour process rather than enter in contracting relationships where both entities remain separate in the coordination of the production of goods and services. Consequently, there is a great deal of debate concerning the benefits and costs of the practice. The Sony-Ericsson case study in Chapter 10 illustrates this debate.

Joint venture

A joint venture is usually a separate legal entity with the partners to the alliance normally being equity shareholders. With a joint venture, the costs and possible benefits from an R&D research project would be shared. They are usually established for a specific project and will cease on its completion. For example, Sony-Ericsson is a joint venture between Ericsson of Sweden and Sony of Japan. It was established to set design manufacture and distribute mobile phones. Previously both firms had been unsuccessful in the handset market. The intention of establishing a joint venture is generally to enable the organisation to 'stand alone'. Illustration 7.2 shows how the Corning Corporation has for many years followed a strategy of developing a range of joint ventures based on its technologies.

Collaboration (non-joint ventures)

The absence of a legal entity means that such arrangements tend to be more flexible. This provides for the opportunity to extend the cooperation over time if so desired. Frequently these occur in many supplier relationships, but they also take place beyond supplier relations. Many university departments work closely with local firms on a wide variety of research projects where there is a common interest. For example, a local firm may be using a carbon-fibre material in manufacturing. The local university chemistry department may have an interest in the properties and performance of the material. Cooperation between the parties may produce benefits for both. Such collaboration is frequently extended and maintained for many years (*see* Illustration 10.2).

R&D consortia

A consortium describes the situation where a number of firms come together to undertake what is often a large-scale activity. The rationale for joining a research consortium includes sharing the cost and risk of research, pooling scarce expertise and equipment, performing pre-competitive research and setting standards (*see* 'Forms of external R&D' in Chapter 9 for a more detailed explanation of this form of strategic alliance).

Illustration 7.2

The Corning Corporation

Corning is unique among major corporations in deriving the majority of its turnover from joint ventures and alliances. The company has a long and impressive heritage: as a specialist glass manufacturer it had its own R&D laboratory as far back as 1908. In the 1930s it began combining its technologies with other firms in other industries, giving it access to a wide variety of growth markets. An alliance with PPG gave it access to the flat glass building market; an alliance with Owens provided access to the glass fibres market and an alliance with Dow Chemicals provided it with an opportunity to enter the silicon products market (recent lawsuits in the United States from people whose silicon breast implants were unsuccessful have forced the Dow–Corning alliance into financial difficulties). Corning now has a network of strategic alliances based on a range of different technologies. These alliances now deliver revenue in excess of its own turnover.

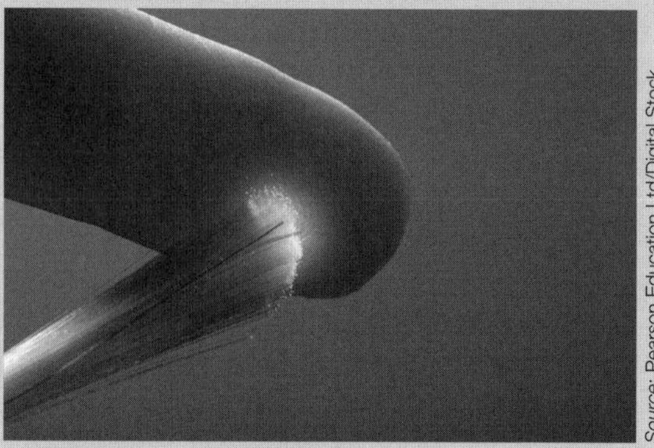
Source: Pearson Education Ltd/Digital Stock

In addition Corning has established a separate division to further develop alliances with firms in the fibres and photonics technologies. Corning Innovation Ventures was established to provide Corning Incorporated with insight and visibility into new technologies and to build future customer partnerships. Corning's unique access to the market and technologies provides partners with guidance to help build and execute a better business plan. The Innovation Ventures team brings together a unique background of technical and marketing skills with 38 years of combined fibre optic and photonic experience within the market leader in optical communications.

In particular, Corning plans to form partnerships with large or small entrepreneurial firms. Such firms may wish to partner with Corning because it is the leader in the optical layer of telecommunications. By utilising its 1,600 scientists, engineers and five major research facilities dedicated to photonic research, any entrepreneur partners are guaranteed access to a wealth of knowledge and experience in photonics and optical fibre. Through the firm's vast network of marketing experience across all its optical product lines, and its extensive customer base at the OEM and carrier level, partners are also granted access to the insight, marketing and commercial experience that has led the firm to its market leadership position.

Source: www.corning.com/innovationventures (2007).

Industry clusters

Michael Porter (1998) identified a number of very successful industry clusters. Clusters are geographic concentrations of interconnected companies, specialised suppliers, service providers and associated institutions in a particular field that are present in a nation or region. It is their geographical closeness that distinguishes them from innovation networks. Clusters arise because they increase the productivity with which companies can compete. The development and upgrading of clusters is an important agenda for governments, companies and other institutions. Cluster development initiatives are an important new direction in economic policy, building on earlier efforts in macroeconomic stabilisation, privatisation, market opening and reducing the costs of doing business.

Porter explains how clusters pose a paradox. In theory, location should no longer be a source of competitive advantage. Open global markets, rapid transportation and high-speed communications should allow any company to source any thing from any place at any time. But in practice, location remains central to competition. Today's economic map of the world is characterised by what Porter calls clusters: critical masses in one place of linked industries and institutions – from suppliers to universities to government agencies – that enjoy unusual competitive success in a particular field. The most famous examples are found in Silicon Valley and Hollywood, but clusters dot the world's landscape. Porter explains how clusters affect competition in three broad ways: first, by increasing the productivity of companies based in the area; second, by driving the direction and pace of innovation; and third, by stimulating the formation of new businesses within the cluster. Geographic, cultural and institutional proximity provides companies with special access, closer relationships, better information, powerful incentives and other advantages that are difficult to tap from a distance. The more complex, knowledge-based and dynamic the world economy becomes, the more this is true. Competitive advantage lies increasingly in local things – knowledge, relationships and motivation – that distant rivals cannot replicate.

Innovation networks

The use of the term network has become increasingly popular. To many it is the new form of organisation offering a sort of 'virtual organisation'. Terms such as 'web' or 'cluster' are also used to describe this or a similar phenomenon (Nadler and Tushman, 1997; DeBresson and Amesse, 1991). Others believe them to be nothing more than a new label for a firm's range of supplier and market relationships. For example, brand management firms like Nike are frequently regarded as network firms. This is because Nike essentially owns and manages the brand and relies on an established network of relationships to produce and distribute its products. It does not own all the manufacturing plant used to manufacture its shoes or all the retail outlets in which its products are sold. It undertakes research, design and development, but has a network of manufacturers in Asia, India and South America. Similarly it has a network of distributors in all the countries in which it operates. Table 7.1 shows the supplier network used by Apple to assemble the iPhone.

There is little consensus in the literature about precisely what an innovation network is or indeed when an innovation network is said to exist, but there is some agreement that a network is more than a series of supplier and customer relationships (Tidd, 2001). Some networks have been described as federated in that a set of loosely affiliated firms work relatively autonomously but none the less engage in mutual monitoring and control of one another (Day and Schoemaker, 2000). Other networks can be viewed more as a temporary web, in which firms coalesce around one firm or a business opportunity. For example, following most natural disasters around the world, a collection of organisations including emergency services, government departments, charities and volunteer organisations quickly work together as a network to tackle the immediate problems. Other networks are sometimes referred to as strategic partnerships and usually evolve from long-standing supplier relationships.

Table 7.1 Assembling the component parts to make an iPhone

Company	Country	Part
1. Samsung	Korea	CPU video processing chips
2. Infineon	Singapore	Baseband communications hardware
3. Primax electronics	Taiwan	Digital camera modules
4. Foxconn International	Taiwan	Internal circuitry
5. Entery Industrial	Taiwan	Connectors
6. Cambridge Silicon	Taiwan	Bluetooth chip sets
7. Umicron Tech.	Taiwan	Printed circuit boards
8. Catcher technology	Taiwan	Stainless metal casings
9. Broadcomm	USA	Touch screen controllers
10. Marvell	USA	802.11 specific parts
11. Apple	Shenzhen China	Assembly; stocks; packs; ships

Through repeated dealings, trust and personal relationships evolve. For example, firms with an established track record in supplying materials, components, etc. to Apple may well find themselves becoming involved in additional activities such as concept testing and product development. This may also include universities, government agencies and competitors.

The United Kingdom's so-called 'motor sport valley', a 100-mile area across southern England centred on Oxford and stretching between Cambridge and Poole, is an interesting example of a loose network or web of firms working within Formula One motor sport. It has a geographic clustering of companies in related industries, a strong focus on innovation and many small flexible manufacturing firms (*see* Illustration 7.3). The point at which a large cluster of firms becomes classified as a 'science park' is a moot point (*see* Chapter 10 for more on science parks). But, in this particular example, unlike 'Silicon Valley' that represents a cluster of firms operating in computer hardware and software industries, the focus of the 'motor sport valley' is on one market – Formula One motor sport.

Illustration 7.3

Lewis Hamilton, McClaren, Red-Bull and the rest make the UK's 'motor sport valley' a world leader

'Motor Sport Valley' is a 100-mile area across southern England centred on Oxford and stretching between Cambridge and Poole; it has many of the features of regionalised, flexible production seen as vital to economic growth in advanced economies (*à la* Silicon Valley, California). These include a geographical clustering of companies in the same sector; high rates of company formation; a strong focus on innovation; emphasis on exports; and flexibility of products and production processes.

With an annual turnover of £6 billion, and supporting over 38,000 jobs, motor sport and performance engineering is one of the UK's industrial success stories. The motor sport industry is also a best practice example of how creativity, engineering, manufacturing and support services can be combined to produce world class radical innovations that have an impact well beyond motor racing. Carbon fibre wheel-chairs, non-slip boots, hi-tech fishing line and the influence of pit-stop crews on the efficient transferral of patients from the operating theatre to intensive care, are all innovations which have their origins in the motor sport industry.

Photo: Schlegelmilch/Corbis

There is 'virtually no other industry in which the need for continual innovation and change is greater than in racing car construction', and that what they see as a surprising degree of flexibility of response at managerial and employee levels plays a large part in the industry's success in the UK.

The competition between the teams helps create a fierce battle for supremacy. Motor sport involves a continuous striving for products and processes to give the winning edge, with knowledge transfer core to the process. Their proximity, within the Valley and at race meetings, also allows the transmission of knowledge through gossip, which plays a much more important role than most realise.

That component suppliers typically work for several teams is seen as beneficial because of the rapid rate of innovation. As long as a team knows it can keep ahead of its rivals, it is not viewed as a problem if the ideas eventually get transferred throughout the industry. An individual team probably has more to gain than lose through the skills which components suppliers learn by servicing a number of different racing car companies.

Source: Delbridge, R. and Mariotti, F. (2009) *Racing for radical innovation: How motorsport companies harness network diversity for discontinuous innovation*, Advanced Institute of Management Research, London.

The 'virtual company'

More recently the idea of a virtual company has begun to emerge. This is where every aspect of the business is outsourced and run by unknown suppliers. Illustration 7.4 shows how the pharmaceutical industry is making progress in this radical way of running a business. However, there are clearly aspects of control that may be lost in such organisations. Other aspects such as intellectual property, skills and know-how may also be lost if everything is outsourced. Illustration 7.4 gives the chilling warning of the business opportunities that may be lost when activities are outsourced. When IBM launched its first PC in 1981 it outsourced the development of the operating system to a small firm called Microsoft!

Illustration 7.4

The virtual organisation

Many business commentators allege that the business organisation of the future will be virtual. But precise definitions of what it means to be a virtual organisation are hard to find. A virtual company resembles a normal traditional company in its inputs and its outputs. It differs in the way in which it adds value during the journey in between.

The virtual organisation has an almost infinite variety of structures, all of them fluid and changing. Most of them need virtually no employees. A New York insurance company was once started from scratch by someone whose overriding aim was to employ nobody but himself. The UK's Virgin Group briefly held 5 per cent of the British cola market with just five employees. This was achieved by tightly focusing on the company's core competence: its marketing. Everything else, from the production of the drink to the distribution of it, was done by someone else.

The virtual organisation has few physical assets, reflecting the fact that adding value is becoming more dependent on (mobile) knowledge and less dependent on (immobile) plant and machinery. The case study at the end of Chapter 12 illustrates how Innocent have built a business with few physical assets. Hollywood is often cited as a template for the virtual organisation. The way that movies have been made since the industry freed itself from the studio system (where everyone was a full-time employee) has been virtual. A number of freelancers, from actors to directors via set builders and publicity agents, come together with a common purpose: to make a movie, to tell a story on celluloid. They then go their separate ways and another (unrelated) bunch of people (with a similar set of skills) comes together to make another movie. And so it goes on, very productively.

Linked to the idea of the virtual organisation is the idea of the virtual office, a place where space is not allocated uniquely to individual employees. People work as and when they need to, wherever space is available. This practice is commonly referred to as hot-desking. The virtual office has the advantage of providing a different vista every day. But it makes it difficult to form close relationships with colleagues.

The process of defining the virtual organisation is a gradual one. As companies withdraw more and more into their core competencies, so they become more virtual. The virtual organisation is able to leverage this core into almost any industrial sector. Thus it can be in the pensions business and the railway business at the same time (as is the Virgin organisation in the UK). It can then rapidly desert any one of those businesses, and equally rapidly move into something completely different by establishing strategic alliances with organisations that have the essential skills that it lacks. It can do this anywhere in the world.

Motives for establishing an alliance

Frequently alliances will have multiple objectives. For example, an alliance may seek to access technology, gain greater technical critical mass and share the risk of future technology development. The European Airbus is a good example of an alliance that has multiple objectives. Table 7.2 lists the most common reasons cited for entering a strategic alliance.

Research by Morrison and Mezentseff (1997) suggests that strategic business alliances will only achieve a sustainable competitive advantage if they involve learning and

Table 7.2 Reasons for entering a strategic alliance

Reasons	Examples
1 Improved access to capital and new business	European Airbus to enable companies to compete with Boeing and MacDonnell Douglas
2 Greater technical critical mass	Alliance (LG Philips) between Philips of the Netherlands and LG Electronics of Korea. Provides access to Philips' technology and lower manufacturing costs in Korea
3 Shared risk and liability	Sony-Ericsson, a joint venture between two electronics firms to try to dominate mobile phone handset market
4 Better relationships with strategic partners	European Airbus
5 Technology transfer benefits	Customer–supplier alliances, e.g. VW and Bosch
6 Reduce R&D costs	GEC and Siemens 60/40 share of telecommunications joint venture: GPT
7 Use of distribution skills	Pixar and Disney; Waitrose and Ocado
8 Access to marketing strengths	NMB, Japan and Intel; NMB has access to Intel's marketing
9 Access to technology	Ericsson gained access to Sony's multimedia technology for third-generation mobile phones
10 Standardisation	Sony licensed their Blue-ray technology to other manufacturers to help secure industry standard over Toshiba's HD DVD
11 By-product utilisation	GlaxoSmithKline and Matsushita, Canon, Fuji
12 Management skills	J Sainsbury and Bank of Scotland; Sainsbury accessed financial skills

Source: D.A. Littler (1993) 'Roles and rewards of collaboration', in Tidd, J., Besant, J. and Pault, K. (eds) (2001) *Managing Innovation*, Wiley, Chichester, p. 51; P.S. Chan and D. Heide (1993) Strategic alliances in technology: key competitive weapon, *Advanced Management Journal*, Vol. 58, No. 4, 9–18; A. Harney (2001) Ambitious expansion loses its shine: analysts change their tune about Sony's dreams and begin to count the costs of the new mobile phone alliance with Ericsson, *Financial Times*, 2 October; R. Budden (2003) 'Sony-Ericsson seeks success with new phones', FT.com, 3 March.

knowledge transfer (*see* Figure 10.6). They design a framework to help such partnerships develop a cooperative learning environment to achieve long-term success. The emphasis on learning helps to develop individual and organisational intelligence, thereby ensuring the future success of the strategic alliance.

The process of forming a successful strategic alliance

The formation of a strategic alliance is a three-step process (*see* Figure 7.2). It begins with the selection of the right partner. This will clearly depend on what is required and the motivation for the strategic alliance. This is usually followed by negotiations based on each partner's needs. The third and final stage is the management towards collaboration. This last step encompasses a wide range of activities, including joint goalsetting and conflict resolution. Moreover, this last stage needs constant work to keep the relationship sound. Aside from collaborative management, the success of a business alliance depends on the existence of mutual need and the ability to work together despite differences in organisational culture.

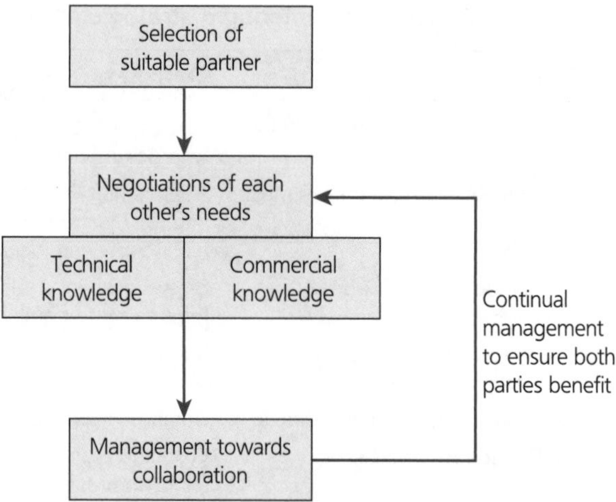

Figure 7.2 The process of forming a strategic alliance

Negotiating a licensing deal

The most common form of alliance is the well-established licensing agreement. Licensing deals are just that – a deal struck between two parties. There is not a correct deal or an incorrect one, simply an agreement where two parties agree to do business that will usually result in benefits for both. For example, the licensing deal struck between Bill Gates and his tiny Microsoft company and the mighty IBM in the 1980s is regarded by many as the one single act of genius that Gates made that helped to launch Microsoft. Similarly the licensing deal struck by J.K. Rowling's agent and the publisher where the author held on to the film rights was another decision of inspired brilliance.

Since most people engaged in deal making are involved in multiple deals at the same time, important aspects can be forgotten or overlooked at any time and for any deal. The following is an inexhaustive list that provides an insight into the areas that need to be agreed upon. Most firms that are involved in licensing will ensure they have people in such positions that are well educated and experienced in dealing with the scientific, legal and business arenas, all at the same time. After all, as experienced negotiators will testify, there is only one thing more expensive than a patent agent and that is a bad patent agent. Simple mistakes can be costly. And what is crucial to one party may not be to the other.

Terms for the agreement

Each licence will have its own specific set of definitions and clear definitions will add great clarity to a licence. All other appropriate terms should be listed and defined. For example, if dealing with a company, is it the company and all its affiliates? All of its subsidiaries? Or only the parent company? Products/processes licensed should be specifically defined as 'Licensed Products' or 'Licensed Processes'. If only certain types of inventions are covered, these need to be referred to as 'Inventions', including the patent number and/or patent application number that is being licensed. The agreement must also specify whether know-how is included.

Licensee, sales, net sales, profit, territory, field, patents, patent rights, intellectual property, and non-profit are examples of other relatively common terms, and there are many more. Once defined, these terms will usually appear, throughout the rest of the contract.

Rights granted

The agreement should also include which intellectual property rights the licence is given under: patent right only or know-how right only or both, and exclusive right, coexclusive with the licensor, or non-exclusive. The licence agreement should also specify the term of the exclusivity and/or non-exclusivity, and whether such a right is irrevocable; and if there is a right to grant sublicences.

Licence restrictions

Either of the parties may also wish to include licensee restrictions concerning the industry or market, territory, prior licensee's rights, and the commercial rights retained by the licensor.

Improvements

The agreement needs to address any improvements made and/or patented (by whom and paid for by whom) during the term of the licence by either the licensor or licensee and what obligations are present in the deal as to whether or not to include future technology under the present licence or to have future technology fall under the reservation of rights to the licensor.

Consideration (monetary value)

The consideration is relatively involved, and can be cut back if equity is not part of the payment for the licence. Royalty, milestone payments, type of currency, determining rate of exchange and equity-ownership issues all need to be considered as this can result in substantial differences in payments. The issue of minimum annual payments is particularly important in the case of an exclusive licence.

Reports and auditing of accounts

The issue of establishing the level of royalties can be tricky. Firm's rely on the licensor to inform them of the actual level of sales achieved. Hence, royalties based on any measure tied to a product's sales needs to be paid to the licensor accompanied by a report stating how the royalty was calculated. The agreement should also specify how often and when these reports (and royalties) are due. Additionally, the right of the licensor to audit the books that generate these reports can be a part of the licence agreement.

Representations/warranties

Certain basic representations and warranties need to be given by each party to the other, such as the ability to enter into the agreement, the validity of the intellectual property and a standard warranty disclaimer.

Infringement

The agreement needs to address issues associated with infringement such as: if the IP is infringed by third parties, how such an infringement will be handled, and if there is a recovery for the infringement, how that will be divided between the licensor and licensee.

Confidentiality

A confidentiality, or non-disclosure, agreement will usually have been signed prior to the licensee agreement to enable exploration of terms of business, etc. This should remain effective during the term of the license agreement.

Arbitration

In the case of a major disagreement about the terms of an agreement, parties may wish to take the issue to arbitration. Arbitration can be carried out in many different ways and it is easier to specify in the agreement the rules to be used for arbitration, before there is an issue to arbitrate. A trade body or other independent organisation could perform this role. This should help avoid expensive legal costs.

Termination

Areas to consider include: the right of either party to end the agreement for no reason at all; the rights of the party that has performed when confronted with a party that refuses to perform; material breach issues; and length of notification of breaching activity and time given to the breaching party to cure the breach before losing rights and/or being charged penalties. Issues dealing with the natural expiration of the licence should be considered, as well. What happens to the know-how (if any) upon the expiration of all patents? And what are the confidentiality provisions?

Risks and limitations with strategic alliances

So far we have addressed only the potential benefits to be gained from strategic alliances. However, a strategic alliance also has a downside. It can lead to competition rather than cooperation, to loss of competitive knowledge, to conflicts resulting from incompatible cultures and objectives, and to reduced management control

(Chan and Heide, 1993). A study of almost 900 joint ventures found that less than half were mutually agreed to have been successful by all partners (Harrigan, 1986; Dacin *et al.*, 1997; Spekman *et al.*, 1996). Illustration 7.5 shows how after more than eight successful years together Pixar and Disney decided to end the joint venture. While the future looks bright for Pixar, Disney's future is less assured.

The literature on the subject of technological cooperation presents a confusing picture. There is evidence to suggest that strategic alliances may harm a firm's ability to innovate. Arias (1995) argues that inter-firm networking may result not only in desired outcomes but also in negative consequences. The creation of closely structured networks of relationships may produce increased complexity, loss of autonomy and information asymmetry. These hazards may ultimately lead to a decreased ability to innovate and participate in technological change.

Illustration 7.5

Setback for Disney as Pixar alliance ends

Michael Eisner's efforts to revive the fortunes of Walt Disney suffered a fresh blow as his hugely successful alliance with Pixar, the animation studio behind *Finding Nemo* and *Toy Story*, collapsed.

The failure will trigger a scramble among other Hollywood studios, which have been angling to take over from Disney as distributor of Pixar's blockbuster movies.

The collapse of the talks with Pixar robs Disney of an important strategic alliance and analysts said it was a serious setback for Mr Eisner, the company's chairman.

Peter Mirsky, an analyst at Oppenheimer in New York, said the Pixar relationship not only generated income from movies but also plugged a hole left by the weakness in Disney's own animation division, for instance by supplying a new crop of popular characters for its theme parks.

Run by Steve Jobs, founder of Apple Computer, Pixar has had an unbroken run of five hit movies which has made it one of the hottest properties in the movie business. Its ground-breaking 3D animation combined with cute characters and storylines have brought comparisons with Disney's own impact on animation in its heyday.

The negotiations foundered despite Disney's willingness to take a far smaller slice of the income from future Pixar films. Disney was also willing to agree a simple distribution deal that would have paid it a basic fee that is far lower than it has accepted on any similar arrangement before, said one person close to the company. At the moment it takes a 12 per cent distribution fee, shares half of the profits from the movies and keeps ownership of Pixar's movies.

In a brief statement, Mr Jobs said: 'We've had a great run together – one of the most successful in Hollywood history – and it's a shame that Disney won't be participating in Pixar's future success.'

Despite losing access to future Pixar films, Disney still has the rights to make sequels to the company's earlier movies, which include *Monsters Inc* and *A Bug's Life*.

Disney buys Pixar in $7.4 billion deal

Walt Disney has now agreed a $7.4 billion (£4.1 billion) deal to buy Pixar, the animation firm behind films including *Toy Story* and *The Incredibles*. Disney's distribution deal with Pixar was due to end in 2006, and it seemed the two would split after failing to agree on how to divide future profits. The loss of Pixar would have been a blow for Disney, as demand for the company's films, as well as DVDs, videos and merchandise, has proved to be very strong. Disney's earnings from Pixar's six films are estimated to be about $3.2 billion.

Sources: R. Waters and P.T. Larsen (2004) Setback for Disney as Pixar alliance ends, *Financial Times*, 29 January. Reprinted with permission.

To avoid these problems, management should anticipate business risks related to partnering, carefully assess their partners, conduct comprehensive resource planning and allocation of resources to the network and develop and foster social networks. All parties should also ensure that the motives for participating are positive, that the networks are as formidable as the alliances within them and that there is a perception of equal contribution and benefits from the parties. Lastly, there should be communication, data sharing, goals and objectives.

The level and nature of the integration appears to be a crucial factor. In some cases the alliance is very tight indeed. For example, Motoman, a robotic systems supplier, and Stillwater Technologies, a tooling and machining company, share the same facility for their offices and manufacturing and their computer and communications systems are linked (Sheridan, 1997). For other firms a loose alliance is far more comfortable.

Research in the area of failure of alliances identifies seven different reasons (Vyas *et al.*, 1995; Duysters *et al.*, 1999):

1 failure to understand and adapt to new style of management required for the alliance;
2 failure to learn and understand the cultural differences between the organisations;
3 lack of commitment to succeed;
4 strategic goal divergence;
5 insufficient trust;
6 operational and or geographical overlaps; and
7 unrealistic expectations.

The formation of strategic alliances by definition fosters cooperation rather than competition. Ensuring competition remains is a major implication of strategic alliances.

Illustration 7.6

Insourcing helps Brompton Cycles to profits rise

Brompton Cycles is the London-based company that makes folding bicycles familiar to health-conscious business people. Sales for 2009 rose almost 27 per cent to £762,521, on a 35 per cent rise in turnover to £11.4m. It is led by Will Butler-Adams, 34. Brompton Bicycle employs 90 people, up from 50 five years ago, and has 120 suppliers, three-quarters of them in the UK. Some 70 per cent of its output is exported to countries including Japan, Spain, Germany, South Korea and the US. The bicycles sell for £550 to £1,000. 'That's a lot for a bicycle, but not for a mode of transport', says Mr Butler-Adams, who came to the company six years ago from the chemicals industry.

'Each bike contains 1,200 parts, 70 per cent of which are unique to our bicycles and which we've designed ourselves', says Mr Butler-Adams.

'Five years ago we made three-quarters ourselves and outsourced the rest; now the proportion is more like the other way around. The change has increased efficiency and enabled us to make more bikes in the same amount of space.'

As a result, Brompton's factory is on course to make 22,500 bikes this year, up from 6,500 in 2000. The goal is to reach an annual output of 50,000 by about 2013.

The company was founded in 1978 by Andrew Ritchie, a former Cambridge University engineering graduate, who remains technical director and a large shareholder but has recently relinquished the top job in the company to the younger man.

Source: Moules, J. (2010) How to keep your best people happy in the saddle, FT.com, 25 October.

The respective government departments of trade and commerce around the world need to be vigilant of the extent to which firms that cooperate are also capable of manipulating the price of products.

There is of course another way: insourcing. Illustration 7.6 shows how Brompton Cycles has brought manufacturing back in house and profits have increased.

The role of trust in strategic alliances

The business and management literature and accepted management thinking are predominantly optimistic in their belief that there is much to gain from strategic alliances and collaborative technology development. This optimism remains largely robust despite substantial failures of high-profile alliances highlighting the difficulties and limitations of such strategic alliances (see Porter, 1987; Bleeke and Ernst, 1992).

According to the strategic management literature, firms with a global presence – in particular those operating in technology-intensive sectors – are increasingly reliant on collaborative technology development. They can no longer continue to rely on the use of traditional means to protect their 'secrets', such as internalisation and legal controls, because they need to become more 'outward-looking' and therefore more receptive in their technology development strategy. By its very nature, collaborative technology development means that sharing knowledge and 'openness' is a precondition for successful organisational learning. Openness and free exchange of information, however, make companies more vulnerable to risks of information leakage. It is in this specific context that the problem of trust emerges most clearly in collaborative technology development. In order to reap the benefits from collaborative technology development, companies or, more precisely, research managers need to be able to trust their partners (Hollis, 1998).

The concept of trust

All forms of collaboration involve an element of risk and require substantial amounts of trust and control. It is the leakage of sensitive information to competitors that is of most concern to firms. Innovative applied research often develops out of the collaboration of firms and research institutions, where this is initiated with the help of previous academic contacts of key players in firms and universities. In this case the selection of, and decision to trust, a partner is typically made on the basis of prior professional and or social knowledge (Liebeskind and Oliver, 1998; Zucker *et al.*, 1996). For example, scientists working at one large firm will have graduated from university with friends who took up similar positions in other large firms. Hence, every scientist will have a small network of scientists largely as a result of university. Firms recognise that all their scientists operate within networks and expect them to exercise their professional judgement. Usually personal knowledge and the desire to protect one's professional reputation are sufficient safeguards to justify a limited-scale disclosure of sensitive information. If the initial collaboration is successful, the scale of collaboration can be increased incrementally and higher levels of mutual trust will be reached (Lewicki and Bunker, 1996).

Trust is not the same as confidence. For example, supporters of football teams are confident that their team will work hard and win some games over the course of the season, but they trust their players, manager and club that collectively the organisation will try to win and that results are not 'fixed' through corruption. Both confidence and trust are based on expectations about the future, but trust entails the exposure to the risk of opportunistic behaviour by others. One can say that an agent exhibits trust when he or she has no reason to believe that the trusted other will exploit this opportunity (Giddens, 1990; Humphrey and Schmitz, 1998).

It is important to keep in mind that trust is practised and exercised between individuals, even if they represent an organisation. Trust is a personal judgement and carries an emotional as well as a cognitive dimension. While trust at the system level is similar to confidence – as there is no choice but to trust the currency to store value – trust in an institution or organisation depends on personal experience with individuals representing the organisation at its contact points (Giddens, 1990). This does not mean that the institutional dimension should be underestimated.

Trust, then, exists at the individual and organisational levels and research has attempted to distinguish different levels and sources of trust (Zucker, 1986; Sako, 1992; Hoecht and Trott, 1999). The bases of trust in alliances are identified in Table 7.3.

The sources of trust production are not mutually exclusive and often work in conjunction. For instance, while membership of an ethnic group (personal-based trust) can be a vital initial advantage for setting up a business, or having studied at a particular university for finding 'open doors', this will not be enough to sustain trust over time. Trust can be initiated as personal trust, but it will have to be 'earned' before long (Humphrey and Schmitz, 1998). Similarly, bestowing trust on to a person or an institution does not mean that methods of limiting the damage from potential 'betrayal' cannot be used. Contractual safeguards, access to legal redress and institutional assurances can have a very positive effect on collaborative business relations as Lane and Bachmann (1996) have shown in their comparison of the role of trust in UK and German supplier relations.

In the context of collaborative R&D, institutional sources of trust production will, however, be of limited use only. It is clearly not possible to rely on institutional-based trust and legal safeguards for the protection of intangible, pre-competitive knowledge against misuse (Sitkin and Roth, 1993). Even if such safeguards were

Table 7.3 Types of trust

Type of trust	Characteristics
Process	Where trust is tied to past or expected exchange, such as reputation or gift exchange
Personal	Where trust is tied to a person, depending on family background, religion or ethnicity
Institutional	Where trust is tied to formal structures, depending on individual or firm specific attributes
Competence trust	Confidence in the other's ability to perform properly
Contractual trust	Honouring the accepted rules of exchange
Goodwill trust	Mutual expectations of open commitment to each other beyond contractual obligations

workable, the necessity to incorporate each little step along the development path of a collaborative research project into a contractual arrangement would cause enormous delays and hence endanger its very success. The level of trust needed here is the one labelled 'goodwill trust' by Sako (1992), where the mutual commitment goes beyond honouring what is explicitly agreed and the trustee can be trusted to exercise the highest level of discretion, to take beneficial initiatives and to refrain from taking unfair advantage even if such opportunities arise (Hoecht and Trott, 1999).

Innovation risks in strategic outsourcing

Outsourcing was originally confined to peripheral business functions and mainly motivated by a cost-saving logic, but has now developed into a routine strategic management move that affects not only peripheral functions, but also the heart of the competitive core of organisations. At the same time, there is a move from traditional outsourcing with one or a small number of key partners and long-term contracts to strategic outsourcing with multiple partners and short-term contracts. Such a strategy is not without risks. Indeed, the literature has identified many risks and limitations with outsourcing (*see* Table 7.4). One in particular needs to be considered carefully here. This risk is closely related to the more general issue of information leakage that arises when business organisations collaborate in order to gain access to knowledge and expertise that they cannot develop on their own. Hoecht and Trott (1999) have demonstrated that there is a trade-off between access to cutting-edge knowledge via collaborative research and technology development in knowledge-intensive industries and the risk of losing commercially sensitive knowledge to competitors. This risk, they argue, cannot be controlled by traditional management approaches and legal contracting alone, but requires the operation of social control and in particular the development of trust to be contained.

Strategic outsourcing goes beyond traditional outsourcing in the sense that competitive advantages are being sought through opening up all business functions, including the core competencies which should provide competitive advantage to

Table 7.4 Main risks identified in the literature

Main negative outcomes	Main references
1 Dependence on the supplier	Alexander and Young (1996); Aubert *et al.* (1998)
2 Hidden costs	Earl (1996); Alexander and Young (1996); Aubert *et al.* (1998); Lacity and Hirschheim (1993); Barthelemy (2001)
3 Loss of competencies	Bettis *et al.* (1992); Martisons (1993); Quinn and Hilmer (1994); Khosrowpour *et al.* (1995); Alexander and Young (1996); Aubert *et al.* (1998); Doig *et al.* (2001)
4 Service provider's lack of necessary capabilities	Earl (1996); Aubert *et al.* (1998); Kaplan (2002)
5 Social risk	Lacity and Hirschheim (1993); Barthelemy and Geyer (2000)
6 Inefficient management	Wang and Regan (2003); Lynch (2002)
7 Information leakage	Hoecht and Trott (2006)

Source: Adapted from Quélin, B. and Duhamel, F. (2003) Bringing together strategic outsourcing and corporate strategy: outsourcing motives and risks, *European Management Journal*, Vol. 21, No. 5, 647–61.

whoever can provide the perceived best solution, internal or external (Quélin and Duhamel, 2003). In contrast to traditional outsourcing, there are no protective boundaries around core activities in the hope that the organisations can maximise their innovative capacity by being an active part of a networked economy. This means that rather than having exclusive arrangements with one or very few service providers over long periods of time which will be expected to offer tailor-made solutions, strategic sourcing arrangements will be with multiple partners over short periods of time (Da Rold, 2001) and with very little protection of internal core competency functions against outsiders.

There is a certain paradox inherent in this approach: a very high level of trust is required for such relationships as the risks involved are substantial while at the same time the conditions for building trust are undermined by a shorter-term orientation with less commitment compared to traditional outsourcing relationships. The risks are significantly higher than with traditional outsourcing: not only is the risk of leakage of commercially sensitive information significantly increased when firms cooperate with multiple partners, but also the very core of the competitive advantage in terms of knowledge, expertise and capabilities will be made dependent on outsiders. There is a danger that the organisations pursuing strategic sourcing may even lose the absorptive capacity required to recognise and exploit new opportunities by themselves.

The reliance on outside providers can be problematic, not only because key areas of expertise may be gradually lost to the outsourcing organisation but also because outside providers may not have the desired leading edge expertise over the long term (Earl, 1996) or may spread their expertise among many clients so that it degrades from 'best in world' to mere industry standard. The problem of information leakage lies at the heart of this dilemma. Companies want exclusivity in their relationships with their service providers, but consultants who work with many clients are unlikely to be able not to be influenced and not to spread the best practice they acquire when working with different client firms. Detailed legal contracts may offer short-term solutions as they can protect tangible outcomes from specific projects undertaken, but not every innovation-related project outcome is tangible and can be clearly defined in legal contracts. Also, consultants are clearly expected to work at the cutting edge of their professional expertise for all of their clients.

In a networked economy, there is hardly any choice for a firm but to have close relationships with more than one service provider. If an industry develops closer networked links among constituent firms and if every single service provider firm entertains more and shorter-term relationships with competing buyer firms, then 'information boundaries' are opened up and long-term relationship commitments are reduced. The predominant boundary relationship with client firms is likely to shift from 'organisational insider' to 'outside agent', as we have discussed above. By entertaining more than one relationship with external service providers itself, the individual buyer firm will have less certainty than before in its exclusive relationships, but at least it would also have the chance to benefit from the more widely shared industry best practice, spread among its competitors by the service providers. The effect might be a levelling out of core skill advantages within the industry, benefiting the industry overall, but eroding the competitive advantage of some of its members. From the point of view of the individual firm, then, the question is how it can maintain a commitment to secrecy and confidentiality from multiple service provider firms while sharing in the benefits of best practice in the industry.

Furthermore, the inability to retain a company's competitive core will not only endanger its future competitiveness, but can also create a serious risk of dependency on outside providers. A crucial question is whether the desired access to 'best in industry' capabilities are sufficient to sustain its competitive advantage, in particular where the provider serves 'many masters' and the particular expertise ceases to be unique and becomes best-practice industry standard. While there is no shortage of advice in the literature on how to manage the risk of dependency from outside providers and suppliers in general (*see*, for instance, Currie and Willcocks (1998) who suggest multi-vendor approaches and shorter-term contracts for handling large-scale long-term total outsourcing contracts with IT/IS providers), the specific problem that access to world-leading expertise via outsourcing may well be compromised by the 'levelling out' of unique advantages when leading service providers spread their world-leading expertise to several clients has not received much attention.

As a consequence of the problem of 'levelling out' of leading edge expertise, the innovation impact of outsourcing is not limited to the issue of core competencies and the need of companies to retain at least the absorptive capacity to exploit innovations that have been developed by outside service providers. There is also the problematic assumption that service providers are always able to infuse best practice into the company. In a traditional outsourcing relationship, a long-term commitment is entered into that 'locks' a company to a service provider for the length of the service contract. The ability to infuse best industry practice may not only depend on the relative competence of the provider, but the service providers may also be restricted in their ability to pass on best practices by confidentiality agreements with previous and other current clients. A significant dilemma emerges: individual firms have a reasoned case against competitors gaining the fruits of their investment and innovation efforts, while at the same time the majority of companies choose outsourcing not least in the hope of gaining such advantages from other firms. This dilemma is mainly left to the service providers and the individual consultants they employ to resolve. It is, however, a very important issue from an organisational innovation perspective. We will see below that this issue becomes even more pressing when companies and industries move away from traditional long-term outsourcing relationships with single service providers to strategic outsourcing, i.e. to much more open, short-term relationships with multiple suppliers involving all business processes.

Eating you alive from the toes up

There are innovation risks associated with outsourcing. The next section examines some of these risks. Within virtually every industrial sector firms are continually under pressure from their shareholders, customers and employees to deliver more profits, to cut costs and to deliver improved products and services. Over the past two decades firms have turned to outsourcing in an attempt to deliver in these areas. This began with outsourcing periphery activities such as catering and cleaning but increased to include maintenance and IT infrastructure. For manufacturing firms the idea of outsourcing to China and India was attractive because of the low labour costs. Some of these firms proved to be so very effective at the manufacturing that they also took on distribution of products. A good example of this is in the personal computer (PC) industry. Since 1976 Acer has been building PCs for others, including

Dell, IBM and Hewlett Packard. This has helped drive the growth of Taiwan's IT industry. With over 25 years of experience in manufacture and assembly Acer is regarded as an expert and leader in its field. It has now decided to develop its own brand of PC: the Acer brand. This will now compete with the very same firms for which it builds PCs.

Many firms believe that many activities can be outsourced, but that their creative knowledge development should be retained. However, even in the R&D and new product development arenas some firms have turned outside for help to:

- obtain additional expertise;
- put together additional resources;
- reduce development costs;
- reduce time to market;
- develop new areas of competencies.

The risk here of course is that once a firm outsources its R&D and new product development (NPD) one is left wondering what does it do? The answer from such a firm is that it owns the brand and will develop and invest in the brand. The danger here of course is that the firm doing the outsourcing may well decide that it too can develop a brand and so eventually does everything. The outsourcing firm has slowly eaten the client firm from the toes up, and finally consumed it.

The use of game theory to analyse strategic alliances

Research using game theory has suggested that some alliance structures are inherently more likely than others to be associated with a high opportunity to cheat, high behavioural uncertainty and poor stability, longevity and performance. Parkhe (1993) argues maintaining robust cooperation in inter-firm strategic alliances poses special problems. The study by Parkhe looked at 111 inter-firm alliances. The findings suggested the need for a greater focus on game-theoretic structural dimensions and institutional responses to perceived opportunism in the study of voluntary inter-firm cooperation.

The development of the VCR industry is littered with strategic alliances formed by various businesses to try to help ensure they gain access to the relevant technology. Unfortunately not all the alliances were successful. Sony embarked on several strategic alliances with competitors in an attempt to try to make its Betamax technology the industry standard. When JVC, Toshiba and others refused, the alliance existed in name only (Baden-Fuller and Pitt, 1996). There are many other examples of alliances failing – some soon after inception, others after a long and successful relationship.

The issue of trust is a critical element in any strategic alliance. By its very nature an alliance, like a marriage, is dependent on all parties working together so that the total outcome is greater than any one party can achieve on its own. It is important to note that trust is usually established over a long period of time, in much the same way as courtship prior to marriage involves understanding one another and building confidence in the relationship. In order to lose trust, however, one must have gained it in the first place. A more serious proposition is that firms may enter a strategic alliance with a lack of trust in the other party. The issue of trust is the underlying theme of the prisoner's dilemma, which is discussed in the next section.

Game theory and the prisoner's dilemma

Source: A. Harrison/Pearson Education Ltd

The prisoner's dilemma: this is probably the most well-known of the games from game theory. Most of us can readily put ourselves in the shoes of the prisoner behind bars, as he wrestles with the dilemma of which answer to give in order to achieve the best outcome.

The extent to which two companies are going to cooperate is a key question for any strategic alliance. This question can be examined using the prisoner's dilemma. It graphically highlights the options facing companies when they embark on a strategic alliance. It illustrates that cooperation is the mutually advantageous strategy but that non-cooperation provides high-risk opportunities to both parties.

The basic form of this game is known as the prisoner's dilemma and gets its name from the following scenario. Suppose two criminals are arrested for drug dealing. The local police chief arrests them both and takes them to the cells for interrogation. They are placed in separate cells and face fierce questioning. The police chief, however, does not have sufficient evidence to gain a conviction. The chief asks Detective Holmes to offer a deal to both criminals. If either confesses, he will receive a minimal sentence for becoming an informer and helping the police. If neither confesses they will both receive a sentence based upon some other lesser charge for which the police chief does have evidence. If they both confess, the court will take this cooperation into account and will probably pass a lighter sentence on both. The game matrix is represented in Figure 7.3, with the relevant years of sentence to be expected.

Both criminals A and B have a dominant strategy. No matter what the other does, both are better off if they confess. The option of 'do not confess' carries with it the risk of spending 10 years in prison. The maximum sentence for confessing is six years with a possibility of only a year. Given this pay-off matrix both criminals should confess. This is the classic form of the prisoner's dilemma.

It has a close relative, which is the repeated game. This is a more realistic interpretation of reality, as few business relationships are one-off events. For example, BMW competes with Volkswagen in a variety of markets now and most likely in the future. With the knowledge that one is to repeat any game played, the options are likely to be different. To return to the criminals locked up in prison: if they both realise that 'squealing' on a fellow-prisoner may bring with it some form of revenge,

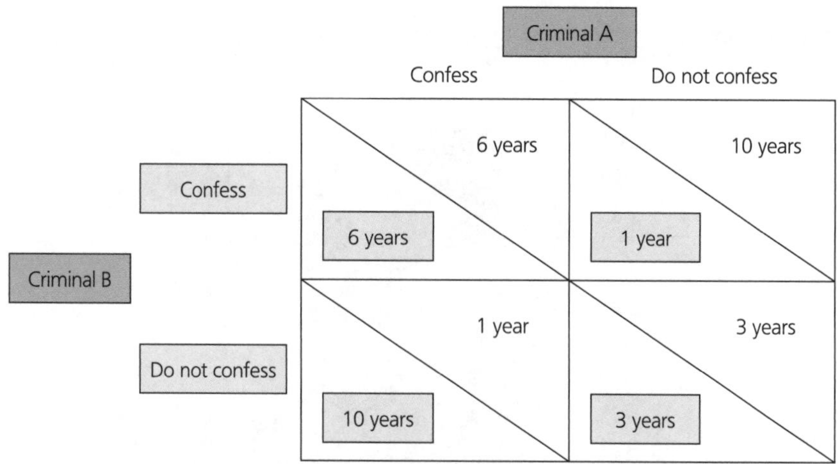

Figure 7.3 Prisoner's dilemma

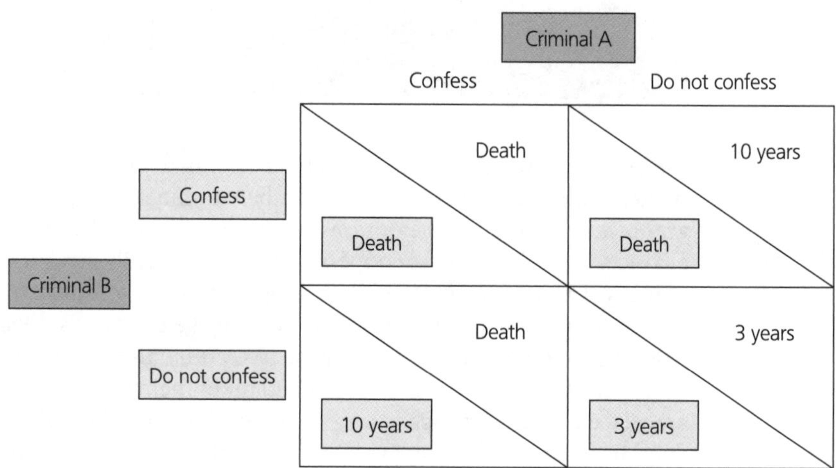

Figure 7.4 The repeated game

such as death, from the prisoner's friends, the range of outcomes changes significantly. The dominant solution is now to play *do not confess*. Figure 7.4 shows the repeated game matrix.

Use of alliances in implementing technology strategy

As we have seen, alliances are often pursued as ways to explore new applications, new technologies or both. By their very nature they confront uncertainty and knowledge asymmetry between the partners. Consequently there are many calls for full explicit agreements with plans to be signed in advance of any collaboration, especially by accountants and lawyers. Yet this can prevent and hinder collaboration because of the lack of familiarity between the partners. What is often required is a more informal approach to enable both parties to learn from each other. Moreover, the collaboration and learning often evolves over time as the parties begin to understand one another better. The benefits can be great indeed, but the costs are often not fully visible. There are significant hidden costs such as management time and energy.

Pause for thought

Many analysts argue strategic alliances are like marriages. But does this mean many of them will end in tears? Is it possible to have a happy ending?

Case study

And the winner is Sony's Blu-ray – the high-definition DVD format war

Christopher Simms and Paul Trott

This case study explores the development of high-definition video and the format war between Sony's Blu-ray and Toshiba's HD DVD. A format war describes competition between mutually incompatible proprietary formats that compete for the same market, typically for data storage devices and recording formats for electronic media. A useful historical example of one of the first format wars was between railway width gauges in the United Kingdom during the Industrial Revolution of the early 1800s. Isambard Kingdom Brunel developed a 2.1m width gauge for his Great Western Railway because it offered greater stability and capacity at high speed. While George Stephenson developed a 1.44m width gauge for the first mainline railway, the Liverpool to Manchester Railway; the de facto standard for the colliery railways where Stephenson had worked. Needless to say the narrower 1.44m gauge won simply because more of this track had been laid, but trains today could be travelling much faster if the wider gauge had been adopted.

The story of the VCR, Betamax, DVD, HD DVD and Blu-ray

Blu-ray Disc (popularly known simply as Blu-ray) is an optical disc storage medium designed to supersede the standard DVD format. Its main uses are for storing high-definition video, PlayStation 3 video games and other data. Blu-ray Disc was developed by the Blu-ray Disc Association, a group representing makers of consumer electronics, computer hardware and motion pictures. The discs have the same physical dimensions as standard DVDs and CDs. The name *Blu-ray Disc* derives from the 'blue laser' used to read the disc. While a standard DVD uses a 650 nanometer red laser, Blu-ray Disc uses a shorter wavelength 405 nm laser, and allows for over five times more data storage on single-layer and over 10 times on double-layer Blu-ray Disc than a standard DVD. During the high-definition optical disc format war, Blu-ray Disc competed with the HD DVD format. Toshiba, the main company that supported HD DVD, conceded defeat in February 2008, and the format war came to an end. In late 2009, Toshiba released its own Blu-ray Disc player. The →

Source: Oliver/Leedham/Alamy Images

two formats have been battling for the growing high-definition share of the £12.3 billion a year global home DVD market. High-definition DVDs offer improved visuals and sound, but also make it harder for content to be illegally copied and pirated. It's a sweet victory for the Sony-backed Blu-ray format. Sony's technically superior Betamax video format lost out to JVC-backed VHS when those formats went head to head in the 1980s.

The story of film and broadcast recording technology for home use dates back to the mid-twentieth century. When television first took off in the 1950s, the only means of preserving video footage was through kinescope, a process in which a special motion picture camera photographed a television monitor. Kinescope film took hours to develop and made for poor quality, and was only useful for the broadcasters themselves. The electronics industry saw opportunities to develop recording technologies and a race developed to create a standard format for doing this. This race continues today.

Overview of the development of the VCR industry

Invented in 1956, the VCR had a lifespan of around 50 years and revolutionised the movie industry, changed television-watching habits, triggered the first 'format wars', and raised new copyright questions, establishing jurisprudence on fair use.

The big electronic companies of the 1950s raced to develop a technology for home recording and playback during the 1950s, seeing a significant opportunity and market gap, and they therefore started working on recorders that used magnetic tape. The first launched player was developed by the Ampex Corporation: however, the world's first magnetic tape video recorder, the VRX-1000 (which was launched in April 1956), had a price tag of $50,000 and expensive rotating heads that had to be changed every few hundred hours. This therefore made it an unviable consumer item, although it was popular with television networks.

Many companies abandoned their research and followed Ampex's lead. RCA pooled patents with Ampex and licensed in the Ampex technology. The new goal for the firms in the industry was to develop a video machine for home use. It had to be solid, low-cost and easy to operate. Sony released a first home model in 1964, followed by Ampex and RCA in 1965. While these machines, and those that followed over the next 10–15 years, were much less expensive than the VRX-1000, they remained beyond the means of the average consumer, and were bought primarily by wealthy customers, businesses and schools. But there was still strong competition to develop a consumer format.

The competition between the companies attempting to develop a consumer format led to the release of three different, mutually incompatible VCR formats: Sony's Betamax in 1975, JVC's VHS in 1976 and the Philips V2000 in 1978. Two of these would come head-to-head in the 1980s in what became known as the First Format War. Before the technology battle could begin, however, the consumer electronics industry had to find an answer to a more pressing problem: content. Where would it come from? What would people watch on their VCRs? At this stage, the industry regarded the VCR's television recording feature as a bonus option of little utility to the average home user: why, they asked, would anyone want to record a TV show and watch it later? They thought movie videos would provide an answer to the content problem, but the movie industry itself was convinced this idea was not to its advantage.

Copyright issues for the VCR

Home video sent the movie industry into a spin. Television had already stolen a big part of its market, and it saw the VCR as a massive new threat. Copyright, the move industry argued, was at stake. Did not the mere recording of a television show constitute an infringement of the copyright owner's rights over reproduction? The studios took the issue to court. In 1976, the year after Sony's release of the Betamax VCR, Universal City Studios and the Walt Disney Company sued Sony, seeking to have the VCR impounded as a tool of piracy.

New communications technology – then as now – has always challenged previous assumptions and jurisprudence in the area of copyright. The first court decision in 1979 went against the studios, ruling that use of the VCR for non-commercial recording was legal. The studios appealed and the decision was overturned in 1981. Sony then took the case to the US Supreme Court, who finally ruled that home recording of television programmes for later viewing constituted 'fair use'. An important factor in the Court's reasoning was that 'time-shifting' – i.e. recording a programme to watch it at another time – did not represent any substantial harm to the copyright holder, nor did it diminish the market for the product.

By then, the VCR had become a popular consumer product and, contrary to their fears, the film studios found themselves to be major beneficiaries of the technology as the sale and rental of movie videos began generating huge new revenue streams. In 1986 alone, home video revenues added more than $100 million of pure profit to Disney's bottom line. The television stations, on the other hand, having found that the 'useless' recording option was a big hit with viewers, faced a different problem. They had to find new ways to keep their advertisers happy now that viewers could fast-forward through the commercial breaks.

Setting the standard: VHS v. Betamax

Meanwhile, the format war between VHS and Betamax was underway. When Sony released Betamax, they were confident of the superiority of their technology and assumed that the other companies would abandon their formats and accept Betamax as the industry-wide technical standard. They were wrong. On their home turf in Japan, JVC refused to comply and went to market with their VHS format. In the European market, Philips did not play along either, but technical problems were to take Philips out of the fight almost before it began.

From where Sony stood, the only clear advantage of the VHS format was its longer recording time. So, Sony doubled the Betamax recording time and JVC followed suit. This continued until recording times were no longer an issue for potential customers, and marketing overtook superior technology as the key to the battle.

Betamax was arguably a superior technology (although debate on this continues today, and many argue that the difference in quality was only really relevant to those using the machines commercially); Beta SP was still used by professional videographers until relatively recently. But what Betamax really needed was market share. Morita (Sony's CEO) blames Betamax's eventual defeat on insufficient licensing. Despite the fact that it was the better product, Betamax never achieved a large enough presence to create consumer preference. VHS had gravity and won the battle.

The two companies were on a par for several years until JVC's VHS format pulled ahead. This was due in part to JVC's broader licensing policy. Counting on increased royalties to make money on their VHS machines, JVC licensed the technology to big consumer electronics companies like Zenith and RCA (a company with significant presence in the United States at the time). As a result, VHS machines became more abundant on the market and prices fell, increasing their consumer appeal.

At about the same time in the early 1980s, video rental shops started springing up on every street corner. Early on, the video shop owners recognised that they would have to make VCRs available for cheap rental to attract a larger client base. The high-quality Betamax machines were more expensive, harder to repair, and the first models were only compatible with certain television sets. So VHS became the obvious choice for the rental shops. Another factor that influenced the outcome is the adult entertainment industry (porn). The size of this industry is enormous and the porn studios' decision to use VHS may also have influenced the outcome. This combined effect of greater availability of machines and increased availability of content on VHS eventually squeezed out Betamax.

Technology development, of course, did not stand still. By 2003 DVD sales had overtaken those of the VCR, signalling the dying days of magnetic tape. Video rental shops, sensitive to market trends, switched to DVD, accelerating the demise of the VCR; eventually leading to a sharp demise in sales of video recorders (VHS). The DVD had advantages in terms of quality, although it lacked the same flexibility and ease of recording that were the case for the VHS format. Today few VCRs are sold (and it is very difficult to find players, with most retailers having stopped selling such machines), and the format is close to being obsolete.

An on-going issue that rumbles on in the background of the format wars is the issue of copyright. It continues to be a key influence in firm's strategic decision making towards the new formats of streaming and downloadable media, as well as the HD disk formats.

The development of DVD

The development of the Laserdisc by Philips in 1969 yielded many of the technologies Sony carried over and utilised when it partnered with Philips to jointly create the CD in 1979. In the early 1990s these two companies then worked closely together again to develop a new high-density disc called the MultiMedia

→

Compact Disc (MMCD was the original name), but their format was eventually more or less abandoned in favour of Toshiba's competing Super Density Disc (SD), which had the vast majority of backers at the time, such as Hitachi, Matsushita (Panasonic), Mitsubishi, Pioneer, Thomson and Time Warner. The two factions cut a deal, brokered by IBM president Lou Gerstner, on a new format: DVD. Toshiba wound up on top after the dust settled in 1995–96, and Sony and Philips, who were not cut in on the standard (and royalties) nearly as much as they would have liked, immediately started work on a next generation system. The Professional Disc for DATA (aka PDD or ProDATA), which was based on an optical disc system Sony had already been developing alongside the existing project, would eventually become the Blu-ray disc. Toshiba, not to be outdone by Philips and Sony, also started work on a new generation system: the Advanced Optical Disc, which eventually evolved into the HD DVD.

Blu-ray DVD vs. HD DVD

After 35 years of optical audio/video disc development history seems to have repeated itself with the launch of the two competing formats of HD DVD and Blu-ray DVD, with both factions attempting to beat one another in order to 'reap the rewards'. The Blu-ray and HD DVD formats were both launched in the early twentieth century, with each format having been developed by competing electronics companies. Sony, alongside Royal Philips Electronics, developed the Blu-ray format, whilst HD DVD was developed by Toshiba, alongside Hitachi.

In 2005 what could be described as 'on going peace talks' between the Blu-ray and HD DVD camps finally dissolved after many attempts to develop a compromise of the next-generation format. This meant that the two companies would have to compete head to head to become the standard for the next generation of video recording and reproduction for the living room.

The two formats are incompatible with one another, despite using lasers of the same type. HD DVD discs also have a different surface layer (the clear plastic layer on the surface of the data, which is the bit you get fingerprints and scratches on) from Blu-ray discs. HD DVD uses a 0.6 mm-thick surface layer, the same as DVD, while Blu-ray has a much smaller 0.1 mm layer to help enable the laser to focus. Herein lie the issues associated with the higher cost of Blu-ray discs. This thinner surface layer is what makes the discs more costly: because Blu-ray discs do not share the same surface layer thickness of DVDs, costly production facilities must be modified or replaced in order to produce the discs. A special hard coating must also be applied to Blu-ray discs, so their surface is sufficiently resilient enough to protect the data a mere 0.1mm beneath – this also drives the cost up. Blu-ray therefore, unlike HD DVD, requires a hard coating on its discs because data is 0.5mm closer to the surface. The polymer coating it uses, called Durabis, was developed by TDK and is supposedly extremely resilient and fingerprint resistant. The added benefit of keeping the data layer closer to the surface, however, is more room for extra layers. This increased cost, which would more than likely lead to increased prices to the consumer, was an issue that would threaten the potential success of the Blu-ray, although the format does hold more data (as shown in Table 7.5 below).

Table 7.5 DVD performance details

Capacity			
Blu-ray		**HD DVD**	
ROM single layer	23.3/25GB	Single layer	15GB
ROM dual layer	46.6/50GB	Dual layer	30GB
RW single layer	23.3/25/27GB	–	–
RW dual layer	46.6/50/54GB	–	–
Highest test	100GB	Highest test	45GB
Theoretical limit	200GB	Theoretical limit	60GB

Film studio support

Not only did each format have to compete to establish themselves as superior in the eyes of the consumer, there was also a separate battle to be won with the movie studios in order to secure eventual success. Table 7.6 shows the different studios and their initial support of each format.

It is also worth noting that in the years prior to the launch of these formats, and immediately afterwards, Sony acquired a number of film studios. Sony was also rumoured to be paying some studios large sums to take on and stick with its format.

A much more difficult factor to unravel is the list of networks (formal and informal) that each group of firms developed. In some cases it was clear, with firms listing associate members of each board. Once again Blu-ray had a longer list of members and interested parties. It seemed Sony had learnt from its mistakes with VCR and it was not going to make the same mistake again (*see* Table 7.7).

Table 7.6 Studios supporting HD DVD and Blu-ray

Studios (movie and game) listed as supporting members	
Blu-ray	**HD DVD**
20th Century Fox	Buena Vista Home Entertainment
Buena Vista Home Entertainment	New Line Cinema
Electronic Arts	Paramount Pictures
MGM Studios	The Walt Disney Company
Paramount Pictures	Universal Studios
Sony Pictures Entertainment	Warner Bros.
The Walt Disney Company	
Vivendi Universal Games	
Warner Bros.	

Table 7.7 Interlinkages and networks between firms

Companies listed as members of the board or managing members	
Blu-ray	**HD DVD**
Apple Computer Corp.	Memory-Tech Corporation
Dell, Inc.	NEC Corporation
Hewlett Packard Company	Sanyo Electric Co.
Hitachi, Ltd.	
LG Electronics Inc.	
Mitsubishi Electric Corporation	
Panasonic (Matsushita Electric)	
Pioneer Corporation	
Royal Philips Electronics	
Samsung Electronics Co., Ltd.	
Sharp Corporation	
Sony Corporation	
TDK Corporation	
Thomson	
Twentieth Century Fox	
Walt Disney Pictures and Television	

→

Whilst the mainstream film studios play a key role in determining the relative success of each format, perhaps as important as the big media conglomerates may be the adult entertainment industry. Most industry analysts agree that US pornographers' decision to adopt the cheap convenient VHS – rather than rival Betamax – when the two systems were introduced in the 1970s killed off Betamax, and sales of pornographic films drove the adoption of video recorders. It may have been Sony's failure to license Betamax that led to its demise but the adult entertainment industry probably also contributed to its demise. Dario Betti, an analyst at London-based digital media consultancy Ovum, says: 'Like it or not, pornography drives each new, convenient visual technology'. Few may be willing to admit it, but sex sells, and there is certainly a case that more convenient nudity (and the pornographers' preferred choice between HD-DVD and Blu-ray) will play some role in determining which of the two formats are, ultimately, successful.

The Sony Playstation

The first Blu-ray player launched by Sony (the primary developer of the Blu-ray format) was actually the Play Station 3 (PS3), which featured the ability to play Blu-ray disks. This gave Sony something of an upper hand for some time, because its PlayStation 3 games console has a built-in Blu-ray player. Sony had therefore sold more than 10 million Blu-ray units while only about 1 million HD-DVD players have been sold, mostly in Japan.

The Playstation 3 was originally launched at a price of around £500, the first 'pure' Blu-ray player was launched later and at a price of around £800. Obviously in comparison to the Playstation this player lacked a number of features, particularly the ability to play games. Interestingly, one of the earliest machines to play HD-DVD was also a games console, the Xbox 360, which was Microsoft's primary competitor against the Playstation (and priced around £200 cheaper). Both of these consoles were notably more expensive than Nintendo's Wii, which was attracting much attention around this time. Despite the high technological performance of both the Playstation and Xbox, Nintendo has been able to gain a majority share in the market (and this is also despite the Playstation's ability to play Blu-ray disks).

Discussion: the winner and the future

Sony's decision to incorporate Blu-ray playback into the PS3 is thought to have been a decisive factor in the format emerging victorious. Ultimately the Blu-ray format won the war to become the next generation of HD player. Another factor that has been linked to this is the 'Wal-Mart effect' – after an announcement from the US retailer that it would only sell Blu-ray movies and players. This retailer has massive power in the US market. With Sony's victory, however, comes another battle: movie downloads. Music downloading destroyed the CD industry; the same may happen in DVD. Why would people go out to the shops to buy disks when they can buy high-definition movies straight away online? What does this suggestion say for the future of Blu-ray?

Interestingly, despite Apple giving its backing to the Blu-ray format; it has yet to produce a single computer with a Blu-ray drive. Instead, Apple seems to be concentrating on movies delivered across the internet, through iTunes and the new Apple TV, rather than on physical discs. So although Blu-ray has won this battle, it may not have won the war. As home internet speeds become faster and consumers get used to video on-demand services, the movie market could undergo a similar change to the music sector, with films downloaded rather than physically bought. Enter a new format war of online video . . .

When Google released the high-quality WebM video format royalty-free to the world, digital video publishers were faced with a conundrum: support the guaranteed royalty-free but slightly lower-quality WebM standard, or the sharper but potentially more expensive H.264 industry standard? The industry divided among the WebM camp, the H.264 supporters, and the true neutrals of the browser world:

- WebM support only: Mozilla Firefox;
- H.264 support only: Microsoft internet Explorer and Apple Safari;
- both: Google Chrome and Opera.

In 2010 the MPEG LA technology licensing body announced that the H.264 standard will join WebM on the royalty-free side of the fence until the end of time or until the standard becomes obsolete, whichever comes first. This makes Google's $133 million buyout of On 2 Technologies seem like a waste of money – that's where the technology for WebM came from, and now there's really no need to provide a royalty-free alternative to the prevailing standard. But few believe that H.264 would be free today if Google had not made that investment.

H.264 is not *entirely* free even now. Free use extends only to services that are free to end users such as Google's YouTube. Apple will still have to pay licence fees for the videos it sells through iTunes. But part of that payment goes back into Apple's own pockets – the company is a longtime backer of and patent contributor to the H.264 standard. Other major beneficiaries of the H.264 licence fee include Microsoft, Cisco Systems and Dolby Laboratories. Keeping the standard relevant and revenue-producing is important to these firms, while Google is not part of the consortium and so has little incentive to support H.264.

Questions

1 What does this case tell us about whether or not it is the best technology and or being first in the market that determines the winner of these product format battles?

2 Illustrate some other business sectors where different formats coexist and some where a single format is preferred.

3 Use the CIM (Figure 1.9) to illustrate the innovation process in this case.

4 Why was the Playstation the first Blu-ray player and subsequently when Blu-ray players were launched, why did the Playstation remain cheaper? Consider possible reasons for this.

5 What additional factors helped Blu-ray win the battle? What role did licensing and networks play in the relative success of each format?

6 What related industries contributed to the format war and how did they influence its outcome?

7 With the increasing popularity and use of downloading films what influence will the DVD format winner play in this related battle.

8 What are the implications for innovation strategy, R&D expenditure and marketing for firms engaged in or likely to be engaged in a format war?

9 List the key factors that seem to determine the eventual winner in industry format wars. Divide these into primary and secondary factors.

Chapter summary

This chapter has explored the role of strategic alliances and how firms are increasingly recognising that alliances provide access to resources that are greater than any single firm could buy. The main purpose was to highlight their growing importance within the world of business. This is further reinforced by the concept of industry clusters and networks. In some knowledge-intensive industries, such as the film industry, the role of alliances has been further developed. In these network industries loose alliances are formed to undertake a project, and when the project is finished the organisation ceases to exist. Linked to the issue of cooperation is the question of intellectual property and in particular the potential problem of information leakage. Many firms are understandably reticent about entering any form of collaboration for they fear losing the small advantage which they perceive they have over their competitors. Trust is frequently at the centre of any decision on whether a firm enters an alliance, and usually trust has to be established over a period of time before firms agree to enter an alliance.

Discussion questions

1 Explain why the car industry seems to have so many strategic alliances.

2 What is meant by 'levelling out of knowledge'? How can firms prevent this happening when engaging in strategic alliances.

3 Considering the case study, discuss some of the wider strategic reasons why firms may wish to enter a strategic alliance.

4 Apple seems to have many strategic alliances and supplier relations. Discuss the extent to which these contribute to its success.

5 Explain some of the risks involved with all strategic alliances.

6 Explain why the repeated game of the prisoner's dilemma is considered to be more useful in predicting behaviour.

Key words and phrases

References

Alexander, M. and Young, D. (1996) Outsourcing: Where's the value?, *Long Range Planning*, Vol. 29, No. 5, 728–30.

Arias, J.T.G. (1995) Do networks really foster innovation?, *Management Decision*, Vol. 33, No. 9, 52–7.

Aubert, B.A., Patry, M. and Rivard, S. (1998) Assessing the risk of IT outsourcing, Working Paper, 98s-16, May, Cirano, Montreal.

Baden-Fuller, C. and Pitt, M. (eds) (1996) *Strategic Innovation*, Routledge, London.

Barthelemy, J. (2001) The hidden costs of IT outsourcing, *Sloan Management Review*, Vol. 42, No. 3, 60–9.

Barthelemy, J. and Geyer, D. (2000) IT outsourcing: findings from an empirical survey in France and Germany, *European Management Journal*, Vol. 19, No. 2, 195–202.

Bettis, R., Bradley, S. and Hamel, G. (1992) Outsourcing and industrial decline, *Academy of Management Executive*, Vol. 6, No. 1, 7–22.

Bleeke, J. and Ernst, D. (1992) *Collaborating to Compete*, John Wiley, New York.

Chan, P.S. and Heide, D. (1993) Strategic alliances in technology: key competitive weapon, *Advanced Management Journal*, Vol. 58, No. 4, 9–18.

Cohen, W.M. and Levinthal, D.A. (1990) A new perspective on learning and innovation, *Administrative Science Quarterly*, Vol. 35, 128–52.

Conway, S. and Stewart, F. (1998) Mapping innovation networks, *International Journal of Innovation Management*, Vol. 2, No. 2, 223–54.

Currie, W.L. and Willcocks, L.P. (1998) Analysing four types of IT sourcing decisions in the context of scale, client/supplier interdependency and risk mitigation, *Information Systems Journal*, Vol. 8, No. 2, 119–43.

Da Rold, C. (2001) 'Buying commodity/access services instead of outsourcing', Gartner Group, Research Note, June.

Dacin, M.T., Hitt, M.A. and Levitas, E. (1997) Selecting partners for successful international alliances, *Journal of World Business*, Vol. 32, No. 1, 321–45.

Day, G.S. and Schoemaker, P.J.H. (2000) *Wharton on Managing Emerging Technologies*, John Wiley, New York.

DeBresson, C. and Amesse, F. (1991) Networks of innovators: a review and introduction to the issues, *Research Policy*, Vol. 20, 363–73.

Doig, S.J., Ritter, R.C., Speckhals, K. and Woolson, D. (2001) Has outsourcing gone too far?, *McKinsey Quarterly*, Vol. 4, 24–37.

Doz, Y. and Hamel, G. (1997) 'The use of alliances in implementing technology strategies', in Tashman, M.L. and Anderson, P. (eds) *Managing Strategic Innovation and Change: A Collection of Readings*, Oxford University Press, New York.

Duysters, G., Kok, G. and Vaandrager, M. (1999) Crafting successful strategic technology partnerships, *R&D Management*, Vol. 29, No. 4, 343–51.

Earl, M. (1996) The risks of outsourcing IT, *Sloan Management Review*, Spring, 26–32.

Faulkner, D. (1995) *International Strategic Alliances*, McGraw-Hill, Maidenhead.

Giddens, A. (1990) *The Consequences of Modernity*, Oxford University Press, Oxford.

Gulati, R. (1995) Does familiarity breed trust? The implications of repeated ties for contractual choice in alliances, *Academy of Management Journal*, Vol. 38, No. 1, 85–112.

Hamel, G. (1991) Competition for competence and inter-partner learning within international strategic alliances, *Strategic Management Journal*, Vol. 12, No. 1, 83–103.

Harrigan, K.R. (1986) *Managing for Joint Venture Success*, Lexington Books, Lexington, MA.

Hoecht, A. and Trott, P. (1999) Trust, risk and control in the management of collaborative technology development, *International Journal of Innovation Management*, Vol. 3, No. 3, 257–70.

Hoecht, A. and Trott, P. (2006) Innovation risks of strategic outsourcing, *Technovation*, Vol. 26, No. 4, 672–81.

Hollis, M. (1998) *Trust Within Reason*, Cambridge University Press, Cambridge.

Humphrey, J. and Schmitz, H. (1998) Trust in inter-firm relations in developing and transition economies, *Journal of Development Studies*, Vol. 34, No. 4, 32–61.

Kaplan, J. (2002) Partners in outsourcing, *Network World*, Vol. 19, No. 11, 41.

Kaufman, A., Wood, C.H. and Theyel, G. (2000) Collaboration and technology linkages: a strategic supplier typology, *Strategic Management Journal*, Vol. 21, 649–63.

Khosrowpour, M., Subramanian, G. and Gunterman, J. (1995) 'Outsourcing organizational benefits and potential problems', in Khosrowpour, M. (ed.) *Managing Information Technology Investments with Outsourcing*, Idea Group Publishing, London, 244–68.

Lacity, M. and Hirschheim, R. (1993) *Information Systems Outsourcing: Myths, Metaphors and Realities*, John Wiley, Chichester.

Lane, C. and Bachmann, R. (1996) The social construction of trust: supplier relations in Britain and Germany, *Organisation Studies*, Vol. 17, No. 3, 365–95.

Lewicki, R.J. and Bunker, B.B. (1996) 'Developing and maintaining trust in work relationships', in Kramer, R. and Tyler, T. (eds) *Trust in Organisations*, Sage, London, 114–39.

Lewis, J.D. (1990) *Partnerships for Profit*, The Free Press, New York.

Liebeskind, J. and Oliver, A. (1998) 'From handshake to contract: intellectual property, trust and the social structure of academic research', in Lane, C. and Bachmann, R. (eds) *Trust Within and Between Organisations: Conceptual Issues and Empirical Applications*, Oxford University Press, Oxford, 118–45.

Lynch, C. (2002) Price vs value: the outsourcing conundrum, *Logistics Management and Distribution Report*, Vol. 41, No. 2, 35.

Martisons, M. (1993) Outsourcing Information Systems: A strategic partnership with risks, *Long Range Planning*, Vol. 26, No. 3, 18–25.

Morrison, M. and Mezentseff, L. (1997) Learning alliances – a new dimension of strategic alliances, *Management Decision*, Vol. 35, Nos. 5–6, 351.

Nadler, D.A. and Tushman, M. (1997) *Competing by Design: The Power of Organisational Architecture*, Oxford University Press, New York.

Nelson, R.R. and Winter, S. (1982) *An Evolutionary Theory of Economic Change*, Harvard University Press, Boston, MA.

Parkhe, A. (1993) Strategic alliance structuring: a game theoretic and transaction cost examination of interfirm cooperation, *Academy of Management Journal*, August, Vol. 36, No. 4, 794.

Porter, M.E. (1987) From competitive advantage to corporate strategy, *Harvard Business Review*, May–June, 43–59.

Porter, M.E. (1998) Clusters and the new economics of competition, *Harvard Business Review*, November–December, 10–24.

Quélin, B. and Duhamel, F. (2003) Bringing together strategic outsourcing and corporate strategy: outsourcing motives and risks, *European Management Journal*, Vol. 21, No. 5, 647–61.

Quinn, J. and Hilmer, F. (1994) Strategic outsourcing, *Sloan Management Review*, Summer, 43–55.

Sako, M. (1992) *Prices, Quality and Trust: Inter-firm Relations in Britain and Japan*, Cambridge University Press, Cambridge.

Sheridan, J. (1997) An alliance built on trust, *Industry Week*, Vol. 246, No. 6, 67.

Sitkin, S. and Roth, N. (1993) Explaining the limited effectiveness of legalistic 'remedies' for trust/distrust, *Organization Science*, Vol. 4, 367–92.

Slowinski, G., Seelig, G. and Hull, F. (1996) Managing technology-based strategic alliances between large and small firms, *Advanced Management Journal*, Vol. 61, No. 2, 42.

Spekman, R.E., Lynn, A.I., MacAvoy, T.C. and Forbes, I. (1996) Creating strategic alliances which endure, *Long Range Planning*, Vol. 29, No. 3, 122–47.

Teece, D. (1998) Capturing value from knowledge assets: the new economy, markets for know-how and intangible assets, *California Management Review*, Vol. 40, No. 3, 55–79.

Tidd, J. (2001) Innovation management in context, organisation and performance, *International Journal of Management Reviews*, Vol. 3, No. 3, 168–83.

Trott, P. and Cordey-Hayes, M. (1996) Developing a 'receptive' environment for inward technology transfer: a case study of the chemical industry, *R&D Management*, Vol. 26, No. 1, 83–92.

Vyas, N.M., Shelburn, W.L. and Rogers, D.C. (1995) An analysis of strategic alliances: forms, functions and framework, *Journal of Business and Industrial Marketing*, Summer, Vol. 10, No. 3, 47.

Wang, C. and Regan, A.C. (2003) Risks and reduction measures in logistics outsourcing, TRB Annual Meeting.

Zucker, L. (1986) Production of trust: institutional sources of economic structure, 1840–1920, *Research in Organisational Behaviour*, Vol. 8, 53–111.

Zucker, L., Darby, M., Brewer, M. and Yusheng, P. (1996) 'Collaboration structure and information dilemmas in biotechnology: organisational boundaries of trust production', in Kramer, R. and Tyler, T. (eds) *Trust in Organisations. Frontiers of Theory and Research*, Sage, London, 90–113.

Further reading

For a more detailed review of the strategic alliances and innovation networks literature, the following develop many of the issues raised in this chapter:

Ahuja, G. (2000) Collaboration networks, structural holes, and innovation: a longitudinal study, *Administrative Science Quarterly*, Vol. 45, 425–55.

Brusoni, S., Prencipe, A. and Pavitt, K. (2001) Knowledge specialization, organizational coupling, and the boundaries of the firm: why do firms know more than they make?, *Administrative Science Quarterly*, Vol. 46, 597–621.

Deeds, D.L., DeCarolis, D. and Coombs, J. (2000) Dynamic capabilities and new product development in high technology ventures: an empirical analysis of new biotechnology firms, *Journal of Business Venturing*, Vol. 15, No. 3, 211–29.

Faulkner, D. (1995) *Co-operating to Compete*, McGraw-Hill International, Maidenhead.

Mason, G., Beltram, J. and Paul, J. (2004) External knowledge sourcing in different national settings: a comparison of electronics establishments in Britain and France, *Research Policy*, Vol. 33, No. 1, 53–72.

Ritala, P. and Hurmelinna-Laukkanen, P. (2009) What's in it for me? Creating and appropriating value in innovation-related competition, *Technovation*, Vol. 29, No. 12, 819–28.

Zeng, S.X., Xie, X.M. and Tam, C.M. (2010) Relationship between cooperation networks and innovation performance of SMEs, *Technovation*, Vol. 30, No. 3, 181–94.

Chapter 8
Management of research and development

Introduction

This chapter shows how R&D is managed as there remains a strong belief that R&D departments are freewheeling places of artistic disorder. Yet, in the large industrialised firm where R&D is institutionalised, it is fully recognised that invention and creativity emerge from the routine of R&D, and innovation follows under management instruction and control. This is not merely understood but also a requirement. For when firms such as Siemens spend annually in excess of $5 billion on R&D, their shareholders would rightly expect that this investment is closely managed and its activities monitored. Moreover, a decent return on these R&D investments is expected. At the end of this chapter is a case study telling the story of the development of Viagra. This helps to illustrate the prominent role given to R&D in technology-intensive industries. But it also shows the key role played by marketing in helping to make the product successful.

Chapter contents

Learning objectives

When you have completed this chapter you will be able to:

- recognise that R&D management is context dependent; the development of a new engine for an aircraft, for example, may take 10 years and involve many different component suppliers; the development of a new domestic cleaning product, however, may take only a few months;
- recognise that the R&D function incorporates several very different activities;
- explain that formal management techniques are an essential part of good R&D management; and
- recognise that investment in R&D must be looked at in the same way as any other investment in the business – the benefits it produces must exceed the costs.

What is research and development?

To many, especially academics, the term research will mean the systematic approach to the discovery of new knowledge. Universities do not usually develop products – unless one considers teaching material as the product of the research. In industry, however, research is a much more generic term and can involve both new science and the use of old science to produce a new product. It is sometimes difficult to determine when research ends and development begins. It is probably more realistic to view industrial R&D as a continuum with scientific knowledge and concepts at one end and physical products at the other. Along this continuum it is possible to place the various R&D activities (*see* Figure 8.1). Later in this chapter we discuss the variety of R&D activities usually found within a large R&D department.

Technology is a commonly used word and yet not fully understood by all those who use it. Hickman (1990) offers a comprehensive classification of technology, used to describe both products and processes. Roussel *et al.* (1991) define technology as the application of knowledge to achieve a practical result. More recently, the term know-how has been used in the management literature to describe a company's knowledge base, which includes its R&D capability.

Research and development has traditionally been regarded by academics and industry alike as the management of scientific *research* and the *development* of new products; this was soon abbreviated to R&D. Twiss (1992: 2) offers a widely accepted definition:

> *R&D is the purposeful and systematic use of scientific knowledge to improve man's lot even though some of its manifestations do not meet with universal approval.*

The recent debates about scientific cloning of animal cells are a good example of what Twiss means by the results of R&D often delivering controversial outcomes. A more contemporary definition is offered by Roussel *et al.* (1991), who define the concept as:

> *To develop new knowledge and apply scientific or engineering knowledge to connect the knowledge in one field to that in others.*

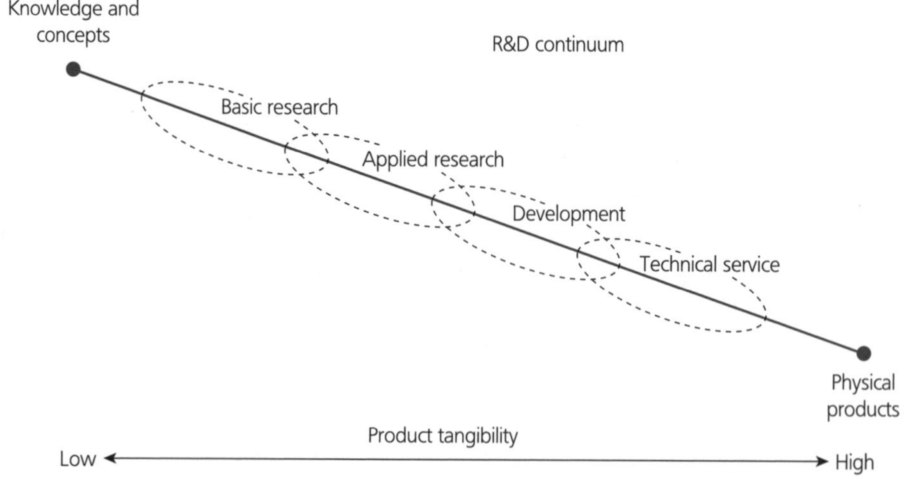

Figure 8.1 The R&D continuum

This definition reflects the more recent view that scientific knowledge is expanding so rapidly that it is extremely difficult for one company to remain abreast of all the technologies that it needs for its products. Companies pull together scientific knowledge from a wide variety of sources. For example, the manufacture of a personal computer will require technology from several different streams including microprocessor technology, visual display technology and software technology. It would be almost impossible for a company to be a technology leader in all of these fields.

The traditional view of R&D

After the Second World War, research and development played an important role in providing firms with competitive advantage. Technical developments in industries such as chemicals, electronics, automotive and pharmaceuticals led to the development of many new products, which produced rapid growth. For a while it seemed that technology was capable of almost anything. The traditional view of R&D has therefore been overcoming genuine technological problems, which subsequently leads to business opportunities and a competitive advantage over one's competitors.

President Kennedy's special address to the US Congress in 1961, in which he spoke of 'putting a man on the moon before the decade was out', captured the popular opinion of that time. Many believed anything was possible through technology. This notion helps to explain one of the major areas of difficulty with R&D. Traditionally, it has been viewed as a linear process, moving from research to engineering and then manufacture. It was US economists and policy makers after the Second World War who were largely responsible for the linear model of science and innovation. This was because statisticians had to measure research spending and this led to the categorisation of science and research (see also Vannevar Bush's *Science: The Endless Frontier* (1945)). That R&D was viewed as an overhead item was reinforced by Kennedy who pledged to spend 'whatever it costs', and indeed enormous financial resources were directed towards the project. But this was a unique situation without the usual economic or market forces at play. Nevertheless, industry adopted a similar approach to that used by the space programme. Vast amounts of money were poured into R&D programmes in the belief that the interesting technology generated could then be incorporated into products. In many instances this is exactly what happened, but there were also many examples of exciting technology developed purely because it was interesting, without any consideration of the competitive market in which the business operated. Hence, many business leaders began to question the value of R&D.

R&D management and the industrial context

As will become clear, there is no single best way to manage R&D. There is no prescription, no computer model that will ensure its success. Each company and every competitive environment is unique and in its own state of change. R&D needs to be managed according to the specific heritage and resources of the company in its competitive industry. While the management of R&D in the aircraft industry is very different from the textile industry, there are, none the less, certain factors and

Illustration 8.1

Industrial R&D has a long history

Many of Europe's largest chemical companies have a long history of funding industrial research. After the end of the First World War several reports were written examining the scope and nature of industrial research in German chemical companies. The following extract is taken from one of these reports:

> *One of the most striking features in the works visited is the application in the broadest sense of science to chemical industry. This is naturally very prominent in the triumvirate of the Bayer, Farbwerke Hoechst and the BASF, but it is equally noticeable in many of the smaller undertakings. The lavish and apparently unstinted monetary outlay on laboratories, libraries and technical staff implies implicit confidence on the part of the leaders of the industry in the ability to repay with interest heavy initial expenditure.*

Source: ABCM (1919) 'Report of the British Chemical Mission on Chemical Factories in the Occupied Area of Germany'.

elements that are common to all aspects of R&D management, almost irrespective of the industry. This chapter will draw on examples from across several different industries. This will help to highlight differences as well as identify commonalties in the management of R&D. Illustration 8.1, taken from a 1919 visit to the occupied territories of Germany, emphasises the very long history of industrial R&D.

At the beginning of this book we discussed one of the most fundamental dilemmas facing all companies, the need to provide an environment that fosters creativity and an inquisitive approach, while at the same time providing a stable environment that enables the business to be managed in an efficient and systematic way. Somehow businesses have to square this circle. Nowhere is this more apparent than in the management of research and development. For it is here that people need to question the accepted ways of working and challenge accepted wisdom.

One may be tempted to think that research, by definition, is uncertain, based around exploring things that are unknown. It cannot therefore be managed and organisations should not try to do so. There is, however, overwhelming evidence to suggest that industrial technological research can indeed be managed and that most of those organisations that spend large amounts of money on R&D, such as Microsoft, IBM, Sony, Siemens and Astra-Zeneca, do so extremely well (*see* Table 8.1). This table of Europe's leading firms in terms of R&D expenditure is part of the DTI's annual R&D Scoreboard. It began in 1992 as a way of raising the profile of R&D in the UK and to try to give recognition to those companies who are investing in the future. The first R&D Scoreboard was sponsored by the *Independent* newspaper as a means of helping to promote the publication (*Independent*, 1992).

Large organisations with more resources can clearly afford to invest more in R&D than their smaller counterparts. Therefore, in order to present a more realistic comparison than that derived from raw sums invested, R&D expenditure is frequently expressed as:

R&D as % of sales = (R&D expenditure/total sales income ´ 100%)

This not only allows comparisons to be made between small and large firms, but also gives a more realistic picture of R&D intensity within the organisation. Across

Table 8.1 Europe's R&D expenditure league (2010)

Rank	Company	R&D spend (£M)	R&D as a % of sales	R&D per employee (£000)	Industrial sector
1	Volkswagen Germany	5,790.00	5.7	17.1	Engineering, vehicles
2	Nokia Germany	4,997.00	12.2	40.6	Electronic and mobile phones
3	SanofiAventis France	4,569.00	15.3	43.6	Pharmaceuticals
4	Siemens Germany	4,282.00	5.6	10.4	Electronic and electrical equipment
5	Daimler Automobiles & parts Germany	4,164.00	5.3	16.1	Engineering, vehicles
6	GlaxoSmithKline UK	4,084.44	12.8	41.3	Pharmaceuticals
7	Robert Bosch Germany	3,578.00	9.4	13.0	Electronic and electrical equipment
8	Astra Zeneca UK	3,090.26	13.5	48.4	Pharmaceuticals
9	Bayer Germany	2,964.00	9.5	27.3	Chemicals
10	EADS The Netherlands	2,878.00	6.7	24.1	Aerospace
11	Alcatel-Lucent France	2,714.00	17.9	34.6	Electronic and electrical equipment
12	BMW Germany	2,448.00	5.1	25.4	Engineering, vehicles
13	Ericsson Sweden	2,401.68	11.9	27.8	Telecommunications
14	Peugeot France	2,314.00	4.8	12.4	Engineering, vehicles
15	Boehringer Ingelheim Germany	2,215.00	17.4	53.3	Pharmaceuticals
16	Finmeccanica Italy	1,926.00	11.7	26.6	Aerospace
17	Philips Electronics The Netherlands	1,714.00	7.4	14.6	Electronic and electrical equipment
18	Fiat Italy	1,692.00	3.4	8.9	Engineering, vehicles
19	Renault France	1,643.00	5.0	13.2	Engineering, vehicles
20	STMC Electronics The Netherlands	1,547.22	26.1	30.0	Semiconductors

Source: http://iri.jrc.ec.europa.eu/research/scoreboard_2010.htm.

Table 8.2 R&D expenditure across industry sectors

Industry sector	R&D expenditure as % of sales
Pharmaceuticals and biotechnology	15.8
Software and computer services	7.4
Fixed line telecommunications	5.1
Technical hardware equipment	5.1
Aerospace and defence	4.2
Automotive and parts	4.1
Electronic and electrical equipment	3.9
Food production	1.7
Banks	1.5
Oil and gas	0.5

Source: www.innovation.gov.uk/rd_scoreboard (2010).

industry sectors there are great differences in expenditure. Table 8.2 shows typical levels of R&D expenditure across different industry sectors. Some industries are technology intensive with relatively high levels of R&D expenditure. The Dyson case study at the end of Chapter 15 shows that even in those industries not normally associated with R&D, the benefits of successful R&D can be large indeed.

The fact that some of the largest and most successful companies in the world spend enormous sums of money on R&D should not be taken as a sign that they have mastered the process. It is important to acknowledge that R&D management, like innovation itself, is part art and part science. Industry may not be able to identify and hire technological geniuses like Faraday, Pasteur or Bell, but many companies would argue that they already employ geniuses who, year after year, develop new patents and new products that will contribute to the future prosperity of the organisation. These same companies would also argue that they cannot justify spending several millions of dollars, pounds or euros purely on the basis of chance and good fortune. This would clearly be unacceptable, not least to shareholders. So while companies appreciate that there is a certain amount of serendipity, there are also formal management techniques that over the years have been learnt, refined and practised and which are now a necessary part of good R&D management.

R&D investment and company success

On a global scale, R&D investment has increased by an average of 23 per cent from 1991 to 2008. R&D expenditure now consumes a significant proportion of a firm's funds across all industry sectors. This is principally because companies realise that new products can provide a huge competitive advantage. Yet comparing national strengths in science and technology is a hazardous exercise, bedevilled by incompatible definitions. While it is relatively easy to measure inputs, it is far harder to measure outputs in terms of quality. Figure 8.2 shows a comparison of share price performance of R&D-intensive firms and the FTSE 100 firms. Clearly the performance of a firm's share price is not necessarily a true guide of performance; it is, none the less, one output. What is worthy of note is that the number of R&D-intensive firms is increasing.

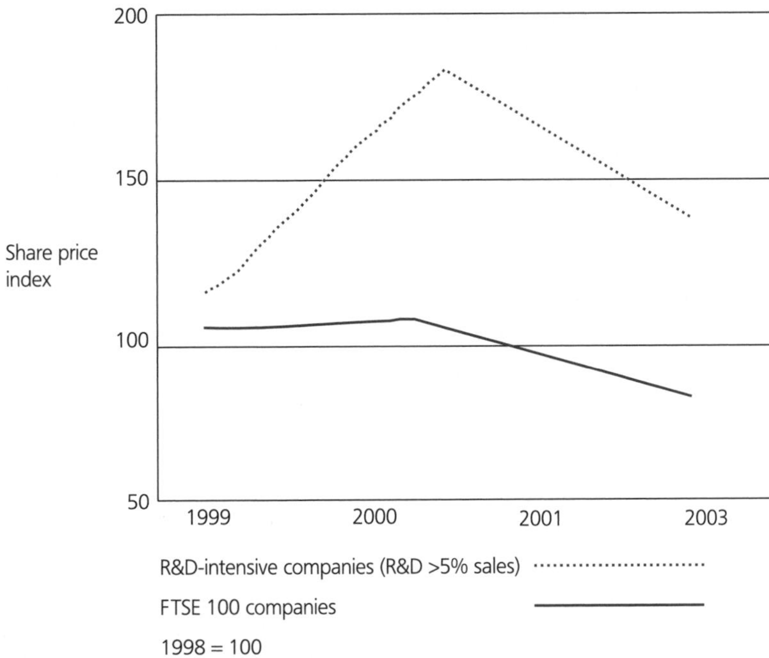

Figure 8.2 Comparison of share price performance of R&D-intensive firms and the FTSE 100 firms

Also, in a study of the German manufacturing industry, Lang (2009) examined the long-term relationship between domestic R&D, knowledge stock and productivity dynamics. He found that 50 per cent of the effects of R&D on the knowledge stock appear within four years.

It is now widely recognised that competition can appear from virtually anywhere in the world. Countries formerly viewed as receptacles for the outputs of factories across Europe are now supplying products themselves. Mexico, Brazil, Malaysia, China and India now supply a wide range of products to Europe, including car components, computer hardware and clothing. Globalisation provides opportunities for companies but it also brings increased competition. The introduction of new products provides a clear basis on which to compete, with those companies that are able to develop and introduce new and improved products having a distinct advantage.

Firms are also uneasy about R&D, or to be more accurate a lack of R&D. Ever since 1982 when ICI completed a study into the effects of stopping product innovation, companies have viewed innovation and R&D investment with some anxiety. They fear that should they stop investment in R&D, and product innovation in particular, the consequences would be severe. The results of the study showed that profits would decline very slowly for around 15 years, before falling very sharply. It is worthy of note that if a similar study were to be undertaken today it is almost certain that the 15-year figure would be halved to approximately eight. The ICI study also posed another important question. How long, it wondered, would it take for profits to recover if after the 15 years the company magically resumed its product innovation at three times its previous rate? The study revealed that it would take another 25 years for profit to recover to the level achieved before the product innovation programme was stopped (Weild, 1986).

These findings reflect the conventional wisdom that has dominated thinking in this field for most of the twentieth century. That is, most companies assume that R&D investment is a good thing; like education in general, it is surely a worthy investment. In the 1980s there was great interest in the concept of technology transfer and the belief that companies could buy in any technological expertise they required. More recent research has highlighted the folly of such arguments (Cohen and Levinthal, 1990; Quintas *et al.*, 1992) and the business community has returned to a view that fundamentally R&D investment is beneficial. The difficulty lies in where precisely to invest; which projects and technology to invest in; and when to stop pouring money into a project that looks likely to fail but could yet deliver enormous profits.

Many international companies, including Unilever, BT and BAE Systems have conducted numerous studies attempting to justify R&D expenditure. This has not been easy because there is no satisfactory method for measuring R&D output. Many studies have used the number of patents published as a guide. This is mainly because it is quantifiable rather than being a valid measure. It is, however, quality not quantity of output that is clearly important. It is worthy of note that most companies would like to be able to correlate R&D expenditure with profitability. At present there is a lack of conclusive evidence to connect the two. Edwin Mansfield (1991) has undertaken many studies concerning the relationship between R&D expenditure and economic growth and productivity. He concludes that:

> *although the results are subject to considerable error, they establish certain broad conclusions. In particular, existing econometric studies do provide reasonably conclusive evidence that R&D has a significant effect on the rate of productivity increase in the industries and time periods studied.*

Furthermore, a study by Geroski *et al.* (1993) did reveal a positive relationship between R&D expenditure and *long-term growth*. This is reinforced by the 2006 R&D scoreboard which concludes that:

> *R&D is a major investment contributing to company success along with other factors like excellent operations and good strategic choices. There are well-established links between R&D growth and intensity and sales growth, wealth creation efficiency and market value.*

This raises an important point. R&D expenditure should be viewed as a long-term investment. It may even reduce short-term profitability. Company accountants increasingly question the need for large sums to be invested in an activity that shows no obvious and certainly no rapid return. Many argue that public money should be used for 'pure research' where there is no clear application. Its outputs could then be taken and used by industry to generate wealth. However, the UK government's recent initiatives to couple science to the creation of wealth, through such programmes as Technology Foresight, seems to suggest that even public money is being directed towards **applied research**. Illustration 8.2 shows how governments encourage firms to invest in R&D.

This raises the issue of evaluating R&D. While few, if any, of the companies listed in Table 8.1 would question the value of R&D, this does not preclude the need for evaluation. How much money should companies invest in R&D? How much should be used for applied research and how much for pure research? These questions will be addressed later in this chapter and in Chapter 9.

Illustration 8.2

R&D tax incentives

In many countries in the world, including Canada, USA and the UK, governments provide tax incentives (in the form of tax credits and/or refund) to businesses to support R&D. These programmes were first introduced in Canada in the 1980s. It is intended to encourage businesses of all sizes – particularly small and start-up firms – to conduct R&D that will lead to new, improved or technologically advanced products or processes. R&D expenditures (already deducted against revenue) may qualify for investment tax credits (i.e. a reduction in income taxes payable), cash refunds or both. Qualified expenditures may include wages, materials, machinery, equipment and some overheads.

Source: Pearson Education Ltd/Nick Rowe/Photodisc

Pause for thought ?

A company generates $1 million profit. How can the R&D director convince the other directors to invest this money in R&D? The sales director will make a strong case that more sales staff will lead to more sales. And the IT director will explain that more investment in IT will help to reduce costs and improve efficiency!

Classifying R&D

Traditionally industrial research has focused on a variety of research activities performed *within* the organisation. This practice was modelled on the research undertaken within universities during the early part of the twentieth century. This was seen as public research financed by public money for the public good. In other words, research undertaken within universities was performed in the pursuit of new knowledge. Its results were publicly available and the commercial exploitation of this knowledge was largely disregarded. For example, Fleming's discovery of penicillin was initially not patented. Industrial research, on the other hand, was specifically intended for the benefit of the company funding the research. Industry's purpose was to grow and make profits and this was to be achieved through the development of new products and new businesses. Hence, industry's expectations of its own research expanded to include the development of knowledge into products (*see* Figure 8.3).

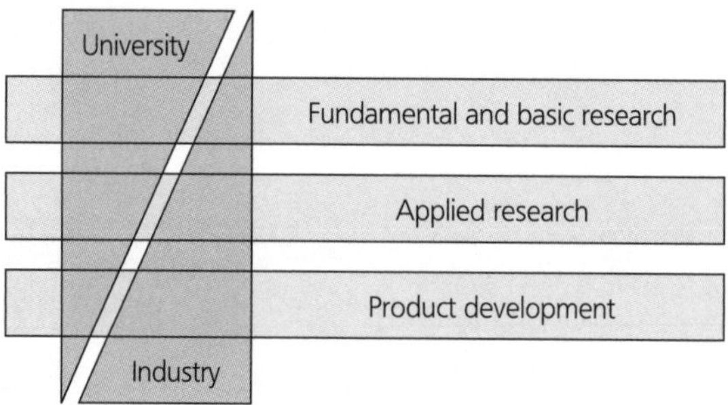

Figure 8.3 Classification of areas of research emphasis in industry and university

Illustration 8.3

EU spending on R&D lags US spending

Europe's spending on R&D is lagging far behind that of the US. Brussels has called for state and private investment to increase by 60 per cent over the next eight years but companies may not rush to meet the challenge

A knowledge gap has opened up over the Atlantic in research and development – one of the key motors of innovation and economic growth.

Europe has fallen well behind the US, as governments and businesses in the European Union fail to keep pace with the expenditure on science and technology of their US counterparts.

Many in Europe fear that achievements such as the sequencing of the human genome, where European scientists made a huge contribution to the work of their US counterparts, could become ever rarer.

The so-called 'Lisbon agenda' is an ambitious set of targets to make Europe the most competitive economy in the world. The EU pledged to increase Europe's state and private investment in R&D by nearly 60 per cent – from the current 1.9 per cent of gross domestic product to 3 per cent within eight years.

Such a rise would bring Europe in line with the US, where R&D investment is 2.6 per cent of GDP and rising fast, and Japan, which already spends 2.9 per cent of its national wealth on research.

The EU is limited in what it can do directly to promote research. It spends only 5 per cent of what national governments will spend on R&D.

A recent study by the European Commission showed that businesses' expenditure on R&D in the US is 73 per cent higher than in the EU and grew nearly three times as fast between 1995 and 1999.

Such a lag in EU businesses' investments accounts for the vast majority of the a 76 billion R&D difference between the US and Europe. 'On current trends, the EU will fall further behind, compromising any chance of reaching the objective agreed at Lisbon', the study concludes. Getting businesses to spend more on R&D at a time of an economic downturn and uncertain stock market conditions is not going to be easy.

Some within the Commission argue that to catch up with the US something stronger is needed: Europe, they argue, should go the American way and build a large venture capital industry.

Across the Atlantic, risk capital has become a vital funding source for technology-based start-ups, while in Europe it accounts for a mere 0.04 per cent of EU GDP. The Commission wants governments to set up schemes to attract venture capital for start-ups.

Over the years industrial research and development has increasingly been guided by the aims of its financiers via its business strategy, and to a lesser extent by the pursuit of knowledge. The main activities of industrial R&D have included the following:

- discovering and developing new technologies;
- improving understanding of the technology in existing products;
- improving and strengthening understanding of technologies used in manufacturing; and
- understanding research results from universities and other research institutions.

The management of R&D can be viewed as two sides of the same coin. On the one side there are research activities, often referred to as fundamental or basic research, and on the other development, usually the development of products. Many industries make a clear distinction between research and development and some companies even suggest that they leave all research to universities, engaging only in development. Figure 8.3 shows the areas of research emphasis in industry and universities. In between the discovery of new knowledge and new scientific principles (so-called fundamental research) and the development of products for commercial gain (so-called development) is the significant activity of transforming scientific principles into technologies that can be applied to products (*see* Illustration 8.4). This activity is called applied research. The development of the videocassette recorder (VCR) shows how, over a period of almost 30 years, industry worked with existing scientific principles to develop a product with commercial potential.

The operations that make up R&D

Figure 8.1 illustrated the R&D operations commonly found in almost every major research and development department. They may have different labels, but within Siemens, Nokia, BMW and Shell such operations are well documented. In smaller organisations the activities are less diverse and may include only a few of these operations. This section explains what activities one would expect to find within each type of R&D operation. To help put these activities in context, Figure 9.5 shows how they relate to the product life cycle framework.

Basic research

This activity involves work of a general nature intended to apply to a broad range of uses or to new knowledge about an area. It is also referred to as fundamental science and is usually only conducted in the laboratories of universities and large organisations. Outputs from this activity will result in scientific papers for journals. Some findings will be developed further to produce new technologies. New scientific discoveries such as antibiotics in the 1940s belong to this research category.

Illustration 8.4

Manipulating known scientific principles through technological development: the VCR story

At the heart of virtually all technologically innovative products lies good fundamental science. The ability to manipulate known scientific principles through technological development is the main research activity of most companies. A good example of this is the VCR industry.

Although videocassette recorders (VCRs) were first introduced in the early 1970s, the story begins long before this date. It was during the 1950s that firms (already in the broadcast industry) began experimenting with existing broadcasting technology to develop a videotape recorder. The front runners were RCA and Ampex in the United States and Toshiba in Japan, all of which had knowledge and experience of television broadcasting technology. In the early 1950s, the RCA team developed a machine that moved a narrow tape at very high speeds past fixed magnetic heads. Meanwhile Toshiba developed a different approach, in which the recording head rotated at high speed while the tape moved past relatively slowly. Toshiba's breakthrough was patented in 1954. Ampex developed a transverse scanner in which four recording heads on a rapidly rotating drum scanned across a two-inch-wide tape.

Ampex was the first to succeed commercially and its videotape recording machine made a huge impact on the broadcasting industry, despite a price of $50,000. Within a few years Ampex had licensed the technology to RCA and Toshiba.

None of the original technology pioneers viewed the idea of producing a product for the mass market as a business opportunity. This baton was to be taken up by three other Japanese firms: JVC, Sony and Matsushita. Spurred on by the success of the other companies, independently they began numerous technical development projects to try to exploit the commercial opportunity of a mass market videotape recorder.

It was only after many failed projects and learning from the mistakes of others that a design emerged in the late 1960s. It was Sony that in 1969 announced the development of a 'magazine-loaded' videotape recorder. JVC soon announced its own slightly different magazine-loaded recorder using half-inch tape as opposed to Sony's one-inch tape. The first Betamax model was offered to the market in April 1975. JVC revealed its VHS technology to its parent company Matsushita and this was launched at the end of 1976.

Source: Duncan Smith/Corbis

The war of the formats is now folklore, especially in business schools around the world. It may be useful to highlight some of the key issues.

The key point is the recording time of the two formats. VHS had a recording time of two hours while Betamax had a recording time of only one hour. Industry experts suggest that technologically the formats were equal. That is, on home commercial television sets the difference in picture quality was nil. In the early years it was Sony and Betamax that pioneered most of the technical developments, but in less than a year the VHS manufacturers had caught up. Another common misconception is that Sony refused to license its Betamax technology. This is not true. It tried from the very beginning to license the technology and have it accepted as standard.

Source: R.S. Rosenbloom and M.A. Cusumano (1988) 'Technological pioneering and competitive advantage: the birth of the VCR industry', in M.L. Tushman and W.L. Moore (eds) *Readings in the Management of Innovation*, HarperCollins, New York; The format war (1988) *Video Magazine*, April.

Applied research

This activity involves the use of existing scientific principles for the solution of a particular problem. It is sometimes referred to as the application of science. It may lead to new technologies and include the development of patents. It is from this activity that many new products emerge. This form of research is typically conducted by large companies and university departments. The development of the Dyson vacuum cleaner involved applying the science of centrifugal forces first explained by Newton. Centrifugal forces spin dirt out of the air stream in two stages (or cyclones), with air speeds of up to 924 miles an hour. This technology led to the development of several patents.

Development

This activity is similar to applied research in that it involves the use of known scientific principles, but differs in that the activities centre on products. Usually the activity will involve overcoming a technical problem associated with a new product. It may also involve various exploratory studies to try to improve a product's performance. To continue with the Dyson vacuum cleaner example, the prototype product underwent many modifications and enhancements before a commercial product was finally developed. For example, the company has launched a cylinder model to complement its upright model.

Technical service

Technical service focuses on providing a service to existing products and processes. This frequently involves cost and performance improvements to existing products, processes or systems. For example, in the bulk chemical industry it means ensuring that production processes are functioning effectively and efficiently. This category of R&D activity would also include design changes to products to lower the manufacturing costs. For Dyson Appliances extensive efforts will be employed in this area to reduce the cost of manufacturing its vacuum cleaner, leading to increased profit margins for the company.

R&D management and its link with business strategy

Planning decisions are directed towards the future, which is why strategy is often considered to be as much an art as a science. Predicting the future is extremely difficult and there are many factors to consider: economic, social, political, technological, natural disasters, etc. The R&D function also has to make some assessment of the future in order to perform effectively. Thus senior R&D managers have to build into their planning process a conscious view of the future. However imprecise, this will include:

- environmental forecasts;
- comparative technological cost-effectiveness;
- risk; and
- capability analysis.

Environmental forecasts

These are primarily concerned with changes in technology that will occur in the future. But this cannot be considered in isolation and other factors such as economic, social and political factors also have to be considered.

- Who will be our competitors in five or 10 years' time?
- What technologies do we need to understand to avoid technological surprises?
- What will be the new competitive technologies and businesses?

Comparative technological cost-effectiveness

It is argued that technologies have life cycles and that after a period further research produces negligible benefit. When this stage is reached a new branch of technology is likely to offer far more promising rewards. This may require a significant shift in resources. Today, for example, many car manufacturers are increasing their research efforts in electrical power technology.

Risk

The culture of the organisation and its attitude to risk will influence decision making. Usually risk is spread over a portfolio of projects and will include some exploratory high-risk projects and some developmental low-risk ones. Planning cannot remove risk but it can help to ensure that decisions are reached using a process of rational analysis.

Capability analysis

It is fairly obvious to state, but companies have to consider their own strengths and weaknesses. This analysis should help them ensure that they have the necessary capabilities for the future.

Integration of R&D

The management of research and development needs to be fully integrated with the strategic management process of the business. This will enhance and support the products that marketing and sales offer and provide the company with a technical body of knowledge that can be used for future development. Too many businesses fail to integrate the management of research and technology fully into the overall business strategy process (Adler *et al.*, 1992). A report by the European Industrial Research Management Association (EIRMA, 1985) recognises R&D as having three distinct areas, each requiring investment: R&D for existing businesses, R&D for new businesses and R&D for exploratory research (*see* Figure 8.4).

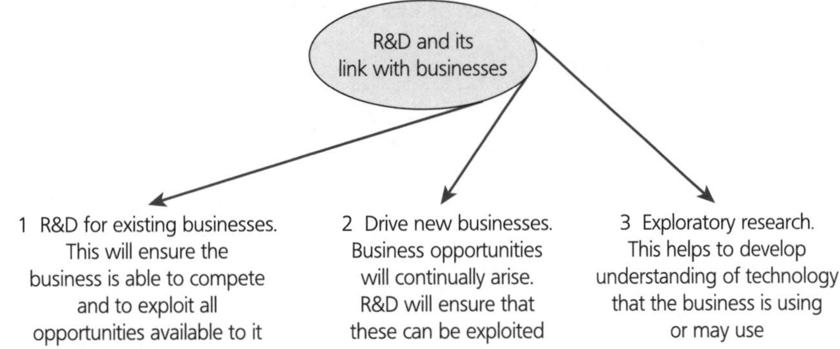

Figure 8.4 The strategic role of R&D as viewed by the business

Source: EIRMA (1985) 'Evaluation of R&D output: working group report, 29', European Industrial research Management Association, Paris; P.A. Roussel, K.N. Saad and T.S. Erickson (1991) *Third Generation R&D*, Harvard Business School Press, Boston, MA.

These three strategic areas can be broken down into operational activities.

Defend, support and expand existing businesses

The defence of existing businesses essentially means maintaining a business's current position, that is, keeping up with the competition and ensuring that products do not become outdated and ensuring that existing products can compete. For example, the newspaper industry has seen numerous technological changes dramatically alter the way it produces newspapers. In particular, the introduction of desktop publishing and other related computer software has provided increased flexibility in manufacturing operations as well as reducing production costs.

Drive new businesses

Either through identification of market opportunities or development of technology, new business opportunities will continually be presented to managers. Sometimes the best decision is to continue with current activities. However, there will be times when a business takes the decision to start a new business. This may be an extension of existing business activities, but sometimes it may be for a totally new product. For example, 3M's unexpected discovery of temporary adhesive technology led to the creation of a completely new business – the Post-It notes.

Broaden and deepen technological capability

The third area is more medium- to long-term strategy. It involves the continual accumulation of knowledge, not only in highly specialised areas where the company is currently operating, but also in areas that may prove to be of importance to the business in the future. For example, Microsoft initially concentrated its efforts on computer-programming technologies. The company now requires knowledge in a wide variety of technologies, including telecommunications, media (music, film and television), sound technology, etc.

Table 8.3 Description of five generations of the R&D process

R&D generations	Context	Process characteristics
First generation	Black hole demand (1950 to mid-1960s)	*R&D as ivory tower*, technology-push oriented, seen as an overhead cost, having little or no interaction with the rest of the company or overall strategy. Focus on scientific breakthroughs.
Second generation	Market shares battle (mid-1960s to early 1970s)	*R&D as business*, market-pull oriented, and strategy-driven from the business side, all under the umbrella of project management and the internal customer concept.
Third generation	Rationalisation efforts (mid-1970s to mid-1980s)	*R&D as portfolio*, moving away from individual projects view, and with linkages to both business and corporate strategies. Risk-reward and similar methods guide the overall investments.
Fourth generation	Time-based struggle (early 1980s to mid-1990s)	*R&D as integrative activity*, learning from and with customers, moving away from a product focus to a total concept focus, where activities are conducted in parallel by cross-functional teams.
Filth generation	Systems integration (mid-1990s onward)	*R&D as network*, focusing on collaboration within a wider system – involving competitors, suppliers, distributors, etc. The ability to control product development speed is imperative, separating R from D.

Source: Nobelius, D. (2004) Towards the sixth generation of R&D management, *International Journal of Project Management*, Vol. 22, 369–75.

Strategic pressures on R&D

The R&D process has changed over the years, moving from a technology-centred model to a more interaction-focused view (Nobelius, 2004). Nobelius describes the R&D process and the five generations it has been through (*see* Table 8.3).

In technology-intensive industries much of the technological resources consumed by a particular business are in the form of engineering and development (often called technical service). These resources can be spread over a wide range of technical activities and technologies. In addition, a firm will have a number of specific areas of technology in which it concentrates resources and builds a technological competence. As one would expect, there is a significant difference between possessing general technical service skills and possessing scientific competence in a particular area. The building and development of technological knowledge competencies take time and demand a large amount of research activity.

Mitchell (1988) suggests there is a trade-off between concentrating resources in the pursuit of a strategic knowledge competence and spreading them over a wider area to allow for the building of a general knowledge base. Figure 8.5 shows the demands on technical resources. The growth of scientific and technological areas of interest to the firm (in particular the research department) pressurises research management to fund a wider number of areas, represented by the upward curve. The need for strategic positioning forces the decision to focus resources and build strategic knowledge competencies, represented by the downward curve. In practice, most businesses settle for an uneasy balance between the two sets of pressures.

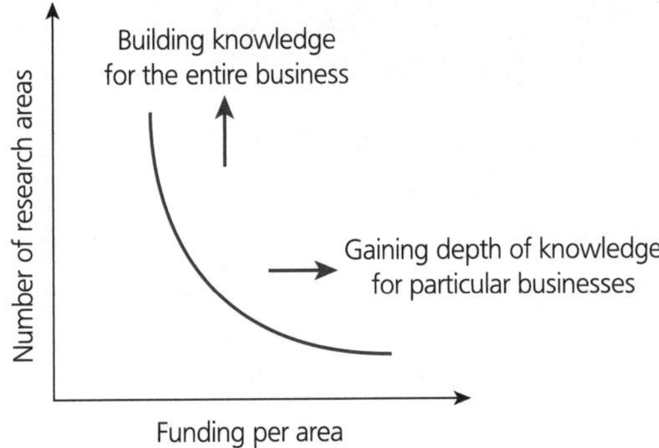

Figure 8.5 Strategic pressures on R&D

Source: Adapted from G.R. Mitchell (1988) 'Options for the strategic management of technology', UNESCO Technology Management, Interscience Enterprises Ltd, Geneva.

The technology portfolio

From an R&D perspective the company's technology base can be categorised as follows:

- core technologies;
- complementary technologies;
- peripheral technologies; and
- emerging technologies.

Core technologies

The core technology is usually central to all or most of the company's products. Expertise in this area may also dominate the laboratories of the R&D department as well as strategic thinking. For example, in the photocopying industry photographic technologies are core.

Complementary technologies

Complementary technologies are additional technology that is essential in product development. For example, microprocessors are becoming essential in many products and industries. For the photocopying industry there are several complementary technologies, including microprocessor technology and paper-handling technology, which enables the lifting, turning, folding and stapling of paper.

Peripheral technologies

Peripheral technology is defined as technology that is not necessarily incorporated into the product but whose application contributes to the business. Computer software often falls into this category. The photocopying industry is increasingly using software to add features and benefits to its products, such as security.

Emerging technologies

These are new to the company but may have a long-term significance for its products. In the photocopying industry, telecommunications technologies may soon be incorporated as standard features of the product.

Innovation in action

For HTC, the maker of the Google phone, respect is more important than fame

HTC is hardly a household name. More have heard of the Google Phone, and as the manufacturer of that phone, the $4.5 billion Taiwanese mobile giant is keen to be recognised for its own products.

As with their competitors, HTC works hard with innovation labs and flexible working practices. But what's interesting is the edge HTC believe it can get from its core cultural value – humility. 'My inspiration comes from Proverbs 15:33; "humility before honour" ', says Cher Wang, cofounder and chairwoman.

'Quietly brilliant' is at the heart of HTC and forms the focus of all marketing activity. 'We don't spend a lot of time worrying about promoting the HTC brand', says John Wang, HTC chief marketing officer. 'We'd rather earn our customers' respect than spend a lot of money on brand recognition.'

Source: Getty/Images/Robert Galbraith/Pool

It comes through in product development. 'Humility is about admitting our own faults. That way we can change and improve', says Wang. 'Our whole organisation is designed to fail. The way to getting a great idea is to have lots of ideas. So our focus is to get these ideas to fail fast and fail cheaply.'

Source: HSBC (2010) 100 Thoughts, HSBC, London.

The difficulty of managing capital-intensive production plants in a dynamic environment

Many manufacturing operations involve the careful management of multi-million-pound production plants. Such businesses have a slightly different set of factors to consider than a company operating the manufacturing plant for say, shoes, which is labour rather than technology-intensive. Hundreds of millions of pounds are invested in a new chemical plant and options open to it in terms of changes in products are limited. This is because a production plant is built to produce one chemical product.

Moreover, the scrapping of an existing plant and the building of a new one may cost in excess of £300 million. There are few companies in the world that could continually build, scrap and rebuild chemical plants in response to the demands of the market and make a profit from such actions. Hence companies operating process plants cannot respond *completely* to market needs.

This particular dilemma faced by companies with large investments in production technology is frequently overlooked by those far removed from the production floor. Young marketing graduates may feel that a company should be able to halt production of one product in order to switch to the production of another offering better prospects. The effect of such a decision may be to bankrupt the company! The chemical industry is increasingly developing smaller, more flexible plants rather than the large, single-purpose plants that have been common since the turn of the twentieth century.

In some industries where investment lies less in the technology and more in the human resources, changes to a production plant are possible.

Pause for thought 

With products incorporating technologies from increasingly diverse fields, is it realistic to continue to believe that firms can continue to be world leaders in all these areas? Maybe they can rely on their suppliers to conduct all the necessary R&D?

Which business to support and how?

It is well understood that technological developments can lead to improved products and processes, reduced costs and ultimately better commercial performance and competitive advantage. The ability to capitalise on technological developments and profit from the business opportunities that may subsequently arise requires a business to be in an appropriate strategic position. That is, it must possess the capability to understand and use the technological developments to its own advantage. This requires some form of anticipation of future technological developments and also strategic business planning. Technological forecasting and planning are fraught with uncertainty. Figure 8.6 illustrates the iterative and continual process involved in the management of research and technology.

The effect of corporate strategy is usually most noticeable in the selection of R&D projects. For example, a corporate decision by Unilever to strengthen its position in the luxury perfume business may lead to the cancellation of several research projects, with more emphasis being placed on buying brands like Calvin Klein. Ideally, a system is required that links R&D decision making with corporate strategy decision making. However, it is common in R&D departments to make decisions on a project-by-project basis in which individual projects are assessed on their own merits, independent of the organisation. This is partly because the expertise required is concentrated in the R&D department and partly due to scientists' fascination with science itself. This used to be the case in many large organisations with centralised

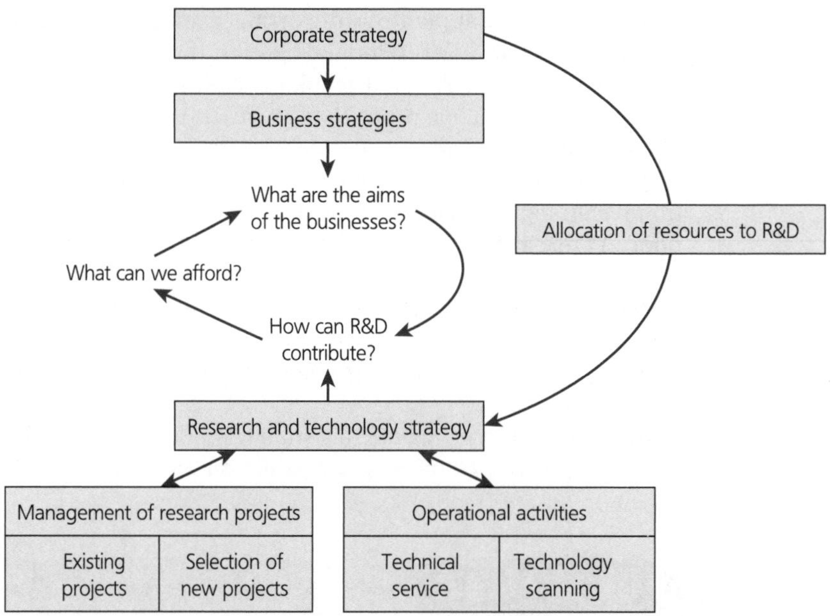

Figure 8.6 The R&D strategic decision-making process

laboratories. Such a decision-making process, however, is only valid when funds are unlimited and this is rarely the case. In practice, funds are restricted and projects compete with each other for continued funding for future years. Not all projects can receive funding and in industrial R&D laboratories projects are cancelled week after week, frequently to the annoyance of those involved.

The flow diagram in Figure 8.6 highlights the need for integration of corporate and R&D strategy. The process of corporate planning involves the systematic examination of a wide variety of factors. The aim is to produce a statement of company objectives and how they are to be achieved. Essentially, a number of questions need to be considered:

- What might the company do?
- What can the company do?
- What should the company do?

This leads to the development of business strategies. At the base of the diagram are the inputs from R&D activities, in particular existing R&D projects and potential projects that may be selected for funding. The organisation must repeatedly ask itself: what are the needs of the businesses? What should R&D be doing? What can R&D do? This process is neither a bottom–up nor a top–down process. What is required is continual dialogue between senior management and R&D management.

While it is tempting to say that technology influences the competitive performance of all businesses, in reality some businesses are more heavily influenced than others. In many mature and established industries, the cost of raw materials is much more of an influence on the competitive performance of the business than are technology developments. For example, the price paid for commodities like coffee, cocoa and sugar can dramatically influence profits in many food industries. Similarly, in the chemical industry the competitive position of petroleum-based plastics is determined by the price paid for the raw material, oil. Consequently, some businesses, especially those operating in mature industries, would be unable to influence their competitive position through technology alone. Even if the business was to substantially increase the level of R&D investment, its competitive position would still be determined by raw material prices.

Several attempts have been made by industry to quantify this factor when considering the level of R&D investment required. Scholefield (1993) developed a model using the concept of **technology leverage**. This is the extent of influence that a business's technology and technology base have on its competitive position. In general, technology leverage will be low when the influence of raw material and distribution costs and economic growth is high. High-volume, bulk commodity products would fall within this scenario.

Technology leverage and R&D strategies

The state of a business in terms of its markets, products and capabilities will largely determine the amount of research effort to be undertaken. Research by Scholefield (1993) suggests that there are essentially two forms of activity for a R&D department, growth and maintenance. Within these two groups it is possible to conduct significantly different types of activity. Hence, these categories can be subdivided into the four groups depicted in Figure 8.7.

A business's expenditure on research activity would normally be reviewed annually or quarterly. The model is used as a guide to establish whether a business's research activity is appropriate for its position. Experience has shown that without such a guide research activity can drift over time, resulting in too much or too little activity appropriate for the business. The model provides the facility for business and research managers to monitor research activity. In practice this involves continual analysis, adjustment and realignment. For example, each quarter a business's executive would meet and discuss quarterly results. During these meetings, its strategic position could be reclassified according to performance and external environmental factors. That is, a business's category may change from, say, 3 to 4 or from 2 to 1.

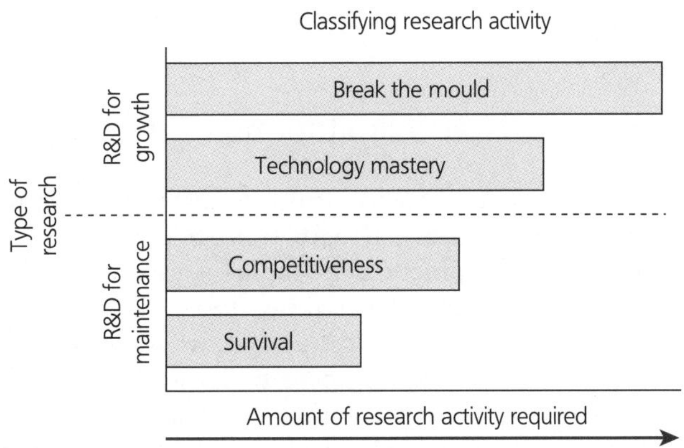

Figure 8.7 Classifying the level of research using technology leverage

Survival

This type of activity is conducted if the decision has been made to exit the business. In such circumstances the role of the R&D department is to ensure its interim survival against technological mishaps to process or product. This would be a reactive problem-solving role and may be termed 'survival research'.

Competitive

If the intention is to sustain the business, then the role of research is to maintain the relative competitive technological position by making improvements to both product and process. For example, in the automotive industry most manufacturers have invested heavily in their own processes and vehicle build-qualities have improved dramatically; so much so that reliability, although still improving, is almost taken for granted by car buyers. The process technologies involved have become widely accepted and used. However, if any one manufacturer allowed its process technologies to fall behind those of its competitors, it would almost certainly provide an advantage to them. The amount of research activity required to maintain a high-technology leverage position, however, will be significantly greater than that required to maintain a low-technology leverage position. Thus it seems reasonable to split this category in two: competitive (low-technology leverage) and competitive (high-technology leverage).

Technology mastery

Incremental growth of a business in a strong position involves improving the product and process relative to the competition. This will clearly involve a level of research activity greater than the competitive position outlined above. It will involve keeping abreast of all technological developments that may affect the business's products or processes. Hence, a much higher level of R&D expenditure will be required.

Break the mould

If the aim is to create a technological advantage then a much higher order of novelty and creativity is required. Following such a strategy will involve developing new patentable technology and may involve a higher level of basic scientific research.

Strengths and limitations of this approach

The model attempts to introduce some theory into what is often an arbitrary competition for research activity. It provides a framework within which discussions may take place. In practice, the model is used to check decisions made by research and business managers, as opposed to being used for dictating decisions. In addition, it includes a technological perspective for classifying a business's strategic position. Many strategic management tools, while paying lip service to the importance of technology, fail to accommodate a technological perspective in the decision-making process. There is an over-emphasis on the financial or marketing perspective (Ansoff, 1968; BCG, 1972; Porter, 1985).

It also shows how the role of strategic technology management and a business's selected growth strategy can influence the business climate within which managers operate. For example, if a strategic decision is taken to exit a business, this will clearly have a profound influence on the nature of activities. One would expect the activities of a business operating in a climate of growth to be different from those of one operating in a climate of decline.

Allocation of funds to R&D

Unlike many other business activities, successful R&D cannot be managed on an annual budgetary basis. It requires a much longer-term approach, enabling knowledge to be acquired and built up over time. This often leads to tensions with other functions that are planning projects and activities. None the less, as was explained earlier in this chapter, R&D has to be linked to the business strategy (see Illustration 8.5).

It is unusual for unlimited funds to be available, hence business functions usually compete with other departments for funds. Marketing will no doubt present a very good case why extra money should be spent on new marketing campaigns; the IT

Illustration 8.5

Are managers at struggling groups right to trim R&D?

The problem

Global carmakers from Ford Motor and Fiat to Honda and BMW are postponing or shelving planned vehicle launches as they cope with the downturn. The moves have raised fears that cuts to research and development budgets will be next – something automakers are traditionally loath to do. Innovation is seen as a vital source of growth, but recession brings tough choices. If managers at struggling manufacturers – whatever the sector – have already made the easy cuts available elsewhere in the business, are they right to look at the scope for savings in R&D? And is there a smart approach to making such savings?

The advice

John Weston, former chief executive of BAE Systems and now chairs Acra Control, MB Aerospace, AWS and learn-direct organisaton UFI

The decision on cuts to R&D has three components. What contribution can R&D make to achieving the cost levels the business requires for survival? What impact will a cut have on employees' morale and commitment? And to what extent will a cut in R&D today affect the company's performance when the recession is over? In businesses where R&D accounts for a larger percentage of revenues there is more scope for cuts. But much of an R&D budget is spent on people, so benefits can only be achieved when engineers are moved to revenue-generating activities. In aerospace and defence, for example, engineers can be redirected to customer-related tasks. For many engineers R&D cuts signal that the company does not truly value engineering. So communication is vital in explaining the rationale and the company's commitment to the future. Companies that protect R&D in a downturn can keep a competitive edge, but each business will find itself in different circumstances. In highly leveraged companies, the decision may be driven by the bankers, and short-term survival may trump all other considerations.

Source: FT.com (2009) 18 February.

department will request more funds for more equipment and valuable training for everyone; and the sales department will almost certainly ask for more salespeople to boost sales. It is a difficult circle to square. A great deal depends on the culture of the organisation and the industry within which it is operating (*see* Chapters 3 and 6). 3M, for example, spends proportionally large sums on R&D, many say too much, especially when one considers its more recent performance (*see* the case study at the end of Chapter 16). Other companies spend very little on R&D but huge amounts on sales and marketing. This is the case for the financial services industry. So one of the most difficult decisions facing senior management is how much to spend on R&D. Many companies now report R&D expenditure in their annual reports. However, while it is now relatively easy to establish, for example, that Volkswagen spent 5.7 per cent of sales on R&D in 2009, exactly how the company arrived at this figure is less clear.

Setting the R&D budget

In practice, establishing the R&D budget for a business is influenced by short-term performance fluctuations and availability of funds, which is, in turn, influenced by the setting of annual budgets. Additionally, budgets are also influenced by the long-term strategic technological needs of the business. It is extremely difficult to establish a basis for the allocation of funds that will be acceptable to all parties. A number of different approaches are used by different companies (*see* below). In practice, businesses use a combination of these methods. In addition, managerial judgement and negotiation will often play a significant role. The portfolio management approach, outlined earlier in this chapter, enables profits from today's successful businesses to be invested into what the company hopes will become the profitable businesses of tomorrow. Many businesses also invest in basic research. This is research that is perceived to be of interest to the company as a whole and of benefit to the organisation in the long term.

There are several key factors that need to be considered when allocating funds to R&D:

- expenditure by competitors;
- company's long-term growth objectives;
- the need for stability; and
- distortions introduced by large projects.

Six approaches can be used for allocating funds to R&D.

Inter-firm comparisons

While R&D expenditure varies greatly between industries, within similar industries there is often some similarity. It is possible to establish reasonably accurately a competitor's R&D expenditure, the number of research personnel employed, etc. By analysing the research expenditure of its competitors, a business is able to establish an appropriate figure for its own research effort. Table 8.4 would suggest that a company trying to establish its R&D budget should consider spending between 14 and 17 per cent of sales on R&D.

Table 8.4 Comparison of R&D expenditure within the European pharmaceutical industry

Company	R&D expenditure as % of sales
Roche (Switz)	16.1
Novartis (Switz)	15.0
Sanofi-Aventis (France)	14.8
GlaxoSmithKline (UK)	14.5
Astra-Zeneca (UK)	14.1

Source: www.innovation.gov.uk/projects/rdrscoreboard (2006).

A fixed relationship to turnover

R&D expenditure can be based on a constant percentage. Turnover normally provides a reasonably stable figure that grows in line with the size of the company. As an example of this method, a company has decided to spend 2 per cent of its annual turnover on R&D. If its turnover is £10 million then its annual R&D expenditure would be £200,000. A criticism of this method is that it uses past figures for future investments.

A fixed relationship to profits

Fixing R&D expenditure to profits is highly undesirable. It implies that R&D is a luxury which can only be afforded when the company generates profits. This method completely ignores the role of R&D as an investment and the likely future benefits that will follow. Often, in fact, poor profits can be turned around with new products.

Reference to previous levels of expenditure

In the absence of any criteria for measurement, a starting point for discussions is likely to be the previous year's expenditure plus an allowance for inflation. In spite of its crudeness, this method is often used in conjunction with one or more of the other methods, especially during negotiations with other functional managers.

Costing of an agreed programme

An R&D manager is concerned with managing research projects, so the allocation of funds for each individual project may seem attractive. This allows him or her to add together the requirements for certain projects and arrive at a figure. Invariably the total will exceed what the department is likely to receive. Negotiations are then likely to ensue, focusing on which projects to cut completely or on which to reduce expenditure.

Internal customer–contractor relationship

In some large multinational companies, the individual business units may pay for research carried out on their behalf by the R&D function. In addition, there is usually some provision for building the knowledge base of the whole organisation. For example, each business manager within the German chemical giant, Bayer, manages his or her own R&D budget but each business must also contribute 10–12 per cent for long-term research. Shell operates a similar programme.

Level of R&D expenditure

Lord Lever's famous quote about advertising expenditure could equally be applied to R&D investment: 'half the money I spend on advertising is wasted, the problem is I don't know which half'. Scientists and technologists would rightly argue that even if the return on investment is not a profitable product, the investment in knowledge is not wasted. Without getting drawn into a philosophical debate on the acquisition of knowledge, the point is that an evaluation of a financial investment in R&D should be subject to the same criteria as evaluations of other investments made by the organisation. However, herein lies the difficulty. There are many short-term returns from an R&D investment, as was made clear above, but there is also a longer-term return. Often technological expertise is built up over many years through many consecutive short-term research projects. It is extremely difficult to apportion the profit to all contributing functions from a product developed over a period of several years. There is also considerable merit in the argument that without the R&D investment there would not have been a product at all. This subject has received a great deal of attention over the past four decades (Williams, 1969; Mansfield *et al.*, 1972; Meyer-Krahmer, 1984; Cordero, 1990; McGrath and Romeri, 1994).

The R&D manager is under the same pressures as the senior management team. They have to ensure that the business has opportunities to exploit for future growth. In reality a few successful projects are usually sufficient to justify the investment.

Virtually all R&D managers are responsible for a portfolio of projects. The aim is to try to select those that will be successful and drop those which will not. The Viagra case study at the end of this chapter highlights the difficulty of project selection. Sometimes it is the project least likely to succeed that turns out to be the next Post-It notes business. One of the most dramatic examples of the high level of uncertainty involved in R&D project evaluations is demonstrated in the Viagra case study below.

Financial forecasts made at the time of R&D project selection are subject to gross errors, either because the development costs turn out to be much higher (rather than lower) or the financial benefits derived from the project are higher or lower than was originally forecast. Such forecasts are clearly of limited value. None the less, some form of financial analysis cannot be avoided. It will certainly be demanded by senior management. Analyses which are unrealistic and have no credibility within the organisation are of limited value. This area of decision making is dominated by personal experience and historical case studies that the company has experienced.

A variety of quantitative and qualitative measurements have been developed to try to help business managers tackle the problem of project selection (Chiesa and Masella, 1996). It remains, however, a combination of uncertain science and experience. Chapter 9 explores how businesses attempt to evaluate R&D projects in terms of whether to continue funding or to drop the project.

Case study

The long and difficult 13-year journey to the marketplace for Pfizer's Viagra

Introduction

There are many stories that have emerged over the years concerning Pfizer's product Viagra. Some of these are true but many are simply fictional stories developed to try to reinforce a particular argument. One of the most common is that Viagra was the result of luck. This case study explores the long 13-year journey from laboratory to the marketplace and explores some of the key challenges faced by Pfizer; most notably, project evaluation considerations, when the available market research evidence suggests a small market for the product. And product launch considerations, when impotence is such an unpopular topic that it is almost impossible for advertisers to refer to it without alienating the very consumer base they are trying to reach.

What is Viagra?

Pfizer's Viagra is now part of business folklore in terms of an example of a successful new product. Viagra is now one of the most recognised brands in the world; it has become a social icon with annual sales in excess of $1.9 billion. And it has transformed Pfizer from a medium-sized pharmaceutical firm into the world's leader. Yet, Viagra was almost dismissed during clinical trials as interesting, but not clinically or financially significant. It is true Viagra was something of an accidental discovery. Scientists testing an angina drug found that as a side effect it seemed to cure impotence in many patients. It did not take long for Pfizer to decide to focus on its unexpected benefit and to develop the product further as an anti-impotence drug. The drug was licensed by the US FDA (Food and Drugs Administration) and launched in the US in April 1998, amidst a huge fanfare of serious and not so serious media hype. At the time many news organisations used attention grabbing headlines often stretching the product's capabilities such as how Viagra could enhance sexual performance. In the first month, 570,000 new prescriptions for Viagra were issued, generating $100 million in revenue. One aspect of the story that frequently seems to get highlighted is that this product was due to serendipity or luck. While this may be true for a very small part of the story, as this case shows the vast majority of the product's success was due to effective management, excellent research and development and very clever marketing.

Unfortunately the serendipity aspect of the Viagra case overshadows the ground-breaking science involved (the Nobel Prize for physiology was awarded to scientists involved in the related research for Viagra) and the effective management by Pfizer of the new product development process. Moreover, this story reinforces in the minds of the public that science and research is dependent on luck. This is misleading at best and at worst dangerous. According to some journalists Viagra owes its existence to serendipity. They argue it started its life as a potential treatment for angina, and was being tested in clinical trials. As an angina treatment, it was pretty useless, but then the researchers began to get reports of some unexpected side effects and hence Viagra was born. This of course is not only incomplete but is misleading. Of course it would be naive to think that the complexities of scientific research will always be accurately relayed to a mass audience, but for medicine and science to be portrayed as scientists playing around in the laboratories in the hope that something will drop from their test tubes is quite simply untrue. If science is not careful Viagra will end up like the discovery of penicillin and therefore antibiotics: that it was all down to luck. Few people realise that while Alexander Fleming discovered penicillin in 1928 it took another *20 years* for scientists Howard Florey and Ernst Chain to develop a method of producing a product that could be used by patients for treatment in the form of antibiotics that we know today.

The true story of Viagra is more complex and illustrates that the research project team had to fight hard for the huge investment that was required to develop the compound into a product. Indeed, it was almost not developed at all. Gill Samuels, was director of science policy at the Pfizer Central Research Site, Sandwich, Kent, and was one of the key developers of Viagra. She was awarded a CBE for services to

→

bioscience in the Queen's 2002 birthday honours list. She recalls some of the problems:

> *Even in the early stages when it was known that we were doing trials in the UK we had patients writing in wanting to participate, and we have had some wonderful letters from patients who participated in those trials. Even before Viagra was launched in the US [in April 1998] we realised that it had a very profound effect. The question was how many of those men who did have erectile dysfunction would actually want to receive treatment for it? It was very, very difficult to predict the absolute numbers. There is no doubt about it that the media interest in Viagra raised the awareness of erectile dysfunction, and probably encouraged men who had the problem, but did nothing about it, to contact their doctor.*
>
> (BBC.co.uk, 2006)

From angina to Viagra

To develop this one successful medicine, scientists screened over 1,500 compounds and spent an estimated £600 million (at today's prices). Furthermore, it took 13 years (1985–1998) to bring Viagra from conception to production. This level of investment is sometimes needed for research, development and to prove that the new medicine is safe and effective. Table 8.5 illustrate the stages from initial concept to final product.

Viagra started life as a medicine intended to treat angina pectoris. Alfred Nobel – an explosives manufacturer from Norway – suffered from angina (angina is defined as brief attacks of chest pain due to insufficient oxygenation of heart muscles). In 1890 he was prescribed nitro-glycerine (called *trinitrin*) to relieve the pain of angina attacks. It is still used today. Over 100 years later, the work of Robert Furchgott, Louis Ignarro and Ferid Murad showed that nitric oxide (NO) was an important signalling molecule in the cardiovascular system. It is released from nerve endings and cells lining the walls of blood vessels. The effect is to make the blood vessel relax, or dilate. It is also involved in the prevention of blood clots. In 1998, they received the Nobel Prize for Physiology. The Nobel prizes were set up by the same Alfred Nobel who had been treated with nitro-glycerine. Building on this knowledge, research by other groups is being undertaken to develop new medicines that moderate the actions of nitric oxide for the treatment of cardiovascular and other disorders (Pfizer, 2005).

Dilating arteries

Researchers started by trying to understand the process of vasodilation (what makes the arteries dilate). They decided to target the action of the new medicine on to the enzyme PDE (*Phosphodiesterase*). This enzyme breaks down the signalling molecule cGMP, which causes vasodilation. By preventing the breakdown of cGMP the new medicine would increase vasodilation. Enzymes have a very specific shape. Viagra fits into the active site and blocks it. This prevents the PDE from breaking down the cGMP, which then stays in the blood and continues to cause vasodilation. The first step to developing the new medicine was to isolate and characterise the PDE enzyme (later called PDE-5). Once the PDE had been isolated, researchers could use it to find out the optimum conditions in which it works and also do tests to find efficient inhibitors. This enables molecules to be modified and designed to affect the enzyme.

Clinical trials

In 1991, following six years of laboratory research, a clinical trial was undertaken in Wales for a compound known as UK-92.480. The findings from the trial on healthy volunteers revealed disappointing results. The data on blood pressure, heart rate and blood flow were discouraging. The R&D project was in trouble. Some patients reported side effects of episodes of indigestion, some of aches in legs and some reported penile erections. This final point was listed merely as an observation by the clinicians involved in the study, at that moment no one said 'wow' or 'great'. Indeed, the decision to undertake trials into erectile dysfunction was not an obvious one. This was partly because the prevailing view at the time was that most erectile dysfunction was psychological and not treatable with drugs. Few people believed it was possible to produce an erection with an injection of drugs. Men, particularly older men who are more likely to suffer from impotence, were treated as if it was their fault, that it was all in the mind and that they should try to accept their sex life was more or less over.

In any large research laboratory there will be hundreds and sometimes thousands of research projects being undertaken at any one time. Each project has to give regular reports on progress to senior R&D managers who continually have to decide with which projects to continue investment and those to stop investment and which new projects to start. In

Table 8.5 The main stages in the development of Viagra

1985	Initial concept	In 1985, scientists at Pfizer decided to develop a medicine to treat heart failure and hypertension. They were looking for a medicine that would vasodilate, or 'open', arteries, lower blood pressure and reduce strain on the heart. They chose to target the medicine to act on an enzyme found in the wall of blood vessels.
1986–1990	Research and development starts	Between 1986 and 1990, hundreds of possible medicines were synthesised and tested in laboratory experiments. The most promising compound was given the code name UK-92.480. It showed properties that suggested it would be a good medicine to treat angina. Research was redirected to look at this heart disorder. The medicine was later called Sildenafil and finally renamed Viagra (Sildenafil citrate).
1991	Volunteer trials	In 1991, healthy volunteers took part in clinical trials to test the safety of Viagra and how the body metabolised the compound. These showed that it was safe. In trials over 10 days, the healthy volunteers reported some unexpected side effects. Male volunteers reported more frequent erections after taking the angina medicine!
1992	Erectile dysfunction	Following the unusual side effects seen in the volunteer trials, researchers switched to looking into using Viagra to treat erectile dysfunction (ED). This serious condition causes psychological and emotional problems that affect many families. Research into using Viagra to treat angina continued but the medicine did not prove powerful enough to be really useful.
1993–96	ED clinical trials start	'Double-blind, placebo controlled' clinical trials started in 1993 to test how well Viagra treated patients with erectile dysfunction. To make the trials a fair test, neither the patients nor their doctors knew if they were receiving the medicine or an inactive placebo. Viagra proved to be a great success.
1997	Licence application	All medicines need to be licensed by the medical authorities before they can be prescribed by doctors. To achieve this, trials must show it is safe and effective. Approval usually takes about 12 months but in the case of Viagra it received its licence in only 6 months.
1998	Licence approval	Viagra was given a licence. It could be used in the treatment of erectile dysfunction in 1998. In its first three months, there were 2.9 million prescriptions for the medicine.

Source: Pfizer.com.

1991 the leader for the Viagra project had to report on progress and the results were disappointing. Essentially the medicine was not effective in treating angina. The senior R&D managers were preparing to drop the angina R&D project due to its disappointing results. It was also considering dropping all studies on the compound even as a possible drug for erectile dysfunction. This was partly because it was not clear that it would have a clinical use. Not all the healthy volunteers had reported erections. Moreover, how would Pfizer be able to conduct trials for such a condition? Furthermore, the market for such a drug was not clear. At that time survey results revealed only 1 in 20 million men suffered from erectile dysfunction; hence even if a medicine could be developed the market would be very small. The R&D team involved in the project eventually managed to gain two years of funding to develop the drug and undertake clinical trials.

One needs to be aware that at the time Pfizer had many drugs under consideration for the treatment of many other conditions such as colonic cancer, diabetes, asthma, etc. These markets were well known and understood. The business case for all of these projects and others could be easily made. Accurate predictions could be made on the number of people who suffered from asthma and what customers would

→

be willing to pay for such drugs. It was not possible to draw up an accurate business case for Viagra due to the uncertainties of the market and the condition. There simply was not a similar drug on the market with which to make a comparison. This made it an even more difficult decision for R&D managers at Pfizer. Fortunately, in 1992 the go ahead was given to provide funds for the continuation of clinical trials into erectile dysfunction (ED). But another problem now faced the team: how to conduct clinical trials in this very sensitive area. Would the team be able to find people willing to participate and discuss their experiences? Fortunately, the team did not experience any major difficulty in recruiting volunteers. While it was true large parts of the population did not feel comfortable in participating, sufficient numbers of people were willing to take part, not least those suffering from ED. The pharmaceutical industry is aware that despite advances in technology and scientific know-how, the odds of a drug candidate's success has not shifted in the past 20 years. Of 12 molecules that Pfizer classes to be its best bets – those drugs that have made it to the verge of clinical testing – only one will make it to market (Michaels, 2001).

Product and market evaluation: decision time!

In 1996 following successful clinical trials the clinical success of the drug and obtaining patent protection did not seem to be in doubt, but that alone is not enough to proceed with the huge investment required to take the drug to market. Major uncertainties remained, especially with the business case:

- What is the size of the market? How many people suffer from ED?
- Could the market be bigger?
- Can we make the market bigger?
- The market for ED is not developed; can it be developed and how?
- Is it a growing market?
- Is there an existing customer base (i.e. current sufferers)?
- Is the potential big enough to warrant the investment?
- Does it support our short-term and long-term plans for the business?

We sometimes need reminding that virtually all businesses are established to make a profit for their investors; hence, most decisions centre on finance. What is the investment and what is the likely return? This decision was no exception. The business case for Viagra was certainly interesting but there were many risks, not least would the product sell and how would Pfizer be able to market the product to a public that, in the US at least, was known to be conservative and prudish about talking about impotence and sex? The likelihood of a television commercial going out at 8 p.m. on ABC or NBC promoting the virtues of Viagra in overcoming impotence was simply unimaginable in the mid-1990s. Hence, there were risks in terms of the size of the market and, even if the market proved to be as big as Pfizer hoped, how would it be able to communicate with this market and promote the product?

Is there a viable marketing plan?

The drug cannot be purchased over the counter; hence men would have to get a prescription from their physician. The challenge for Pfizer then was to encourage men to go to their doctor and ask for treatment. This poses a significant challenge. The marketing campaign would need to focus on education and raising awareness of the condition. Impotence, however, is such an unpopular topic that it is almost impossible for advertisers to refer to it without alienating the very consumer base they are trying to reach. The audience would need reprogramming. While sex sells, it was important to numb the audience and society with educating material: an audience made up of sensitive males with problems that are often highlighted as the butt of many jokes. The consumer had to be reprogrammed to look at the situation in a new light. In order to do this, a large amount of money had to be there for the product launch and the subsequent advertising that ties to it.

After much debate and discussion Pfizer decided to attempt to create a sense of pride in the consumer through the opposite sex's testimonials of newly found happiness and through mainstream sports stars that epitomise the definition of manliness. The Viagra ads eventually selected by Pfizer tried to break through men's reluctance to address the issue by using celebrity spokesmen who embody respectability (politician Bob Dole); athleticism (NASCAR driver Mark Martin, Brazilian footballer Pele and Texas Rangers baseball player Rafael Palmeiro); and virility (Hugh Hefner). Altogether, Pfizer spent more than

$100 million on endorsements, television advertising, online marketing and sports event sponsorship. The celebrities encouraged men to fix the problem – as they would fix headache with Aspirin. The campaign earned Viagra brand-name recognition approaching that of Coca-Cola and has led to a saturation of Viagra jokes and spam emails.

Some analysts argue Pfizer made a critical error by selecting Bob Dole as its advertising spokesperson. Dole, in his 70s, was clearly the market for Viagra. But he was not the target. The target is the 50-year-old married man who is having trouble, but is terrified of asking his doctor. Positioning the product for older men tells younger men that Viagra wasn't for them. Viagra would have been wiser choosing younger, more macho-looking men to help remove the stigma of ED and make younger men feel more comfortable talking about the problem and product. Today, you do see much younger male models in the Viagra ads.

Launch

At the launch, the priority for Pfizer was to retain control over the brand image, ensuring that it was positioned as Pfizer wanted it to be and that accurate information was given to the public. A campaign estimated to be costing tens of millions of dollars on consumer-orientated advertising in popular magazines such as *Time*, *Life* and *Newsweek* was undertaken. The enormous level of pre-launch publicity that Viagra had generated was not necessarily a good thing. The publicity was out of Pfizer's control, meaning that it could be inaccurate and/or damaging to the brand image. The thousands of jokes made about the brand could well have had a negative effect, making patients embarrassed about owning up to an impotence problem and asking for the drug. Pfizer waited until the worst of the publicity had died down before launching its campaign to make sure that its message was heard properly and that the drug was taken more seriously. This, along with all the media hype, had led to a rapid take-up after its introduction.

Sales continued to grow as the product was progressively launched on worldwide markets. In 1998 total sales had reached $776 million, $1,016 million by 1999 and $1,344 million by 2000, representing over 5 per cent of human drug sales for Pfizer. The 2000 Annual Report proclaimed that more than 300 million Viagra tablets have been prescribed for more than 10 million men in more than 100 countries: Viagra had become a worldwide brand in a very short period of time.

Source: Pearson Education Ltd/Photodisc

All the US publicity was heard in Europe and made the European market a little more difficult to enter. When Viagra was eventually licensed in Europe late in 1998, the UK health minister pronounced that Viagra would not be made available on the National Health Service (NHS). This had a lot to do with NHS priorities: impotence is not high on the list, apparently, and there were fears about the cost to the NHS if all the hype produced the same sort of level of demand as in the US. There were fears that it would cost the NHS £1 billion per year if it was available on demand. Although some relaxation has subsequently taken place, and doctors are allowed more say in prescribing the drug, it is still not readily available on prescription. Impotence in itself is not enough for free treatment – it must be caused by specific medical conditions such as diabetes.

Viagra's advertising campaigns were never the key to its success, however. Because of its unique clinical function, Viagra became an immediate cultural point for all issues relating to virility, male sexuality, and aging, and through this continual popular referencing, much more than the effects of its $100 million advertising budget, Viagra has achieved a level of brand recognition that is reserved only for superstar drugs like Tylenol and Prozac. Indeed, Viagra continues to be a constant source of office jokes and comments for late night talk show hosts. More than simply spreading the word on what Viagra is, the enormous street and media buzz that Viagra has inspired has established Viagra's image overwhelmingly in terms of power and efficacy as the remedy for impotence.

→

Competition

The greatest challenge to Viagra came when Pfizer lost some of its patent protection. The main or active ingredient in Viagra is sildenafil, and potential competitors Eli Lilly and Icos Corporation challenged the legitimacy of the original patent issued in 1993. The court ruled that the knowledge on which it had been based was already in the public domain in 1993 and that the patent was now restricting research by other companies. Other companies would now be able to sell drugs that treat impotence by blocking PDE-5, a chemical, although Pfizer retains a patent on the active ingredient in Viagra – meaning that direct copies of the drug itself will not be permitted. In January 2002, the Court of Appeal (UK) had agreed with an earlier High Court ruling that knowledge covered by the Pfizer patent on the 'PDE-5 inhibitor' was already in the public domain. Similarly in 2004 Pfizer faced increased competition in China after Beijing overturned its domestic patent for the main ingredient in Viagra. Although the molecular structure of Viagra was still protected, the main active ingredient was now open to competitors. The first serious challenge came from Uprima after it received its European licence in 2001. Its makers, Abbott Laboratories, based in Illinois, USA, claimed it worked more quickly than Viagra, with fewer side effects and cost less than £5 for both low and high dosage tablets. Quick action can help spontaneity, unlike Viagra which has to be taken at least an hour before sex.

Pfizer continued with its legal battles as it attempted to prevent competitors copying key elements of the drug. GlaxoSmithKline, the Anglo-American group, and its German partner Bayer were relying on Vardenafil to revive their flagging share prices (Firn and Tait, 2002). Critics argued that Pfizer's goal was simply to delay competitive entry for Viagra as long as possible, and if the patent were actually to stick, that would simply be additional profits.

In 2003 the competition for Viagra increased noticeably when Viagra came third in the first independent comparison with its two new competitors. According to the research, 45 per cent of the 150 men involved in the trial preferred Eli Lilly's Cialis, while 30 per cent voted for Levitra, jointly marketed by GlaxoSmithKline and Bayer. The findings are likely to play an important part in the fierce marketing battle between the four pharmaceutical groups over treatments for impotence. Pfizer said the research was not scientifically rigorous (Dyer, 2003).

The challenge for the competitors is different to that faced by Pfizer. Viagra is already a well-known remedy for impotence in the popular imagination; alternative drugs are fighting an uphill battle against the power of the Viagra brand. The marketing challenge that faced the makers of Cialis and Levitra is that they would have to re-establish the problem of impotence – a problem that many consumers see as already having been solved by Viagra – in order to offer their products as a cure. But because Viagra already exists, Levitra and Cialis would have to rely on advertising to increase their market share, and since ED appears to be a distasteful topic, advertisers decided to concentrate on enhancing ED's image, rather than its products' image. Cialis differentiates itself from both Viagra and Levitra by offering a 36-hour window of efficacy. This beats Viagra's and Levitra's four to eight-hour period, and allows Cialis to focus its advertising on timing rather than performance. All three advertising campaigns ultimately suggest the discomfort, shame, embarrassment, and fear that surround sex in general, and the lack of any compassionate, humane, truthful discourse on sexual dysfunctions in our culture. Sex appears as a paranoid game where invisible spectators cheer winners and boo losers.

Conclusions

By virtually all measures this product has been universally successful for Pfizer, transforming it from a large pharmaceutical firm into the world's leading pharmaceutical firm. The actual market for this type of drug is now known to be far greater than the original market research data had revealed. This is a cautionary tale of the need sometimes to encourage innovation and support scientific freedom in the face of evidence to stop the project.

Viagra was the first-mover and first-prover in this category. However, Viagra has not been quick to respond to competitive scientific advancements in erectile dysfunction drugs. It takes Viagra anywhere from 30 minutes to an hour to work but Levitra, launched in 2001, improves upon that by working in 16 minutes. And Cialis, also launched in 2001, improves upon Levitra by being able to last up to 36 hours. Indeed, competitors argue Pfizer has already conceded defeat by introducing a loyalty programme

Table 8.6 Sales of impotence drugs

Impotence drug: brand	Sales (2003)
Levitra (vardenafil)	$131m
Viagra (sildenafil)	$1.88bn
Cialis (tadalafil)	$203m

which they argue is not about building a long-term relationship with their patients as Pfizer's marketing director says. Rather, they see it as a scheme by Pfizer to get the most out of the Viagra brand and it will continue to lose market share to better, more effective options from Levitra and Cialis. The erectile dysfunction market grew 3.5 per cent from 2003 to be worth $1.95 billion in 2005 and is almost entirely composed of sales from the three brands: Viagra (sildenafil), Cialis (tadalafil) and Levitra (vardenafil). Table 8.6 reveals the continued dominance of Viagra.

One aspect of this case study that is seldom discussed is the extent to which Pfizer has benefited from raising disease awareness. A lot of money can be made from healthy people who believe they are sick. Pharmaceutical companies are able to sponsor diseases and promote them to prescribers and consumers, a practice sometimes known as 'disease mongering' (i.e. widening the boundaries of treatable illness in order to expand markets for those who sell and deliver treatments). Within many disease categories informal alliances have emerged, comprising drug company staff, doctors and consumer groups. Ostensibly engaged in raising public awareness about under-diagnosed and under-treated problems, these alliances tend to promote a view of their particular condition as widespread, serious and treatable. Because these 'disease awareness' campaigns are commonly linked to companies' marketing strategies, they operate to expand markets for new pharmaceutical products. Alternative approaches – emphasising the self-limiting or relatively benign natural history of a problem, or the importance of personal coping strategies – are often played down or ignored. As the late medical writer Lynn Payer observed, disease mongers 'gnaw away at our self-confidence' (Payer, 1992). For example, a double-page advertisement in the Sydney *Morning Herald*'s *Weekend Magazine* told Australians recently that 39 per cent of men who visit general practitioners have ED. The 39 per cent claim in the advertisement was referenced to an abstract of a survey finding. However, another recent Australian study, not cited in the advertisement, estimated that erection problems affected only 3 per cent of men in their 40s, and 64 per cent of men in their 70s. The advertisement's fine print cited a host organisation, Impotence Australia, but did not mention that the advertisement was funded by Pfizer (Moynihan *et al.*, 2002). The key concern with 'disease mongering' is the invisible and unregulated attempts to change public perceptions about health and illness to widen markets for new drugs.

Source: Dyer, G. (2003) Pfizer hits back at results of research on Viagra, *Financial Times*, 17 November; Firn, D. and Tait, N. (2002) Pfizer loses legal battle to protect Viagra patent, *Financial Times*, 18 June; Michaels, A. (2001) Pfizer R&D unable to sustain group growth rate, *Financial Times*, 12 September; Moynihan, R., Heath, I. and Henry, D. (2002) Selling sickness: the pharmaceutical industry and disease mongering, *BMJ*, 13 April, Vol. 324, No. 7342, 886–91; Payer, L. (1992) *Disease-mongers*, John Wiley, New York, Pfizer (2005) www.Pfizer.com.

Questions

1 Was Viagra the result of serendipity or is this journalistic licence to help sell a story, where the real story is a complex one of difficult decisions full of risks?

2 Explain why it was so necessary to ensure marketing was involved in the early stages of this new product development project.

3 Explain how, despite the enormous resources of Pfizer, a lack of available information made the evaluation of the new product proposal so very difficult.

4 Explain how the Viagra case needs to be viewed as a successful example of excellent applied science but also an excellent example of good marketing.

5 How can Pfizer manage the threat posed to Viagra by new entrants to the market?

6 How has Pfizer helped create a market for Viagra and thereby contributed to disease mongering?

Chapter summary

This chapter has introduced the substantial subject of R&D management and some of the challenges that it presents. Emphasis has been placed on highlighting the wide range of different activities undertaken by most R&D functions. Formal management techniques were shown to be an essential part of good R&D management. Companies are unable to justify spending millions of dollars purely on the basis of chance and good fortune. The issue of investment in R&D and industry comparisons was another area of discussion.

The link between R&D and the strategic management activities of the business was also discussed in some detail. This presents its own set of challenges in terms of deciding in which areas to invest and what type of R&D investment to follow. Most companies try to manage a balance of activities, but it is important to be aware of the nature of the pressures placed on management.

Discussion questions

1 Discuss whether R&D should be viewed just like any other expenditure, and hence should deliver a positive return for the investor.

2 Explain why R&D functions are often thought as freewheeling places of disorder, yet in reality R&D is routine and follows many procedures.

3 Explain how two firms, A and B, in the same industry, investing the same in R&D as a percentage of sales, can perform so differently. Firm A delivers three new patents and two new successful products; whereas firm B fails to deliver anything.

4 Consider a firm of your choice. Examine what its level of expenditure on R&D could be. What should it be? And what is its actual expenditure?

5 Use CIM (Figure 1.9) to illustrate the innovation process in the Viagra study.

6 Firms investing in R&D in the many countries in the world receive tax credits. How can countries encourage further R&D investment?

7 Describe a balanced portfolio of R&D projects for Nokia. This should incorporate its technology portfolio.

8 What are the advantages and disadvantages from cutting R&D in a downturn?

Key words and phrases

R&D as a percentage of sales *276*

Applied research *280*

Basic research *283*

Technical service *285*

Technology portfolio *289*

Core technologies *289*

Complementary technologies *289*

Peripheral technologies *289*

Emerging technologies *289*

Technology leverage *293*

References

Adler, P.S., McDonald, D.W. and MacDonald, F. (1992) Strategic management of technical functions, *Sloan Management Review*, Winter, 19–37.

Ansoff, H.I. (1968) *Corporate Strategy*, Penguin, Harmondsworth.

BCG (1972) *Perspectives on Experience*, Boston Consulting Group, Boston, MA.

Bush, V. (1945) *Science: The Endless Frontier*, A Report to the President.

Chiesa, V. and Masella, C. (1996) Searching for an effective measure of R&D performance, *Management Decision*, Vol. 34, No. 7, 49–58.

Cohen, W.M. and Levinthal, D.A. (1990) A new perspective on learning and innovation, *Administrative Science Quarterly*, Vol. 35, No. 1, 128–52.

Cordero, R. (1990) The measurement of innovation performance in the firm: an overview, *Research Policy*, Vol. 19, No. 2, 10–21.

EIRMA (1985) Evaluation of R&D output: working group report, 29, European Industrial Research Management Association, Paris.

Geroski, P., Machin, S. and van Reenen, J. (1993) The profitability of innovating forms, *Rand Journal of Economics*, Vol. 24, 198–211.

Hickman, L.A. (1990) *Technology*, McGraw-Hill, Maidenhead.

Independent (1992) R&D Scoreboard, 10 June, 20.

Mansfield, E. (1991) Social returns from R&D: findings, methods and limitations, *Research, Technology Management*, November/December, 24.

Mansfield, E., Raporport, J., Schnee, J., Wagner, S. and Hamburger, M. (1972) *Research and Innovation in the Modern Corporation*, Macmillan, London.

McGrath, M.E. and Romeri, M.N. (1994) The R&D effectiveness index, *Journal of Product Innovation Management*, Vol. 23, No. 2, 213–20.

Meyer-Krahmer, F. (1984) Recent results in measuring innovation output, *Research Policy*, Vol. 13, No. 3, 12–24.

Mitchell, G.R. (1988) Options for the strategic management of technology, *UNESCO Technology Management*, Interscience Enterprises Ltd, Geneva.

Nobelius, D. (2004) Towards the sixth generation of R&D management, *International Journal of Project Management*, Vol. 22, 369–75.

Porter, M.E. (1985) *Competitive Advantage: Creating and Sustaining Competitive Advantage*, Free Press, New York.

Quintas, P., Weild, D. and Massey, M. (1992) Academic–industry links and innovation: questioning the science park model, *Technovation*, Vol. 12, No. 3, 161–75.

Roussel, P.A., Saad, K.N. and Erickson, T.S. (1991) *Third Generation R&D*, Harvard Business School Press, Boston, MA.

Scholefield, J.H. (1993) The development of a R&D planning model at ICI, *R&D Management*, Vol. 23, No. 4, 20–30.

Twiss, B. (1992) *Managing Technological Innovation*, 4th edn, Financial Times Pitman Publishing, London.

Weild, D. (1986) 'Organisational strategies and practices for innovation', in Roy, R. and Weild, D. (eds) *Product Design and Technological Innovation*, Open University Press, Milton Keynes.

Williams, D.J. (1969) A study of the decision model for R&D project selection, *Operational Research Quarterly*, Vol. 20.

Further reading

For a more detailed review of the R&D management literature, the following develop many of the issues raised in this chapter:

Day, G.S. and Schoemaker, P.J.H. (eds) (2000) *Wharton on Managing Emerging Technologies*, John Wiley, New York.

Howells, J. (2008) New Directions in R&D: Current and Prospective Challenges, *R&D Management*, Vol. 38, Issue 3, pp. 241–52.

Lang, G. (2009) Measuring the returns of R&D – An empirical study of the German manufacturing sector over 45 years, *Research Policy*, Vol. 38, No. 9, 1438–45.

Trott, P. and Hartmann, D. (2009) Old wine in new bottles, *International Journal of Innovation Management*, Vol. 13, No. 4, 1–22.

Von Hippel, E. (2005) *Democratizing Innovation*, MIT Press, Boston, MA.

Xu, Q., Chen, J., Xie, Z., Liu, J., Zheng, G. and Wang, Y. (2007) Total Innovation Management: a novel paradigm of innovation management in the 21st century, *The Journal of Technology Transfer*, Vol. 32, 9–25.

Chapter 9
Managing R&D projects

Introduction

The past 10 years have witnessed enormous changes in the way companies manage their technological resources and in particular research and development. Within industrial R&D the effect is a shift in emphasis from an internal to an external focus. Contract R&D, R&D consortia and strategic alliances and joint ventures now form a large part of R&D management activities.

The need to provide scientific freedom and still achieve an effective return from any R&D investment, however, remains one of the most fundamental areas of R&D management. The use of formal planning techniques for R&D is viewed by many as a paradox: the introduction of any planning mechanism would surely stifle creativity and innovation. And yet R&D departments do not have unlimited funds, so there has to be some planning and control. This chapter explores the problems and difficulties of managing R&D projects within organisations.

The case study at the end of this chapter explores the phenomenon of *CSI: Crime Scene Investigation*. It has been one of television's greatest success stories of all time and is a huge hit all over the world. Yet, few people recognise that it was a UK scientist – Alec Jeffreys – who driven by curiosity, uncovered a technique for DNA fingerprinting.

Chapter contents

Learning objectives

When you have completed this chapter you will be able to:

- recognise the changing nature of R&D management;
- recognise the factors that influence the decision whether to undertake internal or external R&D;
- recognise the value of providing scientific freedom;
- examine the link with the product innovation process;
- recognise the significance of evaluating R&D projects; and
- explain how prior knowledge affects a firm's ability to acquire externally developed technology.

Successful technology management

Organisations that manage products and technologies and have been built on a strong research and development base are constantly looking for opportunities to diversify horizontally into new product markets. Their strategic management activities seek to mobilise complementary assets to successfully enter those markets. For example, Apple's knowledge of manufacturing small hand-held music players (iPods) enabled it to move into the manufacture of mobile phones. Similarly, in production-based technologies, key opportunities lie in the technological advances that can be applied to products and production systems, enabling diversification vertically into a wider range of production inputs. The injection-moulding process has had many adaptations, enabling its use in an increasing range of manufacturing techniques. However, companies do not have a completely free choice about the way they manage their technologies (Pavitt, 1990: 346):

> *In many areas it is not clear before the event who is in the innovation race, where the starting and finishing lines are, and what the race is all about. Even when all these things are clear, companies often start out wishing to be a leader and end up being a follower!*

There are two key technology risks that technology managers have to evaluate (Malerba and Orsenigo, 1993; Breschi and Malerba, 1997; Dosi, 1988). First, 'appropriability risks' reflect the ease with which competitors can imitate innovations (*see* Chapter 6). They are typically managed through patent and copyright protection or through controlling complementary assets (such as branding, distribution, specialised services, etc.), as discussed by Teece (1986). In the pharmaceutical industry, for example, patent protection is relatively effective because minor changes in the structure of therapeutic drugs can have major consequences for their operation in the human body (Gambardella, 1995). As a result, drug discovery firms are able to specialise in highly risky activities without needing to develop complementary assets to protect their innovations.

The second risk is 'competence destruction'. This reflects the volatility and uncertainty of technical development that vary greatly between technologies, both in terms of the technological trajectories (*see* Chapter 6) being followed and market acceptance. Where technological uncertainty is high, it is difficult to predict which investments and skills will be effective and firms have to be able to change direction at short notice. Consequently, the managers of firms attempting to develop radically discontinuous innovations are faced with the need to attract and motivate expert staff to work on complex problems when unpredictable outcomes may involve redundancy and/or organisational failure.

These two kinds of technology risk tend to be inversely related. Investments in developing highly uncertain technologies are usually undertaken when appropriability risks are limited (e.g. intellectual property protection is available, such as pharamaceuticals and software), while firms developing innovations that are more open to such risks tend to focus on more cumulative and predictable technologies (e.g. food industry and other fast-moving consumer goods (FMCG) areas). Companies racing to produce highly radical, discontinuous innovations have to be flexible in their use of key resources, such as highly expert technologists, and in changing direction, while those developing more imitable technologies have to develop complementary competencies (branding, distribution) and integrate them through organisational routines. By making innovations more customer-specific and bundling additional services with them, such companies increase their organisational specificity and limit the ease with which they can be imitated (e.g. Coca-Cola, Unilever). However, these kinds of entrepreneurial technology firms are more organisationally complex than radically innovative companies and have to develop stronger coordinating organisational capabilities (Mason *et al.*, 2004; Casper and Whitley, 2004).

The above discussions reveal the weaknesses in some of the commonly accepted views of technology strategy promoted by many business schools and management consultants. It is not helpful to the organisation to try to predetermine whether its technology strategy should be to lead or to follow, to develop a product or a process. Technology cannot be developed to order or acquired to fill a position in a matrix. It can only be successful if it is fully integrated into the company's business. This means that the company needs a range of complementary assets in other areas such as marketing and distribution, in order to exploit its technology successfully. Developing these skills and capabilities and integrating them into the company takes time. Often these characteristics will be determined by the company's size, its previous activities and its accumulated competencies. However, it is these latter factors and not the company's strategy that will determine whether it will successfully exploit its technology.

As virtually all practitioners realise, there is no easy formula for success. In a review of the literature on technology management, Pavitt (1990) identified the following necessary ingredients for successful technology management:

- the capacity to orchestrate and integrate functional and specialist groups for the implementation of innovations;
- continuous questioning of the appropriateness of existing divisional markets, missions and skills for the exploitation of technological opportunities; and
- a willingness to take a long-term view of technological accumulation within the firm.

Innovation in action

Be transparent

A problem online retailers face, as opposed to their bricks and mortar counterparts, is that customers can't touch and feel exactly what they are buying.

This gap is compounded in industries like floristry where, despite tempting brochure shots, florists often can't guarantee exactly what they are sending because of variations in availability. The resulting 'transparency gap' creates nervousness in customers. This in turn presents opportunity.

New Zealand-based florists Roses are Red have addressed this by sending customers a digital photograph of the exact bouquet they have sent. And if customers aren't completely happy with it, they can have a full replacement.

Source: HSBC (2010) 100 Thoughts, HSBC, London.

The changing nature of R&D management

R&D activities have changed dramatically since 1950. The past 10 years have witnessed enormous changes in the way companies manage their technological resources and in particular their research and development. There are numerous factors that have contributed to these changes (*see* Illustration 9.1) the key factors are:

- *Technology explosion*. It is estimated that 90 per cent of our present technical knowledge has been generated during the past 60 years.
- *Shortening of the technology cycle*. The technology cycle includes scientific and technological developments prior to the traditional product life cycle. These cycles have been slowly shortening, forcing companies to focus their efforts on product development. For example, the market life of production cars has decreased from approximately 10 years in the 1960s to approximately six years in the 2000s. In some cases a particular model may be restyled after only three years.
- *Globalisation of technology*. East Asian countries have demonstrated an ability to acquire and assimilate technology into new products. This has resulted in a substantial increase in technology transfer in the form of licensing and strategic alliances.

In addition the following specific changes are facing R&D managers today:

- the increasingly distributed and open nature of networked research and innovation;
- the growth of externally sourced R&D (and, as a consequence, the relative decline in internally generated R&D) within firms;
- overcoming barriers towards the increased productivity and effectiveness of R&D;
- the continued globalisation of R&D, particularly in terms of its spread and reach, associated with R&D offshoring;
- the relative shift from manufacturing-centred R&D towards more service-orientated R&D;
- R&D projects are being managed with the aid of more continuous feedback and information evaluation from stakeholders and sponsors – thereby strengthening the joint role of R&D performers and their clients.

Source: Howells (2008); Brzustowski *et al.* (2010)

Figure 8.3 showed the traditional areas of research activity for universities and industry. University emphasis has been on discovering new knowledge, with industry exploiting these discoveries in the form of products. The past decade has seen a significant increase in collaborative research, with industry sponsoring science departments in universities and engaging in staff exchanges with university departments.

The effect of these macro-factors is a shift in emphasis within industrial R&D from an internal to an external focus. In a study of firms in Sweden, Japan and the United States, Granstrand *et al.* (1992) revealed that the external acquisition of technology was the most prominent technology management issue in multi-technology corporations. Traditionally, R&D management, particularly in Western technology-based companies, has been management of internal R&D. It could be argued that one of the most noticeable features of Japanese companies since the Second World War has been their ability successfully to acquire and utilise technology from other

Illustration 9.1

Finding a new blockbuster drug has become harder now R&D is more complex, more expensive and more time-consuming

The world's drugs companies are coming to terms with a difficult conundrum in research and development: despite huge advances in technology and scientific know-how, R&D productivity seems to have stalled.

By some measures, productivity could even be said to have declined. This is in spite of the much-trumpeted unravelling of the human genome, speedier computing, breakthroughs in biochemistry and, most important, billions of dollars more being thrown at the effort by ever-larger, merged drug behemoths.

The large pharmaceuticals companies' amazing growth in the 1980s and 90s was fuelled by a series of drugs that they turned into blockbusters. But they now realise that their current R&D effort is not enough to sustain that growth. One explanation for falling R&D productivity is that the quick hits – in gastrointestinal disorders or heart disease, for example – have already been made. GlaxoSmithKline built its fortune on the ulcer drug Zantac while Eli Lilly's Prozac for the treatment of depression made it billions.

Diseases that have yet to be conquered with blockbusters – Alzheimer's, or the various forms of cancer, for example – have been much harder nuts to crack.

There have been considerable technical and scientific advances, most notably in biotechnology, genomics and related fields. But everyone seems to have underestimated how long it will take for the greater knowledge to result in medicines.

Finding molecules that have a beneficial effect on humans has always been somewhat haphazard. All drugs are trying to affect the body in one of two ways: they either enhance a chemical process or stop it.

Greater understanding of our genetic make-up is also leading to ideas for drugs that can correct DNA deficiencies before they have caused damage or more precisely identify people at risk from certain conditions.

However, these advances are recent and all target the start of the R&D process. Even without any unexpected obstacles, companies would take a few years yet to turn them into a flow of drugs at the other end of the pipeline.

But there are unexpected obstacles. The first is poisonous – or toxicological – side effects. As we learn more about the body's biochemistry, we can strive to test better what pathways a drug will disrupt aside from those that it was intended to. Too much chemical action on the side and you may have the medicinal equivalent of chopping off a head to cure a headache.

Advances in biochemistry and genetics mean there are now far more body interactions to study. There are also many more drugs on the market than before and research is required into how each new drug will interact with existing ones. Companies are developing the high-throughput screening for toxicology but it has been a slow process.

Ultimately, the screening will be more productive because drug candidates will fail earlier in the R&D process, thus saving money that would otherwise have been spent on clinical trials. But at the moment the faster techniques are in their infancy.

After a drug candidate is successful in its toxicology trials, it still has to be tested in humans – the trials are increasingly subject to criticism, with medical journals warning that the promise of big financial rewards is compromising independence. And with companies and regulators more mindful of side effects, clinical trials are becoming larger and taking longer, another reason why R&D costs are rising. In areas yet to see significant breakthroughs, such as stroke or cancer, large numbers of patients have to be studied for a long time and the effectiveness of a drug is sometimes hard to prove.

Source: A. Michaels (2001) Quick-hit chemistry becomes elusive, *Financial Times*, 12 September. Reprinted with permission.

companies around the world. Granstrand *et al.* (1992) suggest that the external acquisition of technology exposes technology managers to new responsibilities. Although this implies that acquiring technology from outside the organisation is something new, this is clearly not the case, as the long history of licensing agreements will show. However, the importance now placed on technology acquisition by technology-based companies reveals a departure from a focus on internal R&D and an acknowledgement that internal R&D is now only one of many technology development options available. The technology base of a company is viewed as an asset; it represents the technological capability of that company. The different acquisition strategies available involve varying degrees of organisational and managerial integration. For example, internal R&D is viewed as the most integrated technology-acquisition strategy with technology scanning the least integrated strategy. Technology scanning is rather narrowly defined by Granstrand *et al.* (1992) as both illegal and legal forms of acquiring technological know-how from outside.

The classification of technology-acquisition strategies offered by Granstrand *et al.* (1992) provides an illustration of the numerous ways of acquiring external technology (*see* Figure 9.1). Other classifications can be found in the technology transfer literature: Auster (1987); Chesnais (1988); Hagedoorn (1990); Lefever (1992). All these studies, however, offer classifications of only the formal methods of technology transfer. They ignore the many forms of informal linkages, alliances and industry associations that are known to exist and that often result in extensive transfer of knowledge and technology (Kreiner and Schultz, 1990; Rothwell and Dodgson, 1991).

The wide range of activities now being expected from R&D departments and the

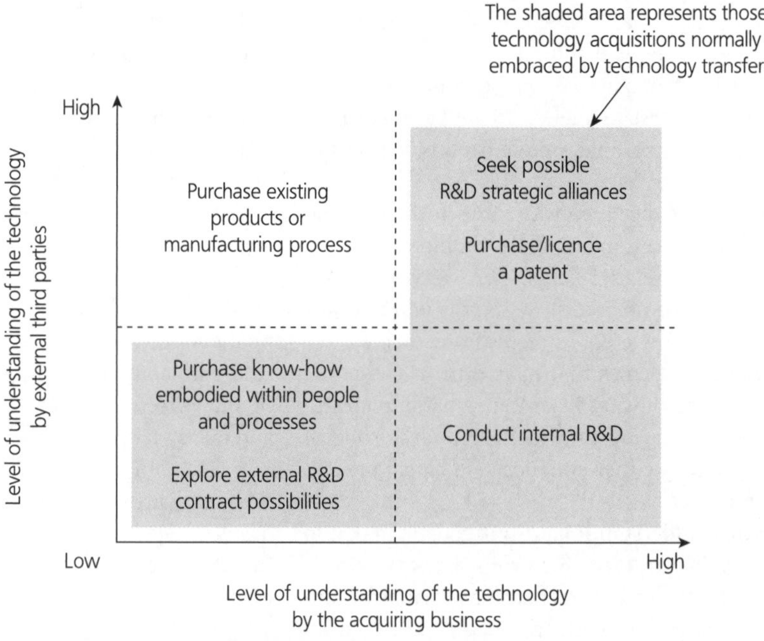

Figure 9.1 Acquisition of external technology/knowledge matrix

demands being placed on them are becoming ever more complex. Particular emphasis is being placed on a company's linkages with other organisations. Networking is now regarded as an effective method of knowledge acquisition and learning (Rothwell, 1992; Tidd *et al.*, 2001; Albertini and Butler, 1995). It is argued that the ability to network in order to acquire and exploit external knowledge enables the firm to enter new areas of technological development. The following areas now explicitly require involvement from the R&D department:

- Industry has expanded its support of university research and established numerous collaborations with university departments (Abelson, 1995).
- Industry has increased the number of technological collaborations. R&D personnel are increasingly being involved in technology audits of potential collaborators.
- Research and development personnel are increasingly accompanying sales staff on visits to customers and component suppliers to discuss technical problems and possible product developments.
- The acquisition and divestment of technology-based businesses have led to a further expansion of the role of R&D. Input is increasingly required in the form of an assessment of the value of the technology to the business.
- A dramatic rise in the use of project management as organisations shift to provide customer-driven results (Englund and Graham, 1999).
- The expansion of industrial agreements, usually in the form of licensing, contract work and consultancy, has resulted in a new area of work for R&D. The rapid growth in knowledge-intensive service firms is clear evidence of this (Kastrinos and Miles, 1995).

The focus of these new areas of work is on external knowledge acquisition and assimilation. This is forcing many companies to reassess the way they manage their R&D. In addition, this increased portfolio of activities requires a different range of skills from the individuals involved. The traditional role of a research scientist as a world expert in a particular field, who uses a convergent, narrow-focus approach to uncover new and cheaper ways of producing chemicals and products, is being replaced by researchers who have additional attributes. These include an ability to interact with a wide variety of external organisations, thereby increasing awareness of specific customer needs, market changes, the activities of competitors and the larger environment. Historically, R&D staff faced alternative definitions of career success and reward in career paths either involving increasing administrative responsibility and a path into managerial hierarchy or one involving increasing prestige as technical specialists. This dual-ladder career structure looks more and more out of place in today's varied and rapidly changing R&D environment.

Organising industrial R&D

The increasing emphasis on knowledge acquisition and assimilation is forcing companies to look for ways to improve their effectiveness in this area. Given the growing use of external sources of technology, the R&D manager now has to determine which form of R&D is most appropriate for the organisation. Figure 9.2 shows the many guises of R&D.

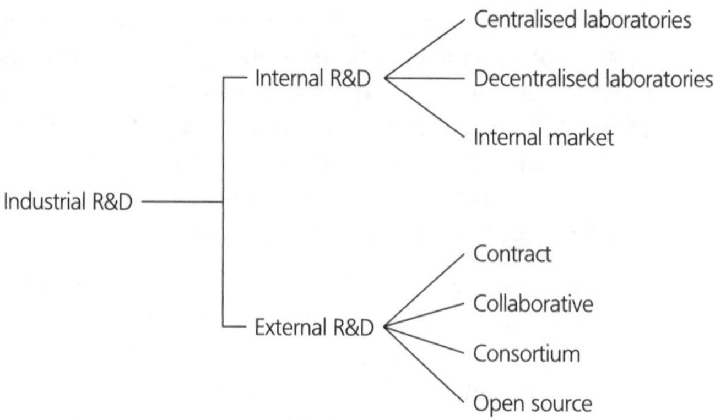

Figure 9.2 Organising industrial R&D

Centralised laboratories

The main advantage with centralised laboratories is critical mass. The idea is that far more can be achieved when scientists work together than when they work alone. Those firms trying to achieve technological leadership often centralise their R&D. There is also the possibility that synergy can result, with technologies from different businesses being employed in different unrelated businesses. 3M argue that they gain synergies between businesses resulting in internal technology transfer by having a centralised R&D laboratory.

Decentralised laboratories

The main advantage of decentralising the R&D function is to reinforce the link with the business, its products and its markets. It is argued that with a large, centralised R&D effort it is often too removed from where the technology is eventually applied. By providing each business or division with its own R&D effort, it is argued that this fosters improved communication and product development. However, the weakness of this closer link is that it can lead to an emphasis on short-term development only.

Internal R&D market

An internal market structure for R&D essentially involves establishing a functional cost centre, where each business pays for any R&D services required. This raises the issue of whether a business is also able to use external R&D services, say from a university. The extent to which this erodes the knowledge base of the organisation, however, is debatable. The limitations of this approach are similar to those for decentralised R&D laboratories.

The acquisition of external technology

So far in this book, we have concentrated on viewing R&D as an activity performed internally by the business. It is necessary, however, to understand that R&D is not necessarily an internal organisational activity. R&D, like any other business function, say marketing or production, can in theory be contracted out and performed by a third party. The previous section highlighted the increasing use of collaborations and strategic alliances to acquire technology (the role of strategic alliances was discussed in detail in Chapter 7). The extent to which it is possible for an organisation to acquire externally developed technology is uncertain and is discussed in Chapters 6 and 10. None the less, many businesses establish research contracts with organisations such as universities to undertake specific research projects.

There is a significant difference between acquiring externally developed technology and external R&D. This difference lies in the level of understanding of the technology involved, often referred to as prior knowledge. To illustrate, the purchase of new computer software will lead to the acquisition of new technology. This is an option available to virtually all businesses, irrespective of their prior knowledge of the technology. However, developing an R&D strategic alliance or an external R&D contract with a third party requires a high level of prior knowledge of the technology concerned. Similarly, the level of prior knowledge of the external third party also influences the choice of method to acquire the technology concerned (Mason *et al.*, 2004).

The matrix in Figure 9.1 offers an insight into the issue of technology acquisition. While the matrix is an oversimplification of a complex subject, it does none the less help to classify the wide range of acquisition options available to companies, from purchasing technology 'off the shelf' to conducting internal R&D. The horizontal axis refers to the level of prior knowledge of the business acquiring the technology. The vertical axis refers to the level of prior knowledge of external third parties.

As was explained in Chapter 3, there are many companies that conduct little, if any, R&D, yet are associated with a wide variety of technology-intensive products. This is particularly the case for supplier-dominated and scale-intensive firms (Pavitt, 1984). Many such companies assemble component parts purchased from other manufacturers and sell the final product stamped with their own brand. Some companies do not even assemble; they simply place their own brand on the purchased product (often called re-badging). In these cases the company concerned usually has commercial and marketing strengths such as service quality and distribution skills. This is similar to own-branding in the grocery market.

The subject of technology transfer is discussed in detail in Chapter 10. It is none the less worth pointing out here that technology transfer usually embraces the activities in the shaded area on the matrix. It is not normally used to describe, say, the purchase of new computer software. Technology transfer is defined as:

> *The process of promoting technical innovation through the transfer of ideas, knowledge, devices and artefacts from leading edge companies, R&D organisations and academic research to more general and effective application in industry and commerce.*
>
> (Seaton and Cordey-Hayes, 1993: 46)

Level of control of technology required

In acquiring externally developed technology, a business must also consider the extent of control over the technology that it requires. For example, if a research project shows promising results that could lead to the development of a new radical

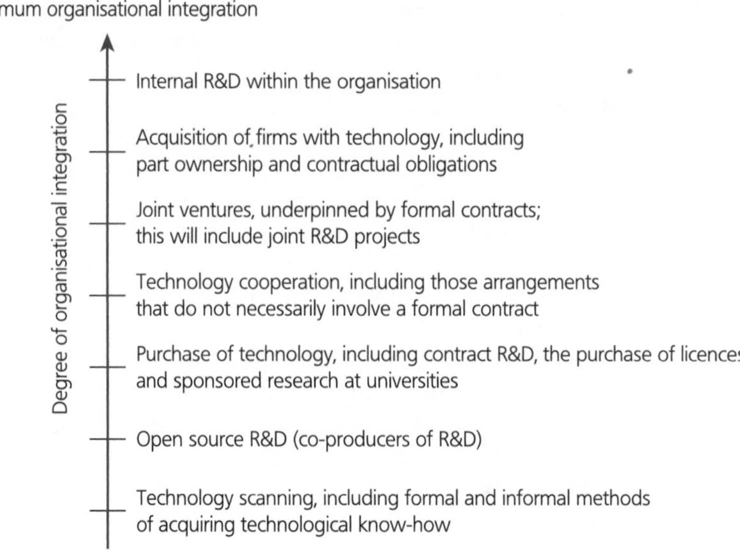

Figure 9.3 Technology acquisition: how much control of the technology is required?

technology with many new product opportunities, it is likely that the business would want to keep such research under close control and thus internal. On the other hand, a project with specific technical problems requiring expertise in an area of technology beyond the scope of the business may be ideally suited to a research contract with a university department. Figure 9.3 shows a classification of technology acquisition methods. You will see that they are classified according to the degree of integration with the organisation.

The particular stage of development of the research, or its position in the technology life cycle, will heavily influence the level of control required. For example, is the research at an early stage without any particular product idea in mind (pre-competitive) or is it near completion and shortly to be incorporated in a new product launch (competitive)? Clearly, competitive research will require careful monitoring to ensure that maximum competitive advantage can be secured.

There may also be occasions when the company does not have the in-house expertise to undertake the research. In this case some form of external R&D will be necessary.

Forms of external R&D

Contract R&D

In those situations where the business has a low level of understanding of the technology (bottom left-hand corner of technology acquisition matrix), contracting the R&D out to a third party is often suitable. University research departments have a long history of operating in this area. However, the use of commercial research organisations is rapidly expanding, especially in the field of biotechnology. This method of R&D is also used in urgent situations, when setting up internal research teams would be too slow.

R&D strategic alliances and joint ventures

This area of management was explored in Chapter 7. At this point it is necessary only to be aware of the key advantages and disadvantages of using strategic alliances. This is a generic term for all forms of cooperation, both formal and informal, including joint ventures. With a joint venture, the costs and possible benefits from an R&D research project would be shared. They are usually established for a specific project and will cease on its completion. For example, Sony and Ericsson formed a joint venture to develop mobile phone handsets. The advantages are usually obvious. In this example, both companies (who were former competitors) were able to share their expertise and reduce the inevitable costs and risks associated with any R&D project. The disadvantages are that either company could inadvertently pass knowledge to the other and receive little in return. It is for this reason alone that many companies still refuse to enter into any form of strategic alliance. It can be usefully explained using game theory principles and in particular the prisoner's dilemma (*see* Chapter 7).

R&D consortia

In this context, R&D consortia are separate from the large-scale technology consortia often found in the Far East. In Japan *keiretsus* (literally meaning societies of business) consist of 20–50 companies, usually centred around a trading company and involving component suppliers, distributors and final product producers, all interwoven through shareholdings and trading arrangements. In South Korea, *chaebols* are similar to *keiretsus* except that they are financed by the government rather than by banks or a trading company and usually the company links are based on family ties (Sakakibara, 2002; Powell, 1996). Such types of business groups are based on common membership and collaborate over a long period of time.

The use of R&D consortia has increased substantially over the past 10 years in both the United States and Europe. Rhea (1991) claims that there have been in excess of 200 R&D consortia registered in the United States since 1984. The European Union offers a number of programmes to encourage R&D cooperation across the Union. One of the most successful, and certainly high-profile, cases is SEMTECH, a consortium of 14 US semiconductor manufacturers. In 1980 nine out of the top 10 silicon chip makers were from the United States. By 1990 five out of the top six were Japanese. SEMTECH was established to try to help the US chip manufacturers. It had substantial funding from the US Defense Department with the aim of creating a viable semiconductor manufacturing equipment and materials industry, thus ensuring that domestic chip producers would not be dependent on Japanese equipment sources. SEMTECH has played a major role in developing successive generations of chip-making technology. By 1995, the US semiconductor industry had experienced a dramatic increase in its share of the world market (Corey, 1997).

Inspired by R&D consortia in advanced countries, Taiwan and the Chinese mainland have sought to develop the cooperative R&D mechanism in their own distinctive contexts. R&D consortia in Taiwan and Public Technological Platforms (PTPs) in the Chinese mainland have unique structural characteristics with their common catch-up goals and have been developing in different ways reflecting the relationships and interaction between academia, industry and government.

One of the potential weaknesses of this concept is the potential for reducing competition. The European Union and the US government spend a great deal of time and money trying to detect those organisations operating a cartel. Harsh penalties are usually enforced on any offending organisation. R&D consortia are closely monitored and have to be registered.

The main advantages of this approach are the ability to reduce costs and risks, the ability to access technologies and to influence industry standards on new technology (the experience of the VCR industry and the computer-operating system industry have shown the potential dangers in having competing industry standards). The main disadvantages are similar to those for joint ventures, in that one party may not be able to gain any technological benefit from the consortia.

Open source R&D

The term 'open source' is taken from the more familiar open source software development which has resulted in many 'free to use' software applications including web browsers, word processing and email. More recently it has been applied to R&D. Distributed or 'open source innovation' in which customers (or anyone else for that matter) are the co-producers of the products and services they consume. Illustration 9.2 shows how Procter & Gamble have used the principles (Dodgson *et al.*; 2006; Chesbrough and Crowther, 2006).

Illustration 9.2

Procter & Gamble's open sourced R&D: Connect & Develop

Most companies are still clinging to the internal innovation model, built on the idea that their innovation must principally reside within their own organisation. This does tend to induce an obsession about secrecy. Not surprisingly, this approach limits both the quantity and quality of ideas, so companies have started to search for new ways of developing new ideas. By 2000, it was clear to P&G that its invent-it-ourselves model was not capable of sustaining high levels of top-line growth. The explosion of new technologies was putting ever more pressure on its innovation budgets. According to P&G, 'Our R&D productivity had levelled off, and our innovation success rate had stagnated at about 35%. Squeezed by nimble competitors, flattening sales, lackluster new launches and falling income P&G had to do something.'

P&G turned to an open source approach. The company has an objective to generate 50 per cent of new product ideas from outside the company. P&G's Collaborative Planning, Forecasting and Replenishment process (CPFR) is a collaborative and transparent process that allows P&G's customers and suppliers to improve its supply chain. Another example is P&G's use of the virtual technology market yet2.com. P&G lists every one of its thousands of patents on yet2.com in the hope that it will facilitate connections and ideas from the outside.

Procter & Gamble launched a new line of Pringles potato crisps in 2004 with pictures and words – trivia questions, animal facts, jokes – printed on each crisp. They were an immediate hit. P&G say: 'In the old days, it might have taken us two years to bring this product to market, and we would have shouldered all of the investment and risk internally. But by applying a fundamentally new approach to innovation, we were able to accelerate Pringles Prints from concept to launch in less than a year and at a fraction of what it would have otherwise cost.'

Source: Chesbrough and Crowther (2006); Dodgson *et al.* (2006).

Open source has also been transferred to other areas ranging from an open source encyclopedia called the Wikipedia and collaborative industrial design such as ThinkCycle to open source aeroplane design, cola recipes, film scripts and beer. The latter was developed with the help of some self-appointed beer aficionados (found on the internet) who created everything from the name of the beer to its packaging and advertising. But perhaps the biggest opportunity for open source innovation lies within the pharmaceutical industry. One of the problems with traditional pharmaceutical R&D is that the patent system effectively blocks outside insights or enhancements to a particular discovery or invention. It also means that there is little or no incentive to develop drugs aimed at people (or countries) with little or no money to spend.

How can open source principles be adopted by commercial organisations? In some ways open source can be thought of as a suggestion box scheme – albeit one with a giant transparent box. A topic is posted on a website, and anyone from industry experts to members of the public can contribute to the solution. Everything is transparent in the sense that all ideas are shared and discussed in public. In some instances, people will do this for nothing, while in others they will ultimately have to be paid in some way.

Some detractors argue that open source R&D is little more than giant focus groups, but there are big differences. The first is sheer scale. Focus groups rarely involve more than a hundred people. Open source can involve thousands and still turn things around faster than more traditional approaches. Second, focus groups usually ask people to react to ideas. Open source asks people for solutions and allows ideas to build cumulatively. Third, focus groups rely on a representative sample of people who are 'ordinary' and by definition uninterested. Open source relies on people who are articulate, passionate and enthusiastic.

Pause for thought

Open source R&D feels a bit like firms undertaking R&D for free with help from anyone willing to contribute. I can see how it works with software because you end up with free software but firms like Procter & Gamble have to sell their products, they can't give them away.

Effective R&D management

Managers of R&D have to try to develop systems and procedures which will enhance the probability of success. To outside observers the research and development process may seem like a random procedure in which inspired scientists, working around the clock, come up with major breakthroughs late at night. It is true that R&D is a high-risk activity, but the process is much less random than it first appears. Over the past 40 years there has been extensive research in R&D management and there is an academic journal dedicated to the subject (*R&D Management*). This research has revealed the presence of certain factors in many successful R&D projects and their absence in many failed projects. Table 9.1 summarises these factors.

Effective R&D management can make a considerable impact on the performance of a company. Illustration 9.3 shows how over a period of 100 years R&D has led to many different applications of a drug.

Table 9.1 Organisational characteristics that facilitate the innovation process and the management of R&D

R&D requirement	Characterised by
1 Growth orientation	A commitment to long-term growth rather than short-term profit
2 Organisational heritage and innovation experience	Widespread recognition of the value of innovation
3 Vigilance and external links	The ability of the organisation to be aware of its technology threats and opportunities
4 Commitment to technology and R&D intensity	The willingness to invest in the long-term development of technology
5 Acceptance of risks	The willingness to include risky opportunities in a balanced portfolio
6 Cross-functional cooperation and coordination within organisational structure	Mutual respect among individuals and a willingness to work together across functions
7 Receptivity	The ability to be aware of, to identify and to take effective advantage of externally developed technology
8 Space for creativity	An ability to manage the innovation dilemma and provide room for creativity
9 Strategy towards innovation	Strategic planning and selection of technologies and markets
10 Coordination of a diverse range of skills	Developing a marketable product requires combining a wide range of specialised knowledge
11 Project management	Good project management skills and systems
12 Market orientation	An awareness of the needs and changing nature of the market

Managing scientific freedom

The idea of applying formal planning techniques to R&D is viewed by many as a paradox. The popular view is that research, by definition, is concerned with uncovering new things and discovering something that previously was unknown. To try to introduce any form of planning would surely stifle creativity and innovation. This leads to one of the most fundamental management dilemmas facing senior managers: how to encourage creativity and at the same time improve efficiency. This dilemma was tackled at a generic level in Chapter 3, so to avoid repetition we will address the problem from an R&D perspective.

R&D managers will argue that the technologist's and scientist's spirit of enquiry must be given room and freedom to exercise. Without the freedom to work on projects that may not appear of immediate benefit to the company, the laboratory may become conservative and uncreative. See the CSI case study at the end of this chapter. Furthermore, it may be difficult to attract and retain the best scientists if they are not allowed to pursue those areas that are of interest to them. There are many disputes between research and technology managers and other senior functional managers concerning the extent of time that scientists and research teams should be able to allocate for personal research programmes.

Illustration 9.3

The continued development of aspirin

Through continued research and development, new uses are continually being found for one of the oldest pharmaceutical products – aspirin. Aspirin was first introduced to the market more than 100 years ago in 1897. It was research into salicin, a compound that is found naturally on willow bark, by Bayer, a large German chemical manufacturer, that led to the development of aspirin as we know it today.

The drug was first used as a treatment for arthritis sufferers. Pharmacologist John Vane received the Nobel Prize for chemistry for uncovering how aspirin relieved arthritis. He showed that prostaglandins are released by the body when cells are injured, triggering the symptoms of inflammation, swelling and pain. Aspirin halts the production of these prostaglandins, hence its effectiveness in treating arthritis.

Aspirin has been shown to have a number of additional effects:

- It acts as an analgesic to ease pain
- It acts as an anti-inflammatory to control inflammation
- It acts as an antipyretic to reduce fever
- By thinning the blood it helps to reduce the danger of blood vessels clotting, thereby helping to prevent strokes and heart attacks
- It has also been shown to help reduce colonic cancer
- It is currently being used in the treatment of Alzheimer's disease.

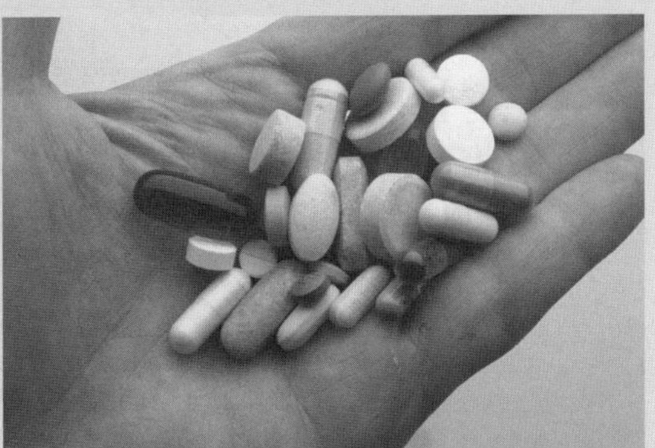

Source: Pearson Education Ltd/Photolink/Photodisc

Source: M. Dobson (1997) A little miracle, *The Sunday Times Magazine*, 16 October.

However, R&D managers are realistic: they recognise that few companies, if any, are going to invest large sums of money solely as an act of faith. There are many formal management techniques that are employed to help to improve the effectiveness and productivity of R&D without necessarily destroying the possibility of serendipity.

Virtually all companies accept that a certain amount of time should be made available for scientific enquiry (after all, there are many examples of such research producing profitable outcomes). The issue is, *how much time*? One approach, adopted by many technology-intensive companies, such as Siemens, 3M, Ericsson and Nokia, is to consider that a company that invests heavily in R&D is, in reality, managing two types of R&D project. This can best be shown schematically as in Figure 9.4, which is an extension of Figure 8.6, and shows a variety of project outcomes, which are explained below in Table 9.2.

The R&D projects are divided into two separate groups. The first group is by far the largest, usually accounting for 90 per cent of the R&D budget. It is established in response to requests from the various businesses and supports and maintains the corporate objectives. In Figure 9.4 these projects are labelled A, B and C. The second group of projects are those generated by the scientists themselves, usually as a result of personal interest in the technology. These are labelled S1 to S5. These projects

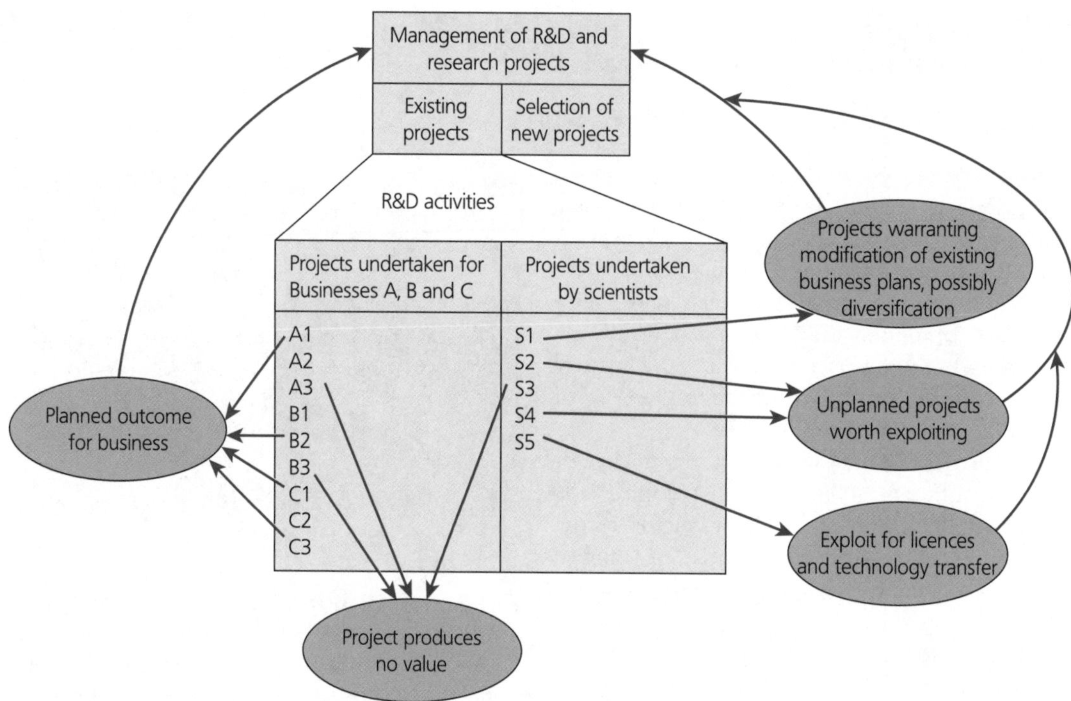

Figure 9.4 Managing scientific freedom within an R&D function

Table 9.2 Research project outcomes

Research	Outcome	Action
Project		
A1, B2, C1 and C3	Planned outcome for the business	Research project produces desired results for business to incorporate into products
A3, B3 and S3	Project produces no immediate commercial value	Results of project will be examined by other research groups to see if the findings can be used; knowledge remains with R&D
S1	Project warrants changing existing business strategy	In exceptional circumstances the findings from a research project can be so unusual and promising that they warrant a change in business strategy to accommodate possible new product ideas
S5	License technology to third party	When the research results produce interesting technology that is beyond exploitation by the business, it may be possible to generate income from licensing the technology to a third party
S2 and S4	Unplanned projects worth exploiting further	The findings from these personal research projects are so interesting that they require further funding and possible inclusion in business research
A2, B1 and C2	Projects lead to further research projects undertaken by scientists	The findings in themselves are of limited commercial value but stimulate further research projects

will be generating technology of a commercial value but free from the constraints of corporate objectives. This latter group of research projects is financed by funds that are allocated at the discretion of the R&D manager or more usually an R&D committee or team. Very often these funds represent about 10 per cent of the total R&D budget. This group of research projects has a variety of labels in industry, including blue-sky research, special projects and personal research. Virtually all major technology-intensive companies accommodate a certain amount of time for individuals to pursue their own research projects. Typically, about 10 per cent of a scientist's time will be spent on autonomous research projects.

Twiss (1992) develops this idea of two types of research project further by suggesting that R&D managers are in effect managing two business activities. The primary activity supports the various businesses and the corporate objectives and the other supports a technology business, involved in generating technology of a commercial value that is unrelated to the corporate objectives.

Skunk works

Technology-intensive companies recognise that if they are to attract and retain the best scientists they have to offer scientific freedom. Moreover, experience has shown that scientists will covertly undertake these projects if autonomy is not provided. There are many examples of exciting technology and successful products that were initiated by scientists operating in a covert manner. In the United States such research projects are referred to as **skunk works** (*see* Illustration 9.4 for an explanation of its origin).

Illustration 9.4

The original skunk works

The name 'skunk works' can be traced back to US aircraft manufacturer Lockheed. It was originally used by Al Capp's 'Li'l Abner' comic strip which featured the 'Skonk works' (sic) where Appalachian hillbillies ground up skunks, old shoes and other foul-smelling ingredients to brew fearsome drinks and other products. Lockheed engineers identified the secret jet aircraft assembly facility as the place where Clarence Johnson was stirring up some kind of 'potent brew'. The skunk works was created by Johnson to design and develop the XP-80 Shooting Star, the US's first production jet aircraft. The nickname stuck, although 'skonk' became 'skunk' in deference to the non-hillbillies working at the Lockheed facility and because Al Capp objected to anyone else using his unique spelling. Cartoonist Capp and the 'Li'l Abner' comic strip departed many years ago, but skunk works is now a registered service mark of Lockheed along with the familiar skunk logo.

Source: Pearson Education Ltd/Photodisc

Source: Lockheed Martin Corporation (1998), www.lmsw.external.lmco.com/lmsw/html/index.html.

The link with the product innovation process

Chapters 6, 7 and 8 have all emphasised the accumulation of knowledge as a key part of the R&D process and the process of developing new products. The link between R&D and new product development is often overlooked or frequently they are treated as separate subjects. In practice the two activities are interlinked. This can be simply shown by looking at the extended product life cycle. This well-known conceptual framework purports to capture some of the stages in a product's life from launch to final withdrawal. What is seldom shown is the series of activities prior to the first stage *introduction*. For some products, most notably aircraft or pharmaceuticals, the lead time prior to launch can be 10 or even 15 years. Figure 9.5 shows the extended product life cycle with some of the key R&D activities incorporated. Mapped on top are the investment and expenditure curves showing the scale of upfront money required in some industries, most notably those with long lead times, as previously discussed.

Many of the models of NPD emphasise the link to the R&D department. In particular, the network model of new product development shown in Figure 12.14 emphasises this continual interaction throughout the development of the product. Knowledge is accumulated over time as an idea for a product is transformed into a research project. The R&D function will be continually consulted on virtually all aspects of the product, including:

- design;
- manufacturing;
- choice of materials to be used;
- required shelf life;
- effects of transportation;
- packaging;
- intellectual property rights; and
- product safety, etc.

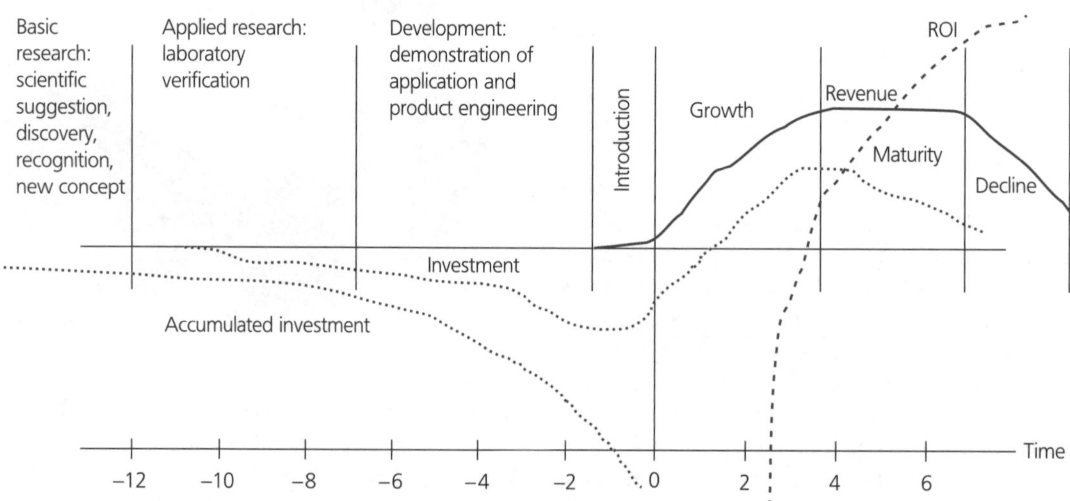

Figure 9.5 Extended product life cycle

It is important to bear in mind that an investment in R&D to develop an existing product further is not generally viewed by product managers as a high-risk activity. The following quote from the brand manager of the makers of one of the leading washing detergents in Europe reflects a commonly held view:

> *We know we can improve the product, our scientists can always improve the product. In fact the launch date for our new improved shampoo has been set but the research is still on-going! The only doubt is the extent of the improvement that our scientists will make.*

A similar example could be drawn from the software industry, which is synonymous with new, improved versions of its software. The key point here is the way R&D investment is viewed. For many firms with years of experience in the management of R&D, an output is expected from their investment in R&D; the only doubt is the detail. Given this perspective on R&D, the following section analyses the range of effects that R&D investment can have on a product's profitability.

The effect of R&D investment on products

Analysis of the products that a company manages will reveal that these contribute in different ways to the overall profit and growth of the company. It is important to recognise that R&D activities can influence this profit contribution in several ways.

Development of existing products

The life cycle of most products lasts for several years. There are some products, especially in the food industry, that seem to have an eternal life cycle. Cadbury's Milk Tray and Coca-Cola are two examples of products that have been on the market for over 100 years. In virtually all other industry sectors, however, a product's market share will slowly fall as competitors compete on price and product improvements (*see* Chapter 12). R&D's role is to extend the life of the product by continually searching for product improvements. The two most common approaches to extend the life of a product are capturing a larger market share and improving profit margins through lowering production costs. For example, the performance of zinc-carbon batteries has improved greatly due to the threat of alkaline batteries like Duracell. This has helped to improve the market share for alkaline batteries. Similarly, personal computer manufacturers such as Dell, Apple, Hewlett-Packard and IBM are continually lowering their production costs in order to ensure that their products compete successfully in the PC market.

Early introduction of a new product

Many companies strive to be technological leaders in their industry. Their aim is to introduce innovative products into the market before the competition to gain a competitive advantage. In some industries, such as pharmaceuticals, this approach is very successful. In other sectors being first to market does not always ensure success (*see* Chapter 11 on Market entry, page 401).

Late introduction of a new product

Deliberately postponing entry into a new market until it has been shown by competitors to be valid reduces the risk and costs. This was the approach used by Amstrad in the European mobile phone market. Furthermore, by deliberately slowing down product launches into the market it is possible to maximise profits. For example, software companies have been very successful in launching improved versions and upgrades every six to nine months.

Long-term projects

Looking further into the future, R&D departments will also be developing products that the public do not yet realise they require. This area also includes starting new initiatives and new areas of research. Technology-intensive companies such as Siemens, Microsoft, Airbus and 3M will be working on products for 2015 and beyond.

Evaluating R&D projects

As was discussed in the above section ('The link with the product innovation process'), virtually all large technology-intensive firms will have many more ideas than it would wish to fund as research projects; the problem as usual is limited resources. Inevitably choices have to be made about which ideas to support and convert to a funded project and which to drop. There have been many studies on this common problem faced by R&D managers (*see* Carbonell-Foulquie *et al.*, 2003; Farrukh *et al.*, 2000; Cooper, 2001). The subject of evaluating research projects is analysed from a marketing perspective in the final chapter of this book on evaluating new product ideas. An R&D perspective is now taken in the following section.

Deciding which projects to select for further resources will inevitably result in dropping others. Typically for every 60 technical ideas considered approximately 12 will receive funding for further evaluation. Of these about six will receive further funding for design and development; half of these will be developed into prototypes and may even go for market testing. But only two will remain for product launch and in most cases only one of these is successful (Babcock, 1996). Figure 9.6 illustrates the drop out rate of project ideas. Dropping an R&D project is theatrically referred to as 'killing a project'. Unsurprisingly it causes considerable anxiety among those involved, especially when one's fellow scientists have been involved with the project for many months or in some cases years. Evaluating research projects, then, is a critical issue.

Evaluation criteria

The evaluation criteria used by businesses varies considerably from industry to industry. There is a considerable body of research devoted to this single area of evaluating research projects. This is not surprising given the long list of famous cases illustrating how many firms rejected projects that later turned into extremely successful products. To this list we must now add that the world's best selling human drug – Pfizer's Viagra – was almost dropped because of the market research findings (*see* Illustration 9.5).

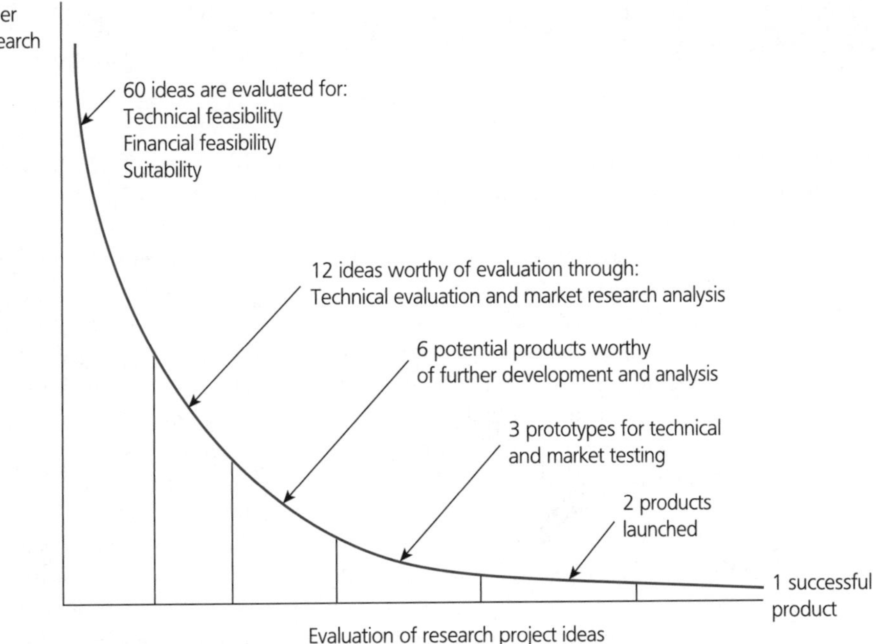

Figure 9.6 Drop out rates for R&D projects

Source: Adapted from D.L. Babcock (1996) *Managing Engineering Technology: An Introduction to Management for Engineers*, 2nd edn, Prentice Hall, London.

We will look at the range of techniques and methods used by firms later, but it is important to recognise that while many firms may state publicy that they adopt quantitative weighted scoring models or specially adapted software to evaluate all project ideas, inevitably, as with so many business decisions, there is an element of judgement. After all, that is what managers are in position to do – make decisions based on their experience and expertise. This is confirmed by a recent study of R&D decision making in the electronic sensors industry by Liddle (2004). He argues that managers continue to rely on rules of thumb and heuristics for the evaluation of research projects:

> *I just think it's a smell test. Does it sound too good to be true? Does it sound truly incremental to what we're doing? Is it something that sounds worthy of the investment of more time?* Extract from an interview with an R&D manager.
>
> (Liddle, 2004: 60)

Whether businesses used formal evaluation models or more informal methods, most will involve some or all of the checklist items shown in Table 9.3. This can be developed further using a weighted checklist or scoring model in which each factor is scored on a scale. A relative weight reflecting the importance of that factor is used as a multiple and the weighted scores for all factors are added.

The new product development literature offers a plethora of screening and decision-making methods and techniques aimed at assisting managers in making this difficult evaluation. Cooper (2001) identifies three broad categories of screening methods:

1 benefit measurement models;
2 economic models; and
3 portfolio selection models.

Illustration 9.5

Pfizer's Viagra almost slipped away!

Pfizer's Viagra is now part of business folklore in terms of an example of a successful new product. Viagra is now one of the most recognised brands in the world; it has become a social icon with sales in excess of $1.9 billion. And it has transformed Pfizer from a medium-sized pharmaceutical firm into the world's leader. However, Viagra was almost dismissed during clinical trials as interesting, but not clinically or financially significant.

The discovery of Viagra was unintended in that in fell out of clinical trials for a new drug being developed for the treatment of angina (angina is defined as brief attacks of chest pain due to insufficient oxygenation of heart muscles). In 1992, following seven years of research, a clinical trial was undertaken in Wales for a compound known as UK-92.480. The findings from the trial on healthy volunteers revealed disappointing results. The data on blood pressure, heart rate and blood flow were discouraging. The R&D project was in trouble. Some patients reported side effects of episodes of indigestion, some of aches in legs and some reported penile erections. This final point was listed merely as an observation; at that moment no one said 'wow' or 'great'. Indeed, the decision to undertake trials into erectile dysfunction was not an obvious one. This was partly because the prevailing view at the time was that most erectile dysfunction was psychological and not treatable with drugs. Few people believed it was possible to produce an erection with an injection of drugs. Pfizer was preparing to drop the angina R&D project due to its disappointing results. It was also considering dropping all studies on the compound even as a possible drug for erectile dysfunction. This was partly because it was not clear that it would have a clinical use. Not all the healthy volunteers had reported erections. How would Pfizer be able to conduct trials for such a condition? Moreover, the market for such a drug was not clear. At that time survey results revealed only 1 in 20 million men suffered from erectile dysfunction; hence, even if a medicine could be developed, the market would be very small. The R&D team involved in the project managed to gain two years of funding to develop the drug and undertake clinical trials. The rest is, as they say, history. Moreover, the actual market for this type of drug is now known to be far greater than the data had revealed. This is a cautionary tale of the need sometimes to encourage innovation and support scientific freedom in the face of evidence to stop the project.

Source: Extracts from www.pfizer.com.

Benefit measurement models

Benefit measurement models are usually derived from a group of well informed and experienced managers identifying variables such as those listed in Table 9.3, and then making subjective assessments of projects. Frequently these variables are brought together in the form of a quantitative or qualitative model that will provide the organisation with a value with which to make comparisons of projects. These models are usually: mathematical, scoring, decision-trees (Holger, 2002).

Financial/economic models

Financial and economic models are the most popular project selection tool. This may not be surprising given that firms are established to make money; however, this type of model is generally accepted as having considerable limitations. This is partly because of the emphasis on financial formulas and their inherent short-term bias. Another

Table 9.3 R&D project evaluation criteria

Criteria	Typical questions
1 Technical	Do we have experience of the technology? Do we have the skills and facilities? What is the probability of technical success?
2 Research direction and balance	Compatibility with research goals? Balance of risk in project portfolio?
3 Competitive rationale	How does this project compare relative to the competition? Is it necessary to defend an existing business? Is the product likely to be superior?
4 Patentability	Can we get patent protection? What will be the implication for defensive research?
5 Stability of the market	How stable is the technology? Is the market developed? Is there an industry standard?
6 Integration and synergy	What is the level of integration of this project relative to other products and raw materials? Will it stand alone?
7 Market	What is the size of the market? Is it a growing market? Is there an existing customer base? Is the potential big enough to warrant the resource?
8 Channel fit	Do we have existing customers who might be interested, or do we have to find new customers?
9 Manufacturing	Can we use existing resources? Will we require new equipment, skills, etc.?
10 Financial	Expected investment required and rate of return?
11 Strategic fit	Does it support our short-term and long-term plans for the business?

Source: Adapted from Seiler, R.E. (1965) *Improving the Effectiveness of Research and Development: Special Report to Management*, McGraw-Hill Book Company, New York. © The McGraw-Hill Companies, Inc.

limitation of financial models is limited accurate future financial data, which inevitably leads to inaccurate estimates of future revenues, etc.

Portfolio selection models

Portfolio models attempt to find those ideas that 'fit' with the business strategy and attempt to balance the product portfolio. They consider a business's entire set of projects rather than viewing new research projects in isolation. The dimension of balance can be:

- *Newness* – how new is the product likely to be? A radically different product, product improvement, repositioning, etc. (*see* Chapter 12).
- *Time of introduction* – is the new product portfolio going to deliver a constant stream or will it be a case of feast and then famine?
- *Markets* – are the different markets and business areas of the company receiving resources proportionate to their size and importance?

Case study

CSI and genetic fingerprinting

The US drama *CSI: Crime Scene Investigation* (CSI) has been one of television's greatest success stories of all time. It is a huge hit all over the world. The show's popularity owes a great deal to the writers and actors who bring the stories to life. But another intriguing element is the cutting-edge technology used by the crime lab in trying to solve crimes. Collecting and analysing DNA evidence tops the list of the lab's forensic toolkit, and its ubiquity in shows like *CSI* and the UK's *Silent Witness* and *Waking the Dead* has increased public awareness to the point that many jurors in real-world courtrooms expect to see DNA evidence presented – whether a case calls for it or not. Indeed, such television programmes as *CSI* have come in for fierce criticism from police chiefs and prosecutors who argue that they portray an inaccurate image of how police solve crimes. There have, however, been some positive outcomes of the so called 'CSI effect' and that is the bringing of science to a mass audience and encouraging interest in science amongst children.

Source: Pearson Education Ltd

The extraordinary growth in the business of DNA fingerprinting has been matched only by the mass appeal of the CSI television shows. In just a few years the industry has grown into a 20 billion dollar technology intensive colossus. But where and when did this all begin? This case study shows how a UK scientist, Alec Jeffreys, driven by curiosity, uncovered a technique for DNA fingerprinting. First we need to look at the background to this development.

Background

In 1865 Gregor Mendel hypothesised that the phenomenon of the inheritance of certain characteristics is due to transferable elements – the gene. Hence, we have Genetics as the study of Inheritance. In 1869 a Swiss biochemist Friedrich Miescher was the first to isolate nucleic acids, the molecular substrates of the genetic code. As time went on more people contributed to our understanding of DNA and inheritance. However, the next major breakthrough came in 1953, when James Watson and Francis Crick discovered the structure of DNA and were able to demonstrate how genetic information encoded in DNA could be passed on from generation to generation. Since the discovery of the structure of DNA in 1953 knowledge of the composition and organisation of the genetic material has accumulated at an astonishing pace. By the early 1980s it had become clear that most human DNA shows very little variation from one person to another. The small percentage that does vary presents enormous potential for fruitful study. The techniques that make it possible to identify a suspect using his or her unique genetic blueprint have only been around since 1985. That's when UK scientist Alec Jeffreys first demonstrated the use of DNA in a criminal investigation. Since then, DNA evidence has played a bigger and bigger role in many nations' criminal justice systems. It has been used to prove that suspects were involved in crimes and to free people who were wrongly convicted. At the heart of DNA evidence is the biological molecule itself, which serves as an instruction manual and blueprint for everything in your body. A DNA molecule is a long, twisting chain known as a double helix. While the majority of DNA doesn't differ from human to human, some 3 million base pairs of DNA (about 0.10 per cent of your entire genome) vary from person to person. In other words, 99.9 per cent of human DNA sequences are the same for everyone, but 0.01 per cent are different enough to tell one person from another. In human cells, DNA is tightly wrapped into 23 pairs of chromosomes. One member of each chromosomal pair comes from your mother, and the other comes from your father. Unless you have an identical twin, your DNA is unique to you. This is what makes DNA evidence so valuable in investigations – it's almost impossible for someone else to have DNA that is identical to yours.

Alec Jeffreys and the development of genetic fingerprinting

In 1984 during routine experiments in his laboratory at Leicester University Alec Jeffreys realised that the X-ray film image he was studying revealed differences and similarities in his technician's family's DNA. He was later to establish that each individual has their own unique genetic profile and how this could be revealed. Working in the laboratory, Sir Alec recalls, he and his technician were simply following their noses. They had 'absolutely no idea' of the applications that would result from the discovery they stumbled upon. 'I have never approached an experiment with a desire to solve a practical problem', he observes, pinning down his moment of discovery to precisely 9.05am on Monday 10 September 1984. 'My forensic thoughts at 8.55 on that morning were precisely zero; they simply were not there. The technology comes first and then the applications, not the other way around, and you see this over and over again' (*Times Higher Education*, 2009).

Interestingly another laboratory had had come up with similar patterns a year previously and binned them because it was not what they wanted. The research laboratory at the University of Leicester was funded by the Lister Institute, a medical charity research organisation that employed Jeffreys as a research fellow. The Lister Institute filed for a patent in 1984 and in November 1984 Jeffreys discussed his findings in public for the first time at a meeting of geneticists in London. The giant chemical company ICI eventually bought the patent from the Lister Institute. In 1987 ICI formed a company called 'Cellmark Diagnostics' specifically to commercially exploit the technology. Professor Jeffreys helped commercialise and popularise the science by coining the inspired phrase genetic fingerprinting and for seeing the forensic implications. 'Cellmark' developed the technology and numerous product applications for the technology. Over the next 20 years it was extremely successful and profitable. Moreover, it has been the forensic science laboratories around the world that have embraced, adopted and further developed this technology.

Curiosity-driven basic research

Alec Jeffreys, along with many other scientific groups, has argued, in terms of many examples, how curiosity-driven research has led to important developments in the interest of society. They argue that basic research is the seed corn of the technological harvest that sustains modern society. Lasers, nuclear magnetic resonance, semiconductors, nanostructures and medical cyclotrons, all subjects of great technological and medical importance, originated in basic physical research. Albert Einstein probably sums this up best with his famous quote: 'I have no special talents. I am only passionately curious.'

The important point here of course is that the model of innovation being advocated is science focused with virtually no concern for the market: the so-called technology push approach. And it is true that progress in research is often made through simple curiosity. Researchers often find different, sometimes greater, riches than the ones they are seeking. For example, the tetrafluoroethylene cylinder that gave rise to Teflon was meant to be used in the preparation of new refrigerants. And the anti-AIDS drug AZT was designed as a remedy for cancer. Frequently, the investigators were interested in some natural phenomenon, sometimes evident, sometimes conjectured, sometimes predicted by theory.

What is significant here is that the road from fundamental discovery to practical application is often quite long, ranging from about 10 years in the example of Nylon to some 80 years in the case of liquid crystals. The role of basic research then is to fill the well of knowledge so that this can be tapped for new technology and new products. Of course few would argue against more research, but there is the small question of who is going to pay. Often it falls to national governments. But elected governments have short time horizons; hence they are interested in a tighter linkage between basic research and national goals.

Firms and their shareholders have even shorter time horizons and it is almost unrealistic to expect firms to put their hands in their pockets to fund research over

→

such long periods of time. But we need to recognise that basic research will continue to provide a stream of ideas and discoveries that will eventually be translated into new products.

Applying the science to develop products and services

To get someone's DNA profile you don't need to sequence their entire hereditary information or genome. The profiling system in use in Britain looks at 11 very small regions of DNA – about one millionth of the total. One of these tells you the person's gender; the other 10 are short tandem repeats or STRs. In lots of places in our so-called 'junk' DNA there are repeating patterns of short sequences of base pairs. The number of times each short sequence is repeated varies from person to person, though within a limited range of, say, 10 to 25. However, the chances of two unrelated individuals having exactly the same number of repeats in all 10 regions used for DNA profiling are one in a billion.

The very first case that utilised DNA fingerprinting was *Sarba* v. *The Home Office* (1985), an immigration case where it was necessary to prove the direct biological relationship between Christianna Sarba and her son Andrew. By comparing Christianna's DNA sample against that of Andrew's and his three legally recognised siblings, a direct biological relationship was shown beyond a doubt. The Ghanian boy was allowed to stay in the country. This captured the public's sympathy and imagination. It was science helping an individual challenge authority. From that moment, Professor Jeffreys entered the realm of celebrity science. The university's switchboard was jammed with calls from people asking him to do tests. One Sunday morning, as he was pruning roses in his front garden, a car drew up and out stepped a lawyer and an immigrant family, begging him to take blood samples. They had driven all the way from London, having heard about DNA fingerprinting. But he was not a licensed phlebotomist and therefore could not agree. (Phlebotomy is the act of drawing blood either for testing or transfusion. It is a skill employed by physicians and many professionals in allied health fields.)

The first forensic application of DNA profiling again caught the public mood after two girls were raped and murdered in the Enderby area of Leicestershire, UK. A man had confessed to one murder but not the other and the police thought genetic profiling might prove him guilty of both. When, against all expectations, he was found innocent of both; the hunt was on to find a genetic profile from the male population of the area that matched samples taken from the two victims. Colin Pitchfork was eventually convicted – after being heard boasting that he had persuaded a friend to give a sample on his behalf. Jeffreys was relieved – not just because a killer had been trapped, but because if the operation had failed, the public's perception of forensic DNA as an effective tool would have been shattered. It is worthy of note that genetic fingerprinting has not made Alec Jeffreys' a fortune. He lives modestly in Leicester with his wife Sue, whom he met when they were teenagers, and they have a cottage overlooking a surfing beach in Cornwall.

DNA profiling and the UK Forensic Science Service

DNA profiling was further developed and fine tuned by Alec Jeffreys and his team in 1985, with the term DNA Fingerprinting being retained for the initial test that compares many small parts of DNA simultaneously. By focusing on just a few of these highly variable parts of DNA, profiling made the system more sensitive, more reproducible, and amenable to computer databasing, and soon became the standard forensic DNA system used in criminal case work and paternity testing worldwide.

The development of DNA amplification opened up new approaches to forensic DNA testing. It allowed automation, greatly increased sensitivity and a move to alternative marker systems. DNA profiling was also further developed by the UK Forensic Science Service in the 1990s, allowing the launch of the UK National DNA Database (NDNAD) in 1995. With highly automated and sophisticated equipment, modern-day DNA profiling can process hundreds of samples each day. The current system developed for the NDNAD, gives a discrimination power of one in over a billion. Under British law, anyone arrested has their DNA profile stored on a database (whether or not they are convicted), which now contains the DNA information of over five million people.

The UK FSS can trace its roots back to the 1930s but it was after the Second World War that forensic science was more widely recognised for its value in crime detection, both by the police and the general public. The Home Office put in place a network of regional laboratories. Changes in the law also changed the profile of the service. DNA profiling is the most significant development yet in forensic science and it was the Forensic Science Service that pioneered the development and implementation of DNA profiling technologies. Almost 10 years after its initial discovery, Mitochondrial DNA (mtDNA) profiling was developed for use on old and degraded material. In 1999 the industry was privatised and the UK FSS had competition from the private sector. LGC Forensics is a major player in the industry and handles a lot of work for the UK police forces. Formerly the state-owned Laboratory of the Government Chemist, LGC Ltd was sold off by the government for £5 million in 1996. In February 2010, LGC was valued at £257 million. It has grown in other ways, too, since privatisation: staff numbers have increased from 270 to more than 1,500.

The FSS designed and built a dedicated unit, to establish the world's first DNA database to permit mouth and hair samples to be taken without consent from individuals who are charged, sported for or convicted of an offence. The database now contains more than four million samples, a volume that is increasing by around 40,000 to 50,000 new samples every month. Today in the UK the national criminal database has had a remarkable impact on criminal investigation. Seventy per cent of all forensic tests done in Britain are DNA tests. If you get a crime scene DNA sample and put it on the database, the odds are that you will find your suspect straightaway. It is the most powerful criminal investigation tool there is. The following shows how (Jones, 2010):

> *In June 2008, a 19-year-old man from Nottingham was arrested for careless and inconsiderate driving. The police took his photograph, his fingerprints and a swab from the inside of his cheek to get his DNA profile. A few months after the DNA profile of the 19-year-old careless driver was uploaded to the database, it was flagged as a close but not perfect match to the profile of the probable killer of Colette Aram. Aram, was 16-years-old when she was abducted, raped and strangled on 30 October 1983 – five years before the careless driver was born! Twenty thousand people were interviewed in the course of the investigation, but the killer wasn't found. In October 2008, on the 25th anniversary of the murder, Nottinghamshire police announced they had new evidence, derived using the latest forensic DNA analysis techniques. They also had the killer's DNA profile. But it didn't match any of the four million profiles on the database. A new tactic was called for. The database was searched again, this time for 'near misses': profiles similar enough to the killer's that they could belong to a member of his family. The DNA of the 300 closest (male) hits was then re-examined, this time looking at markers on the Y-chromosome: as all the DNA on this is passed from father to son, it's a very good indicator of familial relationships between men. The markers on the 19-year-old careless driver's Y-chromosome came up as a match for the killer's. His father and two uncles were arrested in April 2009. The careless driver's father, Paul Hutchinson, a 51-year-old newspaper delivery agent, was charged with Colette Aram's murder. He pleaded guilty and on 25 January 2010 was sentenced to life imprisonment.*

Collecting DNA evidence and the CSI effect

Standard turnaround times – from crime scene exhibit to DNA profile – have gone down from three months to three weeks to three days. When necessary analysis can be done in a matter of hours. It has also become possible to generate profiles from ever smaller or more degraded DNA samples. A lot of the material that is analysed comes in as swabs taken by police investigators and scene of crime officers, but finding and removing the human tissue from objects isn't always straightforward. The objects in question are frequently things such as cigarette ends, gloves, hats, drink cans, but sometimes there are larger objects, too. Different objects present different challenges: a cigarette end is likely to have plenty of DNA on it, but it may come from more than one person, if the cigarette has been shared, and chemicals in the paper or filter can interfere with the profiling process. There is also the potential difficulty of linking the cigarette to the crime in court. Just because the suspect smoked a cigarette found at the crime scene doesn't mean he committed the crime, or that he was even there: the cigarette could have been brought along on someone's shoe. So the condition of the cigarette end has to be documented: does it look freshly stubbed out, or is it dirty and flattened? A blood-stained hammer may be easier to link to the crime, but getting the DNA profile of the last person to have wielded it

→

presents a whole new set of problems. This raises another issue, which is time and quality of examinations. Detecting evidence is often linked to available time; so if somebody's got all day to look at an item then they're more likely to find something than someone who spends only an hour analysing it. This has nothing to do with technology but simple procedure and professionalism.

For many years, fingerprints were the gold standard for linking suspects to a crime scene. Today, the gold standard is DNA evidence because DNA can be collected from virtually anywhere. Even a criminal wearing gloves may unwittingly leave behind trace amounts of biological material. It could be a hair, saliva, blood, semen, skin, sweat, mucus or earwax. All it takes is a few cells to obtain enough DNA information to identify a suspect with near certainty.

For this reason, law enforcement officials take unusual care at crime scenes. Police officers and detectives often work closely with laboratory personnel or evidence collection technicians to make sure evidence isn't contaminated. This involves wearing gloves and using disposable instruments, which can be discarded after collecting each sample. When investigators find a piece of evidence, they place it in a paper bag or envelope, not in a plastic bag. This is important because plastic bags retain moisture, which can damage DNA. Direct sunlight and warmer conditions may also damage DNA.

The *CSI* series is known for its unusual camera angles, editing techniques, hi-tech gadgets, detailed technical discussion, and graphic portrayal of bullet trajectories, blood spray patterns, organ damage, methods of evidence recovery (e.g. fingerprints from the inside of latex gloves), and crime reconstructions. This technique of shooting extreme close-ups, normally with explanatory commentary from one of the characters is referred to in the media as the 'CSI shot'. Many episodes feature lengthy scenes in which experiments, tests or other technical work is portrayed in detail, usually with minimal sound effects and accompanying music. The CSI Effect suggests that the television programme and its spin-offs, which wildly exaggerate and glorify forensic science, affect the public, and in turn affect trials either by (a) burdening the prosecution by creating greater expectations about forensic science than can be delivered or (b) burden the defence by creating exaggerated faith in the capabilities and reliability of the forensic sciences.

Another criticism of the show is the depiction of police procedure, which some consider to be decidedly lacking in realism. For instance, the show's characters not only investigate crime scenes ('process', as their real-world counterparts do), but they also conduct raids, engage in suspect pursuit and arrest, interrogate suspects, and solve cases, areas which fall under the responsibility of uniformed officers and detectives, not CSI personnel.

Some police and district attorneys have criticised the show for giving members of the public an inaccurate perception of how police solve crimes. Victims and their families are coming to expect instant answers from showcased techniques such as DNA analysis and fingerprinting, when in real life processing such evidence can take days or even weeks. District attorneys suggest that the conviction rate in cases with little physical evidence has decreased, largely due to the influence of *CSI* on jury members. However, it is not all negative; recruitment and training programmes have seen a massive increase in applicants, with a far wider range of people now interested in something previously regarded as a scientific backwater.

What often goes unmentioned is the long tedious process from physical evidence to convicted criminal. The physical evidence itself is only part of the equation. The ultimate goal is the conviction of the perpetrator of the crime. So while the CSI hero scrapes off the dried blood without smearing any prints, lifts several hairs without disturbing any trace evidence and smashes through a wall in the living room, he is also considering all of the necessary steps to preserve the evidence in its current form, what the laboratory can do with this evidence in order to reconstruct the crime or identify the criminal, and the legal issues involved in making sure this evidence is admissible in court.

Conclusions

This case has shown the impact of DNA fingerprinting on the world and the forensic world in particular. It has been considerable; helped in no small way by the success of the *CSI* television series. And yet the story of the scientist who uncovered DNA fingerprinting is largely unknown. But, this is not unusual and indeed is arguably the norm for most scientific advancements. Scientific development itself rarely produces fame or fortune. It is the application of this science that usually leads to fortune and to a lesser extent fame.

The success, however, of DNA fingerprinting has led to problems in the world of prosecution and a phenomenon known as the prosecutor's fallacy. The fallacy here is the idea that as the DNA profile generated from stains found at a crime scene matches the suspect's DNA profile, and as there is only a one in a billion chance of it also matching someone else's profile, then there is a one in a billion chance that the suspect is innocent. But DNA evidence simply cannot, on its own, tell you whether or not someone is guilty. The prosecutor's fallacy stems, in general, from a misunderstanding of how statistics work. In the case of DNA, however, it may be exacerbated by an almost mystical belief in the molecules' power to solve all identification and criminal investigation problems.

This case also provides an insight into the debate on the extent of curiosity-driven research. Sir Alec Jeffreys argues the importance of continuing to allow researchers to conduct 'unfettered, fundamental, curiosity-driven' research that has led to some of the most important discoveries, including his own. Firms with large R&D budgets may be able to fund some basic research, but with its long time horizons much of the funding for basic research will remain in the hands of national governments. Applied research, with its eye on the market and potential applications of the technology, is very different from curiosity-driven research. Such research is full of directions, priorities and time frames. Alec Jeffreys argues such an approach tends to direct scientists towards establishing and solving obvious problems. This may be true, but as far as the firm is concerned the research must deliver a return for the shareholders and this will usually involve new products and services.

Another issue that the case raises is whether scientists today are exploited by the system. For example, compare Alec Jeffreys with James Watt. While Jeffreys was responsible for developing DNA fingerprinting – it belonged to the Lister Institute who paid for the research – and it was ICI (now Astra-Zeneca) who made it into a kit that the police and forensic science service could use. The large profits from the discovery of genetic fingerprinting do not go to the scientist who discovered it, they go to Astra-Zeneca, and the many other firms that followed. James Watt, on the other hand, financed his own laboratory at Glasgow University out of the profits he made selling steam engines to coal owners. He made a fortune in the eighteenth century, one which enabled him to maintain his independence as a scientist. Not all scientists today are able to maintain their independence and many seek funding from industry for their research.

Sources: *Times Higher Education* (2009) The small scientist, 3 September; Jones, T. (2010) The rise of DNA analysis in crime solving, *Guardian*, 10 April, Weekend, 24.

Questions

1 What are the benefits of undirected research (curiosity-driven research)?

2 Should firms undertake undirected or curiosity-driven research or should all research be linked to products and businesses?

3 Show how this case illustrates the power and influence of radical innovation and incremental innovation.

4 Given the contribution to society that DNA fingerprinting has made, why is Alec Jeffreys not a household name?

5 Explain why the adoption of technology in this case seems to have happened very quickly.

6 Discuss how this case illustrates benefits and limitations of the public understanding of science.

7 Discuss the impact of the *CSI* phenomenon.

8 Explain the prosecutor's fallacy and why it is a problem.

Note: This case study has been written as a basis for class discussion rather than to illustrate effective or ineffective managerial or administrative behaviour. It has been prepared from a variety of published sources, as indicated, and from observations.

Pause for thought 

Would you participate in a clinical trial? If not, what would encourage you to participate: money, limiting risk, a trial the results of which may help a friend's suffering?

Chapter summary

This chapter has focused on the key activities of R&D management. It has shown that these have changed significantly over the past few decades. Emphasis has traditionally been placed on internal R&D, but now there is an increase in the use of external R&D. This presents another set of challenges. In particular, when acquiring externally developed technology, a business must also consider the extent of control that it requires over the technology. The need to provide scientific freedom for R&D personnel and the benefits that this brings were also considered.

R&D plays a considerable role in the product innovation process. Indeed, there is often continual interaction with R&D throughout the development of the product. Finally, the chapter considered the various ways of funding the R&D activity. The approach adopted will significantly affect the way R&D is perceived within and outside the company.

Discussion questions

1. Explain how Dyson Appliances Ltd could exploit externally sourced R&D.
2. Examine the degree of control required by a firm over its technology portfolio. Are there certain components or technologies that should remain in-house?
3. Discuss the benefits and limitations of open source R&D.
4. What is meant by scientific freedom and why is it important? How would you react to a Skunk works in your firm?
5. Discuss the relative shift from manufacturing-centred R&D towards more service-orientated R&D.
6. Explain why many product managers do not view an investment in R&D as a high-risk activity. Indeed, for some it seems they are certain of a positive result.
7. Explain the product development process in the pharmaceutical industry.

Key words and phrases

Globalisation of technology *314*
Centralised laboratories *318*
Decentralised laboratories *318*
R&D consortia *321*
Open source R&D *322*
Scientific freedom *324*
Skunk works *327*
Extended product life cycle *328*
Evaluating R&D projects *330*

References

Abelson, P.H. (1995) Science and technology policy, *Science*, Vol. 267, No. 27, 1247.

Albertini, S. and Butler, J. (1995) R&D networking in a pharmaceuticals company, *R&D Management*, Vol. 25, No. 4, 377–93.

Auster, E.R. (1987) International corporate linkages: dynamic forms in changing environments, *Columbia Journal of World Business*, Vol. 22, No. 2, 3–6.

Babcock, D.L. (1996) *Managing Engineering Technology: An Introduction to Management for Engineers*, 2nd edn, Prentice Hall, London.

Breschi, S. and Malerba, F. (1997) 'Sectoral innovation systems: technological regimes, Schumpeterian dynamics, and spatial boundaries', in Edquist, C. (ed.) *Systems of Innovation: Technologies, Institutions and Organizations*, Pinter, London, 130–55.

Brzustowski, T., Butler, J., Leung, F., Linton, J.D. and Smith, J. (2010) Emerging and new approaches to R&D management: selected papers from The R&D Management Conference 2008, Ottawa, *R&D Management*, Vol. 40, 1–3.

Carbonell-Foulquie, P., Munuera-Aleman, J.L. and Rodriquez-Escudero, A.I. (2003) Criteria employed for go/no-go decisions when developing successful highly innovative products, *Industrial Marketing Management*, June.

Casper, S. and Whitley, R. (2004) Managing competences in entrepreneurial technology firms: a comparative institutional analysis of Germany, Sweden and the UK, *Research Policy*, Vol. 33, No. 1, 89–106.

Chesbrough, H. and Crowther, A.K. (2006) Beyond high tech: early adopters of open innovation in other industries, *R&D Management*, Vol. 36, No. 3, 229–36.

Chesnais, F. (1988) 'Multinational enterprises and the international diffusion of technology', in Dosi, G., Freeman, C., Nelson, R., Silverberg, G. and Soete, L. (eds) *Technical Change and Economic Theory*, Pinter, London, 496–572.

Cooper, R.G. (2001) *Winning at New Products*, 3rd edn, Perseus Publishing, Cambridge, MA.

Corey, E.R. (1997) *Technology Fountainheads: The Management Challenge of R&D consortia*, Ziff-Davis/Harvard Business School Press, Boston, MA.

Dodgson, M., Gann, D. and Salter, A. (2006) The role of technology in the shift towards open innovation: the case of Proctor & Gamble, *R&D Management*, Vol. 36, No. 3, 333–46.

Dosi, G. (1988) Sources, procedures, and microeconomic effects of innovation, *Journal of Economic Literature*, Vol. 26, No. 3, 1120–71.

Englund, R.L. and Graham, R.J. (1999) From Experience: linking projects to strategy, *Journal of Product Innovation Management*, Vol. 16, 52–64.

Farrukh, C., Phaal, R., Probert, D., Gregory, M. and Wright, J. (2000) Developing a process for the relative valuation of R&D programmes, *R&D Management*, Vol. 30, No. 1, 43–53.

Gambardella, A. (1995) *Science and Innovation: The US Pharmaceutical Industry During the 1980s*, Cambridge University Press, Cambridge.

Granstrand, O., Bohlin, E., Oskarsson, C. and Sjoberg, N. (1992) External technology acquisition in large multi-technology corporations, *R&D Management*, Vol. 22, No. 2, 111–33.

Hagedoorn, J. (1990) Organisational modes of inter-firm co-operation and technology transfer, *Technovation*, Vol. 10, No. 1, 17–30.

Holger, E. (2002) Success factors of new product development: a review of the empirical literature, *International Journal of Management Reviews*, Vol. 4, No. 1, 1–40.

Howells, J. (2008) New Directions in R&D: Current and Prospective Challenges, *R&D Management*, Vol. 38, No. 3, 241–52.

Kastrinos, N. and Miles, I. (1995) Knowledge base, technology, strategy and innovation in environmental services firms, paper presented at R&D Management Conference, 20–2 September, *Knowledge, Technology and Innovative Organisations*, Pisa, Italy.

Kreiner, K. and Schultz, M. (1990) Crossing the institutional divide: networking in biotechnology, paper for the tenth International Conference, *Strategic Bridging to Meet the Challenge of the 90s*, Strategic Management Society, Stockholm, 24–27 September.

Lefever, D.B. (1992) Technology transfer and the role of intermediaries, PhD thesis, INTA, Cranfield Institute of Technology.

Liddle, D. (2004) R&D Project Selection at Danahar, MBA Dissertation, University of Portsmouth.

Malerba, F. and Orsenigo, L. (1993) Technological regimes and firm behaviour, *Industrial and Corporate Change*, Vol. 2, 45–71.

Mason, G., Beltramo, J.P. and Paul, J.-J. (2004) External knowledge sourcing in different national settings: a comparison of electronics establishments in Britain and France, *Research Policy*, Vol. 33, No. 1, 53–72.

Pavitt, K. (1984) Sectoral patterns of technological change: towards a taxonomy and theory, *Research Policy*, Vol. 13, 343–73.

Pavitt, K. (1990) What we know about the strategic management of technology, *California Management Review*, Spring, 17–26.

Powell, W.W. (1996) 'Trust based forms of governance', in Kramer, R.M. and Tyler, T.R. (eds) *Trust in Organisations*, Sage, London, 246–60.

Rhea, J. (1991) New directions for industrial R&D consortia, *Research Technology Management*, September–October, 16–19.

Rothwell, R. (1992) Successful industrial innovation: critical factors for the 1990s, *R&D Management*, Vol. 22, No. 3, 221–39.

Rothwell, R. and Dodgson, M. (1991) External linkages and innovation in small and medium-sized enterprises, *R&D Management*, Vol. 21, No. 2, 125–36.

Sakakibara, M. (2002) Formation of R&D consortia: industry and company effects, *Strategic Management Journal*, Vol. 23, 1033–50.

Seaton, R.A.F. and Cordey-Hayes, M. (1993) The development and application of interactive models of technology transfer, *Technovation*, Vol. 13, No. 1, 45–53.

Teece, D. (1986) Profiting from technological innovation: implications for integration, collaboration, licensing, and public policy, *Research Policy*, Vol. 15, 285–305.

Tidd, J., Bessant, J. and Pavitt, K. (2001) *Managing Innovation*, 2nd edn, John Wiley & Sons, Chichester.

Twiss, B. (1992) *Managing Technological Innovation*, 4th edn, Financial Times Pitman Publishing, London.

Further reading

For a more detailed review of the R&D management literature, the following develop many of the issues raised in this chapter:

HSBC (2010) 100 Thoughts, HSBC, London.

Lakemond, N., Berggren, C. and van Weele, A. (2006) Coordinating supplier involvement in product development projects: a differentiated coordination typology, *R&D Management*, Vol. 36, No. 1, 55–66.

Leifer, R. (2000) *Radical Innovation*, Harvard Business School Press, Boston, MA.

Lichtenthaler, U. and Ernst, H. (2006) Attitudes to externally organising knowledge management tasks: a review, reconsideration and extension of the NIH syndrome, *R&D Management*, Vol. 36, No. 4, 367–86.

Phillips, W., Lamming, R., Bessant, J. and Noke, H. (2006) Discontinuous innovation and supply relationships: strategic dalliances, *R&D Management*, Vol. 36, No. 4, 451–61.

Roussel, P.A., Saad, K.N. and Erickson, T.J. (1991) *Third Generation R&D*, Harvard Business School Press, Boston, MA.

Tsai, K.-H. and Wang, J.-C. (2007) Inward technology licensing and firm performance: a longitudinal study, *R&D Management*, Vol. 37, No. 2, 151–60.

Chapter 10
Open innovation and technology transfer

Introduction

Information is central to the operation of firms. It is the stimulus for knowledge, know-how, skills and expertise and is one of the key drivers of the innovation process. Most firms are involved with a two-way flow of knowledge wrapped up as technology in the form of a product or process. Those companies that spend the most on R&D are also some of the biggest licensors of technology; and dynamic, innovative firms are likely to buy in more technology than their static counterparts. This chapter examines the complex subject of technology transfer, increasingly being referred to as knowledge transfer. It explores its role in the innovation process and its influence on organisational learning. The case study at the end of this chapter provides evidence to illustrate the benefits of technology transfer in the mobile phone industry.

Chapter contents

Learning objectives

When you have completed this chapter you will be able to:

- recognise the importance of the concept of technology/knowledge transfer with respect to innovation management;
- provide a summary of the process of technology/knowledge transfer;
- examine the various models of technology transfer;
- assess the importance of internal organisational factors and how they affect inward technology transfer;
- explain why a 'receptive' environment is necessary for technology transfer;
- identify the different barriers to technology transfer; and
- recognise how tacit knowledge links technology transfer and innovation.

Background

The industrialised world has seen a shift from labour- and capital-intensive industries to knowledge- and technology-based economies. As competition has increased in markets throughout the world, technology has emerged as a significant business factor and a primary commodity. Knowledge, transformed into know-how or technology, has become a major asset within companies. Technology is vital for a business to remain competitive. In rapidly evolving markets such as electronics and bio-technology, new products based on new technology are essential. Even in mature markets, new technology is necessary to remain competitive on cost and quality.

In the 1960s, 1970s and 1980s many businesses favoured the internal development of technology. But today, with the increasing technological content of many products, many organisations consider internal development too uncertain, too expensive and too slow for the rapid technological changes that are occurring in the market. These drawbacks can be traced to a more fundamental cause – the increasing complexity of technologies and the increasing range of technologies found within products. This has led to a shortening of product life cycles with replacement technologies rapidly succeeding others. The rising costs of conducting R&D have forced many organisations to look for research partners. In addition, companies are finding it increasingly difficult to sustain R&D capability over all areas of their business as the complexity of these areas increases. Internal R&D is increasingly focused on core competencies (*see* Prahalad and Hamel, 1990). R&D in all other business activities is progressively covered by collaborations, partnerships and strategic alliances. While the activity is not new – Alfred Marshal noted the extensive linkages between firms in his work in 1919 (CEST, 1991) – the extent of collaboration appears to be on the increase. Hagedoorn (1990), for example, has shown a marked rise in the amount of collaboration between firms during the 1980s and 1990s.

Many large firms operate in several technology fields and are often referred to as multi-technology corporations (MTC). It is extremely difficult and expensive for such corporations to be technological leaders in every technology within their scope. More and more companies are looking for outside sources of either basic technology to shorten product development time, or applied technology to avoid the costs and delay of research and development. In addition, avoiding 're-inventing the wheel' appears to be high on the list of corporate objectives. Previously, there was one well-known exception to this and that was where a competitor was undertaking similar research. Under these circumstances duplication of research was regarded as inevitable and thus acceptable. However, numerous recent technological collaborations between known competitors, for example IBM and Apple, General Motors and BMW, would suggest that even this exception is becoming less acceptable to industry.

The search for, acquisition and exploitation of developed technology is clearly of interest to virtually all sectors of industry, but it is of particular interest to R&D-intensive or science-based industries. A US government study on technology transfer stated: 'Corporations trade in technology in world markets just as they do in other goods and services' (DFI International, 1998: 93).

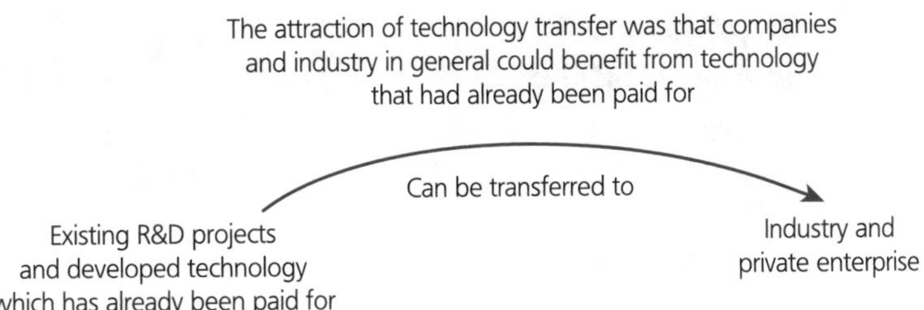

Figure 10.1 The economic perspective of technology transfer

The dominant economic perspective

It was in the 1980s that governments around the world began to recognise the potential opportunities that technology transfer could bring. This was based on a simple economic theory. Technology which has already been produced, and hence paid for by someone else, could be used and exploited by other companies to generate revenue and thereby economic growth for the economy (*see* Figure 10.1).

It was with this theory in mind that governments began encouraging companies to be involved in technology transfer. They set up a whole variety of programmes trying to utilise technology that had been developed for the defence or space industries (*see* below 'Models of technology transfer'). They also encouraged companies to work together to see if they could share technology for the common good. Furthermore, since 1980, the transfer of technology from universities to private industry has become big business, particularly in the United States. For example, during 2003 technology transfer revenues were approximately $1.3 billion, and more importantly, the economic benefits that flowed from the technologies that were transferred into the private sector were estimated to have exceeded $41 billion in value. Technology transfer, as a university enterprise, only came into existence with the passage of the Bayh-Doyle Act or University and Small Business Patent Procedures Act in 1980. The Bayh-Doyle legislation (sponsored by two senators, Birch Bayh of Indiana and Robert Doyle of Kansas) created an emerging industry by transferring ownership for any intellectual property that was developed with federal research funding to the developing institution. This transfer of ownership allowed universities the right to license or sell their intellectual property rights to industry for further development and profitable commercialisation. Thus, this legislation cleared the way for technology transfer to become a factor both in driving the US economy and contributing to the greater social good. Twenty-five years later, universities have become increasingly adept at developing and transferring their technology.

The alleged panacea for industry's problems did not materialise. Looking back, some still argue that it was a commendable theory, it just did not seem to work in practice. Others argue that the theory was flawed and would never work in practice (Seaton and Cordey-Hayes, 1993); this is discussed below in the section on 'Limitations and barriers to technology transfer'. There were, however, many benefits that emerged from the energetic interest in technology transfer. One of them was the realisation that successful collaboration and joint ventures could be achieved even with competitors.

Pause for thought 

While it may be possible in theory to buy technology with little prior knowledge of it, surely it would be extremely difficult to exploit it without prior knowledge?

Open innovation

It should now be clear that the need for external linkages and connectivity is a major factor influencing the management of innovation. Furthermore, Chesbrough (2006) argued recently that the process of innovation has shifted even further from one of closed systems, internal to the firm to a new mode of open systems involving a range of players distributed up and down the supply chain (*see* Figure 10.2). This seems to be supported by the increasing application of network theory into more and more areas of business management (Parkhe *et al.*, 2006).

This chapter illustrates the strong link within the innovation process between the external environment of the firm and the internal environment of the firm. It examines and explores knowledge flows within the innovation process. It illustrates how the 'open innovation' paradigm builds on previous research and is presented as opportunities for the management of innovation. It confirms that accessing and utilising these flows of knowledge is a fundamental part of the innovation process. The process of accessing and transferring technology, then, is becoming increasingly crucial within innovation and new product development. In a recent study of 203 laboratories of Japanese firms located in Japan the findings revealed how an open innovation policy can contribute to the laboratory's R&D performance by facilitating external collaborations by the laboratories Asakawa *et al.* (2010).

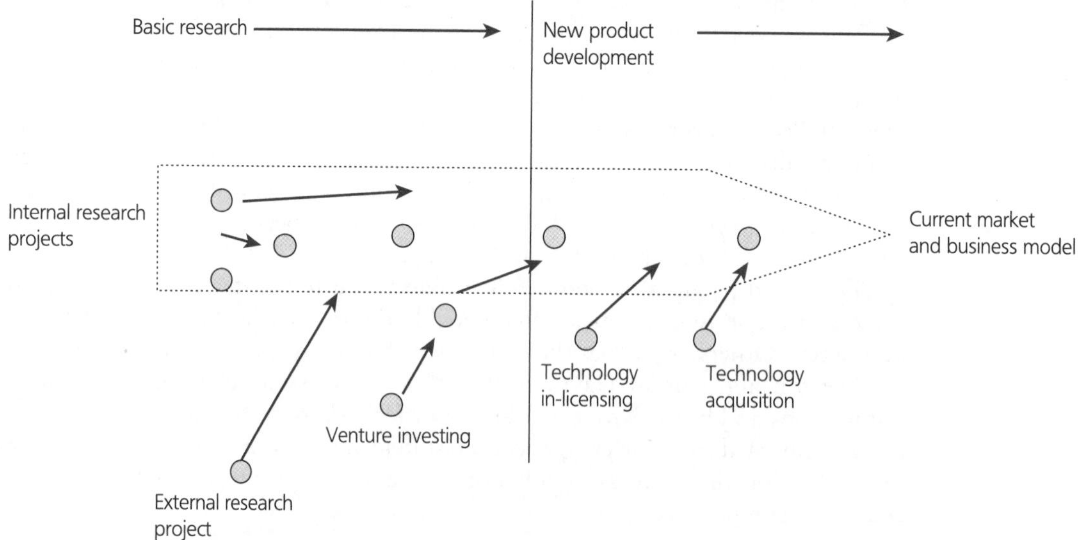

Figure 10.2 Chesbrough's open innovation approach

Table 10.1 Contrasting 'closed innovation' principles and 'open innovation' principles

Closed innovation principles	Open innovation principles
The smart people in our field work for us.	Not all of the smart people work for us so we must find and tap into the knowledge and expertise of bright individuals outside our company.
To profit from R&D, we must discover, develop, produce and ship it ourselves.	External R&D can create significant value; internal R&D is needed to claim some portion of that value.
If we discover it ourselves, we will get it to market first.	We don't have to originate the research in order to profit from it.
If we are the first to commercialise an innovation, we will win.	Building a better business model is better than getting to market first.
If we create the most and best ideas in the industry, we will win.	If we make the best use of internal and external ideas, we will win.
We should control our intellectual property (IP) so that our competitors do not profit from our ideas.	We should profit from others' use of our IP, and we should buy others' IP whenever it advances our own business model.

Source: Chesbrough, H. (2003) *Open Innovation: The new imperative for creating and profiting from technology*, HBS Press, Boston, MA.

Chesbrough (2003) presents six notions that lie behind the so called closed model of innovation (*see* Table 10.1). However, while the dichotomy between closed innovation and open innovation may be true in theory, it does not really exist in industry today. Unmistakably, Chesbrough has been very successful in popularising the notion of technology transfer and the need to share and exchange knowledge. Indeed, it seems that in using a business strategy perspective the open innovation concept may have reached new audiences (e.g., CEOs of technology-intensive companies) that for so many years the innovation and R&D literatures failed to reach. The fact that large multinational companies such as Procter & Gamble and Philips have incorporated the principles of open innovation and facilitate conferences and publications on the subject deserves admiration and praise. In essence, it has created real-life laboratories (playgrounds) in which the mechanisms of open innovation can be studied in great detail (see, for example, Hacievliyagil, 2007 and Hacievliyagil *et al.*, 2008).

Open innovation is currently one of the most debated topics in management literature. There are many unanswered questions: how relevant is it to firms? And how should firms implement open innovation in practice (Chiaroni *et al.*, 2009)? Furthermore, the open innovation paradigm is not without its critics. While Chesbrough (2003, 2006) acknowledges the rich source of antecedents to the 'open innovation paradigm' there may be many scholars of R&D management and innovation management who would argue that this so-called paradigm represents little more than the repackaging and representation of concepts and findings presented over the past 30 years (see Trott and Hartmann, 2009). More recently, Dahlander and Gann (2010) reviewed a wide range of studies on the topic of open innovation and concluded that openness seems to manifest itself in two inbound processes: sourcing and acquiring technology, and two outbound processes, revealing and selling technology. This suggests that fundamentally the activities being undertaken by firms have changed little.

Introduction to technology transfer

The concept of technology transfer is not new. In the thirteenth century Marco Polo helped introduce to the Western world Chinese inventions such as the compass, papermaking, printing and the use of coal for fuel. In more recent years, the concept has generated an enormous amount of debate. Many argue that it was a change in US law which led to the surge of interest in the subject. The passage of the landmark National Cooperative Research Act (NCRA) of 1984 officially made cooperation on pre-competitive research legal. This, plus the Bayh-Doyle Act in 1980, certainly helped raise the profile of the concept of technology transfer (Werner, 1991).

> *Technology Transfer is the application of technology to a new use or user. It is the process by which technology developed for one purpose is employed either in a different application or by a new user. The activity principally involves the increased utilisation of the existing science/technology base in new areas of application as opposed to its expansion by means of further research and development.* (Langrish *et al.*, 1982)

One of the main problems of research into technology transfer is that over the years the term has been used to describe almost any movement of technology from one place to another, to the ridiculous point where the purchase of a car could be classified as an example of technology transfer. It is true that the technology in question may take a variety of forms – it may be a product, a process, a piece of equipment, technical knowledge or expertise or merely a way of doing things. Further, technology transfer involves the movement of ideas, knowledge and information from one context to another. However, it is in the context of innovation that technology transfer is most appropriate and needs to be considered. Hence, technology transfer is defined as:

> *The process of promoting technical innovation through the transfer of ideas, knowledge, devices and artefacts from leading edge companies, R&D organisations and academic research to more general and effective application in industry and commerce.*
> (Seaton and Cordey-Hayes, 1993: 46)

Information transfer and knowledge transfer

It was suggested at the beginning of this chapter that information is central to the operation of firms and that it is the stimulus for knowledge, know-how, skills and expertise. Figure 10.3 helps distinguish information from knowledge and know-how according to its context. It is argued that it is the industrial context which transforms knowledge into action, in the form of projects and activities. It is only when information is used by individuals or organisations that it becomes knowledge, albeit tacit knowledge. The application of this knowledge then leads to actions and skills (projects, processes, products, etc.). Consider Illustration 10.1.

Pause for thought 

The famous Delft blue and white pottery in Holland developed in the sixteenth century and was copied from the original Chinese blue and white pottery. Similarly, the UK Wedgwood pottery developed in the nineteenth century was an imitation of the Delftware. Is this technology transfer or illicit copying?

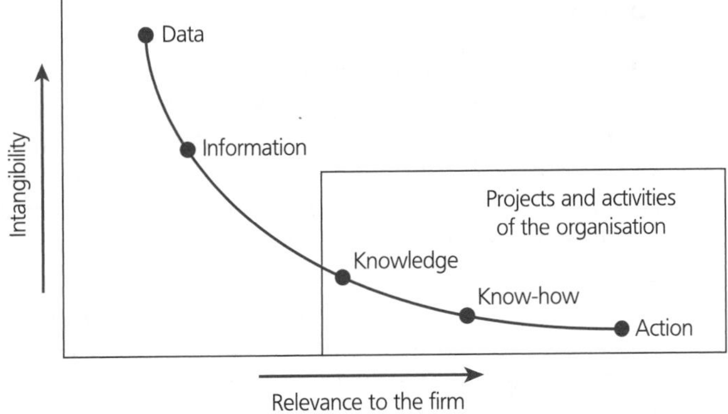

Figure 10.3 The tangibility of knowledge

Source: Adapted from M. Cooley (1987) *Architect or Bee? The Human Price of Technology*, Hogarth Press, London. Used by permission of the Random House Group Limited and with kind permission from Professor M. Cooley.

Illustration 10.1

Pilkington, information and knowledge

Materials have different melting points; for example, glass is molten at 1,500°C whereas tin is molten at 180°C. On its own, this is information that can be found in most metallurgy books. Provide an industrial context and the information is transformed into knowledge, know-how and expertise.

Pilkington pioneered the manufacturing process of 'float glass'. This essentially involves heating sand to 1,500°C and forcing it out through rollers and over a pool of molten tin to cool prior to being cut to size. This patented process is now universally used by every glass manufacturer in the world. Pilkington developed the process in the 1950s and 1960s and then licensed it to every glass manufacturer in the world. For an entire year, however, the pilot plant had produced nothing but scrap glass. After many operating difficulties, production engineers eventually succeeded in getting the process to work. The company made so much money out of licensing the process that it was able to purchase what was at that time the largest glass manufacturer in the world.

Source: Pearson Education Ltd/Image Source Ltd.

Models of technology transfer

A wide variety of models of technology transfer have been used over the years, particularly in the past 20 years (Dorf, 1988). The following section examines some of these models and offers examples of their application.

Licensing

Essentially, licensing involves the technology owner receiving a licence fee in return for access to the technology. Very often the technology in question will be protected by patents. The details of each licensing agreement will vary considerably. Sometimes the licensor will help the licensee in all aspects of development and final use of the technology. In other cases, the amount of involvement is minimal.

Mutual self-interest is the common dominator behind most licensing contracts, as it is in other business contracts. Licensing is the act of granting another business permission to use your intellectual property. This could be a manufacturing process which is protected by patents or a product or service which is protected by a trademark or copyright. Licensing is the main income generator for the British Technology Group (BTG), a FTSE 100 listed company. It helps businesses and universities generate income from their intellectual property through the licensing of technology to third parties.

Licences to competitors constitute a high percentage of all licences extended; Microsoft's Windows-operating system is a case in point. These normally arise out of a desire on the part of the competitor to be free of any patent infringement in its development product features or technology. They are also due to the owner of the patent seeking financial gain from the technology.

The licensee must be careful to evaluate the need for and the benefits likely to accrue from the technology before making the commitment to pay. Technology which is only marginally useful, or which may be quickly superseded by new developments in the field, may not be worth a multi-million-dollar licensing agreement. Many companies with sufficient R&D resources believe that patents can be legally breached through creative use of technology.

Other reasons for licensing are (Rothberg, 1976; Brown 2007):

- to avoid or settle patent infringement issues;
- to diversify and grow through the addition of new products;
- to improve the design and quality of existing products;
- to obtain improved production or processing technology;
- to ensure freedom of action in the company's own R&D programme (patents held by other companies may inhibit R&D activities);
- to save R&D expense and delay;
- to eliminate the uncertainty and risk involved in developing alternative processes and technology;
- to accommodate customer needs or wishes; and
- to qualify for government and other desirable contracts.

Science park model

Science parks are a phenomenon that originated in the United States. The idea is to develop an industrial area or district close to an established centre of excellence, often a university. The underlying rationale is that academic scientists will have the opportunity to take laboratory ideas and develop them into real products. In addition, technology- or science-based companies can set up close to the university so that they can utilise its knowledge base. In the United States, where science parks have existed for 40 years, the achievements have been difficult to quantify. Examples are

Silicon Valley, a collection of companies with research activities in electronics, and the 'research triangle' in North Carolina, which has several universities at its core. In the United Kingdom, one of the first science parks to be established was the Cambridge Science Park. Over the past 20 years, this has grown into a large industrial area and has attracted many successful science-based companies. Many other universities have also set up their own science parks, such as Southampton, Warwick and Cranfield. It is worth noting that the science park notion separates the innovation process: the R&D is conducted at the science park but manufacturing is done elsewhere (Link and Link, 2003; Dabinett, 1995). Business parks, however, combine all activities.

Intermediary agency model

These come in a variety of forms and range from Regional Technology Centres (RTC) to university technology transfer managers. Their role, however, is the same: they act as the intermediary between companies seeking and companies offering technology.

Directory model

During the explosion of interest in technology transfer during the 1980s, many new companies sprang up in an attempt to exploit interest in the subject. Companies such as Derwent World Patents, Technology Exchange, NIMTECH and Technology Catalysts offered directories listing technology that was available for licence. Some universities in the United States also produced directories of technology available from the university's own research laboratories. (For an example of the type and range of patents available, *see* Derwent World Patents at www.patentexplorer.com/.)

Knowledge Transfer Partnership model

Previously called 'the teaching company scheme' this UK Research Council-funded programme aims to transfer technology between universities and small companies. This is achieved through postgraduate training. Students registering for a two-year MSc at a university are linked to a local company-based research project. The student studies part time for two years with the university, say two days a week, and the other three days are spent at the company working on the project. The university provides support to the student and offers other expertise to the company. These programmes continue to be very successful and has an impressive 30-year track record (see Illustration 10.2).

Ferret model

The ferret model was first used by Defence Technology Enterprises (DTE). DTE resulted from a joint initiative between the UK Ministry of Defence (MOD) and a consortium of companies experienced in encouraging, exploiting and financing new technology. The *raison d'être* of DTE was to provide access to MOD technology and generate commercial revenue. This was achieved through the use of so-called

Illustration 10.2

Cult carmaker Morgan links with universities to generate success

Morgan Motor Company, the centenarian British car manufacturer, has defied the difficulties of the global automobile industry with record sales of its cult sporty convertibles.

Turnover, 60 per cent of which comes from exports, is expected to hit a new high of £28.6 million for 2010. Unlike its larger peers, Morgan only makes cars that people have ordered, pre-selling build slots and taking sizeable deposits to secure commitment from customers. For those buying a Morgan, this means a wait of up to a year for their set of wheels, but the business model has protected Morgan from the risk of masses of unsold stock that have become the bane of its much larger peers. It is a point not missed by Charles Morgan, managing director and grandson of the company's founder: 'Our approach might not be fashionable, but we don't have a situation like some of the other companies in our industry where they have a workforce twice as big as they want', he says. 'We have never gone for volume.'

Morgan is planning to add a couple of extra positions to the 165-person workforce at its factory in the idyllic surroundings of the Malvern Hills. This will help the company raise production to a new high of 850 cars a year. Little seems to have changed on the production line since the company first started making cars there in 1909, with chassis still assembled on wooden blocks and moved by hand around the building. However, Mr Morgan notes that the method of production is not what slows down delivery. 'A lot of the things you put into a luxury car have a three- or five-month order time', he says. 'If it takes us longer than a year to complete a vehicle, however, we are deeply efficient.'

The one thing Morgan orders in advance is its engines from BMW. And it is under the bonnet that Morgan has strived to match the best in the world.

Source: Morgan Motor Company

Each Morgan is also fitted with the latest generation ABS braking system, providing stopping times that are better than a Ferrari, according to Bosch, its supplier. Morgan also collaborates with a number of UK universities and is one of the most successful beneficiaries of the government's Knowledge Transfer Partnership, aimed at linking academic innovation with industry. Its AeroMax and SuperSports lines are the world's first superformed aluminium cars, making them at least 20 per cent lighter than their rivals.

'With the AeroMax we have started to attract a completely different sort of customer', Mr Morgan says. 'We are still selling the little four-door £26,500 sports car to the guy who has just retired and always promised himself a Morgan, but we are also finding people who want a second car down at the villa in France.'

Morgan plans to build on its success with an electric car, whose on-board power generation provides a range of 1,000 miles, due for launch in 2012. It has also started taking orders for its EvaGT, a four-seater sports saloon that was shown for the first time at the Pebble Beach Concours d'Elégance in California this month.

'What we aim to do is to produce a traditional British sports car without the unreliability', Mr Morgan says.

Source: Moules, J. (2010) Cult carmaker Morgan defies the gloom, FT.com, 22 August. Reprinted with permission.

'ferrets', qualified scientists and engineers who would ferret around for interesting defence technology that could have wider commercial opportunities. The company ceased trading in 1989.

Hiring skilled employees

One of the oldest methods of technology transfer, and one of the most effective according to many research managers, is hiring people with the necessary skills and knowledge. For R&D managers who wish to establish a range of research projects in an area of technology where the company has limited knowledge or experience, this is one of the fastest methods of gaining the necessary technology. People are either recruited from other organisations, including competitors, or from university research departments that have relevant expertise. These people will bring to the organisation their own knowledge, and the ways of working and methods used by their previous organisation – some of which may be replicable, others may not. The role of individual and organisational learning is explored towards the end of this chapter.

Technology transfer units

In the 1980s the US Federal Labs and other research-based organisations, including universities, established industrial liaison units and technology transfer units to bring in technology from outside and/or to find partners to help exploit in-house developments. In the United States, academia has always been subject to financial pressures to generate funds. In Europe, however, universities have traditionally relied on government to fund their needs. With an ever-decreasing pool of resources, universities have recognised the potential benefits from exploiting in-house technology. This has also led to the growth in science parks. Technology transfer units use elements of the intermediary and licensing models.

One of the most successful examples of this approach is the British Technology Group (BTG), a state-owned corporation that was set up to commercialise as much state-funded research as possible, including that undertaken by universities. It was previously known as the National Research Development Corporation. It became so successful and profitable that in 1993 BTG was sold to private investors and it is now operating as a successful public limited company with a FTSE 100 listing. Its main activities are the licensing of new scientific and engineering products to industry and providing finance for the development of new technology (*see* www.btg.co.uk).

Research clubs

This is a UK Department of Trade and Industry (DTI) funded programme which tries to bring companies together with common interests in particular research areas. Some conduct collaborative research, others exchange information, knowledge and/or experience. This approach adopts the science park model of technology transfer. One of the most successful clubs is the M62 Sensors and Instrumentation Research Club, so called because it originated from a group of companies along the M62 motorway in the north-west of England.

European Space Agency (ESA)

The ESA offers access to space research in virtually all fields of science and technology. This is achieved using a combination of three models: the intermediary agency model, the directory model and the ferret model.

Consultancy

This area has experienced rapid growth from a non-existent base in the early 1980s to a multi-billion-dollar industry today. Although it is management consultancy groups that receive a great deal of attention from the business sections of the quality press, it is the lesser-known technology consultants that have been used and continue to be used by many science-based organisations. Very often they were formerly employed in a research capacity within a large organisation. After developing their knowledge and skills in a particular area of science, they offer their unique skills to the wider industry. R&D research groups within large organisations will often contact several consultants prior to establishing a research project in a particular field related to the consultant's area of expertise. Consultants are able to offer help, advice and useful contacts to get the research project off to a flying start. Frequently they will remain part of the research group during the early years of the project. This is a very popular method of technology transfer and essentially adopts the hiring skilled employees model.

Limitations and barriers to technology transfer

The management of technology transfer has not been entirely straightforward, as is demonstrated in the range of technology transfer mechanisms that have been developed over the last 20 years or so. Research into technology transfer suggests that this is because emphasis has been on providing information about access to technology (Seaton and Cordey-Hayes, 1993). While the provision of technical ideas is a necessary part of technology transfer, it is only one component of a more complex process. Research at the Innovation and Technology Assessment Unit, Cranfield University, has led to the development of a comprehensive conceptual framework that has helped develop understanding of the complex nature of inward technology transfer and knowledge accumulation.

The conceptual framework, shown in Figure 10.4, views technology transfer and inward technology transfer as a series of complex interactive processes as opposed to a simple decision process. It breaks down the transfer process into a series of subprocesses. The initial framework was developed following a study of the role of intermediaries in the technology transfer process. A mismatch was identified between the needs of potential innovators and the activities of information-centred technology transfer intermediaries (Lefever, 1992). This deficiency was illuminated through the use of the conceptual framework: Accessibility–Mobility–Receptivity (AMR). The research revealed that while much effort appeared to have been directed at providing access to technology, little effort had been aimed at understanding the needs of organisations acquiring technology developed outside the organisation.

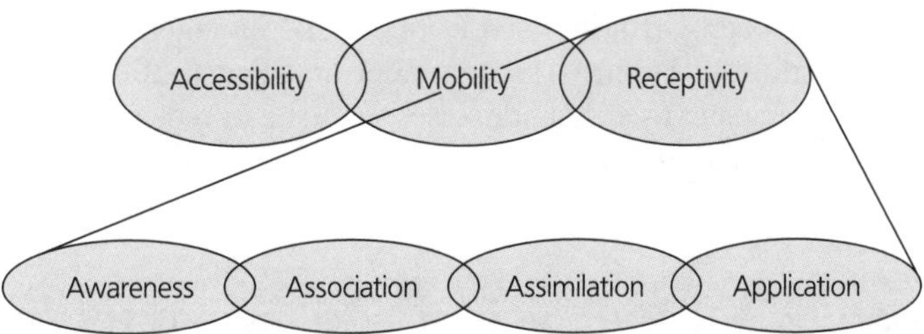

Figure 10.4 Conceptual framework of technology transfer and inward technology transfer

An organisation's overall ability to be aware of, to identify and to take effective advantage of technology is referred to as 'receptivity'.

The original framework has since been developed further to show the elements which constitute the inward transfer of technology from the viewpoint of the receiving organisation. Figure 10.4 breaks down the receptivity element into four further components. This has provided a useful theoretical framework from which to analyse the notion of technology and knowledge transfer. It is important, however, to understand that this overarching conceptual framework has limitations as a concept. These limitations are a consequence of the fact that, while it expresses the nature of the internal organisational processes and identifies a number of key areas that constitute such processes, it does not itself operationalise these processes. Hence, it functions as a vantage point from which to explore the issues involved.

Subsequent research has uncovered the nature of some of the internal processes of inward technology transfer and has provided an insight into how they affect an organisation's ability to capture, assimilate and apply technology to commercial ends (Trott and Cordey-Hayes, 1996). Research by Macdonald (1992) identified the difficulty of applying other people's technology and the need for this technology to be in such a form that the organisation can reap some benefit. This highlights the importance of viewing technology development as a combination of knowledge, skills and organisations (all embodied in 'organisational know-how') rather than the economist's view of technology as an artefact to be bought and sold. Chapter 6 portrayed the notion of assimilation as an internal knowledge accumulation process, which offers an explanation of how organisations are able to use, manipulate and retain knowledge.

NIH syndrome

One of the best-known barriers to technology transfer is the not-invented-here (NIH) syndrome. This is defined as the tendency of a project group of stable composition to believe that it possesses the monopoly of knowledge in its field, leading it to reject new ideas from outsiders to the likely detriment of its performance (Katz and Allen, 1988). It is general folklore among R&D professionals that groups of scientists and engineers who have worked together for many years will begin to believe that no one else can know or understand the area in which they are working better than they do. In some cases this attitude can spread across the whole R&D function, so that the effect is a refusal to accept any new ideas from outside. This syndrome has been so widely discussed since it was first uncovered that, like many diseases, it has been virtually wiped out. R&D managers still need to be vigilant to ensure that it does not recur (Lichtenthaler and Ernst, 2006).

The next section addresses the issue of receptivity and, in particular, how an organisation's own internal activities affect its ability to transfer technology successfully.

Internal organisational factors and inward technology transfer

Danhof (1949) may be described as one of the first attempts to explore the inward technology transfer process. In his study of the adoption of innovations by industrial companies he identified four different types of company:

- Innovators: the first firms to adopt a new idea.
- Initiators: the firms that adopted the idea soon after the innovators.
- Fabians: the firms who adopted the idea only after its utility was widely acknowledged in the industry.
- Drones: the last firms to adopt new ideas.

This study revealed that there was considerable difference in the responsiveness of organisations to take up externally developed technology. A similar conclusion was drawn by Kroonenberg (1989) following a study of 3,000 firms in The Netherlands. He suggests that small and medium-sized enterprises (SMEs) can be classified into one of three groups:

1 technology-driven SME;
2 technology-following SME; and
3 technology-indifferent SME.

Both of these studies reveal clear distinctions between firms in either their ability or their willingness to adopt new technology. Establishing the precise nature of the activities that are required to ensure that organisations can either remain as innovators or become innovators has been the subject of numerous studies. Carter and Williams's (1959) study of technically progressive firms uncovered a number of shared characteristics within organisations that facilitate innovation. In a comprehensive review of the technology transfer literature, Godkin (1988) suggests that these same factors would foster technology transfer. The factors are shown below:

- high quality of incoming communication;
- a readiness to look outside the firm;
- a willingness to share knowledge;
- a willingness to take on new knowledge, to license and to enter joint ventures;
- effective internal communication and coordination mechanisms;
- a deliberate survey of potential ideas;
- use of management techniques;
- an awareness of costs and profits in R&D departments;
- identification of the outcomes of investment decisions;
- good-quality intermediate management;
- high status of science and technology on the board of directors;
- high-quality chief executives; and
- a high rate of expansion.

Godkin's classification is one of the earliest studies, specifically on technology transfer, to recognise that the existence of certain activities within the recipient organisation is necessary for successful technology transfer. This point will be explored in detail in the following two sections.

Innovation in action

Source: WineSide

Think small

Persuading wine drinkers to be adventurous and try more high-end wines has traditionally been hard. Tentative consumers tend to stick to wines at the £5 mark and only pay more for a limited number of the most famous brands.

A French start-up, WineSide, has come up with an alternative. They offer a variety of 6cl sealed glass tubes sold individually or in boxes through retailers and their website. These packs encourage novice wine enthusiasts to sample GrandCru wines and gain confidence – without breaking the bank.

WineSide also markets its tubes to restaurants in 10cl sizes. This allows restaurants to offer high quality wine by the glass without having to open a whole bottle.

Source: HSBC (2010) 100 Thoughts, HSBC, London.

Absorptive capacity: developing a receptive environment for technology transfer

As was shown above, many of the traditional technology transfer mechanisms concentrate on providing access to technology, with little effort directed towards understanding the needs of organisations acquiring externally developed technology. The early literature on inward technology transfer centred on the ability of organisations to access technological knowledge (Gruber and Marquis, 1969) and their subsequent ability to disseminate this information effectively. Allen's work in the 1960s on the role of gatekeepers within organisations exemplifies this (*see* Allen, 1966, 1977; Allen and Cohen, 1969). Seaton and Cordey-Hayes (1993) argue that there has been little thought and research aimed at the difficulties of exploiting externally developed technology. They suggest that this is because technology transfer has largely been seen in terms of providing access to technology. They emphasise the need to view technology transfer as a process.

The notion of receptivity advocated by Seaton and Cordey-Hayes (1993) suggests that there are certain characteristics whose presence is necessary for inward technology transfer to occur. In a similar vein, but within an R&D context, Cohen and Levinthal (1990) put forward the notion of 'absorptive capacity'. In their study of the US manufacturing sector they reconceptualise the traditional role of R&D investment as merely a factor aimed at creating specific innovations. They see R&D expenditure as an investment in an organisation's absorptive capacity and argue that an organisation's ability to evaluate and utilise external knowledge is related to its prior knowledge and expertise and that this prior knowledge is, in turn, driven by prior R&D investment.

Absorptive capacity is often touted as being important for the success of open innovation. Yet different absorptive capacities may be required for inbound versus outbound open innovation. In a study of how multiple firms participated in the development of a groundbreaking anti-influenza drug, Newey (2010) found that firms needed to develop both supplier- and customer-types of absorptive capacity. Inbound open innovation involved customer absorptive capacity and outbound innovation required supplier absorptive capacity. In each case absorptive capacity needed to be leveraged differently.

Seaton and Cordey-Hayes (1993) argue that inward technology transfer will only be successful if an organisation has not only the ability to acquire but also the ability effectively to assimilate and apply ideas, knowledge, devices and artefacts. Organisations will only respond to technological opportunity in terms of their own perceptions of its benefits and costs and in relation to their own needs and technical, organisational and human resources. The process view of inward technology transfer, therefore, is concerned with creating or raising the capability for innovation. This requires an organisation and the individuals within it to have the capability to:

- search and scan for information which is new to the organisation (awareness);
- recognise the potential benefit of this information by associating it with internal organisational needs and capabilities;
- communicate these business opportunities to and assimilate them within the organisation; and
- apply them for competitive advantage.

Table 10.2 4A conceptual framework of technology transfer

Activity	Process
Awareness	Describes the processes by which an organisation scans for and discovers what information on technology is available
Association	Describes the processes by which an organisation recognises the value of this technology (ideas) for the organisation
Assimilation	Describes the processes by which the organisation communicates these ideas within the organisation and creates genuine business opportunities
Application	Describes the processes by which the organisation applies this technology for competitive advantage

These processes are captured in the following stages: awareness, association, assimilation and application. This four-stage conceptual framework (4A) is used to explore the processes involved in inward technology transfer (*see* Table 10.2).

Identifying external technology: the importance of scanning and networking

Scanning by individuals on behalf of the organisation is often regarded as an informal and unassigned activity. But in order for individuals to practise the process effectively, organisations must recognise its value (Tidd *et al.*, 2001, Afuah, 2003). However, it is because organisations are unaware of its value that they do not provide support for the process. Research by Oakley *et al.* (1988) on the subject of the search for technical knowledge argues that small firms in particular do not recognise the importance of external technical contacts, suggesting that they do little if any technology scanning.

It has long been recognised that a key characteristic of technically progressive firms is the high quality of their incoming information. In 1959 Carter and Williams reported this in almost 200 firms over a wide range of industries. Many other studies have since demonstrated the importance of external information for successful innovation. For example, SPRU's Project SAPPHO confirmed the need for high-quality external linkages (Rothwell *et al.*, 1974; Peters and Waterman, 1982; CEST, 1991).

The process of searching for and acquiring technical information is a necessary activity for organisations in order to maintain their knowledge base (*see* Johnson and Jones, 1957). This can be effectively achieved by scanning the technological environment, either through the scientific literature or through interactions with other people (often called networking). Thus, innovation within firms is a process of know-how accumulation based on a complementary mix of in-house R&D and R&D performed elsewhere, obtained via the process of technology scanning.

Research at Aston University has also shown that organisations that do not possess boundary-spanning individuals (scanning) will be restricted in the degree to which the organisation becomes aware of and assesses the relevance of innovations in the first place (Newell and Clark, 1990). In a study of biotechnology firms, Fabrizo (2009) found the enhanced access to university research enjoyed by firms that engage in basic research and collaborate with university scientists leads to superior searches for new inventions and provides advantages in terms of both the timing and quality of search outcomes (see also Kang and Kang, 2009).

Given the importance of an awareness of external information and the role of technological scanning and networking, awareness is seen as the necessary first stage in the inward technology transfer process.

In order for an organisation to search and scan effectively for technology that will match its business opportunities, it needs to have a thorough understanding of its internal organisational capabilities. This can be effectively achieved via internal scanning and networking, which will enable it to become familiar with its internal activities. The coupling of internal technology scanning with external technology scanning activities can be seen in Figure 10.5 (*see* Trott (1998) for a more detailed explanation of the development of this model).

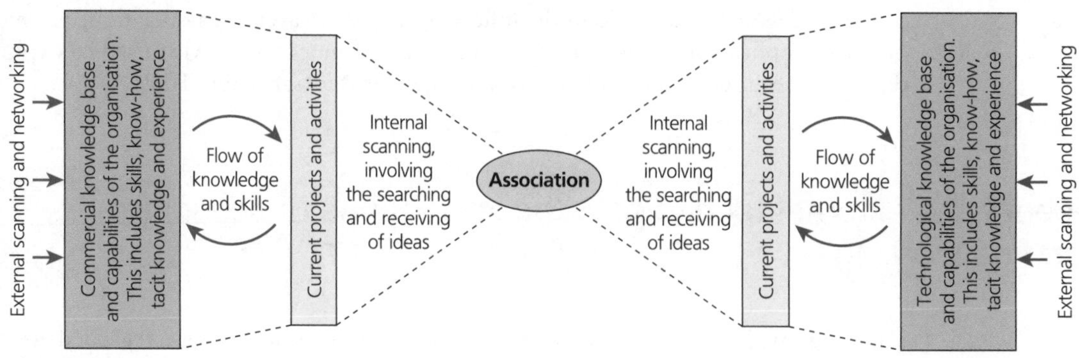

Figure 10.5 A conceptual framework for the development of genuine business opportunities

Linking external technology to internal capabilities

External scanning without a full understanding of the organisation's capabilities and future requirements is likely to produce much 'noise' along with the 'signal'. 'Tuned scanning', achieved through the internal assimilation of an organisation's activities, as opposed to 'untuned scanning', will produce a higher 'signal-to-noise' ratio (Trott and Cordey-Hayes, 1996).

Inward technology transfer, however, involves more than identifying interesting technology; it is necessary to match technology with a market need in order to produce a potential opportunity for the business. The scanning process needs to incorporate commercial scanning as well as technology scanning so that technological opportunities may be matched with market needs (*see* Figure 10.5).

Such levels of awareness increase the probability of individuals being able to develop and create associations on behalf of the organisation between an internal opportunity and an external opportunity. This process of association is the second stage in inward technology transfer.

Chapter 6 emphasised the importance of recognising that the knowledge base of an organisation is not simply the sum of the individual knowledge bases. Nelson and Winter (1982) argue that such learning by doing is captured in organisational routines. It is these internal activities undertaken by an organisation that form the third stage in the process, assimilation.

Managing the inward transfer of technology

The final stage in the inward technology transfer process is the application of the business opportunity for competitive advantage. This is the stage where the organisation brings about commercial benefit from the launch of a new product or an improved product or manufacturing process. In science-based organisations a combination of credibility and respect, coupled with extensive informal and formal communications among individuals within the organisation, facilitates this process (referred to as an internal knowledge accumulation process). This is not to disregard totally the presence of external influences.

Even in science-based industries few companies are able to offer their researchers total scientific freedom, untouched by the demands of the market. R&D programmes are therefore focused on the business aspirations of the company and its future markets. These are usually set out using the most applicable technology. There is not a constant need for new ideas in technologies beyond these programmes – there are clearly resource limits on R&D departments. Inevitably there will be crisis points, where the competition brings out something involving new technology. At these times, there is usually full management commitment and money is invariably made available to bring in new technology quickly to respond to the competition. Here the inward technology transfer processes generally works well due to total commitment from all levels within the organisation.

Where technology is introduced on a more routine basis, a decision has to be made about spending money on a prototype or a demonstrator. The assimilation phase is usually dominated by who will put up the money to try out the new technology. This raises the question: what is the business need and who has the budget to address it and, moreover, do they have any money that can be diverted from something they are already doing to implement this new technology?

Technology transfer and organisational learning

Several different pieces of research have identified a number of stages that form an inherent part of the knowledge transfer process (Trott and Cordey-Hayes, 1996; Gilbert, 1996; Cordey-Hayes *et al.*, 1996). These must occur if the process of knowledge transfer and thus organisational learning is to be complete. While each organisation conducts its activities in different ways, members of that organisation soon adopt the company's way of operating. Organisational know-how is captured in routines, such as particular ways of working. The relationship between knowledge transfer between individuals and groups and the whole organisation may be expressed as two interlinked systems, as in Figure 10.6.

In order for inward technology transfer to take place, members of the organisation must show an awareness of and a receptivity towards knowledge acquisition. Individual learning involves the continual search for new information of potential benefit to the organisation. This frequently challenges existing procedures. Individuals must be continually scanning the internal and external environments for relevant information that can be used to develop associations with internal knowledge. Over time these associations, coupled with additional internal knowledge, can lead to the creation of genuine business opportunities. Having created these opportunities the knowledge can be said to be assimilated at the individual and work group level (this is shown in Figure 10.6 as the first stages in the process of organisational learning). At this point the organisation has not accepted the change, nor has it learnt: knowledge has not been transferred, it remains within the work group. However, the idea is implicitly accepted in its adoption by the individual/group.

In order for the organisation to learn, the knowledge must be assimilated into the core routines of the organisation. That is, the knowledge becomes embedded in skills and know-how. It is during application by the work group that knowledge transfers from the individual to the organisation. However, before this knowledge can be assimilated into the core routines of the organisation, there needs to be explicit

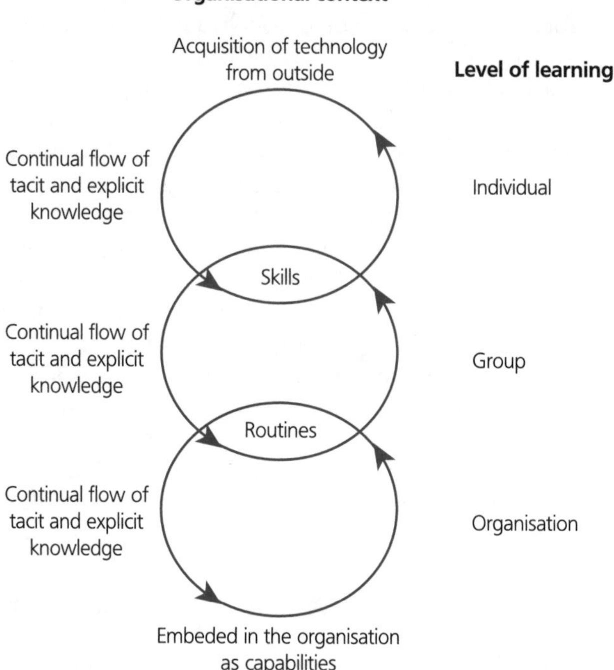

Figure 10.6 Interlinking systems of knowledge-transfer relationships

acceptance by the organisation. There are many examples of individuals bringing technology into an organisation that they believe to be beneficial and yet it does not become accepted by all or part of the organisation. A simple but useful example is that of different versions of software. Several people may have a preference for a certain spreadsheet package, but usually only one version is adopted.

The way in which the learning cycles link together is illustrated in Figure 10.6. In the manner of double-loop learning, the individual and organisational cycles are interrelated and interdependent (Argyris and Schon, 1978). The learning process forms a loop, transferring knowledge from individual into the group. The process of assimilation and adoption of this new knowledge within the inner cycle moves the knowledge into the wider environment and thus into the loop of organisational learning. The role of assimilation has a slightly different emphasis within the individual loops. Assimilation in the individual and group learning cycle refers to assimilation of knowledge from an external source, which may then be applied within the company. Assimilation in the wider cycle relates to assimilation of technology into the core routines of the organisation, which is evidenced by a behavioural change within the organisation. It is only when assimilation in the wider cycle has occurred that learning has truly taken place.

Case study

Sony-Ericsson mobile phone joint venture dependent on technology transfer

This case study provides an excellent example of why firms engage in technology transfer. It provides practical evidence to illustrate the benefits of technology transfer and licensing. The case also illustrates the difficulty of operating in a highly competitive and rapidly developing industry. The joint venture (JV) established by Sony and Ericsson takes time to develop, but eventually the JV has some success. Big questions remain however, for the firm. Is the mobile handset market one in which it can succeed? Or is it simply too competitive?

Introduction

In April 2001 Ericsson, the Swedish telecommunications equipment group, and Sony of Japan established a joint venture in mobile phones. The venture, based in London, brought together the two companies' loss making handset businesses. The news was generally accepted as good for both companies. It would combine Sony's consumer products expertise with Ericsson's extensive knowledge of mobile phone networks. Ericsson is the world's leading maker of wireless networks. It would give Ericsson access to Sony's multimedia technology, branding expertise and knowledge acquired from Japan's early start in third generation mobile phone technology. Sony would gain access to Ericsson's telecommunications technology and its distribution. The two companies hoped to create a market leader to threaten the dominance of Nokia of Finland within five years. In 2000 the two companies together shipped 50 million or $7.2 billion worth of mobile phones, giving them a 12 per cent market share and third position after Nokia of Finland and Motorola of the United States.

The wider business environment, however, was extremely challenging. At the start of the new century despite the huge growth in mobile phones few handset manufacturers were making profits. Nokia was the clear market leader and was producing a profit but Motorola, Philips, Sony, Ericsson, Siemens, Matsushita, Mitsubishi and others were struggling to deliver profits. Indeed, Ericsson made a loss of £1.6 billion on handsets in 2000 and the group announced thousands of job losses. Ericsson suffered from poor handset design, delays in getting them to market and failure to anticipate a market shift to low-end phones. Sony was in a different position. It had well-designed phones but a much smaller global market share – less than 2 per cent – but the impending launch of 3G phones would provide an enormous opportunity for Sony to exploit its multimedia technology portfolio. In particular liquid crystal display technology, digital camera, and music and video technology, all of which are expected to be driving forces behind the launch of 3G.

Rationale of alliance for Sony

The strategic alliance with Ericsson is part of an ambitious expansion led by Nobuyuki Idei, chairman and chief executive, to transform Sony into a global media, communications and network conglomerate. Sony has invested in semiconductors and broadband technology, an online bank and issue a tracking stock to give So-net, its internet service provider, the means to acquire other ISPs. But, Sony has delivered disappointing financial results for investors over the past few years and Sony will need to accelerate the pace of other changes within the company and develop further new products or else it will fall behind in the next generation of products.

The move into a new business area such as mobile phones is welcomed by investors who argue that Sony has been too slow to move away from its traditional businesses such as music stereos, televisions, VCR, DVD and camera recorders. At the same time, market conditions have deteriorated: in consumer electronics, the weakening of consumer confidence after the September 11 (2001) attacks on the US has come on top of already sluggish demand and falling prices.

Certain products, such as low-end stereos made by Aiwa, Sony's 61 per cent-owned subsidiary, are increasingly dominated by low-cost Chinese and South Korean manufacturers. In addition the games division, which in 1998 accounted for 44 per cent of operating

→

profits, has been mired in losses. Increasing competition from Nintendo's GameCube and Microsoft's Xbox will put further pressure on Sony's PlayStation2.

Rationale of alliance for Ericsson

For Swedish-based Ericsson, the venture will give it access to Japanese knowledge of third-generation technology, this should help it compete in the fiercely competitive handset market. While Ericsson has been dominant in providing technology for the network market, it has increasingly struggled to stay in the top league among handset producers. Ericsson has a long history in microelectronics and its customers come not just from the telecoms industry, but from a variety of other sectors, including avionics, computing, military and space. Nonetheless, Ericsson has been badly hit by the downturn in the global telecoms equipment market, and it accumulated huge losses in the mobile phone businesses. The group recorded an underlying loss of more than $980 million in 2000. Ericsson Microelectronics supplies Ericsson and other customers. It employs 2,500 people and has annual sales of more than SKr5 billion. The division makes a range of products such as radio frequency power transistors, as well as chips designed to support 'Bluetooth', a wireless communications standard. Manufacturing is carried out in Sweden, California, Texas and China while design centres are located in Sweden, Norway, the UK and the US. The business has its headquarters in Kista, a high-technology suburb and major centre of Ericsson operations just north of Stockholm.

The business of making handsets has changed beyond all recognition in recent years from a niche, high-tech activity to the world's biggest consumer electronics industry. As rivals have jumped on the gravy train and developed markets have neared saturation, mobile phones have become commodity items where efficient manufacturing becomes a vital part of staying ahead. In particular, Nokia has demonstrated that the two most important factors in a successful handset business are fashion and speed to market. This is because suppliers have become increasingly reliant on the replacement market since the majority in many countries owns a phone. Ericsson has been grappling with this for some time but has continually failed to find the magic formula for churning out fashionable models fast enough to keep up with changing technology. Notwithstanding the joint venture with Sony Ericsson intends to retain a large research and development division focusing on handsets, which is vital to ensure its network business stays in touch with consumer demands.

How does mobile phone technology work?

Few people realise that a mobile phone is much more like a radio than a conventional wired telephone. Indeed, mobile phone technology is a development of radio technology rather than wired telecommunications technology. That is, it picks up signals from transmitters. The mobile phones we use today were developed from 'business' radio communication devices such as those as used by taxi firms and emergency services. These allow one party to talk at a time. You push a handset button to talk then release the button to listen. The use of the word 'over' was used to indicate the end of a message. This eliminated echo problems, which took many years to solve before natural, full duplex communications was possible. This proved to be an extremely difficult technical problem to overcome. Simplex, used in business radio, shares a single frequency for both people talking. With mobile phones technology the transmitting and receiving frequencies are different, and offset from each other to prevent interference.

Each mobile phone requires a cellular system. When we say a cellular system, it means a division of a city or town into small cells. Each cell has a base station that consists of a tower and a small building containing radio equipment, this allows widespread frequency reuse across an area, so that millions of people can use mobile phones concurrently. Each cell is typically sized at and covers about a 10 square mile radius.

Cellular technology uses a principle called frequency reuse to greatly increase customers served. Low powered mobiles and radio equipment at each cell site permit the same radio frequencies to be reused in different cells, multiplying calling capacity without creating interference. This spectrum efficient method contrasts sharply with earlier mobile systems that used a high-powered, centrally located transmitter, to communicate with high-powered, car-mounted mobiles on a small number of frequencies, channels which were then monopolised and not reused over a wide area.

There is a requirement to have a large number of base stations in a city of any size to make mobile

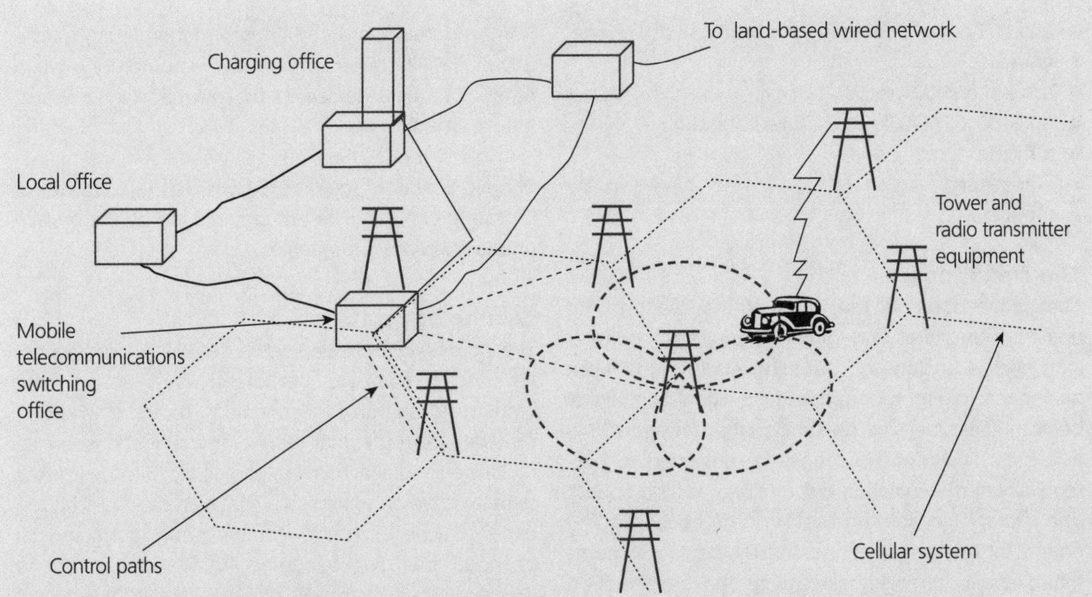

Figure 10.7 A simplified cellular technology system

phones function conveniently. A typical large city can have hundreds of towers placed in certain regions to cover most of the areas completely. Central offices called the Mobile Telephone Switching Offices (MTSOs) handle all of the phone connections to the normal land-based phone system, and controls all of the base stations in the region. Each network operator, such as Vodaphone, O2, Virgin and Orange in the UK runs one (see Figure 10.7).

Moving from cell to cell within a network

All mobile phones have special codes related to them. These codes are used to identify the phone's owner, phone and the service provider that they use. Here is what happens when you use your mobile phone.

When a person first turns on their phone, it listens for a System Identification Code (SID) on the control channel. This is a unique frequency that the phone and base station use to send signals to another about things like call set-up and channel changing. If the phone can't find any control channels to listen to, then it's out of range and will display on the phone a 'no service' message. When it receives the SID, the phone matches up to the SID programmed into the phone. If the SIDs match, the phone realises that the cell it is corresponding with is part of its home system. The phone also transmits a registration request, along with the SID, and the MTSO keeps track of your phone's location in a database – this way it is known what cell you are in when it wants to ring your phone. The MTSO gets the call that is calling you and it tries to find you by looking in its system to see which cell you are in. The call is sent to you at that time. You are now talking by two-way radio to a friend!

As you travel and move near the end of your cell, your cell's base station sees that your signal strength is diminishing. In the meantime, the base station in the cell you are moving closer to sees your phone's signal strength increasing. The two base stations coordinate with each other through the MTSO and, at some point, your phone gets a signal on a control channel telling it to change frequencies. This hand-off switches your phone to the new cell without interruption to you and your call. As you travel, the signal is passed from cell to cell.

Inside a mobile phone handset

Mobile phones are some of the most intricate devices people play with on a daily basis. Modern digital cell phones can process millions of calculations per second in order to compress and decompress the voice stream. The mobile phone comprises the following key individual parts:

→

- a circuit board containing the brains of the phone;
- an aerial;
- a liquid crystal display (LCD);
- a keyboard (similar to a TV remote control);
- a microphone;
- a speaker;
- a battery.

The circuit board

The circuit board is the heart of the system. The analogue-to-digital and digital-to-analogue conversion chips translate the outgoing audio signal from analogue to digital and the incoming signal from digital back to analogue. The digital signal processor (DSP) is a highly customised processor designed to perform signal-manipulation calculations at high speed. The microprocessor handles all of the housekeeping chores for the keyboard and display, deals with command and control signalling with the base station and also coordinates the rest of the functions on the board.

The ROM and Flash memory chips provide storage for the phone's operating system and customisable features, such as the phone directory. The radio frequency (RF) and power section handles power management and recharging, and also deals with the hundreds of FM channels. Finally, the RF amplifiers handle signals travelling to and from the aerial.

The display has grown considerably in size as the number of features in mobile phones have increased. Most current phones offer built-in phone directories, calculators, music and games. And many of the phones incorporate some type of PDA or web browser.

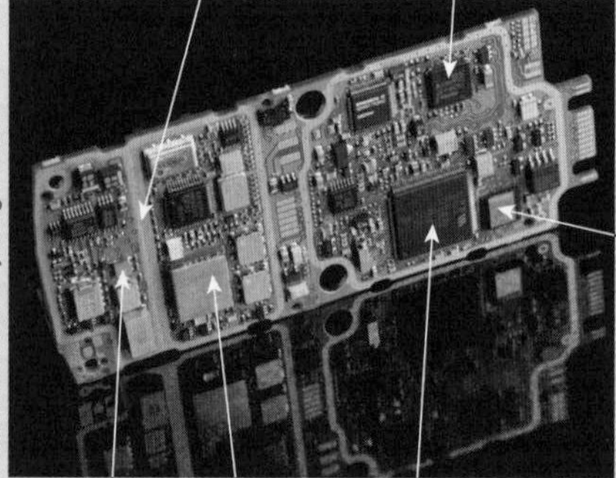

Source: David J. Green/Alamy Images

Some phones store certain information, such as the SID and MIN codes, in internal Flash memory, while others use external cards that are similar to Smart Media cards.

Mobile phones have such tiny speakers and microphones that it is incredible how well most of them reproduce sound. The battery, is used by the mobile phone's internal clock chip.

Technology transfer

The increasing technological content of mobile phones, as illustrated above, has forced many firms in the industry to search for technology partners who can provide the additional technology required such as multi-media, digital camera, games etc. For these firms to try to develop expertise in these areas would be too expensive and too slow for the rapid technological changes that are occurring in the mobile phone market. Indeed, the mobile phone market is an excellent example of the increasing complexity of technologies and the increasing range of technologies found within products. This has led to a shortening of product life-cycles within the mobile phone market. Many users now change their handset after 18 months to two years. In addition, companies are finding it increasingly difficult to sustain R&D capability over all areas of their business as the complexity of these areas increases. Internal R&D is increasingly focused on core competencies, while R&D in all other business activities is progressively covered by collaborations, partnerships and strategic alliances.

Ericsson is the world leader in mobile phone networks and has a long established reputation in the microelectronics industry stretching back over 50 years. Hence, it has extensive knowledge and expertise of mobile phone technology. Sony on the other hand does not, but it does have an extensive portfolio of other technologies that may be useful in third and fourth generation mobile phones. Some of Sony's technology portfolio includes the following:

- HDTVs, Flat-panel Plasma and LCD WEGA® TVs, FD Trinitron® WEGA® CRT televisions, CRT rear projection TVs, and Grand WEGA® LCD rear projection televisions;
- DVD-video players/recorders, VCRs, Super Audio CD players, and home theatre-in-a-box systems;
- hi-fi components (AV receivers), shelf systems and speakers;

- Walkman® personal stereos, MiniDisc Walkman® players/recorders and personal digital music players;
- Handycam® camcorders;
- Cybershot® and Mavica® digital still cameras;
- Memory Stick® flash media;
- VAIO® desktop and notebook computers;
- CLIÉ™ handheld devices;
- video conferencing products;
- visual imaging products;
- professional digital photography systems;
- e-communication and digital signage;
- OEM Li-ion and li-polymer batteries;
- semiconductor devices, including Sigma RAM memory, ICs, CCD sensors, optical comm. ICs, GPS and cellular/PCs ICs.

New products emerge from Sony Ericsson

In 2002, one year after its launch, Sony Ericsson unveiled its first six new handset models, including three with colour screens and one with a built-in camera. At the time Nokia, the market leader, did not have a colour screen phone on the market, although it was planning to launch a camera-phone by the middle of 2002. Sony Ericsson said it would launch its first 3G handset by the end of 2002. It also unveiled an alliance with Sony's film business to provide games on its new colour screen phones, which would be based on the films *Men in Black* and *Charlie's Angels*. Further new handset models were planned to utilise Sony's product design strengths. In 2002 the launch of next generation mobile services (so called third generation (3G)), were being held up by the financial difficulties of many operators and technical delays in the development of new handsets. The 3G phones were expected to drive demand for a wider range of applications on mobile phones.

In 2003 Sony Ericsson announced disappointing end of year results. Its market share did not achieve 6 per cent in 2002, compared with a 7–10 per cent target, forcing its owners to plough extra cash into the start-up after it failed to reach profitability as planned. The results placed Sony Ericsson fifth in terms of market share. The company president, Katsumi Ihara admitted: 'Last year wasn't a good year for Sony Ericsson, we expected a better business market at the beginning of the joint venture.' But failure is not an option for 2003, he says. 'We cannot accept the fact that Sony Ericsson can continue to lose money. We need to turn around the business.'

He points to three main causes of the poor performance;

- problems integrating teams from Sony and Ericsson;
- market share losses in China;
- strong competition in the US.

The picture in 2003 was very different to the one painted in 2001 when the two firms got together. The product and brand skills of Sony and the telecommunication and distribution skills of Ericsson were thought to be an ideal marriage. Competing with market leaders Nokia, Motorola and Samsung has proved extremely tough. And now other handset makers such as Alcatel and Sagem are beginning to deliver new products into an already crowded market place. The signs are worrying for Sony Ericsson. There may be job losses ahead. Alcatel and Sagem have much lower market share figures than Sony Ericsson and yet they are both able to deliver profits. Without the success of its T68 handset, which it inherited from the old Ericsson design team, market share would have been several percentage points lower. Kurt Hellström, former Ericsson chief executive and Sony Ericsson chairman, caused further controversy by suggesting that the Swedish group could halt further investment in the joint venture if there was no evidence of a turn-round. The joint venture is a long way short of becoming the market leader as was suggested at its launch in 2001 and Sony Ericsson desperately needs to show that it can manufacture a broad range of compelling phones as it tries to revitalise its flagging market share.

In 2003 there were signs of a change of fortunes: market share in China climbed on the back of sales of its low-end T100 phone and its upmarket colour screen T68. Also, newly launched handsets such as its top-of-the-range P800 phone, sold well in early trials. Combined with the launch of 'more cute and sexy' models including camera phones 'in all price segments'. In addition to new products Sony Ericsson is looking to trim costs by moving more handset production to China and cutting other operational expenses.

Good news at last

In 2003 the Sony and Ericsson joint venture reported its first quarterly profit since its inception in 2001. Sony Ericsson's sales rose to €1.3 billion. This improvement was particularly due to high demand for its new

→

camera phones in Japan and to the success of its T610 series. In 2004 it launched five new mobile phones with in-built cameras to take advantage of the growing demand for sending and receiving pictures over mobile handsets. Its Z200 and Z600 Clamshell handsets also proved extremely popular. It is also planning to launch a series of very low-cost, entry-level phones for markets such India, China and Brazil.

Sony Ericsson is planning to take more of its mobile phone manufacturing plants under its own control to smooth out supply chain problems and help it take market share. It is in talks to raise its stake in Beijing Ericsson Putian Mobile Communication, a manufacturing facility outside Beijing, and could consider other similar deals in the future. The company is keen to avoid a repeat of 2002, when it failed to take full advantage of booming pre-Christmas demand for phones because of component shortages, and lost market share. However, the decision to bring more factories under direct control is a reversal of parent company Ericsson's policy – in 2001 just before setting up the joint venture – of outsourcing all its handset manufacturing to companies such as 'Flextronics'. About 30 per cent of Sony Ericsson phones are produced in factories controlled by the company while 70 per cent of production is outsourced. Sony Ericsson is aiming for 50 per cent production in factories controlled by the company.

Using the iconic Walkman brand to compete

The Sony Walkman become one of the world's most familiar brands. It emerged first in the late 1970s and attained an unparalleled position as the most recognised consumer electronic good throughout the 1980s and 1990s. Even with the emergence of MP3 technology and the shift of music from cassettes and CDs to files, the Walkman brand has power. It is for this reason that Sony has reused the Walkman in as many formats as possible to try and capitalise on the brand awareness that the Walkman still achieves. The Walkman branding came back in a big way at the beginning of 2006 with the release of a range of Walkman branded Sony Ericsson phones that attempted to capture the era of music player capability within mobile handsets. The Sony Ericsson W580i Walkman offers music, the internet, pictures, organiser functions and calls. There is a Walkman button on the phone that takes you directly to the music. One interesting feature of the W580i is a pedometer that keeps track of your movement, whether you are running or walking.

Competition continues to increase

The mobile phone handset market is one of the world's most fiercely contested markets. The reasons for this are long and varied. One clear reason is that many technology forecasters see the handset as the future hub of virtually all technology; with people accessing all forms of media via their handset. Nokia, the world leader in handsets has faced fierce competition not just from Sony Ericsson, but from Samsung, Motorola and others. In 2005 Nokia sold 265 million handsets worldwide, but even so its global market share has fallen from 38 per cent to 30 per cent in 2004. In contrast Sony Ericsson has made progress towards its goal of becoming the industry's number three manufacturer by generating more revenue than Samsung Electronics during 2006. Sony Ericsson leapfrogged LG Electronics to become the industry's number four during 2006. Miles Flint, president of Sony Ericsson, hailed 2006 as an 'extraordinary year'. Sony Ericsson recorded sales of €11 billion for 2006, up 51 per cent on 2005. Pre-tax profit for 2006 was €1.3 billion, up 160 per cent. The launch in January 2007 of the iPhone by Apple will add even further competition to this dynamic market.

In November 2008, in a decision that surprised many, the world's largest mobile phone maker decided to pull out of one of the world's biggest cellular markets. Nokia announced that it was withdrawing from the Japanese market. This market is arguably the most competitive mobile phone market in the world. The company was active in Japan in the 1990s, supplying handsets for the country's proprietary second-generation PDC networks. Nokia's decision probably says more about the Japanese market than it does about Nokia. Handsets from NEC, Fujitsu, Sharp, Panasonic and other domestic makers, which are typically developed in close cooperation with carriers and highly tuned to local tastes, are most popular in Japan and no foreign phone maker enjoys the same level of popularity in Japan than it does in other major markets.

2008 was another fiercely competitive year for all the handset manufacturers. Although global mobile handset shipments grew in 2008, Motorola, Sony Ericsson and Apple all lost market share to stronger competitors. Emerging markets in Asia and Africa drove the surge in growth in 2008, compensating

Table 10.3 Global handset market share

	2008		2009	
	Millions of units	**Market share**	**Millions of units**	**Market share**
Nokia	122	41.00%	103.2	37.80%
Samsung	45.7	15.40%	52.3	19.20%
LG	27.7	9.30%	29.8	10.90%
Motorola	28.1	9.50%	14.8	5.40%
Sony Ericsson	24.4	8.20%	13.8	5.10%
Others	49.4	16.60%	59.1	21.60%
Total	297.3	100.00%	273	100.00%

Source: Strategy Analytics.

for sluggish demand in developed regions of North America and Western Europe.

The first quarter results for 2008 reveal difficult times for the big brands. While still a newcomer to the mobile handset market, Apple saw global handset shipments fall sharply, from 2.3 million units to 1.7 million units. This resulted in the first decline in the company's market share, which dropped from 0.7 per cent to 0.6 per cent. Third placed Motorola suffered yet more woes as its market share dropped sharply from 12.4 per cent to 9.7 per cent, while Sony Ericsson experienced a decline from 9.4 per cent to 7.9 per cent. Market leader Nokia saw its share remain unchanged at 40 per cent. It has been the Korean firms of LG and Samsung that have increased their market shares. Improved handset portfolios have enabled LG to grow at almost four times the annual industry average, while Samsung grew two times faster (*see* Table 10.3).

Handset sales in 2010 continued to be positive, due to a strong growth in global smartphone sales and also the continuing uptake of unbranded low cost mobile devices in emerging markets. The handset sector also saw the Google Android OS continue to rise in popularity, overtaking the iOS for third position on a global level. The rise of the smartphone is at the expense of the more traditional players however, which are now beginning to feel the impact of the competitive threats from iPhone and Google Android.

Conclusions

The case illustrates how two large multi-technology firms such as Sony and Ericsson, operating in several technology fields found it extremely difficult and expensive to be technological leaders in every technology within their scope. It shows how Sony and Ericsson used technology transfer to enhance their own technology portfolio to shorten product development time and to avoid the costs and delay of research and development.

The longer-term problem for Sony Ericsson is that it operates in a highly volatile market, that of the technology fashion market. The problem is that fashionable status is ephemeral. Buyers of trendy goods – such as the latest mobile phones – quickly switch to the next 'well cool' item. In the case of handsets, it is usually within 12 to 18 months. One of the questions for Sony Ericsson, is whether it can retain shoppers when they tire of their Sony Ericsson phone. Will they stick with the brand or move to one of its competitors? How much money is Sony-Ericsson willing to invest in branding?

Sony Ericsson plans to continue to supply a full range of phones, from cheap to expensive. Putting all its efforts into just one segment may make more sense. If Sony Ericsson can master how to keep fashion victims interested, it may yet become a successful niche player and capture more market share. But this is a very competitive market and Sony and Ericsson may decide that there are other markets that could prove more profitable.

Mobile technology is rising rapidly as hardware and software companies face a new competitive landscape. The smartphone, along with the tablet computer, is pulling the attention of software developers and consumers away from desktop computers and laptops. As phones become smarter, software and services are becoming the critical differentiating factor, as in

→

1982 when Microsoft's MS-DOS operating system took the lion's share of value from IBM personal computers. In the most compelling devices, software and services have been integrated with hardware to form a whole, as with Research in Motion's BlackBerry and Apple's iPhone. But the rapid ascent of Android, which now powers devices from the Verizon Droid to Samsung's new Galaxy S, shows the power of software. Taking the market share figures at face value, talk of a duopoly between Apple and Android is premature, since Nokia and Research in Motion still beat them in sales of smartphones. But the momentum, particularly at the expensive end of the market, is with iPhones and Android phones. The global market share of the Symbian platform backed by Nokia fell in 2009 while the iPhone OS rose to 15 per cent from 11 per cent in 2009. Android grew rapidly, supported by mobile operators without the iPhone, rising from 2 per cent to 10 per cent.

Finally, the network operators that subsidise and sell handsets have a vested interest in diversity. The iPhone has been a sales success for those operators who dealt with Apple, but Apple has been able to drive a hard bargain with network operators on subsidies and other terms. For that reason, network operators have been supporting Android to regain bargaining power with Apple.

An interesting side story to this case is the technology development of cellular technology. It seems that the technology existed for many years and was extremely slow to develop. If one considers that 'one-way business radio' has been around for 50 years. It seems funding to develop the technology was not forthcoming because people did not perceive how popular cellular radio would become nor how cheap the service would eventually be. If anyone had suspected such a great demand then funding would certainly have flowed much earlier. In the 1970s and 1980s cellular technology was thought of as an evolution of early radio telephones, a better way to provide a few people with a telephone for their cars. It was not thought that cellular technology would revolutionise communications for everyone.

Sources: C. Brown-Humes and M. Nakamoto (2001) Ericsson and Sony explore tie-up, *Financial Times*, 20 April; C. Brown-Humes and C. Daniel (2001) Ericsson plans microelectronics division sell-off: unit hit by fall in mobile phone market, *Finanical Times*, 20 August; R. Budden (2003) Sony-Ericsson seeks success with new phones', www.FT.com, 3 March; A. Harney (2001) Ambitious expansion looses its shine, *Financial Times*, 2 October; M. Pesola (2004) Sony-Ericsson to raise control, *Finanical Times*, 10 March; D. Roberts and C. Brown-Humes (2001) Ericsson nears surrender in handset battle, *Financial Times*, 26 January. A. Parker (2007) Sony Ericsson edges ahead of Samsung. FT.com site, 17 January; Nokia (2010) FT.com, 21 September.

Questions

1. Ericsson is the world leader in mobile phone networks and has many years of experience of handsets. Explain how Sony's technology portfolio has helped the joint venture.
2. Use the CIM (Figure 1.9) to illustrate the innovation process in this case.
3. Explain why Sony and Ericsson were finding it increasingly difficult to sustain R&D over all of their businesses?
4. Explain why Ericsson is maintaining a large R&D division focusing on handsets when its joint venture with Sony is also conducting R&D and product development of handsets?
5. Discuss why the mobile phone handset market seems to be more like the fashion industry.
6. Many firms are outsourcing more and more of their activities and focusing on core activities. What are the advantages for Sony Ericsson in bringing manufacturing back under its control?
7. What are the advantages and disadvantages of outsourcing?
8. This is a fierce industry in which to try to compete. Should Sony Ericsson quit?
9. What is the market share/profitability of the Apple iPhone in this market?

Chapter summary

Technology transfer has a significant impact on the management of innovation. The process is concerned with facilitating and promoting innovation. The increasing use of strategic alliances means that its importance is set to increase. This chapter has introduced the subject of technology transfer and examined various models of the process. Most models of technology transfer emphasise access to technology rather than trying to understand the receptivity issues of the receiving organisation. The case study showed how effective technology transfer can be in contributing to a firm's success in very competitive conditions.

Discussion questions

1 How does technology transfer differ from simply purchasing technology?

2 Explain the limitations of many of the models of technology transfer.

3 Explain how a firm's internal activities affect its ability to acquire external technology.

4 What opportunities does 'open innovation' offer to the R&D function?

5 To what extent is open innovation 'old wine in new bottles'?

6 Explain why any technology transferred to an organisation needs to be embedded into its core routines.

7 Explain how firms can improve their absorptive capacity?

Key words and phrases

Open innovation *348*
Knowledge transfer *350*
Technology transfer *351*
Licensing *352*
Organisational learning *355*
Receptivity *356*
NIH syndrome *357*
Scanning and networking *361*

References

Afuah, A. (2003) *Innovation Management*, 2nd edn, Oxford University Press, Oxford.

Allen, T.J. (1966) Performance of communication channels in the transfer of technology, *Industrial Management Review*, Vol. 8, 87–98.

Allen, T.J. (1977) *Managing the Flow of Technology*, MIT Press, Cambridge, MA.

Allen, T.J. and Cohen, W.M. (1969) Information flow in research and development laboratories, *Administrative Science Quarterly*, Vol. 14, No. 1, 12–19.

Argyrs, C. and Schon, D.A. (1978) *Organisational Learning*, Addison-Wesley, Reading, MA.

Asakawa, K., Nakamura, H. and Sawada, N. (2010) Firms' open innovation policies, laboratories' external collaborations, and laboratories' R&D performance, *R&D Management*, Vol. 40, 109–23.

Carter, C.F. and Williams, B.R. (1959) The characteristics of technically progressive firms, *Journal of Industrial Economics*, March, 87–104.

Centre for Exploitation of Science and Technology (CEST) (1991) *The Management of Technological Collaboration*, March, Manchester.

Chiaroni, D., Chiesa, V. and Frattini, F. (2009) The Open Innovation Journey: How firms dynamically implement the emerging innovation management paradigm, *Technovation*, Vol. 30, 3, 34–43.

Chesbrough, H. (2003) *Open Innovation: The new imperative from creating and profiting from technology*, HBS Press, Boston, MA.

Chesbrough, H. (2006) 'Open innovation: a new paradigm for understanding industrial innovation', in Henry Chesbrough, Wim Vanhaverbeke and Joel West (eds) *Open Innovation: Researching a New Paradigm*, Oxford University Press, Oxford, 1–12.

Cohen, W.M. and Levinthal, D.A. (1990) A new perspective on learning and innovation, *Administrative Science Quarterly*, Vol. 35, No. 1, 128–52.

Cordey-Hayes, M., Trott, P. and Gilbert, M. (1996) 'Knowledge assimilation and learning organisations', in Butler, J. and Piccaluga, A. (eds) *Knowledge, Technology and Innovative Organisations*, Guerini e Associati, Italy, 131–44.

Dabinett, G. (1995) 'Economic regeneration in Sheffield', in Turner, R. (ed.) *The British Economy in Transition*, Routledge, London.

Dahlander, L. and Gann, D. (2010) How open is innovation?, *Research Policy*, Vol. 39, No. 6, 699–709.

Danhof, C. (1949) *Observations on Entrepreneurship in Agriculture: Change and the Entrepreneur*, Harvard Research Center on Entrepreneurship History, Harvard University Press, Cambridge, MA.

DFI International (1998) Short- and long-term implications of technology transfer, *China Technology Transfer Report*, DTI International, London, 93–8.

Dorf, R.C. (1988) Models for technology transfer from universities and research laboratories, *Technology Management*, Vol. 1, Interscience Enterprises Ltd, Geneva.

Fabrizio, K. (2009) Absorptive capacity and the search for innovation, *Research Policy*, Vol. 38, No. 2, 255–67.

Gilbert, M. (1996) Technological change as a knowledge transfer process, PhD thesis, INTA, Cranfield University.

Godkin, L. (1988) Problems and practicalities of technology transfer: a survey of the literature, *International Journal of Technology Management*, Vol. 3, No. 5, 597–603.

Gruber, W.H. and Marquis, D.G. (1969) *Factors in the Transfer of Technology*, MIT Press, Cambridge, MA.

Hacievliyagil, N.K. (2007) The Impact of Open Innovation on Technology Transfers at Philips and DSM, M.Sc. Thesis, Faculty of Technology, Policy & Management, Delft University of Technology.

Hacievliyagil, N.K., Auger, J.-F., Maisonneuve, Y. and Hartmann, D. (2008) The position of virtual knowledge brokers in the core process of open innovation, *International Journal of Knowledge, Technology and Society*, Vol. 3, No. 5, 47–60.

Hagedoorn, J. (1990) Organisational modes of inter-firm co-operation and technology transfer, *Technovation*, Vol. 10, No. 1, 17–30.

Johnson, S.C. and Jones, C. (1957) How to organise for new products, *Harvard Business Review*, May–June, Vol. 35, 49–62.

Kang, K. and Kang, J. (2009) How do firms source external knowledge for innovation? Analysing effects of different knowledge sourcing methods, *International Journal of Innovation Management*, Vol. 13, No. 1, 1–17.

Katz, R. and Allen, T. (1988) 'Investigating the NIH syndrome: a look at the performance, tenure and communication patterns of 50 R&D project groups', in Tushman, W.L. and Moore, M.L. (eds) *Readings in the Management of Innovation*, HarperCollins, New York.

Kroonenberg, H.H. van den (1989) Getting a quicker pay-off from R&D, *Long Range Planning*, Vol. 4, 22, 51–8.

Langrish, J., Evans, W.G. and Jerans, F.R. (1982) *Wealth from Knowledge*, Macmillan, London.

Lefever, D.B. (1992) Technology transfer and the role of intermediaries, PhD thesis, INTA, Cranfield Institute of Technology.

Lichtenthaler, U. and Ernst, H. (2006) Attitudes to externally organising knowledge management tasks: a review, reconsideration and extension of the NIH syndrome, *R&D Management*, Vol. 36, No. 4, 367–86.

Link, A.N. and Link, K.R. (2003) On the growth of science parks, *Journal of Technology Transfer*, Vol. 28, 81–5.

Macdonald, S. (1992) Formal collaboration and informal information flow, *International Journal of Technology Management*, Special Issue on Strengthening Corporate and National Competitiveness through Technology, Vol. 7, Nos. 1/2/3, 49–60.

Nelson, R.R. and Winter, S. (1982) *An Evolutionary Theory of Economic Change*, Harvard University Press, Boston, MA.

Newell, S. and Clark, P. (1990) The importance of extra-organisational networks in the diffusion and appropriation of new technologies, *Knowledge: Creation, Diffusion and Utilisation*, Vol. 12, No. 2, 199–212.

Newey, L. (2010) Wearing different hats: How absorptive capacity differs in Open Innovation, *International Journal of Innovation Management*, Vol. 14, No. 4, 703–31.

Oakley, R.P., Rothwell, R. and Cooper, S.Y. (1988) *The Management of Innovation in High Technology Small Firms*, Frances Pinter, London.

Parkhe, A., Wasserman, S. and Ralstan, D. (2006) New frontiers in network theory development, *Academy of Management Review*, Vol. 31, No. 3, 560–8.

Peters, T. and Waterman, R.H. (1982) *In Search of Excellence: Lessons from America's Best Run Companies*, Harper & Row, New York.

Prahalad, G. and Hamel, C.K. (1990) The core competence of the corporation, *Harvard Business Review*, Vol. 68, No. 3, 79–91.

Rothberg, R. (1976) *Corporate Strategy and Product Innovation*, Free Press, New York.

Rothwell, R., Freeman, C., Horsley, A., Jervis, V.T.P., Robertson, A.B. and Townsend, J. (1974) SAPPHO updated: Project SAPPHO phase II, *Research Policy*, Vol. 3, 258–91.

Seaton, R.A.F. and Cordey-Hayes, M. (1993) The development and application of interactive models of technology transfer, *Technovation*, Vol. 13, No. 1, 45–53.

Tidd, J., Bessant, J. and Pavitt, K. (2001) *Managing Innovation*, 2nd edn, John Wiley & Sons, Chichester.

Trott, P. (1998) Growing businesses by generating genuine business opportunities: a review of recent thinking, *Journal of Applied Management*, Vol. 7, No. 2, 111–22.

Trott, P. and Cordey-Hayes, M. (1996) Developing a 'receptive' environment for inward technology transfer: a case study of the chemical industry, *R&D Management*, Vol. 26, No. 1, 83–92.

Trott, P. and Hartmann, D. (2009) Old wine in new bottles, *International Journal of Innovation Management,* Vol. 13, No. 4, 1–22.

Werner, J. (1991) Can collaborative research work? Success could spawn 'collateral benefits' for all industries, *Industry Week*, Vol. 240, No. 13, 47.

Further reading

For a more detailed review of the technology transfer literature, the following develop many of the issues raised in this chapter:

Chiaroni, D., Chiesa, V. and Frattini, F. (2009) The Open Innovation Journey: How firms dynamically implement the emerging innovation management paradigm, *Technovation*, Vol. 30, No. 3.

Dodgson, M., Gann D. and Salter, A. (2006) The role of technology in the shift towards open innovation: the case of Procter & Gamble, *R&D Management*, Vol. 36, No. 3, 333–46.

Fleming, L. and Waguespack, D.M. (2007) Brokerage, Boundary Spanning, and Leadership in Open Innovation Communities, *Organization Science*, Vol. 18, No. 2, 165–84.

Harryson, S.J. (2008) Entrepreneurship through relationships – navigating from creativity to commercialisation, *R&D Management*, Vol. 38, No. 3, 291–310.

HSBC (2010) 100 Thoughts, HSBC, London.

Jacobides, M.G. and Billinger, S. (2006) Designing the boundaries of the firm: From 'make, buy, or ally' to the dynamic benefits of vertical architecture, *Organization Science*, Vol. 17, No. 2, 249–61.

Kang, K. and Kang, J. (2009) How do firms source external knowledge for innovation? Analysing effects of different knowledge sourcing methods, *International Journal of Innovation Management*, Vol. 13, No. 1, 1–17.

Newey, L. (2010) Wearing different hats: How absorptive capacity differs in Open Innovation, *International Journal of Innovation Management*, Vol. 14, No. 4, 703–31.

West, J., Vanhaverbeke, W. and Chesbrough, H.W. (2006) 'Open innovation: A research agenda', in H.W. Chesbrough, W. Vanhaverbeke and J. West (eds) *Open innovation: Researching a new paradigm*, Oxford University Press, Oxford, 285–307.

Part Three
New product development

This final part reviews and summarises the nature and techniques of new product development. It looks at the process of developing new products and examines many of the new product management issues faced by companies.

Product and brand strategy is the subject of Chapter 11, it addresses the positioning of the product and the importance of brand strategy on the success of any new product. In particular, it examines the influences on product planning decisions and the role of marketing management. All of these heavily influence any decision to develop new products.

Our understanding of the new product innovation process has improved significantly in the past 30 years. During this period numerous models have been developed to help explain the process. These are examined in Chapter 12. Many of these models identify the role of market research to be significant in developing successful new products. Chapter 13 examines the significant role of packaging in new product development. We turn from products to services in Chapter 14 and examine the development of new services. The role of market research is addressed again in Chapter 15, but this time it explores whether there are times when market research may hinder the development of new products.

Chapter 16 moves from the conceptual to the operational level and analyses the particular challenges faced by the new product manager. Taking a practitioner viewpoint, it investigates the activities that need to be undertaken and how companies organise the process. Emphasis is placed on the role of the new product team and the chapter closes with a look at 3M, the innovating machine.

Chapter 11
Product and brand strategy

Introduction

The products developed by an organisation provide the means for it to generate income. But there are many factors to consider in order to maximise the product's chance of success in competitive environments. For many technology-intensive firms their approach is based on exploiting technological innovation in a rapidly changing market. Other firms, especially those involved in fast-moving consumer goods (FMCG), will be more focused on meeting and supplying products to meet the rapidly changing needs of their customers. All firms have to consider the market in which they are competing, the nature of the competition and how their capabilities will enable their products to be successful. The positioning of the product and the brand strategy selected are of particular importance and also reflect the subject of this chapter. The case study at the end of this chapter tells the story of how a firm developed a tooth whitening product. It illustrates many of the npd activities within the firm.

Chapter contents

Learning objectives

When you have completed this chapter you will be able to:

- explain how product strategies contribute to a firm's performance;
- recognise that new products serve a variety of purposes depending upon what is seen to be the strategic imperative;
- examine the concept of platforms in new product development;
- assess the importance of brand strategy in product development;
- explain how differentiation and positioning contribute to a product's success in the market place; and
- recognise the importance of marketing research for the effective development of new products.

Capabilities, networks and platforms

The company's core capabilities, and those that it can develop or acquire, bound what it can accomplish. However, a broader view brings in the notion of distinctive capabilities. This is wider than technical or operations competence. These broader capabilities include an organisation's 'architecture' and this embraces the network of relationships within, or around, the firm. These relationships might cover customers, suppliers, distributors or other firms engaged in related activities. This leads to the perspective that product development, and the competitive rivalry of which it is usually a part, can sometimes be better understood as undertaken by networks of partnerships and alliances rather than by individual, isolated producers (Delbridge and Mariotti, 2009).

Chapter 7 introduced the concept of networks and explained that their composition can vary widely. In some high-technology industries a horizontal alliance of competitors or firms might dominate, and perhaps they form a consortium for the research and development of a technology. For example, Kodak, Fujifilm, Minolta, Nikon and Canon were allied in the development of the Advanced Photo System. In other industries it might be a vertical arrangement between suppliers, manufacturers, distributors and possibly even customers. It can be a formal agreement, a loose collection of understandings or a system 'managed' by a powerful member.

Saying this of capabilities leads to complications. If networks are competing, rather than individual firms, then the activities across the network need to be coordinated. Sometimes it is the manufacturer that is dominant and leads and controls the network, as in the motor industry. Sometimes it is a distributor that takes the lead and initiates new product categories, as in food retailing. On occasion a large customer can dominate, show the need for a new product and encourage suppliers to innovate, as in the health service or defence industries. How effectively this leadership and coordination are undertaken influences substantially what products are developed and how they are developed. Another consideration is that the network members may have a collection of varied motives for being party to the relationship. Through time they may come to stress other motives that may result in their becoming less interested in the network's aims and less willing to cooperate. The network leader therefore needs to spend some time monitoring motives and encouraging, or inducing, full cooperation between all network members. If the network is established for the development of a technology then the partners have other sets of problems once the technology is available. How do they share the results and how do they each go on to establish distinctive, competitive products?

Choosing appropriate partners for the network and keeping them focused are important attributes for network leadership. Developing and refining the network's innovative ability is crucial, and this is not restricted to technical innovation because innovation in business processes and in distribution can also have a large impact.

Capabilities change. Without continuous attention they can become ineffectual or redundant, as the technology or the market requirement moves on. Alternatively, capabilities may be enhanced through internal development, through external acquisition and through the bringing together of new partnerships and alliances so that the network's capability is deeper or wider. Most capabilities thrive through continuity: through continuous incremental enhancement around a technology or a set of related technologies. This is in keeping with the idea of organisational heritage introduced in Chapters 1 and 3.

Innovation in action

Let your customers join your team

Sometimes the best talent isn't just within your own walls. 'Crowdsourcing' allows you to engage customers in new product design.

British drinks firm Firefly took this idea to heart and last year asked customers to design their new drink, including the flavour, label design and name. The result is 'Britannia', a raspberry, blackberry and Bramley apple drink, which went on sale in 2010.

'We had so many wonderful entries, it was hard for us to choose, so we got customers to vote for their favourite', says cofounder Marcus Waley-Cohen. 'The winning design is just what we were looking for – fun, creative, and well rounded!'

Source: HSBC (2010) 100 Thoughts, HSBC, London.

Product platforms

Emphasis upon continuity in the development of capabilities is also consistent with the idea of an evolving **product platform** that a 'product family' shares. Muffatto and Rovedo (2000) use the car industry as the classic example of this idea where several individual models may share the same basic frame, suspension and transmission. As they say, 'a robust platform is the heart of a successful product family, serving as the foundation for a series of closely related products' (p. 31). The Sony Walkman gives another illustration, with its 160 variations and four major technical innovations between 1980 and 1990, all of which were based upon the initial platform (Jones, 1997). Black & Decker rationalised its hundreds of products into a set of product families, with consequent economies throughout the chain from procurement to distribution and after-sales service. In all these cases the evolution of the product platform, along with the evolution of the requisite capabilities, is central to the product development strategy.

This notion may have originated in engineering but it can be applied widely. Mobile phone handsets, food, cosmetics, clothing and furniture manufacturers can be seen to have product platforms and families. Johnson & Johnson and its development of the Acuvue disposable contact lenses provides another example. Thomas (1995) points out that many people needing vision correction did not wear traditional hard or soft contact lenses because of the discomfort and the cleaning requirements. Acuvue uses high quality soft contact lenses sold at a sufficiently low price to allow disposal after a week, without cleaning. This distinctive advantage, which was clearly relevant to many consumers, led to the successful launch that defined a new market segment. The original product became the basic platform for continuing innovation that is leading to other new offerings in Johnson & Johnson's vision care product family.

Sometimes entirely new platforms and entirely new capabilities are required. Step changes in the product or manufacturing technology, in the customer need or in what the competition offers, and how it offers it, can demand radical rather than incremental change. The risk is all the more if that means the adoption of new technologies, outside the firm's traditional arena.

Source: Getty Images/Mark Elias/Bloomberg

The car industry was the first to utilise the product platform concept. It has since been adapted in other industries.

If we return to the car industry we see that today products are developed from multiple brand product platforms. Furthermore, products of different brands are developed from inter-firm platform projects. For example, Figure 11.1 shows the Volkswagen Audi Group (VAG) inter-firm product platform development. This shows the one platform supporting several different brands with very different strategic objectives. When the car industry began using product platforms the objective was to obtain commonality and benefits of scale within the company boundary. The basic idea was to differentiate all the components visible to the customer, while at the same time sharing components and production processes across product models (Wheelwright and Clark, 1992; Mohr *et al.*, 2010). Some 20 years later, however, the application of the product platform concept is causing concern for many industry analysts, who believe the search for commonality has gone too far at

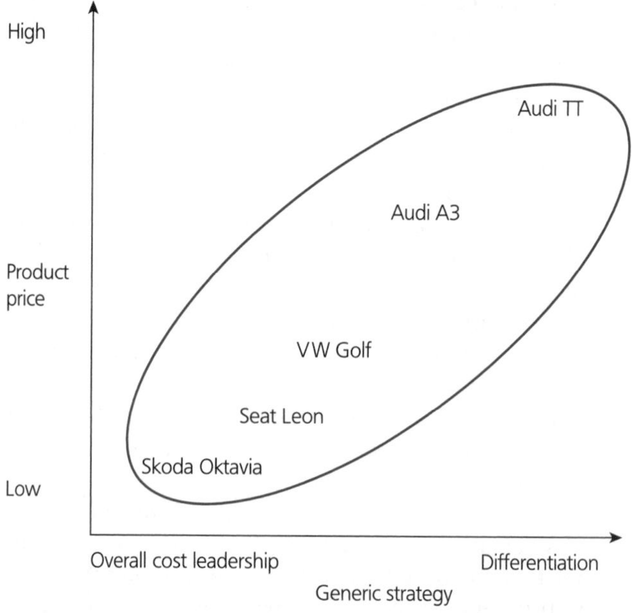

Figure 11.1 VAG inter-firm product platform development

Illustration 11.1

Nestlé Polos: a new flip top for a new product

Nestlé recently launched a new confectionary product: Polo Holes. The bits left over when the famous mints are pressed. Robinson Plastic Packaging has delivered a transparent, food-grade poplypropylene tube for the launch of this new product. The pack features a flip-top closure with Polo embossing. Robinson Plastic Packaging is part of the Robinson Group and is a dedicated moulder of closures, components and containers for the food, drinks and confectionery industries.

the expense of brand distinctiveness. The illustration in Figure 11.1 shows how the product platform operates across a wide variety of models/brands with different strategies and significant price gaps between the models/brands. According to Muffatto and Rovedo (2000) and Mohr *et al.* (2010) the benefits gained through using product platforms are:

- reduced cost of production;
- shared components between models;
- reduced R&D lead times;
- reduced systemic complexity;
- better learning across projects; and
- improved ability to update products.

When used across firms and models there are many challenges presented. According to Kim and Chhajed (2000) in practice it is difficult to achieve optimum or best solution. Inevitably compromises are sought between engineers and designers from the different brands resulting in decisions that are not in the interest of either brand. Moreover, with inter-firm product platforms some of the sought-after gains such as shared components between models and reduced complexity were not achievable because of the constraint of factory sequencing or architectural structure of the brand.

Illustration 11.2 shows how Nokia has struggled to compete with Apple because it has had too many devices operating on slightly different platforms that require developers to write slightly different code.

Product planning

The product planning process takes place before substantial resources are applied to a project. Product planning considers the range of projects that a firm might pursue and over what time frame. It is closely linked to the broader business strategy of the firm and addresses such questions as:

- What product development projects will be undertaken?
- What is the mix of the portfolio of projects (discontinuous new products; platform products; derivative products)?
- What is the timing and sequence of the projects?

The product planning activity clearly requires substantial input from research and development (R&D). It is this link to the technology portfolio of the firm that is so important and needs careful management (*see* Chapters 8 and 9). Deriving a set of products which customers perceive as useful and worth buying may be fortuitous, but more often it is the result of deliberate, systematic endeavour. Organisations choose to compete in one or more product markets using a specified range of technologies (the technology portfolio). They seek to have a set of balanced capabilities that will enable them to match market opportunities by developing attractive market offerings, which customers perceive as conveying valuable benefits. How well they accomplish this, compared with competitors, is a major determinant of success.

The product plan identifies the portfolio of products to be developed by the organisation. The planning process considers product development opportunities from many sources, including marketing, R&D, customers, current product teams and competitor analysis. Usually large firms will have more opportunities than resources to fund and the key question facing product planners is which projects to fund.

The product plan is regularly updated to reflect the changing competitive environment. Indeed, a surprise new product launch by a competitor frequently results in a major change to a firm's product plan. This was the case for Hoover when it responded quickly to Dyson's bagless vacuum cleaner. Product planning decisions generally involve senior management of the firm and form part of the ongoing strategy process. When considering product development opportunities they are usually classified as four types:

- *New product platforms*. This type of project involves a major development effort to create a new family of products based on a new, common platform. From an R&D perspective this would be seen as developing a new core technology. The new platform would be used to help existing products compete. An example of this would be Kodak's move into digital photography.
- *Derivatives of existing platforms*. Projects of this type develop an existing platform usually to ensure existing products are updated. This will either provide them with an advantage over the competition or make sure they can compete with the competition. Honda have been extremely successful in utilising their product platform of small petrol engines and applying this technology to a wide variety of market applications from lawn mowers to motorcycles and from outboard motors for boats to chainsaws.
- *Incremental improvements to existing products*. These projects may only involve adding or modifying features of existing products to keep the product line current and competitive. Frequently this may be improving the packaging or reducing the manufacturing cost of producing the product or changing the design slightly. While such changes may seem small they can often have significant impact on sales. The change from see-through cellophane to foil packaging by Walker's made a huge impact on sales. *See also* Nestlé Polos in Illustration 11.1.
- *Fundamentally new products (discontinuous products)*. These projects involve radically different product or production technologies and may help to take the firm into new and unfamiliar markets. Such projects are inherently more risky but may help to secure the long-term future of the firm. This was the case for W.L. Gore & Associates following the development of its breathable fabric 'Gore-Tex'. This new technology has enabled the firm to enter new fabric-based markets. Previously its portfolio of products covered the areas of medical, electronic and industrial.

Illustration 11.2

Apps crucial in Nokia's fight for customers

Stephen Elop, who is due to take over as chief executive of Nokia next week, bounded on to the stage at the end of the Finnish handset maker's annual trade show in London to award one developer $1m for his winning mobile phone application.

'Fundamentally at Nokia we are capable of building great devices and getting them out there. But without you guys we can't create vibrancy within the ecosystem', Mr Elop told an audience gathered to see the winners of Nokia's apps developers awards. 'It isn't just that I love developers, it's that you guys bring the system to life.' Mr Elop's words highlight the key challenge he faces – how to drive demand for the company's products and keep customers.

Source: Alamy Images/Pixellover RM9

Nokia is still the world's largest handset maker by volumes, but it has seen its market share eroded at the bottom end by cheap Asian devices and at the top by Apple's iPhone and smartphones that operate on Google's open source Android platform.

For Apple having an attractive apps library has been critical to the rapid takeup of its iPhones and has allowed it to grab the lead in the smartphones market. Apple, which launched the iPhone in 2007, now boasts 225,000 apps in its store.

'If you have spent a few hundred quid on apps for one handset, you are likely to be captive to that product', says Fred Huet, managing director at Greenwich Consulting.

Google's Android platform, which is expected to be available on more handsets than Apple's very soon, is now becoming increasingly attractive to developers too. It has about 80,000 apps. Yet Nokia's Ovi store has just 13,000 apps.

Kooaba, a Swiss group that has developed a digital recognition app, says that a key issue for developers has been the expense of creating apps for each of the different operating systems.

Part of Nokia's problem has been that until now it has had too many devices operating on slightly different platforms that require developers to write slightly different code. In addition, the revamped Symbian platform that operates its smartphones is only now beginning to match rivals in terms of functionality and is less popular with consumers.

Developers have also been better able to monetise their apps for the iPhone and Android. Adam Leach, principal analyst at Ovum, says that Apple has benefited from having a single platform but also a product that excited app developers just as much as consumers. He says that part of what Nokia needs to do is 'to inspire developers to write apps for them'.

Nokia claims the quality of its apps is more important than quantity, but recent moves by the group suggest otherwise. This week the company announced plans to make it 'easier and more lucrative' for developers to build apps for its phones. These include improving its QT development kit so that there are far fewer codes required to develop apps for Nokia's Symbian smartphones. 'Apple only has the iPhone. Nokia has lots of devices and lots of customers but until now it has been more difficult to develop apps . . . Technology like QT is very interesting

→

because it will allow convergence of development across Nokia's phones', says Anthony Saunier, a development engineer for Newscape, creator of a 3D tourist map app.

But perhaps the most significant advance is that Nokia has signed a series of deals that will allow customers to buy apps through their phone operator's billing. Apple, Google and Nokia all currently pay developers 70 per cent of any revenues from app sales bought in their stores and take a 30 per cent cut themselves. If a Nokia consumer uses operator billing the split is 60/40, with the additional 10 per cent going to operators.

George Linardos, vice-president products/media at Nokia, says that there has to be a business case for apps to succeed. 'Only a small percentage make any revenue.' Whether that will be enough to help Nokia attract developers remains to be seen, but analysts say the apps battle will be crucial for handset makers as they fight for customers.

Source: Telecoms (2010) FT.com, 16 September. Reprinted with permission.

Pause for thought 

How do product platforms differ from umbrella brands such as Nestlé or Kellogg's?

Product strategy

New product strategy is part of a web of strategies. It is linked to, and its objectives are derived from, marketing strategy, technology strategy and the overall corporate strategy. These other strategies provide the role, the context, the impetus and the definition of the scope of new product strategy.

Competitive strategy

New products are not needed just because they are new products. They are required because they serve a customer need and an organisation need. The organisation need will be articulated in the organisation's strategy and there might be comments about striving to lead in the technology, or to be the key innovator, in its mission statement. However, much new product development is not concerned with new-to-the-world innovations, and this is partly because many companies are followers and not leaders in their technology. NPD for a follower can be very different from NPD for a leader. New products perform different roles at different times for different companies. They serve a variety of purposes depending upon what is seen to be the strategic imperative.

Competitive strategy may drive new product planning on a short-term or long-term basis. In the shorter term a defensive posture may suggest that product variants are needed to shore up a declining market share, which is perhaps attributed to a competitor's aggressive new product activities. A reactive strategy could entail filling out product lines with different product sizes or added features that may be intended to deter a new entrant to the market, by not leaving unattended small market segments to be used as an entry point by the new competitor. Such minor product changes could also be employed to secure distributors' loyalty, because they are then able to carry a full range of the product and so be less inclined to stock rival offerings. Imitative products may be brought out, copying competitors, for similar reasons. In these kinds of situations where the new product is a minor modification, however new the advertising proclaims it to be, it is unlikely that the full, classic NPD process would be engaged. There may be little or no research, and market testing may be restricted to determining acceptable price levels or to choosing between alternative advertising messages.

In the longer run competitive strategy may seek a more profound contribution from new products. A strategy may look for new product categories to be developed, within the same or a related technology, or in a new technology area. These new products may appeal to the organisation's traditional customer base or seek new customer segments. This more radical product development would more likely be subject to thorough marketing and technical research, development and testing.

New products can also perform a learning function for the organisation. The development of a pioneering new product platform may at first be tentative, and several alternative concepts for new platforms may be investigated simultaneously. Uncertainties surround such ventures because the new platform may require the development of costly new competencies, while simultaneously the nature and the scale of the market opportunity are illusory. The firm may need to develop both new knowledge and new skills in technical, operations and marketing areas. The adequacy of the search for, and the acquisition of, these new skills and knowledge will mark out the leaders.

Product portfolios

Another set of strategic considerations concerns the overall portfolio of products. Analysing the organisation's total collection of products by viewing it as a portfolio, as in an investment portfolio, may give fresh insights. This approach was initiated by the share–growth matrix, or Boston Matrix, which used market share and market growth as dimensions against which to plot the positions of products. A typology was derived with high and low values for each of the two dimensions so that the four quadrants could be contrasted. For example, products classified as high share/high growth could be contrasted with those deemed to be low share/low growth. Prospects could also be investigated by comparing where products are positioned presently, where they might be in the future with no change in strategy, and compared with some desired positions. Analyses of this kind might suggest some strategic issues. A clustering of the portfolio in one quadrant might be viewed as unbalanced, and an absence of any products in the two high-growth quadrants might be thought unhealthy.

Such a simple depiction has attracted controversy and alternative models have been suggested using multi-factor dimensions that are composites of variables, such as business strength and market attractiveness. Most of the derivations still employ two dimensions because they can be displayed with ease, but more complex, and some say more realistic, models are multi-dimensional. All these models share a similar aim: to give the strategist an overview that could reveal current or potential problems or opportunities in the product strategy.

This portfolio approach might also be applied to the product families and the platforms upon which they are built, although the selection of appropriate variables to describe the space can be a problem. Thought might be given to the extent to which a wide range of words might be usefully employed to indicate the dimensions, such as: robust, innovative, sophisticated, flexible, generic, evolving, traditional. For example, using relative sophistication (ranging from very sophisticated to unsophisticated) and flexibility (from very flexible to very inflexible) as descriptors of two dimensions might show the majority of product platforms to be unsophisticated and inflexible, with possibly one isolated platform that is sophisticated and flexible. Without qualification that probably means little and it leads to no great revelation. Being unsophisticated is not necessarily a bad thing; it may be just what the customer needs. Regarding the other dimension, a very flexible product platform is not necessarily a good thing; it may result in too many compromises that lead to products that are not specialised enough for customer applications. Several such 'mapping' exercises might be tried using different descriptors. A supplementary analysis might trace connections between platforms, any spin-off from them and in addition bring in a time dimension.

Nothing conclusive can be expected from these analyses: they are probing and investigative. The process of taking this broader view of the portfolio draws attention to issues that, with deeper analysis, could be significant. It is this identification of issues that can be critical and can be creative. It can flout any fixation with norms and conventions, which can flourish readily within organisations, and it can underline the point that approaches to product strategy development must be original if they are to lead to distinctive new market offerings.

The competitive environment

The external environment constrains what can be done, for example within the bounds of current understanding of a technology. Sometimes the external environment dictates what must be done, for example following the introduction of a new piece of legislation protecting an aspect of the natural environment. It can present possibilities and opportunities, such as a breakthrough in an enabling technology or the new affluence of consumers that allows them to be prepared to pay more for products in a particular category. The external circumstances can also pose threats and problems, as when a competitor introduces a significant product advance, or when another rival closes access to materials or to distributors, through its acquisition of companies in those activities.

Close analysis of the present situation in the market is fundamental, along with speculations about how it might progress and because of the potential importance of external events and conditions some type of environmental monitoring, in a strategic sense, has become a key exercise in strategy search. Assessments of the present situation can be extended to conjectures about future environments, and in some industries, such as aerospace or pharmaceuticals, this may require a very long-term view. A range of alternative future scenarios may be built around these conjectures, indicating guesses about what the organisation sees to be the aspects of its environment carrying the most stress. These speculations might deal with some of the following issues.

1 Estimates would be needed about the way the technology will change, and this could be more or less rigorous. It could involve some brainstorming within the organisation and it could seek various forms of external advice from government agencies, research centres, consultants and universities.
2 Estimates might also be made about how the industry competitive structure may alter. Are the same competitors likely to be contending in the market in the future? Are there any indications that any are preparing some kind of strategic shift? Will any withdraw or reduce their activities within the industry? Will there be changes in how companies compete and the positioning they seek in the market? Will there be any new entrants from other industries, or from other countries? Unexpected arrivals in the industry, especially if they are well funded, well managed and they come with a significant innovation, can be particularly troublesome. That was the case when Mars entered the ice cream business and quickly secured a significant market share.
3 Another area of concern could be how any regulatory framework may evolve and this could include the extent to which it would limit activities in the future or open new possibilities.
4 Customer needs may be a further area in which to speculate. Will they become more demanding and require better materials and better performance in the products they use? Will they perceive some emerging technology as a substitute? Will they have new kinds of needs and will there be new kinds of customers?

Taking various combinations of these factors could yield a series of scenarios, and the investigation of the implications for the organisation of each of them could indicate important issues requiring attention. Such future scenarios may throw up attractive or unattractive situations and the organisation may then attempt to do what it can to prepare itself, and to do what it can to increase the likelihood of the former while inhibiting the latter. This will help to shape ideas about the potential role for new products and the scope of the problems and opportunities that they are intended to address.

Differentiation and positioning

Product strategy will express how the organisation seeks to differentiate itself, and distance itself, from its competitors and it will be the bedrock of its market positioning. It is axiomatic that for new products to be successful in the market they need to be perceived to be beneficial by prospective buyers. The benefit needs to stand out, to be distinctive and attractive. This distinction needs to be relevant to buyers, and it needs to be seen to be relevant by them. It is pointless being distinctive in a way that consumers believe to be irrelevant or incomprehensible. This point is illustrated in the case study at the end of this chapter.

Differentiation

Broadly, the **product differentiation** sought by competitors could be based upon cost, with a value-for-money proposition, or it could be based upon superior quality, which might encompass better materials, better performance, new features, uncommon availability or better service. A useful perspective on product differentiation is provided by Levitt's idea of product augmentation (Levitt, 1986). He suggests that there are four levels on which products can be considered:

1 *The core product* comprises the essential basics needed to compete in a product market; a car needs wheels, transmission, engine and a rudimentary chassis.
2 *The expected product* adds in what customers have become accustomed to as normal in the product market; for a car this would be a reasonably comfortable interior and a range of accessories.
3 *The augmented product* offers features, services or benefits that go beyond normal expectations.
4 *The potential product* would include all the features and services that could be envisaged as beneficial to customers.

An interesting implication of this categorisation is that it can demonstrate that the position is dynamic because customer expectations change. In the example of the car, where would air conditioning be placed in these categories? Until recently it would have been an augmentation for mass-market vehicles, but it has now become a standard expectation in new cars. Competition drives up consumer expectations. One rival introduces something new and, if it meets customer acceptance, other rivals follow. In consequence augmentations become expectations, and this ratchet effect means there is no equilibrium until the full potential has been realised. Even then changes to the technology, or to another technology, might release an entirely new kind of potential, so that the process continues.

Another implication is that as firms migrate upwards in this process they leave market opportunities for others to exploit. There may be niche markets left for 'unbundled' products or services making low-cost, basic offers with no frills. Airlines are an example.

The choice of differentiation strategy is pivotal. It reaches back to core capabilities and it reaches forward to positioning strategy. The differentiation will not be effective unless it is rooted firmly in the organisation's capabilities, or in the capabilities of the network delivering the new product. Similarly, the positioning of the product in the market needs to be built upon, and needs to be consistent with, the differentiation strategy (*see* Figure 11.2).

Product positioning

Product positioning refers to the perceptions customers have about the product. It is a relative term that describes customer perceptions of the product's position in the market relative to rival products. It is founded upon understanding how customers discriminate between alternative products and it considers the factors customers use in making judgements or choices between products in the market being investigated. These are referred to as the customer's evaluative criteria and they may be the product's physical attributes, but they can include customer assessments about whom the product is meant for, when, where and how it is used and aspects of the brand's 'personality' (e.g. innovative, functional, old-fashioned, exclusive, frivolous, fun).

Positioning studies begin with determining a relevant set of products. The criterion for inclusion is that they must be perceived by customers to be choice alternatives. Then a list of determinant attributes is generated; that is a list of attributes

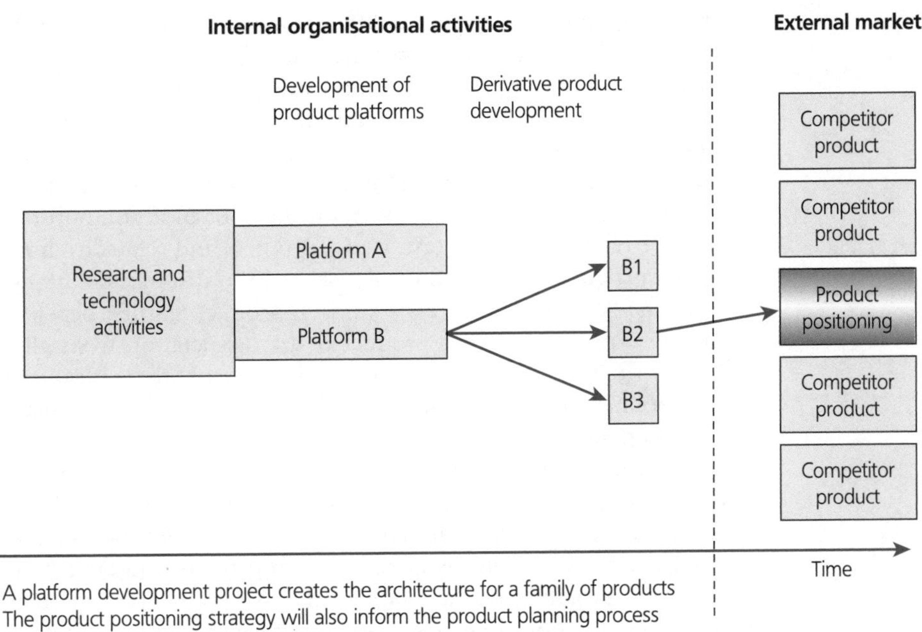

Figure 11.2 Platform development creates the architecture for a family of products

that are salient or the most important to customers in discriminating between the alternatives. With this framework customers' perceptions and preferences are then collected. This could be by survey using a structured questionnaire. Respondents would be asked to scale their feelings about each product on each attribute. They could also be asked their preferred level for each attribute. The output can be portrayed in a diagram (sometimes called a brand map or a perceptual map) showing the locations of each product against the attributes (the dimensions) and relative to the preferred level (the ideal point). This is most readily understood if the analysis is restricted to two dimensions. For example, for a food product the dimensions might be nourishment and calory count and respondents could rate all the brands they know in the category from high to low on these. Some brands may be seen to be highly nourishing with a high calory count and some not so nourishing with a low calory count. Illustrations can be found in Moore and Pessemier (1993) and in Mohr *et al.* (2010).

Such a study would show the proximity of, or the distance between, the perceived positions of the products considered. This might show the positions to be crowded in one area, or well spaced. If an ideal point, that is the customers' preferred position, is introduced then the relative distance of each product from this ideal can be measured. If these relative distances accord reasonably with the relative market shares of the products then it could be assumed that the dimensions chosen are a fair representation of the way customers choose in this market. Generally it would be expected that the higher market shares would be won by products nearer to the ideal point.

Customers may be far from unanimous about these perceptions and preferences. If the observations were widely scattered then further research would be needed to understand how customers make their evaluations, and perhaps other dimensions might be tried. If there were several clusters of preferences, each in a different part of the map, this might indicate different market segments. In the food example above, there could be one group preferring a very nourishing product with a low calory count, and another group wanting something nourishing with a high calory count. Mapping product positions against these two ideal points might then reveal one segment to be well served with many products, but an opening for a new product near the other ideal point where there may be no major existing brands.

Positioning strategy depends upon the choice of an appropriate base. This base must be relevant and important to customers and related to how they make choices in that product field. It should also attempt to distance the brand from the positions of rivals. Wind (1982) offers six bases: product feature, benefits, use occasion, user category, against another product or by dissociation from all the other products. Crawford (1997) adds parentage (. . . because of where it comes from), manufacture (. . . because of how it is made) and endorsement (. . . because people you respect say it is good).

Selecting an appropriate positioning can make the difference between success and failure. It determines what the organisation tells the market about the product, whom it tells and how it tells it. Motorcycle producers take various positions. Piaggio's Vespa scooter is aimed at young riders and latterly at women. Suzuki is also now targeting women as a distinctive segment. Some of the most expensive machines are now aimed at older men with a revived interest in motorcycling and higher discretionary income. For most products there may be a host of features, benefits and applications; few, if any, products have a single feature, a singular benefit and one narrow application. Choosing from among the possibilities can lead to creative and unique solutions and consequentially to a highly differentiated strategy. For example, Procter & Gamble (P&G) position two identical products, in terms of specification, very differently (*see* Table 11.1). 'Sure' is targeted in the US at young males between 18 and 25, while 'Secret' is targeted at young females between 12 and 24. The brands clearly have different packaging and marketing communications to reflect their target market and positioning. This simple example illustrates the significance of positioning in modern marketing, especially in FMCG. Positioning can also result in costly mistakes with products being positioned in strange ways that consumers neither understand nor find credible. As the market grows and matures it may become necessary to consider repositioning. The original

Table 11.1 A comparison of the product specifications of two of P&G's successful brands

	Sure®	Secret®
Price	$2.98	$2.98
Weight	1.7oz	1.7oz
Ingredients	Aluminium Zirconium Trichlorohydrex Gly Cyclomethicone Dimethicone Polyethylene Silica Propylene Carbonate	Aluminium Zirconium Trichlorohydrex Gly Cyclomethicone Dimethicone Polyethylene Silica Propylene Carbonate
Patent No.	5,069,897 5,000,356	5,069,897 5,000,356

differentiation could become less effective as competitors crowd in, or as new types of buyers with different expectations adopt the product. A repositioning exercise could focus upon some reformulation of the product, some change to the image projected, a realignment of the segments targeted or a change to the distribution channels employed.

Competing with other products

Deschamps and Nayak (1995) in their best-selling book on products and brands *Product Juggernauts: How Companies Mobilize To Generate A Stream of Winners* argued that one factor differentiates great companies from the others and that is the products they sell. In a study of leading products they argued that even in basic industries such as chemicals and minerals, suppliers always found ways of differentiating their products from those of their competitors. Deschamps and Nayak identified five distinct product strategies that firms have used in competition, these are shown in Table 11.2.

As products compete with one another they are thus compared with one another. This leads to selection criteria and buyer behaviour. The latter is a subject and a

Table 11.2 Product strategies

Product strategy	Firm	How?
Product proliferation	Honda Procter & Gamble	On entering the European motorcycle market Honda offered an enormously wide range of engine sizes. When launching their disposable nappy Proctor & Gamble offered a wide range of sizes and gender-specific products.
Value	BMW Toyota	BMW offer a high-quality product with emphasis on reliability. It is not the most expensive and emphasis is on value for money. Similarly Toyota use the same product strategy in different market segments.
Design (outward appearance)	Sony Apple	Both Sony and Apple emphasise good design in all of their products, frequently pioneering unique styles and offering elegance and easy-to-use products.
Innovation	3M Merck Philips	3M and more recently Merck and Philips have developed reputations for product innovation. This is based on a strong technology culture. This is distinct from design, in that while the product may incorporate a new outward appearance it is the use of new technology that is the focus of the strategy.
Service	American Express Tesco	Both American Express and Tesco continue to be at the forefront of service development. Historically American Express pioneered many service offerings. More recently Tesco (UK retail grocer) compete by continually offering new and improved services to their customers. Their competitors always seem to be trying to catch up.

Source: Deschamps, J.P. and Nayak, P.R. (1995) *Product Juggernauts: How Companies Mobilize To Generate A Stream of Winners*, Harvard Business School Press, Boston, MA.

Table 11.3 Product performance criteria

Product performance factors	
1 Performance in operation	10 Ease of maintenance
2 Reliability	11 Parts availability and cost
3 Sale price	12 Attractive appearance/shape
4 Efficient delivery	13 Flexibility and adaptability in use
5 Technical sophistication	14 Advertising and promotion
6 Quality of after-sales service	15 Operator comfort
7 Durability	16 Design
8 Ease of use	17 Environmental impact
9 Safety in use	

Source: Baker, M. and Hart, S. (1989) *Product Strategy and Management*, Prentice Hall, Harlow.

textbook in its own right and beyond the scope of this book. It is necessary to note, however, that most models of buyer behaviour recognise two kinds of factors – objective and subjective. Objective factors may or may not be tangible but they must be quantifiable and measurable. By contrast, subjective factors are intangible and are influenced by attitudes, beliefs, experience and associations that the decision maker holds towards the product. If we leave the subjective criteria to the behavioural sciences and turn our attention to the objective criteria it soon becomes clear that to discriminate between products a performance criteria is required. Many of us would recognise such a list of factors, for we have probably drawn up such a list when going to purchase a personal computer or a car. For the most part, however, such performance criteria do not play a large part in our buying decisions. In industrial markets the reverse is the case and such criteria are the norm. Indeed, in many instances buyers will forward their performance criteria to a list of suppliers and await a quote detailing price, warranties, delivery, etc. Table 11.3 shows typical product performance criteria commonly used by buyers in assessing a product.

Objective product characteristics enable firms to be grouped together so that the whole economy may be classified. The Standard Industrial Classification Manual was first published in the United States in 1945. SIC codes now form part of an international system, making it possible to make precise comparisons between products and services between countries.

Pause for thought 

To what extent is it possible to have several different product strategies within the same firm?

Many products may appear objectively similar, such as washing machines. This group of products are often made to a standard size (typically 600mm wide; 500mm depth and 1,000mm high). Other performance criteria such as load capacity and spin speed can all be compared; but subjective information is supplied to the customer via branding. The process of branding can take many forms and is not restricted to physical products. Moreover, successful brands are not easily copied.

For example, Dyson did not file for patents in the United States, yet through branding has been able to offer a unique product to consumers that competitors have struggled to imitate.

Managing brands

To many, especially the cynical, the word brand is associated with a collection of gimmicks and a lot of advertising to convince the public to buy one manufacturer's product rather than another. To others brands are simply products with brand names or logos. This is partly correct, but there is more to a brand than simply advertising. Even after a huge advertising expenditure a firm would have very few customers if the product in question was faulty or of poor quality. Brands are commonly described in the literature as a multiple-level pyramid, with basic physical attributes forming the base, upon which rests the tangible benefits, the emotional benefits, the brand personality characteristics, with the soul or core of the brand at its apex. Moreover, its not just the marketing function that contributes to the brand, as Illustration 11.3 shows.

A successful brand combines an effective product, distinctive identity and added values as perceived by customers. For some brands that have been managed effectively this can translate into a life of over 100 years and over 200 years in some cases. Table 11.4 illustrates just how long some of the most well known brands have been with us.

Brands and blind product tests

There has been substantial research on the subject of whether consumers are able to recognise brands that they buy frequently from intrinsic attributes alone (taste or smell). The results reveal that from cigarettes to peanut butter and from cola to beer subjects are not capable of recognising their usual brand (Riezebos, 2003). Given these findings one might ask why consumers continue to pay a premium for particular

Table 11.4 Market introduction of brands

Twining	1706	Adidas	1920
Schweppes	1798	Volvo	1926
Levis	1850	Durex	1929
Heineken	1864	Mars	1932
Agfa	1873	McDonald's	1937
Coca-Cola	1886	Playboy	1953
Philips	1891	Benetton	1965
Pepsi-Cola	1898	Nike	1972
Persil	1907	Body Shop	1976
Nivea	1911	Swatch	1982
Boeing	1916	Eternity	1988

Illustration 11.3

The role of brand in the price–quality trade-off

FT

Price seems so self-evidently to be the reason why goods and services sell that marketers must occasionally feel there is not a great deal more they can add. In sectors as diverse as airlines, call centres, vehicles, electronics, supermarkets and public sector cleaning contracts, low prices attract customers – it is as simple as that.

All companies must deliver a satisfactory quality at an attractive price. But beyond that, the aim is to generate a kind of emotional attachment to a name, a level of confidence in a proposition. According to Mike Snapes, executive chairman of Hillary's Group, the window blinds specialist, 'Repeat business is far cheaper to generate than new business, so it is a question of what you surround the product with – the product is now about the overall experience of buying. Do the fitters keep their promises, do they sort out problems quickly, is the process "low hassle"?'

A lack of repeat business can be a sign of trying to do things on the cheap.

Price attracts, but it does not necessarily retain. Raman Roy, chairman and managing director of Wipro Spectramind, India's largest call-centre outsourcing company, has repeatedly emphasised it is not solely lower costs that are spurring the Indian call-centre market. 'They will come for the lower price, but they will stay for the quality of service', he claims.

Innovation is invariably a longer-term aim. In the shorter term, many companies would far rather pull off what Interbrew achieved with Stella Artois: selling an everyday French beer to the British as a 'reassuringly expensive' premium product.

Collective assumptions are shaky enough for companies to exploit: 'Price and quality are all to do with the perspective of the consumer. There is a widespread belief that price reflects something objective, but that assumption may let us down as any number of blind tests tend to show', says Dr Sue Eccles, lecturer in marketing at Lancaster University.

Price may be the most firmly established notion in the mind of many customers when they make a decision. Quality is more ethereal – 'acceptable' quality is often good enough. But invariably consumers are willing to pay more to reduce the 'risk factors' involved in a purchase.

When buying something significant, such as a car or clothes, customers are turned away from a low price/acceptable quality product because of social risks. A premium is attached to products with a low social risk/desirability value. The decision becomes one of identity. This explains why issues of 'brand value' and even 'brand experience' play such a dominant role in corporate life.

Calls to increase pricing transparency have produced reams of new information that is easily comparable on the internet; as a result, consumers are better informed.

Yet the arena of perception, the emotional and psychological space inhabited by products, remains a critical factor in the marketing mix.

Source: S. Overell (2003) The importance of 'brand value', FT.com, 19 May. Reproduced with permission.

brands when they cannot taste the difference. Illustration 11.3 discusses the role of brand value.

Mudambi *et al.* (1997) suggest that branding is based on random utility theory, where customers form preferences based on their perception of attributes. Decisions are then made upon these preferences with customers selecting the product with highest expected value or utility. This overview of the branding system is captured in Figure 11.3, with the degree of branding affecting buyer perception and attitudes, buyer behaviour and brand financial performance, and thereby affecting branding strategy.

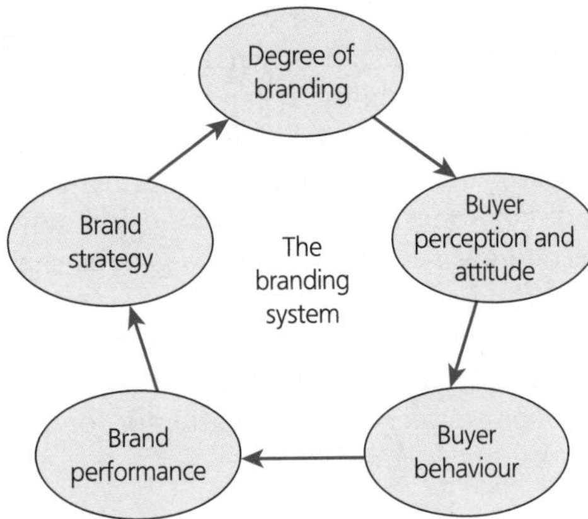

Figure 11.3 Branding system

The brand manager and the firm have to decide the extent to which they wish to invest in their brand and thereby develop it. Such considerations will involve all aspects of the marketing mix and in turn will obviously affect buyer perception. Buyers will then consider the benefits and values that are being promoted and make choices. In the case study at the end of the chapter the firm could use brand endorsement to launch the product. These choices will affect the returns to the firm and will determine investment decisions for the future of the brand. This is the subject of brand strategy, which we turn to now.

Brand strategy

Brand strategy is the spearhead of the organisation's competitive intentions. It carries the company or product name into the market and shows how it is positioning itself to compete. It involves choices between having no brand name at all, so that the product is sold as a commodity, and the attempt to develop a distinctive brand name with a distinctive set of associations and expectations. In the latter case there are further options. The product could be sold to another party for them to place their trademark or branding on it, or alternatively the complete product, or major components, could be bought in and then company-branded. There are more choices with the brand name itself. Should the company have a single brand for all its products, such as Kellogg's, or a range of apparently unconnected brands, such as Procter & Gamble? Should it establish a corporate brand as an umbrella with a series of sub-brands under the umbrella, such as Ford? Or should it have a mixed brand strategy with elements of all these approaches?

On one level such consideration might appear to be quite trivial. What's in a name? Think about chocolate confectionary. If Cadbury's decides to launch a new chocolate bar with no Cadbury's identification then would market acceptance be achieved? Will consumers trust it? Will they take the risk and make a first purchase? In any event they probably would not be given the chance to buy because it would not gain sufficient acceptance by distributors. It might achieve limited distribution but it may take a great deal of time to reach full national, let alone international, distribution.

The brand name itself is really a summary; it can stand for a great deal more. It can represent the sum of what people know about the product and its usefulness, quality and availability. It can be surrounded with associations, negative or positive, about how it can be used, where it can be used and the occasions on which it is used. It can be symbolic and loaded with imagery about the kinds of people who use the brand. For some well-known brands the few letters in their names can be triggers to wide-ranging perceptions. Focus groups can talk for hours with just the prompt of a few brand names.

It is not just in consumer markets that this power of the brand name is apparent. Inspection of any trade magazine reveals its prevalence in all kinds of markets, and component makers now also attempt to ensure that their brand is evident in advertising and packaging.

Pause for thought

The Consumers' Association produce the magazine *Which?* This conducts regular independent product performance tests on a variety of consumer products. Why is this objective evaluation of a wide range of consumer products not always referred to when consumers make purchases of a durable good?

Given the significance of brands it is surprising that so many firms make careless mistakes with regard to their brands. According to Helen Rubenstein many firms do not recognise how their departments affect the delivery of the brand. Figure 11.4 helps to show how brands interact with different parts of the organisation: it shows **internal and external brand contracts**. At the centre of this wheel is the finance department as it is guided by the chief executive, who sets financial targets and determines the business objectives. Clearly the finance department has a significant impact on the brand development, in particular the degree of investment in brand development.

Brand extensions

A **brand extension** is the use of an established brand name on a new product in the same product field or in a related field. The brand name might also be stretched to an unrelated product field. A simple brand extension would be when a new or unconventional size is brought out, so that the original brand name is given a prefix (e.g. Giant, Jumbo, Fun), or for some technical products this could be a new alphanumeric code. Operating within the same product field, but attempting to attract a new market segment, the extension might have a modified design and there could be added words to the brand name indicating whom it is intended for, such as for men or for women. Daily newspapers extended publication to Sunday and have branded sections, all carrying the original brand name in some way. In the case of an extension to a business computer package it could specify a new application type in the branding.

More radical extensions occur when the brand is stretched or carried into unrelated product fields. Some newspapers, such as the *Daily Telegraph*, started direct

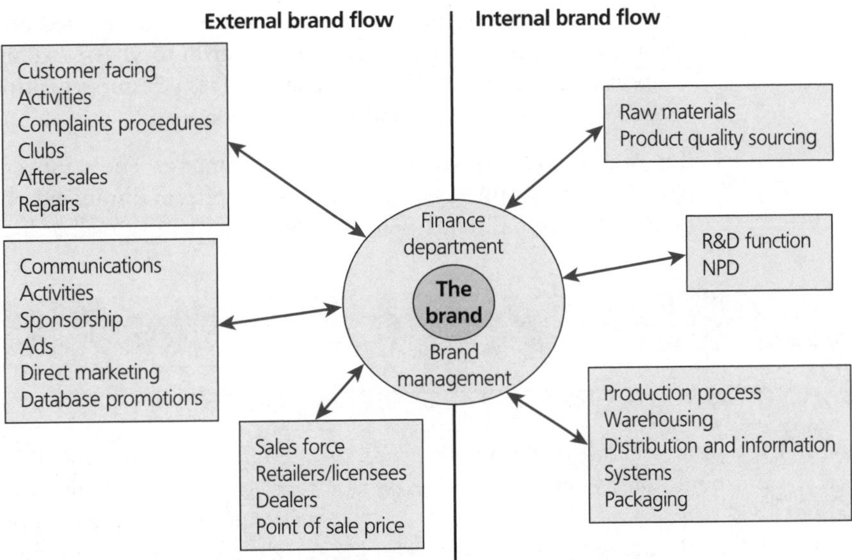

Figure 11.4 Internal and external brand contacts

Source: H. Rubenstein (1996) 'Brand first management', *Journal of Marketing Management*, Vol. 12, 269–80.

marketing operations selling their own brand of clothing. Several fashion houses, such as Boss and Calvin Klein place their brand name wide and far across a range of luxury goods. Wilkinson Sword sell razors and gardening tools under the same brand. Canon market cameras and copiers. Philips use their brand name in diverse electrical and electronic industries. And the Virgin brand name is carried on an airline, a railway, a cola, a retail chain and in insurance.

The rationale behind a brand extension strategy is to take advantage of potential carry-over effects from the original brand. If the original is both well known and well regarded then it probably has a pool of goodwill among consumers and distributors. The extension would be planned to dip into that pool. Three kinds of carry-over effects may be relevant:

1 *Expertise*. If the original had established and maintained itself, probably over a fairly long period, as the best available for that application or usage, then it is likely to have accrued a reputation for high-level competence in its field. Users may feel very comfortable and assured in making repeat buys. This may have been promoted actively and the company may have sought to have itself perceived to be the acknowledged consultant in its area. An extension that was complementary to the original, and of the same quality, would have its introduction eased owing to a halo-effect. Consumers would know the name already and would have positive expectations, and they may believe that the company that they trusted would not bring out a poor new product. The extension benefits from a trusting relationship established by the original.
2 *Prestige*. Some brands have enviable images and some consumers may believe that these images confer status on those that use them. Some brands benefit from particular kinds of associations and symbolism and they may have become, for some people, the only acceptable product to have in some situations. This does not just apply to consumer markets; organisational buyers can sometimes be just as subjective.

3 *Access*. A well-established original may have developed and held good access to the best suppliers and to the best distributors. An extension would capitalise upon these relationships and it may have a better reception to its initial launch than a new brand that had no reputation.

But brand extensions can also be problematic. The connection with the original brand can be strained and the carry-over effects diminished or eliminated. Bic was famous for its ballpoint pens. Its extension to disposable lighters worked because

Illustration 11.4

Old brands, new brands and stretching brands

The top 10 branded items bought in UK grocers have been around, on average, for 70 years, as Table 11.5 shows.

In this list of successful and relatively old products (eight out of 10 are 50 years old) it seems to suggest that being first into the market is an advantage. However, the challenge for the brand manager is how to remain appealing while maintaining your heritage. It maybe a little bit like growing up and getting older: a few grey hairs can add dignity, but if you don't take care of yourself you can easily look old and tired.

Multinational brand management firms like Procter & Gamble, Unilever and Beiersdorf know only too well that many grocery products fail, hence they recognise the value tied up in existing brands; especially those with a long heritage.

Table 11.5 Top 10 grocery products/years

Brand	Years in market
1 Coca-Cola	106
2 Warburtons	22
3 Walkers Crisps	58
4 Cadbury Dairy Milk	101
5 Hovis	116
6 Nescafé Instant	68
7 Andrex toilet tissue	64
8 Kingsmill	16
9 Robinsons	69
10 Lucozade	77

Source: Nielsen.

Marketing professionals have long recognised that strong brand names that deliver high sales and profits have the potential to create new product categories. But, the risks involved are high, and brand stretching exercises can easily backfire. Not only can they be costly in that the money spent on a parallel product could be lost if customers are not interested. If the new launch goes wrong, it can even damage the credibility of the original product.

Brand stretching refers to the use of an established brand name for products in unrelated markets. When done successfully it has several advantages. Customers will associate the quality of the original product with the new and are more likely to trust it. Launch costs are usually lower and customer awareness can build more quickly. For branding experts, the general rule of thumb is that if the brand extension contributes more value than the original core product it ultimately tends to fail. Pierre Cardin was criticised for over-extending its brand and lost credibility for exactly this reason. Holiday firm Club Med once launched a shower gel called Club Med and a unisex cologne of the same name. The idea had been pioneered by Disney at its theme parks, selling dolls of giant cartoon characters the children had just met in the flesh. The rationale – a good experience on holiday would be recreated at home. This is what marketing people refer to as 'memorialising' the good experience.

Further reading: Reuben, A. (2006) BBC News-on-line (November 24) http://news.bbc.co.uk/; International Advertising Association UK (2008) Old Brands New Tricks, New Brands Old Tricks, www.iaauk.com.

people still saw them as consistent with the original in being inexpensive, disposable, functional products. But its extension into perfumes failed. Guinness withdrew its Guinness Bitter, and once it did try an apparently contradictory idea with a new version of its original stout called Guinness Light.

In some markets brand extensions are added which contribute little and at times they can be harmful to the original. They can clutter the market and confuse the consumers. A series of lacklustre extensions, and no really new product development, can undermine the credibility of the company among distributors, customers and city analysts. For a closer look at brand extensions and brand stretching see Illustration 11.4.

Market entry

Decisions about how and when to enter the market can make a substantial difference to the new product's prospects. This is illustrated with Microsoft's entry into the video sharing market to compete with Yahoo and Google (see Illustration 16.2). Timing the entry to the market can make or break an innovation. Thoughtless positioning, with little or no distinction, can be harmful to the long-term prospects, whereas astute positioning can have a very positive effect. Entry scale, and in particular obtaining and maintaining a strong market presence with high levels of market exposure, can ease the product introduction and stimulate the market's evolution. These three factors are explored in this section.

Entry timing has received particular attention. Commonly it is assumed that early entry is desirable and there is evidence that 'pioneers' accrue 'first mover advantages'. They are able to influence customer expectations and shape how customers make evaluations of products in the new field. They can suggest to consumers the criteria they should employ in making their judgements, and products that are later entrants are then evaluated on that basis. Pioneers can set the standards, establish a distinctive quality position, take the lead in the continuing evolution of the technology, and gain valuable experience in manufacturing and distribution (Buzzell and Gale, 1987). In many mature markets the leaders are those that were the pioneering entrants. However, being too early can be as much of a disadvantage as being too late. A weak, tentative first mover, without the motivation or resources to grow the market, can spend years making losses only to be superseded by a stronger 'fast follower'. Green *et al.* (1995) caution that 'simple nostrums, such as early entry is best, can be dangerous oversimplifications'.

Those that come to the market early, but after the pioneer, can be successful. Procter & Gamble was not the pioneer in disposable napkins or in biological washing powders, but its Pampers and Ariel brands dominate these markets. Japanese competitors displaced Ampex, the pioneer in VCR technology (*see* Table 6.2 for a long list of followers who became leaders). For example:

> It was Creative Industries that launched the first Digial Audio Player (DAP) in 2000. It was a 6GB hard drive based player called the Creative NOMAD Jukebox. But Creative did not become the market leader. In October 2001, Apple unveiled the first generation iPod, a 5 GB hard drive based DAP with a 1.8″ Toshiba hard drive. The iPod was initially popular within the Macintosh community. In July 2002, Apple introduced the second generation update to the iPod. It was compatible with Windows computers. The iPod series has become the market leader in DAPs.

Illustration 11.5

Media and blog buzz for the Apple iPod Hi-Fi

As the product manager for the Apple iPod, how do I maximise the buzz and measure the impact of my new product launch?

The Solution from Biz360

We analysed blog posts and media articles to prepare for the launch and monitor its impact. In preparation we researched the key influencers in both media and blogs, the competitive landscape, and the key messages to our target buyer. During the launch were able to measure the impact that the positive buzz created in both media and blogs and the number of target consumers we reached and how effective we were at getting our key messages across.

Did the launch impact the market?
Yes (20× increase MediaSignal)

How many consumers did we reach?
187 million

Did the launch impact key media influencers?
1.5 billion impressions in the top media segment

Did we affect both a national and local audience? How large was that impact?
922 million national media impressions; 94 million in local metros

Did we reach influential Apple bloggers?
231 mentions from Top-60 Blogs

Source: www.biz360.com (2006).

Positioning decisions can be influential and the digital camera industry illustrates this point. Eastman Kodak was the first firm to produce a digital camera for consumers in 1994. It offered 24-bit colour and the ability to connect to a desktop computer via a simple serial cable to download images directly. Today, the market is crowded by firms such as Fuji, Cannon, Olympus, Hewlett-Packard, Nikon and Minolta. Sony is the market leader in terms of market share, but competition is fierce due to the mobile phone. Demand for digital cameras, which record images on memory chips instead of film, continues to grow as consumers become more comfortable with capturing, storing and printing their images. Eastman Kodak pioneered this market but has not dominated it. Indeed, competitors reacted so swiftly that there was little to distinguish the products in the marketplace.

Scale of entry affects how the product performs and how the market evolves. High levels of effort and resource commitment can stimulate market evolution and a critical factor in this is market exposure. Getting prospective customers talking and thinking about the product is vital. This may mean the establishment of a strong 'market presence' through press articles, blogs, advertising, participation at exhibitions and a highly visible presence in distribution channels. Illustration 11.5 shows how an advertising agency created buzz for the launch of the Apple iPod Hi-Fi.

Launch and continuing improvement

From a business perspective the innovation is not a success until it has established and fixed its place in the market. That depends upon how it is launched, its reception by customers and the continuing attention given to its improvement. The earlier discussion of market entry showed some key factors relevant to the launch strategy, but the act of putting the product on to the market is not an end: it is the beginning of a new phase. Close and constant monitoring of the reactions of customers, distributors and competitors is required to inform the proceeding strategy.

Having the product on the market allows the validation or the rejection of important estimates or assumptions about customer attitudes and behaviour that would have been made during development. It could also reveal unanticipated problems or opportunities. What do customers now understand about the product and has comprehension of its benefits spread in the predicted way? Are there still difficulties? Are they using the product in the ways envisaged? Have customers found problems in using the product that had not come to light before? Do they use it as much as expected and as frequently as expected? Are any potential customers holding back because they see risk in adopting the product, perhaps delaying their acceptance in anticipation of further developments in the technology? Are there enough of those for it to be a problem? Do customers perceive the benefits that were promised, and are these as important to them as hoped originally? Are the benefits now seen as interesting but irrelevant? And are there any problems with the product itself that customers have revealed? Unravelling these questions and dealing effectively with their implications will condition how the prospects for the product evolve.

Many assumptions will also have been built into the operations and marketing plans. Do they stand up? Was the desired positioning achieved, and was that the right positioning decision? Is it now too narrowly defined on a relatively unimportant dimension? Was it conveyed appropriately to distributors and customers? Were the pricing and distribution plans appropriate? Are customer problems being handled efficiently and is the right level of customer service in place? On all these issues the organisation should be learning and responding, tracking and improving.

Thought about how the product and the market will evolve from the launch might give attention to three areas:

1 *Product platform evolution and brand extensions.* What is the next generation of the product? Can the basic product platform be enhanced and should this lead to brand extensions?
2 *Market evolution.* How rapidly will the innovation be diffused? Will there be a lengthy introductory period before any rapid growth? Will new market segments become apparent or can they be created? How should the geographic scope be widened?
3 *Competitive evolution.* How soon will competitors arrive? How predictable is their entry? What distinction, if any, will they bring? What kind of positioning and entry scale are they considering? What entry barriers are in place to deter rivals?

Inauguration is not enough. To be effective the innovation must be well founded in the market and receive customer acceptance, if not their acclaim, and plans need to be made to secure, deepen and widen its market position from the initial launch.

Withdrawing products

Pruning the product range can be an important part of managing the portfolio. Chronic poor sales performance would be a first indicator that consideration should be given to withdrawing products. Prior to that decision careful assessments would be needed of the reasons for the poor performance, of the possible future trends and of the costs and benefits of continuing or withdrawing. In Toyota's case with several of its brands it seems the firm had few options other than to organise a complete product recall, as Illustration 11.6 shows.

Investigations could first focus on how well the organisation had managed its efforts. It may have lost market share, in which case a series of questions could be

Illustration 11.6

How to avoid making a drama out of a crisis

FT

The brand careering off the road is **Toyota**'s. Chilling recordings of the phone calls made by distressed drivers to the emergency services – sometimes from people behind the wheel of an out-of-control car – have been repeated on TV programmes for months now. Proof, if any were needed, that there is such a thing as bad publicity.

The Japanese carmaker has been strongly criticised for its response to this crisis, and the embarrassing recall of several Toyota models. 'Speed of response, transparency of message and visibility are the three key principles to successful crisis management', says Basil Towers, founding partner of Hesleden, a reputation management consultancy. 'Toyota arguably failed on all three.'

For a brand built on the key elements of quality and reliability, the events of the past few months have been disastrous. Worse, the at times slow and almost grudging response to that criticism the company displayed – at least initially – seems to have done it even more harm. US politicians leapt on to the opportunity to kick a foreign business when it was down.

So if Toyota offers us a case study in how not to react to a crisis and protect your brand, which examples are more helpful? The gold standard in brand protection remains the 1982 case of Johnson & Johnson's Tylenol painkiller.

For once the scare stories put out by the media had some substance to them. Seven people living in the Chicago area died after taking Tylenol, the top-selling painkiller in the US, which had been contaminated with cyanide.

Johnson & Johnson did not go into denial. Senior managers did not get into a non-communicative huddle and hope the problem would go away. Instead, the company quickly took the difficult and financially painful decision to recall more than 30 million bottles of the drug. It kept up a regular flow of information – the 'transparency and visibility' recommended by Hesleden above – and introduced new safety measures, including improved tamper-proof packages.

Source: Corbis/John Lamm/Transtock

When the new batches of safe Tylenol started reappearing on the pharmacy shelves, the company opted to take another financial hit by offering discount coupons. But the public was convinced. The Tylenol brand was intact, regaining 70 per cent of its market share within five months. It is still the number one brand today.

Mattel, the US toymaker, had to own up to severe problems with its Chinese manufacturers in the summer of 2007. It went into hyper-communication mode. After a product recall announcement a team of 16 press officers contacted dozens of US media outlets. A conference call with senior executives was arranged.

Robert Eckert, Mattel's chief executive, did 14 TV interviews in one day, as well as conducting many phone calls with reporters. He got the tone of contrition and candour just right, apologising for his company's recall of faulty toys.

'I'm disappointed, I'm upset, but I can assure your viewers that we are doing everything we can about the situation', Mr Eckert said on CNN. 'Every production batch of toys is being tested, and we'll continue to enforce the highest quality standards in the industry.' In one week, Mattel dealt with more than 300 media requests in the US alone. Their faith in the company intact, shoppers stuck with the brand.

PepsiCo was also praised for its open and robust reaction to a crisis in 1993. It was claimed that syringes had been found in cans of diet Pepsi. When an arrest was made after a police investigation, the company was happy to publicise it. It also produced a video made at one of its factories showing how such tampering was impossible.

The so-called syringe problem was in fact a hoax, carried out clumsily by various individuals around the country. There was nothing wrong with the company's production procedures, as they were able to show. Pepsi reacted fast partly because it already had a plan of action in place ready to deal with a case of product tampering.

Clearly it is possible to take action quickly and explain to a worried public that a perceived problem is being dealt with. But of course, wise managers try to make sure that, as far as possible, they avoid sudden, unexpected crises in the first place. This, too, is part of the business of protecting the brand and the corporate reputation.

Hesleden's Mr Towers raises a few questions about the Toyota debacle which, had they been answered sooner, might have prevented a lot of the subsequent damage:

'Did/does Toyota engage in systematic scenario planning and simulation to stress test or benchmark its responses to crises?', he asks.

'Did/does its business leaders recognise the importance of the broadest level of stakeholder engagement and transparency? To what extent is Toyota reviewing its approach to the crisis and the lessons it can learn?'

Unexpected disasters can hit any company at any time. But as some have shown, the brand can still be protected and repaired. You do not have to make a drama out of a crisis.

Source: Stern, S. (2010) How to avoid making a drama out of a crisis, FT.com, 28 April.

posed. Is manufacturing cost out of line with others in the industry? Has there been any decline in quality relative to rivals? Has the product kept up with any evolution in the technology? Have marketing efforts tailed off? Fixing any problems that emerge from these analyses might give the product a new lease of life, and this may be associated with a repositioning exercise. However, if nothing significant is signalled then other possibilities would need to be examined.

If market share was constant but sales were none the less in chronic decline, then this could indicate that the industry, or the particular product form, was past maturity and entering decline. Predictions about the future industry trend might confirm a pessimistic outlook and the firm would have to decide if it should withdraw quickly, more gradually or try to maintain a position in what may be a much smaller industry in the future.

Exit costs would feature strongly. There may be a complex manufacturing economy within the company with shared processes involving many products. The arbitrary removal of one may throw into jeopardy the economics of the remainder, and so it could be that the product was continued so long as it made some contribution to overheads. The firm may also become an involuntary survivor in the industry because contractual obligations tie it in. These contracts may be with suppliers, customers, distributors or other partners in the network. An inflexible manufacturing plant could also tie it. Reputation could be another issue. The company may not wish to undermine the confidence placed in it by customers or distributors. For example, customers may have high switching costs if they had to buy alternative products and may become resentful if they dropped the product. If the product is part of a wide portfolio then the whole range might suffer if the organisation's reputation were to be damaged.

Alternatively the firm may decide to make an active commitment to stay in the declining industry in anticipation of increasing market share.

Managing mature products

As growth slows and the level of competition intensifies, profit margins will come under pressure. Product and brand managers will need to make decisions on the medium- and long-term futures of the brand. **Mature products** usually make up the majority of a firm's source of cash-generative lines (hence the term cash cow in portfolio planning). Profit margins may decline due to increasing numbers of competitive products, cost economies used up, decline in product distinctiveness, etc. Frequently, with the loss of profit margins, industries tend to stabilise with a set of entrenched competitors. Indeed, the low margins act as a barrier to entry and those firms remaining in an industry can generate sustained profits over a long period in the maturity and decline stages of a product's life cycle. For example, the 35mm film processing industry is declining rapidly with the introduction of digital photography. Soon there will probably be a few suppliers only remaining in this once enormous market. Agfa, Fuji and Kodak will probably establish positions in this declining market. Indeed, within the maturity and decline stages of a product's life cycle Schofield and Arnold (1988) distinguish four phases to the mature phase of the traditional product life cycle:

- late growth;
- early maturity;
- mid-maturity; and
- late maturity.

They argue that firms need to be able to recognise the early signs of late growth usually characterised by aggressive price cutting. This continues into the early stages of maturity when the market becomes saturated with little or no opportunity for growth. At this stage firms are forced into taking tactical decisions regarding additional services and promotions. It is also important for firms to be vigilant for changes that take place in the market concerning segments: some segments may decline rapidly while others may still be growing. As the market moves towards mid- and late maturity customers are seen as more discerning and less loyal. Schofield and Arnold argue that several strategies are available to firms managing mature businesses and there are several positive factors:

- price is not important to everyone and probably not to the majority;
- industries that evolve gradually offer time and space for careful strategy selection;
- the market is stable;
- niches, once secured, require fewer resources to defend them; and
- sustainable real or perceived advantage in cost or performance will attract new business.

In a study of mature brands Beverland *et al.* (2010) found that product innovation is vital to ongoing brand equity and has been responsible for revitalising many brands, including Apple, Dunlop Volley, Mini and Gucci.

Case study

Developing a new product for the teeth whitening market

Nestled alongside the Olympic Park in the heart of Munich's industrial district, to the north of the city, sits Munich Gases: a German industrial gas company with a long history of supplying gases and liquids to firms across Europe. Its product range is dominated by liquid oxygen which it supplies to health care markets and carbon dioxide which it supplies to the drinks and beverages industry. With a market capitalisation of €10 billion Munich Gases is one of the industry leaders. It also has a proud history of successful R&D which has helped to maintain its dominant position over the past 80 years. This case study tells the story of how Munich Gases uncovered a multi-billion dollar market opportunity for whitening teeth, and explored how best to exploit it.

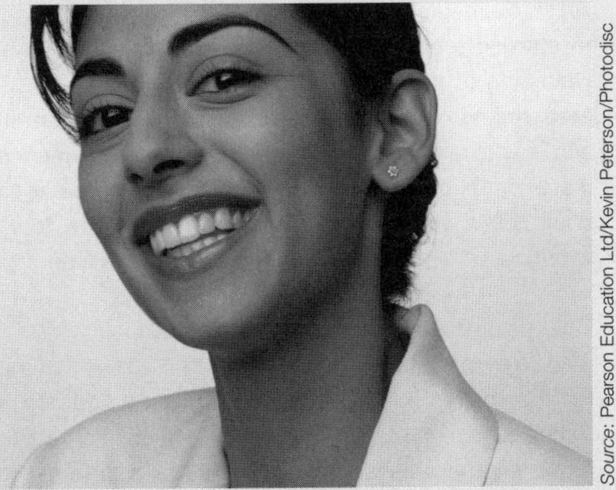
Source: Pearson Education Ltd/Kevin Peterson/Photodisc

A portfolio of R&D projects

Munich Gases employs almost 48,000 employees working in more than 100 countries worldwide. In the 2009 financial year it achieved sales of €11.211 billion. The strategy of the Group is geared towards 'sustainable earnings-based growth and focuses on the expansion of its international business with new forward-looking products and services'. Munich Gases offer a wide range of compressed and liquefied gases as well as chemicals and it is therefore an important and reliable partner for a huge variety of industries. Its products are used, for example, in the energy sector, in steel production, chemical processing, environmental protection and welding, as well as in food processing, glass production and electronics. It is also investing in the expansion of its fast-growing health care business, i.e. medical gases, and it is a leading global player in the development of environmentally friendly hydrogen technology. It has an annual R&D budget of €100 million. Recently it faced the decision of whether to invest 10 per cent of this budget in a single project – teeth whitening.

Amongst over 100 R&D projects running within Munich Gases' R&D department was one that was exploring applications for the use of plasma as a cleaning agent. Plasma is the fourth matter. Matter can be either solid, liquid, a gas or a fourth type, plasma, which is actually the most common in the universe. Plasma is an ionized gas capable of conducting electricity and absorbing energy from an electrical supply. Man-made plasma is generally created in a low-pressure environment. (Lightning and the Aurora Borealis are naturally occurring examples of plasma.) When a gas absorbs electrical energy, its temperature increases causing the ions to vibrate faster and 'scrub' a surface. Plasma has been used for many years to clean surfaces, for example, in semiconductor processing, plasma cleaning is commonly used to prepare a wafer surface prior to wire bonding. Removing contamination (flux) strengthens the bond adhesion, which helps extend device reliability and longevity. Plasma, therefore, is an effective way to clean without using hazardous solvents. For the past year a research team at Munich Gases has been exploring the viability of incorporating plasma for cleaning and whitening teeth.

Artificial plasmas can be created when energy is added to a gas, perhaps using an electrical field or a laser. The resulting matter can behave differently when it comes into contact with other particles. While many artificially created plasmas are extremely hot – for example, the flame on an arc welder – advances in recent years have allowed the creation of much cooler plasmas. This, in turn, has opened the possibility of using them on the human body, where they could offer a very precise way of targeting tiny areas.

→

In this case, the properties of the plasma are harmful to bacteria, without affecting the surrounding tissue.

This project at Munich Gases was quickly established following the uncovering of a patent submitted by the University of Southern California (USC) in 2009 which claimed scientists at the USC had used plasma to sterilise teeth and one of the side-effects was a whitening of the teeth. When Munich Gases uncovered and read it they were so intrigued by the patent and its possibilities that they quickly established a team of researchers to explore whether the idea could be a viable business opportunity. The team was given 12 months and a budget of €1 million.

The plasma teeth cleaning project

Twelve months had now passed and it was now time for the research project to report its findings to a panel of senior management. The panel wanted to know whether this technology would be of interest to Munich Gases. The project had caused much discussion amongst the R&D personnel – some believing that the company was mad to spend €1 million on a crazy idea, and others simply curious as to whether plasma could indeed work.

The project leader Thomas Wolfgang presented the findings. He explained that when thinking of plasma, the first thing that comes to mind is temperature. Most people know, and all scientists should know, that high temperatures are required to turn gas into this state. He finished his introduction by suggesting that the findings after 12 months confirmed that it is possible to use plasma to clean teeth. The panel were fascinated, they all smiled full of excitement and anticipation. Wolfgang began to explain some basic principles about how plasma cleaning uses ion excitation as a cleaning process. He explained that when a gas absorbs electrical energy, its temperature increases causing the ions to vibrate faster. In an inert gas, such as argon, the excited ions can bombard a surface ('sandblast') and remove a small amount of material. In the case of an active gas, such as oxygen, ion bombardment as well as chemical reactions occur. As a result, organic compounds and residues volatilise and are removed.

Wolfgang went on to explain that his team had recently created a new plasma laboratory instrument, which uses the matter to destroy bacterial bio-films on teeth, the main cause of them turning yellow. The micro-organisms also contribute to bad breath. He explained that it may be described as a tiny, plasma blowtorch that breaks apart the sticky bonds that holds plaque to a tooth. However, unlike the hot plasma at the centre of stars and lightning bolts, this plasma torch is no warmer than room temperature. At present, his research team had only used the torch to sterilise a tooth during a root canal, but according to Wolfgang they already have some more exciting uses in mind. He showed the board a short film of some of the experiments. The laboratory instrument resembled a tiny purple blowtorch, with a pencil-sized jet of plasma coming out of it. Remarkably it had the ability to annihilate bacteria with outstanding efficiency. In a study experts show that bacteria tend to come together in a slimy matrix, which boosts their ability to resist attackers. However, the new instrument renders any kind of matrix completely useless to the micro-organisms, and destroys them. In one experiment bacterial colonies grown in the root canal of an extracted human tooth fell prey to the plasma tool so fast, that when the team analysed the surface of the canal using scanning electron microscopes, they found a near pristine surface. Heat sensors placed on the tooth also revealed that its temperature only rose by about five degrees during a 10-minute test fire with the plasma tool, which means that it remains well within tolerable pain limits for humans.

Wolfgang explained that there were real and perceived health risks; and these were considerably different. Given that this method was using essentially cold plasma the risks were minimal. But, he acknowledged that the association of heat with plasma is so strong that there may be a negative reaction to the product based on ignorance or lack of knowledge. Either way this was a problem that would have to be addressed. It may mean that a part of the marketing communication budget will need to cover education.

Wolfgang saved his compelling arguments and convincing slides until last. This was a series of slides of teeth. The teeth were from pigs. As it was not possible to use or even get access to the teeth of humans Wolfgang had to test the product on the nearest substitute which was pigs teeth. The slides revealed some dramatic changes in colour following exposure to the plasma. Discoloured yellow teeth noticeably changed to a shade of white. Wolfgang had to explain that white like any other colour has hundreds of different shades including cream, off-white, ivory, brilliant white, etc., all of which are

Table 11.6 Project analysis

Progress of project	% of analysis complete
Market overview	90
Market study	
Expert interviews	
Internal interviews	
Customer view	
Intellectual property	60
IP review	
Patent filing	
IP strategy	
Regulatory	100
Regulatory review	
Regulatory plan	
Technology/risk assessment	60
Assessment and mitigation	
Efficacy tests	
Risk plan	
Product development	95
Laboratory prototype	
Initial concepts/designs/proposition	
Route to market	70
Conceptualisation and road map	
Partners	
Value proposal	

natural shades of teeth that can be found amongst the population of human beings.

The meeting had to consider whether to invest €10 million in this project. Such a decision would of course be at the expense of other projects not being funded. Munich Gases considered a commonly used framework for evaluating R&D projects. This was made up of six key areas indicating how much of the analysis was complete (*see* Table 11.6).

Market overview for plaque, periodontal (gum) disease and whitening

Wolfgang put up a slide showing the competitive space for a variety of products and techniques currently available and used by people to combat periodontal disease. It seemed there was a clear need for an effective simple cleaning product. For example, people were aware of the benefits of flossing but few people actually regularly flossed their teeth because of the difficulty. Currently there is a clear trade-off between ease of use and efficacy. Thus things easy to use are not very effective. It was however the issue of teeth whitening that seemed to be grabbing most people's attention. Several members of the panel were amazed at the possibility that plasma could actually whiten teeth. And it was specifically this benefit that the marketing manager believed was of most interest. He argued that whitening was a growing and lucrative market. He also argued that there were few if any easy to use effective whitening products available. The dentist present confirmed that the most commonly used effective whitening was a bleach-based process, where users essentially bathed their teeth in a solution of bleach for a couple of hours a day. Products in this category typically were of the format of a plastic tray that is held around the teeth to ensure the solution/gel is in contact with the teeth.

The Marketing Manager was Thomas Haas he gave some details of the world toothpaste market. First he put up a slide showing how the market has a number of specific segments including: Regular Toothpaste, Anti-Caries Toothpaste, Children's Toothpaste, Desensitising Toothpaste, Gum Protection Toothpaste, Multi-Benefit Toothpaste, Tartar Control Toothpaste, Whitening Toothpaste and others. He then went on to explain that toothpaste is one of the most dynamic segments of the oral care market:

> *The frequency of product launches in existing segments of the market contributes to continuous evolution of the toothpaste market. Increase in sales of oral hygiene products in major markets worldwide has largely resulted from growing awareness of hygiene and product innovation. New advancements have led to the launch of a variety of high-priced, value-added multifunctional products in several oral care categories such as toothpastes and toothbrushes. Whitening toothpastes and products offering multiple functions are driving growth in the dentifrices segment. Currently, for major toothpastes, averting tooth decay is not sufficient, which usually guarantee benefits such as fresher breath, healthier gums and whiter teeth. Technological advancements in recent years have altered the toothpaste segment to one that offers additional benefits besides just fighting cavities to customers. This made manufacturers roll out products with a lot of additional features that were not available previously.*

He cautioned that entry into this market or related markets would be difficult given the extent of

→

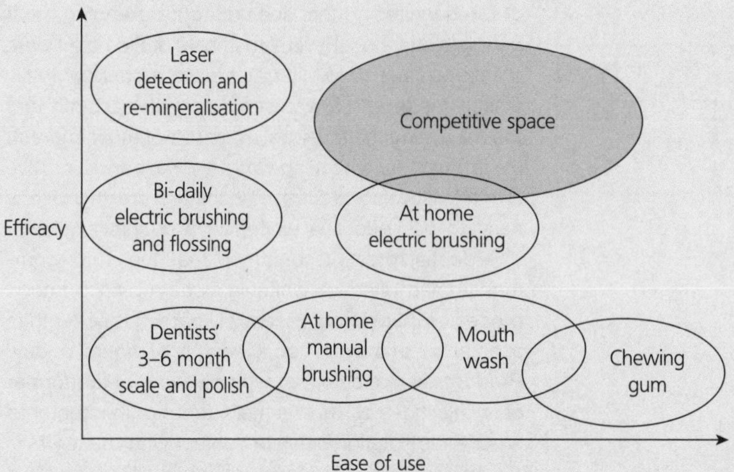

Figure 11.5 Competitor map: prevention and therapy of periodontal disease

competitors and the fact that some of these firms are multinational firms with huge power such as Colgate-Palmolive, GlaxoSmithKline, Henkel AG & Co., Johnson & Johnson, Procter & Gamble and Unilever.

Thomas Haas then went on to argue that this power also presents opportunities especially when it comes to licensing technology. Powerful brand management firms with international brands to defend are always looking for opportunities to steal a march on their competitors. Exclusive access to a unique technology would provide such an opportunity. This made all the panel smile.

Thomas then gave the panel an example of a small company of three employees based in Maine, USA, that developed a new product in the teeth cleaning market. The company launched the product in a few 'Wal-mart' stores in the USA. Sales were impressive. Immediately, Procter & Gamble took an interest and approached the company with an offer. After several months of negotiation the small company agreed to sell the business for a staggering $165 million up-front with an 'earn-out' payment in three years based on a formula pegged to financial results. The up-front payment alone was nearly four times annual sales of $43 million. The deal required the three employees to work developing the business inside P&G for three years.

Consumer market or professional market

Discussions continued for another hour with a wide variety of views being expressed. The dental scientists felt more research was required to prove and fully explain precisely how the plasma was whitening teeth. Some of the business development managers felt that teeth whitening was a fad and that the product should be specifically marketed as a cleaning tool. There was one key issue that dominated the discussion towards the end of the meeting and that centred on whether to target the professional market, i.e. dentists, or the consumer market with a simple to use micro cylinder product. Such cylinders were commonly incorporated into pen type torches, and were used in soldering in the jewelry industry.

In many ways the professional market would be easier to reach and Munich Gases could work with a few lead users to develop the most appropriate product. Such a product would use much larger cylinders of plasma as these would be in a regulated market used by professional dentists in their surgeries only.

The head of R&D tried to summarise the arguments:

Look both options are feasible. It seems to me that we need to examine the type of business model that we wish to build. The professional market offers less risk, we could also build in an annual service to the product. This may include replacement parts and filters, for example. It also offers the opportunity for repair and maintenance and an after sales service. We could also license the product to dentists without them necessarily having to pay upfront. This all sounds very attractive. On the other hand the consumer market does offer the potential for big riches. We all know the margins and mark-ups available on consumer products. I mean hundreds of per cent. Also we have the possibility of designing in replacement cartridges and follow the Gillette razor model or the ink jet cartridge model. This is where the original product is sold at a minimal price, but where complimentary products such as cartridges are sold with significant margins. The major profits lie in the replacement cartridges.

Smiles emerged all round the table. This was beginning to look like an opportunity to print money – lots of it.

Marcus Leitz was the Head of R&D. He explained that ink jet printer manufacturers have gone to extensive efforts to make sure that their printers are incompatible with lower cost after-market ink cartridges and cartridge refilling. This is because the printers are often sold at or below cost to generate sales of proprietary cartridges which will generate profits for the company over the life of the equipment. Indeed, this business model is so successful that it has become known as the razor-cartridge business model.

The licensing option

There was another option that the panel had to consider. This was simply licensing the technology without forming a business. A technology licensing agreement grants a licensee the right to utilise specific technologies, patents, software, know-how or product designs. In a typical technology licence agreement, a running royalty fee based on licensed product sales revenue is paid to the licensor on a periodic basis. Stephan Boch was Licensing Manager for Munich Gases and had an impressive track record of securing some very profitable licensing deals for Munich Gases. Unsurprisingly he was enthusiastic about the licensing option. He explained how licensing would allow Munich Gases to gain revenue from their plasma technology by licensing it to other companies so that it may be integrated into an end-product. The success of the model rests on secure intellectual property protection, which he said we have. This option would allow Munich Gases to exit at this stage of the development without any further additional costs. The innovation itself is clearly not yet a complete product, and will need to be integrated into a product to be of value for the end-user (consumer or professional). Members of the panel were now interested in this option.

Stephan Boch went on to explain that this was not a short-term solution; this would be a long-term agreement because all parties must exchange certain (confidential) information. Boch argued that any licensing arrangement can be structured in different ways, with upfront payments by the licensee or with payments that are revenue-dependent. In this case Munich Gases could argue for funding to develop the technology to the point where it becomes a suitable add-on to the offering of its licensee partner. Royalty fees may accompany licensing revenue on a per-unit-sale basis, or the parties may use some other transparent means of measuring usage of the licensed technology. An important consideration in structuring licensing agreements is the portion of income derived from licensing revenue versus that deriving from royalties. Royalty revenue is dependent on the selling ability of the party integrating the licensed technology, and the size of the addressable market for the end-product.

The R&D Manager was critical:

My understanding is that licensing works well in situations where developing an entire product independently is not feasible. But, in our case it is feasible. The trade-off is that since the product comprises only one element of a complete product, it may hinder the development of a strong company profile for Munich Gases, unless a co-branding option is available.

The room fell silent. The temperature in the room was rising and making a decision was not going to be easy. Some people were going be angry and upset if the decision goes against them.

Maria Klaus was Marketing Manager for Munich Gases. She had a different view of how the project should develop.

I see things differently from Stephan, she said. I think we can build a business around this technology. The consumer product offers the potential for big rewards. I can vision a hand-held small plasma toothbrush in bathrooms all over Europe; a product that is in addition to their existing tooth brush that the whole family can use to whiten and clean their teeth. We could build a brand that becomes synonomus with clean teeth. The business could extend the brand in to other markets and become the market leader. Equally the professional product also offers another route to a

→

Selecting a business model

1. **Value proposition** – a description of the customer problem, the product that addresses the problem, and the value of the product from the customer's perspective.
2. **Market segment** – the group of customers to target, sometimes the potential of an innovation is unlocked only when a different market segment is targeted.
3. **Value chain structure** – the firm's position and activities in the value chain and how the firm will capture part of the value that it creates in the chain.
4. **Revenue generation and margins** – how revenue is generated (sales, leasing, subscription, support, etc.), the cost structure, and target profit margins.
5. **Position in value network** – identification of competitors, partners and any network effects that can be utilised to deliver more value to the customer.
6. **Competitive strategy** – how the company will attempt to develop a sustainable competitive advantage, for example, by means of a cost, differentiation, or niche strategy.

Source: Chesbrough, H. and Rosenbloom, R.S. (2002) The Role of the Business Model in Capturing Value from Innovation: evidence from Xerox Cooperation's technology spin-off companies, *Industrial and corporate change*, Vol. 11, No. 3, 529–55.

successful business. This offers less financial reward but, significantly for Munich Gases, this is less risky and less costly, but none the less could raise huge profits for us, especially in the after-sales services.

Maria Klaus went on to explain that in her view it was the business model that they constructed and selected that would ultimately influence the outcome of discussions. She put up a slide which identified six components of any business model. A long discussion ensued about what type of business model would be desirable. Her second slide showed the theoretical options that could be constructed (*see* Table 11.7). There were 16 business models, but there were three categories that were

Table 11.7 The 16 detailed business model archetypes

Basic business model archetype	What type of asset is involved?			
	Financial	Physical	Intangible	Human
Creator	1 Entrepreneur (serial entrepreneurs)	2 Manufacturer (VW automobiles)	3 Inventor (Trevor Bayliss)	4 Human creator (illegal)
Distributor	5 Financial trader (investment banks)	6 Wholesaler/retailer (Tesco; Amazon)	7 IP trader (Logicalis)	8 Human distributor (illegal)
Landlord	9 Financial landlord (banks; insurance companies)	10 Physical landlord (hotel; car rental)	11 Intellectual landlord (publisher; brand manager)	12 Contractor (Federal Express; management consultancy)
Broker	13 Financial broker (insurance brokers)	14 Physical broker (eBay; estate agents)	15 IP broker (3i)	16 HR broker (employment agent)

Source: Weill, P. *et al.* (2005).

applicable for this business. Munich Gases can be classified as a creator and there were three types of assets involved: entrepreneur; manufacturer and inventor.

Decision time

The R&D Manager was chairing the meeting and after two hours he decided to bring the panel members back to focus on the decision that was in front of them. We need a decision today he explained. The board will want to know our recommendation. They will back our decision and release the €10 million, but we need to be clear and unambiguous, we cannot say we think 'a' is right but it could be 'b'.

Yes or no to an investment of €10 million? And which particular product, market and business model?

This case raises many questions and not all the information is available to answer them. None the less, decisions have to be taken on the best available information at a given point in time. It is always possible to delay the decision until all the information you require is available but this may cost the business in terms of losing a position of advantage to a competitor who decides to enter the market.

Sources: Weill, P., Malone, T.W., D'Urso, V.T., Herman, G. and Woerner, S. (2005) *Do Some Business Models Perform Better than Others? A Study of the 1000 Largest US Firms*, Sloan School of Management, Massachusetts Institute of Technology, Working Paper No. 226.

Questions

1 Should Munich Gases invest €10 million in this new product project?

2 What other factors may yet decide the fate of this project?

3 Which market should Munich Gases select? The consumer product market or professional/business market?

4 Sketch out five different possible business models. Of these determine which is the most profitable and which is most likely to succeed?

5 How will the powerful toothpaste brand owners react?

6 Should Munich Gases secure an entry into the market with one of Europe's leading multiples (e.g. Lidl, Tesco, Carefour, Aldi)?

7 Should Munich Gases secure the endorsement of one of Europe's leading toothpaste brands (e.g. Aquafresh; Signal; Macleans) before entering the market?

8 How can the firm reassure uneasy consumers about the safety of plasma in their mouths?

Chapter summary

Deciding how and on what basis a company wishes to compete with its competitors is of central concern to all companies. Firms need to consider a wide range of factors in order to maximise the product's chance of success in competitive environments. This chapter has shown that a company has to identify the specific ways it can differentiate its products in order to gain competitive advantage.

First and foremost, it has to consider the market in which it is competing, the nature of the competition and how its capabilities will enable its products to be successful. The concept of platforms in new product development was introduced as a way of developing product groups for the future. The positioning of the product and the brand strategy selected were also shown to be of particular importance. Finally, marketing research offers extensive opportunities in terms of information provision. The effective use of this information often leads to the successful development of new products.

Discussion questions

1. If there was a strategic alliance between competitors for the development of a new technology then what are the strategic issues for these firms once that technology becomes available?
2. Apply the notion of product platform to service industries. How relevant is it to financial services or to hotels? What are the issues that would need to be investigated if an idea emerged in a firm in those industries for a novel platform that had no connection with what was done before in that industry?
3. Would you agree that product portfolio analysis is too simplistic to be of much value?
4. Trace the connections between differentiation strategy, core capabilities and positioning strategy. How are they relevant to new product planning?
5. Are brand extensions as relevant in industrial markets as in consumer markets? Do they have a strategic role or are they short-term tactical exercises?
6. It seems Toyota has been successful at recalling some of its cars for modifications, without damaging the Toyota brand. How has it achieved this?
7. Apply CIM (Figure 1.9) to the case study at the end of this chapter to illustrate the innovation project.
8. Examine whether it is only the launch of technology intensive products that can benefit from the use of 'blog buzz' or whether all product launches could benefit.

Key words and phrases

References

Beverland, M.B., Napoli, J. and Farrelly, F. (2010) Can All Brands Innovate in the Same Way? A Typology of Brand Position and Innovation Effort, *Journal of Product Innovation Management*, Vol. 27, 33–48.

Buzzell, R.D. and Gale, B.T. (1987) *The PIMS Principles*, The Free Press, New York.

Crawford, C.M. (1997) *New Products Management*, 4th edn, Irwin, Burr Ridge, IL.

Deschamps, J.P. and Nayak, P.R. (1995) *Product Juggernauts: How Companies Mobilize To Generate A Stream of Winners*, Havard Business School Press, Boston, MA.

Doyle, P. (1995) Marketing in the new millennium, *European Journal of Marketing*, Vol. 29, No. 13, 23–41.

Green, D.H., Barclay, D.W. and Ryans, A.B. (1995) Entry strategy and long-term performance: conceptualization and empirical examination, *Journal of Marketing*, October, 1–16.

Jones, T. (1997) *New Product Development*, Butterworth Heinemann, Oxford.

Kim, K. and Chhajed, D. (2000) Commonality in product design: cost saving, valuation change and cannibalisation, *European Journal of Operational Research*, Vol. 125, No. 3, 602–21.

Levitt, T. (1986) *The Marketing Imagination*, The Free Press, New York.

Mohr, J., Sengupta, S. and Slater, S. (2010) *Marketing of High-Technology Products and Innovations*, 3rd edn, Prentice Hall, Harlow.

Moore, L.M. and Pessemier, E.A. (1993) *Product Planning and Management*, McGraw-Hill, New York.

Mudambi, S., Doyle, P. and Wong, V. (1997) An exploration of branding in industrial markets, *Industrial Marketing Management*, Vol. 26, 433–46.

Muffatto, M. and Roveda, M. (2000) Developing product platforms: analysis of the development process, *Technovation*, Vol. 20, No. 11, 617–30.

Riezebos, R. (2003) *Brand Management: A Theoretical and Practical Approach*, Prentice Hall, Harlow.

Schofield, M. and Arnold, D. (1988) Strategies for mature business, *Long Range Planning*, Vol. 21, No. 5, 69–76.

Thomas, R.J. (1995) *New Product Success Stories*, John Wiley, New York.

Urban, G.L. and Hauser, J.R. (1993) *Design and Marketing of New Products*, 2nd edn, Prentice-Hall, Englewood Cliffs, NJ.

Wheelwright, S.C. and Clark, K.B. (1992) *Revolutionising Product Development*, The Free Press, New York.

Wind, Y. (1982) *Product Policy*, Addison-Wesley, Reading, MA.

Further reading

For a more detailed review of the product and brand management literature, the following develop many of the issues raised in this chapter:

Barczak, G., Griffin, A. and Kahn, K.B. (2009) PERSPECTIVE: Trends and Drivers of Success in NPD Practices: Results of the 2003 PDMA Best Practices Study, *Journal of Product Innovation Management*, Vol. 26, No. 1, 3–23.

Belliveau, P., Griffin, A. and Somermeyer, S. (eds) (2002) *The PDMA ToolBook for New Product Development*, John Wiley & Sons, New York.

Biemans, W.G., Griffin, A. and Moenaert, R.K. (2007) Twenty Years of the *Journal of Product Innovation Management*: History, Participants, and Knowledge Stocks and Flows, *Journal of Product Innovation Management*, Vol. 24, 193–213.

Biemans, W., Griffin, A. and Moenaert, R. (2010) In Search of the Classics: A Study of the Impact of *JPIM* Papers from 1984 to 2003, *Journal of Product Innovation Management*, Vol. 27, 461–84.

HSBC (2010) 100 Thoughts, HSBC, London.

Lundbäck, M. and Karlsson, C. (2005) Inter-firm Product Platform Development in the Automotive Industry, s. 155–181, *International Journal of Innovation Management*, Vol. 9, No. 2, 155–81.

Mohr, J., Sengupta, S. and Slater, S. (2010) *Marketing of High-Technology Products and Innovations*, 3rd edn, Prentice Hall, London.

Zirpoli, F. and Camuffo, A. (2009) Product architecture, inter-firm vertical coordination and knowledge partitioning in the auto industry, *European Management Review*, Vol. 6, No. 4, 250–64.

Chapter 12
New product development

Introduction

Few business activities are heralded for their promise and approached with more justified optimism than the development of new products. Successful new products also have the added benefit of revitalising the organisation. Small wonder then that the concept of new product development (NPD) has received enormous attention in the management literature over the past 20 years. The result is a diverse range of literature from practitioners, management consultants and academics. This chapter explores this literature and examines the various models of NPD that have been put forward. It also explains the importance of NPD as a means of achieving growth.

The case study at the end of this chapter features one of the fastest growing brands in Europe – innocent. Its range of 'smoothies' and other beverages has propelled it into the top flight of brands. The case explores how this start-up firm acquired funding and developed its products.

Chapter contents

Learning objectives

When you have completed this chapter you will be able to:

- examine the relationship between new products and prosperity;
- recognise the range of product development opportunities that can exist;
- recognise that a new product is a multi-dimensional concept;
- identify the different types of models of NPD;
- provide an understanding of the importance of external linkages in the new product development process.

Innovation management and NPD

When one considers a variety of different industries, a decline in product innovations is matched only by a decline in market share. For example, Table 6.2 illustrates that across a wide variety of industries product innovation has led to winning market share and leadership.

This chapter looks at the exciting process of developing new products. Part One of this book has highlighted the importance of innovation and how the effective management of that process can lead to corporate success. To many people new products are the outputs of the innovation process, where the new product development (NPD) process is a subprocess of innovation. Managing innovation concerns the conditions that have to be in place to ensure that the organisation as a whole is given the opportunity to develop new products. The actual development of new products is the process of transforming business opportunities into tangible products.

Innovation in action

Hero Honda – Just4her

When Indian scooter maker Hero Honda introduced a scooter specifically targeted at women, it went beyond a 'feminised product'. To start with, it opened up 22 dedicated women-only scooter 'Just4her' showrooms across the country. With an all-female sales staff, the entire showroom is designed to make women buyers feel more at ease.

The company is working on creating all-women teams of mechanics. It's also introduced the Lady Rider Club, the first of its kind, offering special benefits that include milestone rewards, personal accident insurance and special events for members.

Source: HSBC (2010) 100 Thoughts, HSBC, London.

Source: Corbis/Larry Williams/Larry Williams and Associates

New product development concerns the management of the disciplines involved in the development of new products. These disciplines have developed their own perspectives on the subject of NPD. These are largely based on their experiences of involvement in the process. Hence, production management examines the development of new products from a manufacturing perspective, that is, how can we most effectively manufacture the product in question? Marketing, on the other hand, would take a slightly different perspective and would be concerned with trying to understand the needs of the customer and how the business could best meet these needs. However, producing what the customer wants may or may not be

Figure 12.1 A variety of perspectives from which to analyse the development of new products

either possible or profitable. The lack of a common approach to the development of new products is due to this multiple perspective. This is illustrated in Figure 12.1. The variety of views presented on the subject is not a weakness. Indeed, it should be viewed as a strength, for these different perspectives illuminate the areas that are left in the dark by other perspectives.

Usually, competition between companies is assessed using financial measures such as return on capital employed (ROCE), profits and market share. Non-financial measures such as design, innovativeness and technological supremacy may also be used.

Theoretically it is possible for a firm to survive without any significant developments to its products, but such firms are exceptions to the norm. Where long-term success is dependent on the ability to compete with others, this is almost always achieved by ensuring that your company's products are superior to the competition.

Product development as a series of decisions

The existing literature on product development is vast. The Brown and Eisenhardt (1995) review provides a comprehensive overview of the literature, and an illustration of the diversity of the literature, largely adopting an organisational perspective, which is arguably the main focus of the existing new product literature. However, other key perspectives on new product development are evident. The reviews by Finger and Dixon (1989a; 1989b) provide an excellent insight into the engineering design literature. The marketing perspective on new product development is reviewed by Green and Srinivasan (1990) and Mahajan and Wind (1992) and Barczak *et al.*, (2009). Arguably the paper by Krishnan and Uldrich (2001) remains one of very few papers that attempts to pull this wide and vast literature together. This review examines product development as a series of decisions. Within the product development project the authors divide the decisions into four categories: concept development; supply chain design; product design; and production ramp-up/launch.

Focusing on the study of Krishnan and Uldrich (2001), within concept development there are five basic decisions to be made:

1 What are the target values of the product attributes?
2 What will the product concept be?
3 What variants of the product will be offered?
4 What is the product architecture?
5 What will be the overall physical form and industrial design of the product?

Within the decisions surrounding supply chain design Krishnan and Uldrich (2001) argue that the following questions are key:

- Which components will be designed specifically for the product?
- Who will design and produce the product?
- What is the configuration of the physical supply chain?
- What type of process will be used to assemble the product?
- Who will develop and supply the process equipment?

New products and prosperity

The potential rewards of NPD are enormous. One only has to consider the rapid success of companies such as Microsoft and Compaq in the rapidly growing home computer industry. Similar success was achieved by Apple, and prior to this IBM, in the early development of the same industry. This example illustrates an important point, that success in one year does not ensure success in the next. Both Apple and IBM experienced severe difficulties in the 1990s.

Research by Cooper (1999) has suggested that, on average, new products (defined here as those less than five years old) are increasingly taking a larger slice of company sales. For 3M, for example, new products contributed to 30 per cent of sales in 2009, for Johnson & Johnson it was 25 per cent of sales in 2009 and for Du Pont a staggering 39 per cent of sales came from new products. The life cycles of products are becoming increasingly shorter. This is clearly evident in the mobile phone handset business where virtually all of Motorola's and Nokia's sales are from products that are less than three years old.

Considerations when developing an NPD strategy

Chapter 6 outlined many of the activities and factors that organisations need to consider in managing a business in the short and long term. In addition, Chapter 11 highlighted many of the factors that a business needs to consider if it is successfully to manage its products. It should be clear that establishing a direction for a business and the selection of strategies to achieve its goals form an ongoing, evolving process that is frequently subject to change. This is particularly evident at the product strategy level (Figure 12.2 illustrates the main inputs into the decision-making process). The process of product strategy was highlighted in Chapter 11 and is the creative process of recognising genuine business opportunities that the business might be able to exploit. It is commonly referred to as 'opportunity identification'.

Ongoing corporate planning

In large organisations this can be a very formal activity involving strategic planners and senior managers with responsibility for setting the future direction of the business. In smaller organisations this activity may be undertaken by the owner of the business in an informal, even *ad hoc* way. For many businesses it is somewhere in the middle of these two extremes. The effects of any corporate planning may be

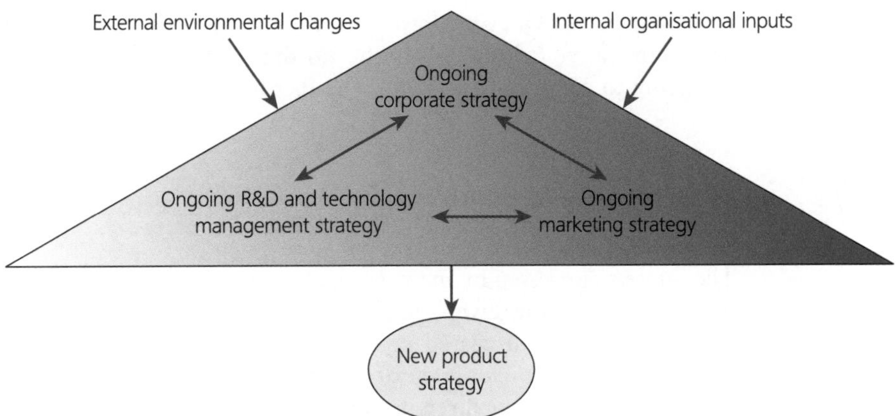

Figure 12.2 Main inputs into the decision-making process

important and long term. For example, the decision by a sports footwear manufacturer to exit the tennis market and concentrate on the basketball market due to changing social trends will have a significant impact on the business.

Ongoing market planning

Decisions by market planners may have equally significant effects. For example, the realisation that a competitor is about to launch an improved tennis shoe that offers additional benefits may force the business to establish five new product development projects. Two of these projects may be established to investigate the use of new materials for the sole, one could be used to develop a series of new designs, one could look at alternative fastenings and one could be used to reduce production costs.

Ongoing technology management

In most science- and technology-intensive industries such as the pharmaceutical and computer software industries, this activity is probably more significant than ongoing market planning. Technology awareness is very high. The continual analysis of internal R&D projects and external technology trawling will lead to numerous technical opportunities that need to be considered by the business. Say that a recent review of the patent literature has identified a patent application by one of the company's main competitors. This forces the business to establish a new project to investigate this area to ensure that it is aware of any future developments that may affect its position. This area is explored in more detail in Chapter 9.

Opportunity analysis/serendipity

In addition to the inputs that have been classified above, there are other inputs and opportunities that are often labelled miscellaneous or put down to serendipity (*see* Chapter 1). The vice-president of 3M remarked that 'chaos is a necessary part of an innovative culture. It's been said that 3M's competitors never know what we are going to come up with next. The fact is neither do we.'

NPD as a strategy for growth

The interest expressed by many companies in the subject of developing new products is hardly surprising given that the majority of businesses are intent on growth. Although, as was discussed in Chapter 11, this does not apply to all companies, none the less the development of new products provides an opportunity for growing the business. (It is worth reminding ourselves that new product development is only one of many options available to a business keen on growth.)

One of the clearest ways of identifying the variety of growth options available to a business is using Ansoff's (1965, 1968) directional policy matrix. This well-known matrix, shown in Figure 12.3, combines two of the key variables that enable a business to grow: an increase in market opportunities and an increase in product opportunities. Within this matrix new product development is seen as one of four available options. Each of the four cells considers various combinations of product–market options. Growth can be achieved organically (internal development) or through external acquisition. A criticism of this matrix is that it adopts an environmental perspective that assumes that opportunities for growth exist – they may not. Indeed, often consolidation and retrenchment need to be considered, especially in times of economic downturn. Each of the cells in the matrix is briefly discussed below.

Market penetration

Opportunities are said to exist within a business's existing markets through increasing the volume of sales. Increasing the market share of a business's existing products by exploiting the full range of marketing-mix activities is the common approach adopted by many companies. This may include branding decisions. For example, the cereal manufacturer Kellogg's has increased the usage of its cornflakes product by promoting it as a snack to be consumed at times other than at breakfast.

	Current products	New products
Current markets	1 Market penetration strategy	3 Product development strategy
New markets	2 Market development strategy	4 Diversification strategy

Figure 12.3 Ansoff matrix

Source: Adapted from I. Ansoff (1965) *Corporate Strategy*, Penguin, Harmondsworth; (1968) *Toward a Strategy of the Theory of the Firm*, McGraw-Hill, New York.

Market development

Growth opportunities are said to exist for a business's products through making them available to new markets. In this instance the company maintains the security of its existing products but opts to develop and enter new markets. Market development can be achieved by opening up new segments. For example, Mercedes decided to enter the small car market (previously the company had always concentrated on the executive or luxury segment). Similarly, companies may decide to enter new geographic areas through exporting.

Product development

Ansoff proposes that growth opportunities exist through offering new or improved products to existing markets. This is the subject of this chapter and, as will become clear, trying to establish when a product is new is sometimes difficult. None the less, virtually all companies try to ensure that their products are able to compete with the competition by regularly improving and updating their existing products. This is an ongoing activity for most companies.

Diversification

It hardly needs to be said that opportunities for growth exist beyond a business's existing products and markets. The selection of this option, however, would be significant in that the business would move into product areas and markets in which it currently does not operate. The development of the self-adhesive notepads (Post-it) by 3M provided an opportunity for the company to enter the stationery market, a market of which it had little knowledge, with a product that was new to the company and the market.

Many companies try to utilise either their existing technical or commercial knowledge base. For example, Flymo's knowledge of the electric lawnmower market enabled it to diversify into a totally new market. Indeed, the introduction of its Garden-vac product led to the creation of the 'garden-tidy' product market. While this is an example of organic growth, many companies identify diversification opportunities through acquisition. For example, in the United Kingdom some of the privatised electricity companies have purchased significant holdings in privatised water companies. The knowledge base being utilised here is the commercial know-how of the provision of a utility service (former public service).

Additional opportunities for diversified growth exist through forward, backward and horizontal diversification. A manufacturer opening retail outlets is an example of forward integration. Backward integration is involvement in activities which are inputs to the business, for example a manufacturer starting to produce components. Horizontal diversification is buying up competitors.

A range of product development opportunities

A development of Ansoff's directional policy matrix was Johnson and Jones's (1957) matrix for product development strategies (*see* Figure 12.4). This matrix

Increasing technology newness →

Increasing market newness ↓

Products objectives	No technological change	Improved technology	New technology To acquire scientific knowledge and production skills new to the company
No market change	Sustain	Reformulation To maintain an optimum balance of cost, quality and availability in the formulae of present products	Replacement To seek new and better ingredients of formulation for present company products in technology not now employed
Strengthened market To exploit more fully the existing markets for the present company's products	Remerchandising To increase sales to consumers of types now served by the company	Improved product To improve present products for greater utility and merchandisability to consumers	Product line extension To broaden the line of products offered to present consumers through new technology
New market To increase the number of types of consumer served by the company	New use To find new classes of consumer that can utilise present company products	Market extension To reach new classes of consumer by modifying present products	Diversification To add to the classes of consumer served by developing new technology knowledge

Figure 12.4 New product development strategies

Source: S.C. Johnson and C. Jones (1957) How to organise for new products, *Harvard Business Review*, May–June, Vol. 35, 49–62.

replaces Ansoff's product variable with technology. It builds on Ansoff's matrix by offering further clarification of the range of options open to a company contemplating product decisions. In particular, the use of technology as a variable better illustrates the decisions a company needs to consider. For example, Johnson and Jones distinguish between improving existing technology and acquiring new technology, the latter being far more resource intensive with higher degrees of risk. Ansoff's directional policy matrix made no such distinction. Similarly, the market-newness scale offers a more realistic range of alternatives. Many other matrices have since been developed to try to help firms identify the range of options available (*see* Dolan, 1993).

The range of product development strategies that are open to a company introduces the notion that a new product can take many forms. This is the subject of the next section.

Illustration 12.1

New products crucial to success for Shimano

As a keen cyclist, Yoshizo Shimano knows all about the importance of keeping in touch with his company's products. Mr Shimano is president of Shimano, the world's biggest maker of bicycle components.

Frequently, he borrows a bike from the company's R&D division to keep in touch with what researchers are up to. 'We won't compete with our customers by building complete bikes. But we must keep in mind how our components are going to be used and have a vision of the product that is safe as well as being fun', he says.

Mr Shimano's interest in trying out bicycles containing his company's components underlines how manufacturers must pay increasing importance to bringing out new products. These must either solve a pressing customer problem or come up with an idea that breaks completely new ground within a few years. In either case, manufacturers' strategies on new product development are crucial to their chances of long-term success in a world where competition is becoming steadily tougher.

In 1921 Shozaburo Shimano established Shimano Iron Works and began production of the bicycle freewheel. Today, some 90 years later, Shimano is a world leader in the manufacture and supply of bicycle parts, fishing tackle and rowing equipment. Sales in 2009 were ¥186 billion and profits were ¥20 billion. Shimano Inc. is the world's largest bicycle component manufacturer. Furthermore:

- Shimano has about a 70–80 per cent share of the worldwide bicycle component market;
- bicycle components make up about 78 per cent of sales while fishing tackle makes up the rest of sales;
- operating margin has increased nicely for the past seven years: from 9 per cent in 2001 to 14.8 per cent in 2007;
- operating margin has averaged about 14 per cent for the past eight years;
- Shimano has a strong history of sponsoring some of the best athletes and cycling teams in the world.

Source: Len Holsborg/Alamy Images

Shimano is quoted on the Tokyo stock exchange, with the family retaining a minority stake.

Mr Shimano says Shimano keeps in touch on product development by talking continually to the 400–500 bicycle manufacturers world-wide it supplies. It makes 13 main types of parts – gears, brake systems and drive chains – each of which can come in up to 100 different variants.

In the early 1990s, the company prospered through the development of products, such as specialist gears, that suited the then fashion for rugged, off-road mountain bikes. Now the mountain bike craze has died away, Mr Shimano says the company is increasing its development of products such as automatic gears that will give cyclists, particularly on congested city roads, safer, smoother rides.

'If the cyclist does not have to bother with changing gears, he can concentrate on other aspects of controlling the bike which is likely to lead to safer journeys', says Mr Shimano.

Source: P. Marsh (2002) New products crucial to success, FT.com, 21 May; Shimano.com (2010).

What is a new product?

Attempting to define what is and what is not a new product is not a trivial task, although many students of business management have had much fun arguing over whether the Sony Walkman was indeed a new product or merely existing technology repackaged. Another example that illustrates this point is the product long-life milk, known in the United States as aspectic milk (sold without refrigeration). This product has been consumed for many years in Europe but it is a relatively new concept for most consumers in the United States. Consumers who drink refrigerated milk may be extremely wary of milk sold from a non-refrigerated shelf. Once again, while clearly this product is not absolutely new, it can be seen that it is more useful from a product manager's perspective to adopt a relativistic view.

It is important to note, as was explained in Chapter 11, that a product is a multi-dimensional concept. It can be defined differently and can take many forms. Some dimensions will be tangible product features and others intangible. Does the provision of different packaging for a product constitute a new product? Surely the answer is no – or is it? New packaging coupled with additional marketing effort, especially in terms of marketing communications, can help to reposition a product. This was successfully achieved by GlaxoSmithKline with its beverage product Lucozade. Today this product is known as a sports drink, yet older readers will recall that the product was originally packaged in a distinctive bottle wrapped in yellow cellophane and commonly purchased at pharmacists for sick children. This

Illustration 12.2

The repositioning of BMW's Mini

The Mini is one of the most established and successful product brands in the automotive industry. It has been in existence for over 45 years and had sold over 4 million units before its highly successful relaunch in 2001. The Mini was designed and manufactured in Britain; the car was launched in 1959 by the British Leyland Motor Corporation. The Mini remained under British ownership until 1994 when BMW acquired the Rover Group; though it later sold off much of the group, BMW kept the Mini. In 1999 the Mini celebrated its 40th birthday and *Autocar* named it the car of the century. The Mini itself remained relatively unchanged from its original launch until it was completely withdrawn from production in 2000. A new Mini and Mini Cooper (designed and manufactured by BMW) were launched in 2001. It has been a very successful project with sales growing from 25,000 units in 2001 to over 200,000 units in 2006 (Arlidge, 2006).

Source: Mini UK

Source: Arlidge, J. (2006) Minis maxi challenge, *Sunday Times*, S3 Business, p. 11, 17 September; Simms, C. and Trott, P. (2006) The perceptions of the BMW Mini brand: the importance of historical associations and the development of a model, *Journal of Product & Brand Management*, Vol. 15, No. 4, 228–38.

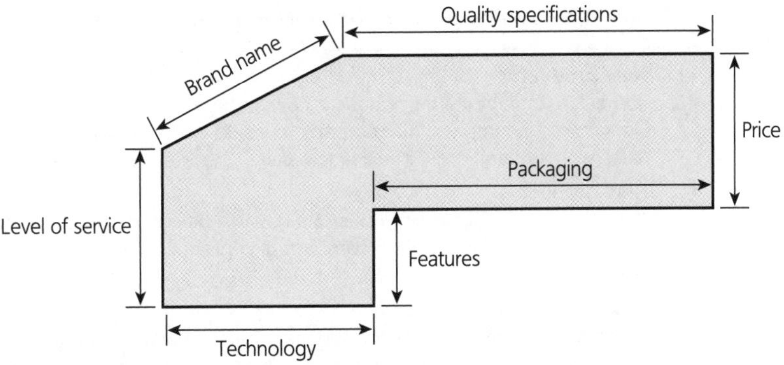

Figure 12.5 A product is multi-dimensional

illustrates the difficulty of attempting to offer a single definition for a new product. (Also, *see* the example of BMW's Mini in Illustration 12.2.)

If we accept that a product has many dimensions, then it must follow that it is theoretically possible to label a product 'new' by merely altering one of these dimensions, for example packaging. Figure 12.5 illustrates this point. In addition Corrocher and Zirulia (2010) found that mobile communication operators used pricing tariffs to develop innovative new services. Each dimension is capable of being altered. These alterations create a new dimension and in theory a new product, even if the change is very small. Indeed, Johne and Snelson (1988) suggest that the options for both new and existing product lines centre on altering the variables in the figure. Table 12.1 shows what this means in practice.

Defining a new product

Chapter 1 established a number of definitions to help with the study of this subject and provided a definition of innovation. In addition, it highlighted a quotation by Rogers and Shoemaker (1972) concerning whether or not something is new. It is useful at this juncture to revisit their argument. They stated that while it may be difficult to establish whether a product is actually new as regards the passage of time, so long as it is perceived to be new it *is* new. This is significant because it

Table 12.1 Different examples of 'newness'

1 Changing the performance capabilities of the product (for example, a new, improved washing detergent)
2 Changing the application advice for the product (for example, the use of the Persil ball in washing machines)
3 Changing the after-sales service for the product (for example, frequency of service for a motor car)
4 Changing the promoted image of the product (for example, the use of 'green'-image refill packs)
5 Changing the availability of the product (for example, the use of chocolate-vending machines)
6 Changing the price of the product (for example, the newspaper industry has experienced severe price wars)

Source: F.A. Johne and P.A. Snelson (1988) The role of marketing specialists in product development, Proceedings of the 21st Annual Conference of the Marketing Education Group, Huddersfield, Vol. 3, 176–91.

Table 12.2 A new product has different interpretations of new

New product A
A snack manufacturer introduces a new, larger pack size for its best-selling savoury snack. Consumer research for the company revealed that a family-size pack would generate additional sales without cannibalising existing sales of the standard-size pack.

New product B
An electronics company introduces a new miniature compact disc player. The company has further developed its existing compact disc product and is now able to offer a much lighter and smaller version.

New product C
A pharmaceutical company introduces a new prescription drug for ulcer treatment. Following eight years of laboratory research and three years of clinical trials, the company has recently received approval from the government's medical authorities to launch its new ulcer drug.

illustrates that newness is a relative term. In the case of a new product it is relative to what preceded the product. Moreover, the overwhelming majority of so-called new products are developments or variations on existing formats. Research in this area suggests that only 10 per cent of new products introduced are new to both the market and the company (Booz, Allen & Hamilton, 1982). New to the company (in this case) means that the firm has not sold this type of product before, but other firms could have. New to the market means that the product has not appeared before in the market. However, the examples in Table 12.2 illustrate the confusion that exists in this area.

The three products in the table are all new in that they did not exist before. However, many would argue, especially technologists, that Product A does not contain any new technology. Similarly, Product B does not contain any new technology although its configuration may be new. Product C contains a new patented chemical formulation, hence this is the only truly new product. Marketers would, however, contend that all three products are new simply because they did not previously exist. Moreover, meeting the needs of the customer and offering products that are wanted is more important than whether a product represents a scientific breakthrough. Such arguments are common to many companies, especially those that have both a strong commercial and technological presence and expertise.

Pause for thought 

Has the BMW Mini been repositioned? Or is it a new product?

For the student of innovation and new product development, awareness of the debate and the strong feelings that are associated with it is more important than trying to resolve the polemics. Indeed, the long-term commercial success of the company should be the guiding principle on which product decisions are made. However, in some industries, the advancement of knowledge and subsequent scientific breakthroughs can lead to possible product offerings that would help certain sections of the population. Commercial pressures alone would, however, prevent these new products from being offered, as we saw in the tooth whitening case study in Chapter 11. The science and technology perspective should therefore not be dismissed.

Pause for thought

Is it possible to create a new product by simply changing the packaging? Does this also apply to the dimension of price?

Classification of new products

There have been many attempts to classify new products into certain categories. Very often the distinction between one category and another is one of degree and attempting to classify products is subject to judgement. It is worthy of note, however, that only 10 per cent of all new products are truly innovative. These products involve the greatest risk because they are new to both the company and the marketplace. Most new product activity is devoted to improving existing products. At Sony 80 per cent of new product activity is undertaken to modify and improve the company's existing products. The following classification (Booz, Allen & Hamilton, 1982) identifies the commonly accepted categories of new product developments.

New-to-the-world products

These represent a small proportion of all new products introduced. They are the first of their kind and create a new market. They are inventions that usually contain a significant development in technology, such as a new discovery, or manipulate existing technology in a very different way, leading to revolutionary new designs such as Dyson's vacuum cleaner. Other examples include Apple's iPad, 3M's Post-it notes and Guinness's 'in-can' system.

New product lines (new to the firm)

Although not new to the marketplace, these products are new to the particular company. They provide an opportunity for the company to enter an established market for the first time. For example, Alcatel, Samsung and Sony-Ericsson have all entered the mobile phone market to compete with market leaders Nokia and Motorola, originators of the product.

Additions to existing lines (line additions)

This category is a subset of new product lines above. The distinction is that while the company already has a line of products in this market, the product is significantly different from the present product offering but not so different that it is a new line. The distinction between this category and the former is one of degree. For example, Hewlett-Packard's colour ink-jet printer was an addition to its established line of ink-jet printers.

Improvements and revisions to existing products

These new products are replacements of existing products in a firm's product line. For example, Hewlett-Packard's ink-jet printer has received numerous modifications over time and, with each revision, performance and reliability have been improved. Also, manufacturing cost reductions can be introduced, providing increased added value. This classification represents a significant proportion of all new product introductions.

Cost reductions

This category of products may not be viewed as new from a marketing perspective, largely because they offer no new benefits to the consumer other than possibly reduced costs. From the firm's perspective, however, they may be very significant. The ability to offer similar performance while reducing production costs provides enormous added-value potential. Indeed, frequently it is this category of new product that can produce the greatest financial rewards for the firm. Improved manufacturing processes and the use of different materials are key contributing factors. The effect may be to reduce the number of moving parts or use more cost-effective materials (*see* Chapter 4). The difference between this category and the improvement category is simply that a cost reduction may not result in a product improvement.

Repositioning

These new products are essentially the discovery of new applications for existing products. This has as much to do with consumer perception and branding as technical development. This is none the less an important category. Following the medical science discovery that aspirin thins blood, for example, the product has been repositioned from an analgesic to an over-the-counter remedy for blood clots and one that may help to prevent strokes and heart attacks.

In practice most of the projects in a firm's portfolio are improvements to products already on the market, additions to existing lines (line extensions), and products new to the firm but already manufactured by competitors (new product lines). Figure 12.6 illustrates the average project portfolio within firms. Here, 70 per cent of new products are improvements, cost reductions and additions to existing lines.

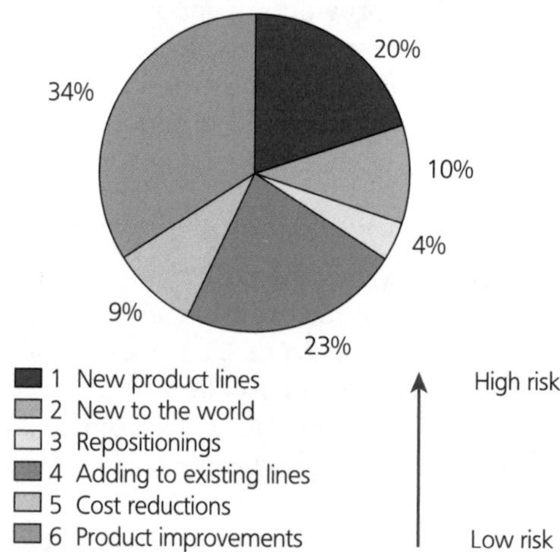

Figure 12.6 The average new product portfolio

Source: Adapted from A. Griffin (1997) PDMA research on new product development practices: updating trends and benchmarking best practices, *Journal of Product Innovation Management*, Vol. 14, 429.

		Product category	
		New	Existing
Brand name	New	New brand	Flanker
	Existing	Brand extension	Line extension

Figure 12.7 Tauber's growth matrix

Source: Tauber, E.M. (1981) Brand franchise extension: new product benefits from existing brand names, *Business Horizons*, Vol. 24, No. 2, 36–41.

Repositioning and brand extensions

The concepts of brand extension and repositioning appear as two distinct elements within classifications of new product development. When it comes to brand extension Tauber's (1981) growth matrix categorises a firm's growth opportunities using two different dimensions: product category, and brand name used. The resulting matrix is shown in Figure 12.7. Tauber makes a key distinction between brand extension and line extension. However, as Ambler and Styles (1997) have shown in a survey of the academic literature, each concept has been given a variety of definitions and the terms are used interchangeably (see Ambler and Styles, 1997). For example, Kotler (1991: 556) defines a brand extension strategy as: 'any effort to extend a successful brand name to launch new or modified products or lines'. Whereas Doyle (1994: 159) is more specific: 'a brand extension means using a brand name successfully established for one segment or channel to enter another one in the same broad market'.

Saunders and Jobber's phasing continuity spectrum (Saunders and Jobber, 1994) illustrates the extent of marketing mix effort required for each of the options open to firms considering new product development (*see* Figure 12.8). Product changes are on the horizontal axis and changes to the rest of the marketing mix are on the vertical axis. Product developments are classified according to the extent of change. This ranges from no change in the upper left-hand quadrant to a new innovative product in the bottom right-hand quadrant. Significantly Saunders and Jobber introduce the notion of tangible and intangible repositioning, and these are distinguished from each other by changes to the physical product. Yet, Bingham and Raffield (1995) identified six positioning alternatives for firms: price, technology, product quality, distribution, image and service. It follows, therefore, that any decision by a firm to alter the perceptual position of a brand (that is, reposition it) will demand careful consideration of all of the brand's attributes (Park *et al.*, 2002). Indeed, Bhat and Reddy (1998) argue in their research on brand positioning that brands can be positioned at a symbolic and/or functional level.

Within FMCG industries product and brand development are considered together. Indeed, according to Yakimov and Beverland (2004), who examined eight brand repositioning case studies, successful brand management firms place the brand at the centre of their organisation and strategy, and build integrated strategies to continually support the brand. While this may be understandable for FMCG, where differences in products is frequently limited, the extent to which this is also the case in non-FMCG goods, and technology-intensive industries in particular, is

Marketing		Product: No change	Product: Modified	Product: Technology change
	No change	**No change** No change	**Facelift** Appearance	**Inconspicuous substitution** Technology Materials Manufacturing
	Modified	**Re-merchandising** Name Promotion Price Distribution Packaging	**Relaunch** Costs Promotion Price Distribution	**Conspicuous substitution** Technology Materials Name Appearance Promotion Price Distribution
	New market/ segment	**Intangible repositioning** Name Promotion Price Distribution Target market Competition	**Tangible repositioning** Name Appearance Costs Promotion Price Distribution Target market Competition	**Neo-innovation** Technology Materials Manufacturing Promotion Price Distribution Target market Competition

Figure 12.8 Saunders and Jobber's phasing continuity spectrum

Source: Saunders, J. and Jobber, D. (1994) Product replacement: Strategies for simultaneous product deletion and launch, *Journal of Product Innovation Management*, Vol. 11, No. 5, 433–50.

less clear. Within technology-intensive industries, such as personal computers, it could be argued that product specification vis á vis price is a more significant factor for consumers.

New product development as an industry innovation cycle

Abernathy and Utterback (1978) suggested that product innovations are soon followed by process innovations in what they described as an industry innovation cycle (*see* Chapter 1). A similar notion can be applied to the categories of new products. The cycle can be identified in a wide variety of industries. New-to-the-world products (Category 1) are launched by large companies with substantial resources, especially technical or marketing resources. Other large firms react swiftly to the launch of such a product by developing their own versions (Categories 2 and 3). Many small and medium-sized companies participate by developing their own new products to compete with the originating firm's product (Category 4). Substantial success and growth can come to small companies that adopt this strategy. Hewlett-Packard has grown into one of the most successful personal computer manufacturers even though it was not, unlike Apple and IBM, at the forefront of the development of the personal computer. As competition intensifies, companies will compete in the market for profits. The result is determined efforts to reduce costs in order to improve these profits, hence there are many cost reductions (Category 5).

Overview of NPD theories

The early stages of the new product development process are most usually defined as idea generation, idea screening, concept development and concept testing. They represent the formation and development of an idea prior to its taking any physical form. In most industries it is from this point onwards that costs will rise significantly. It is clearly far easier to change a concept than a physical product. The subsequent stages involve adding to the concept as those involved with the development (manufacturing engineers, product designers and marketers) begin to make decisions regarding how best to manufacture the product, what materials to use, possible designs and the potential market's evaluations.

The organisational activities undertaken by the company as it embarks on the actual process of new product development have been represented by numerous different models. These have attempted to capture the key activities involved in the process, from idea to commercialisation of the product. The representation of these tasks has changed significantly over the past 30 years. For example, the pharmaceutical industry is dominated by scientific and technological developments that lead to new drugs; whereas the food industry is dominated by consumer research that leads to many minor product changes. And yet the vast majority of textbooks that tackle this subject present the NPD process as an eight-stage linear model regardless of these major differences (Figure 12.9 shows how the process is frequently presented). Consequently this simple linear model is ingrained in the minds of many people. This is largely because new product development is viewed from a financial perspective where cash outflows precede cash inflows (*see* Figure 12.10). This graph shows the cumulative effect on cash flow through the development phases, from the build-up

Figure 12.9 Commonly presented linear NPD model

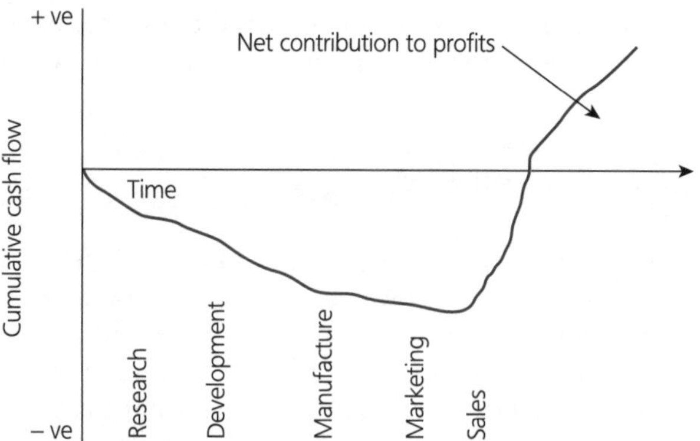

Figure 12.10 Cash flows and new product development

of stock and work in progress in the early stages of production, when there is no balancing in-flow of cash from sales, to the phase of profitable sales which brings the cash in-flow.

Virtually all those actually involved with the development of new products dismiss such simple linear models as not being a true representation of reality. More recent research suggests that the process needs to be viewed as a simultaneous and concurrent process with cross-functional interaction (Hart, 1993; Barczak *et al.*, 2009).

For the reasons outlined above, the different perspectives on NPD have produced a wealth of literature on the subject (Brown and Eisenhardt, 1995; Barczak *et al.*, 2009). In addition, the subject has attracted the attention of many business schools and business consultants, all interested in uncovering the secrets of successful product development. Numerous research projects have been undertaken including indepth case studies across many industries and single companies and broad surveys of industries (e.g. Ancona and Caldwell, 1992; Clark and Fujimoto, 1991; Dougherty, 1990; Biemans *et al.*, 2007).

As a result, research on new product development is varied and fragmented, making it extremely difficult to organise for analysis. Brown and Eisenhardt (1995) have tackled this particular problem head on and have produced an excellent review of the literature. In their analysis they identify three main streams of literature, each having its own particular strengths and limitations (*see* Table 12.3). These streams have evolved around key research findings and together they continue to throw light on many dark areas of new product development.

While this is an important development and a useful contribution to our understanding of the subject area, it offers little help for the practising manager on how he or she should organise and manage the new product development process. An analysis of the models that have been developed on the subject of new product development may help to identify some of the activities that need to be managed.

The fuzzy front end

Within the new product development literature the concept of the so-called 'fuzzy front end' is the messy 'getting started' period of new product development processes. It is at the beginning of the process, or 'the front end', where the organisation develops a concept of the product to be developed and decides whether or not to invest resources

Table 12.3 The three main streams of research within the NPD literature

	Rational planning	Communication web	Disciplined problem solving
Aim/objective/title	Rational planning and management of the development of new products within organisations	The communication web studies the use of information and sources of information by product development teams	Disciplined problem solving focuses on how problems encountered during the NPD process were overcome
Focus of the research	The rational plan research focuses on business performance and financial performance of the product	The communication web looks at the effects of communication on project performance	The third stream tries to examine the process and the wide range of actors and activities involved
Seminal research	The work by Myers and Marquis (1969) and SAPPHO studies (Rothwell *et al.*, 1974) was extremely influential in this field	Thomas Allen's (1969, 1977) research into communication patterns in large industrial laboratories dominates this perspective	The work by the Japanese scholars Imai *et al.* (1985) lies at the heart of this third stream of literature

Source: S.L. Brown and K.M. Eisenhardt (1995) Product development: past research, present findings and future directions, *Academy of Management Review*, Vol. 20, No. 2, 343–78.

in the further development of an idea. It is the phase between first consideration of an opportunity and when it is judged ready to enter the structured development process (Kim and Wilemon, 2002; Koen *et al.*, 2001). It includes all activities from the search for new opportunities through the formation of a germ of an idea to the development of a precise concept. The fuzzy front end disapears when an organisation approves and begins formal development of the concept.

Although the fuzzy front end may not require expensive capital investment, it can consume 50 per cent of development time and it is where major commitments are typically made involving time, money and the product's nature, thus setting the course for the entire project and final end product. Consequently, this phase should be considered as an essential part of development rather than something that happens 'before development', and its cycle time should be included in the total new product development cycle time.

There has been much written in the NPD literature about the need to involve customers at an early stage in the process and to integrate them into the process in order to fully capture ideas (Cooper, 1999; von Hippel, 1986; Brown and Eisenhardt, 1995; 1998; Thomke, 2003). Despite this, customer involvement in NPD has been limited and largely passive in most industries (Weyland and Cole, 1997). There are many reasons for this limited utilisation of consumers in NPD and some have touched on above, but perhaps the most limiting factor is the disconnection between customers and producers.

Nowadays, technology enables an innovative way of involving and integrating customers to the product development process. In this context, it is here that new technologies, most notably in the form of 'toolkits', offer considerable scope for improving connection between consumers and producers. Franke and Piller's (2004)

Table 12.4 Customer roles in NPD

Customer role	NPD phase	Key issues/managerial challenges
Customer as resource	Ideation	Appropriateness of customer as a source of innovation Selection of customer innovator Need for varied customer incentives Infrastructure for capturing customer knowledge Differential role of existing (current) and potential (future) customers
Customer as co-creator	Design and development	Involvement in a wide range of design and development tasks Nature of the NPD context: industrial/consumer products Tighter coupling with internal NPD teams Managing the attendant project uncertainty
	Product testing	Enhancing customers' product/technology knowledge Time-bound activity Ensuring customer diversity
Customer as user	Product support	Ongoing activity Infrastructure to support customer–customer interactions

Source: Adapted from Nambisan, S. (2002) Designing virtual customer environments for new product development: Toward a theory, *Academy of Management Review*, Vol. 27, No. 3, 395.

study analysed the value created by so-called 'toolkits for user innovation and design'. This was a method of integrating customers into new product development and design. The so-called toolkits allow customers to create their own product, which in turn is produced by the manufacturer. An example of a toolkit in its simplest form is the development of personalised products through uploading digital family photographs via the internet and having these printed on to products such as clothing or cups, etc., thereby allowing consumers to create personalised individual products for themselves. User toolkits for innovation are specific to given product or service types and to a specified production system. Within those general constraints, they give users real freedom to innovate, allowing them to develop their custom product via iterative trial and error (von Hippel, 2001; Franke and Piller, 2004).

Nambisan (2002) offers a theoretical lens through which to view these 'virtual customer environments'. He considers the underlying knowledge creation issues and the nature of the customer interactions to identify three roles: customer as resource; customer as co-creator and customer as user. These three distinct but related roles provide a useful classification with which to examine the process of NPD. This classification recognises the considerably different management challenges for the firm if it is to utilise the customer into the NPD process (*see* Table 12.4).

Time to market

Time to market (TTM) is the length of time it takes from a product being conceived to it reaching the market place. TTM is important in industries where products are outdated quickly. A common assumption is that TTM matters most for innovative products, but actually the first mover often has the luxury of time, while the clock is clearly running for the followers. TTM can vary widely between industries, say 15 years in aircraft and six months in food products. Yet, in many ways it is a firm's

TTM capability relative to its direct competitors that is far more important than the naked figure. While other industries may be much faster, they do not pose a direct threat – although one may be able to learn from them and adapt their techniques.

As usual there are some other factors that need to be considered when analysing a firm's TTM. For example, rather than reaching the market as soon as possible, delivering on schedule may be more important: to have the new product available for a trade show could be more valuable. Many managers argue that the shorter the project the less it will cost, so they attempt to use TTM as a means of cutting expenses. Unfortunately, a primary means of reducing TTM is to staff the project more heavily, so a faster project may actually be more expensive. Finally, as we have seen throughout this chapter, the need for change often appears midstream in a project. Consequently, the ability to make changes during product development without being too disruptive can be valuable. For example, one's goal could be to satisfy customers, which could be achieved by adjusting product requirements during development in response to customer feedback. Then TTM could be measured from the last change in requirements until the product is delivered. The pursuit of pure speed of TTM may also harm the business (Cooper and Edgett, 2008).

Agile NPD

Flexible product development is the ability to make changes to the product being developed or in how it is developed, even relatively late in the development process, without being too disruptive. Consequently, the later one can make changes, the more flexible the process is; and the less disruptive the change is, the greater the flexibility. Change can be expected in what the customer wants and how the customer might use the product, in how competitors might respond, and in the new technologies being applied in the product or in its manufacturing process. The more innovative a new product is, the more likely it is that the development team will have to make changes during development. In his book *Flexible Product Development* (2007) Preston Smith uses the software industry to show that having an agile NPD process enables the firm to adapt to changing markets. These days many industrial new product development (NPD) software projects apply agile methodologies, such as *Scrum, eXtreme Programming (XP)* and *Feature-Driven Development (FDD)*. Petri Kettunen from Siemens studied some of these systems and found that agility in embedded software product development can be further enhanced by following typical NPD principles (Kettunen, 2009).

Models of new product development

Among the burgeoning management literature on the subject it is possible to classify the numerous models into eight distinct categories:

1 departmental-stage models;
2 activity-stage models and concurrent engineering;
3 cross-functional models (teams);
4 decision-stage models;

5 conversion-process models;
6 response models;
7 network models and
8 outsourced (see Chapter 16).

Within this taxonomy decision-stage models and activity-stage models are the most commonly discussed and presented in textbooks. Figure 12.13 (later) is an example of an activity-stage model and Cooper's stage-gate model is an example of a decision stage model.

It is worthy of note that there are many companies, especially small specialist manufacturing companies, that continue to operate a craftsman-style approach to product development. This has been the traditional method of product manufacture for the past 500 years. For example, in every part of Europe there are joinery companies manufacturing products to the specific requirements of the user. Many of these products will be single, one-off products manufactured to dimensions given on a drawing. All the activities, including the creation of drawings, collection of raw materials, manufacture and delivery, may be undertaken by one person. Today, when we are surrounded by technology that is sometimes difficult to use never mind understand, it is possible to forget that the traditional approach to product development is still prevalent. Many activities, moreover, remain the same as they have always been.

Departmental-stage models

Departmental-stage models represent the early form of NPD models. These can be shown to be based around the linear model of innovation, where each department is responsible for certain tasks. They are usually represented in the following way. R&D provides the interesting technical ideas; the engineering department will then take the ideas and develop possible prototypes; the manufacturing department will explore possible ways to produce a viable product capable of mass manufacture; the marketing department will then be brought in to plan and conduct the launch. Such models are also referred to as 'over-the-wall' models, so called because departments would carry out their tasks before throwing the project over the wall to the next department (*see* Figure 12.11).

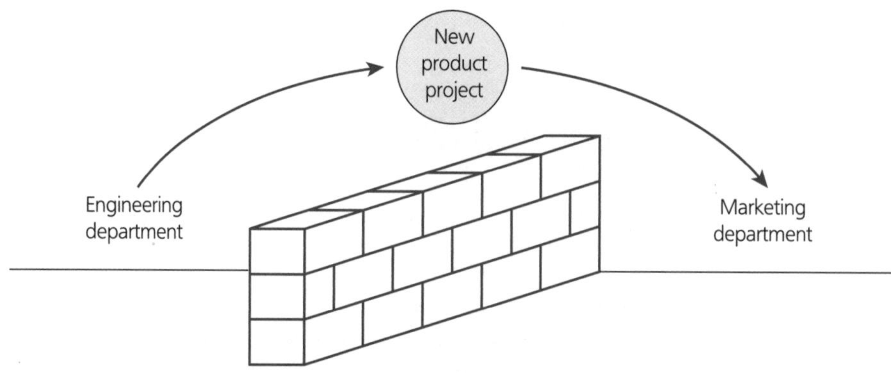

Figure 12.11 Over-the-wall model

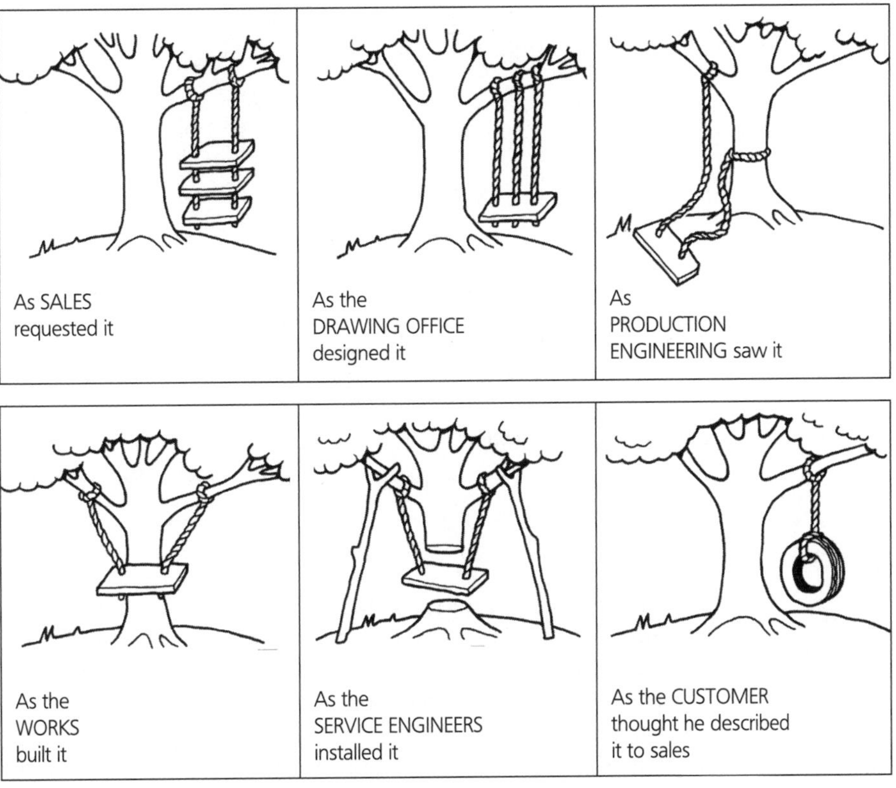

Figure 12.12 Mike Smith's secret weapon: the salutary tale of 'How not to design a swing, or the perils of poor coordination'

Source: C. Lorenz (1990) *The Design Dimension*, Blackwell Publishing Ltd, Oxford.

It is now widely accepted that this insular departmental view of the process hinders the development of new products. The process is usually characterised by a great deal of reworking and consultation between functions. In addition, market research provides continual inputs to the process. Furthermore, control of the project changes on a departmental basis depending on which department is currently engaged in it. The consequence of this approach has been captured by Mike Smith's (1981) humorous tale of 'How not to design a swing, or the perils of poor coordination' (*see* Figure 12.12).

Activity-stage models and concurrent engineering

These are similar to departmental-stage models but because they emphasise activities conducted they provide a better representation of reality. They also facilitate iteration of the activities through the use of feedback loops, something that the departmental-stage models do not. Activity-stage models, however, have also received fierce criticism for perpetuating the 'over-the-wall' phenomenon. More recent activity-stage models (Crawford, 1997) have highlighted the simultaneous nature of the activities within the NPD process, hence emphasising the need for a

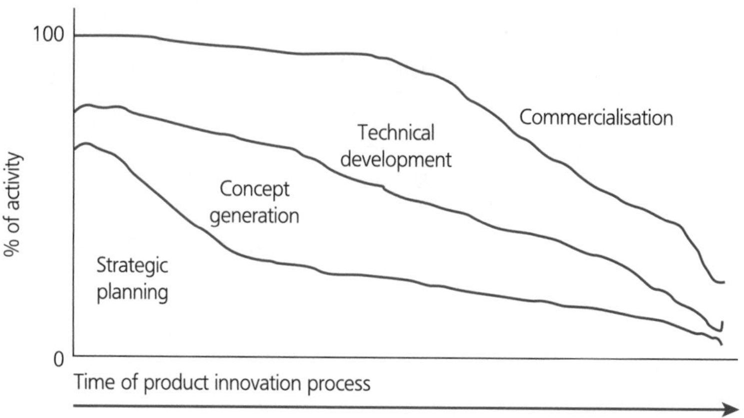

Figure 12.13 An activity-stage model

Source: From *New Products Management*, 5th edn (Crawford, C.M. 1997), © The McMcGraw-Hill Companies, Inc.

cross-functional approach. Figure 12.13 shows an activity-stage model where the activities occur at the same time but vary in their intensity.

In the late 1980s, in an attempt to address some of these problems, many manufacturing companies adopted a concurrent engineering or simultaneous engineering approach. The term was first coined by the Institute for the Defense Analyses (IDA) in 1986 (IDA, 1986) to explain the systematic method of concurrently designing both the product and its downstream production and support processes. The idea is to focus attention on the project as a whole rather than the individual stages, primarily by involving all functions from the outset of the project. This requires a major change in philosophy from functional orientation to project orientation. Furthermore, technology-intensive businesses with very specialist knowledge inputs are more difficult to manage. Such an approach introduces the need for project teams.

Cross-functional models (teams)

Common problems that occur within the product development process revolve around communications between different departments. This problem, specifically with regard to the marketing and the R&D departments, is explored more fully in Chapter 16. In addition, projects would frequently be passed back and forth between functions. Moreover, at each interface the project would undergo increased changes, hence lengthening the product development process. The cross-functional teams (CFT) approach removes many of these limitations by having a dedicated project team representing people from a variety of functions. The use of cross-functional teams requires a fundamental modification to an organisation's structure. In particular, it places emphasis on the use of project management and interdisciplinary teams.

Decision-stage models

Decision-stage models represent the new product development process as a series of decisions that need to be taken in order to progress the project (Cooper and Kleinschmidt, 1993; Kotler, 1997). Like the activity-stage models, many of these models also facilitate iteration through the use of feedback loops. However, a criticism of these models is that such feedback is implicit rather than explicit. The importance of the interaction between functions cannot be stressed enough – the use of feedback loops helps to emphasise this.

Stage-gate process

This is a widely employed product development process that divides the effort into distinct time-sequenced stages separated by management decision gates. It has been popularised by Robert Cooper's research in this area (Cooper, 1999; www.prod-dev.com/stage-gate). Multifunctional teams must successfully complete a prescribed set of related cross-functional tasks in each stage prior to obtaining management approval to proceed to the next stage of product development. The framework of the stage-gate process includes work-flow and decision-flow paths and defines the supporting systems and practices necessary to ensure the ongoing smooth operation of the process.

As with any prescribed approach the stage-gate process suffers from a number of limitations:

- The process is sequencial and can be slow.
- The whole process is focused on end gates rather than on the customer.
- Product concepts can be stopped or frozen too early.
- The high level of uncertainty that accompanies discontinuous new products makes the stage-gate process unsuitable for these products.
- At each stage within the process a low level of knowledge held by the gatekeeper can lead to poor judgements being made on the project.

Conversion-process models

As the name suggests, conversion-process models view new product development as numerous inputs into a 'black box' where they are converted into an output (Schon, 1967). For example, the inputs could be customer requirements, technical ideas and manufacturing capability and the output would be the product. The concept of a variety of information inputs leading to a new product is difficult to criticise, but the lack of detail elsewhere is the biggest limitation of such models.

Response models

Response models are based on the work of Becker and Whistler (1967) who used a behaviourist approach to analyse change. In particular, these models focus on the individual's or organisation's response to a new project proposal or new idea. This approach has revealed additional factors that influence the decision to accept or reject new product proposals, especially at the screening stage.

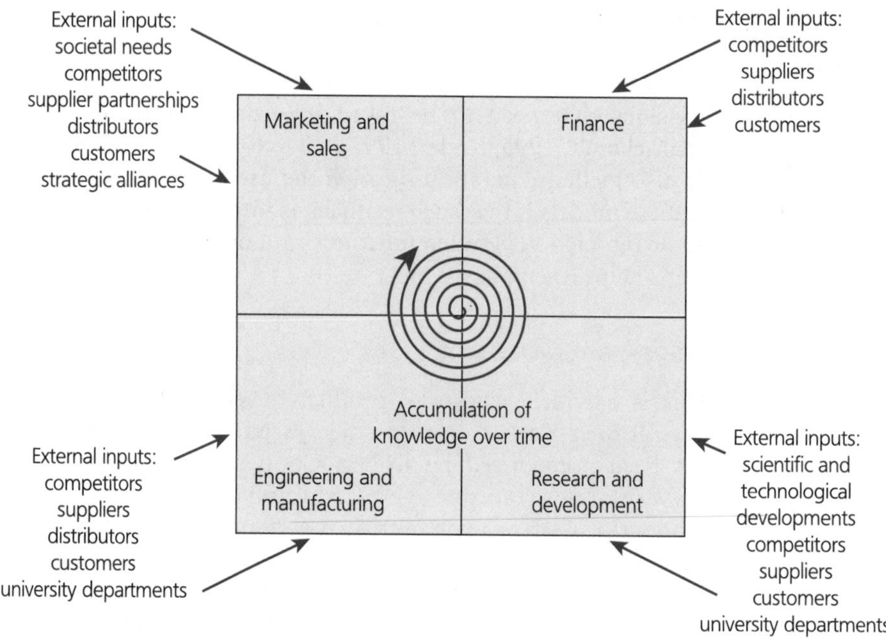

Figure 12.14 A network model of NPD

Network models

This final classification of new product development models represents the most recent thinking on the subject. The case studies in Chapters 7 and 10 highlight the process of accumulation of knowledge from a variety of different inputs, such as marketing, R&D and manufacturing. This knowledge is built up gradually over time as the project progresses from initial idea (technical breakthrough or market opportunity) through development. It is this process that forms the basis of the network models (these models are explored more fully in Nonaka and Takeuchi, 1995).

Essentially, network models emphasise the external linkages coupled with the internal activities that have been shown to contribute to successful product development. There is substantial evidence to suggest that external linkages can facilitate additional knowledge flows into the organisation, thereby enhancing the product development process. These models suggest that NPD should be viewed as a knowledge-accumulation process that requires inputs from a wide variety of sources. The model in Figure 12.14 helps to highlight the accumulation of knowledge over time. This may be thought of as a snowball gaining in size as it rolls down a snow-covered mountain.

Pause for thought

Linear models are simple and hence dominate NPD, but they do not reflect reality.

Case study

Launching innocent into the growing fruit smoothie market

Introduction

Since launching the business in 1999, innocent has not only witnessed the rise of its own business, but also the growth of the smoothie market and the rise of competitors. Whilst being the market leader (UK market share of 72 per cent by their own calculation), the 2005 purchase of the number two smoothie brand, PJ Smoothies, by the multinational PepsiCo firm means that innocent can expect fierce competition as it attempts to be the dominant smoothie brand in Europe. This case study tells the story of how innocent developed a business idea into a product and launched it into the UK market with very limited funds. At that time the smoothie market was in its infancy, although innocent was not the first into the market and could not benefit from any early entrant advantages. None the less, the launch of the product coincided with the rapid growth of the market, especially in the form of own-label smoothies from Sainsbury, Tesco and M&S.

The fruit smoothies market

Fruit smoothies are a fruit-based beverage (usually 100 per cent crushed fruit and very little else). According to the advertisements they are nutritious and versatile, and are an excellent way of grabbing a quick meal. Smoothies have been popular in health-conscious California for many decades. They are generally low in fat and calories and make an excellent drink and/or snack especially at lunchtime. innocent is now the brand leader in the UK smoothie market, generating revenue of £80 million annually. Pete & Johnny's – the first UK smoothie company – has annual sales of £13 million while private-label brands make up around one-third of the market. innocent's timing has been lucky or astute. As concern grows over rising levels of obesity in Europe, consumers are paying more attention to what they eat and drink and multinational food and beverage companies are trying to tap into changing consumer tastes by selling healthier products. Californians had been consuming fruit smoothies for a number of years before the concept was exported to the UK. It is Harry Cragoe, founder of PJ Smoothies, who is generally regarded as the first entrant into the UK in 1994. Harry had been living in California and had enjoyed fruit smoothies for lunch; when he returned to the UK he realised this drink was not available. But importing a fresh product and transporting it 8,000 miles across the world proved to be extremely difficult. Indeed, the first few years of operating were full of problems. Initially the smoothies were simply imported in large containers. They were frozen and there were problems of them not defrosting or still being frozen when they were put on the shelves. Not surprisingly the product was twice as expensive as other drinks at the time. Many experienced traders were doubtful such a product could succeed in such a highly competitive market. Eventually, however, Cragoe was able to establish production in Newark, Nottinghamshire, which has solved many of the initial logistical problems.

The success of the PJ Smoothie business is remarkable and unusual in that very little money has been spent on marketing and market research. This is even more remarkable for a fast moving consumer good. Cragoe is a critic of traditional market research, arguing that 'I've never spent a penny on market research because you end up looking at it too religiously. The growth we have experienced is purely from word of mouth. People have tasted the products and told their friends. We also tried to get away from bad labelling, deciding instead to use just pictures of apples and oranges. We have always tried to be fun, relevant and interesting with our packaging.' Cragoe insists that tasting the product is the best way to experience whether it is good or bad and this has led to even more growth. He believes that 99 per cent of people like the taste and pass on the message.

Source: Innocent Ltd

→

innocent and developing a new product concept

Hot on the heels of PJ Smoothies was innocent smoothies. In 2005 innocent drinks was the fastest growing food and drinks company in the UK; it was launched in 1999, and the company has grown into the No. 1 smoothie brand in the UK with 240 staff and an £80 million turnover. It has gone from making three recipes of smoothie to seventeen different drinks. Through constant innovation and refusal to compromise, innocent continues to make an unrivalled range of totally natural fruit drinks that taste good and have health benefits. But the road to success was far from simple.

The beverage market is fiercely competitive, dominated by global players such as Coca-Cola and Pepsi. The range of beverages available is also vast, from bottled water to carbonated drinks in all flavours. The fruit smoothie product being launched was perishable, with a very short shelf life, and with a price tag at almost £2 a bottle it was four times that of other beverages on the shelf. Achieving success was not going to be easy.

The beginnings of the business idea stretch back many years and is the result of a friendship started at university. Richard Reed, Adam Balon and Jon Wright left university and went into the obligatory milk-round professions – one into advertising, two into management consultancy. Four years later, they were still talking about their business ideas, although they still had no product. One idea they all liked and enjoyed was fruit smoothies. They all enjoyed a fruit smoothie for lunch and all had enjoyed making them at home with fresh soft fruit and an electric blender. At the time there were very few smoothies on the shelf. In 1998, during their spare time from work and sometimes during their time at work the three friends began planning their business idea of fruit smoothies. During this time they continued trying out recipes on friends and developing their business plan. At the end of that time they spent £500 on fruit, turned it into smoothies and tested their drinks on visitors to the Jazz on the Green festival in London. Their much-recounted scenario goes like this:

We put up a big sign saying, 'Do you think we should give up our jobs to make these smoothies?' and put out a bin saying 'YES' and a bin saying 'NO' and asked people to put the empty bottle in the right bin (see Figure 12.15). At the end of the weekend the 'YES' bin was full so we went in the next day and resigned.

(innocentdrinks.co.uk)

Figure 12.15 innocent's own form of concept testing

But the launch of the business took much longer than they had realised; first, there was the problem of funds. How should the entrepreneurs raise money? The options were as follows.

Raising money

When it comes to financing a business, there are two basic types of funding: debt and equity. Loans are debt financing; you borrow money and must pay it back, with interest, within a certain timeframe. With equity funding, you raise money by selling a portion of your ownership in the company. This is the traditional route for people wishing to fund a start-up business, with friends and family probably the most common form of debt financiers; others are: banks, finance companies, credit unions, credit card companies and private corporations. Taking out a business loan allows the owners to remain in control of the company and not answer to investors. Getting a loan is also usually faster than searching out investors. Professional investors review thousands of investment opportunities each year, and only invest in a small fraction. Another benefit of debt financing is that as a firm repays its debts so it builds creditworthiness. This makes the business more attractive to lenders in the future.

Overall, debt financing is typically cheaper than equity financing because the firm only pays interest and fees, and retains full ownership of the company.

Equity financing

Selling equity means taking on investors and being accountable to them. Many small business owners raise equity by bringing in relatives, friends, colleagues or customers who hope to see their businesses succeed and get a return on their investment. Other sources of equity financing include venture capitalists, which are professional investors willing to take risks on promising new businesses. These investors include individuals with substantial net worth, corporations and financial institutions (this is the group highlighted in the BBC television programme *Dragons' Den*). Most investors do not expect an immediate return on their investment, but they would expect the business to be profitable in three to seven years. Equity investors can be passive or active. Passive investors are willing to offer capital but will play little or no part in running the company, while active investors expect to be heavily involved in the company's operations. Personality conflicts can arise in either arrangement. Equity financing is not cheap: investors are entitled to a share of the business's profits indefinitely. Conversely, small business owners who may have difficulty securing a traditional loan or are comfortable sharing control of their business with partners may find equity financing a mutually beneficial arrangement.

Venture capital is a widely used phrase that few people properly understand. It typically refers to investment funds or partnerships (and, increasingly, venture capital divisions within large corporations) that focus on investing in new, promising start-up and emerging companies. Venture capitalists (VCs) have invested in some of today's most famous corporate names, including Apple, Genentech, Intel and Compaq. Typically, the investment is in company stock – the venture capitalist gets an ownership interest for the money invested. Beyond supplying the company with money, the VC also provides assistance and expertise with business planning – bringing industry knowledge, experience in growing businesses and expertise in taking the company public some day. Entrepreneurs should be wary, venture capitalists' primary motive is to make a lot of money on their intended investment. Furthermore, most venture capitalists are interested only in businesses that can grow very big. So, if you're a small grocery store, you should seek funds elsewhere.

Fortunately, the founders of innocent benefited from very good educations and had many business contacts from over four years working in advertising and management consultancy; hence it was not long before they were in touch with venture capitalists. Eventually Maurice Pinto, a wealthy American businessman, invested £250,000 and became the fourth shareholder in the group, retaining a 20 per cent stake. The money provided salaries for the three entrepreneurs, office space, cash to buy production capacity at bottling plants, promotional material and labelling for the bottles.

Product development and growing the business

While on the surface this new business venture may seem slightly unusual, and the three founders would probably very much like to think that business is unique, the development of their fruit smoothie product follows the well-documented process from concept to commercialisation (*see* Figure 12.9).

Generation of new product concepts

The three founders of innocent had been exploring and planning starting their own business ever since they met at university. They had even tried a few crazy ideas, including a gadget that would prevent baths from overflowing. It was the fruit smoothie concept, however, that seemed to appeal to the three founders the most; this is probably largely due to the fact that they were developing a new product for people like them: young urban professionals who wanted a healthy lunchtime drink to go with their sandwich. In many large cities across Europe and the US lunch for most is a sandwich. And when buying your sandwich most people usually buy a drink to wash it down. Also, the UK Government Health Department was promoting the benefits of eating more fruit and vegetables. This was a publicity campaign that innocent could use to its advantage.

Idea screening

Having a new product concept is a long way from a commercially successful new product. Moreover, this was not a completely new product; fruit smoothies had been on the market for several years, hence, innocent was entering an established market, albeit a relatively new one. Their challenge was to become

→

more successful than the existing players. To do this they believed their product had to be different. They were able to achieve this through clever and very different forms of promotion. In many ways they were developing the whole fruit smoothie market, without realising it at the time.

The main purpose of screening ideas is to select those that will be successful and drop those that will not – herein lies the difficulty. Trying to identify which ideas are going to be successful and which are not is extremely difficult. Screening product ideas is essentially an evaluation process. It occurs at every stage of the new product development process and involves such questions as:

1. Do we have the necessary commercial knowledge and experience?
2. Do we have the technical know-how to develop the idea further?
3. Would such a product be suitable for our business?
4. Are we sure there will be sufficient demand?

From here more detailed evaluation checklists can be drawn up, such as the one in Table 12.5.

Concept testing

innocent had already proved to themselves – with their unusual form of product testing using bins – that their target market liked the product. None the less, starting a company from scratch is daunting. There's little room for error so the product has to be pitched in exactly the right way. Given that this was a crowded market, innocent drinks realised early on that the product had to stand out on the shelf. Packaging is a critical issue, especially in FMCG markets. innocent decided to develop something different. A friend of the three founders was hired to look after branding. Once again a great deal of emphasis was placed on the fact that the three founders belonged to the target market and decisions were made based on their own thoughts and ideas, despite a lack of branding experience. Indeed, innocent confessed in interviews with the press that 'our user testing was done on people we knew. We'd email our friends with packaging designs.' None the less, the company has always sought advice and expertise from external experts; for example, Turner Duckworth designed the original bottle shape. innocent also used an agency for an advertising campaign in Ireland.

Design has played a big role in the product's success, from the logo and shape of the bottles to the delivery vans. Careful consideration of design and packaging has contributed to the success of the business. The brand was totally unknown so innocent had to rely on people being intrigued enough to try the product. It is not a cheap drink, so it had to appeal to the consumer and it had to stand out and look like something you would want to pick up. Finally, like all beverage producers, innocent relied on the taste to be sufficiently good to ensure a repeat purchase.

Prototype development

Given that the three founders were the target market – young (they were all in their mid-twenties), urban office workers (they all worked in central London), affluent (they all had very well paid jobs) – identifying what would appeal was simply a question of asking themselves: What do we like? They wanted to emphasise the purity and naturalness of the product, which is made completely from fresh fruit. This is a key point because most fruit drinks are made from concentrated juice with water – and perhaps sweeteners, colours and preservatives – added. innocent wanted to offer pure fruit juice. This had significant manufacturing implications and problems, as they later discovered. They also wanted a bottle that would sit easily in the hand for the 'grab-a-sandwich' crowd and they wanted to introduce an element of fun. Lacking any kind of knowledge about the design process or how to go about finding and developing

Table 12.5 Simple evaluation checklist

	Evaluation criteria
1	Technical abilities
2	Competitive rationale
3	Patentability
4	Stability of the market
5	Integration and synergy
6	Market: growth and competition
7	Channel fit
8	Manufacturing
9	Financial
10	Longer term strategic fit

the right image, the company was forced to use external experts and keep things simple. According to innocent the logo, which resembles an apple with a halo, or a person with a halo depending on how you look at it, was sketched on a serviette in felt-tip pen.

The creation of a brand image is crucial here, and especially so for products in FMCG markets. For all new entrants into an existing market the aim is to try to get existing users to change to your brand of fruit smoothie and to try to attract new buyers who currently purchase bottled water or Coca-Cola, for example. The brand image developed and carefully nurtured by innocent is one based on fun, and an almost hippie approach to life. This is reflected in the packaging, promotion and logo used for the product.

Another interesting point is that due to the high raw material costs and high production costs, initially the product offered was relatively expensive – three or four times as much as lunchtime beverage alternatives.

Market testing

Fruit is sourced from all over the world, and regular sampling is conducted at innocent's test kitchen to ensure that only the most flavoursome varieties are used in the drinks. Recipes created in the kitchen at their London offices are tested on people in surrounding office buildings. Once approved, the drinks are manufactured by one of four independent manufacturers in the UK and sold in outlets across the UK and Europe. The smoothies, which appeal to consumers whom innocent describe as 'slightly more female, slightly more affluent, slightly younger', are priced at the high end of the fruit juice market, selling for £1.79 to £1.99 in 'on the go' plastic bottles, and for £3.29 to £3.49 in larger take-home cartons. innocent has also recently launched a childrens' range, retailing at 99p.

Launch and promotion

Having developed their idea, the three founders then ran into numerous other operational difficulties that meant the launch of the product took much longer than expected. They encountered barriers, including various experts who told them their idea would not work. In particular this was because the product's shelf life was too short. Arguments then ensued about whether or not to include preservatives or additives to lengthen its life. Ignoring most of the expert advice, innocent created a range of smoothies made from 100 per cent pure and fresh fruit. Careful quality controlled production methods and the latest packaging technology gave it the longest possible shelf life.

Their first foray into the market was very modest. Out to Lunch, the local sandwich shop round the corner from their office in Ladbroke Grove, agreed to stock a few of their drinks. They supplied 20 bottles and, when they checked later, found that the drinks had sold out. Indeed, most of their early sales were through local delicatessens and sandwich shops, but it was not long before Coffee Republic, also a young and growing business, agreed to stock innocent drinks in their eight or nine shops.

innocent has not spent large sums of money on television, press or radio promotion. Emphasis is placed on packaging design and retailers who stock and shelf the product. Advertising copy tends to be witty and straightforward, as does other communications material. The relationship with retailers has been built up through regular communication, including a newsletter, which combines product information and fun stories. Each communication is intended to reinforce the unique brand image innocent has built for itself. The copy on the labelling is intended to break down the barriers between manufacturer and customer, using humour. For example, the 'this water' labels have a section called fruit corner, which gives the fruit a personality while also explaining why it's good for you. See the following example about the apple:

> *Apples have a long history. God put them in his garden so that Adam and Eve would have something to talk about on that awkward first date. But it all went tragically wrong; indeed, the reason why you and I feel sinful thoughts is because of that pesky apple. But apples have done a lot to improve their public image since then. William Tell did some tricks with one a few hundred years ago, and there was the one that fell out of a tree and hit Archimedes on the head, prompting him to discover fire later that day. Marvellous.*
>
> (innocentdrinks.co.uk)

Future growth

Growth for many businesses can cause problems and sometimes cause a firm to fail; usually this is because it overstretches to expand, borrows money →

and then runs into cash flow problems. innocent was careful not to fall into this well-known trap despite its dramatic growth. innocent adopted a cautious approach with the national multiples such as Tesco and Sainsbury, despite the lure of multi-million-pound orders. To begin with innocent would only supply a few of the multiples stores and as sales grew and revenue came in so the production would be increased. This is a much slower approach to growth and can sometimes allow competitors to enter the market or allow the multiples themselves to develop own-label versions. None the less, innocent adopted the prudent approach, which seems to have paid off.

innocent now employs 240 people and has slowly expanded along the line of industrial units rented by the company. innocent recorded turnover of £80 million in 2006 and is growing at an annual rate of 50 per cent to 60 per cent. innocent now supplies most of the major supermarkets and this year became Britain's leading brand of smoothie, selling, they calculate, about 72 per cent of the 50 million downed annually by British drinkers. If imitation is the sincerest form of flattery then innocent's founders should feel very pleased. The refrigerated shelves of the nation's supermarkets are filled with own-label versions of some of the company's best sellers such as its yogurt, vanilla bean and honey 'thickie'. But this could present a serious challenge to the firm. innocent would not be the first manufacturer to lose out to own-label multiples like Sainsbury, Tesco and Asda.

There would also seem to be many opportunities for future growth. innocent are still aware that while the business has grown extremely fast there are still plenty of people who have not yet tasted innocent drinks. innocent is continuing to extend its product line with new flavours of smoothies and a new product launched in 2003 called Juicy Water, whose packaging was designed by Coley Porter Bell. innocent's main market is still the UK and Ireland, which accounts for 90 per cent of its sales, but its smoothies are also sold in The Netherlands, Belgium, Luxembourg and France. It eventually plans to expand within and beyond Europe. 'We have the trademark registered in every country that we think it can become business relevant.' These include the US, Australia, New Zealand, China, India and countries in South America.

Like any growing business, maintaining innocent's internal culture as the company expands is going to be a challenge. Much will depend on the rate of growth and whether the company will be able to control this growth. Clearly, employing the right people as the business expands, both in the UK and overseas, will be one of the significant challenges.

Many analysts argue that innocent is one of a new breed of virtual food and drink companies. Such companies develop the brand and outsource production. There's a division of labour between the owner of the brand and the manufacturer. Other such firms include: Green & Black's, the organic chocolate company; Duchy Originals, which sells organic foods; and Gu Chocolate Puds. These smaller food companies have found there is demand for products made with natural or organic ingredients and low in fats, sugars and salts. While larger food companies have been altering product ingredients to try to address consumer concerns, smaller companies have been quicker at creating products that meet specific demands. The success of these companies in identifying changes in consumer tastes has made them attractive acquisition targets; for example, in May 2005 Green & Black's was bought by Cadbury Schweppes for £20 million.

PepsiCo enters the smoothie market

In 2005 the maker of Pepsi dramatically entered the UK smoothie market with the purchase of the British smoothie and fruit juice brand PJ Smoothies. PepsiCo UK did not reveal the price it paid for the business, based in Newark, Nottinghamshire. PJ, launched in 1994, founded the British smoothie market and has become its leading brand. PepsiCo said PJ Smoothies is the only major brand that produces its own 100 per cent fruit smoothies.

Between 1998 and 2004, PJ spent £4 million developing the brand. It remained the top smoothie brand in terms of volume, with most of its sales in Britain. PJ was launched in the Irish Republic in 2003.

PepsiCo UK said it would maintain PJ's operational structure and manufacturing would continue at Newark. It said the move would give it a significant presence in the rapidly growing premium juice market. PepsiCo said PJ, which now has a 19 per cent market share, would complement its existing drinks brands Tropicana and Copella.

Pete & Johnny Smoothies have recently undertaken a major rebranding programme, with a new logo that

Table 12.6 Smoothies brands (market value and market share)

	2007 £m	% share	2008 £m	% share	2009 £m	% share	2007–09 % point different
Innocent	150	71	120	71	100	80	–33
PJs*	25	12	10	6	na	na	na
Tropicana Smoothies	8	4	15	9	3	2	–63
Ella's Kitchen	1.5	1	2.2	1	2.5	2	67
Others	4	2	5	3	4	3	–
Own-labels	22	10	18	10	16	12	–28
Total	**210**	**100**	**170**	**100**	**125**	**100**	**–40**

*brand discontinued in late 2008.

Source: Mintel Group 2011 Smoothies, UK, 2010, Market share.

is stronger, more modern and presents a clearer image. The PJ's rebranding is designed to maximise shelf impact and re-emphasise the company logo, which now incorporates different fruit for different blends. The reverse of the label carries humorous copy and cartoons, illustrating Pete & Johnny's adventures over the past ten years. In addition, PJ's is introducing a groundbreaking 500ml smoothie bottle in response to consumer demand. The market shares for smoothies is shown in Table 12.6.

The global recession has blown a cold wind through the UK smoothies market. During the recession people have understandably tried to cut their costs. The high-priced fruit smoothies have consequently suffered. In addition people have tended to abandon new products for ones they know and trust. For example, in 2010 Pepsi, Robinsons squash and the childrens' drink Fruit Shoot were among Britvic's best-selling brands. According to some analysts the UK smoothies market has fallen by 30 per cent in value. More worrying is that premium high street brands such as Waitrose and M&S have introduced own label competing products. The future for innocent looks more difficult now than at any time in the past five years.

Conclusions

innocent's turnover has increased from £35 million in 2004 to £80 million in 2006 and in 2005 the company overtook P&J Smoothies as brand leader. The success of innocent is remarkable partly because this is such a competitive market in which some of the world's largest brands operate and partly because this success has been achieved unconventionally with minimal use of traditional advertising and promotional techniques. The development and launch of their business and new product in particular follows a conventional approach from concept to market, but innocent has used some very different approaches along the way. According to innocent there are some important factors that have contributed to its success. These are:

1. Keeping your potential customer's tastes, lifestyle and personality clearly in view.
2. Keeping designs simple and practical and concentrating on the quality of the product can be the key to standing out in an overcrowded market.
3. The brand image has to consistently reflect the product and the company's values.
4. Getting the product, packaging and marketing design right before diversifying and expanding will help establish the product.
5. How should innocent respond to falling sales and market share?

The founders of innocent perhaps project an image of being hippies who have emerged from a travelling caravan to start a drinks business and who are now investing all the profits into Third World social programmes. However, these friends had a privileged upbringing (one of them attending Winchester College, one of the world's most expensive private schools), gained even more knowledge from four years at university and then gained a further four years of practical experience working for large corporate city firms in London advising others on how to run a business. Although the promotional material might suggest a 'devil may care' attitude to life, the

→

three were involved in meticulous planning of their business idea. For example, even when they had decided on their business idea and began planning it, they adopted a cautious approach by negotiating two months' leave from their employers as opposed to simply leaving employment.

Turning to another company and a similar scenario, but this time with ice cream, two self-confessed hippies built an ice cream brand in the 1980s on their socially conscious image – Ben & Jerry's 'all natural' ice cream – and then sold to the conglomerate Unilever for $326 million. While innocent are sticking to their values of doing something they can be proud of, whilst keeping an eye on the commercial side of things too, we can see from Ben & Jerry's example that there is always the potential for a 'hippie' brand to be sold for a huge amount of money.

Source: AC Nielsen Scantrack Total Market, 4 weeks to WE 30 October 2004; Cummings, L. (2005) Just an Innocent business?, BBC News Online: Business, 23 August; Wiggins, J. (2005) An Innocent making its way in the big bad world of health, FT.com, 22 August; Wiggins, J. (2009) Tried and trusted brands give smoothies and bottled water a hard time, FT.com, 15 July.

Questions

1 innocent are very clear about the image it wishes to project to the public. This is one based on being different, fun-loving and having a care-free approach to life. This hippie-style image has helped the brand become acceptable to the young urban professionals at which it is aimed. But beneath the surface of this image there is evidence of a business that could be characterised as single-minded, profit driven and very business orientated. Where is the evidence of the latter?

2 The success of the business is partly based on extremely good communications with retailers. How is this achieved?

3 What type of financing did innocent secure? Does it matter?

4 Would you sell the company to Coca-Cola for £400 million? As one of the shareholders you could pocket tens of millions of pounds. If not, why not?

5 innocent benefited from a key advantage: what was this and explain how it helped in the product development process.

6 How is innocent 'virtual' and how is this different from traditional food and drink manufacturers? What advantages and disadvantages does this provide?

7 Use CIM (Figure 1.9) to illustrate the innovation process.

Chapter summary

This chapter has considered the relationship between new products and prosperity and shown that new product development is one of the most common forms of organic growth strategies. The range of NPD strategies is wide indeed and can range from packaging alterations to new technological research. The chapter stressed the importance of viewing a product as a multi-dimensional concept.

The later part of the chapter focused on the various models of NPD that have emerged over the past 50 years. All of these have strengths and weaknesses. By their very nature, models attempt to capture and portray a complex notion and in so doing often oversimplify elements. This is the central argument of critics of the linear model of NPD, that it is too simplistic and does not provide for any feedback or concurrent activities. More recent models such as network models try to emphasise the importance of the external linkages in the NPD process.

Discussion questions

1 Explain why the process of new product development is frequently represented as a linear process and why this does not reflect reality.

2 Explain why screening should be viewed as a continual rather than a one-off activity.

3 Discuss how the various groups of NPD models have contributed to our understanding of the subject of NPD.

4 To what extent has BMW repositioned the Mini?

5 Examine the concept of a multi-dimensional product; how is it possible to create a new product by modifying the price dimension?

6 The software industry seems to have a very flexbile NPD process enabling changes to be made to the product at any time. Consider whether this approach could be applicable for a car production line or mobile phone handset products.

7 Explain why time to market may be less important than a flexible NPD process.

8 Discuss the strengths of network models of NPD.

Key words and phrases

References

Abernathy, W.L. and Utterback, J. (1978) 'Patterns of industrial innovation', in Tushman, M.L. and Moore, W.L. (eds) *Readings in Management of Innovation*, HarperCollins, New York, 97–108.

Allen, T.J. (1969) Communication networks in R&D laboratories, *R&D Management*, Vol. 1, 14–21.

Allen, T.J. (1977) *Managing the Flow of Technology*, MIT Press, Cambridge, MA.

Ambler, T. and Styles, C. (1997) Brand development vs new product development: Towards a process model of extension decisions, *Journal of Product and Brand Management*, Vol. 6, No. 1, 13–26.

Ancona, D.G. and Caldwell, D.F. (1992) Bridging the boundary: external processes and performance in organisational teams, *Administrative Science Quarterly*, Vol. 37, 634–65.

Ansoff, I. (1965) *Corporate Strategy*, Penguin, Harmondsworth.

Ansoff, I. (1968) *Toward a Strategy of the Theory of the Firm*, McGraw-Hill, New York.

Becker, S. and Whistler, T.I. (1967) The innovative organisation: a selective view of current theory and research, *Journal of Business*, Vol. 40, No. 4, 462–69.

Bhat, S. and Reddy, S.K. (1998) Symbolic and functional positioning of brands, *Journal of Consumer Marketing*, Vol. 15, No. 1, 32–43.

Bingham, F.G. and Raffield, B.T. (1995) *Business Marketing Management*, South Western Publishing, Cincinnati, OH.

Booz, Allen & Hamilton (1982) *New Product Management for the 1980s*, Booz, Allen & Hamilton, New York.

Brown, J.S. and Eisenhardt, K.M. (1998) *Competing on the Edge – Strategy as Structured Chaos*, Harvard Business School, Boston, M.A.

Brown, S.L. and Eisenhardt, K.M. (1995) Product development: past research, present findings and future directions, *Academy of Management Review*, Vol. 20, No. 2, 343–78.

Clark, K. and Fujimoto, T. (1991) *Product Development Performance*, Harvard Business School Press, Boston, MA.

Cooper, R.G. (1999) From experience: the invisible success factors in product innovation, *Journal of Product Innovation Management*, Vol. 16, No. 2, 115–33.

Cooper R.G. and Edgett, S.J. (2008) Maximizing productivity in product innovation, *Research Technology Management*, March.

Cooper, R.G. and Kleinschmidt, E.J. (1993) Major new products: what distinguishes the winners in the chemical industry?, *Journal of Product Innovation Management*, Vol. 10, No. 2, 90–111.

Corrocher, N. and Zirulia, L. (2010) Demand and innovation in services: The case of mobile communications, *Research Policy*, Vol. 39, No. 7, 945–55.

Craig, A. and Hart, S. (1992) Where to now in new product development?, *European Journal of Marketing*, Vol. 26, 11.

Dolan, R.J. (1993) *Managing the New Product Development Process*, Addison-Wesley, Reading, MA.

Dougherty, D. (1990) Understanding new markets for new products, *Strategic Management Journal*, Vol. 11, 59–78.

Doyle, P. (1994) *Marketing Management and Strategy*, Prentice-Hall, Englewood Cliffs, NJ, 159–65.

Finger, S. and Dixon, J.R. (1989a) A review of research in mechanical engineering design, part I: Descriptive, prescriptive, and computer-based models of design processes, *Research in Engineering Design*, Vol. 1, No. 1, 51–68.

Finger, S. and Dixon, J.R. (1989b) A review of research in mechanical engineering design, part II: Representations, analysis, and design for the life cycle, *Research in Engineering Design*, Vol. 1, No. 2, 121–37.

Franke, N. and Piller, F. (2004) Value creation by toolkits for user innovation and design: The case of the watch market, *Journal of Product Innovation Management*, Vol. 21, No. 6, 401–16.

Green, P.E. and Srinivasan, V. (1990) Conjoint analysis in marketing: New developments with implications for research and practice, *Journal of Marketing*, Vol. 54, No. 4, 3–19.

Hart, S. (1993) Dimensions of success in new product development: an exploratory investigation, *Journal of Marketing Management*, Vol. 9, No. 9, 23–41.

IDA (1986) *The Role of Concurrent Engineering in Weapons Systems Acquisition*, report R–338, IDA Washington, DC.

Imai, K., Ikujiro, N. and Takeuchi, H. (1985) 'Managing the new product development process: how Japanese companies learn and unlearn', in Hayes, R.H., Clark, K. and Lorenz C. (eds) *The Uneasy Alliance: Managing the Productivity–Technology Dilemma*, Harvard Business School Press, Boston, MA, 337–75.

Johne, F.A. and Snelson, P.A. (1988) The role of marketing specialists in product development, Proceedings of the 21st Annual Conference of the Marketing Education Group, Huddersfield, Vol. 3, 176–91.

Johnson, G. and Scholes, K. (1997) *Exploring Corporate Strategy*, 4th edn, Prentice Hall, Hemel Hempstead.

Johnson, S.C. and Jones, C. (1957) How to organise for new products, *Harvard Business Review*, May–June, Vol. 35, 49–62.

Kettunen, P. (2009) Adopting key lessons from agile manufacturing to agile software product development – A comparative study, *Technovation*, Vol. 29, Nos 6–7, 408–22.

Kim, J. and Wilemon, D. (2002) Focusing the fuzzy front end in new product development, *R&D Management*, Vol. 32, No. 4, 269–79.

Koen, P., Ajamian, G., Burkart, R., Clamen, A., Davidson, J., Ámore, R.D., Elkins, C., Herald, K., Incorvia, M., Johnson, A., Karol, R., Seibert, R., Slavejkov, A. and Wagner, K. (2001) Providing clarity and a common language to the 'fuzzy front end', *Research Technology Management*, March–April, 46–55.

Kotler, P. (1997) *Marketing Management*, Prentice-Hall, Englewood Cliffs, NJ.

Krishnan, V. and Ulrich, K.T. (2001) Product development decisions: A review of the literature, *Management Science*, Vol. 47, No. 1, 1–21.

Mahajan, V.E. and Wind, J. (1992) New product models – Practice, shortcomings and desired improvements, *Journal of Product Innovation Management*, Vol. 9(June), 128–39.

Myers, S. and Marquis, D.G. (1969) Successful industrial innovation: a study of factors underlying innovation and selected firms, National Science Foundation, NSF 69–17, Washington.

Nambisan, S. (2002) Designing virtual customer environments for new product development: Toward a theory, *Academy of Management Review*, Vol. 27, No. 3, 392–413.

Nonaka, I. and Takeuchi, H. (1995) *The Knowledge Creating Company*, Oxford University Press, Oxford.

Park, J.-W., Kim, K.-H. and Kim, J. (2002) 'Acceptance of brand extensions: interactive influences of product category similarity, typicality of claimed benefits, and brand relationship quality', in Broniarczyk, S. and Nakamoto, K. (eds) *Advances in Consumer Research*, Vol. 29, Association for Consumer Research, Valdosta, GA.

Rogers, E. and Shoemaker, R. (1972) *Communications of Innovations*, Free Press, New York.

Rothwell, R., Freeman, C., Horlsey, A., Jervis, V.T.P., Robertson, A.B. and Townsend, J. (1974) SAPPHO updated: Project SAPPHO phase II, *Research Policy*, Vol. 3, 258–91.

Saren, M. (1984) A classification of review models of the intra-firm innovation process, *R&D Management*, Vol. 14, No. 1, 11–24.

Saunders, J. and Jobber, D. (1994) Product replacement: Strategies for simultaneous product deletion and launch, *Journal of Product Innovation Management*, Vol. 11, No. 5, 433–50.

Schon, D. (1967) Champions for radical new inventions, *Harvard Business Review*, March–April, 77–86.

Smith, P.G. (2007) *Flexible product development: building agility for changing markets*, John Wiley and Sons, New York.

Smith, M.R.H. (1981) Paper presented to the National Conference on Quality and Competitiveness, London, November, reported in *Financial Times*, 25 November.

Tauber, E.M. (1981) Brand franchise extension: new product benefits from existing brand names, *Business Horizons*, Vol. 24, No. 2, 36–41.

Thomas, R.J. (1993) *New Product Development*, John Wiley, New York.

Thomke, S.H. (2003) *Experimentation Matters: Unlocking the Potential of New Technologies for Innovation*, Harvard Business School Press, Boston, MA.

von Hippel, E. (1986) Lead users: a source of novel product concepts, *Management Science*, Vol. 32, No. 7, 791–805.

von Hippel, E. (2001) Perspective: User toolkits for innovation, *The Journal of Product Innovation Management*, 18, 247–57.

Weyland, R. and Cole, P. (1997) *Customer Connections*, Harvard Business School Press, Boston, MA.

Yakimov, R. and Beverland, M. (2004) Brand repositioning capabilities: Enablers of ongoing brand management, Australia and New Zealand Marketing Academy (ANZMAC) Conference, 27 November–1 December, University of Wellington, Victoria, NZ.

Zirger, B.J. and Maidique, M.A. (1990) A model of new product development: an empirical test, *Management Science*, Vol. 36, 876–88.

Further reading

For a more detailed review of the new product development literature, the following develop many of the issues raised in this chapter:

Barczak, G., Griffin, A. and Kahn, K.B. (2009) PERSPECTIVE: Trends and Drivers of Success in NPD Practices: Results of the 2003 PDMA Best Practices Study, *Journal of Product Innovation Management*, Vol. 26, No. 1, 3–23.

Belliveau, P., Griffin, A. and Somermeyer, S. (eds) (2002) *The PDMA ToolBook for New Product Development*, John Wiley & Sons, New York.

Biemans, W., Griffin, A. and Moenaert, R. (2007) Twenty Years of the Journal of Product Innovation Management: History, Participants, and Knowledge Stocks and Flows, *Journal of Product Innovation Management*, Vol. 24, 193–213.

Biemans, W., Griffin, A. and Moenaert, R. (2010) In Search of the Classics: A Study of the Impact of *JPIM* Papers from 1984 to 2003, *Journal of Product Innovation Management*, Vol. 27, 461–84.

Grindling, E. (2000) *The 3M Way to Innovation: Balancing people and profit*, Kodansha International, New York.

HSBC (2010) 100 Thoughts, HSBC, London.

Chapter 13
Packaging and product development

Introduction

Packaging is rarely the first issue one cites when we are asked to consider the reasons why some firms are successful. Yet, when one strolls into McDonald's for a morning cup of coffee one cannot separate the beverage from its packaging: the cup, the lid, the stirrer and the bag in which you carry away your hot drink. The packaging's colourful imagery helps reinforce the brand of McDonald's and does much more, such as: keeps the drink warm; helps to reduce spillage through a lid; enables you to hold the drink without scalding your hand; enables you to add milk and sugar to suit your personal preference. While this is a very simple illustration it reminds us of how easy it is to overlook packaging and its role in product development.

This chapter examines the role of packaging in the product development process and illustrates the importance of packaging in the development of new products in the fast-moving consumer goods (FMCG) sector. It provides a case study at the end showing how packaging helped transform engine oil retailing.

Chapter contents

Learning objectives

When you have read this chapter you will be able to:

- understand the contribution packaging can make to the new product development process;
- recognise the wide range of packaging systems available;
- recognise the significance of the interface between product and channel members;
- recognise how packaging can provide significant scope for added-value benefits; and
- demonstrate what impact packaging has on product development, brand management and channel management.

Wrapping and packaging products

Packaging and its products touch all our lives every day. It is inextricably bound up with all kinds of industries, both large and small. The world packaging industry is estimated to be $500 billion (WPO, 2008). It is most heavily used across food and drink, healthcare, cosmetics and other consumer goods. Packaging is a vital tool in the marketing mix, too often ignored by companies, but usually more is annually spent on this as on above-the-line advertising and promotions. Moreover, every product requires packaging; hence the packaging industry is one of the largest sectors in the world economy.

When it comes to packaging Japan and its long history of craftsmen and designers are unsurpassed in their beautiful and delicate wrappings of even the most fragile of products. Hideyuki Oka's best-selling book *How to Wrap Five Eggs* is a feast of 244 beautiful photographs of traditional delicate Japanese packaging (Oka, 1989). For example, there is an illustration of rope wrapping of dried fish, which provides ventilation, thereby preserving the fish for up to six months and it is possible to unwrap just a bit at a time. The skills necessary to produce such exquisite wrapping and packaging of products are remarkable, the passing of which we all will surely lament. The eminent American designer (George Nelson) in the foreword of this book asks:

> *If the craftsmen and designers of old Japan could create beauty with their materials are we today to accept defeat when faced with ours?*

In Europe, one of the oldest and simplest forms of packaging, which was the norm in the nineteenth and early part of the twentieth centuries, was to wrap the product in paper. Very few products are still sold this way, even fewer food products. One product that has continued to be packaged in this way, despite fierce competition from substitute products, is butter. It continues to be offered as a block form simply wrapped in paper. Such simple packaging is rarely selected by many firms today; indeed in most other product categories the world of packaging has changed considerably. In those cases where the product has been competing in the marketplace for many years it has been the development of its packaging that has enabled it to remain competitive, sometimes allowing the product to remain relatively unchanged (*see* Table 13.1). For example, at the beginning of the twentieth century washing

Table 13.1 Maintaining brand leadership through packaging developments, while the product remains unchanged

Brand	Position in 1935	Position in 2010
Hovis	1	1
Heinz Soup	1	1
Kellogg's Cornflakes	1	1
McVitie's Digestives	1	1
Cadbury Dairy Milk Chocolate	1	1
Schweppes Mixers	1	1
Coca-Cola	1	1

Source: Nielsen.

detergent was originally sold in paper bags; this was later changed to cardboard boxes, and then plastic bags and more recently resealable plastic containers.

Packaging is a frequently overlooked aspect of managing products. It is not, however, overlooked by those involved in the daily ordering, shipping, storage and display of products. Retailers in particular have the daily, sometimes hourly, task of ripping open boxes and lifting consumer products on to supermarket shelves. When one is in daily contact with a wide range of consumer products like this one soon appreciates the importance of packaging. Dented cans, torn boxes and leaky bottles cost P&G, the world's largest producer of fast-moving consumer goods, over £50 million a year. It is very much aware of the impact of packaging on its profits. In the late 1990s P&G decided to tackle this issue and changed its policy on so-called 'unsaleables', those products that have damaged packaging. This change in policy had enormous implications for retailers. It introduced a no-returns policy and placed the responsibility of disposing of unsaleables with the retailers. In addition, P&G would pay a quarterly lump sum to retailers based on estimates of unsaleables likely to occur (Narisetti, 1997). The impact on all retailers was significant, but this serves as a reminder of how the issue of packaging affects businesses on a daily basis. In his eleventh edition of *Marketing Management*, Phillip Kotler suggested that packaging was so significant that many marketing managers have called it a fifth P along with price, product, place and promotion (Kotler, 2003: 436).

Packaging has evolved significantly from its uses by primitive societies to carry food and water. Glass containers first appeared in Egypt in 2000 BC and later the French emperor Napoleon awarded 12,000 francs to the winner of a contest to find a better way to preserve food, which led to a crude method of vacuum-packing (Croft, 1985). Today, where there is competition in virtually all product categories, packaging is often the consumer's first point of contact with the actual product and so it is essential to make it attractive and appropriate for both the product's and the customer's needs. Here then is the first challenge facing any product manager: to ensure the package for the product serves its functional purpose and acts as a means of communicating product information and brand character.

Illustration 13.1 shows how even for an established international brand like Timotei the significance of packaging continues to play a part in the brand's growth. Failure to recognise this would have serious implications for the brand's future.

Illustration 13.1

Why Timotei is packaged differently in India

Over the past five years Unilever has been steadily increasing sales of its international brand of shampoo: Timotei. European readers may be surprised to learn that consumers in India prefer to purchase their shampoo in individual sachets rather than in bottles. Unilever has tried to offer Timotei in a variety of size bottles but consumers prefer the individual sachets. It is true there are a number of explanations for this type of behaviour. First, there is the economics dimension that needs to be considered; that is, the up-front investment in a bottle of shampoo, which may sit around on a shelf for many weeks. Second, and most importantly for this group of consumers, is that the small individual sachet provides the correct amount of shampoo without the need to measure out the required quantity!

Source: BBC Radio 4, 'In Business', 6 February 2003.

Arla's yogurt for children: Bob the Builder yogurt pots

Source: Bob the Builder is © 2007 HIT Entertainment Limited and Keith Chapman. With permission.

If anyone is in any doubt about the importance of packaging in FMCG consider Arla's yogurt for children. The strawberry-flavoured yogurt is contained in a yogurt pot shaped in the style of *Bob the Builder*, BBC television's very successful children's series: a new product created entirely from a change in packaging of the yogurt. Clearly Arla of Denmark considers that the substantial royalty payments are worth it to secure increased sales of its yogurt (www.Arlafoods.com). Furthermore, the future of the packaging industry looks exciting, with new technologies offering many opportunities for growth. The use of intelligent packaging systems that sense and register changes in the pack contents are now being introduced by food manufacturers. And brand-protection devices such as radio frequency identification (RFID) tags are being added to packaging to prevent counterfeiting (Hancock, 2003).

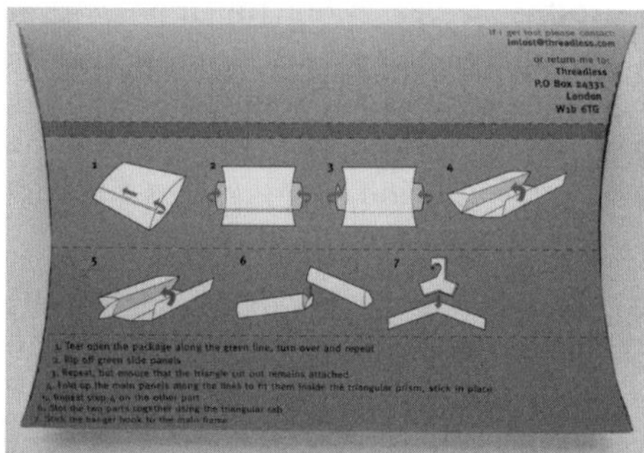

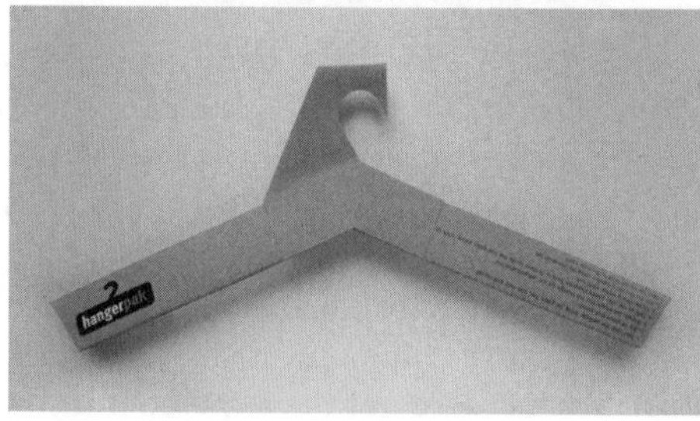

Source: Steve Haslip

HangerPak is the brainchild of designer Steve Haslip and has been designed specifically for the online market.

Packaging is also contributing to the increase in online retailing. For example, HangerPak, the brainchild of designer Steve Haslip, is designed specifically for the online market.

The basic principles of packaging

The three basic principles of packaging are shown in Figure 13.1; they are:

1 protection (and tamper proofing);
2 containment; and
3 identification.

These basic principles need to be met with all packaging at optimal overall cost. Clearly it is always possible to have improved packaging but at what cost and do the benefits enjoyed justify the additional cost? For example, Kellogg's packaging for its cereals has changed very little since the 1930s; indeed, today Kellogg's continues to use a cardboard box. The brand manager could, for example, use an aluminium box or a steel box or a polyurethane container (maybe it should), but the firm has decided that the additional cost would not be most advantageous for the firm. In addition there are many examples of products where the packaging cannot be separated from the product (*see* Illustration 13.2 on page 462).

Protection

Packaging has a primary role in preserving product integrity by protecting the product against potential damage from climatic, bacteriological and transit hazards, plus any other hazards to which the product is likely to be exposed on its journey from manufacturer to the end consumer. UK multiples recognise that many products perish in the very last stages of their journey following purchase by the consumer. Typically products are accidentally dropped in the supermarket car park during loading into the car or they are attacked by pets or young children in the home prior to reaching the safety of the cupboard!

Tamper-proof packaging

Food producers and retailers have experienced commercial terrorism within their own stores. Sainsbury experienced several attempts in the 1990s to blackmail it out

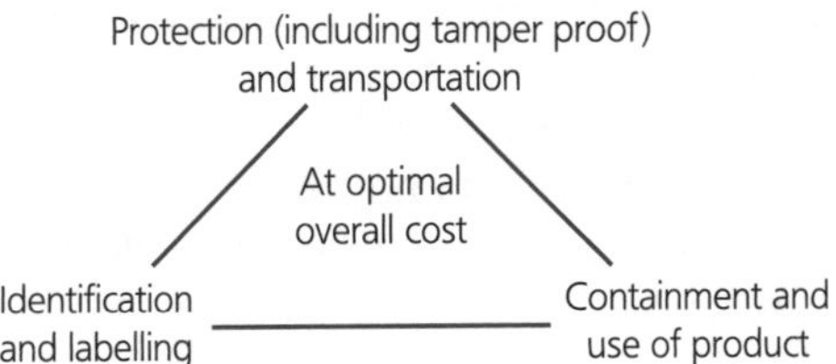

Figure 13.1 The basic principles of packaging

Source: Adapted from B. Stewart (1996) *Packaging as an Effective Marketing Tool*, Kogan Page, London.

Illustration 13.2

When the packaging is an integral part of the product

Books are probably the clearest example of where the packaging forms part of the product. In this case the cover helps to achieve the three basic objectives of packaging: containment, identification and protection. Significant resources are devoted to the task of devising a cover that will help sell a book. See the case study at the end of Chapter 4.

The Guinness 'in-can' system is another good example of a product that cannot be separated from its packaging; it is the particular packaging system that delivers the final product to the consumer. Indeed, it was the development of the product's packaging that itself led to a new product.

Jiff Lemon is one of the few brands to mimic nature quite so unashamedly. Its packaging is in the shape of the fruit and allows the consumer to squeeze it without producing any wastage, and unlike real lemons has excellent storage properties.

Dulux solid emulsion overcomes the problem of dripping paint for the consumer. However, there was a 10-year gap between development of the solid emulsion and the development of the pack that allows access by the roller rather than having to empty the contents of the tin into a roller tray.

The toothpaste pump was developed in Sweden. This type of packaging is the norm for most toothpaste brands. It is an example of a packaging system coming to the aid of an outmoded, inefficient system for dispensing paste.

of millions of pounds. Baby food manufacturers such as Cow & Gate and Heinz were pioneers in developing tamper-proof packaging. All of their food products are now sold with tamper-proof packaging, which indicates any tampering to consumers and resellers. These baby food manufacturers use glass jars and metal jar tops with pop-up discs showing when a jar has been opened. In addition, extra labelling on the package warns consumers not to purchase the product if the pop-up disc is visible (Morgan, 1997). Illustration 13.3 on page 464 shows how new packaging designs are helping to save lives.

Containment

The second principle of any packaging is that of containment, which may seem almost too obvious for consideration. This may help to explain why this basic principle is often overlooked. It is during the use of the product by the consumer that issues of containment become all too visible. Fluids such as milk, orange juice and hairspray are obvious examples of products that require a package that contains the product after it has been initially used. Hence, there is a requirement for such packaging to have dispensing and resealing features. Effective containment clearly involves ensuring the pack does not leak, fall apart or otherwise annoy the end user. Caps that do not reseal properly, bags that split on opening, and cartons that fall apart are irritants, and they deter repeat purchases. As consumers we have all struggled to peel the aluminium foil lid off a yogurt pot. In frustration we use more force, only to send the entire contents on to the floor or worst still down the front of our shirt. Similarly, we have all cut our fingers on the cardboard cartons of cereal boxes as we struggle to enter the box without ripping the top of the box.

Pause for thought 

Packaging does not seem to be covered by marketing textbooks. Yet with many FMCGs packaging is integral to the product! Why is this?

Identification

The third basic principle underlying any form of packaging is that of identification, frequently referred to as labelling. It would be unusual to find an aisle of brown cardboard boxes sitting on shelves in a store but this would be the interesting experience if products were to go unidentified or unlabelled. Canned food produce is a clear example of the importance of identification. Without the wraparound paper label all tins would appear identical, hence the need to inform the consumer what is inside the packaging. In many fast-moving consumer goods categories great efforts are made to display the actual product or part of the product to the consumer. This role of packaging includes:

- information on how the product is used;
- establishment of brand identity; and
- promotion of sale.

Identity is not simply a function of graphics; it can also be a function of shape. Shape can provide the unique brand identity for a product, or it can place the product in a specific market sector. For example, computer software is an intangible product, but by using a paint tin as packaging for a drawing and paint computer software product Jenkins & Hall Rucker, Rucker Design Group has helped reinforce the tangibility of art (Morgan, 1997).

The underlying principle that ties these three cornerstones of packaging together is that of optimal overall cost. This is an important concept for its implications are far beyond the basic unit cost of the packet. Whatever product is to go inside the package, it has to be filled or placed inside in an efficient operation or significant costs will be incurred at this stage. Similarly, if the packet design leads to difficulties or poor performance in storage, this will add to the overall costs. It should be clear that selecting the optimal package design to meet all the differing requirements is not a simple task.

Labelling

As well as the functional requirements, the label also has to provide information on the following:

- source of the product;
- contents;
- how to use the product;
- universal product code (UPC) or bar code (used by retailers and producers for price and inventory control purposes);
- warnings;
- certifications;

- how to care for the product;
- nutritional information;
- type and style of the product; and
- size and number of servings.

A famous anecdote that is often told to reinforce the importance of packaging, and labelling in particular, concerns the ability of labelling to double sales of a product. The story goes that some of the world's leading fast-moving consumer goods manufacturers were intrigued by an email which they had received that claimed to be able to double sales. Eventually the firm was contacted and after the payment of appropriate sums of money it revealed that by simply using the word 'repeat' on the package consumers would consume double the amount. Whether one believes the story or not, the reverse is certainly true. Labelling also serves to promote the product; however, marketing communication is beyond the scope of this book (*see* Fill (2002) *Marketing Communications: Context, Strategies and Applications*; Pickton and Broderick (2002) *Integrated Marketing Communications*).

Illustration 13.3

Childproof packaging – new designs could save lives

New packaging designs have been developed that could save lives and make 'childproof' containers more user-friendly for adults.

A collaboration involving psychologists, engineers and designers has led to the development of radical but practical new child-resistant closure (CRC) designs.

Because they are easier for adults to open, the containers will discourage the decanting of medicines into unsafe packaging – a practice which currently causes an estimated 10,000 cases/year of accidental poisoning in the UK, mostly involving small children.

The initiative was commissioned by the Faraday Packaging Partnership, which is funded jointly by the Engineering and Physical Sciences Research Council (EPSRC) and the DTI. Those taking part included the University of Sheffield Packaging Research Group and 3D consultants Factory Design.

First, the project team carried out a consumer survey involving volunteers aged between 20 and 84. Ninety per cent of those who took part reported having difficulty opening traditional childproof containers, e.g. the 'squeeze hard and turn' design, with the over-50s experiencing frequent problems. The research showed that most difficulties were caused by lack of physical strength.

These results underlined the need for an innovative design approach focusing on the end-user and on real-world situations. The team therefore set out to design packaging that was physically easy to open, even for the elderly or infirm, but which required actions to be thought through in a way that a small child would not be capable of.

Based on this philosophy, the team produced three revolutionary designs:

- 'Slide': a container with three buttons that must be aligned to release the lid.
- 'Tri': a container with three buttons that must be pressed gently but simultaneously.
- 'Poke': a tube with an internal catch that can only be released by an adult-length finger.

Patents have been filed and the team now aim to grant manufacturing licences to commercial organisations. Pauline King of the Faraday Packaging Partnership says: 'Our objective is to enable these more practical, safer CRC designs to make life easier for a significant proportion of the population.'

Source: EPSRC, November 2006.

Characteristics of packaging

Packaging provides significant scope for product and brand managers to develop their products. In its most simple form new packaging provides opportunities for making the product available in different quantities. Take a product like milk; it is available in a wide range of forms including: 4-pint containers, 2-litre containers, 1-litre containers, 1-pint containers, 1/2-pint containers and single vacuum-cup sachets for use by the trade in cafes, etc. This wide range of different size of packaging enables the product to be offered to different market segments: the 1/2-pint cardboard package is targeted at the snack/lunch box segment, whereas the larger 4-pint plastic container is targeted at the family home-use segment. Moreover, by considering carefully how your product is offered and used in the market it is possible to gain significant product design advantages. One of the most famous packaging developments occurred in the toilet cleaning products category. The appropriately named Toilet Duck product recognised that by changing the shape of the bottle it was possible to help consumers use the product. The angled spout with a swan-neck shape convinced shoppers that this product would make cleaning toilets easier. This change in pack design from the standard upright-shaped bottle revolutionised this product range; now all products in this category have adopted similar shaped packaging. Table 13.2 offers a summary of some of the development opportunities that are available to virtually all FMCG products.

Dispensing

Table 13.5 (p. 475) illustrates a number of products that suffer from poor dispensing. Many manufacturers have attempted to improve this aspect of their products packaging. Most ground roast coffee packaging contains a plastic measuring scoop to facilitate dispensing into a percolator machine; the same cannot be said for rice or other dried pasta products where consumers are unsure about correct quantity. Similarly, few people would buy a shower-gel product if it did not incorporate a hook from which to hang the product in the shower, thereby facilitating dispensing.

Storage

Easy product storage is one aspect of packaging purpose that can offer considerable development opportunities. In this case storage refers to storage of the pack by the

Table 13.2 FMCG packaging purpose and development considerations

Package purpose	Development considerations
Dispense	Access; portion control, e.g. built in measure; pouring
Storage	Stackability; location: refrigerator, bathroom, kitchen
Stability	Storage life, especially after opening
Handling	Ease of use for intended purpose
Opening/resealing	Appropriate to task, i.e. frequency of use
After use	Secondary use (e.g. as storage container)
Disposal	Ease of disposal

consumer after purchase. One would rightly question the wisdom of glass containers for products that are frequently used in a bathroom. Similarly the packaging for tinned food facilitates stacking and storage. It is therefore necessary to think through the use of a product rather than simply consider on-shelf appearance, notwithstanding this aspect of merchandising.

Stability

Stability in this case does not refer to physical stability of the package in terms of whether it remains upright; this is covered under storage. Stability in this case refers to shelf-life. There are some obvious examples of packaging development to lengthen the shelf-life for products such as aseptic packaging for milk and orange juice. Bread manufacturers have also developed foil packaging in an attempt to improve the shelf-life of the product after opening. Conversely, pharmaceutical manufacturers are in search of almost the opposite objective: packaging that will deteriorate the product as soon as the shelf-life has expired. One of the concerns of pharmaceutical manufacturers is the use of drugs, such as antibiotics, by consumers long after their shelf-life has expired, hence they are developing packaging that turns an unappealing black colour.

Handling

Effective pack **handling** is also an important issue to consider in adding value and consumer convenience. The built-in carrying handle on a 2-litre or 4-litre milk carton is an obvious example where without it simply taking the product from the shelf would be problematic. Conversely, glass bottles of wine are frequently dropped on their journey from shelf to the safety of the consumer's car. Initial pack handling, then, needs careful consideration when developing packaging, but so too does the ability to direct the product to do its job. Producers of baby products have long recognised this important element in pack design. For example, Johnson & Johnson understand that where baby personal care products are concerned ease of use is essential because at least one hand will be holding the baby.

Opening/resealing

Many products, once opened, require resealing for use at another time; whether it is a 250-gram tub of yellow spread that has a plastic lid or a shampoo bottle with a screw cap, the ability to reseal and reopen a package is a fundamental requirement for many products. Packaging engineers and designers need to think through the product's use from the consumer's viewpoint in order to design-in appropriate resealing to the packaging system. An example where this element of packaging has helped manufacturer's add value to their offering is in carbonated drinks – 333-ml cans of carbonated drinks such as Coca-Cola, Pepsi and Irn-Bru retail for 25 per cent less than their screw-cap plastic 333-ml bottle equivalents. Consumers are willing to pay a premium for the ability to drink, seal and reopen the product.

Illustration 13.4

Packaging and waste

In the UK we bury 16 million tones of waste in landfill sites each year and packaging alone accounts for over a quarter of all this waste. Almost all national governments in the EU are giving the environment and energy conservation extra priority. Energy and environmental policy is quickly moving up the political agenda. Environmental policy is also a red-hot issue for private companies too. In fact, major changes have already been implemented at most enterprises, both horizontally across the various sectors and vertically through the supply chain. Environmentally aware businesses now have specific targets and strategies to reduce their impact to a minimum.

Source: Pearson Education Ltd/Tracey Montana/Photodisc

Retailers

In the UK the big retailers such as Tesco, Sainsbury, ASDA and M&S have all been introducing targets to reduce packaging and waste. M&S has pledged to reduce the number of plastic bags it gives away and to reduce its food packaging by 25 per cent. In the USA, too, change is occurring. In 2007 in the stores of US retailer 'Target' iPod carrying cases came wrapped in cardboard. This seemingly irrelevant change – when coupled with new packaging on several hundred other items – adds up to a significant environmental impact that critics charge is long overdue. The powerful US retailer asked its packaging vendor to replace the clamshell with a recyclable cardboard package with a small plastic window. This single change will prevent an estimated 5,000 pounds of PVC from entering landfills each year.

The consumer

Several consumer associations have become involved and have actively participated in the environmental debate. One of the more vociferous of these is the Women's Institute (WI) in the UK. They organised a day-of-action, when groups of WI members travelled to various stores and shopped as normal shoppers. The difference that day was that the women removed all the packaging that they believed was superfluous in relation to the product's needs and left it at the checkout (something that has subsequently prompted one retailer to test waste bins for excess packaging).

This stunt resulted in extensive media coverage and in one day the WI had successfully demonstrated a highly effective way of making retailers more aware of the waste issue. However, more thought-provoking was the packaging that the WI women removed. Almost without exception it was the secondary and tertiary packaging – the paper and cardboard sleeves as well as the display packaging that sat outside the primary packaging of tray and lid. In the main, the WI identified fruit and vegetable as over-packaged.

There are environmental benefits in recycling packaging creating so called closed loops. As in the case of PET plastic, trays and bottles can be collected after they have served their purpose as packaging and the consumer has discarded them. After collection, the packaging can be cleaned washed and ground into flakes of a size and quality that enables them to be mixed and reintroduced into the raw materials stream. The original PET can be reused to make new packaging. PET material that contains recycled plastic is referred to as RPET, 'R' for 'Recycled'. This process is increasingly being used in packaging factories across Europe.

Further reading: Harcourt-Webster, A. (2007) How green is your High Street? BBC Money Programme, http://news.bbc.co.uk/ (27 June).

After use and secondary use

The use of some packaging for storage containers has a long heritage and is recognised by many brand managers. The round tins used to package and store loose tobacco have been used by households all over the world for a variety of secondary uses. One of the world's oldest producers and distributors of tea, Twinings, have frequently used their loose tea tins as a promotional incentive. Consumers see value in purchasing the product to obtain a useful steel storage tin complete with hinged lid. At the most basic level, many households reuse polyethylene carrier bags as waste-bin liners.

Disposal

The ability to dispose of packaging easily with the minimum of fuss is a consumer convenience that is often overlooked as an opportunity to add value. The obvious example where disposal takes a high priority is in diapers or nappies. In this case the introduction of a use and dispose product made this necessary but unpleasant activity more convenient for the consumer. In other FMCG areas, there are many opportunities for development. Many plastics-film materials in particular resist disposal in the waste-bin by expanding rather than being compressed. Similarly the 2-litre or 4-pint milk containers take up considerable space in the waste-bin. Moreover, it is at this stage where environmental concerns are most obvious as consumers begin to consider where the refuse will go next. This subject, however, is vast and beyond the scope of this chapter or book.

Having developed an improved pack design it is necessary to communicate this to consumers, especially if this developed advantage is not obvious. This area of brand management and marketing communications is beyond the scope of this book and readers should consult texts such as: Kotler (2003) *Marketing Management*; Fill (2002) *Marketing Communications*; and Pickton and Broderick (2002) *Integrated Marketing Communications*.

Product rejuvenation

All markets inevitably experience periods of both growth and decline. Product managers have been very successful in intervening to help their products increase market share and extend their life in the marketplace. None the less, as growth slows and products enter maturity, profit margins to the firms and their owners, in particular, will begin to decline. The firms will be putting the product managers under pressure to regain those margins. The product managers will hopefully already have new product development projects in place, but they may wish also to consider rejuvenating the existing product. Developing the packaging is an activity that is frequently overlooked in favour of increased promotional activity or more radical product development activity. Rogers (1962) cites a number of reasons why profit margins decline:

- increasing number of competitive products leading to over-capacity and intensive competition;

- market leaders under pressure from smaller companies;
- strong increase in R&D to find better versions of the product;
- cost economies used up;
- decline in product distinctiveness;
- dealer apathy and disenchantment with a product with declining sales; and
- changing market composition where the loyalty of those first to adopt begins to waver.

Packaging development provides a relatively inexpensive way of rejuvenating a product. Johnson and Jones's (1957) product–market matrix offers an excellent classification of nine opportunities for growth (*see* Figure 12.4). Packaging, however, is not mentioned. Since this time, technology has developed rapidly and the opportunities now available to packaging engineers is simply breathtaking. It is possible to use virtually any material and improved printing techniques provide further flexibility. Illustration 13.5 shows the breathtaking assortment of packaging systems available to the product manager considering packaging for what one might consider as straightforward: some pills. Alas, even here the options are considerable.

Indeed, the packaging industry has been one of the fastest growing industries over the past 20 years. A simple but effective illustration of the industry and revenues involved can be found by referring to some trivia from the UK's *Sunday Times* 'Rich List'. Each year this national newspaper produces a list of the wealthiest people in Britain. In 2011 Hans Rausing was thirteenth on this list; he is part of the family behind the Tetra Pak empire (*Sunday Times*, 2011). One of the industry's leaders is Smurfit-Stone Container Corporation (Nasdaq: SSCC). It is the world's largest integrated producer of paperboard and paper-based packaging products. In the year 2000 68 per cent of Smurfit-Stone's operating revenue was generated from containerboard and corrugated container sales; consumer packaging, which includes folding cartons and boxboard mills, accounted for 12 per cent; speciality packaging accounted for 8 per cent; and recycling, 5 per cent.

Illustration 13.5

We need a bottle for our pills, what can you do?

The answer is, quite a lot. The following gives an indication of the extent of this variety on offer to the product or brand manager:

- Clic reversible cap child-resistant vials (very small medicine bottle);
- Clear-Vu Screw-Loc child-resistant vials;
- Clear-Vu PET plastic graduated oval bottles;
- ointment jars, dropper bottles, amber glass oval bottles;
- amber glass pill vials and square jars;
- child-resistant and regular continuous thread closures;
- HDPE wide-mouth pharmaceutical rounds; and
- Sani-Glas graduated flint glass oval bottles
- plus many more . . .

D. Luce & Son Inc., a wholesale distributor of prescription packaging and pharmacy supplies since 1943, offers a wide variety of glass and plastic containers, and closures.

Source: www.essentialsupplies.com.

Innovation in action

Target image buyers

Given that sales of luxury vehicles have plummeted during the recession, it is odd to see Ford so upbeat about the launch of the latest Ford/Harley-Davidson tie-up, the F-150 Truck.

'Despite the recession, image buyers remain', explains Matt O'Leary, Director, Corporate Strategy for Ford, 'These customers buy based on what the product represents.' The F-150 adds a sprinkling of Harley magic to what is Ford's top-selling truck; seats crafted from Harley biker leather and cloisonné badges, for example. It is a very loyal customer base. Ford has sold 74,000 such co-branded trucks since the partnership began.

'We find out what the customer values; what they like, want, and what they wish they had, and we go from there', says O'Leary. 'No-one understands their customers better.'

Source: HSBC (2010), 100 Thoughts, HSBC, London.

New product opportunities through packaging

Continual analysis of the market in which current products operate should provide many opportunities for developing the product/brand. This is one of the fundamental responsibilities of the brand manager; in much the same way as scientists are expected to remain up to date with scientific developments in their field, so too must brand managers. With this in mind brand managers should be reviewing opportunities continually. Frequently, the decision not to proceed with a business opportunity may be correct, but as was stated earlier, in virtually all cases improvements to a product's packaging are always possible. For example, it is usually possible to improve the way a product is displayed on the shelf or to improve the opening or resealing, etc. Frequently the changes will be minor, but sometimes a change in packaging can lead to a completely new market for the brand. Take the example of 'Celebrations', the new assorted chocolate product from Mars. This has proved to be an extremely successful new product for Mars and has helped the firm establish itself in the chocolate gift-box market; a segment previously unexploited and dominated by its competitors Nestlé with Quality Street and Cadbury with Roses. If ever there was an example of the power of packaging in new product development this was it (*see also* Illustration 13.6).

Altering the packaging of a product can considerably change the target market and the way a product is used. The example of carbonated soft drinks is useful here. Lemonade offered in glass bottles suggests high quality and is aimed at the adult market. Lemonade in PET bottles and aluminium cans is offered to the children's market, whereas PVC bottles are usually targeted at the family 2-litre take-home market. Table 13.3 illustrates the wide range of packaging systems used in a single product category.

Illustration 13.6

Take away coffee: its all about the packaging

Hutamaki is not a name that one would immediately associate with Costa Coffee, McDonald's, Pret A Manger and Starbucks. But this company, based in Finland, is one of the world's biggest manufacturers of paper cups and supplies cups to all of the above retail coffee outlets.

Hutamaki has worked with its customers to develop paper cups for coffee that offer the customer an improved cup. First it has developed lids with drinking spouts. It has developed corrugated sleeves for the cups that help prevent heat conduction and prevent scalding of the hand. All of these relatively minor product developments have delivered huge profit margins to their customers as end-users seem to be willing to pay more for a coffee in a smart take-away paper cup than they are for coffee in a china cup and saucer.

Source: Pearson Education Ltd/Naki Kouyioumtzis

Table 13.3 A wide variety of packaging systems are used for soft drinks

Packaging system	Benefits and limitations
Glass bottle	Indicated high quality, can be clear or coloured; not suitable for children's drinks; rigid structure for graphics; recyclable.
PET (Polyethylene terephthalate) bottle	Can be clear or coloured; resealable, suitable for carbonated soft drinks; unbreakable, recyclable, rigid structure for graphics.
PVC (Polyvinyl chloride) bottle	More opaque than PET; less rigid; can have a handle incorporated; cheap; unbreakable.
Aluminium can	Particularly suitable for carbonated soft drinks; unresealable; effective structure for graphics; recyclable.
Steel-mix can	Particularly suitable for carbonated soft drinks; unresealable; effective structure for graphics; recyclable; cheaper than aluminium.
Tetra Pak carton	Ideal for children's drinks; variety of pack sizes; cheap; unresealable; appropriate for long-life drinks; recyclable.

Product and pack size variation

Product and brand managers are constantly searching for ways to increase sales, especially when this is linked to their personal remuneration. By aligning pack sizes with particular consumer lifestyles it is possible to increase growth through market development. For some consumers making less frequent trips to the store suits their

Illustration 13.7

Dulux emulsion paint – new package development

It is attention to the detail and painstaking analysis that frequently leads to effective results. This was the case when ICI, owner of the Dulux paint brand, began looking at ways to try to differentiate its product from that of the competition. After all, paint is hardly a new product – it has been around for hundreds of years. There have been developments in paint technology such as the introduction of emulsion paint and, more recently, the move to more aqueous-based paints. None the less, in 2000 when product managers at Dulux began reviewing their emulsion product it was, as usual, the ability to differentiate the brand among the competition that would allow it to charge a premium for its product and increase its market share. The emulsion market is crowded and competition from DIY store brands such as B&Q, Homebase, Wickes, etc. is fierce. Furthermore, many consumers perceive emulsion to be a commodity product such as coffee, and so the argument goes: 'coffee is coffee – why would anyone pay more for one type of coffee?'. But, as all students of marketing know, this is precisely the role of brand management to develop the brand and position it in the marketplace so that consumers are willing to pay a premium for it. With this in mind Dulux emulsion brand and product managers set about examining their product.

They started by examining the end use of a tin of emulsion paint. The paint is probably going to be used by homeowners decorating their own property. The influence of successful television programmes such as the BBC's *Changing Rooms* cannot be overlooked. Frequently, the house will be furnished and the task is to improve the appearance of the room. None the less, avoiding spillage and mess is a high priority of users. Indeed, they will usually put down sheets of newspaper and dustsheets to avoid drips of emulsion on furniture (so called non-drip paints have been on the market for many years but drips still occur). The tin will need a handle to facilitate lifting and carrying from floor to stepladder etc. The lid must be secure to enable users to close with confidence it will not leak and yet must be able to be reopened. Frequently, the user will struggle with a screwdriver to open the tin. When this has been achieved the user searches for a stick or maybe the same screwdriver to stir the contents of the tin. Those studying carefully will not have forgotten the lid, which needs to be placed somewhere, paint-side up! Hopefully, where someone will not walk on it or put their hand on it. And let us not forget the stick that was used to stir the emulsion, where does that now go? When the emulsion is used, excess emulsion has to be removed from the brush by scraping it across the top of the tin. This causes paint to build up in the rim that eventually overflows down the side of the tin or hardens slowly, making resealing the lid difficult. After the painting is complete the tin will be stored in the garage.

This analysis of emulsion paint in use quickly revealed to Dulux brand and product managers that the existing packaging was failing in many areas and numerous opportunities existed to create consumer benefits through packaging improvements. Not all of these have been developed and some will be developed over time because brand managers have to consider *optimal overall cost* (*see* Figure 13.1):

- a genuine 'non-drip' emulsion paint;
- change tin to enable access to tin with roller;
- a hinged lid;
- provision of stirring stick;
- safety catch on lid to reassure closure;
- indicator on tin showing when past shelf-life; and
- transparent tin showing colour of contents.

busy schedule; others who have more time to shop and operate with restricted budgets may opt for smaller pack sizes. For large families large pack sizes are bought frequently because consumption is high, whereas for older people living alone the reverse may be true.

Opportunities for size alterations are relatively straightforward for the manufacturer of 'free flowing' consumables such as food and personal care products in the form of liquids, granules and powders. The situation is different with unit products such as disposable nappies or a confectionary chocolate bar. The implications in this category are much more significant and are similar to those of a new product introduction. Indeed, the introduction by Mars of its Celebrations product was essentially a product/pack size alteration.

There is a strong association in the eyes of the consumer between larger pack size and economy; however, there are some obvious restrictions in terms of how large a pack should be, such as:

- weight and ease of carrying home;
- storage space within the home;
- product usage versus shelf-life;
- capital outlay; and
- ease of dispensing product from large container.

Clearly larger packs carry a weight penalty and there is a limit to what a consumer can be expected to carry home. Packaging for baby nappies and washing detergents almost excludes those without a car to carry the product home.

Another area where large packs are used is in promotions, where packs are frequently sold with a 25 per cent free content. Once again for 'free flow' consumables (such as cereals or shampoo) this is a relatively easy option to exploit, but for unit consumables, such as confectionary chocolate bars, the implications are akin to a new product introduction.

The example of the Mars 'Celebration' new product illustrates the opportunities that exist in exploiting smaller product/pack varieties. Small containers are often associated with 'precious' products, and indeed many 'exclusive' brands of perfume are packaged in this way. The travel market is another segment where small containers have obvious advantages. One product that utilises both small packaging and product variants is Kellogg's cereal variety pack. This product provides the fascination of miniaturised products of their full-size counterparts, and product variants within one unit pack. Variety packs provide opportunities for manufacturers to move less popular products.

Packaging systems

Whether one is considering the packaging for a new product or reviewing the packaging of an existing product it is worth remembering that all packaging can be improved. There is, however, the optimal overall cost to consider (*see* Figure 13.1 earlier). The type of materials used and the package system selected are inextricably linked together, particularly when one considers the high-volume automated production lines that will be used for FMCGs. Any large-scale capital expenditure will require careful analysis and justification, hence product and brand managers need an understanding of the variety of packaging systems available. Table 13.4 provides a summary of the most common forms of packaging and their key attributes in FMCGs. Table 13.5 shows some of the most common irritating forms of packaging according to consumers.

Pause for thought 

Is the success of Mars 'Celebrations' confectionary all due to the packaging?

Table 13.4 **Packaging systems**

Packaging system	Product example	Key attributes
Steel and aluminium tins and cans	Carbonated soft drink.	Unresealable (single serve); effective structure for graphics; recyclable.
Folding cartons	Frozen cheesecakes; cereal boxes; Easter eggs.	Versatile; final shape often a box but features such as handles can be added; cardboard engineering and new coatings provide additional opportunities.
Rigid boxes	Polystyrene boxes for chicken pieces and minced beef.	Still used for premium products; stackability; separate lid.
Hanging-pack formats:	Popular within the DIY market.	Inexpensive; ideal for small low-cost items.
– Blister packs	Children's small toys; batteries.	Versatile blister from PVC usually mounted on to a backing card.
– Skin packs	Often used in promotions to put two products together, e.g. jar of coffee and a packet of biscuits.	Versatile blister from PVC, similar to above without the backing card mount; forms a 'covering skin' around the product.
– Cartons	Small cartons of DIY products such as screws, nails, etc.	All advantages of cartons plus ability to hang.
Flowraps	Chocolate bars.	Inexpensive, good graphics available; variety of films available.
Glass bottles and jars	Premium products; wine; baby food.	Traditional, facilitates tamper proofing.
PVC bottles and jars	Personal care products; carbonated drinks.	More opaque than PET; less rigid; can have a handle incorporated; cheap; unbreakable.
PET bottles and jars	Premium personal care products; carbonated drinks.	Can be clear or coloured; resealable; unbreakable; recyclable; rigid structure for graphics.
Flexible tubes	Toothpaste; pharmaceutical creams.	Convenience of application; resealability.
Thermoform/ fill/seal	Yogurt pots; pharmaceutical products.	Simple; facilitates in-house packaging; cost-effective.
Composite containers	Pringles.	A spirally wound paper-based tube with plastic end caps.
Bags	Potato chips; rice; sugar; fertiliser; retailer carrier bags.	Wide variety of finished products available from high-quality paper carrier bag with rope handle to thin polyethylene carrier bag.

Table 13.5 Ten of the most irritating packages

	Product package	Problem/difficulty
1	4-pint milk plastic containers	Leakage
2	Single-portion vacuum-formed cup for milk	Difficult to open
3	Biscuit wraps	Difficult to open
4	Frozen vegetables in bags	Cannot reseal
5	Sugar, flour and rice bags	Cannot be resealed
6	Compact discs that are tightly shrink-wrapped	Difficult to open
7	Vacuum-packed roasted coffee	Difficult to open and to dispense
8	McDonald's Happy Meals	Excessive packaging
9	Pickled onions in glass jar	Difficult to remove screw-top lid
10	Toothpaste tube	Excessive waste, unable to access all the contents

Source: P. Trott (2006) Packaging and new product opportunities, University of Portsmouth Business School, Student Survey.

Retailer acceptance

When considering a product's packaging it is desirable, if not essential, to get input from members of the distribution channel from an early stage. After all, it is resellers and wholesalers who have to handle, store and deliver the product to the retailer. Consideration must therefore be given to storage space, ease of stacking and handling. A triangular-shaped box may be an interesting design for a new brand of soup but if distributors and resellers have difficulty storing and stocking it they may decide not to purchase it and stock it in their stores.

For a new product to become successful it must, of course, be accepted by the final user, but success is also dependent on acceptance of the new product by the channel members through whom it passes in reaching the final customers. Whereas final users are most concerned about how the product will perform when used, channel members are much more interested in how the product will sell, whether it will be easy to stock and display and, most important, whether it will be profitable. This is especially the case when it comes to consumables, which is the business of the supermarkets. Such retailers are overwhelmed by products that consumers hardly ever buy. Research from Kurt Salmon Associates found that almost 25 per cent of the 30,000 products in a typical supermarket sell less than one unit a month. And 85 per cent of the sales are generated by just 7 per cent of the products (Schiller *et al.*, 1996). No wonder retailers are sceptical of more new products.

Levels of anxiety increase still further for manufacturer brands when they consider the rise of the distributor brands or store brands. Distributor brands or store brands sell in supermarkets typically for about 10–20 per cent less than manufacturers' brands, yet the profit margins realised by supermarkets are usually about 10–15 per cent higher than for manufacturers' brands. A significant amount of shelf space is given over to the store's own brands, thus making any request for additional shelf space more likely to be rejected.

While the manufacturer may view the idea of having 10 flavours of ice cream as an excellent marketing idea, the retailer would prefer fewer flavours as they see different flavours simply competing with one another and not contributing to turnover. From the retailer's perspective they want to:

- stock only product lines that sell;
- reduce quantity purchased; and
- stock goods that produce high levels of profit.

Retailers do recognise that they have to offer a service to the consumer and so they have to stock a variety of products, but manufacturers must recognise that the retailer will frequently see things differently. Understanding the problems retailers face will help in developing effective packaging. For example, one needs to consider how a retailer would prefer (probably intends) to stock and display the goods. Consider a pizza. Is this product to be displayed lying flat on a shelf with the facing edge being the side of the box or is to be displayed standing on its end with the full pizza facing outwards? The manufacturer may prefer the exciting toppings on the pizza to be facing out, but the retailer may argue that a lack of shelf space prevents this option from being considered. Such constraints may force manufacturers to alter their packaging.

Revitalising mature packaged goods

The idea of the product life cycle implies that the brand will eventually die, but there is no reason why a brand should die if it is attached to a product people want to buy. One only has to look around at the brands on our shelves and one is immediately struck by the longevity of many brands (*see* Chapter 11). None the less, many brands do lose sales and become labelled mature or, worse, old! In such circumstances brand managers need to use a variety of tools and skills if they are to successfully revitalise these mature goods. There are three key areas that need to be addressed:

- reminding consumers about the brand;
- improving where the product is sold; and
- improving the packaging.

The first of these is largely a promotional tactic and beyond the scope of this book. According to Wansink and Huffman (2001) it is the simple act of promoting an old brand, which consequently results in significant increases in sales. It is almost as if the consumer has forgotten about the brand and, when they are reminded of its existence, they buy it because they have not had it for a while.

Illustration 13.8

Packing in freshness with foil at Walkers Crisps

Walkers was founded in 1948 in Leicester, England. It sold potato chips (crisps) at a price premium because it argued that its crisps were fresher than the competition. This small but significant price premium enabled the firm to spend more on advertising than the competition, which in turn drove up sales. In 1989 PepsiCo acquired Walkers and set about expanding the brand. PepsiCo identified that Walkers would be able to reinforce their freshness advantage through improving the packaging of their product. The standard packaging across the industry for crisps was see-through cellophane. Walkers introduced foil packaging, which kept the product fresher for longer. Moreover, it was seen as an innovative product development and indeed was promoted as such. By 1994 Walkers was the biggest food brand in the United Kingdom in terms of unit sales. Since this development Walkers have developed the brand further by using Gary Lineker (UK soccer hero) and later Michael Owen (England international soccer player) to promote the brand.

Source: K.L. Keller (2003) *Building, Measuring and Managing Brand Equity*, 2nd edn, Prentice-Hall, Englewood Cliffs, NJ.

Case study

Halfords Motor Oil – redesign and rebranding of an existing product

Introduction

Halfords is Britain's number one retailer of car parts, cycles and accessories. With over 400 stores in Britain, it attracts more than 1.2 million customers through its doors every week and is one of the largest non-food retailers in the UK. It boasts around 12,000 product lines, an annual turnover of in excess of £500 million and a company history spanning more than a century; many analysts view it as a British business institution.

For many British car users, especially the DIY enthusiast, when they require something for their car Halfords would be one of the first retailers they would consider. Yet, surprisingly, in the 1990s Halfords own brand of motor oil did not sell well and preliminary market research revealed that it was not valued highly by its customers. Some executives at Halfords considered it surprising that, given that oil was largely a commodity product like bread and milk, sales of their own-brand oil was disappointing. The company set out to investigate what could be done to increase sales.

Source: Pearson Education Ltd/Studio 8

Background

Founded as a local hardware store in Birmingham in 1892 by F.W. Rushbrooke, Halfords has since grown

→

to establish its position as the leading retailer of car parts, cycles and accessories in the UK. It was not until 1965 that the business became known as Halfords Limited. The years that followed saw Halfords open its 300th store and become part of the Burmah Group in 1969. The business moved to a custom-built head office and warehouse in Redditch, Worcestershire, where it remains to this day.

The 1980s was a decade of change for Halfords, as it was one of the first retail groups to make the move from the high street to edge-of-town locations, recognising customers' needs for bigger stores, more choice and convenient parking. It also introduced its well-known blue, red and white corporate identity. Two more changes of ownership followed with the Ward White Group purchasing the business in 1984 and then the acquisition of the Group by The Boots Company in 1989. Since then, Halfords has gone from strength to strength, leading the revolution in out-of-town retailing, generating consistent growth in sales and profits over the last 10 years and clearly establishing itself as the UK market leader. In April 2000, Rod Scribbins became managing director, overseeing the rollout of the company's ambitious 'Arcade' superstore programme. Within 'Arcade' stores customers benefit from added features including sub-shops for Bikehut, Audio Parts, Ripspeed and Touring. More product ranges, specialist staff who are enthusiasts in their particular areas and a brighter, more contemporary shopping environment are all changes that have been introduced.

In September 2002, Halfords was acquired by CVC Capital Partners from The Boots Company and Rod Scribbins was appointed chief executive. Halfords head office employs 600 people, supporting over 400 stores with a total staff of 9,000.

The problem

As is often the case in such apparent positive positions, all is not well in the Halfords garden. Scratch beneath the surface and problems and missed opportunities abound. One in particular is the focus of this study: motor oil. Given that Halfords is the largest retailer of motor oil in the UK one might expect sales of its own brand of motor oil to be significant. This, however, was not the case; indeed, sales from its own brand were very disappointing. This is somewhat surprising given that sales from store brands in the UK are generally good. That is, compared with some European countries the UK consumer has a favourable view towards store brands and in many product categories, from clothes to food, consumers readily purchase a store brand. Why then not motor oil? Moreover, Halfords saw this as a business opportunity they wished to exploit, but how? Was there something particularly unusual about motor oil? Who were the competitors? What were the other brands? Was this a market in which Halfords could be competitive? So many questions, and at present so few answers. The one question that had been answered by the managing director of Halfords was that the business should exploit this opportunity.

Design brief

Halfords decided that it did not have sufficient expertise in-house to tackle the task of exploring the task of rebranding and repackaging a major product. The firm commissioned the international design group Pentagram with a brief to redevelop its brand of motor oil. This would probably involve redesigning the container, relabelling it and repositioning it in the market. The decision to use an external agency is not uncommon and is the approach followed by most large retailers. Such product design expertise is rarely found in-house and such projects are commonly contracted to third-party experts.

Research

The brief to Pentagram was clear, but before the firm could start it needed to understand the situation better. Indeed, it needed to be sure that it was going to address the problem and not a symptom of the problem. Pentagram undertook its own market research on retailing motor oil and undertook a series of in-depth interviews with consumers in the form of focus groups to try to uncover some of the issues surrounding motor oil.

The team soon uncovered that the industry is confronting a number of changes. In particular there is an overall decline in sales as modern cars require less servicing and less frequent top-ups and changes. On the other hand, within this declining market premium grade motor oils rather than standard grade are becoming more prevalent. Furthermore, the industry is dominated by some of the largest firms in the world, most notably the world's oil companies. Over many years these firms have developed a range of brands that are synonymous with motoring. This association is reinforced through extensive advertising and sponsorship of motoring events, in particular Formula One motor racing. Indeed, most oils carried 'flashy' Grand Prix-style branding. It seemed that this did nothing to help consumers select the correct oil. The brand leaders in Europe are:

- BP and Castrol;
- Shell Oils; and
- Exxon (Esso) Mobil.

BP recently announced a major sponsorship deal with David Beckham, as the *Guardian* recently announced (Day, 2002):

> *Not content with posing smothered in baby oil for a magazine cover shoot, David Beckham has signed up to endorse an oil more associated with the grime of the garage – BP's Castrol brand. The England and Real Madrid football star has signed a two-year sponsorship deal with oil giant BP to promote the Castrol lubricant.*

The Pentagram team next had to investigate the product in terms of what it does.

What motor oil does in your engine

Motor oil lubricates the hundreds of moving parts in your engine to keep them from wearing out before their normal lifetime. It must also help to cool the engine, and keep hot combustion gases out of the crankcase. And it cleans up water, soot, carbon, lead salts and acids that get into every engine. Thus, the right motor oil helps the engine run better and last longer.

To help oil do these jobs better, certain chemicals, called additives, are put into it. For example, cleaning additives called detergents or dispersants grab dirt and sludge particles as they are generated in the engine and hold them in suspension until they are removed when you change the oil. Other additives fight oxidation, rust, corrosion and foaming to prolong engine life. But additives are used up in doing their work, and can only be replaced by changing the oil. To summarise, engine motor oil is required for:

- lubrication of the moving engine parts to prevent wear;
- reducing friction;
- maintaining engine cleanliness;
- protecting against engine rust and corrosion;
- cooling engine parts;
- sealing combustion gases;
- permitting easy starting; and
- extending engine life.

Different types of engine oil

There are different types of oil and consumers have to pick the oil that is best for their own usage and application. They have to choose an oil depending upon how they use their car, and the outdoor temperature they are driving in.

Outdoor temperature

As the temperature changes, the viscosity or fluidity of the oil changes. Think of the oil in the engine as being like molasses in a bottle. When the bottle of molasses is removed from the refrigerator, it is very thick or viscous and moves slowly. But if it is warmed up, it becomes thinner and flows easily. The same is true of oil in an engine. When it is cold, the oil will be thick. If it is too thick, it may not even allow the engine to turn over and start. On the other hand, if it is too thin, it may allow the engine to start but it could be too thin when the engine warms up to do its work properly.

Viscosity measurements designate thickness and thinness

To tell consumers how thick or thin an oil is, the Society of Automotive Engineers (SAE) has established a viscosity classification that appears on the top of oil cans. The numbers consumers see go from 5W, which would be for very thin oil used in extremely cold weather conditions, up to a 50, which would be for very thick oils that have special uses such as very hot applications or racing engines. These numbers designate the SAE viscosity grade. Most people use a multi-graded oil that covers the highest and lowest temperatures that will be encountered.

This background information was useful and helped the team paint a picture of the product, the brands and the market. It also revealed that 50 per cent of cars required premium grade oil, yet 75 per cent of sales was standard grade. It seemed that many consumers were not buying the correct oil; moreover, Halfords was not selling its most profitable lines.

It was now necessary to uncover the views of consumers; in particular, the team were aware that

➔

many motorists did not buy motor oil and left this to the annual service of their car. What soon became clear following discussions with retailers was that there were essentially three types of buyers of motor oil:

1. DIY enthusiast – regular purchaser of motor oil. This group undertook their own servicing of their vehicle.
2. DIY part-timer. This group did not service their own vehicle but regularly checked their vehicle and would top-up their engine with oil if necessary.
3. Emergency. This group only purchased oil in an emergency.

The Pentagram team soon recognised that the largest retail purchasers of motor oil was the DIY group. The DIY part-timer with limited knowledge tended to purchase the branded product, whereas the DIY enthusiast, armed with more knowledge, would make their purchase decision based on performance and price. This was the group that the Pentagram team decided would be most likely to purchase the Halfords store brand. Even here, however, price itself would be insufficient. There needed to be additional qualities that would convince the DIY enthusiast to select the Halfords brand ahead of the branded oils.

Consumer testing

Pentagram set up a series of consumer focus groups to try to explore the issues that influence purchase and to explore how consumers use the oil. The discussions soon revealed that price was a significant factor in the decision-making process. Many questioned the high price of the manufacturer's brand. Yet, when asked about store-branded oil, few had even tried it. Indeed, knowledge about the properties and performance of motor oil was low and many were buying the incorrect oil for their car. Interestingly the Halfords brand seemed to hold up well under analysis and was regarded as a trusted brand. These findings were confirmed in other focus groups. This presented some interesting challenges for the Pentagram team. Consumers feel the leading manufacturer brands of oil are expensive, yet few had tried the store brands. Also, there was an opportunity to offer some clear relevant product information regarding performance and selection of oil. Yet the Halfords brand was highly regarded and many consumers regularly purchase store brands in other product areas. The studies looking at how consumers used the oil revealed little other than problems with pouring a heavy 5-litre container. This was well documented and almost an accepted part of the process of using motor oil. But, maybe this was a way for Halfords to challenge the leading brands. It was also noticed that it seemed the only way to determine how much oil was in a can was to lift it up and feel the weight. If the Halfords brand of oil could solve the pouring problem and make this task simple, provide a viewer for oil level and offer some better information and labelling regarding properties and performance, maybe this would encourage people to try the Halfords brand.

New packaging

Pentagram decided to look closely at the possibility of improving considerably the dispensing of oil from the container into the engine. Further studies revealed that the problem seemed to centre on the inability to accurately direct the flow of oil. A longer neck like a teapot spout would help, but so would a better hand position on the can to control the flow of oil in much the same way as one would using a bottle (*see* Figure 13.2). The packaging designers came up with the idea of an additional long spout that could be attached to the neck of the container. This would certainly improve direction of flow. The problem with this was the additional cost of screw threads on the detachable long spout. Also, in tests consumers suggested it was unnecessarily fiddly to have to unscrew and screw on another spout. The obvious solution was a long spout for pouring that was integral to the container in some way, but how? Eventually the designers developed the 'pull-up teapot pouring spout'. The traditional screw cap top has been replaced with a push-on top; this reduces cost by dispensing with the need for a screw thread. A ring tab is then pulled, revealing a long neck about 50 cm in length, giving sufficient direction in pouring (*see* Figure 13.2). In addition the handle for the container is in line with the spout, helping to direct the flow of oil. The issue of labelling was solved simply by offering three types of motor oil. A premium-grade oil for most 16-valve petrol engines, a diesel grade for diesel engines and one for standard grade. The three

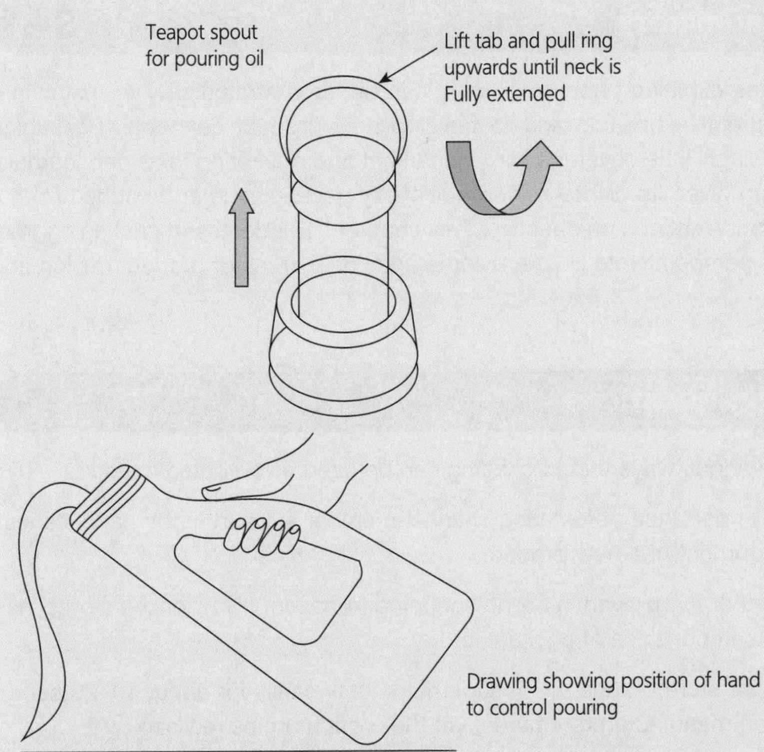

Figure 13.2 Drawings for new packaging of oil container

different oils were offered in three different colours, making them different and distinguishable on the shelf. The final container also incorporated a viewer for oil level. All these packaging attributes propelled the Halfords brand up the sales league, and many of the leading manufacturer brands have been forced to incorporate them into their own brands. After one year, volume of sales increased by 18 per cent, its value by 44 per cent and profits by 54 per cent (PSAG, 1997).

Discussion

This case clearly illustrates the value of packaging and labelling in product development. The motor oil itself remained unchanged, but the packaging and labelling of the oil was considerably altered, enabling Halfords to resposition its oil as a slightly more upmarket store-brand oil. Initial sales were very encouraging and if copying is viewed as a form of flattery then Halfords is surely content.

Reference: Day, J. (2002) *Media Guardian*, 30 April.

Questions

1. Discuss how Halfords used packaging as a strategic tool.
2. Should Halfords have explored the possibility of developing a new brand of motor oil?
3. Use the attributes in Table 13.2 to explore whether more radical packaging could be developed for this product category.
4. Arguably this was a product whose sales were declining and could have been dumped. Can you think of any other 'mature' products that could benefit from an investment in packaging design?
5. Use the CIM (Figure 1.9) to illustrate the innovation process in this case.

Note: This case has been written as a basis for class discussion rather than to illustrate effective or ineffective managerial or administrative behaviour. It has been prepared from a variety of published sources, as indicated, and from observations.

Chapter summary

This chapter has explained how packaging can be used strategically to maintain a product's competitive position and to develop new product concepts. Packaging receives surprisingly little coverage in management and marketing texts and journals; this is surprising given its pivotal role. Traditionally packaging is approached from a marketing communications perspective. This chapter has addressed packaging from the producer's perspective to illustrate some additional areas of product design and development.

Discussion questions

1. Explain the various ways that packaging can be used as a strategic tool.
2. Discuss the importance of fostering channel-member support in the early stages of the development of a new product.
3. Discuss whether the growth in online shopping (Amazon, eBay, online stores) has increased the importance of packaging.
4. Private label or store brands sell in supermarkets typically for about 10–20 per cent less than manufacturers' brands, yet the profit margins realised by supermarkets are usually about 10–15 per cent higher than for manufacturers' brands. Explain why both parties need each other.
5. Select a package of any consumable product. Assess its contribution to brand equity. Justify your decisions.
6. Name an example of a brand article where product design is actively deployed to communicate the brand values. Discuss which brand values are involved and how product design is used.
7. Discuss how packaging can be used to enhance a brand's image and provide some examples.
8. Discuss the factors that may lead to declining profit margins for mature products and how packaging can help.

Key words and phrases

The basic principles of packaging *461*
Dispensing *465*
Storage *465*
Stability *466*
Handling *466*
Opening/resealing *466*
After use and secondary use *468*
Disposal *468*
Product rejuvenation *468*
Product and pack size variation *471*
Retailer acceptance *475*
Revitalising mature packaged goods *476*

References

Croft, N. (1985) Wrapping up sales, *Nation's Business*, October, 41–2.

Fill, C. (2002) *Marketing Communications: Context, Strategies and Applications*, 3rd edn, Prentice Hall, London.

Hancock, M. (2003) *Consumer Technologies will Spur Growth in Profit through Innovation*, PIRA, London.

Johnson, S.C. and Jones, C. (1957) How to organise for new products, *Harvard Business Review*, May–June, Vol. 35, 49–62.

Kotler, P. (2003) *Marketing Management*, 11th edn, Prentice Hall, London.

Morgan, C.L. (1997) *Packaging Design*, Watson-Guptill, New York.

Narisetti, R. (1997) P&G to stores: keep the dented Crisco cans, *Wall Street Journal*, 21 March, 5.

Oka, Hideyuki (1989) *How to Wrap Five Eggs*, Weatherhill, Tokyo.

Pickton, D. and Broderick, A. (2002) *Integrated Marketing Communications*, Prentice Hall, London.

PSAG (1997) Packaging Solutions Advice Group (PSAG). 'Pack to the Future' is a series of discussions on design, branding and packaging issues hosted by the Packaging Solutions Advice Group. 'Strategic Shifts in Retail Brands' was held at the Design Show at the Business Design Centre on 28 October 1997.

Rogers, E. (1962) *Diffusion of Innovations* (3rd edn, 1983; 4th edn 1995), The Free Press, New York.

Schiller, Z., Burns, G.L. and Miller, K. (1996) Make it simple, *Wall Street Journal*, 9 September, 98.

Stewart, B. (1996) *Packaging as an Effective Marketing Tool*, Kogan Page, London.

Sunday Times (2011) Sunday Times Rich List 2011, 8 May.

Trott, P. (2003) Packaging and new product opportunities, University of Portsmouth Business School, Working Paper Series No. 00123.

Wansink, B. and Huffman, C. (2001) Revitalising mature packaged goods, *Journal of Product and Brand Management*, Vol. 10, No. 4, 228–42.

World Packaging Organization (WPO) (2008) *Market Trends and Developments*, World Packaging Organization, 17 April.

Further reading

For a more detailed review of the packaging management literature, the following develop many of the issues raised in this chapter:

Ampuero, O. and Vila, N. (2006) Consumer perceptions of product packaging, *Journal of Consumer Marketing*, Vol. 23, No. 2, 100–112.

HSBC (2010) 100 Thoughts, HSBC, London.

Kumar, N., Scheer, L. and Kotler, P. (2000) From market driven to market driving, *European Management Journal*, Vol. 18, No. 2, 129–41.

Shavinina, L. (2003) *The International Handbook on Innovation*, Elsevier, Oxford.

Underwood, R.L. (2003) The communicative power of product packaging: creating brand identity via lived and mediated experience, *Journal of Marketing Theory and Practice*, Vol. 11, No. 1, 62–77.

Underwood, R.L. and Klein, N. (2002) Packaging as brand communication: effects of product pictures on consumer responses to the package and brand, *Journal of Marketing Theory and Practice*, Vol. 10, No. 4, 58–69.

Wells, L.E., Farley, H. and Armstrong, G.A. (2007) The importance of packaging design for own-label food brands, *International Journal of Retail & Distribution Management*, Vol. 35, No. 9, 677–90.

World Packaging Organization (WPO) (2008) *Market Trends and Developments*, World Packaging Organization, 17 April.

Chapter 14
New service innovation

Introduction

In Europe and the USA services now account for an increasing share of the gross domestic product of these economies, yet compared to new product development we know relatively little about managing innovation within services. This chapter explores the growth in services and helps to explain some of the factors behind this shift in the balance of activities within economies. It identifies the pivotal role played by technology in facilitating the development of many new service opportunities, most notably internet-related technologies. This chapter also examines how new services are created and what firms need to do to enhance their new service development activities. Finally the case study at the end of this chapter illustrates how eBay has used service innovation to grow the business and profits for the firm.

Chapter contents

Learning objectives

When you have completed this chapter you will be able to:

- recognise the reasons for the growth in services;
- recognise the wide range of different types of services;
- explain how new services have led to the creation of new business models;
- examine the pivotal role technology plays in new service innovation;
- explain the role of a classification of service innovations; and
- explain the role of the consumer in the new service development process.

The growth in services

The term knowledge-based economy has been introduced to characterise some of the main changes in the development of economies over the past 20 years. In the most advanced service economies in the world, such as the United States and the United Kingdom, services now account for up to three-quarters of the wealth and 85 per cent of employment (Tidd and Hull, 2003). Within the EU services now account for 60 per cent of GDP (Eurostat, 2006). But when it comes to innovation how should we view services?

Traditionally the literature has viewed services as different from products; this is because 'innovation theory' has been developed around science and technological development. The intangibility of services clearly makes it difficult for the traditional view to embrace or understand innovation within services. But the development of internet-based firms, such as eBay (*see* case study at end of chapter) with its community of users driving the development of new services, is clear evidence of innovation outputs within services – even if technology is a key antecedent.

The influence of technology in general and information communication technologies in particular cannot be overstated. In virtually all industries there has been a huge growth in specialist knowledge and skills being made available to firms. For example, in civil engineering and architecture, where previously much of the input came from the architect, now the architect employs a range of specialists from, for instance, fire engineering, acoustic engineers, lighting designers, etc. A new range of disciplines have emerged offering specialist knowledge and skills. This has been replicated in virtually all industries (Salter and Gann, 2003).

Growth in knowledge-intensive business services (KIBS)

Occasionally one would be forgiven for thinking that in these advanced developed economies services had replaced all manufacturing activities, and there had simply been a huge growth in coffee bars, smoothie bars and hair salons. The truth is that the development of these economies has led to a massive increase in the amount of specialised business services which now provide critical inputs to firms in all sectors. It is this area of the economy (United States and Europe) that has witnessed huge expansion and development. It is not simply that people are spending more time and money in hair salons (though that may also be true). It is these knowledge-intensive business services (KIBS) that are the key behind the development of the service side of the economies. KIBS include traditional professional business services such as accountancy and law, but also a new generation of KIBS. Illustration 14.1 shows how the provision of very specialist services to the oil industry has led to huge growth for Halliburton and Schlumberger, the world market leader for oil services.

The growth in information communication technologies during the 1980s and the development of the internet in the 1990s and into the twenty-first century has led to enormous sums of money being spent by firms in order to ensure that they are equipped to compete. In addition, the introduction of some of these business systems, such as enterprise resource planning systems (ERP), have led to significant reductions in costs and improvements in efficiency. If one then adds to the KIBS the huge growth in entertainment industries, including the gaming industry (Xbox,

Illustration 14.1

Huge growth in oil services

FT

Providing services to oil companies has been an even better business than finding and producing oil in recent years. Since the start of 2003, Exxon Mobil's shares have roughly doubled; those of Royal Dutch Shell's, now the runner-up among Western oil majors, have risen about 40 per cent. But shares in Halliburton and Schlumberger, the world market leader for oil services, have more than tripled. Scarcity of equipment and skilled personnel at a time of bumper investment in oil exploration and production have sent the costs of oil services soaring. BP estimated its cost inflation was 14 per cent last year, and oil services companies were among the beneficiaries.

Source: *Financial Times*, 13 March 2007. Reprinted with permission.

Source: Pearson Education Ltd/Digital Vision

Nintendo, PlayStation, PC games, etc.), the new online gambling industry (PartyGaming, Gaming Corporation) and the more recent social networking industry (which includes Myspace, Bebo and Facebook), one begins to recognise just how much change and growth there has been to economies over the past 10 years. In painting this picture of change that continues to take place in developed economies around the world, we also need to include the two biggest internet players, eBay and Google, and we all recognise the enormous impact the online auction firms and the internet search engine firms have on our lives.

Pause for thought

With previously internal activities now being simply outsourced, is the growth in services simply a mirage?

Outsourcing and service growth

Outsourcing has become very widespread in the last decade and has moved on from limited applications where peripheral business functions are 'outsourced' to much more vital business functions being outsourced today, such as IT support (Jennings, 1997; Quélin and Duhamel, 2003). Despite the rather mixed record of large-scale long-term total outsourcing deals with single suppliers in particular in the IT/IS industry (Lacity and Willcocks, 1998), such contracts are still entered into in significant numbers. The academic literature has identified a number of expected gains that companies can derive from outsourcing. These include:

- the reduction of operational costs (Lacity and Hirschheim, 1993);
- the ability to transform fixed costs into variable costs (Alexander and Young, 1996);
- the ability to focus on core competencies (Quinn and Hilmer, 1994);
- access to the industry-leading external competencies and expertise (Kakabadse and Kakabadse, 2002).

There seems little doubt that the growth in services is linked to this enormous growth in outsourcing, with many firms now buying in 'services' that were previously undertaken in-house. So, whether it's catering facilities within schools now being bought from local providers by the County Education Authority or whether it's a firm buying in information technology (IT) support rather than providing the service themselves, the evidence is overwhelming that this growth in outsourcing has contributed to the growth in services (Davies, 2003). Coupled to this debate, however, is the suggestion that manufacturers are now moving into highly profitable knowledge-intensive services. This is certainly the case at IBM which has moved successfully from manufacturer to service solution provider with its profits now being dominated by IT services (*Financial Times*, 2007). For some firms, lower production costs in India and China are forcing them downstream into the provision of services. For other firms, like IBM and Ericsson, it is recognition that they can offer added value market offerings to their customers by providing additional services. Within sectors of complex products and systems (CoPS) buyers are outsourcing non-core activities and focusing on the provision of services to the final customer. In the pharmaceutical industry, for example, clinical trials that were previously undertaken by the firm are now outsourced to clinical trial specialist firms. Illustration 14.2 shows how firms including Nokia, Yahoo, Cisco and Merck are all outsourcing activities to India.

Illustration 14.2

India and globalisation: spending rockets to match returns

At the height of the internet bubble in 2000, when computer scientists were scarce in California's Bay Area, Yahoo toyed with the idea of looking further afield for software engineers. The internet company set up a small office in Bangalore – in 2003 its office's head count was fewer than 20 people. Today the Bangalore office has 1,000 computer scientists and engineers in what is Yahoo's largest research and development centre outside its California headquarters.

'We wanted to see whether we could acquire talent to help us out', says Venkat Panchapakesan, chief executive of Yahoo India research and development, who moved from Silicon Valley to India.

'We were just looking for people to do analytics and data mining. We weren't looking to build products. But in the last few years we've been ramping up what we can do here', he says.

Now Yahoo's R&D operation in Bangalore takes on advanced work, such as developing new services for Yahoo users that might be launched globally.

Yahoo is continuing to add employees to its R&D centre in India 'because of the volume of work that needs to get done', says Mr Panchapakesan. Current numbers account for 10 per cent of Yahoo's global workforce.

India's spending on R&D in 2004 was $24 billion, ranking it eighth in the world, according to a report from the Organisation for Economic Co-operation and Development (OECD) last year. According to the organisation, China spent $94 billion on research and development in 2004, placing it fourth behind the US, the EU and Japan.

Until 2001, the total amount spent on R&D in India was only $2.9 billion, with businesses accounting for 45 per cent and the rest coming from government, according to a report from Evalueserve, a research and analystics firm based in Delhi.

However, multinational and large Indian companies have stepped up investment in R&D, with more than 220 multinationals and 130 domestic companies currently engaged in advanced work in India. R&D investment from for-profit companies has grown from $1.3 billion in 2001 to $6.5 billion in 2005, representing annual growth of 50 per cent.

Those figures are expected to continue increasing. Evalueserve estimates that total R&D spending will grow to $27.5 billion by 2010, and mushroom to $119 billion by 2020, or about 2.7 per cent of GDP, bringing India close to levels of R&D investment in the US and Japan.

Large pools of highly skilled, English-speaking engineers and computer scientists hired at lower cost than in the developed world are an important factor. Yet companies are setting up R&D centres for reasons that go beyond cost savings.

Source: © Lindsay Hebberd/Corbis

Cisco, the world's largest maker of network switches and routers, has made one of the largest R&D commitments to India.

Booming business at India's technology and outsourcing companies is driving demand for network equipment and routers. But overall growth across many sectors, whether retail or real estate, contributes to demand.

'Cisco chose India as the location from which to expand its globalisation vision because India has a highly skilled workforce, supportive government, innovative customers and world-class partners', said John Chambers, chief executive, in India last month.

While India's strength in innovation has been focused on software, R&D for hardware is beginning to grow.

India is the world's largest mobile phone market and has spurred telecom groups such as Nokia to set up R&D centres in addition to factories. In 2005, French telecom group Alcatel opened a research centre in Chennai to design and develop broadband wireless products.

Alcatel holds a 51 per cent stake in the CDOT Alcatel Research Centre – a joint venture with the Centre for Development of Telematics, the Indian Government's telecom technology development centre.

For Yahoo, Cisco and Alcatel, R&D done in India is aimed at the global market. Alcatel is designing products for India and 'subsequently for the world market'.

R&D for India's auto industry is also receiving a strong push from both government and companies to make Indian vehicles globally competitive and to develop lower-cost technology for exports. Indian automakers such as Mahindra & Mahindra, and Maruti Udyog which is a joint venture with Suzuki of Japan, are investing heavily in R&D.

As part of a joint government and private-sector initiative, about $400 million will be spent on testing, research and development centres for the auto industry across the country. The first centre of the National Automotive Testing and

→

R&D Infrastructure Project (Natrip) is expected to open next year.

A patent law enacted by India last year has also rekindled interest from multinational pharmaceutical companies. Global drugmakers exited India years ago because it did not grant pharmaceutical products patents.

But as part of World Trade Organisation negotiations, India last year brought into force a regime that gave stronger and broader protection to intellectual property rights.

Some drugmakers are dipping their toes back into India and forming 'research-based' partnerships that allow them to help bring down soaring costs of developing original drugs.

Pharmaceutical giant Merck last November announced a partnership with Advinus Therapeutics, backed by Tata, one of India's largest conglomerates. Merck and Advinus will work together on early-stage drug development for metabolic disorders, with Merck retaining the right to advance research into late-stage clinical trials.

'Now that the intellectual property environment is more favourable, we see Indian scientists turning their attention to the challenges and opportunities of drug discovery', says Dr Merv Turner, senior vice-president.

Merck has no plans to build a bricks-and-mortar R&D centre in India, but it is keen to form other links in India as it 'seeks external research partnerships to complement its own research'.

Source: Amy Yee (2007) *Financial Times*, 26 January. Reprinted with permission.

There is, however, also an emerging literature that highlights the weaknesses and risks associated with large-scale outsourcing arrangements, in particular where non-peripheral business functions are concerned. This highlights the risk of becoming dependent on a supplier (Alexander and Young, 1996); Barthelemy (2001) draws our attention to the hidden costs of outsourcing and authors such as Doig *et al.* (2001) and Quinn and Hilmer (1994) identify the possibility of a loss of vital know-how, in particular with respect to core competencies, as a major risk factor in outsourcing. There is also the problem of selecting the most suited supplier/service provider and their longer-term ability to offer the capabilities that are needed in particular in business environments with rapid technology change (Earl, 1996). Another risk that is often overlooked is linked to the broader area of information leakage that arises when business organisations collaborate in order to gain access

Table 14.1 Main outsourcing risks identified in the literature

	Main negative outcomes of outsourcing	Research evidence
1	Dependence on the supplier	Alexander and Young (1996); Aubert *et al.* (1998)
2	Hidden costs	Earl (1996); Alexander and Young (1996); Aubert *et al.* (1998); Lacity and Hirschheim (1993); Barthelemy (2001)
3	Loss of competencies	Bettis *et al.* (1992); Martinsons (1993); Quinn and Hilmer (1994); Khosrowpour *et al.* (1995); Alexander and Young (1996); Aubert *et al.* (1998); Doig *et al.* (2001)
4	Service provider's lack of necessary capabilities	Earl (1996); Aubert *et al.* (1998); Kaplan (2002)
5	Social risk	Lacity and Hirschheim (1993); Barthelemy and Geyer (2000)
6	Inefficient management	Wang and Regan (2003); Lynch (2002)

Source: Adapted from Quélin, B. and Duhamel, F. (2003) Bringing together strategic outsourcing and corporate strategy: outsourcing motives and risks, *European Management Journal*, Vol. 21, No. 5, 647–61.

to knowledge and expertise that they cannot develop on their own. Research by Hoecht and Trott (2006) has demonstrated that there is trade-off between access to cutting-edge knowledge via collaborative research and technology development in knowledge-intensive industries and the risk of losing commercially sensitive knowledge to competitors. This risk, they argue, cannot be controlled by traditional management approaches and legal contracting alone, but requires the operation of social control and in particular the development of trust to be contained. Table 14.1 offers an overview of the main risks identified in the literature.

Different types of services

The service sector is vast and it varies considerably from public services in the form of state-funded education for 97 per cent of children in the United Kingdom to specialist business services in the form of internet website design and maintenance. Each sector of the service economy (such as leisure, charities, public services, financial services) has its own set of specific challenges. Yet, at the same time, the distinctions between some of these sectors is blurring. Some charities and not-for-profit organisations are offering their services to compete with the private sector. Healthcare provision is a prime example. Similarly, some public-funded organisations such as the BBC offer their services in the commercial world and generate large revenue streams. Table 14.2 offers a classification of services and

Table 14.2 Typology of services

	Business-to-business services (traditional)	Business-to-business services (KIBS)	Consumer services	Internal firm services	Public services	Not-for-profit services
Description	Services provided for businesses	Specialist services provided to businesses	Services provided to individuals	Services provided by internal functions	Services provided by local and national government	Services provided by charities
Examples	Accountancy Legal advice Training	Management consultancy IT consultancy	Shops Hotels Banking	Finance Personnel IT	Health Education Leisure	Hospices Counselling Aid agencies
Customers	Frequently purchased by professionals, who may not be end users	Frequently purchased by professionals, who may not be end users	Health and beauty Purchased by consumer of the service	Consumers of the service have no choice of provider	Prisons Funded Purchased by consumer of the service	Funded through charities, maybe government grants; consumers chosen or choose
Challenges	Providing high-quality tailored and personal service	Providing high-quality services to businesses that have high purchasing power	Providing a consistent service to a wide variety of customers	Delivering customised, personal service, and demonstrating value for money	Delivering acceptable public services against a backcloth of political pressures	Balancing needs of volunteers, donors and overwhelming needs of customers

Source: Adapted from Johnston, R. and Clark, G. (2005) *Service Operations Management*, 2nd edn, Prentice Hall, Pearson Education Limited, Harlow.

includes professional business services, such as accountancy, and public services, such as libraries. This overview helps demystify the service notion. It clarifies the different sectors within services and illustrates the different challenges facing each sector.

From the perspective of innovation, however, we are less concerned with the type of organisation or even the industry sector in which it operates. We are more concerned with how the service is managed and in particular how it is designed and operated. In order to investigate this area it is useful to separate out the wide range of services undertaken. For example, services in Table 14.2 range from bespoke specialist industry services to homogenised customer services found within fast-food restaurants. One way is to use the two key parameters: volume of transactions within a certain amount of time and the variety of tasks to be carried out by a given set of people and processes. At one end of the spectrum is a service we are all familiar with: that of fast-food restaurants where the volume is high and process variety is low. This type of service can be clearly classified as a commodity. Whereas at the other end of the spectrum we have specialist business services such as internet website design, where the volume is low and process variety is very high (the designer can draw upon a limitless amount of imagination). Johnston and Clark (2005) have developed a simple matrix which helps to capture the different types of service processes (*see* Figure 14.1). On the vertical axis is process variety and on the horizontal axis is volume per unit, with fast-food restaurants sitting in the bottom right-hand quadrant as a commodity service process and internet website design sitting in the top left-hand corner. It is capability-based service processes where the provider frequently works with the customer to clarify the problem and/or to develop a customised solution, such as management consultants and web designers.

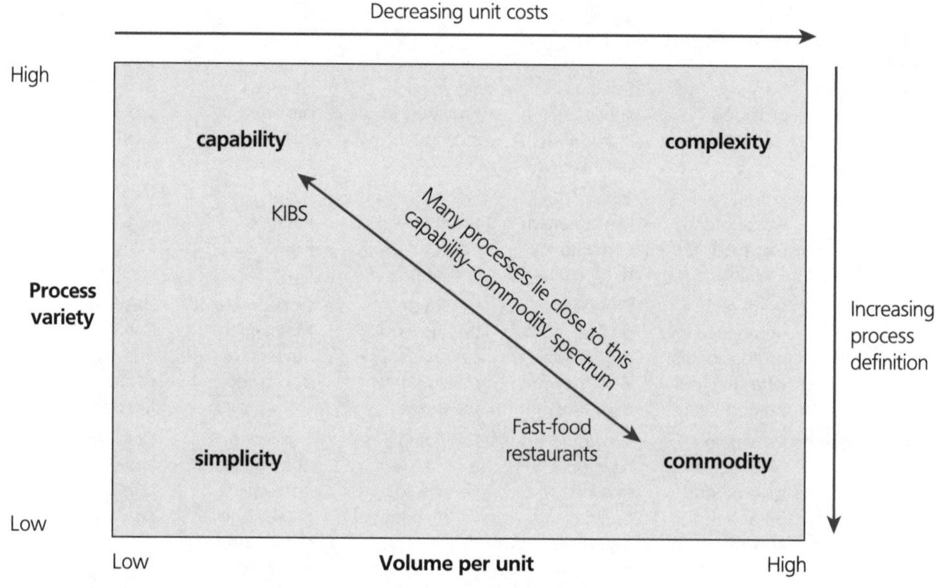

Figure 14.1 Four main types of service processes

Source: R. Johnston and G. Clark (2005) *Service Operations Management*, 2nd edn, Prentice Hall, Harlow. Reproduced with kind permission.

Technology and new service development

Business opportunities based on new technology developments have been (and continue to be) identified and exploited by entrepreneurial individuals, leading to the creation of multinational businesses. Indeed, technology has become the most significant enabler of innovation in services. The application of different technologies in the context of existing service products has changed the way services are delivered and thereby gave rise to the development of highly innovative service products. For example, the internet technology that gave rise to the development of e-commerce has brought radical transformations in consumers' shopping practices. In contrast to the increasing significance of technology in the development of innovative services in practice, the literature has largely overlooked and failed to explain the role technology plays in the development of new services (Menor *et al.*, 2002; Boone, 2000). Technology changes the nature of service development in many ways: it can reduce the tasks of service developers by empowering customers with certain technical mechanisms such as user toolkits. Therefore, the effect of technology is evident in transforming the roles of both employees and customers. Within this framework, technology also increases the organisational socialisation by easing the connectivity between service developers and customers (cf. Bitran and Pedrosa, 1998). Indeed, new service development processes that have traditionally been undertaken by marketing departments has now to involve technology teams in the development of technology-based services. Technology may also transform the structure of new service development processes. Service firms that have insufficient capabilities to develop a particular technological service may outsource service production. Illustration 14.2 shows how a wide variety of firms are utilising skills and resources in India to deliver and develop services.

New services and new business models

For many years the innovation literature overlooked the concept of new service innovation. Innovation was deemed to require a new physical 'thing'. But the world of business suggested new services could deliver potentially even more significant changes than new products – they could deliver new business models. The one caveat here is that frequently the new service is underpinned by a new technology application. None the less, there are a range of firms that have introduced new services that have completely changed an industry sector. Customers are usually unable to conceptualise or visualise the benefits of revolutionary new products, concepts and technologies. A good example here is the online auction concept; eBay was not the first but it slowly became the dominant player. Ryanair was the first in the European market to offer a budget airline service, where the price of an airfare was cut in return for a cut-down service. Ryanair identified that within Europe the short flying times meant that customers did not always value the extra tariff for additional services and preferred a discounted ticket price over extra services. Within the airline industry others, most notably FlyBe, have continued with new service innovations. In 2006 FlyBe launched the first online check-in facility – Q-Buster. It was also the first to provide customers with the online ability to select seats in advance. Table 14.3 illustrates how other service innovations have revolutionised an industry sector.

Table 14.3 A range of new services that also create new business models

Company	Industry sector	New service/new business model
eBay	Online auction	A new way of buying and selling through a community of individual users
Ryanair	Airline	A new way of consuming air travel with no-frills service and emphasis on economy
Amazon	Retailer	New way to buy goods – online retailer
Napster; iTunes	Music retailer	New way to buy and download music
Google	Internet search engine	A fast way to search for information on the internet
PartyGaming	Online gambling, e.g. poker	Gambling and gaming from the comfort of your own home
Facebook	Social networking	A community of users online who can chat and share music, images, news from their own home
YouTube	Online video and film archive	A community of users sharing home-made video clips plus recorded favourite clips from movies

Pause for thought

It seems services are so diverse that they cover almost every aspect of business. Even tangible products, such as cars, are now wrapped in services. Should we separate services from products?

Characteristics of services and how they differ from products

Within the marketing literature many differences between goods and services are discussed. Significantly, these differences are referred to as characteristics of services and are identified as intangibility, heterogeneity and simultaneity, i.e. the three key characteristics that distinguish services from products, with interaction with the consumer the key distinguishing characteristic in service development. Moreover, the literature suggests that, while offer development, process development and market development occur simultaneously, in those industries where services dominate it is process development that is significant. Frequently this has involved a fundamental rethink and redesign of business processes resulting in radically new offerings, such as the purchase of airline seats using the internet, including the ability to select one's preferred seat on the aircraft at the time of making the reservation (*see* Table 14.3). Whichever service one considers, it involves a number of activities which, when linked together, can be described as a process. Figure 14.2 shows the key characteristics of services. In a study of the top 500 service firms and top 100 financial firms in Taiwan, Jaw *et al.* (2010) found that service characteristics of heterogeneity and perishability and market orientation positively influence a firm's resources and innovation.

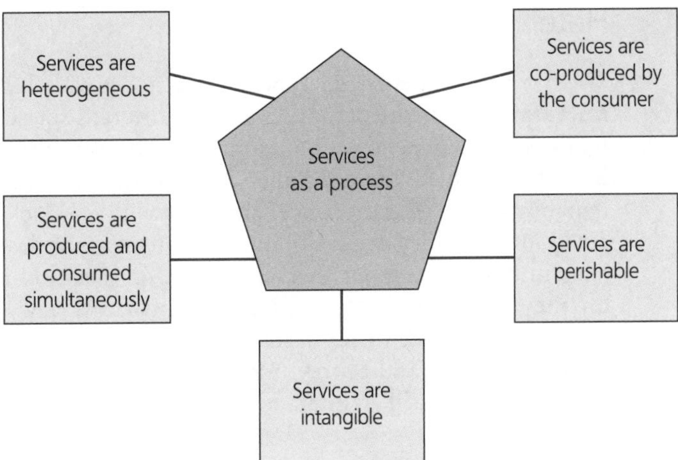

Figure 14.2 Services as a process

Intangibility

Services are intangible deeds, processes and performances. It is not possible to see, feel, taste or touch services in the same manner as tangible products. While service firms are paid to perform a function, manufacturing firms generate tangible products that are bought to provide a function (cf. Tidd and Hull, 2003). There may be some tangible aspects of services but the result of the service experience is intangible performances. For example, the purchase of an item of clothing via the online auction firm eBay will hopefully result in both parties being satisfied: the seller receives their money and the buyer receives their goods. All via the website, which can be seen but cannot be touched. Given this intangible nature of services, it is difficult to test them during concept development. For this reason, the testing of new services usually end up in the actual market (Easingwood, 1986). However, the level of technology used in a service innovation increases the possibility of concept testing and prototyping phases of new service development.

It is often easier and quicker to develop and modify services compared to tangible products and processes. It is for this reason that for most firms new service development is an ongoing and informal activity where new services are developed through time in response to the changes in client needs or competitive offerings (*see* the eBay case study at the end of this chapter). In addition, they often tend to evolve throughout a trial and error process due to the ease of modifying services. This also facilitates and speeds up imitation in services. As new services cannot be protected with patents, new service concepts or development processes can be easily copied by competitors. This can reduce the new service development efforts or at least force service firms to diminish innovation investment. For this reason, innovation in services often results in small and incremental changes in processes and procedures and development of 'me too' services rather than radically new ones. Finally, research by De Brentani (1991) uncovered that service firms have much less incentive to employ costly and time-consuming product development activities compared to physical product firms, partly due to ease of imitation and partly due to the difficulty (if not impossibility) of attaining long-term competitive edge.

Heterogeneity

We have all experienced repeat visits to service-based organisations, such as a restaurant or hairdresser, and received different service experiences. This is because many services depend on human interaction. In other words, services are produced by both suppliers and consumers. As a result, service development efforts may not match with service experience. Heterogeneity and lack of standardisation of services result in difficulties in developing accurate concept descriptions and can create problems in concept testing. Yet, the degree of variation in heterogeneity also depends on the amount of standardisation in services. The standardisation of a service, on the other hand, varies in line with the amount of technology applied at the user interface (Johne and Storey, 1998). However, in the context of technology-based services, there is still an interaction of individuals with the service interface. Although technology-based services tend to enhance the standardisation of services from the supplier side, service experience may still vary due to the technical deficiencies and customer-oriented problems. Customer education and staff training (i.e. service development team and service encounters) have a vital importance in enhancing the consistency of service experiences and quality of service development processes. For technology-based services, it is also vital to ensure the maintenance of the system to enable coherent service experiences. The eBay case study at the end of this chapter illustrates how early technical problems encountered by eBay caused the site to close for a few days. This not only resulted in loss of income to eBay but also enormous anger and frustration to buyers and sellers.

Simultaneous production and consumption

Services are produced and consumed simultaneously whereas tangible products are produced, sold and consumed at different times. In services, interaction of customers and staff is an important part of service experience. Besides physical and operational characteristics of using services, attitudes, behaviour and appearance of people involved in service delivery have significant influences on perceptions of a service (Cowell, 1988). For this reason, it is also critical that the new service development process involves both employees and customers (Zeithaml and Bitner, 2003). In service businesses, the operations staff play both an operational and a marketing role. Their feedback and suggestions, obtained from knowledge gained during interaction with customers, provide an important source of new ideas for new service development (Cowell, 1988; Zeithaml and Bitner, 2003). Therefore, customers' role in new service development is much more crucial than in the development of physical products.

Perishability

Services cannot be saved, stored, resold or returned. Therefore, there is lack of ownership in services. Managing supply and demand or capacity planning is more difficult in services compared with physical products (Zeithaml and Bitner, 2003). Service development concerns more than the design of the service delivery. It should also involve the processes that assist service firms when they face fluctuating demand.

With technology-based services such as internet banking, problems concerning perishability of services often arise due to technical flaws. For example, a common occurrence for us all of a service that perishes is when we visit an ATM only to find it out of order. Service firms that cannot manage their capacity planning process and human resources efficiently eventually suffer from economic loss. For example, how many times do customers walk into stores and walk out again because of the long queues at the pay-desk?

Classification of service innovations

In services, often it is not feasible to distinguish product and process innovation due to the simultaneous production and consumption of services. The service product is the core of the new service offering consisting of the essential functional benefit(s) conveyed by the service. Service process innovation, on the other hand, is a new service delivery system (cf. Gadrey *et al.*, 1995). Boone (2000) states that process technology innovation is often utilised to increase efficiency (reducing operational costs) and effectiveness (i.e. reducing time costs, improving quality and increasing flexibility) of firms and their offerings. Innovation in services does not always necessitate changes in the core service-offering characteristics. A service innovation can involve integration of an existing core service offering and innovative service process. For example, during the last two decades, the internet has emerged as the most innovative service process. The effects of the internet-based technologies on the way that businesses compete and manage their operations in general have also been profound (Barnes *et al.*, 2003). For this reason, many service firms have been exploring ways to exploit the internet in delivering their existing service products (*see* Table 14.2).

It much the same way as new products are classified dependent on level of newness, services have been classified depending on the level of change. Lovelock's (1984) classification is the most widely known and usefully illustrates the different levels of change that can occur within service innovation (*see* Table 14.4). On the other hand, the typology developed by Booz, Allen & Hamilton (1982), which explains different types of product innovation, is the most extensively applied classification in the context of both new services and new products. The innovation typologies suggested by Lovelock (1984) and Booz, Allen & Hamilton (1982) overlap with each other (Johne and Storey, 1998) (*see* Table 14.4). Both typologies make a distinction between radical and incremental innovations. Yet, they are rather limited in explaining the role of technology in the identification of different innovation types. Furthermore, the diffusion of innovations literature concerns the objective newness of an innovation, rather than the perceived newness of an idea, practice or physical object (Rogers, 2005).

The new service development process

New service development can be defined as the overall process of developing new service offerings from idea generation to market launch (Goldstein *et al.*, 2002). Offer development is a combination of the development of core product/service attributes (i.e. product or service development) and the processes by which consumers

Table 14.4 Typologies for innovations

Booz, Allen & Hamilton (1982)	Lovelock (1984)
New-to-the-world products: New products that not only represent a major new challenge to the supplier, but which are also seen to be quite new in the eyes of customers	**Major innovation**: New services for markets as yet undefined; innovations usually driven by information and computer-based technologies
New product lines: New products which represent major new challenges to the supplier	**Start-up business**: New services in a market that is already served by existing services
Additions to existing product lines: New products that supplement a company's established product lines, so rounding out the product mix	**New services for the market presently served**: New service offerings to existing customers of an organisation (although the services may be available from other companies)
Improvements and revisions to existing products: New products that provide improved performance and so replace existing products	**Service line extensions**: Augmentations of the existing service line such as adding new menu items, new routes, and new courses
Repositionings: Existing products that are targeted to new markets or market segments	**Service improvements**: Changes in features of services that are currently being offered
Cost reductions: New products that provide similar performance at a lower cost of supply	**Style changes**: The most common of all 'new services'; modest forms of visible changes that have an impact on customer perceptions, emotions and attitudes, with style changes that do not change the service fundamentally, only its appearance

Source: Ozdemir, S. (2007) An Analysis of Internet Banking Adoption in Turkey: Consumer, Innovation and Service Developer Dimensions, Ph.D thesis, University of Portsmouth.

evaluate, purchase and consume the service (i.e. product or service augmentation development). Similarly, due to the nature and distinctive characteristics of services, when developing a new service emphasis should not only be given to its core attributes but it should also be given to the existence of other supplementary services (cf. Papastathopoulou *et al.*, 2001). Although product augmentation or a supplementary service often brings incremental changes, it can differentiate the core service and add value to it by providing innovative support processes. This can be seen in the internet economy, where providing value added services to customers constitutes the basis of differentiation. For example, the ability to print off your boarding pass at home prior to taking a flight can remove one of the most frustrating aspects of flying: queuing.

None the less, relative to new product development (NPD), the service innovation concept is little studied. This is despite the fact that the service component has become an integral part of most manufactured products. For example, the purchase of a motor car now involves a wide range of service offerings including finance, breakdown cover, warranty, etc. In recent years, more attention has been given to innovation in services (Dolfsma, 2004; Tidd and Hull, 2003), with some research expressing severe doubts about applying concepts developed in NPD to the service sector, arguing that precisely how innovation occurs in service sectors remains unclear (e.g. Sundbo, 1997).

Today our understanding of the process of service innovation is mainly dominated by NPD models. The well-known NPD process suggested by Booz, Allen & Hamilton

Table 14.5 Four dimensions of service innovation by eBay

Four service dimensions	Illustration
New service concept	Online auction community of traders
New client interface	Introduction of payment system that helps eBayers trade more easily – Paypal
New service delivery system	Huge investment in technology infrastructure to improve reliability and performance
Technological options	Introduction of voice over internet protocol service – SKYPE

Source: Adapted from Den Hertog, P. (2002) Knowledge-intensive business services as co-producers of innovation, *International Journal of Innovation Management*, Vol. 4, No. 4, 491–528.

(1982) has been the most widely applied model in the context of service innovation. However, both the linear and more interactive models of NPD insufficiently emphasise the significance of customers and cannot capture the dynamic process of consumer involvement in the creation of innovative services. It is widely accepted that gaining an understanding of the factors that are likely to influence customer evaluations of a new product or service and how customers are likely to relate to it is necessary for ensuring a successful market outcome.

The internet has provided the mechanism through which many more industries can now develop offerings. Indeed, the development of a service 'offer' requires far more attributes to be brought into consideration than for a tangible product. Nowhere is this more clearly visible than in the eBay case study at the end of this chapter. It is this technology dimension that now forms such a significant part of service development. This was recognised by Den Hertog (2002), who offers four dimensions of service innovations all of which are influenced by the technological options available. These are: service concept, new client interface, new service delivery system and technological options. Table 14.5 illustrates how eBay has exploited these four dimensions.

Pause for thought

It seems much of the growth in services can be attributed to the exploitation of new technology, such as the internet. Are these really services or are they products?

New service development models

The marketing literature argues that because product development processes have not been employed in the development of new services, and because of the distinctive nature and characteristics of services, the process has been haphazard or ad hoc (cf. Boone, 2000; Menor *et al.*, 2002). However, although new product development models represent a useful framework for studying the development of new services, more research is required to integrate the influence of the unique characteristics of services into the process of new service development. New service development models are derived from the process models that were initially created for the development of manufactured products (Fitzsimmons and Fitzsimmons, 2000).

Indeed, researchers have emphasised that, with few exceptions, it is useful to integrate the models created in the study of product development into those dealing with service development (Lovelock, 1984; Boone, 2000). The applicability of these models depends on the nature of different services.

Sequential service development models or stage-gate models

The majority of new service development models are based on the new product development framework suggested by Booz, Allen & Hamilton (1982). This viewed the process as a sequence of stages to be undertaken during new product development. These stages include new product development strategy, idea generation, screening and evaluation, business analysis, development, testing and commercialisation (Figure 14.3 offers an illustration of such a sequential model). The number of these stages varies across different studies. Similarly, a widely applied approach has been the stage-gate model that was initially suggested by Cooper (1990) and has been used to conceptualise service activities (Stevens and Dimitriadis, 2005). Besides different stages of the product development process, the model also includes certain gates where decisions are given on the basis of the information generated in the previous groups of activities. Therefore, these gates represent the review points for the preceding stages (Phillips *et al.*, 1999). Stage-gate models suggest a more comprehensive and action-oriented process compared to their predecessor – sequential new product development models. However, the common point of these models is that both are characterised by a sequence of a linear progression of activities (Bullinger *et al.*, 2003; Stevens and Dimitriadis, 2005). Indeed, limitations of these models derive from their

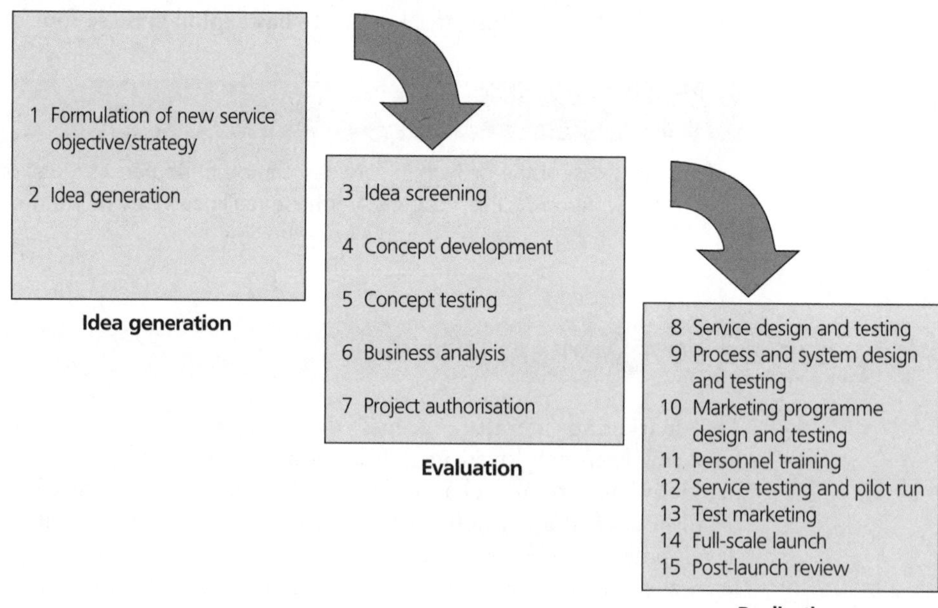

Figure 14.3 The service innovation process – a sequential model

Source: Adapted from Scheuing and Johnson, 1989.

sequential nature. One of the most important limitations is that they are very costly, time consuming and overly bureaucratic processes (Bullinger *et al.*, 2003; cf. Stevens and Dimitriadis, 2005; cf. Vermeulen and Dankbaar, 2002). Each stage of the process is needed to be completed before proceeding to the subsequent stage. For this reason, they do not allow for parallelisation of the activities. Furthermore, because of the time-consuming nature of the process, the new market opportunity identified at the beginning may no longer exist when the product is commercialised (May-Plumlee and Little, 1998). In addition, their structured and inflexible pattern gives very little chance for adaptation of the process to special service or project-specific features (Bullinger *et al.*, 2003). Sequential models also increase the communication problems across different departments in the design and development processes. With stage-gate models, a failure in a particular gate may result in dropping potentially successful products.

New product or service development is an iterative process that also proceeds after the commercialisation or market launch stage. In this context, new product development models that characterise the process as being iterative in nature have also been applied in the context of services. These models are also referred to as spiral models or interactive models. They are more sophisticated models compared to linear models of product development as each stage is repeated several times, which gives provision for feedback (Bullinger *at al.*, 2003). The new service development model suggested by Johnson *et al.* (2000) conceptualises iterative stages of the service development process (*see* Figure 14.4). Indeed, actors, systems and technology of the process are identified as playing a significant role in the process of NSD.

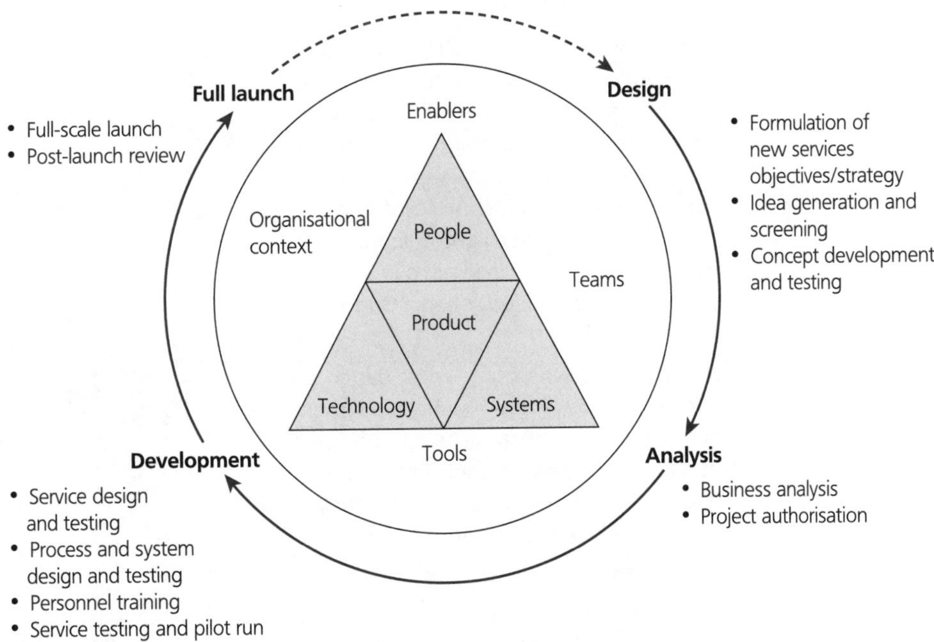

Figure 14.4 The new service development cycle

Source: Adapted from Johnson *et al.* (2000) 'A critical evaluation of the new service development process: Integrating service innovation and service design', in J.A. Fitzsimmons and M.J. Fitzsimmons (eds) *New Service Development: Creating Memorable Experiences*, Sage Publications, London.

However, the model still includes the limitations of sequential development processes as mentioned previously.

Concurrent service development models

Concurrent service development or simultaneous engineering overcomes the limitations of the sequential type of models and offers more flexible ways of developing innovative services. Essentially it enables the parallelisation of the activities. The objective of this approach is to consider the whole service development processes rather than individual stages. In concurrent service development, communication is improved and expertise of all departments is employed. Therefore, these types of service development processes are relatively faster and less costly compared to sequential service development models (May-Plumlee and Little, 1998; cf. Vermeulen and Dankbaar, 2002). It also avoids potential design errors that may arise in the future stages. However, specialisms of different people from different departments may also create problems during collaborative working, as these people frequently do not speak the same 'language' and they may have little understanding about each other's activities (Vermeulen and Dankbaar, 2002). This in turn may lead to an increase in time to market and costs (cf. Vermeulen and Dankbaar, 2002).

Innovation in action

Hire a husband

The seismic demographic shifts of age, race and gender are easy to notice, but some of the most important shifts take place below the surface. Spotting these changing social patterns can lead to brilliant business opportunities. A Melbourne DIY enthusiast had such a light-bulb moment. He was hard at work fixing things at home when his wife's friend joked, 'Can I hire your hubby?'

Source: Pearson Education Ltd/Gareth Boden

Hire a Hubby was born. What began as a local service is now Australia's largest handyman business. The purple-clad hubbies, who are all security checked, can now be seen in the UK as the company is being franchised worldwide.

The key to its success lies in capitalising on the gap caused by the changing role of men who no longer define themselves by their practical skills, but rather by their parenting and work successes.

Source: HSBC (2010) 100 Thoughts, HSBC, London.

Service innovation and the consumer

One important characteristic of services that distinguishes them is that customers are co-producers of services. Therefore, the role customers play in services is more crucial relative to manufacturing products. Importantly, Nambisan (2002) identified three different methods of customer involvement in the new product development process: customer as resource, customer as co-producer and customer as user. Table 14.6 illustrates further ways consumers can provide input to the new service development process at every stage. Traditionally, quality function deployment (QFD) has been the most widely known method employed during this stage. QFD has been defined as a system that is capable of linking customer requirements to design characteristics of the product or service through certain market research methods such as direct discussion or interviews, surveys, focus groups, customer specifications, observation etc. (cf. Zeithaml and Bitner, 2003; see also Chapter 4).

Table 14.6 Customers' input into the new service development process

	New service development stages	Activities performed by the customer
1	Strategic planning	Thoughts and feedback on long-term plans
2	Idea generation	State needs, problems, criticise existing services; identify gaps in the market; state service requirements; state new service adoption criteria
3	Idea screening	Suggest desired features, benefits and attributes; show reactions to concepts; show level of purchase intent for concepts; indication of sales and market size
4	Business analysis	Possible feedback on financial data, including profitability of concepts; also pricing levels
5	Formation of cross-functional team	Either participate in team selection or even form part of the team
6	Service design and process system design	Review and jointly develop 'blueprints'; suggest improvements by identifying weak or fail points; observe service delivery trial by personnel
7	Personnel training	Observe and participate in simulated service delivery process and suggest improvements
8	Service testing and pilot	Participate in a simulated service delivery process and suggest final improvements and design changes
9	Test marketing	Provide feedback on the marketing plan; detailed comments about marketing mix – suggest improvements
10	Commercialisation	Adopt the service as a trial; feedback about overall performance of the service along with improvements; word of mouth communication to other potential customers

Source: Adapted from Allam, I. and Perry, C. (2002) A customer-oriented new service development process, *Journal of Services Marketing*, Vol. 16, No. 6, 515–34.

Consumer user toolkits

There has been much written in the NPD literature about the need to involve customers at an early stage in the process and to integrate them into the process in order to fully capture ideas (Cooper, 1999; von Hippel, 1986; Brown and Eisenhardt, 1995, 1998; Thomke, 2003). Despite this, customer involvement in NPD has been limited and largely passive in most industries (Weyland and Cole, 1997). There are many reasons for this limited utilisation of consumers in NPD, but perhaps the most limiting factor is the disconnection between customers and producers. Another reason is that research within marketing has shown for many years that gaining valuable insight from consumers about innovative new market offerings, especially discontinuous new products, is extremely difficult and can sometimes lead to misleading information (Trott, 2001; King, 1985; Tauber, 1981; Martin, 1995; Hamel and Prahalad, 1994). Indeed, frequent responses from consumers are along the lines of 'I want the same product, only cheaper and better'. Von Hippel (1986) has suggested that consumers have difficulty in understanding and articulating their needs and describes this phenomenon as 'sticky information'; that is, information which is difficult to transfer (similar to the notion of tacit knowledge). Recent research, however, has shown that 'user toolkits' can facilitate the transfer of so-called 'sticky information' and have enabled firms to better understand the precise needs and desires of customers. Given these difficulties of utilising consumers effectively in the new service development process, how then should firms proceed?

The earlier section on technology may provide some indications. Today, technology enables innovative ways of involving and integrating customers to the product and process development process. In this context, it is here that new technologies, most notably in the form of 'toolkits', offer considerable scope for improving connection between consumers and producers. Franke and Piller's (2004) study analysed the value created by so-called 'toolkits for user innovation and design'. This was a method of integrating customers into new product development and design.

The so-called toolkits allow customers to create their own product, which in turn is produced by the manufacturer. An example of a toolkit in its simplest form is the development of personalised products through uploading digital family photographs via the internet and having these printed on to products such as clothing or cups, thereby allowing consumers to create personalised individual products for themselves. User toolkits for innovation are specific to given product or service type and to a specified production system. Within these general constraints, they give users real freedom to innovate, allowing them to develop their custom product via iterative trial and error (von Hippel, 2001; Franke and Piller, 2004). Research by Thomke and von Hippel (2002) found that toolkits are particularly useful when market segments are shrinking and customers are increasingly asking for customised products. However, employment of toolkits can lead to increasing supplier costs. For example, Jeppesen (2005) found that using toolkits may be costly for suppliers due to the increased need for consumer support. This is largely due to overcoming difficulties faced by consumers. He further revealed that under these conditions consumer communities that enable consumer-to-consumer interaction can facilitate problem solving concerning the usage of toolkits in the consumer domain, thereby reducing operational costs.

The idea of integrating users into the design and production process is a promising strategy for companies being forced to react to the growing individualisation of demand (Franke and Piller, 2004). Over the past few years many more firms have turned to the internet as a mechanism for communicating with their customers. Significantly, the internet enables manufacturers to communicate directly with their customers without the need for intermediaries such as retailers and wholesalers. In some product category areas, most notably software related ones, the internet provides the opportunity for firms to interact with customer groups and for customers to interact with customers (as eBay does with its 'community' of users). Powerful user networks can be established around product ideas, technology ideas or, most significantly, company capabilities. That is, genuine new product opportunities may be developed. This is especially so in dynamic markets where new technologies are emerging that may offer considerable advantage to firms, as in the case of online gambling, online auctions, social networking and internet banking.

Consumer testing of services

Customers also embrace the role as users in the development of new services. The role of users in this process is testing new services. As was mentioned earlier, due to the intangible nature of services, it is often easier to modify services relative to manufactured products. For this reason, consumers often test services following their market launch rather than during the initial stages of service development. For example, one of the fastest growing parts of the services sector is the software industry and it has been using lead users as active testers of their new service offerings for many years. Microsoft has been Beta testing the initial versions (prototypes) of their new software with voluntary users. Indeed, the employment of Beta testing has given rise to the emergence of online user communities that provide collaborative assistance to service firms in developing their new offerings. Internetworking giant Cisco even gives its customers open access to its information, resources and systems through an online service that enables the company's customers to engage in a dialogue. In this way, customers who access Cisco's knowledge base and user community assist other customers to solve the problems they encountered (Prahalad and Ramaswamy, 2000). Yet, involving consumers only at the end of the service development process has received criticisms from the marketing literature (van Kleef *et al.*, 2005). For example, in the field of UK commercial banking, Athanassopoulou and Johne (2004) revealed that most successful developers communicated with their lead users throughout the new service development process whereas less successful ones concentrated their communication at the end of the process.

Case study

Developing new services at the world's most successful internet-based company, eBay

This case study explores the remarkable success of eBay and illustrates how its continual development of new services has enabled it to remain the world's leading auction site and deliver extraordinary financial results for investors.

Introduction

Founded in September 1995, eBay is The World's Online Marketplace for the sale of goods and services by a diverse community of individuals and small businesses. This eBay community includes more than 100 million registered members from around the world. According to Media Metrix, people spend more time on eBay than any other online site, making it the most popular shopping destination on the internet. On an average day, there are millions of items listed on eBay. People come to eBay to buy and sell items in thousands of categories from collectibles like trading cards, antiques, dolls and housewares to practical items like used cars, clothing, books, CDs and electronics. Buyers have the option to purchase items in an auction-style format or items can be purchased at a fixed price through a feature called Buy It Now. Currently, eBay has local sites that serve Australia, Austria, Belgium, Canada, France, Germany, Ireland, Italy, Korea, The Netherlands, New Zealand, Singapore, Spain, Sweden, Switzerland, Taiwan and the United Kingdom. In addition, eBay has a presence in Latin America and China through its investments in MercadoLibre.com and EachNet respectively.

eBay, Inc. is possibly the most successful web-based enterprise in existence; eBay has a market capitalisation of $35 billion and, by way of illustration, eBay's quarterly profits are similar to Amazon's annual profits (Birchall, 2006; Nuttall, 2006). The San Jose, California, based company is universally known and is synonymous with the auction model of online selling. eBay was pivotal in helping to facilitate buying and selling between individuals and businesses. The industry leader also created one of the first trusted online commercial communities, whereby the exchange between sellers and buyers is regulated by the evaluations and recommendations of each. Although eBay has spawned many imitators, as well as a spate of other web destinations with auction capabilities, it continues to dominate the auction industry and remains on the leading edge in innovation with models such as fixed-price and half-price sales.

How eBay works

The internet auction site's rise from local flea-market to global trading powerhouse has been accompanied by one of the most consistent track records of any US company. As revenues soared from $86 million in 1996 to $3.3 billion in 2004, eBay was consistently posting better than expected financial performances. The result was a share price that stood out even by the heady standards of internet stock prices. Its ability to generate cash was always superior to Yahoo and Google.

Figure 14.5 illustrates how eBay works. It is essentially the same as that of a physical auction. Prior to bidding or listing an item for sale, buyer and seller must register with eBay. All items listed by eBay can be viewed by all including non-registered users, but to trade (i.e. buy or sell) you must register. Figure 14.5 shows the process for a typical trade:

1 Item is listed.
2 A seller's track record of selling is made available to all.
3 Potential buyers can bid.
4 Sellers view buying track record of buyers.
5 eBay notifies winning bidder and seller of winning bid.
6 Payment made and goods shipped.
7 Buyers and sellers leave feedback on each other.

eBay receives its income from charging sellers a small fee to display items and then also taking a small

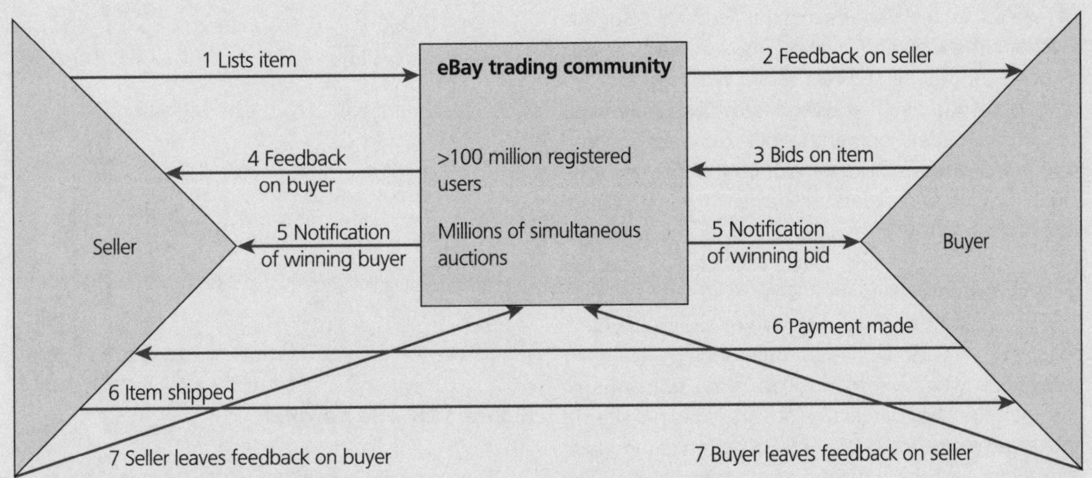

Figure 14.5 How eBay works

percentage of the winning bid. For example, it costs very little to display items of low value such as a novel. A seller may display a novel (including a digital image of the book) for a few pence (approximately 20p). The move into higher-value items such as automobiles has provided eBay with substantial additional income. eBay charges a vendor £6 to display a vehicle which may sell for several thousand pounds. eBay will then also take a small percentage of this winning bid.

The entire system is based upon trust and there is clearly an opportunity for rogue traders to operate and steal money from genuine traders. The use by eBay of the feedback system allows vendors and buyers to view the trading record of each other before agreeing to trade. This helps genuine traders to determine authentic traders from rogue ones. New traders will have to establish themselves as genuine before others will trade with them. This is possible by agreeing to pay for goods prior to receiving them or, if one is a vendor, forwarding goods prior to receiving the money.

The birth of eBay

eBay was born in September 1995. Its original name was AuctionWeb. The idea fell out of a discussion between Pierre Omidyar a 30-something French-born computer programmer and his fiancée, who was an avid Pez collector (sweet dispensers). With the help of his friend Jeff Skol, Mr Omidyar launched AuctionWeb; it was incorporated in 1996 and changed its name to eBay in 1997.

After a year of trading, however, the start-up company was struggling to develop quickly. Worryingly for the founders there were many competitors (including Yahoo's own online auction site) and the technology and internet were developing and changing rapidly. Omidyar and Skol needed significant amounts of money if they were to make eBay successful. In 1997, Pierre Omidyar drove to Silicon Valley's Sand Hill Road to seek venture capital funding for his fledgling online flea market. Though it was growing at 40 per cent a month – without any marketing – and enjoyed 30 per cent margins, eBay also needed professional management. Competition was intense: there were 150 other auction sites, many of them free, unlike eBay's fee-based service. Mr Omidyar had no PowerPoint presentation and no business plan and his company's computer server was down – meaning there was no active website for him to showcase. This was not a good start for Mr Omidyar, but within four weeks *Benchmark*, a venture capital firm, had agreed to invest $6.7 million, valuing eBay at about $20 million. According to Benchmark it seems Mr Odimyar recognised that he needed help. In particular, it required better qualified people to run the business. In addition to their investment Benchmark offered its services and its industry contacts. Benchmark's investment generated a return of $4.5 billion, probably the greatest profit ever

→

generated in the venture capital industry. But the investment paid off for eBay too. Indeed, it was Benchmark that helped recruit Ms Whitman as CEO and Mr Swette as chief operating officer, now head of corporate development. While no one doubted that the business model developed (connecting individual buyers and sellers online and taking a cut of the transaction) was excellent, it was the development of this to a public offering which has enabled eBay to become the giant it is today.

The appointment of Ms Whitman as CEO is regarded universally as an outstanding move by eBay. She was able to develop eBay from one of the many auction websites into the leading site. In those early days of 1997 the eBay site was in black and white and the typeface was basic courier. The company was called eBay and the website was called AuctionWeb, but both brands appeared on the site. The eBay web pages appeared amateurish compared to what Ms Whitman was used to at P&G, Disney and Hambro; many thought she would not join, but she did. After Mr Omidyar explained eBay's impressive growth rate, margins and profitability, Ms Whitman realised the potential. Furthermore, when Mr Omidyar explained that people had met their best friends on eBay, there was an emotional connection to the site and the eBay community. Ms Whitman joined the company on 2 January 1998. One of her first major decisions was to reject an offer to merge with rival auction site 'Onsale', and instead began to prepare for an Initial Public Offering (IPO). The company had just 35 employees, and she began filling senior management positions. She hired auditors and set up the selection process for investment banks to lead the offer. By September 1998 she, Mr Omidyar and Gary Bengier, eBay's then chief financial officer, began three weeks of roadshows to investors. That autumn eBay enjoyed a sensational IPO – the fifth most successful IPO ever. The shares began trading on Nasdaq on 24 September at $18. By the close of trading they had nearly trebled to $47 (Abrahams and Barker, 2002). The cash raised was immediately put to work. While eBay's peers burned their start-up cash, eBay became a phenomenon – a Silicon Valley company that has always made a profit and is the world's most successful internet group. Moreover, the profit potential was huge; eBay had almost no cost of goods, no inventories, few marketing costs and no large capital expenditure (*see* Figure 14.6).

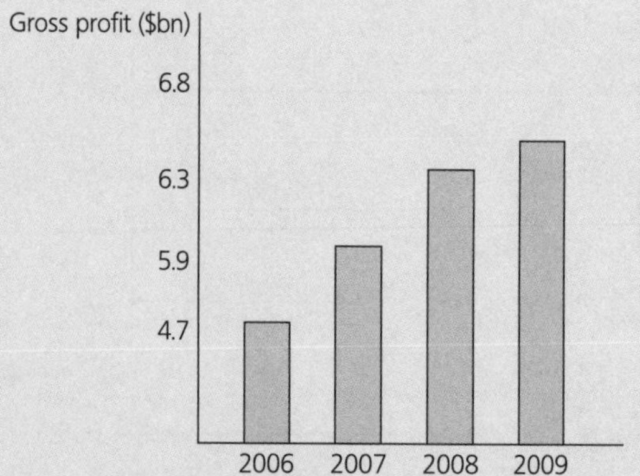

Figure 14.6 eBay profits

Everything seemed to be set fair and then in 1999 eBay suffered one of its worst disasters – in June the site went down for 22 hours, and did not work well for four days. During that summer, the senior management team questioned whether it could scale up the business to provide a site that would be available to the world. Significantly the team began to question and doubt their own technology. It was clear that eBay would need to invest heavily in its technology platform on which the entire business rested.

The business model

The business model developed by eBay is unique and has evolved over time as the business has grown. The founders' intentions was that eBay should be made up of a community and this vision has helped shape the business. According to the chief operating officer, Brian Swette, the business has grown by constantly responding to what the users have wanted. It is the eBay community that has designed the business model. eBay supports the desire to respond to the user community by employing approximately 5,000 people, about half of whom are involved in customer support and about 20 per cent of whom are in technology. eBay does not need to spend large sums of money trying to understand what their customers want because their customers constantly request and suggest changes. For example, in 2003 over 100,000 messages from users were posted each week in which tips were shared and system glitches highlighted. The technology systems that eBay has introduced over time enables the company to trace every move of every potential customer, this yields rich information which can be acted upon. In addition, category managers for eBay play a crucial role in the company's development. Unlike other positions, say product managers in large firms, these roles involve listening, adapting and enabling. It is the category managers' responsibility to develop tools to help users buy and sell more effectively.

How to grow the business?

In 1999, one year into the role as CEO, the challenges facing Ms Whitman were daunting. To achieve the ambitious growth targets eBay had set itself she needed to transform eBay. Opportunities for growth existed in all four quadrants of Ansoff's growth share matrix (*see* Figure 14.7). As always, the key decision was which ones to invest in? In which order? And when?

There was a need to develop eBay's carboot or garage sale community and expand the number of different audiences the company serves. In particular eBay needed to consider moving into sectors with higher average selling prices, such as cars, boats and even houses. eBay needed to consider increasing the range of formats, shifting from auctions to fixed-price sales – without alienating traditional customers. Another area for growth was new sellers, particularly big corporations, while raising the amount of revenue from each transaction – all without giving her competitors an opportunity to expand market share. Finally, eBay needed to exploit international opportunitites.

The development of new services

International

Between 2000 and 2005 eBay expanded internationally, and had country-specific sites in the UK, Germany, Japan, Italy and Australia and in 2005 purchased a majority stake in Korea's largest online auction site.

Online payment system: Paypal

In 2002 eBay purchased Paypal, the world's largest online payment system, in an all-stock deal worth about $1.37 billion. The deal was eBay's largest investment to date and it was recognition by eBay that Billpoint, its own payment system, had been unsuccessful. Furthermore, about 60 per cent of Paypal's revenues were generated on eBay; hence there was a natural association between the two firms. The acquisition of Paypal will allow eBay to expand beyond its core auction services. eBay and Paypal have both prospered because their strategies capitalised on the internet's strengths. eBay has employed the 'network effect', in which new customers are added at almost zero marginal cost and to the benefit of other users. Together, eBay and Paypal can enhance the internet's potential by reducing the

	Current products/services	New products/services
Current markets	1 Market penetration strategy Try to get existing users to spend more	3 Product development strategy Wireless Develop sectors such as introduce car sales, boat sales etc. Fixed-price shops Paypal: payment system providing commission on sales
New markets	2 Market development strategy Attract new vendors such as large corporations Develop international sites in significant markets such as Germany, Japan	4 Diversification strategy Skype: VOIP Enabling communication among community

Figure 14.7 Ansoff's growth matrix identifying opportunities for growth for eBay

→

number of steps for buyers. This should accelerate the number of transactions, thereby improving revenues (for an interesting story on what happened to the $1.3 billion see Illustration 1.4).

One of the main risks facing Paypal was its dependence on eBay for 60 per cent of its revenues. eBay has acquired a fast-growing business – with analysts forecasting a 50 per cent earnings growth rate over three years (2003–06) – albeit one with lower margins. It should now be able to increase its overall commission on transactions that include online payment, as well as brushing up Paypal's act and expanding abroad. This helps eBay address the threat from bilateral transactions between merchants and customers that cut out the middleman. In this case these made up the other 40 per cent of Paypal's revenues (Moules and Abrahams, 2002).

Wireless

Offering the ability for customers to use eBay on the move and via wireless technology is a natural development of the firm's technology. In most ways the eBay product has the necessary components to be a success in wireless markets: it delivers highly personalised content that is time sensitive in nature. A wireless service from eBay should appeal to the well-heeled big-ticket item bidders least likely to have free time during their hectic professional life to track auctions on their PCs. However, one important consideration with any wireless software program – still a novelty for most consumers – is that it has to have a simple interface. Such a service would enable eBay to charge a premium and many believe eBay customers would be willing to pay a small monthly sum if it increases their chances of landing that item of pop culture ephemera on which they had set their heart (Phillips, 2002).

eBay shops

In 2004 eBay began offering commercial sellers the concept of a shop on the site, where they could direct consumers to view more of their merchandise. This has proved extremely popular for the large sellers.

Voice over internet protocol (VOIP) and Skype

In October 2005 eBay purchased Skype, the internet telephone service, for $2.6 billion, which was by any measure a risky venture. Skype is an internet voice company offering voice over internet protocol (VOIP). This enables users to talk for free over the internet. Skype produced $50 million of revenues in the third quarter of 2006 (Nuttall, 2006). eBay wanted to move beyond its core e-commerce business, potentially putting it on a collision course with Google and Yahoo. This would provide eBay with the opportunity to add a voice calling feature to its existing online network and would allow it to charge fees to merchants for generating sales leads with merchants paying every time a potential customer clicks on a link in an online listing to initiate a voice call.

There is little doubt that eBay has at least 500,000 sellers, many of whom are entrepreneurial, quick to copy best practices, and used to working with new forms of software. Indeed, they are motivated by money. The acquisition of Skype and the use of VOIP should enable eBay to offer its call transfer functionality, which can bypass traditional private branch exchange networks, thereby enabling small companies to acquire enterprise-style communications systems for a meagre amount. Further opportunities should exist, for example sellers could direct details and similarly automate information content, such as allowing potential buyers to watch a video of the product free of charge via Skype. Similarly, calls coming into an auction will have caller ID of potential buyers, feedback of buyers, and could concurrently provide additional information back, such as details of other auctions.

This isn't even a full list of benefits of the link-up between eBay and Skype. There is also the potential to link Skype and eBay user profiles to databases on other services and create new communities and communication tools. Initially, however, Skype enables a much broader platform. Furthermore, the link up of Skype/eBay/Paypal develops a platforming strategy for conversational markets. Thus, connected to different application platform interfaces developers might design their own 'softphones', enterprise solutions, or even 'pay to call you' channels – a Skype equivalent of premium telephone services (*see* Figure 14.8).

Dangers, threats and challenges

Competition

While eBay is the internet's most successful business, the internet is none the less currently dominated by the two biggest search engine companies: Yahoo and Google. Also, there is disenchantment within certain parts of eBay's user community. This is largely because eBay is moving away from its 'user community'

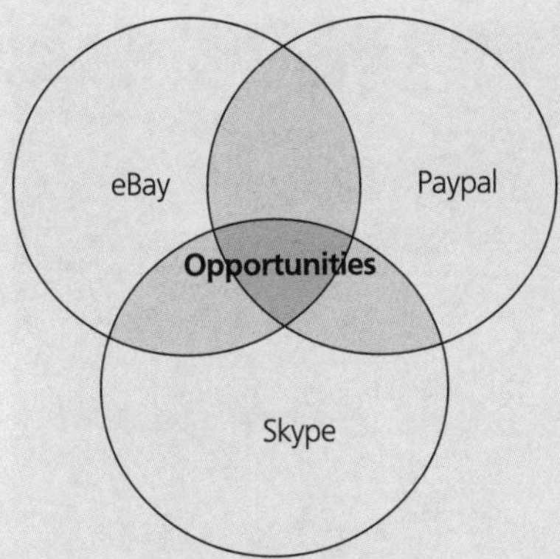

Figure 14.8 New opportunities for eBay

model to a more mainstream market. The question is whether rivals – principally Amazon.com and Yahoo – can take advantage. Amazon is trying to convert its big customer base – 23 million active customer accounts in 2006 – to the lucrative area of person-to-person trading. In Amazon's case, this is focused on outsiders selling second-hand books at a fixed price for a fee – an area that now accounts for about 17 per cent of its US transactions. There is a danger that Amazon could start eroding eBay's liquidity through aggressive pricing. That would hit eBay's margins, though the company hopes to raise operating margins from the current 25–28 per cent to 30–35 per cent by 2005, says Rajiv Dutta, chief financial officer. That would partly be achieved by raising the amount charged for each transaction or through additional services. At present, however, the competitive threat seems low as neither Yahoo nor Amazon can rival the number of buyers on eBay.

Maturing markets and slow growth

After a run of more than six years as a public company, during which it consistently turned in financial results that made every other dotcom firm green with envy, in 2005 eBay's earnings came up short. The slowdown was particularly acute in the US and Germany, its biggest markets. In the US, revenue growth slowed to 24 per cent, from 29 per cent, prompting fears it would be hard to keep the long-term growth rate above the promised 20 per cent. eBay's non-US business slowed even faster, from 82 to 64 per cent. Worse, the company's rock-solid profit margins showed uncharacteristic signs of erosion. eBay's much-admired business model has enabled it to keep its gross profit margins above 80 per cent. But heavier spending on marketing, including the first TV campaigns in countries like the UK and China, ate into operating profit margins, cutting them by one point to 30.4 per cent. eBay spent more than $300 million in 2005 to improve growth opportunities, with most of this spending taking the form of higher marketing costs. It spent $100 million (£53 million, €77 million) in expanding its presence in China in a race to dominate what is likely to become the world's biggest internet market (Waters, 2005b).

Fixed-price sales

The move in 2004 to sell an increasing number of goods at fixed prices, rather than through auction, was seen as controversial among some suppliers. So too has the strategy of attracting large corporate sellers – such as IBM, now the biggest supplier – which has raised fears among smaller, traditional clients. Such moves risk antagonising the 'power sellers', the army of entrepreneurs that have formed the bedrock of eBay's sellers and make their living trading on the site. They provide the liquidity that makes eBay the dominant online auctioneer. Many sellers welcome the changes because of the new buyers they attract to the site. Others, however, believe corporations will get special treatment from eBay – and destroy its culture.

Cash rich

With $1 billion already on the balance sheet and projected free cash flow of $1 billion a year by 2005, eBay will one day have to decide how to spend it. One opportunity is the personal communication market because eBay has no related presence in the instant messaging, chat or email services.

Fraud

The continual coverage in the popular media of fraud on the internet in general and criminals using eBay to amass ill-gotten gains clearly does not help eBay. But, there are so many millions of users who have very positive experiences of using the site that it seems unlikely that existing users will be put off using the online auction site. Should one of its competitors develop a more fool-proof trading model, however, this would be a serious threat to the business.

The press is full of stories of people with bad experiences of using eBay. Vendors have placed

→

articles for sale and have been shocked at the number of people who make a successful bid but, when the time comes to pay up, disown their bid. And, significantly, there is no recourse. Meanwhile, eBay has collected its fee and leaves vendors high and dry. Indeed, sellers and buyers have never seen an invoice from eBay for its fees. The bidder may get a black mark against their name, but that is irrelevant as they can easily get a new pseudonym and continue playing games with other vendors.

In 2005 Visa, Microsoft and eBay announced a global service to combat identity theft on the internet, especially 'phishing' incidents. Phishing refers to the practice of emails being sent to users purporting to be from institutions such as their bank and urging them to click on a web link to update their online account information. The link leads to a fake website where inputting details risks giving fraudsters access to actual bank accounts. This new network is a response to concerns from within the industry that consumers were reducing their online shopping and one-fifth refused to work with their financial institutions via the internet. The new network allows companies targeted by phishing attacks to report them to a central database. Then others devising software to alert users or block them from phishing sites, such as Microsoft, would be immediately notified by the network, enabling them to update their programs (Nuttall, 2005).

Shill bidding

In 2007 a *Sunday Times* investigation claimed the practice of shill bidding was widespread on eBay. A shill is an associate of a person selling goods or services who pretends no association to the seller and assumes the air of an enthusiastic customer. The intention of the shill is to encourage other potential customers, unaware of the set-up, to purchase said goods or services. The word 'shill' is probably related to 'shillaber', a word of obscure early twentieth-century origin with the same meaning. eBay tried to reassure customers and stated that any such fraudulent bidding is strictly prohibited on their auction site (*Sunday Times*, 2007).

Ebay bans negative seller views

In 2008 eBay announced a major change to its business model. eBay said problems were occurring, and slowing down trade, when buyers left negative comments about sellers who then retaliated with

Photo: © George Hall/Corbis

their own views. From May 2008 those selling on eBay will not be able to leave unfavourable or neutral messages about buyers. The decision, which will affect users worldwide, has angered many sellers. Sellers feel it will leave them unprotected. Critics of the changes argue that by taking away a seller's right to complain about a problem buyer they will have very little recourse for action when a sale goes wrong. Moreover, they argue that by still allowing buyers to leave dissenting comments about sellers, eBay has skewed the whole trading process. However, eBay believes the change is necessary and is putting in additional tools to protect sellers and promote a fair marketplace:

- Sellers can add buyer requirements to their listings to prevent unwanted bidders. Sellers can block buyers with too many policy violations, unpaid items or who are not registered with PayPal. This can help dramatically reduce the number of unpaid items.
- Sellers can require buyers to pay right away. If you use Buy It Now, sellers require buyers to pay you immediately using PayPal.
- Sellers have an easy way to report problems with buyers. Sellers can use the seller reporting hub to report an unpaid item, feedback extortion, or any other problem with a buyer.

Conclusions

In addition to managing eBay, Meg Whitman also serves on the Board of Directors of Procter & Gamble and Dream Works Animation. According to *Forbes* magazine, Whitman is currently worth an estimated $1.3 billion. She is one of only seven women to have been repeatedly ranked among the world's most influential people by *Time Magazine*. Whitman is a multi-billionaire and one of the richest female CEOs in the world. Whitman donated more than $30 million to her alma mater, Princeton University, which has allowed the construction of the university's sixth residential college, Whitman College.

Meg Whitman has transformed eBay from a purely domestic group that held auctions in 300 categories into a global enterprise, operating in 18 countries and offering 16,000 categories. She has expanded the range of goods sold from mainly collectibles – Beanie Babies dolls accounted for 8 per cent of items sold at the time of the IPO – to include used cars, motorcycles, computers, time-share holiday homes and even golf tee-off times. A Gulfstream corporate jet has been sold on eBay for $4.9 million. However, eBay risks alienating its customers and the whole eBay community by introducing fixed-price sales. IBM is now its biggest customer. This move away from auction and into mainstream sales goes against the principles on which eBay was established.

eBay should start to address the fraud issue. The introduction of deposit accounts would help overcome the problem of bogus bidders. The deposit account would enable a percentage of the successful bid to be automatically deducted or eBay could make an automatic deduction from users' credit cards. It seems there are people who use the eBay site as a sort of free internet game, making bids but with no intention of buying. While eBay can produce statistics showing how many auctions are successful, the numbers give no indication of how many sellers actually get paid.

The purchase of Skype raises many opportunities. Will eBay block potential in the adult market – an area where a great many developers see potential? Especially when history teaches us that from the VCR industry to the internet the adult industry has been at the forefront of developing technologies and markets.

VOIP, the online payment system (Paypal) and the eBay community should create new experiences and encourage new developer solutions at the intersection of the three businesses. How open the enlarged business is to the innovation in the developer community could well determine its success. There is a shared opportunity for the company and independent developers. eBay will undoubtedly find ways to achieve a return on the huge investment it has made in Skype, but the rewards could be all the richer if it opens the platform to outside influences. It is worthy of note that what was a weakness for eBay – its technology – has now become a strength.

During her 10 years with the company Meg Whitman oversaw expansion from 30 employees and $4 million in annual revenue to more than 15,000 employees and $8 billion in annual revenue when she stepped down in 2008. In February 2009, Whitman announced her candidacy for Governor of California, becoming the third woman in a 20-year period to run for the office. She won the Republican primary in June 2010. She spent more of her own money on her candidacy than any other self-funded political candidate in US history, spending about $160 million total. However, in the November 2 election, Whitman lost to Jerry Brown.

Sources: Abrahams, P. and Barker, T. (2002) Companies and Finance: Inside eBay, *Financial Times*, 11 January; Birchall, J. (2006) Amazon shares plunge after drop in profits, FT.com, 25 July; Moules, J. and Abrahams, P. (2002) Companies and Finance, the Americas: eBay set to buy Paypal for $1.37bn, FT.com, 9 July; Nuttall, C. (2005) Visa, Microsoft, eBay combat 'phishing', FT.com, 14 February; Nuttall, C. (2006) Companies International: eBay sales and profits top forecasts, *Financial Times*, 19 October; Phillips, S. (2002) Case study: eBay, FT.com, 20 November; *Sunday Times*, 28 January 2005, pp. 1–2; Waters, R. (2005) eBay beats Wall Street expectations, *Financial Times*, 20 October; Waters, R. (2005b) eBay chief takes the rough with the smooth, *Financial Times*, 18 April. BBC (2008) BBC News.co.uk/eBay to ban negative seller views, 5 February; *Sunday Times*, 28 January 2007, The eBay bidscam, www.thetimesonline.co.uk.

Questions

1 eBay is one of the only major internet-based firms to consistently make a profit from its inception. What is eBay's business model? Why has it been so successful?

2 Other major websites, like Amazon.com and Yahoo, have entered the auction marketplace with far less success than eBay. How has eBay been able to maintain its dominant position?

3 Why did eBay ban the leaving of negative feedback on sellers? What has been the impact of this change?

→

4 eBay makes every effort to conceptualise its users as a community (as opposed to, say, 'customers' or 'clients'). What is the purpose of this conceptual difference and does eBay gain something by doing it?

5 eBay has long been a marketplace for used goods and collectibles. Today, it is increasingly a place where major businesses come to auction their wares. Why would a brand name vendor set up shop on eBay?

6 Many analysts have argued that by moving to fixed-price sales eBay is risking alienating its traditional community of garage/carboot traders. How can eBay stop becoming just another site for selling?

7 Given the growth opportunities available to eBay, which ones and in which order should it develop?

Chapter summary

This chapter has explored the area of new service innovations. It should be clear from the chapter that there is a considerable overlap between product development and service development. There are clear differences between products and services, most notably that with services the consumer is co-producer, but so many products now incorporate services that it is sometimes unclear why we treat them separately. The chapter has reviewed the wide range of services within the economy and also shown how new technology is providing a driving force for many new services. This is illustrated very clearly in the eBay case study at the end of the chapter.

Discussion questions

1 Discuss the differences between product innovation and service innovation.

2 What are the factors that have led to the increase in services?

3 How has new technology contributed to the growth in services?

4 Discuss how some new services have created new business models.

5 Explain why manufacturing firms are increasingly involved in offering services. Discuss some examples.

6 Explain the key roles played by the consumer in new service development.

7 Explain how various groups of people in the organisation might use a service blueprint?

Key words and phrases

Intangibility *488*

Knowledge-intensive business services (KIBS) *488*

Outsourcing *489*

New service development *495*

New service development models *501*

Sequential service development *502*

Concurrent service development *504*

Co-producer *505*

Consumer user toolkits *506*

References

Alexander, M. and Young, D. (1996) Outsourcing: Where's the Value?, *Long Range Planning*, Vol. 29, No. 5, pp. 728–30.

Athanassopoulou, P. and Johne, A. (2004) Effective communication with lead customers in developing new banking products, *The International Journal of Bank Marketing*, Vol. 22, No. 2, 100–125.

Aubert, B.A., Patry, M. and Rivard, S. (1998) *Assessing the risk of IT outsourcing*, Working paper, 98s-16, May 1998, Cirano Montreal.

Barnes, D., Mieczkowska, S. and Hinton, M. (2003) Integrating operations and information systems in e-business, *European Management Journal*, Vol. 21, No. 5, 626–34.

Barthelemy, J. (2001) The hidden costs of IT outsourcing, *Sloan Management Review*, Vol. 42, No. 3, 60–69.

Barthelemy, J. and Geyer, D. (2000) IT outsourcing: findings from an empirical survey in France and Germany, *European Management Journal*, Vol. 19, No. 2, 195–202.

Bettis, R., Bradley, S. and Hamel, G. (1992) Outsourcing and industrial decline, *Academy of Management Executive*, Vol. 6, No. 1, 7–22.

Bitran, G. and Pedrosa, L. (1998) A structured product development perspective for service operations, *European Management Journal*, Vol. 16, No. 2, 169–89.

Boone, T. (2000) 'Exploring the link between product and process innovation in services in new service development', in Fitzsimmons, J.A. and Fitzsimmons, M.J. (eds) *New Service Development: Creating Memorable Experiences*, Sage Publications, London, 92–107.

Booz, Allen & Hamilton (1982) *New products for management for the 1980s*, Booz, Allen & Hamilton, New York.

Brown, S.L. and Eisenhardt, K.M. (1995) Product development: past research, current findings and future directions, *Academy of Management Review*, Vol. 20, No. 2, 343–78.

Brown, S.L. and Eisenhardt, K.M. (1998) *Competing on the edge: Strategy as structured chaos*, HBS Press, Boston, MA.

Bullinger, H.J., Fahrich, K.P. and Meiren, T. (2003) Service engineering – methodological development of new service products, *International Journal of Production Economics*, Vol. 85, No. 3, 275–87.

Cooper, R.G. (1990) New products: what distinguishes the winners, *Research and Technology Management*, Vol. 33, No. 6, 27–31.

Cooper, R.G. (1999) From experience: the invisible success factors in product innovation, *Journal of Product Innovation Management*, Vol. 16, No. 2, 115–33.

Cowell, D.W. (1988) New service development, *Journal of Marketing Management*, Vol. 3, No. 3, 296–312.

Davies, A.C. (2003) 'Are firms moving downstream into high-value service?', in Tidd, J. and Hull, F. (eds) *Service Innovation: Organisational Responses to Technological Opportunities and Market Imperitives*, Imperial College Press, London, 321–42.

De Brentani, U. (1991) Success factors in developing new business services, *European Journal of Marketing*, Vol. 25, No. 2, 33–59.

Den Hertog, P. (2002) Knowledge-intensive business services as co-producers of innovation, *International Journal of Innovation Management*, Vol. 4, No. 4, 491–528.

Doig, S.J., Ritter, R.C., Speckhals, K. and Woolson, D. (2001) Has outsourcing gone too far?, *McKinsey Quarterly*, No. 4, 24–37.

Dolfsma, W. (2004) The process of new service development – issues of formalisation and appropriability, *International Journal of Innovation Management*, Vol. 8, No. 3, 319–37.

Earl, M. (1996) The risks of outsourcing IT, *Sloan Management Review*, Spring, Vol. 37, No. 3, 26–32.

Easingwood, C.J. (1986) New product development for service companies, *Journal of Product Innovation Management*, Vol. 4, No. 2, 264–75.

Eurostat (2006) See European Union (2006).

European Union (2006) *European Innovation Scoreboard: Comparative analysis of innovation performance*, Brussels, retrieved 3 February 2007 from European Union website: www.proinno-europe.eu/doc/EIS2006_final.pdf.

Financial Times (2007) IBM's bounceback, FT.com site, 19 January.

Fitzsimmons, J.A. and Fitzsimmons, M.J. (2000) *New Service Development: Creating Memorable Experiences*, Sage Publications, London.

Franke, N. and Piller, F. (2004) Value creation by toolkits for user innovation and design: The case of the watch market, *Journal of Product Innovation Management*, Vol. 21, No. 6, 401–416.

Gadrey, J., Gallouj, F. and Weinstein, O. (1995) New modes of innovation: How services benefit industry, *International Journal of Service Industry Management*, No. 6, 4–6.

Goldstein, S.M., Johnston, R., Duffy, J. and Rao, J. (2002) The service concept: the missing link in service design research?, *Journal of Operations Management*, No. 20, 121–34.

Hamel, G. and Prahalad, C.K. (1994) Competing for the future, *Harvard Business Review*, Vol. 72, No. 4, 122–8.

Hoecht, A. and Trott, P. (2006) Innovation risks of strategic outsourcing, *Technovation*, Vol. 26, No. 4, 672–81.

Jaw, C., Lo, J. and Lin, Y. (2010) The determinants of new service development: Service characteristics, market orientation and actualizing innovation effort, *Technovation*, Vol. 30, No. 4, 265–77.

Jennings, D. (1997) Strategic guidelines for outsourcing decisions, *Journal of Strategic Change*, Vol. 6, 85–96.

Jeppesen, L.B. (2005) User toolkits for innovation: consumers support each other, *Journal of Product Innovation Management*, Vol. 22, No. 4, 347–62.

Johne, A. and Storey, C. (1998) New service development: A review of the literature and annotated bibliography, *European Journal of Marketing*, No. 32, 184–251.

Johnson, S.P., Menor, L.J., Roth, A.V. and Chase, R.B. (2000) 'A critical evaluation of the new service development process: Integrating service innovation and service design', in Fitzsimmons, J.A. and Fitzsimmons, M.J. (eds) *New Service Development: Creating Memorable Experiences*, Sage Publications, London, 1–32.

Johnston, R. and Clark, G. (2005) Service Operations Management, 2nd edn, Prentice Hall, Pearson Education Ltd, Harlow.

Kakabadse, A. and Kakabadse, N. (2002) Trends in outsourcing, *European Management Journal*, Vol. 20, No. 2, 189–98.

Kaplan, J. (2002) Partners in outsourcing, *Network World* , Vol. 19, No. 11, 41.

Khosrowpour, M., Subramanian, G. and Gunterman, J. (1995) 'Outsourcing organizational benefits and potential problems', in Khosrowpour, M. (ed.) *Managing Information Technology Investments with Outsourcing*, Idea Group Publishing, London, 244–68.

King, S. (1985) Has marketing failed or was it never really tried?, *Journal of Marketing Management*, Vol. 1, No. 1, 1–19.

Lacity, M. and Hirschheim, R. (1993) *Information Systems Outsourcing: Myths, Metaphors and Realities*, John Wiley, Chichester.

Lacity, M. and Willcocks, L. (1998) An empirical investigation of information technology sourcing practices: lessons from experience, *MIS Quarterly*, Vol. 22, No. 3, 363–408.

Lovelock, C.H. (1984) 'Developing and implementing new services', in George, W.R. and Marshall, C.E. (eds) *Developing New Services*, American Marketing Association, Chicago, 44–64.

Lynch, C. (2002) Price vs value: the outsourcing conundrum, *Logistics Management and Distribution Report*, Vol. 41, No. 2, 35.

Martin, J. (1995) Ignore your customer, *Fortune*, Vol. 1, No. 8, 121–5.

Martinsons, M. (1993) Outsourcing information systems: A strategic partnership with risks, *Long Range Planning*, Vol. 26, No. 3, 18–25.

May-Plumlee, T. and Little, T.J. (1998) No-interval coherently phased product development model for apparel, *International Journal of Clothing Science and Technology*, Vol. 10, No. 5, 342–64.

Menor, L.J., Mohan, V.T. and Sampson, S.E. (2002) New service development: Areas for exploitation and exploration, *Journal of Operations Management*, Vol. 20, No. 2, 135–57.

Nambisan, S. (2002) Designing virtual customer environments for new product development: toward a theory, *Academy of Management Review*, Vol. 27, No. 3, 392–413.

Papastathopoulou, P., Avlonitis, G. and Indounas, K. (2001) The initial stages of new service development: A case study from the Greek banking sector, *Journal of Financial Services Marketing*, Vol. 6, No. 2, 147–61.

Phillips, R., Neailey, K. and Broughton, T. (1999) A comparative study of six stage-gate approaches to product development, *Integrated Manufacturing Systems*, Vol. 10, No. 5, 289–97.

Prahalad, C.K. and Ramaswamy, V. (2000) Co-opting customer competence, *Harvard Business Review*, Vol. 78, No. 1, 79–87.

Quélin, B. and Duhamel, F. (2003) Bringing together strategic outsourcing and corporate strategy: outsourcing motives and risks, *European Management Journal*, Vol. 21, No. 5, 647–61.

Quinn, J. and Hilmer, F. (1994) Strategic outsourcing, *Sloan Management Review*, Summer, 43–55.

Rogers, E.M. (2005) *Diffusion of innovations*, 5th edn, Free Press, New York.

Salter, A. and Gann, D. (2003) Sources of ideas for innovation in engineering design, *Research Policy*, Vol. 32, 1309–24.

Scheuing, E.E. and Johnson, E.M. (1989) New product development and management in financial institutions, *International Journal of Bank Marketing*, Vol. 7, No. 2, 17–21.

Stevens, E. and Dimitriadis, S. (2005) Managing the new service development process: towards a systematic model, *European Journal of Marketing*, Vol. 39, No. 1/2, 175–98.

Sundbo, J. (1997) Management of innovation in services, *The Service Industries Journal*, Vol. 17, No. 3, 432–55.

Tauber, E.M. (1981) Brand franchise extension: New product benefits from existing brand names, *Business Horizons*, Vol. 24, No. 2, 36–41.

Thomke, S. (2003) *Experimentation Matters: Unlocking the Potential of New Technologies for Innovation*, Harvard Business School Press, Boston, MA.

Thomke, S. and von Hippel, E. (2002) Customers as innovators: A new way to create value, *Harvard Business Review*, Vol. 80, No. 4, 74–81.

Tidd, J. and Hull, F. (2003) 'Managing service innovation: Variations of best practice', in Tidd, J. and Hull, F. (eds) *Service Innovation: Organizational Responses to Technological Opportunities and Market Imperatives*, Imperial College Press, London, 1–34.

Trott, P. (2001) The role of market research in the development of discontinuous new products, *European Journal of Innovation Management*, Vol. 4, No. 3, 117–25.

van Kleef, E., van Trijp, H.C.M., Luning, P., *et al.* (2005) Consumer research in the early stages of new product development: A critical review of methods and techniques, *Food Quality and Preference*, Vol. 16, No. 3, 181–201.

Vermeulen, P. and Dankbaar, B. (2002) The organisation of product innovation in the financial sector, *The Service Industries Journal*, Vol. 22, No. 3, 77–98.

von Hippel, E. (1986) Lead users: a source of novel product concepts, *Management Science*, Vol. 32, No. 7, 791–805.

von Hippel, E. (2001) Perspective: user toolkits for innovation, *Journal of Product Innovation Management*, Vol. 18, No. 4, 247–57.

Wang, C. and Regan, A.C. (2003) *Risks and Reduction Measures in Logistics Outsourcing*, TRB Annual Meeting.

Weyland, R. and Cole, P. (1997) *Customer Connections*, Harvard Business School Press, Boston, MA.

Zeithaml, V.A. and Bitner, M.J. (2003) *Services Marketing: Integrating Customer Focus Across the Firm*, 3rd edn, McGraw-Hill, New York.

Further reading

For a more detailed review of the innovation management literature, the following develop many of the issues raised in this chapter:

Allam, I. and Perry, C. (2002) A customer-oriented new service development process, *Journal of Services Marketing*, Vol. 16, No. 6, 515–34.

Hipp, C. and Grupp, H. (2005) Innovation in the service sector: The demand for service specific innovation measurement concepts and typologies, *Research Policy*, Vol. 34, No. 4, 517–35.

HSBC (2010) 100 Thoughts, HSBC, London.

Jaw, C., Lo, J. and Lin, Y. (2010) The determinants of new service development: Service characteristics, market orientation and actualizing innovation effort, *Technovation*, Vol. 26, No. 4, 265–77.

Johnston, R. and Clark, G. (2005) *Service Operations Management*, 2nd edn, Prentice Hall, London.

Tidd, J. and Hull, F. (2003) 'Managing service innovation: Variations of best practice', in Tidd, J. and Hull, F. (eds) *Service Innovation: Organizational Responses to Technological Opportunities and Market Imperatives*, Imperial College Press, London, 1–34.

von Hippel, E. and Katz, R. (2002) Shifting innovation to users via toolkits, *Management Science*, Vol. 48, No. 7, 821–33.

Chapter 15
Market research and its influence on new product development

Introduction

The role and use of market research in the development of new products is commonly accepted and well understood. There are times, however, when market research results produce negative reactions to discontinuous new products (innovative products) that later become profitable for the innovating company. Famous examples such as the fax machine, the VCR and James Dyson's bagless vacuum cleaner are often cited to support this view. Despite this, companies continue to seek the views of consumers on their new product ideas. The debate about the use of market research and, more importantly, what type of research should be used in the development of new products is long-standing and controversial. This chapter will explore these and other related issues. It also provides a case study which shows how Dyson pursued 'unpopular' designs that later become the industry standard.

Chapter contents

Learning objectives

When you have completed this chapter you will be able to:

- understand the contribution market research can make to the new product development process;
- recognise the benefits and weaknesses of consumer new product testing;
- recognise the powerful influence of the installed base effect on new product introductions;
- understand the significance of discontinuous products; and
- recognise the role of switching costs in new product introductions.

Market research and new product development

Business students in particular are very familiar with the well-trodden paths of arguments about the need for market research. Indeed, they are warned of the dangers and pitfalls that lie ahead if firms fail to conduct sufficient market research. Compelling and potentially alarming stories are used to highlight the importance of market research. One of these is presented in Illustration 15.1.

Chapters 11 and 12 outlined the activities involved in the development of new products. In this chapter it is necessary to examine in more detail some of these activities and to identify areas of potential difficulty. Figure 12.9 outlined the key activities of the new product development process. Within the product concept generation stage, however, there is a significant amount of internal reviews and testing. Figure 15.1 expands this stage into a series of further activities. As can be seen from the diagram, it is extremely difficult to delineate between the activities of concept testing, prototype development and product testing. The activities are intimately related and interlinked. There is a considerable amount of iteration. Product concepts are developed into prototypes only to be quickly redeveloped following technical inputs from production or R&D. Similarly, early product prototypes may be changed almost on a daily basis as a wide variety of market inputs are received. This could include channel members who have particular requirements and early results from consumer tests may reveal a number of minor changes that can be made simply and quickly by prototype designers.

Yet, we also recognise that consumers frequently have difficulty articulating their needs. This has recently been confirmed by two CEOs. Steven Jobs, CEO of

Illustration 15.1

The traditional view of new product testing

FT

McDonald's recently admitted to making a big mistake with a new product. Several years ago it was considering launching the McPloughman's, a cheese and pickle salad sandwich. The McPloughman's was developed to compete with the UK's supermarket chains in the cold sandwich market. Unfortunately, had the company conducted market research it would have found that this product was not highly desirable. Indeed, their customers did not want the product and their staff were embarrassed to sell it. From now on, said the company, rather than relying on 'gut-feeling' that it knew what its customers wanted McDonald's intended to conduct rigorous fact-based market research.

Source: Pearson Education Ltd/Burke Triolo Productions/Brand X Pictures

Source: *Financial Times*, 28 October 1994. Reprinted with permission.

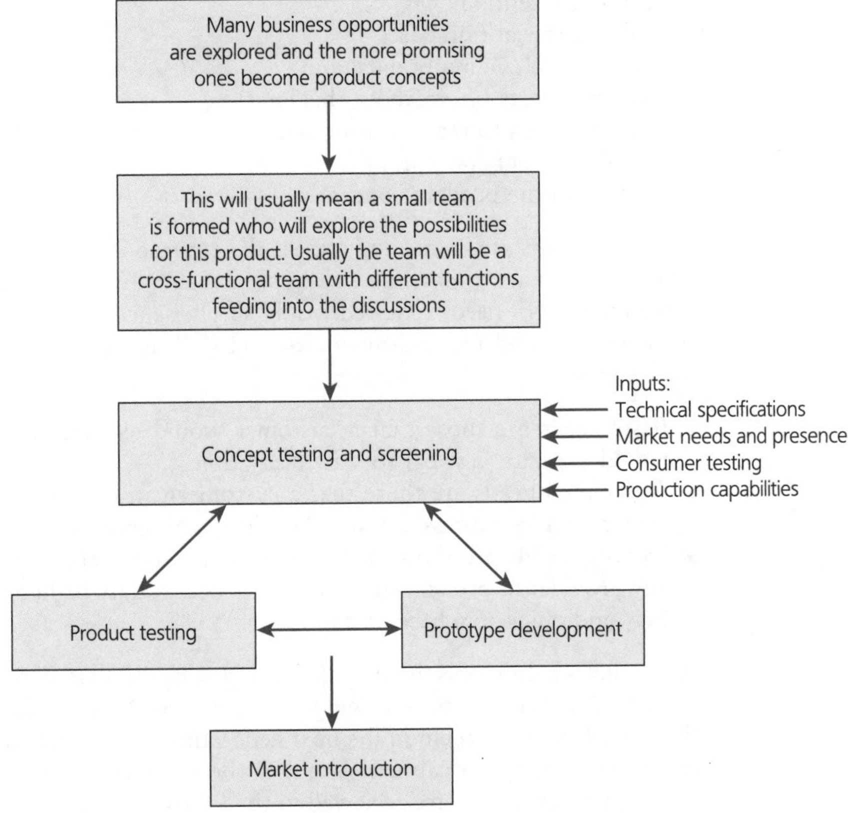

Figure 15.1 New product concept and prototype testing

Apple, in an interview with *Fortune* magazine (2008) said: 'Apple does no market research, and in fact just wants to "make great products".' And Bart Becht, CEO of Reckitt Benckiser, said in an interview with the *Sunday Times* (2008): 'Consumers are not very good at imagining what they might want to buy if it were available . . . consumers are not very innovative.' The issue here is clear. There are some firms who wish to lead the public with new products, for they believe that the public do not know what is possible and market research frequently reinforces this lack of knowledge.

The purpose of new product testing

The main objective here is to estimate the market's reaction to the new product under consideration, prior to potentially expensive production and promotional costs. To achieve this objective it is necessary to consider a number of other factors:

1 The market:
current buying patterns;
existing segments; and
customer's view of the products available.

2 Purchase intention:
   trial and repeat purchase;
   barriers to changing brands; and
   switching costs (more about this later).
3 Improvements to the new product:
   overall product concept; and
   features of the product concept.

All these factors are linked and are usually covered in consumer new product testing and referred to as *customer needs and preferences*. This, however, raises an important issue: the type of needs required would surely depend on the type of product under consideration and the consumer. King (1985) argues needs can be classified into three types:

- Basic needs are those that a customer would expect. For example, a customer would expect a new car to start every time.
- Articulated needs are those that a customer can readily express. For example, a customer may express a desire for additional features on a motor vehicle.
- Exciting needs are those that will surprise customers and are not being met by any provider at present. In the example here it may be finance packages enabling easy and quick purchase of a new car.

While this is helpful it is the so-called 'exciting needs' that all new product developers want to uncover. For success will surely come to those who are able to understand these needs and use them in the next generation of new products. This, however, is extremely difficult to capture. Some of the techniques and concepts used in consumer product testing are reviewed in the following sections.

Testing new products

Have you ever been stopped in a supermarket and asked for your opinion on a new food product? This is more than a diversion from the chore of shopping – you could be tasting the next big product. For example, all food manufacturers hope it will be their company that will develop the next 'Flora' or 'Sunny Delight' (two of the most successful new food products of the past ten years). In-store tasting is a serious business and millions of pounds are spent on this activity to create new foods that will tempt consumers. This is the accepted and well-known face of consumer research. Indeed, the food industry is one of the most prolific developers of new products and a heavy user of consumer research. Frequently the process involves enhancing an existing winner or repackaging tried and tested products. 'Flora' was one of many 'yellow spreads' but the brand has become so successful that it has been extended to other product lines including cheese.

Food manufacturers are continually seeking to add value to their products. This clearly enhances their profit margins, but competition in food retailing is fierce and retailers have been able to put pressure on manufacturers to keep prices down. Indeed, during 1999 and 2000 average food retail prices actually fell. Initially manufacturers pushed down their own costs in an attempt to improve margins, but when these could be reduced no further manufacturers turned to new product development to

Illustration 15.2

Robinsons Fruit Shoot

Fruit Shoot from Robinsons was launched in 2001 and is now a £72.7 million super brand (July 2006). It achieved value sales growth of 44 per cent from 2003–04. Its success has been attributed to the unique design and packaging of the drink. Prior to Fruit Shoot, most children's drinks were packaged in paper board cartons with straw. Fruit Shoot revolutionised the market by using a colourful resealable plastic bottle. In the UK, Fruit Shoot was bought by 41 per cent of all households with kids in 2005–06 and achieves 98 per cent awareness among children, according to Britvic. During 2003 and 2004 Fruit Shoot incorporated two new flavours and this redesign promises to maintain and continue the strong growth of the brand.

Source: www.Britvic.com (2004 and 2007).

enable them to add value and command a higher price. Frequently the success of the product lies in the packaging, as Illustration 15.2 shows.

Put crudely, to command a higher price a manufacturer of, say, baked beans will have to develop different forms of packaging, add curry, meat balls, etc., all of which will have been tested by the taste buds of consumers first. But if a product is not liked by consumers, should it always be dumped and labelled 'bad idea'? In the food industry a disliked new flavour crisp may indeed be a 'bad idea' and a potential flop if the product gets to market, but in other industries initial rejection by consumers may not be a good indication of future success. The Dyson case study at the end of this chapter is a good illustration of a successful product that was initially rejected by manufacturers, retailers and some consumers, yet it turned out to be a success. There are, of course, many other well-known cases such as the fax machine. Peter Drucker once observed that 'one can use market research only on what is already in the market'. He supported his point by saying that American companies failed to put the fax machine on the market 'because market research convinced them there was no demand for such a gadget'.

Techniques used in consumer testing of new products

The following is a brief guide to some of the research techniques used in consumer testing of new products. Some products and services go through all the stages listed, but few do or should go through all these. The techniques would have to be adapted to meet the specific requirements of the product or service under consideration.

Concept tests

Qualitative techniques, especially group discussions, are used to obtain target customer reactions to a new idea or product. Question areas would cover:

- understanding and believability in the product;
- ideas about what it would look like;
- ideas about how it would be used; and
- ideas about when and by whom it might be used.

This would help to reveal the most promising features of the new product, and groups to whom it might appeal. It might be argued that the assessment of *purchase intent* is the primary purpose of concept testing, so that products and services with poor potential can be removed. The most common way to assess purchase intention is to provide a description of the product or take the product to respondents and ask whether they:

- definitely would buy;
- probably would buy;
- might or might not buy;
- probably would not buy; or
- definitely would not buy.

Test centres

These are used for product testing when the product is too large, too expensive or too complicated to be taken to consumers for testing. One or more test centres will be set up and a representative sample of consumers brought to the test centre for exposure to the product and questioning about their reaction to it. See the development of the tooth whitening product in the case study at the end of Chapter 11.

Hall tests/mobile shops

These are commonly used for product testing or testing other aspects of the marketing mix such as advertising, price, packaging, etc. A representative sample of consumers is recruited, usually in a shopping centre, and brought to a conveniently located hall or a mobile caravan, which acts as a shop. Here they are exposed to the test material and asked questions about it.

Product-use tests

These are frequently used in business-to-business markets. A small group of potential customers are selected to use the product for a limited period of time. The manufacturer's technical people watch how these customers use the product. From this test the manufacturer learns about customer training and servicing requirements. Following the test the customer is asked detailed questions about the product including intent to purchase.

Trade shows

Such shows draw large numbers of buyers who view new products in a few days. The manufacturer can see how buyers react to various products on display. This technique is convenient and can deliver in-depth knowledge of the market because the buyers' views may differ considerably from those of the end-user consumers.

Monadic tests

The respondents are given only one (hence the name) product to try, and are asked their opinion of it. This is the normal situation in real life when a consumer tries a new product and draws on recent experience with the product they usually use, to judge the test product. The method is not very sensitive in comparing the test product with other products because of this.

Paired comparisons

A respondent is asked to try two or more products in pairs and asked, with each pair, to say which they prefer. This is less 'real' in terms of the way consumers normally use products, but does allow products to be deliberately tested against others.

In-home placement tests

These are used when an impression of how the product performs in normal use is required. The product(s) are placed with respondents who are asked to use the product in the normal way and complete a questionnaire about it. Products may be tested comparatively or sequentially.

Test panels

Representative panels are recruited and used for product testing. Test materials and questionnaires can be sent through the post, which cuts down the cost of conducting in-home placement tests. Business-to-business firms may also have test panels of customers or intermediaries with whom new product or service ideas or prototypes can be tested.

When market research has too much influence

It is argued by many from within the market research industry that only extensive consumer testing of new products can help to avoid large-scale losses such as those experienced by RCA with its Videodisc, Procter & Gamble with its Pringles and General Motors with its rotary engine (Barrett, 1996). Sceptics may point to the issue of vested interests in the industry, and that it is merely promoting itself. It is, however, widely accepted that most new products fail in the market because consumer needs and wants are not satisfied. Study results show that 80 per cent of newly introduced products fail to establish a market presence after two years (Barrett, 1996). Indeed, cases involving international high-profile companies are frequently cited to warn of the dangers of failing to utilise market research (e.g. Unilever's Persil Power and R.J. Reynold's smokeless cigarette).

Given the inherent risk and complexity, managers have asked for many years whether this could be reduced by market research. Not surprisingly, the marketing literature takes a market-driven view, which has extensive market research as its key driver. That is, find out what the customer would like and then produce it (the market-pull approach to innovation). The benefits of this approach to the new product development process have been widely articulated and are commonly understood (Cooper, 1990; Kotler, 1998). Partly because of its simplicity this view now dominates management thinking, but unfortunately this sometimes goes beyond the marketing department. The effect can be that major or so-called discontinuous innovations are rejected or accepted based on consumer research.

Advocates of market research argue that such activities ensure that companies are consumer oriented. In practice, this means that new products are more successful if they are designed to satisfy a perceived need rather than if they are designed simply to take advantage of a new technology (Ortt and Schoormans, 1993). The approach taken by many companies with regard to market research is that if sufficient research is undertaken the chances of failure are reduced (Barrett, 1996). Indeed, the danger that many companies wish to avoid is the development of products without any consideration of the market. Moreover, once a product has been carried through the early stages of development it is sometimes painful to raise questions about it once money has been spent. The problem then spirals out of control, taking the company with it. Illustration 15.3 highlights many of the difficulties facing firms introducing new products.

The issue of market research in the development of new products is controversial. The marketing literature has traditionally portrayed new product development as essentially a market/customer-led process, but paradoxically, many major market innovations appear in practice to be technologically driven, to arise from a technology seeking a market application rather than a market opportunity seeking a technology. This, of course, is the antithesis of the marketing concept, which is to start with trying to understand customer needs. The role of market research in new product development is most clearly questionable with major product innovations, where no market exists. First, if potential customers are unable adequately to understand the product, then market research can only provide negative answers (Brown, 1991). Second, consumers frequently have difficulty articulating their needs. Hamel and Prahalad (1994: 8) argue that customers lack foresight; they refer to Akio Morita, Sony's influential leader:

> *Our plan is to lead the public with new products rather than ask them what kind of products they want. The public does not know what is possible, but we do.*

This leads many scientists and technologists to view marketing departments with scepticism. Frequently they have seen their exciting new technology rejected due to market research findings produced by their marketing department. Market research specialists would argue that such problems could be overcome with the use

Illustration 15.3

Neuromarketing accesses subconscious views on products and brands

Last month, I surrendered my subconscious to analysis. A red swimming cap was stretched over my head, long grey wires stuck to my skull and my innermost thoughts fed into a computer as I nervously watched an advertisement for Volkswagen.

In turn, the computer told a team of researchers which scenes I paid attention to, what I responded to emotionally and what I would go away remembering.

It was a far cry from the marketing industry's traditional method of finding out what consumers think about their brands: asking them.

The problem is, when gathered in traditional focus groups, respondents can be swayed by those sitting next to them or by the presence of researchers. Alternatively, they may be unable to articulate their responses accurately. As a result, an increasing number of marketers now prefer to analyse the response of peoples' brainwaves to brands and advertisements by using the latest developments in neuroscience.

In recent months, these techniques have not just been applied to the marketing of finished products, but also to product development. 'It's about uncovering new undiscovered needs', says Martin Lindstrom, author of *Buyology*, who has been studying the development of neuromarketing since its inception seven years ago. 'A lot of manufacturers are struggling as it's easy to come up with ideas consumers don't feel they need.'

He cites the example of dishwasher tablets. Consumers are attracted to tablets embedded with a blue ball because, subconsciously, they believe they clean better. However, when asked in the context of traditional marketing methods, they claim no preference about colour.

'The main reason why [traditional market research often] fails is that we look at things from a conscious point of view', says Mr Lindstrom. 'We ask: "Do you like the brand?" We ask the consumer to be incredibly rational and we know today from neuroscience that 85 per cent of the decisions we make are made by the unconscious part of brain.'

Neuromarketers believe their work will be especially useful for products consumers find hard to describe – particularly when they need to know consumers' reactions to smell, taste and touch.

According to Neurofocus, the global market leader in neurological testing, consumer goods companies are even creating their own in-house testing units that mock up supermarkets. They can use them to change everything from shelf positioning to point-of-sale advertisements with the flick of a switch and monitor the shopper's brain during the few seconds it takes to select a product.

But some advertisers fear this adherence to science could stamp out 'light bulb' ideas and destroy creativity in the industry.

Neurofocus argues that mind-reading actually helps sell original thinking to companies that would otherwise stick with tried-and-tested methods.

Source: Kuchler, H. (2010) Marketing industry turns to mind-reading, FT.com, April 11.

of 'benefits research'. The problem here is that the benefits may not be clearly understood, or even perceived as a benefit by respondents. King (1985: 2) sums up the research dilemma neatly:

> *Consumer research can tell you what people did and thought at one point in time: it can't tell you directly what they might do in a new set of circumstances.*

In Illustration 15.4, from GlaxoSmithKline, consumer healthcare highlights the difficulties of trying to understand consumer research.

Illustration 15.4

GlaxoSmithKline

FT

GSK have known for many years that consumers are fickle. Many years after the launch of its very successful Aquafresh striped toothpaste GlaxoSmithKline undertook consumer research to try to explore product development opportunities. Some of the findings were surprising. Consumers questioned the need or benefit of having stripes in the paste. Yet, in store trials, when given the opportunity to purchase a single colour paste consumers continued to purchase the striped toothpaste. A similar reaction was recorded when consumers were asked about flavouring of the toothpaste. Consumers suggested that they would prefer a wider variety of flavours such as strawberry or banana rather than mint, yet when other flavours were offered few consumers purchased them. The product manager emphasised the need to check consumer rhetoric with their actions.

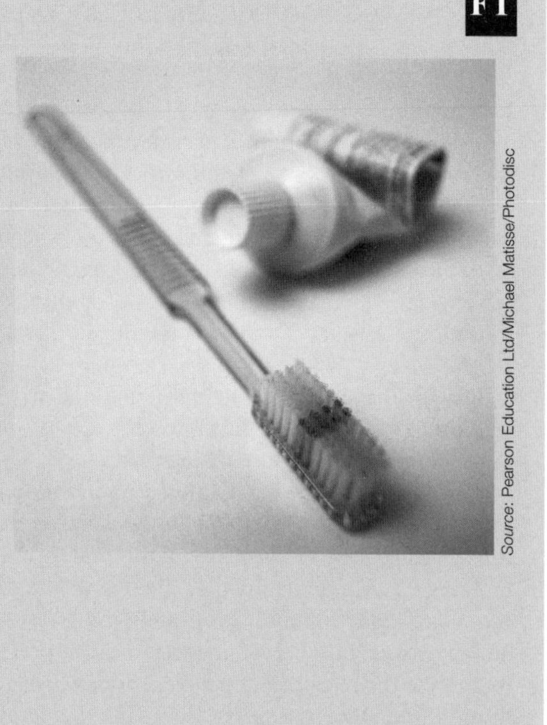

Source: Pearson Education Ltd/Michael Matisse/Photodisc

Source: P. Trott and A. Lataste (2003) The role of consumer market research in new product decision-making: some preliminary findings from European firms, Entrepreneurship, Marketing and Innovation Conference, University of Karlsrühe, 8–9 September, conference proceedings.

Discontinuous new products

Major innovations are referred to as discontinuous new products when they differ from existing products in that field, sometimes creating entirely new markets and when they require buyers to change their behaviour patterns. For example, the personal computer and 3M's Post-it notes created entirely new markets and required consumers to change their behaviour. Such products usually require a period of learning on the part of the user. Indeed, sometimes the manufacturer has to explain and suggest to users how the product should and could be used. Rogers' (1995) study on the diffusion of innovations as a social process argues that it requires time for societies to learn and experiment with new products. This raises the problem of how to deal with consumers with limited prior knowledge and how to conduct market research on a totally new product or a major product innovation. The two major difficulties are:

1 the problem of selection of respondents; and
2 the problem of the understanding of the major innovation.

Confronted with a radically new technology, consumers may not understand what needs the technology can satisfy, as was the case with the fax machine or the Post-it note. This is because consumers are not able to link physical product characteristics with the outputs of the innovation. For example, when consumers first saw a fax machine all they saw was a bulky expensive machine that looked like a copier. They were not able to imagine using it, hence they were not receptive to the new idea. Research has shown that experts are better able to understand potential benefits than those with less product knowledge. The type of research technique selected is crucial in obtaining accurate and reliable data.

Market research and discontinuous new products

In the case of discontinuous product innovations, the use and validity of market research methods is questionable (von Hippel and Thomke, 1999; Elliot and Roach, 1991). As far back as the early 1970s Tauber (1974) argued that such approaches discourage the development of major innovations. It may be argued that less, rather than more, market research is required if major product innovations are required. Such an approach is characterised by the so-called technology-push model of innovation. Products that emerge from a technology-push approach are generated with little consideration of the market. Indeed, a market may not yet exist, as with the case of the PC and many other completely new products. Frequently, consumers are unable to understand the technology in question and view new products as a threat to their existing way of operating. Martin (1995: 122) argues that:

> *customers can be extremely unimaginative . . . trying to get people to change the way they do things is the biggest obstacle facing many companies.*

Many writers on this subject argue that potential consumers are not able to relate the physical aspects of a major innovative product with the consequences of owning and using it (Ortt and Schoormans, 1993). Others argue that while market research can help to fine-tune product concepts it is seldom the spur for an entirely new product concept. Consequently most conventional market research techniques deliver invalid results (Hamel and Prahalad, 1994).

More recently, new approaches are being recognised in the area of discontinuous product innovations. One technique adopts a process of probing and learning, where valuable experience is gained with every step taken and modifications are made to the product and the approach to the market based on that learning (Lynn *et al.*, 1997). This is not trial and error but careful experimental design and exploration of the market often using the heritage of the organisation. This type of new product development is very different from traditional techniques and methods described in most marketing texts.

Circumstances when market research may hinder the development of discontinuous new products

Product developers and product testers tend to view the product offering in a classical layered view, where the product is assumed to have a core benefit and additional attributes and features are laid around it, hence layered view. Saren and

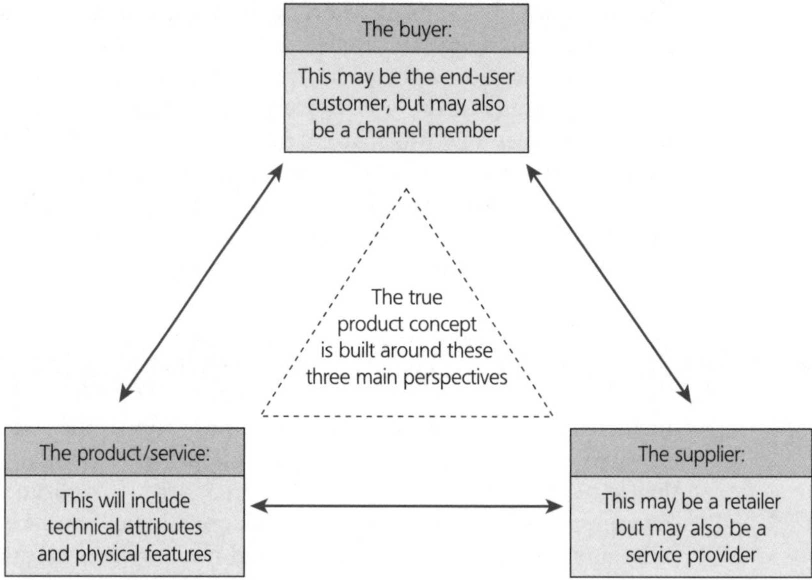

Figure 15.2 The tripartite product concept

Source: Adapted from M.A.J. Saren and N. Tzokas (1994) *Proceedings of the Annual Conference of the European Marketing Academy*, Maastricht.

Tzokas (1994) have argued that much of the problem is due to the way we view a product. They state that we often view it in isolation from:

- its context;
- the way it is used; and
- the role of the customer–supplier relationship.

This contributes to misleading views on new products. Figure 15.2 illustrates the tripartite product concept that captures the three views highlighted by Saren and Tzokas. The significance of this alternative view is that it highlights the reality of any product's situation. That is, product developers and product testers need to recognise that a product will be viewed differently by channel members than by end-users. For example, end-users will be concerned about how the product will perform, whereas channel members are more interested in how the product will *sell*, whether it will be easy to *stock and display* and, most important, whether it will be *profitable*. The Dyson case study at the end of this chapter illustrates the difficulties in trying to convince retailers to stock a new, slightly unusual product with which they are not familiar.

Technology-intensive products

Adopting a technology-push[1] approach to product innovations can allow a company to target and control premium market segments, establish its technology as the industry standard, build a favourable market reputation, determine the industry's

[1] The technology-push approach to NPD centres on trying to deliver the most effective technology available.

future evolution, and achieve high profits. It can become the centrepiece in a company's strategy for market leadership. It is, however, costly and risky. Such an approach requires a company to develop and commercialise an emerging technology in pursuit of growth and profits. To be successful, a company needs to ensure its technology is at the heart of its competitive strategy. Merck, Microsoft and Dyson have created competitive advantage by offering unique products, lower costs or both by making technology the focal point in their strategies. These companies have understood the role of technology in differentiating their products in the marketplace. They have used their respective technologies to offer a distinct bundle of products, services and price ranges that have appealed to different market segments. Such products revolutionise product categories or define new categories, such as Hewlett-Packard's laser-jet printers and Apple's (then IBM's) personal computer. These products shift market structures, require consumer learning and induce behaviour changes, hence the difficulties for consumers when they are asked to pass judgement.

This is particularly the case if the circumstances relate to an entirely new product that is unknown to the respondent. New information is always interpreted in the light of one's prior knowledge and experience. In industrial markets the level of information symmetry about the core technology is usually very high indeed (hence the limited use of market research), but in consumer markets this is not always the case. For example, industrial markets are characterised by:

- relatively few (information-rich) buyers;
- products often being customised and involving protracted negotiations regarding specifications;
- and, most importantly, the buyers usually being expert in the technology of the new product (i.e. high information symmetry about the core technology).

In situations of low information symmetry consumers have difficulty in understanding the core product and are unable to articulate their needs and any additional benefits sought. Conversely, in situations of high information symmetry consumers are readily able to understand the core product and hence are able to articulate their needs and a wide range of additional benefits sought, for example in tasting new food products.

Furthermore, discontinuous product innovations or radical product innovations frequently have to overcome the currently installed technology base – usually through displacement. This is known as the installed base effect. The installed base effect is the massive inertial effect of an existing technology or product that tends to preclude or severely slow the adoption of a superseding technology or product. This creates an artificial adoption barrier that can become insurmountable for some socially efficient and advantageous innovations. An example of this is the DVORAK keyboard, which has been shown to provide up to 40 per cent faster typing speeds. Yet the QWERTY keyboard remains the preference for most users because of its installed base, i.e. the widespread availability of keyboards that have the QWERTY configuration (Herbig *et al.*, 1995).

The idea of being shackled with an obsolete technology leads to the notion of switching costs. Switching is the one-time cost to the buyer who converts to the new product. Porter (1985) notes that switching costs may be a significant impediment to the adoption of a new consumer product. Buyer switching costs may arise as a result of prior commitments to a technology (a) and to a particular vendor (b) (Jackson, 1985). Computer software is an obvious example where problems of compatibility frequently arise. Similarly, buyers may have developed routines and procedures for dealing with a specific vendor that will need to be modified if a new relationship is established. The effect of both types of switching costs for a buyer is a disincentive to explore new vendors. There is a clear dilemma facing firms: market research may reveal genuine limitations with the new product but it may also produce negative feedback on a truly innovative product that may create a completely new market. The uncertainty centres on two key variables:

1 information symmetry about the core technology between producer and buyer; and
2 the installed base effect and switching costs.

Breaking with convention and winning new markets

There is evidence to suggest that many successful companies were successful because they were prepared to take the risky decision to ignore their customers' views and proceed with their new product ideas because they passionately believed that it would be successful. Subsequent success for these new products suggested that the firm's existing customers were unable to peer into the future, recognise that a different product or service would be desirable and articulate this to the firm. On reflection this seems a lot to ask of customers, and indeed is extremely difficult.

Between 1975 and 1995, 60 per cent of the companies in the *Fortune* 500 listing were replaced. Irrespective of their industry, new entrants either created new markets or recreated existing ones. Compaq overtook IBM to become the world's largest manufacturer of personal computers; Dyson overhauled Hoover's established position of market leader to become the new market leader in vacuum cleaners; Xerox lost out to Canon, which quickly became the bestseller in copiers; and there are many other examples. So why is it that established highly respected firms fail to recognise the future? In the cases already mentioned hindsight suggests that more resources should have been devoted to innovation, but that is not all. Established businesses that have been successful for many years also develop comfortable routines and become complacent. Hierarchies, systems, rulebooks and formulae work pretty well for controlling and improving the efficiency of repeated actions. They are hopeless for inventing, experimenting with and developing something that has never happened before (*see* 'The dilemma of innovation management', Chapter 3). Furthermore, a growing number of academics (Christensen, 1997; Hamel and Prahalad, 1994) argue that a particular problem exists because firms rely too heavily on market research and that some of the techniques reinforce the present and do not peer into the future. It is well known that market research results often produce negative reactions to discontinuous new products (innovative products) that later become profitable for the innovating company. Indeed, there are some famous examples such as the fax machine, the VCR and James Dyson's bagless vacuum cleaner. Despite this, companies continue to seek the views of consumers on their new product ideas. The debate about the use of market research in the development of new products is long-standing and controversial.

In his award-winning 'business book of the year'[2] Clayton Christensen (1997) investigated why well-run companies that were admired by many failed to stay on

[2] Christensen (1997) was awarded the *Financial Times* business book of the year award in 1999.

Illustration 15.5

Closures for the wine industry: the customer does not know best

Consumers made it clear time and again that they did not want a screw-cap on their bottle of wine. They preferred the theatre of the cork and pop. Yet the international wine brands and retailers were determined to show customers that screw-cap was better: 75 per cent of wine sales in Australia and New Zealand are now screw-cap (see the case study at end the of Chapter 6).

top of their industry. His research showed that in the cases of well-managed firms such as Digital, IBM, Apple and Xerox, 'good management' (sic) was the most powerful reason why they failed to remain market leaders. It was precisely because these firms listened to their customers and provided more and better products of the sort they wanted that they lost their position of leadership. He argues that there are times when it is right not to listen to customers. Indeed, many companies share the same ideas about who their customers are and what products and services they want. The more that companies share this conventional wisdom about how they compete, the more they fight for incremental improvements in cost reductions and quality, and the more they avoid the discontinuous disruptive new products. Illustration 15.5 highlights the dangers of falling into this trap.

It is not surprising that many firms try to meet the needs of their customers. After all, successful companies have established themselves and built a successful business on providing the customer with what he or she wanted. IBM and Hoover, for example, became very good at serving their customers. But when a new, very different, technology came along these companies struggled. These large successful companies have been fighting known competitors for many years through careful planning and reducing costs. Suddenly they were faced with a completely different threat: new, smaller firms doing things differently and using unusual technologies. In IBM's case it was personal computers and in Hoover's case it has been bagless vacuum cleaners. Table 15.1 illustrates a wide range of products that were initially rejected by consumers, but went on to be successful.

If sufficient care is not exercised by managers, market research can be used to support conservative product development decision making. The previous sections have highlighted the difficulty faced by many managers in the field of new product development. In many crucial new product development decisions, the course of action that is most desirable over the long run is not the best course of action in the short term. This is the dilemma addressed in the debate about short-termism, that is, an emphasis on cutting costs and improving efficiencies in the immediate future, rather than on creativity and the development of innovative new product ideas for the long term. What is of concern is not the desire to cut costs but the apparent disregard of the implications and damage that such policies may bring about, and in particular the neglect of the company's ability to create new business opportunities for the future well-being of the company.

To return to a point made earlier by Akio Morita, Sony's influential leader. Morita argued that the public did not know what was possible and it was the firm that should lead the customer. This point is explored more fully by Hamel and Prahalad (1994: 108) who argue that firms need to go beyond customer-led ideas if

Table 15.1 Products that were initially rejected by consumers but went on to be successful

New product	Year	
Fax machines	1960s	Initially rejected by consumers who could not see any application for this product.
Microcomputers	1960s	Initially consumers could not foresee all the potential uses for microcomputers.
Benson & Hedges Gold cigarettes	1970s	Gallagher launched this product in the UK in 1978. Early consumer tests revealed indifferent support, yet the product was eventually a huge commercial success and brand leader in the UK.
Baileys Irish Cream Liqueur	1980s	Early consumer trials of this product suggested that it was not liked by consumers.
Dyson bagless vacuum cleaner	1990	Consumer research by retailers led them to believe consumers did not want a vacuum cleaner that displayed dirt collected in a transparent container. In fact consumers later preferred this design.
Chryslers PT Cruiser	1990s	Actually this product was not rejected, but Chrysler interpreted its consumer research as a niche product rather than a mass volume product. Hence, sales production could not match demand.
Screw-cap wine bottle closures	2000	Wine bottlers bowed to the demand of large retailers (buyers) to incorporate screw-caps. Consumers initially rejected screw-caps, but many now prefer it.

Source: A dirty business, *Guardian* 16/03/1999, copyright Guardian News & Media Ltd 2010.

they wish to be successful in the future. They are brutal in their criticism of customers' ability to peer into the future:

> *Customers are notoriously lacking in foresight. Ten or fifteen years ago, how many of us were asking for cellular telephones, fax machines and copiers at home, 24 hour discount brokerage accounts, multivalve automobile engines, video dial tone, etc.?*

Successful companies of the future will be those that are part of its creation. This means developing products that will be used in the future. Companies need to continually challenge existing products and markets. This can be achieved by pushing at the boundaries of current product concepts. Some firms have recognised this and are putting the most advanced technology they have available into the hands of the world's most sophisticated and demanding customers. IBM and Xerox have learnt through bitter experience what it is like to lose out to newcomers with new ideas and new technology. They know that today's customers may not be tomorrow's.

Using a simple two-by-two matrix (Figure 15.3) showing needs and customers, Hamel and Prahalad have shown that however well a company meets the articulated needs of current customers, it runs a great risk if it does not have a view of the needs customers cannot yet articulate: in other words the products of the future.

All this raises the problem of how to deal with consumers with limited prior knowledge and how to conduct market research on a totally new product or a major product innovation. In their research analysing successful cases of discontinuous product innovations, Lynn *et al.* (1997) argue that firms adopt a process of probing and learning. Valuable experience is gained with every step taken and modifications are made to the product and the approach to the market based on that learning.

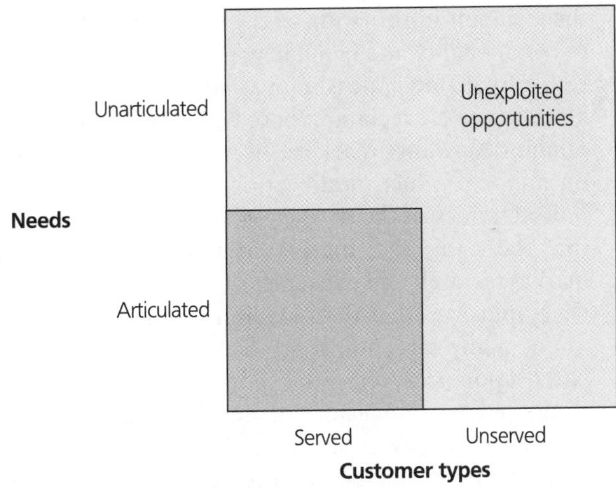

Figure 15.3 Gaining new customers of the future

Source: S. Hamel and C.K. Prahalad (1994) Competing for the future, *Harvard Business Review*, Vol. 72, No. 4, 122–8.

This is not trial and error, but careful experimental design and exploration of the market often using the experience and heritage of the organisation. This type of new product development is very different from traditional techniques and methods described in marketing texts.

Technology intensive products present similar difficulties. Nyström (1990) described high-tech markets as marketing dependent and technologically driven. Unfortunately, there is evidence that this linkage is not often recognised by organisations (Gupta *et al.*, 1985). High-tech markets are characterised as complex. In addition, they exist under rapidly changing technological conditions which lead to shorter life cycles and the need for rapid decisions. The importance of speed in high-tech markets is driven by increasing competition and the continually evolving expectations of customers. All of this is compounded by higher levels of risk for both the customer and the producer. Herein lies the problem: highly innovative products have an inherent high degree of uncertainty about exactly how an emerging technology may be formulated into a usable product and what the final product application will be. Market vision, or the ability to look into the future and picture products and services that will be successful, is a fundamental requirement for those firms wishing to engage in innovation but also very problematic (Van der Duin, 2006). It involves assessing one's own technological capability and present or future market needs and visioning a market offering that people will want to buy. While this may sound simple it lies at the heart of the innovation process and focuses attention on the need to examine not only the market but the way the new product offering is used or consumed.

When it may be correct to ignore your customers

Many industry analysts and business consultants are now arguing that the devotion to focus groups and market research has gone too far (Christensen, 1997; Martin, 1995; Francis, 1994). Indeed, the traditional new product development process of market research, segmentation, competitive analysis and forecasting, prior to passing the resultant information to the research and development (R&D) department, leads to commonality and bland new products. This is largely because the process constrains rather than facilitates innovative thinking and creativity. Furthermore, and more alarming, these techniques are well known and used by virtually all companies operating in consumer markets. In many of these markets the effect is an over-emphasis on minor product modifications and on competition that tends to focus on price. Indeed, critics of the market-orientated approach to new product development argue that the traditional marketing activities of branding, advertising and positioning, market research and consumer research act as an expensive obstacle course to product development rather than facilitating the development of new product ideas.

For many large multi-product companies it seems the use of market research is based upon accepted practice in addition to being an insurance policy. Many large companies are not short of new product ideas – the problem lies in deciding in which ones to invest substantial sums of money (Cooper, 2001; Liddle, 2004), and then justifying this decision to senior managers. Against this background one can see why market research is so frequently used without hesitation, as decisions can be justified and defended. Small companies in general, and small single-product companies in particular, are in a different situation. Very often new product ideas are scarce; hence, such companies frequently support ideas based upon their intuition and personal knowledge of the product.

The significance of discontinuous new products is often overlooked. Morone's (1993) study of successful US product innovations suggests that success was achieved through a combination of discontinuous product innovations and incremental improvements. Furthermore, in competitive, technology-intensive industries success is achieved with discontinuous product innovations through the creation of entirely new products and businesses, whereas product line extensions and incremental improvements are necessary for maintaining leadership (Lynn *et al.*, 1997). This, however, is only after leadership has been established through a discontinuous product innovation. This may appear to be at variance with accepted thinking that Japan secured success in the 1980s through copying and improving US and European technology. This argument is difficult to sustain on close examination of the evidence. The most successful Japanese firms have also been leaders in research and development. Furthermore, as Cohen and Levinthal (1990, 1994) have continually argued, access to technology is dependent on one's understanding of that technology.

Pause for thought 

Ignoring your customers' views seems like a very high risk strategy, especially for an ambitious new manager; and if the product eventually fails, so might the career of the new manager!

Striking the balance between new technology and market research

Market research can provide a valuable contribution to the development of innovative products. The difficulties lie in the selection and implementation of research methods. It may be that market research has become a victim of its own success, that is, business and product managers now expect it to provide solutions to all difficult product management decisions. Practitioners need to view market research as a collection of techniques that can help to inform the decision process.

The development and adoption process for discontinuous or complex products is particularly difficult. The benefits to potential users may be difficult to identify and value, and usually because there are likely to be few substitute products available it is difficult for buyers to compare and contrast. Sometimes product developers have to lead buyers/consumers and show them the benefits, even educate them. This is where some marketing views suggest the process is no longer customer led or driven by the market, and they would argue that what is now occurring is a technology-push approach to product development. Day (1999) suggests that on closer examination there are a number of false dichotomies here:

- that you must either lead or follow customers;
- that you cannot stay close to both current and potential customers; and
- that technology-push cannot be balanced with market-pull.

It is true, as we have seen in this chapter, that customers respond most positively to what is familiar and comfortable and that customers view the high costs of new technology (including switching costs) in a largely negative way. Firms need to try to understand how customers will view innovations in the marketplace; this may include adoption influences such as consumption pattern, product capability and technological capability (Veryzer, 2003). Valid good management should be capable of selecting the appropriate market research techniques to avoid superficial consumer reactions. A thorough understanding of all aspects of the market and the needs of users should inform managers that it is possible to provide customers with what they want and lead them through education.

The argument about current markets and future markets is powerfully made by both Christensen (1997) and Hamel and Prahalad (1994). The suggestion here is that firms become myopic towards their current customers and fail to see the larger slowly changing market. The case of IBM in the 1980s is often given here. It surely is a responsibility of senior management to try to understand the wider and future environment of the firm. This may be very easy to record, but in practice it is extremely difficult to carry out. There are real dangers for all firms here. For example, discontinuous new technologies may require huge changes for firms, and one can see that for many the easy option is to hope the new technology fails and the firm can carry on as normal. Failure to change and adopt may result in more cases like IBM, Xerox, Hoover and many financial service firms that failed to respond to online banking. Once again it should be possible for a well-run company to fully exploit its current markets and develop and enter the markets of the future. For example, both Kodak and Fuji have exploited the massive changes in the photographic market with the introduction of digital photography.

Finally, the arguments about market-pull or technology-push never seem to go away. But readers of this book should now be clear that this is a stale argument. What is required is an understanding of innovation. While it is clear that in some industries the role of science and technology is far greater than in other industries, innovation requires inputs from both. It is true there are many firms in the pharmaceutical sector that argue that their approach to product development is to start with brilliant science and to look for ways of using it in new drugs; and that the role of marketing and sales is to develop sales of these products. While this approach may work for a few, even in this industry sector there are many firms that operate differently. Some of the most successful pharmaceutical firms including GlaxoSmithKline, Pfizer and Merck work very closely with buyers and users to develop new drugs and to improve many existing ones. Indeed, the success of one of the world's bestselling drugs, Viagra, is surely testament to the benefits of working closely with the market.

Innovation in action

Self-service is growing in some industries. What other sectors can it be applied to?

MiNiBAR, in the heart of Amsterdam, is a self-service bar. When you arrive, a concierge gives you the key to your own fridge which is stocked with beer, wine, spirits and snacks. You and your friends help yourselves over the course of the evening, and settle up your account before leaving. The mini-bars are stocked from the back, making for easy restocking. It's simply extending the concept of the hotel mini-bar to the high street of course – but it's new and is bound to attract interest.

From the customer perspective, it's fun, convenient and there's no more queuing at the bar. From a business perspective it also means fewer staff members, and more customers can be accommodated because less space is taken up by the bar.

Source: HSBC (2010) 100 Thoughts, HSBC, London.

The challenge for senior management

Innovation is clearly a complex issue and sometimes it is a concept that sits uneasily in organisations. Indeed, some writers on the subject have argued that organisations are often the graveyard rather than the birthplace for many innovations. Applying pressure on product managers to seek high profits from quick volume sales rather than develop business opportunities for the future is a common mistake made by senior management. Similarly a heavy reliance on market research to minimise risk when developing new product ideas also contributes to an early grave for product ideas. The use of financial systems that minimise risk and avoid investment in more long-term projects is another common preference, which frequently emanates from senior management.

Correcting such ills will never be easy, but given the strategic importance of innovation it is a challenge senior management must take up. The adjustments which need to be made in order to encourage innovation in large companies may break some of the established rules of corporate life. They will require changes to internal systems and structures and the culture of the organisation. However, without such changes, potential innovations will continue to be squeezed out by the system, and thus rob the company of the most effective means of survival (Brown, 1991).

Case study

Dyson, Hoover and the bagless vacuum cleaner

This case study illustrates many of the obstacles and difficulties of launching a new product. The product in question used new technology that was initially rejected by existing manufacturers. It was priced at more than double that of existing products, but eventually captured more than 50 per cent of the UK vacuum cleaner market in less than four years.

Source: © A. Harrison/Pearson Education Ltd

Introduction

Conventional wisdom would surely suggest that Dyson Appliances Ltd would fail within a few months. After all, it appeared to be a small company with an eccentric manager at its helm, trying to sell an over-priced product of limited appeal in a very competitive market with less expensive, conventional, mass-market products made by respected manufacturers whose names were, quite literally, household words. The result was very different. The story of the Dyson bagless vacuum cleaner is not a classic tale of 'rags to riches'. The charismatic inventor James Dyson was afforded many privileges and opportunities not available to most. It is, none the less, a fascinating story and illustrates many of the difficulties and problems faced by small businesses and 'lone inventors'; and demonstrates the determination, hard work and sacrifices necessary in order to succeed. The cliché *against the odds*, which Dyson (1998) used as the title of his autobiography, is certainly appropriate and tells the story of the development and launch of the first bagless vacuum cleaner – the Dyson DC01.

This case raises several significant research questions in the field of innovation management. First, how and why did senior executives at leading appliance manufacturers across Europe, such as Electrolux, Bosch and Miele, decide not to utilise the technology offered to them by Dyson? Second, how and why did senior buyers for many retail chains across the United Kingdom fail to recognise the potential for the DC01? Third, technology transfer experts would point out that the Dyson vacuum cleaner is a classic case of technology transfer – a technology developed for one industry, i.e. dust extraction from sawmills, is applied to a different use in a new industry. Hence, it is technology transfer that needs to be championed and supported further by governments. Fourth, as a mechanism for protecting intellectual property, it seems that patents depend on the depth of your pocket. That is, they are prohibitively expensive and are almost exclusively for the benefit of large multinational organisations. What can be done to help small businesses without such large pockets and unlimited financial resources? And finally, many commentators would argue Dyson was successful partly because he had some influential contacts that he had established – he was fortunate. But there may be a hundred failed Mr Dysons littering the business highways who did not have such contacts. How can governments try to facilitate inventors like Dyson and ensure that more innovations succeed (thereby developing the economic base of their country)?

Reaping the rewards from technological innovation

Since Dyson's entry into the domestic appliance market two of the largest world players in the vacuum cleaner market have responded to the challenge laid down by James Dyson's bagless vacuum cleaner, launched in the United Kingdom in 1993. Dyson now accounts for a third of all vacuum cleaner sales in the United Kingdom. In 1998 Dyson Appliances

→

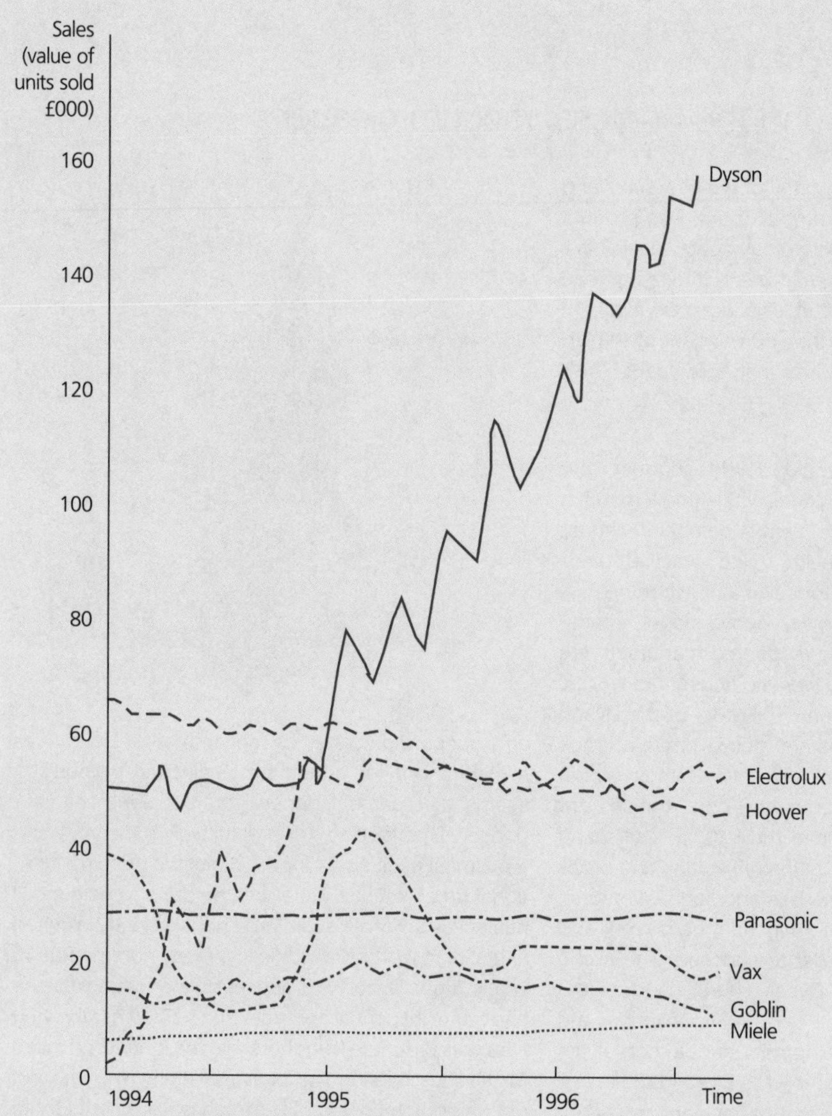

Figure 15.4 The spectacular growth of Dyson

sold nearly 1.4 million units worldwide. Revenues for the year were £190 million but, surprisingly, net income was £29 million – 15 per cent of sales (*see* Figure 15.4).

Background

Prior to the development of the bagless vacuum cleaner James Dyson had already demonstrated his prowess as a designer and businessman. He was responsible for the 'ballbarrow', a wheelbarrow that revolutionised that market by using a ball rather than a wheel. This was to provide the financial foundation for the development of the bagless vacuum cleaner. That particular experience taught James Dyson many lessons. One in particular is worth mentioning. The patents for the ballbarrow were owned by the company that James Dyson helped to set up. He eventually parted with this company but unfortunately lost all control of the patents as they belonged to the company and not to himself. Dyson was determined that any future patent would personally belong to him and not a company.

For those who may not recall their British social and economic history, Hubert Booth developed the first vacuum cleaner at the end of the nineteenth century. Vacuum technology uses the principle of a vacuum (the absence of everything, even air). Vacuum cleaners actually create a partial vacuum, or more accurately, an area of reduced air pressure as air moves outward within the fan. Airflow is created as air with normal air pressure moves towards the area with the reduced air pressure. A few years later in 1902 the British Vacuum Cleaner Company was offering a vacuum cleaning service to the homes of the affluent and wealthy. A large horse-drawn 5-hp engine would pull up outside your home and a hose would be fed into the house where it would begin to suck out all the dust. By 1904 a more mobile machine was available for use and was operated by domestic servants. As popularity of the technology increased, additional manufacturers began entering the market. Electrolux introduced a cylinder and hose vacuum cleaner in 1913 and in 1936 Hoover an upright cleaner with rotating brushes. This was known as the Hoover Junior and was the bestselling vacuum cleaner in the United Kingdom. Indeed, virtually all vacuum cleaners since this time are variations on that Hoover Junior design. That was until the late 1970s and early 1980s when James Dyson developed a vacuum cleaner using cyclonic forces and avoided the need for a bag to collect dust.

When it comes to cleaning performance, there is a tendency to look primarily at the power of the suction motor and the amount of bristles on the brush roll. While these are important considerations, the quality and size of the paper bag are very important factors as well. The paper bag in a vacuum cleaner consists of a special paper enclosure into which the dirt and air are directed as part of the filtering system. The paper used is specially processed to permit the air to pass through it while retaining as much of the dust and dirt as possible. The quality of the bag's filter media affects both its ability to retain the fine dust and allergens and its ability to allow air to flow easily through it. The size of the bag will also affect how easily the air flows. A good-quality paper bag is a very important vacuum cleaner component, which needs to be regularly replaced. The Dyson vacuum cleaner maintains its performance during the vacuuming process because it has no bag, hence there is no reduction in suction due to clogging of the pores of the bag, a feature that is characteristic of the bagged cleaners.

The development of a bagless vacuum cleaner

It is the bag component of a vacuum cleaner that Dyson focused on to revolutionise the vacuum cleaner appliance industry. Put simply he tackled the key dilemma for vacuum cleaners – how to collect dirt and dust, yet at the same time allow clean air to pass through. This was achieved by abandoning the use of bags to collect dirt. Instead he adapted the use of centrifugal forces. Many of us will have enjoyed cyclonic forces personally. One of the oldest fun rides at fairgrounds involves a large drum in which people stand with their backs against the outer wall. When the drum spins the floor is lowered and people remain pressed against the outer wall. The exhilaration and excitement clearly results from being forced against a wall, unable to move one's head or arms due to the huge forces that are created. Yet the fascinating aspect here is that the drum's speed is no more than 33kph (20mph).

It is this principle that is used to separate the heavy dust particles from the air, allowing the clean air to continue through the machine. The air, which has no mass, is not forced against the side walls of the container and takes the easiest route in the centre and thus out through the hole at the bottom (*see* Figure 15.5). This approach had been used in a variety of industries to collect dust, for example, in sawmills, but this was on a large scale (30m by 10m) and involved substantial pieces of equipment. The difficulty was applying this technology to a small domestic appliance.

If anyone still thinks that innovation is about waking up in the morning with a bright idea and shouting 'Eureka!' they should consider carefully James Dyson's difficult road to success. Between 1978 and 1982 he built over 1,000 prototype vacuum cleaners, spent over £2 million and experienced many years of sweat and headaches before eventually developing a successful prototype. But this was merely the start of an even longer project to get manufacturers to buy the licence to manufacture. Indeed, over 10 years later Dyson decided to mass produce the product for the UK market himself.

The story begins in 1978 with James Dyson at home with his young family helping with some of the

→

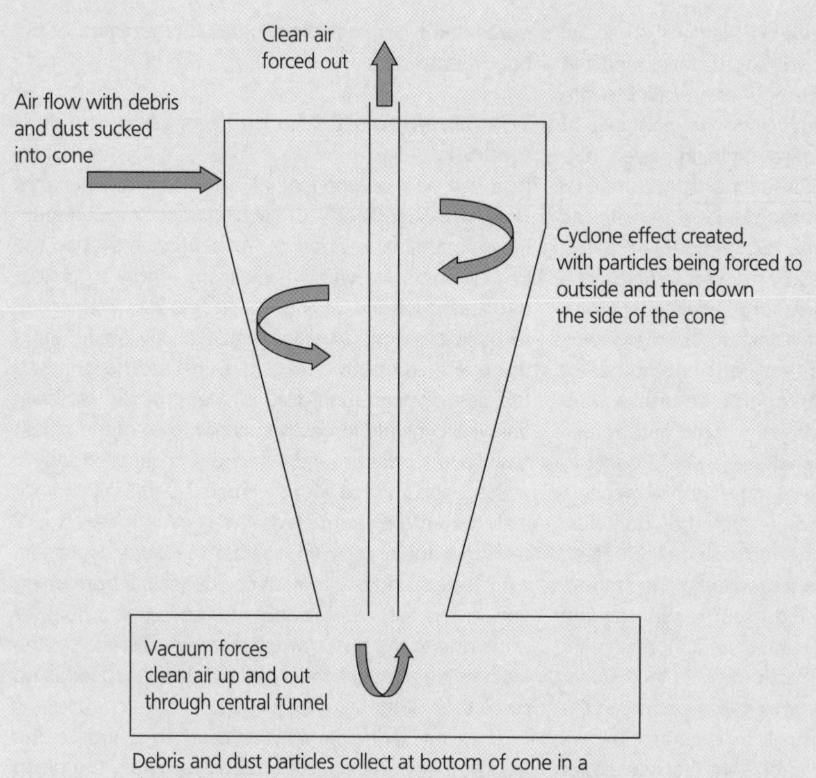

Figure 15.5 Basic operating principle of Dyson bagless vacuum cleaner

chores around the home. Like many families at the time, the Dysons owned a Hoover Junior upright vacuum cleaner. Dyson noticed that when a new bag is fitted to the vacuum cleaner it works well, but quickly loses much of its suction. He soon had the vacuum cleaner in pieces on his workbench and was amazed to realise that the standard vacuum cleaner technology relied on holes in the bag to allow clean air to pass through. As soon as these clogged up (which starts to occur immediately) suction begins to deteriorate. Moreover, he quickly discovered that all bagged vacuum cleaners operate on the same principle. How, then, can this limitation be overcome? The idea came to Dyson while he was investigating a problem at his ballbarrow factory. To improve toughness the product was powder-coated and then heated. This involved spraying the powder coating, which was messy. To overcome this problem an industrial vacuum cleaner was required. The suppliers of the powder coating informed Dyson that most of their larger customers use cyclones to collect the powder. Such cyclones are also used in a variety of industrial settings such as sawmills to extract dust from the air. This information was the beginning of what turned out to be a 15-year project.

Cyclonic cleaning systems separate the dust particles from the airflow by spinning the air within a separation chamber. The Dyson system operates as follows.

Any dirt and air enters the nozzle near the floor and travels through the hose towards the separation chambers. It first enters the primary dirt-separation chamber where the larger dirt particles are deposited. From there the air with the remaining fine dirt and dust travels to the cyclonic chamber. Once in the cyclonic chamber, the spinning action separates most of the fine dirt and dust particles from the airflow. The spinning causes centrifugal force to act upon the dust particles, moving them outward while the air exits from the inner part of the chamber (*see* Figure 15.5).

The Dyson vacuum cleaner uses two cyclones and several filters to capture dirt and dust. While the first cyclonic chamber captured large dust particles some fine dust particles were escaping with the air. The answer was a second, smaller, cyclone and Dyson spent many months developing this idea. The key problem was in the application of the theory, that is, having dust pass through one cyclone and then another, all in a small domestic appliance. After months, and eventually years, of further trials and errors the development of a cyclone within a cyclone was born (the dual cyclone). As dirt and air is sucked into the machine the first cyclone separates the large dust particles and these come to rest at the bottom of the canister. The remaining air and fine dust (including cigarette smoke) is then carried into a second cyclone which separates the even finer dust particles from the air.

The technology also uses several replaceable filters to remove even smaller particles of dust. Since the air is quite clean, it is then allowed to flow through the motor to cool it. After leaving the motor the air is filtered by a HEPA (High Efficiency Particulate Air) exhaust filter to remove even more fine particles and carbon from the motor brushes before it leaves the vacuum cleaner.

In search of a manufacturer – 'don't let them get you down'

Thanks to experience gained with other products, most notably the ballbarrow, Dyson was able to ensure that patent applications were in place prior to negotiations. This is essential if you wish to ensure that large multinational companies are not going to steal your intellectual property. From Dyson's experience he would argue that they would probably try to steal it regardless of any protection one held.

Dyson was offering a licence to manufacturing companies that included exclusive rights to his patents. In return Dyson would receive a percentage of their profits from the sale of the manufactured product. Dyson was looking for a five- to ten-year licence with a royalty of 5 per cent of the wholesale price and £40,000 up front. In addition he was offering his help in the development of the product from its prototype form. Unfortunately Hoover, Electrolux, Goblin, Black and Decker, AEG, Vax and many others all declined. There were many different reasons given. Sometimes the companies appeared to be arrogant and dismissed Dyson as a 'loony crank'. What was surprising was that throughout, companies appeared to be obsessed with finding fault with the product. On other occasions the company expected Dyson to hand over the patents for very little financial reward. Frequently there were difficulties in agreeing to meet. This was due to problems of protecting the intellectual property that would flow from a meeting between the R&D experts of the company in question and Dyson.

Many of the objections, limitations and problems with the prototype may have been justified. One may even argue that the agreement sought by Dyson was ambitious. There is also one other key issue – the bags. The Dyson product was proposing to eliminate vacuum bags, but this was a very profitable business for vacuum cleaner manufacturers. They were unlikely to relish this prospect.

Breaking through in Japan

If things were not going well in the United Kingdom and Europe fortunately Dyson had a breakthrough in Japan. Apex Inc. agreed, after several arduous weeks of negotiations, to a licence to manufacture and sell in Japan. The product was to be called 'G-Force'. The successful licensing of the technology to a Japanese manufacturer in the late 1980s helped Dyson to secure much-needed revenue at a time when he was beginning to consider throwing in the towel. This small level of income also provided the encouragement he needed to start planning the establishment of manufacturing facilities in the United Kingdom. What is interesting about the licensing arrangement in question is that Dyson was uncertain that licensing revenues received reflect the true sales figures. As with all licensing and royalty agreements, there is a significant element of trust required. For example, authors trust their publishers that sales of their book will be accurately recorded and appropriate royalties paid. There is, however, the small matter of who establishes the level of sales. This, of course, is taken by the publisher who then pays the royalties to authors. This 'high-trust' relationship also operates with other licensing agreements where royalties are paid per item sold.

Entering the UK market and manufacturing in the United Kingdom

With a small amount of revenue starting to trickle in Dyson decided that it was time to start in Britain. The existing appliance manufacturers had expressed no interest, hence Dyson planned to manufacture the

→

product in Britain by offering the product to existing contract manufacturers. Essentially Dyson decided to offer a series of contracts to two existing manufacturing companies, one to mould the component parts and another to assemble. For the existing moulding and assembly companies it was additional capacity. Unfortunately the companies selected by Dyson caused further problems. First, the quality of the completed product was not acceptable to Dyson. Second, the companies seemed to be squeezing Dyson's work in between existing long-standing contracts. In the end Dyson decided that he would prefer to manufacture and assemble the product himself. He purchased the moulds from the plastic moulding company and attempted to establish a factory in the United Kingdom, the rationale being that this would at least ensure that he was in control of his own destiny and would not have to rely on others. Further difficulties, however, were encountered by Dyson. First, he found that it is extremely difficult to borrow money – even with a proven successful product. Dyson explored the possibility of setting up a factory in an area where government development grants are available. For example, he tried South Wales but David Hunt, the then Welsh Office Minister, refused his application for a grant.

The project had now consumed 12 years of his life and had cost £2 million. Once again Dyson was forced to consider whether it was all worth it.

After months of negotiations Dyson's local bank manager agreed to lend him some more money and he was able to set up his manufacturing factory in Wiltshire. Soon Dyson was producing his own product in his own factory and the first Dyson bagless vacuum cleaner rolled off the production line in 1992.

Trying to sell to the retailers

Armed with a shiny new DC01 under his arm James Dyson began visiting the large UK white-goods retailers such as Currys, Dixons and Comet to arrange sales orders. Unfortunately Dyson was disappointed at their reaction. Quite simply, the retailers were not convinced that the UK consumer would be willing to pay possibly three times as much for a vacuum cleaner. Moreover, Dyson's bagless product was twice the price of the brand leader. The response was almost universal:

> *Consumers are very happy with this one – why should they pay twice as much for yours? And anyway, if your idea was any good Hoover or Electrolux would have thought of it years ago.*

Eventually, several of the home catalogue companies agreed to feature the product. In addition, an electricity board shop in the Midlands also agreed to stock a few products. Initially, sales were slow but gradually they increased. Eventually John Lewis, the national department store, agreed to take the product. From here sales began to take off.

In terms of marketing and promoting the product what is interesting is that, to date, the company has spent virtually nothing on promotion. Dyson has always adopted a strong product orientation and has believed that if a product is good enough it should require very little promotion. It is this approach which Dyson adopted for the bagless vacuum cleaner. Despite the use of revolutionary technology Dyson decided against large advertising budgets and instead relied upon a few press releases and features in newspapers.

The competition responds

With Dyson beginning to challenge the once-comfortable dominant position of Electrolux and Hoover, both companies mounted a strong defence of their products' technology, claiming that their traditional vacuum cleaning technology was more effective than the Dyson. Much of the debate, usually via press advertisements, centred on cleaning effectiveness. Hoover and Electrolux were able to make some headline-grabbing claims, in particular, that their products had more suction power and, hence, were better. Certainly the traditional vacuum cleaner with a bag had an initial high level of suction power, but this was necessary because the bag soon clogged up, reducing the level of suction. There are two different ways of viewing cleaning effectiveness. The most common use has to do with the ability of a vacuum cleaner to pick up dirt from the surface being cleaned. The other is the ability of the filtering system to clean the air so that a minimum amount of dirt and allergens is recirculated back into the home. The variable that is significant in a vacuum cleaner, however, is the flow of air and is measured in cubic metres per minute (CMM). It is one of the most important aspects of vacuum cleaner performance. Airflow

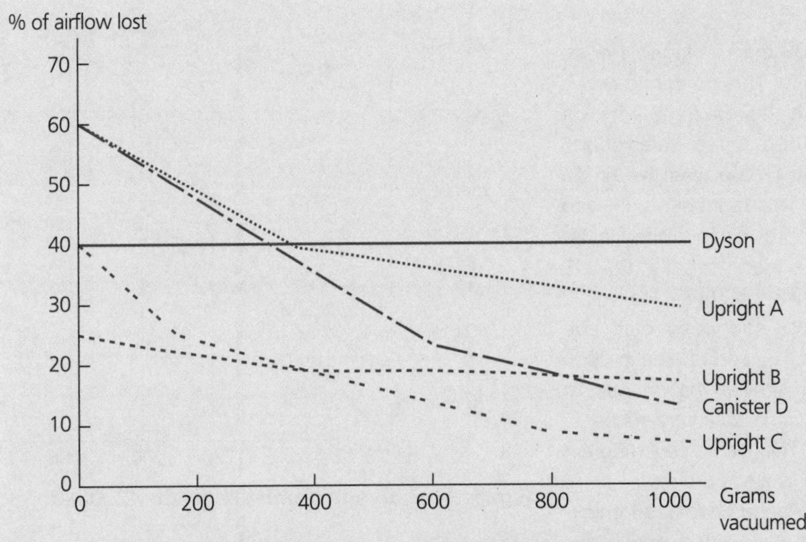

Figure 15.6 Cleaning performance of five vacuum cleaners

in a vacuum cleaner is inversely proportional to the total resistance within the system and directly proportional to the suction created by the suction motor.

Figure 15.6 depicts cleaning performance after vacuuming 1,000 grams of ASTM (American Society for Testing and Materials) Test Dirt. You will see that the Dyson machine maintains a steady airflow while other 'bagged' machines lose airflow.

Hoover's bagless vacuum cleaner

With sales and market share continuing to decline (*see* Table 15.2) Miele and Hoover attempted to fight Dyson in the vacuum cleaner market by developing similar bagless vacuum technologies. Hoover embarked on a technology transfer exercise to utilise technology first developed for the oil industry. The centrifugal force technology (similar to that used by Dyson) was used to separate gas or sand from crude oil. This technology has now been applied to Hoover's range of Triple Vortex vacuum cleaners in an attempt to compete with Dyson's own patented centrifugal force technology (www.Hoover.co.uk). Interestingly, Hoover's technology dispenses with the need for any filters. This may provide the advantage Hoover requires to re-establish itself as a key player in the vacuum cleaner market. Dyson, however, claimed that Hoover's technology copied its patents and sued Hoover for patent infringement in March 2000, eventually winning around £3 million in damages.

Table 15.2 With sales declining Miele and Hoover have attempted to take on Dyson in the vacuum cleaner market

	Volume (%)	Value (%)
Dyson		
Total market	33.5	53.5
Upright	51.6	66.9
Cylinder	13.6	29.8
Hoover		
Total market	12.3	9.2
Upright	16.5	10.2
Cylinder	8.2	7.1
Miele		
Total market	2.1	2.6
Cylinder	6.1	10.4

Source: A dirty business, *Guardian*, 16 March 1999.

Dyson has had several legal battles with his competitors over patent infringement and advertising standards. In January 2000 the Advertising Standards Association (ASA) ruled in favour of Dyson regarding an advertisement from Electrolux that claimed its vacuum cleaner was the most powerful. The ASA ruled that power of the motor was no indication of vacuum cleaner effectiveness (*Sunday Times*, 2000).

→

Hitting the big time

In 2002 Dyson entered the US market. In 2004 sales reached almost 1 million units. This contributed to a surge in profits at Dyson, which were £102.9 million in 2005, more than double 2003's figure. Sales efforts have continued and in 2006 Dyson was the brand leader in the United States. This has been achieved with no intellectual property protection in the United States. Unusually Dyson decided to enter the US market without any patent protection. He relied on the brand's strength that had been built and developed over the previous 10 years. Sales in 2006 were 1.5 million units. Dyson revealed that success in the United States was partly down to a very successful $30 million ad campaign. This was a very different strategy to that used in the UK and Europe.

More recently Dyson Appliances has been enjoying continued and improved success in one of the fiercest markets of all – Japan. Indeed, in 2006 Dyson overtook Toshiba to become the third biggest vacuum brand in Japan. This success is due to the Dyson DC12, a small digital machine designed especially for Japanese consumers. For Dyson Appliances Ltd success continues largely due to success in overseas markets. In Japan, the hand-held DC12 was the biggest selling carpet cleaner last year, outdoing such Japanese brands as Sharp and Sanyo. This helped push profits in 2006 past the £100 million barrier for the first time. The group's annual report reveals that the inventor awarded himself a £30 million dividend on top of his £29 million salary following a 9 per cent rise in annual sales and a 19 per cent pre-tax profits boost, to £115 million. Profits have almost trebled in four years, when the group made pre-tax profits of £43 million. This is largely because of success in the United States and Japan. Turnover has rocketed from £2.4 million in 1993 to £515 million. Its exports have increased three-fold in the past three years, now accounting for 80 per cent of turnover (*see* Figure 15.7).

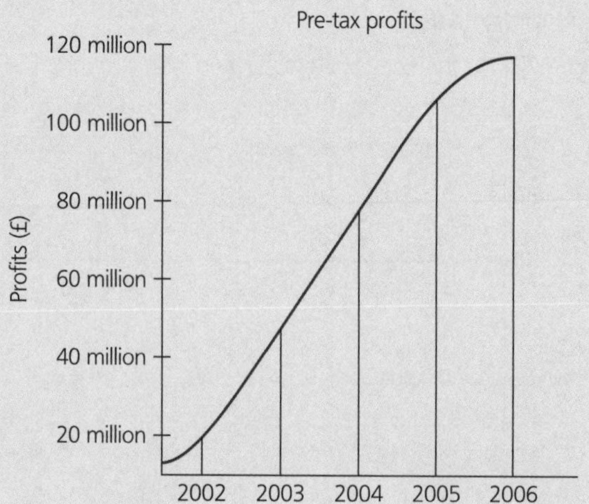

Figure 15.7 Dyson's pre-tax profits (2002–06)

Conclusions

James Dyson certainly believes it was worth it in the end. But during the 15-year period there were probably many occasions when he felt like giving up or more likely would have sold out for a few hundred thousand pounds. The period 1980–92 was very difficult, not just for himself but also for his family, and enormous pressures were placed on them. Fortunately they survived; arguably someone without the background, resources and contacts would have failed. Many people have great ideas but only a few achieve success. Very often it is due to the determination of the individual involved; sometimes events seem to conspire against even the best efforts of the individual.

Dyson invests heavily in R&D and believes that this is the key to success. Not all firms support this view. The level of investment in R&D varies considerably. The high value he places on creativity sets Dyson apart from other firms and helps to explain his insistence on maintaining what in Britain are considered insanely large annual investments in research and development. Nearly 17 per cent of revenues regularly goes to supporting the company's R&D efforts, a figure some ten times greater than the average in the United Kingdom. As a result of these ongoing research expenditures, a company that started with just one product now offers more than a dozen – all either upright or canister vacuum cleaners, each a more refined and technologically advanced model than its predecessors.

Reference: Dyson, J. (1998) *Against the Odds*, Orion Books, London; *Sunday Times* (2000) Dyson bags ruling on Electrolux, Business Section, 24 January, 1; Wallop, H. (2006) Dyson cleans up with £31m payday, *Daily Telegraph*, 1 November, Business Section, 4.

Questions

1 Explore the key problems Dyson had to overcome.

2 Characterise the type of innovation and new product development in the mature vacuum cleaner market prior to Dyson. Are there other industries in this situation?

3 Manufacturing the product has turned out to be hugely profitable, yet this was not the original plan; why not?

4 Explain the rationale behind Electrolux and Hoover's decision not to purchase the licence from Dyson. Given Hoover's recent development of the *Triple Vortex* how do you assess this decision? What level of royalty would have been reasonable for both parties – that is, Dyson and Hoover?

5 Why is negotiating a licence for a new product so difficult?

6 How can businesses try to ensure that their senior managers (both buyers and new business development managers) do not dismiss exciting technology and with it potentially profitable business?

7 What is the role of patents? To what extent is it an effective system for protecting intellectual property?

8 Not all firms invest in R&D. What should be the level of expenditure on R&D for a firm?

9 Explain the very different market entry strategy used for the United States?

Note: This case has been written as a basis for class discussion rather than to illustrate effective or ineffective managerial or administrative behaviour. It has been prepared from a variety of published sources, as indicated, and from observations.

Chapter summary

This chapter has shown that great care must be exercised in market research, for there are times when market research results produce negative reactions to discontinuous new products (innovative products) that later become profitable for the innovating company. Like any activity that contributes to new product development, it has strengths and weaknesses. Many of these weaknesses are highlighted when the new product is discontinuous. Finally, some new products have particularly difficult problems to overcome if they are to be successful, like high switching costs. If these are recognised in advance, however, it is possible to overcome even these significant challenges.

Discussion questions

1 Explain why consumer market testing might not always be beneficial.

2 We are told that many new products fail, but is this because many firms are impatient? Discuss whether firms should allow more time for their product to be adopted and whether they would end up with a successful product.

3 Explain why discontinuous new products present a different challenge.

4 Show why the more radical the innovation, the greater the pertinence of qualitative market research techniques (e.g. customer visits and focus groups).

5 Examine whether there do exist innovations, typically radical, where market research of almost any kind is premature, not cost-justified or of limited value.

6 Discuss the advantages of the tripartite product concept in developing new products.

7 Discuss the dilemma faced by all firms of trying to listen to customers' needs and wants and yet also trying to develop new products for those customers that they do not yet serve.

8 Explain why some writers argue that organisations are the graveyard of product innovations rather than the birthplace.

Key words and phrases

Market research *524*
Concept testing *528*
Discontinuous new products *532*
Tripartite product concept *534*
Installed base effect *535*
Switching costs *535*

References

Barrett, P. (1996) The good and bad die young, *Marketing*, 11 July, 16.

Brown, R. (1991) Managing the S curves of innovation, *Journal of Marketing Management*, Vol. 7, No. 2, 189–202.

Christensen, C.M. (1997) *The Innovator's Dilemma: When New Technologies Cause Great Firms to Fail*, HBS Press, Cambridge, MA.

Cohen, W.M. and Levinthal, D.A. (1990) A new perspective on learning and innovation, *Administrative Science Quarterly*, Vol. 35, No. 1, 128–52.

Cohen, W.M. and Levinthal, D.A. (1994) Fortune favours the prepared firm, *Management Science*, Vol. 40, No. 3, 227–51.

Cooper, R.G. (1990) New products: What distinguishes the winners, *Research and Technology Management*, November–December, 27–31.

Cooper, R.G. (2001) *Winning at New Products*, 3rd edn, Perseus Publishing, Cambridge, MA.

Day, G.S. (1999) *The Market Driven Organisation*, The Free Press, New York.

Elkind, P. (2008) The trouble with Steve Jobs, *Fortune*, 5–8, 5 March.

Elliot, K. and Roach, D. (1991) Are consumers evaluating your products the way you think and hope they are?, *Journal of Consumer Marketing*, Vol. 8, No. 1, 5–14.

Fortune (2008) Steven Jobs, Apple, 3 March.

Francis, J. (1994) Rethinking NPD: giving full rein to the innovator, *Marketing*, 26 May, 6.

Guardian (1999) A dirty business, 16 March, 22.

Gupta, A.K., Ray, S.P. and Wilemon, D.L. (1985) R & D and Marketing Dialogue in High-Tech Firms, *Industrial Marketing Management*, Vol. 14, 289–300.

Hamel, G. and Prahalad, C.K. (1994) *Competing for the future*, Harvard Business Review, Vol. 72, No. 4, 122–8.

Herbig, P., Howard, C. and Kramer, H. (1995) The installed base effect: implications for the management of innovation, *Journal of Marketing Management*, Vol. 11, No. 4, 387–401.

Jackson, B.B. (1985) *Winning and Keeping Industrial Customers*, Lexington Books, Lexington, MA.

King, S. (1985) Has marketing failed or was it never really tried?, *Journal of Marketing Management*, Vol. 1, 1–19.

Kotler, P. (1998) *Marketing Management*, Prentice Hall, London.

Laurance, B. (2008) Reckitt Benckiser cleans up with research to boost global sales, *Sunday Times*, Business p. 3, 17 February.

Liddle, D. (2004) R&D Project Selection at Danahar, MBA Dissertation, University of Portsmouth.

Lynn, G.S., Morone, J.G. and Paulson, A.S. (1997) 'Marketing and discontinuous innovation: The probe and learn process', in Tushman, M.L. and Anderson, P. (eds) *Managing Strategic Innovation and Change, a Collection of Readings*, Oxford University Press, New York, 353–75.

Martin, J. (1995) Ignore your customer, *Fortune*, Vol. 8, No. 1, 121–25.

Morone, J. (1993) *Winning in High-tech Markets*, Harvard Business School Press, Cambridge, MA.

Nyström, H. (1990) *Technological and market innovation: strategies for product and company development*, Wiley, Chichester.

Ortt, R.J. and Schoormans, P.L. (1993) Consumer research in the development process of a major innovation, *Journal of the Market Research Society*, Vol. 35, No. 4, 375–89.

Porter, M.E. (1985) *Competitive Advantage*, Harvard Business School Press, Cambridge, MA.

Rogers, E. (1995) *The Diffusion of Innovation*, The Free Press, New York.

Saren, M.A.J. and Tzokas, N. (1994) *Proceedings of the Annual Conference of the European Marketing Academy*, Maastricht.

Sunday Times (2008) 17 February.

Tauber, E.M. (1974) Predictive validity in consumer research, *Journal of Advertising Research*, Vol. 15, No. 5, 59–64.

Van der Duin, P.A. (2006) *Qualitative futures research for innovation*, Eburon Academic Publishers, Delft, The Netherlands.

Veryzer, R. (2003) 'Marketing and the development of innovative products', in Shavinina, L. (ed.), *The International Handbook on Innovation*, Elsevier, Oxford.

von Hippel, E. and Thomke, S. (1999) Creating breakthroughs at 3M, *Harvard Business Review*, Vol. 77, No. 5, 47–57.

Further reading

For a more detailed review of the role of market research in new product development, the following develop many of the issues raised in this chapter:

Hamel, G. and Prahalad, C.K. (1994) Competing for the future, *Harvard Business Review*, Vol. 72, No. 4, 122–8.

HSBC (2010) 100 Thoughts, HSBC, London.

Hutlink, E.J., Hart, S., Henery, R.S.J. and Griffin, A. (2000) Launch decisions and new product success: an empirical comparison of consumer and industrial products, *Journal of Product Innovation Management*, Vol. 17, No. 1, 5–23.

Kumar, N., Scheer, L. and Kotler, P. (2000) From market driven to market driving, *European Management Journal*, Vol. 18, No. 2, 129–41.

Swink, M. (2000) Technological innovativeness as a moderator of new product design integration and top management support, *Journal of Product Innovation Management*, Vol. 17, No. 1, 208–20.

Chapter 16
Managing the new product development process

Introduction

The popular phrase 'actions speak louder than words' could be a subtitle for this chapter. While the previous five chapters in the third part of this book helped to identify some of the key factors and activities involved in the new product and service development process, it is the execution of these activities that will inevitably lead to the development of new market offerings. The focus of this chapter is on the management of the project as it evolves from idea into a physical form. Many companies have become very good at effective NPD, demonstrating that they are able to balance the many factors involved. The case study at the end of this chapter analyses how 3M has built a reputation for innovation and is frequently referred to as 'the innovation machine'.

Chapter contents

Learning objectives

When you have completed this chapter you will be able to:

- examine the key activities of the NPD process;
- explain that a product concept differs significantly from a product idea or business opportunity;
- recognise that screening is a continuous rather than a single activity;
- provide an understanding of the role of the knowledge base of an organisation in the new product development process; and
- recognise that the technology intensity of the industry considerably affects the NPD process.

New products as projects

Globalisation is a major market trend today, one characterised by both increased international competition as well as extensive opportunities for firms to expand their operations beyond current boundaries (*see* Chapter 7). Effectively dealing with this important change, however, makes the management of global new product development (NPD) a major concern. To ensure success in this complex and competitive endeavour, companies must rely on global NPD teams that make use of the talents and knowledge available in different parts of the global organisation. Thus, cohesive and well-functioning global NPD teams become a critical capability by which firms can effectively leverage this much more diverse set of perspectives, experiences and cultural sensitivities for the global NPD effort (Salomo *et al.*, 2010).

Over the past 50 years a large number of models and methods have been developed to help improve a company's performance in new product development (Craig and Hart, 1992). However, despite the positive influences these models may have on companies' efforts, Mahajan and Wind (1988) have shown low rates of usage in their study of *Fortune* 500 companies. More recently, Nijssen and Lieshout (1995) have shown in their study of companies in The Netherlands that the use of NPD models has a positive effect on profits.

The previous chapters have outlined some of the conditions that are necessary for innovation to occur and have shown various representations of the new product development process. However, while these conditions are necessary, they are

Table 16.1 NPD terminology

NPD terminology	Definition
The fuzzy front end	The messy 'getting started' period of new product development processes. It is the front end where the organisation formulates a concept of the product to be developed and decides whether or not to invest resources in the further development of an idea (*see* page 434).
Business opportunity	A possible technical or commercial idea that may be transformed into a revenue-generating product.
Product concept	A physical form or a technology plus a clear statement of benefit.
Screening	A series of evaluations, including technical, commercial and business assessments of the concept.
Specifications	Precise details about the product, including features, characteristics and standards.
Prototype/pilot	A tentative physical product or system procedure, including features and benefits.
Production	The product produced by the scale-up manufacturing process.
Launch	The product actually marketed, in either market test or launch.
Co-joint analysis	A method for deriving the utility values that consumers attach to varying levels of a product's attributes.
Commercialisation	A more descriptive label would be market introduction, the phase when the product is launched and hopefully begins to generate sales revenue.
Commercial success	The end product that meets the goals set for it, usually profit.

insufficient in themselves to lead to the development of new products. This is because, as with any internal organisational process, it has to be managed by people. The concepts of strategy, marketing and technology all have to be coordinated and managed effectively. Inevitably, this raises issues in such areas as internal communications, procedures and systems. This is where the attention turns from theory and representation to operation and activities.

We have seen that a product idea may arise from a variety of sources. We have also seen that, unlike some internal operations, NPD is not the preserve of one single department. And it is because a variety of different functions and departments are involved that the process is said to be complicated and difficult to manage. Furthermore, while two separate new products may be similar generically, there will frequently be different product characteristics to be accommodated and different market and technology factors to be addressed. To be successful new product development needs to occur with the participation of a variety of personnel drawn from across the organisation. This introduces the notion of a group of people working as a team to develop an idea or project proposal into a final product suitable for sale. The vast majority of large firms create new project teams to work through this process. From initial idea to launch, the project will usually flow and iterate between marketing, technical and manufacturing groups and specialists. The role of the new project team is at the heart of managing new products and is the focus of the case study at the end of this chapter. Additionally, NPD has developed its own jargon and Table 16.1 offers an overview of source of the key terminology.

The Valley of Death

The Valley of Death is used as a metaphor to describe a discrete segment of development between research and product development. It is associated with a relative lack of resources and expertise in the front end of product innovation. The metaphor suggests that there are relatively more resources on each side of the valley: on one side in the form of research expertise and on the other side commercialisation expertise and resources.

The concept of the Valley of Death is shown in Figure 16.1. The *y*-axis maps resource availability, while the *x*-axis reflects the level of development. As Figure 16.1 suggests, if an idea makes it through the valley to NPD, there is adequate resource availability to take the idea to market. In a study of product development projects (Markham *et al.* 2010) found that a variety of interlocking roles are identified that move projects from one side to the other. The study revealed that significant development takes place before projects enter into a firm's formal product development process. Also, the roles of champion, sponsor and gatekeeper are seen as major actors that work together to develop and promote projects for introduction into the formal NPD process. Champions make the organisation aware of opportunities by conceptualising the idea and preparing business cases. Sponsors support the development of promising ideas by providing resources to demonstrate the project's viability. Gatekeepers set criteria and make acceptance decisions. Clearly companies need to be aware of the Valley of Death and must develop the skills and make resources available to master the front end of product innovation to ensure products do not die in the valley.

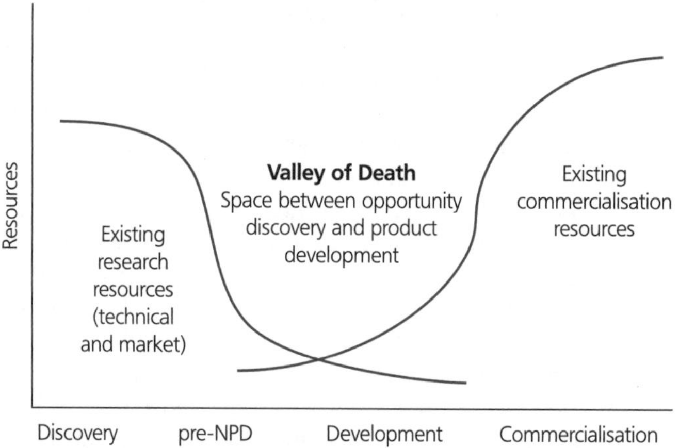

Figure 16.1 The Valley of Death

The key activities that need to be managed

The network model of NPD shown in Figure 12.14 represents a generalised and theoretical view of the process. To the practising manager, however, this is of limited practical use. Business managers and the managers of project teams need to know what particular activities should be undertaken. From this practitioner standpoint it is more useful to view the new product development process as a series of linked activities.

Figure 16.2 attempts to identify and link together most of the activities that have been associated with the NPD process over the years. This diagram represents a generic process model of NPD. It is not intended to be an actual representation of the process as carried out in a particular industry. Rather, it attempts to convey to the practitioner how the key activities are linked together to form a process. Some of these labels differ between industries and a good example of this is in the pharmaceutical industry. Final testing of a product is referred to as the clinical trial, where the product is used by volunteers and the effects carefully monitored. In the automotive industry final testing may involve the use of consumers trying the product for the first time and offering their reflections on the design and ergonomics.

One of the most comprehensive studies on new product success and failure was undertaken by Cooper in 1979. In this study 12 activities were identified: initial screening; preliminary market assessment; preliminary technical assessment; detailed market study; financial analysis; product development; product testing (in-house); product testing (with customer); test marketing; trial production; full-scale production; and product launch. Since this study a number of different studies have highlighted the importance of some of these activities over others. Other studies have shown that firms frequently omit some of these activities (Cooper, 1988a,b; Sanchez and Elola, 1991). Students of new product development are left with an unclear picture of which activities are necessary and which are performed. The answer is context-dependent and, in particular, industry-dependent. Some industries no longer use test marketing, for example, whereas for others it is still a very important activity. This is explained below.

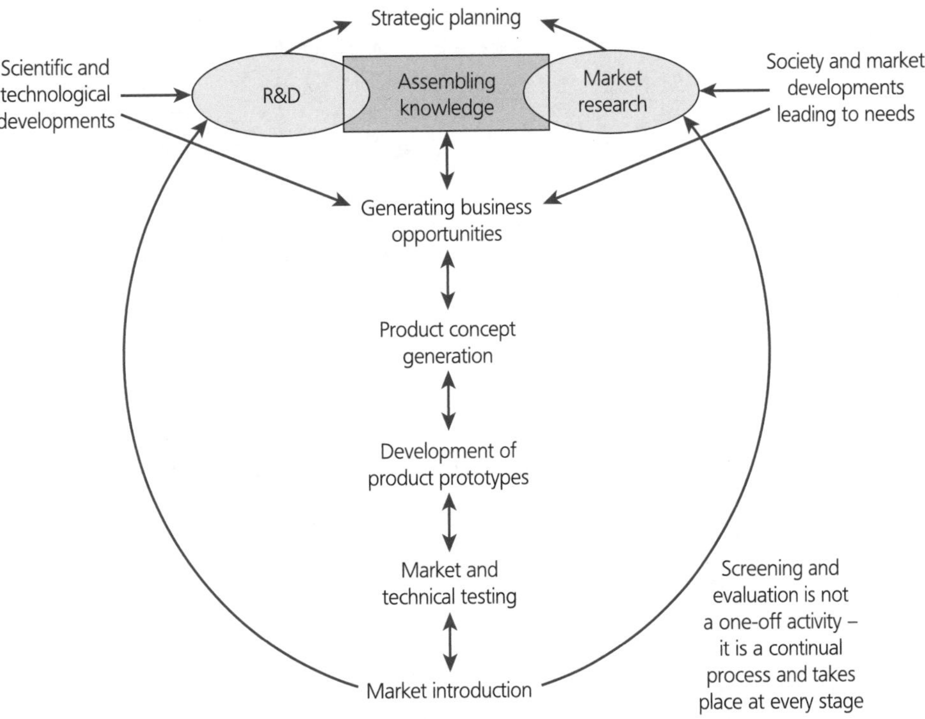

Figure 16.2 The NPD process as a series of linked activities

This section will examine the activities that need to be performed by businesses and NPD teams. The early activities are defined as the 'assembly of knowledge' and the 'generation of business opportunities'. These activities usually occur before a physical representation of the product has been developed. Up to this point costs have been relatively low, especially when compared to subsequent activities. These activities, defined here as product concept development and development of product prototypes, transform what was previously a concept, frequently represented by text and drawings, into a physical form. The product begins to acquire physical attributes such as size, shape, colour and mass. The final activities are market and technical testing and market introduction. It is worthy of note that these activities may occur at an earlier stage and that any of these activities can occur simultaneously.

Chapter 12 reviewed the wide range of models that have been developed to try to further our understanding of this complex area of management. Hopefully you will recognise the new product development process as a series of activities that transform an opportunity into a tangible product that is intended to produce profits for the company. In practice, the process is difficult to identify. Visitors who ask to see a company's NPD process will not see very much because the process is intertwined with the ongoing operation of the business. Furthermore, the process is fluid and iterations are often needed. Developments by competitors may force a new product idea due for impending launch back to the laboratory for further changes. The model in Figure 16.2 highlights many of the important features and also identifies the importance played by the external environment. From an idea or a concept the product evolves over time. This process involves extensive interaction and iteration, highlighted by the arrows in the diagram.

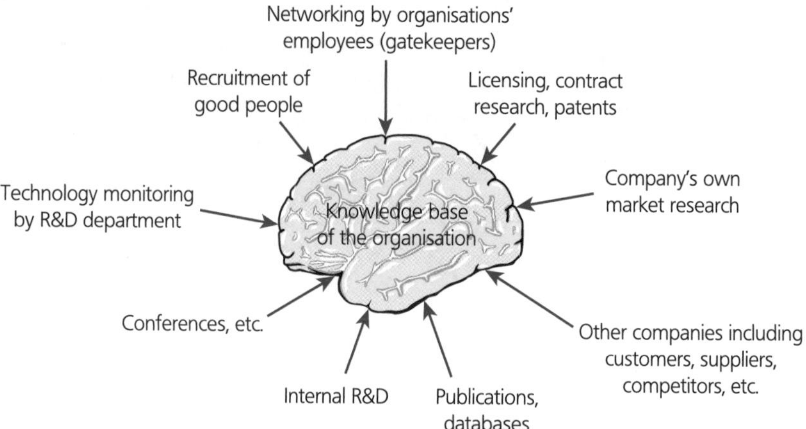

Figure 16.3 Maintaining an organisation's knowledge base

Assembling knowledge

The vast majority of marketing textbooks fail to identify the first activity of the NPD process, the assembling of knowledge (Kotler, 2003; Brassington and Pettitt, 2003). It is from an organisation's knowledge base that creativity and ideas for new products will flow. Chapter 6 emphasised the importance of an organisation's knowledge base in underpinning its innovative ability. Without the continual accumulation of knowledge, an organisation will be hindered in its ability to create new product ideas. Figure 16.3 shows a wide range of activities that together help to maintain a company's knowledge base.

Innovation in action

Simple! Sample

Handing out samples is a well-tried route for gaining advocacy and feedback on a new product. But getting your products into the hands of influential customers can be tricky, much less getting detailed feedback.

A new store in Japan has taken a more rigorous approach. Sample Lab! in Tokyo is dedicated to sampling. Its customers, mainly young women, pay a small annual fee to try out a wide range of products like cosmetics, food and alcoholic drinks.

'The concept of going into a retail store and being able to shop absolutely free, exchanging no money whatsoever, is unique', says Anthony James, founder and Global General Manager. 'Nothing is behind glass. You can try, touch, or taste anything in the store.' They are now planning to offer this concept around the world.

Source: HSBC (2010) 100 Thoughts, HSBC, London.

The generation of business opportunities

The generation of business opportunities is the next activity in the process of new product development. This was discussed in Chapters 6 and 12. You should

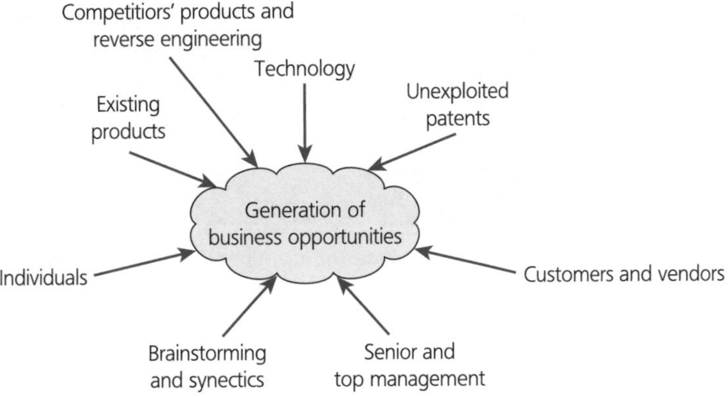

Figure 16.4 Sources of business opportunity

therefore be aware of the concept, even if the process is not fully clear. This stage in the NPD process is also referred to as opportunity identification (OI). It is the process of collecting possible business opportunities that could realistically be developed by the business into successful products. This definition contains several caveats, which helps to explain the difficulty that businesses faces. New product ideas can emerge from many sources, as illustrated in Figure 16.4. Although this classification is not intended to be exhaustive, the figure identifies many of the key sources for product ideas which are explained below.

Existing products

Many new ideas will come from a company's existing range of products. Very often small changes to a product result in the development of new lines and brands. This was the case for Unilever, which since 1930 has added detergents to its original product line of bar soap. It has also developed new brands of detergent from its original detergent Persil, such as Surf.

Competitors' products and reverse engineering

We examined the concept of reverse engineering in Chapter 6. It is worth restating here that competitor analysis provides a valuable source of ideas for developing and improving a firm's own products. Indeed, this is the principle of competition which helps to drive up quality and choice and drive down price. A useful illustration here of how competing firms in a market closely follow each other is the mobile phone handset market. The introduction of a camera to the handset by Nokia was soon imitated by Sony-Ericsson, Motorola, Samsung and the others. Similarly the introduction of an MP3 player into the handset by Motorola was quickly followed by the others. Reverse engineering can help firms quickly see how their competitors' design, engineering and manufacturing is being deployed in a device and this can help speed up the new product development process.

Technology

The most obvious source of ideas is the company's own R&D department which is funded to research technology and develop new product ideas. It is also the responsibility of the R&D department to keep abreast of external technological developments of interest to the company. This is frequently referred to as technology assessment. Opportunities for the transfer of technology to the company need to be continually reviewed. This is explored in further detail in Chapters 9 and 10.

Pause for thought 

When is reverse engineering copying? What is wrong with copying?

Unexploited patents

For those companies that invest heavily in R&D, the development of patents is part of the day-to-day operation of a busy research and development laboratory. Many of these patents could be used in the eventual development of a new product; many, however, will not. Research and development laboratories continually scan patent databases, such as Derwent in the United States, for listings of interesting patents. In so doing, they can identify patents that have not yet been exploited and use them to develop new product ideas. This highlights and emphasises an earlier point made in Chapter 6 about the dual benefits of investment in R&D. In order to scan, search and identify interesting and potentially useful patents, a company needs to be knowledgeable in that area. Without this prior knowledge scanning patent databases would be akin to looking at a foreign language that one does not understand.

Customers

Eric von Hippel's (1988) famous study of medical equipment manufacturers and users identified that the highest percentage of new product ideas originated with customers (the users). It has, however, since been suggested that this was a particular trait of that industry. It is, none the less, an important contribution to the debate about the origin of new product ideas. Indeed, in many other industries, especially fast-moving consumer goods (FMCG) industries, consumers are carefully studied to try to identify possible product ideas. For example, Procter & Gamble and Unilever continually visit consumers in their homes to watch and analyse the way they clean their furniture and do the laundry. Such studies have produced numerous product ideas. In addition, customer complaints about products are an excellent source of ideas. Many product packaging improvements have been the result of customer complaints. For example, many of the multiples have responded to complaints from customers about leaking liquid containers, such as those for milk and orange juice, and have developed improved packaging as a result.

Salesforce

Vendors (sales representatives) are a particularly good source of new product ideas. Gordon (1962) has shown the important role played by this group in generating new business opportunities. They spend a large part of their time with customers discussing their own products and learning about competitors' products. Many companies insist that their sales representatives provide weekly reports on all the companies they have visited, noting any possible product development opportunities. For example, sales representatives from Shell, BP and Hoecht frequently visit manufacturing companies which use chemicals in their manufacturing operations. It is during discussions with these manufacturers about the effectiveness of the chemicals that ideas for product modifications are generated. Several new chemicals have been developed for specific companies and later launched nationally or internationally as a new product.

This raises an important point about the role of sales representatives, especially in technology-intensive industries. They are expected to be qualified scientists or engineers who subsequently undergo extensive commercial training in marketing and sales. Such highly trained people are in stark contrast to the popular image of a sales representative often depicted as a smooth-talking second-hand car salesman!

Senior and top management

Many company leaders have taken personal responsibility for technological innovation in their companies. As far back as the 1950s, Alistair Pilkington continued to push the float glass process in Pilkington Glass against severe opposition. His idea was eventually successful. Akio Morita adopted a similar approach at Sony with the development of the Walkman, even though initial market research suggested that there was limited demand for such a product. However, not all leaders are successful. Edwin Land, former CEO of Polaroid, pushed his idea of instantly developed movies against fierce opposition, but the product was a major failure.

Those companies that have developed a reputation for innovation and new product development, such as Siemens, Nokia and 3M, rely on their senior management to concentrate on providing an environment for innovation to flourish. This is emphasised in the case study at the end of this chapter.

Brainstorming and synectics

Brainstorming is a creativity exercise used with groups of about six to eight people. The idea is for people to use their own imagination and creativity and to build on the ideas of others in the group. There is usually a chairperson who asks for and records ideas relating to a specific problem. People within the group are encouraged to be liberal and uninhibited with their suggestions. A slightly more involved and subtle approach called synectics has been developed by Gordon (1962), who suggests that if the problem under investigation remains a secret, more imaginative ideas will flow.

Individuals

In addition to the R&D department, sales representatives and marketers, product ideas can originate from areas not usually associated with product development. Accountancy departments, secretarial support staff and contract hire personnel have all been identified as originators of ideas for new products. Many inventors have remarked, after the event, that the original idea was conceived outside company time and far away from the company. Everyone has the ability to be creative.

Developing product concepts: turning business opportunities into product concepts

This activity involves transforming a list of ideas into potential product concepts. In some cases the identification of an opportunity is sufficient to reveal the product required. For example, a paint manufacturer may uncover a need for a new form of paint that will not drip on to carpets and clothes, is easy to apply, will wash off users' hands and clothes if spilt and is hard-wearing like conventional paints. In other cases the concept is clear but the details need to be added. For example, a domestic appliance manufacturer may discover that some of its customers have expressed interest in a domestic water-cleaning device. In this case, the manufacturer is clear that the appliance will need to be fitted in the home but much more information is required. Sometimes it may not be clear at all what form the product will take. For example, a chemical manufacturer may uncover an opportunity in the treatment of water for industry. The eventual product could take many different forms and use many different technologies, chemical treatment, mechanical treatment, etc. The idea is a long way from an actual product.

For a product idea to become a new product concept, Crawford and Di Benedetto (2008) argue that three inputs are required: form, technology and need.

- *Form*: This is the physical thing to be created (or in the case of a service, the sequence of steps by which the service will be created). It may still be vague and not precisely defined.
- *Technology*: In most cases there is one clear technology that is at the base of the innovation (for the 3M Post-it it was the adhesive; for the instamatic camera it was the chemical formulation which permitted partial development in light).
- *Need*: The benefits gained by the customer give the product value.

The following example illustrates this point. A mobile phone handset manufacturer may uncover the idea for incorporating a digital music player into its current range of handsets. All the details for the product at this stage remain unclear (some known, others not). This is simply an idea or a product concept. Once the concept starts to accumulate more information the project team may be able to sketch out possible forms for it. Clearly this will be influenced by the technology available from within the firm and what is available outside in the form of licensing or in the form of alliances (*see* Figure 16.5).

It is important to remember that an idea is just that, an idea, whereas a concept is the conjunction of all the essential characteristics of the product idea. This usually incorporates form, technology and need but lacks detail. The underlying message here is that product ideas without details are often more like dreams and wishes. For example, an aircraft manufacturer may wish for a noise-free aircraft engine, or a pharmaceutical company may wish for a cure for AIDS.

The screening of business opportunities

Screening product ideas is essentially an evaluation process. It is important to note that it is not a single, one-off activity as portrayed in many textbooks. It occurs at every stage of the new product development process (and is covered in Chapter 9 under 'Evaluating R&D projects') and involves such questions as:

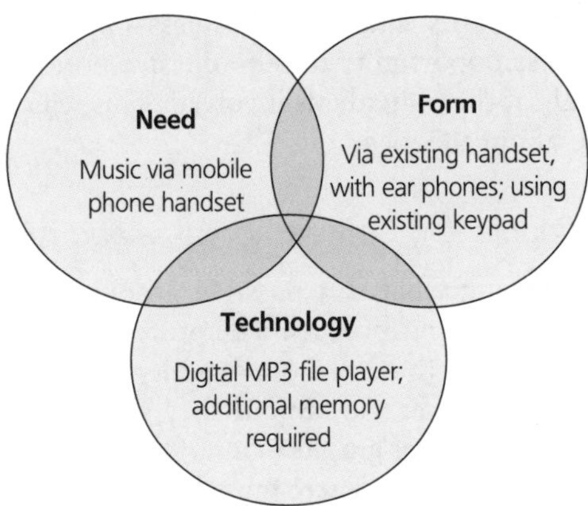

Figure 16.5 A new product concept

- Do we have the necessary commercial knowledge and experience?
- Do we have the technical know-how to develop the idea further?
- Would such a product be suitable for our business?
- Are we sure there will be sufficient demand?

To help with this activity firms often turn to product lead-users and product experts (Ozer, 2009). The main purpose of screening ideas is to select those that will be successful and drop those that will not – herein lies the difficulty. Trying to identify which ideas are going to be successful and which are not is extremely difficult. Many successful organisations have made serious errors at this point. The Research Corporation of America (RCA) identified the huge business opportunity of radio and television but failed to see the potential for videocassette recorders (VCR). Kodak and IBM failed to see the potential in photocopying but Xerox did not. The list grows each year and while the popular business press are quick to identify those companies which make a mistake they are not so quick to praise those companies

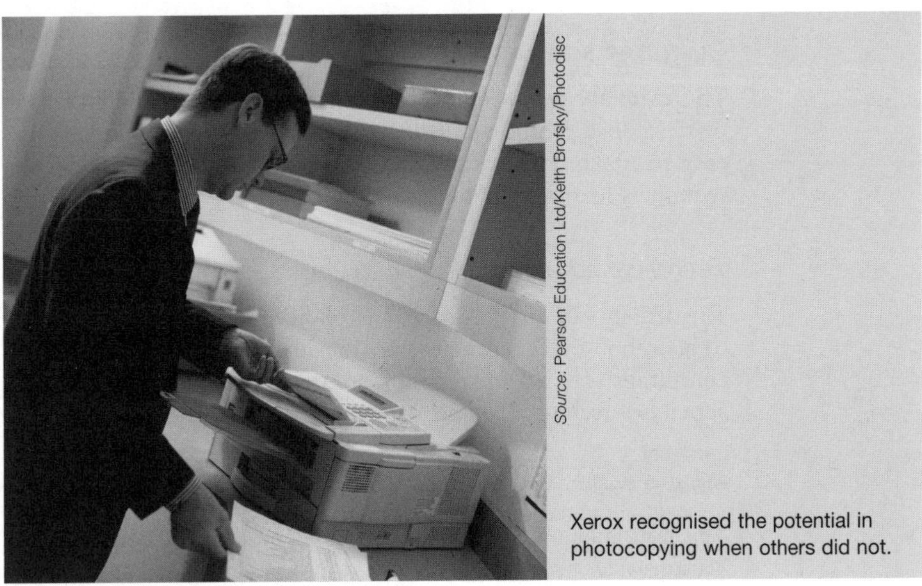

Source: Pearson Education Ltd/Keith Brofsky/Photodisc

Xerox recognised the potential in photocopying when others did not.

which identify successful business opportunities. 3M, for example, recognised a business opportunity in self-adhesive notes. Even here, persistence was required on behalf of the individuals involved. This was because, initially, the company was not sure about the idea.

Distinguishing between dreams and reality

Recognising what is a possible product and what is fantasy is an important part of the screening process. There are many examples of businesses rejecting a new product idea (business opportunity) because they did not believe it would work. Some of these are so famous they are known outside the world of business: Xerox and the computer graphical interface; Dyson and the bagless vacuum cleaner; Whittle and the jet engine. There must be a distinction between those opportunities that the business could develop into a product and those which it could not, and recognition of those that are likely to generate revenue and those that will not.

Market research will clearly provide valuable market analysis input at this stage to help in the decision process. This is covered in Chapter 9 along with other activities often associated with the screening activity, such as concept testing, product testing, market testing and test marketing. Organisations use a variety of different labels for very similar activities. The following represents an overview of many of the activities associated with the screening process.

Initial screen, entry screen or preliminary screen

This represents the first formal evaluation of the idea. Each of the ideas that came from the pool of concepts has to be given an initial screen. This will involve a technical feasibility check and marketing feasibility test, plus a comparison with the strategic opportunity. This would include evaluating whether the particular product would fit with the business's existing activities. The advantage of early screening is that it can be done quickly and easily and prevents expenditure on product ideas that are clearly not appropriate.

Customer screen, concept testing

This can vary between informal discussions with potential customers and feedback on developed prototypes. Concept testing is extremely difficult and mistakes are very easy to make. People have difficulty reacting to an entirely new product concept without a learning period, as discussed below.

Technical screen, technical testing

This activity can vary from a few telephone calls to technical experts to extensive analysis by an in-house R&D department or an analysis by a third party such as an independent consultant (often a university laboratory). This chapter and Chapter 9 discuss the activity of technical testing during which evaluations are continually undertaken.

Final screen

This normally involves the use of scoring models and computer assessment programs. Various new product ideas are fed into the program and a series of questions and assessments, with different weightings, are made, resulting in a scoring for each. One of the most serious criticisms of scoring models is their use of weights, because these are necessarily judgemental.

Business analysis

This may involve the construction of preliminary marketing plans, technical plans, financial reviews and projected budgets. All of these may raise potential problems that were previously unforeseen. It is not uncommon for new products to reach the mass-production stage only to encounter significant manufacturing difficulties, often when production is switched from one-off prototypes to high-volume manufacture.

New technology product blogs

Lead users and early adopters are often blogging or reading and commenting on blogs. Blogs, which are characterised by postings, links and readers' comments, create a virtual 'community' of blogger and readers. Members self-select, and then the community gels around a theme or idea, product, industry, hobby or any other subject. While community creation is one chief function of blogs, the information-sharing, entertainment, or self- or value-expressive functions are also important. Thus, new product development (NPD) managers can glean a great deal of information about what these audiences are thinking. The significance of blogging to NPD managers also lies in the shift of focus from being separate from to being immersed in these communities. Immersion enhances the potential of close relationships, sharing experiences and co-creating value with blogging communities through innovation. Droge *et al.* (2010) studied the roles of blogs in new product development. They found that people voluntarily join new product blogging communities, and if the manager of that product is not 'present' (at least as an observer of this 'straw poll'), an entire new product marketing agenda can be set by the community. Implicitly or explicitly, blogs can position the value proposition of the product in a prime target audience's mind. Such positioning could be advantageous or disastrous as far as the NPD manager is concerned.

Development of product prototypes

This is the phase during which the item acquires finite form and becomes a tangible good. It is at this stage that product designers may develop several similar prototypes with different styling. Manufacturing issues will also be discussed such as what type of process to use. For example, in the case of a tennis racket, engineers will discuss whether to manufacture using an injection-moulding or compression-moulding process. During this activity numerous technical developments will occur. This will include all aspects of scientific research and development, engineering development and design, possible technology transfer, patent analysis and cost forecasts.

Rapid prototyping

Reducing the time to develop products is a top priority for firms, especially in consumer markets. Pamela Buxton (2000) argues that time to market is no longer measured in years but months. In the food industry 'own label' development is extremely rapid. Brand management firms like Procter & Gamble, Unilever and Biersdorf have all reduced their product development times. Ten years ago development took eighteen months to two years. Now this has been cut to six to nine months. Industry analysts now argue that it is better to get to the market 90 per cent correct and grab the market opportunity rather than wait longer and enter the market 100 per cent correct (Buxton, 2000). It is not only the FMCG industries that are under pressure to reduce NPD times. Domestic appliance manufacturers such as Siemens, Hoover and AEG are also responding to the need to get new products into the marketplace more quickly.

One area that has seen a significant development is the area of rapid prototyping. This is the process of developing a range of prototypes quickly for consideration by the firm. Stereolithography (SLA) is the most widely used rapid prototyping technology. Stereolithography builds plastic parts or objects a layer at a time by tracing a laser beam on the surface of a vat of liquid photopolymer. This class of materials, originally developed for the printing and packaging industries, quickly solidifies wherever the laser beam strikes the surface of the liquid. Once one layer is completely traced, it is lowered a small distance into the vat and a second layer is traced right on top of the first. The self-adhesive property of the material causes the layers to bond to one another and eventually form a complete, three-dimensional object after many such layers are formed.

Stereolithography allows you to create almost any 3-D shape you can imagine. If you can get it into a computer-aided design (CAD) program, you can probably create it. Hoover used stereolithography during the development of its Vortex vacuum cleaner. This helped it get a product from drawing board to the retailer in 12 months. It was able to develop a range of prototype vacuum cleaners and test them before deciding on the most suitable design. Once produced, the object has the strength of polystyrene plastic. Which means that it can be drilled, mounted and cut. It enables the firm to try out the prototype in actual use. For example, a chair manufacturer will produce different arm-rest shapes using stereolithography and try them out on actual chairs to see how they feel.

The basic stereolithography process goes like this:

- create a 3-D model of your object in a CAD program;
- a piece of software chops the CAD model up into thin layers – typically 5–10 layers per millimeter;
- the 3-D printer's laser 'paints' one of the layers, exposing the liquid plastic in the tank and hardening it;
- the platform drops down into the tank a fraction of a millimetre and the laser paints the next layer; and
- this process repeats, layer by layer, until the model is complete.

It is not a particularly quick process. Depending on the size and number of objects being created, the laser might take a minute or two for each layer. A typical run might take 6–12 hours.

Stereolithography is generally considered to provide the greatest accuracy and best surface finish of any rapid prototyping technology. Over the years, a wide range of materials with properties mimicking those of several engineering thermoplastics have been developed. Limited selectively colour-changing materials for biomedical and other applications are available, and ceramic materials are currently being developed. The technology is also notable for the large object sizes that are possible.

Technical testing

Closely linked to the development of product prototypes is the technical testing of a new product. It is sometimes difficult to distinguish between where prototype development finishes and testing begins. This is because in many industries it is frequently an ongoing activity. Take the motor vehicle industry as an example. Engineers may be developing a new safety system for a vehicle. This might involve a new harness for the seat belt and a new airbag system. As the engineers begin designing the system they will be continually checking and testing that the materials for the belt are suitable, and that the sensors are not so sensitive that the airbag is inflated when the vehicle goes over a bump in the road. There will, of course, be final testing involving dummies and simulated crashes, but much of the technical testing is ongoing.

Market testing and consumer research

These activities have been covered in Chapter 15, so they will only be dealt with briefly here. The traditional approach to NPD involved a significant stage devoted to market testing. Developed products were introduced to a representative sample of the population to assess the market's reaction. This was usually carried out prior to a full-scale national launch of the product. This was the commonly accepted approach, especially in fast-moving consumer goods industries such as confectionery, household products, food and drink. More significantly, manufacturers have emphasised the need to be first into the market and have often skipped the test market. Linked to this is the fear that a test market may reveal a new product to competitors who may be able to react quickly and develop a similar product. Furthermore, the use of direct marketing and the internet has seen many new products being introduced via these developing channels.

In today's fiercely competitive marketplace products tend to go straight from consumer research and product development to national launch:

> *Marketers claim that consumer research techniques are now so sophisticated that full-blown tests are no longer necessary. Besides, once they have invested in R&D plus new plant, and created an advertising campaign, they might as well go national immediately. The fixed costs are so high that you might as well get on with it, says Mark Sherrington of marketing consultancy Added Value.* (*Management Today*, 1995)

The debate about the benefits and limitations of consumer research has raged for many years (*see* Chapter 15 for much more on this). Put simply, critics associated with the consumerism movement claim that most new products are actually minor variations of existing products. They further argue that consumers are not able to peer into the future and articulate what products they want. They suggest that the major innovations of the twentieth century, such as electricity, frozen food, television, microcomputers and telecommunications, have been the result of sustained technological research uninhibited by the demands of consumers. Marketers, on the other hand, argue that without consumer research technologists will produce products

Illustration 16.1

Be wary of consumer research

If consumer research had been conducted at the turn of the century, the responses garnered from people as they walked along dusty dirt tracks meandering across the meadows of England would have halted research into the motor car. If asked whether they would like to have a noisy, dirty machine that would be responsible for thousands of deaths and cause enormous amounts of pollution, their answer would probably have been 'no thank you'. Chapter 15 explores the issue in more detail.

Source: © Kirsti J. Black/Corbis

that are not what the market wants. There are many examples to support both arguments. The Sony Walkman is often cited by those critical of consumer research, since the product was initially rejected on the basis of insufficient features such as the ability to record, etc. Similarly, the Disk camera, developed by Eastman Kodak between 1980 and 1988, is used by supporters of consumer research to highlight the potential disaster of not seeking consumers' views. It was a very small instamatic camera designed to appeal to those seeking a simple-to-use machine. Unfortunately, it produced grainy photographs.

Research by Christensen and Bower (1995) and Daily (1996) suggests that listening to your customer may actually stifle technological innovation and be detrimental to long-term business success. Ironically, to be successful in industries characterised by technological change, firms may be required to pursue innovations that are not demanded by their current customers. The results of this study suggest that managers may sometimes be wise to ignore the advice of their existing customers, who are primarily interested in incremental product improvements. This argument of not relying too heavily on the market derives further support from research conducted by Schmidt (1995) (*see* Illustration 16.1). This revealed that for industrial products, technical activities are more important than marketing activities such as market assessment, detailed market study, product testing with customer and test marketing. Indeed, Schmidt argues that inadequate focus on the technical activities and excessive focus on marketing activities and the marketing concept are myopic.

How virtual worlds can help real-world innovations

By integrating users of virtual worlds into an interactive new product development process, companies can tap customers' innovative potential using the latest technology. Connecting the emerging technology of virtual worlds allows unique and inventive opportunities to capitalise on users' innovative potential and knowledge. The concept of avatar-based innovation may provide firms with new, original possibilities and enable them to take advantage of virtual worlds for innovation management. The latest advances of information and communication technologies enrich the interaction process and can improve new product development processes. Virtual worlds allow producers and consumers to swarm together with like-minded individuals to create new products and permit companies to find an audience to test, use and provide feedback on the content and products they create. A few path-finding companies have experimented with avatars as a source of innovation. In particular, the initiatives of Osram, Steelcase, Mazda and Toyota seem to have truly linked the concepts of open innovation and virtual worlds to employ the interactive technology for new product development. In a study of avatar-based innovation, Kohler *et al.* (2009) found that in order to fully realise the potential of avatar-based innovation, companies need to create a compelling open innovation experience and consider the peculiarities of virtual worlds.

Market introduction

Commercialisation is not necessarily the stage at which large sums of money are spent on advertising campaigns or multi-million-pound production plants, since a company can withdraw from a project following the results of test marketing.

It is important to remember that for some products, say in the pharmaceutical business, the decision to finance a project with 10 years of research is taken fairly early on in the development of the product and this is where most of the expense is incurred. With other fast-moving consumer goods, like foods, advertising is a large part of the cost, so the decision is taken towards the launch phase.

Launch

We must not lose sight of reality. Most new products are improvements or minor line extensions and may attract almost no attention. Other new products, e.g. a major cancer breakthrough or rapid transport systems without pollution, are so important that they will receive extensive television news coverage. Illustration 16.2

Illustration 16.2

Microsoft's Bing fights Google for market share

One year after its launch, Microsoft's rebranded search engine has made less than spectacular gains against its rivals. It has a market share of about 10 per cent, compared to 70 per cent for Google and 15 per cent for Yahoo.

Bing was launched in 2009 by Steve Ballmer, chief executive, at a West Coast technology conference with the aim of enabling 'people to find information quickly and use the information they've found to accomplish tasks and make smart decisions'. However, its underlying aim was to reverse the market-share losses suffered by its predecessor Live Search. Bing sought to set itself apart from Google's plain search-box home page and catch-all results with a striking full-page image and channels of interest such as shopping and travel. A funky and expensive advertising campaign accompanied the launch. Just five months later Microsoft said its US unique visitors had risen by 16 per cent to 83 million, while its share of internet searches had grown by 1.9 percentage points to 9.9 per cent.

Source: C. Nuttall (2010) Year-old Bing searches for share, FT.com, 24 May.

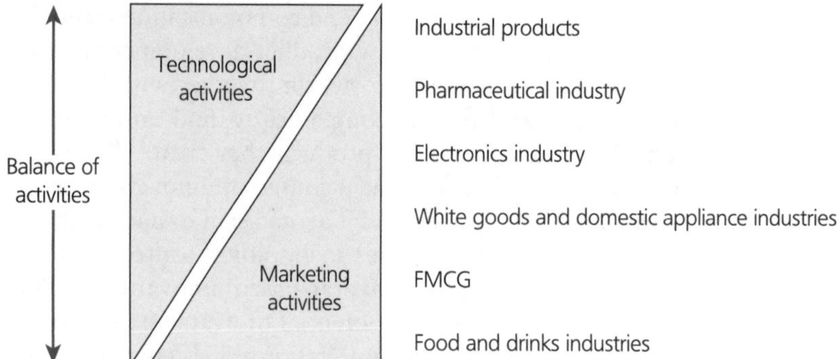

Figure 16.6 Classification of new product development activities across different industries

shows Microsoft's new product launch of Soapbox, its attempt to compete with YouTube and Yahoo for a part of the video-sharing market. The promotion for this was naturally almost entirely web based.

NPD across different industries

It has been stressed throughout this book that innovation and NPD in particular are context dependent. That is, the management of the process is dependent on the type of product being developed. A simple, but none the less useful, way of looking at this is to divide the wide range of activities involved in the development of a new product into technical and marketing activities. Figure 16.6 shows the NPD activities divided into the two categories. Against this are placed a variety of industries to illustrate the different balance of activities. It becomes clear that industrial products (products developed for use by other industries), such as a new gas-fired electricity generator, have many different considerations from those of a new soft drink. In the latter case there will be much more emphasis on promotion and packaging, whereas the electricity generator will have been designed and built following extensive technical meetings with the customer concentrating on the functional aspects of the product. Clearly, in between these two extremes the balance of activities is more equal. In a recent study of NPD involving 12 firms across a variety of industries, Olson *et al.* (1995) found that cross-functional teams helped shorten the development times of truly innovative products. More bureaucratic structures may provide better outcomes for less innovative products.

Organisational structures and cross-functional teams

Industrialists and academics have for many years been interested in the subject of how organisations are structured and the relationships that occur between individuals and functions. The nature of the industry in general and the product being developed in particular will significantly influence the choice of structure. Moreover, the organisation structure will considerably affect the way its activities are managed. It is not possible to alter one without causing an effect on the other. For example, the introduction of concurrent engineering techniques means that companies will need to be less reliant on functional operations and adopt the use of project management and cross-functional teams. Organisational structures and teams will therefore be examined together in this section.

The use of cross-functional teams increases creativity in new product development leading to shorter development time and higher product innovativeness. Research in new product development has identified a number of organisational practices associated with supporting organisational creativity in cross-functional teams including frequent and open communication, building organisational slack, attitude to risk, and top management commitment (Bunduchi, 2009).

Teams and project management

The use of teams within organisations is certainly nothing new. In sport, having between five and fifteen individuals all working together has been the foundation for games all over the world. Similarly, within organisations teams have been used for many years, especially on large projects. In industry, however, the concept of having teams of individuals from different functions with different knowledge bases is a recent development. Jones (1997) suggests that in the field of medicine the practice of having a group of experts from different functions working together on a project has been around for many years. In manufacturing industries the use of cross-functional teams has occurred in parallel with the introduction of concurrent engineering.

New product project teams in small to medium-sized organisations are usually comprised of staff from several different functions who operate on a 'part-time' basis. Membership of the project team may be just one of the many roles they perform. In larger organisations, where several projects are in progress at any one time, there may be sufficient resources to enable personnel to be wholly concerned with a project. Ideally, a project team will have a group of people with the necessary skills who are able to work together, share ideas and reach compromises. This may include external consultants or key component suppliers.

Functional structures

Unlike the production, promotion and distribution of products, NPD is a cross-disciplinary process and suffers if it is segregated by function. The traditional functional company structure allows for a strong managerial layer with information flowing up and down the organisation. Each function would usually be responsible for one or more product groups or geographical areas (*see* Figure 16.7).

Another common approach used by many large manufacturing companies is to organise the company by product type. Each product has its own functional activities. Some functions, however, are centralised across the whole organisation. This is to improve efficiency or provide common features (*see* Figure 16.8). This type of structure supports the notion of product platforms (*see* Chapter 11) where a generic group of technologies are used in a variety of products. Sony, Philips and Nokia all have

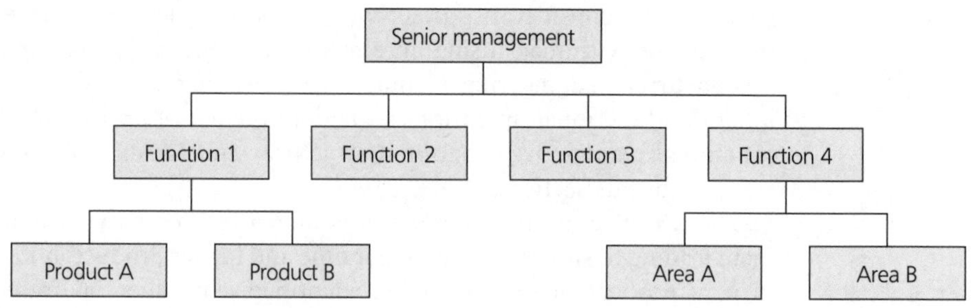

Figure 16.7 Functional company organisation

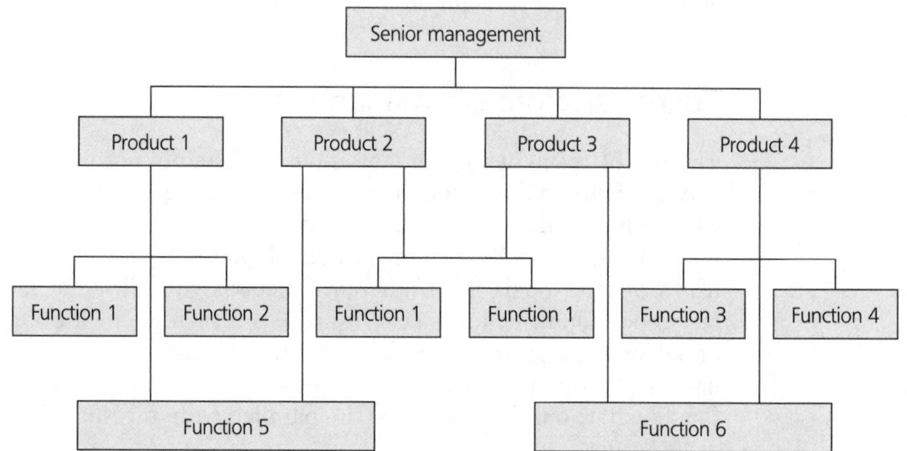

Figure 16.8 Functional company: diversification by product with centralised functions

centralised R&D activities where the majority of products are developed, allowing for a high degree of technology transfer between product groups. This is one of the key arguments in favour of a centralised R&D function, of which more later.

It is important to note that while many organisations have clearly defined company structures, closer inspection of the actual activities within these companies will invariably reveal an informal structure that sits on top of the formal structure. This is made up of formal and informal communication channels and networks that help to facilitate the flow of information within the organisation (*see* Figure 16.9).

Matrix structures

The use of a matrix structure requires a project-style approach to NPD. Each team will comprise a group of between four and eight people from different functions. A matrix structure is defined as any organisation that employs a multiple-command system including not only a multiple-command management structure but also related support mechanisms and associated organisational culture and behaviour patterns (Ford and Randolph, 1992).

Matrix structures are associated with dual lines of communication and authority (Tushman and Nadler, 1978; Lawrence *et al.*, 1982). They are seen as cross-functional

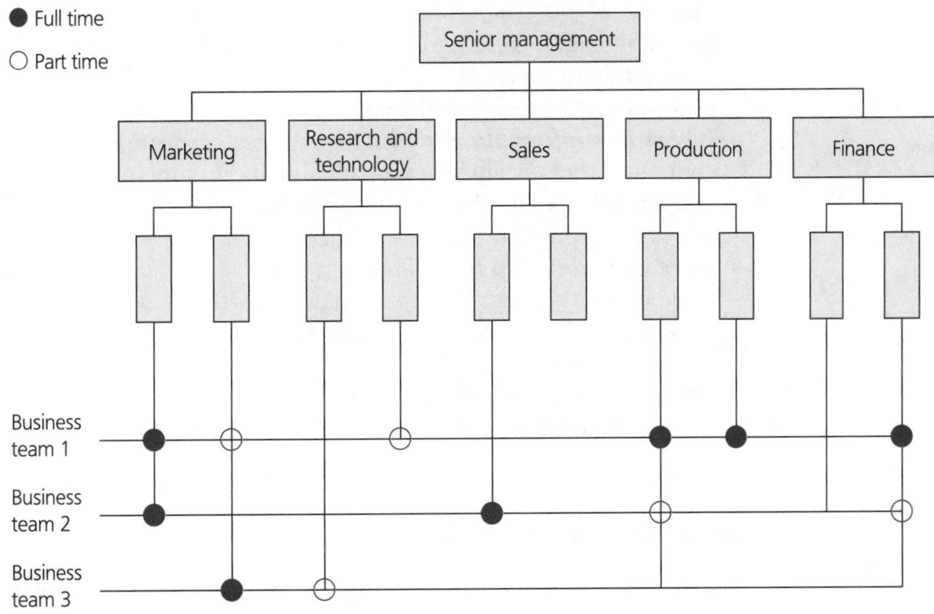

Figure 16.9 Matrix structure at Siemens

because they involve bringing people together from two or more separate organisational functional areas. This can be seen in Figure 16.9, which shows the matrix structure at Siemens. The traditional hierarchy is functional, while the horizontal overlay consists of business areas known as business teams. Business team 1 comprises one full- and one part-time member from marketing, one part-time member from R&D, two full-time members from production and one full-time member from finance. Between them this group would manage a number of projects. There would be a team leader for each business team. However, this person would not necessarily be, and often is not, the most senior member of the group. The choice of business team leader is based on the type of project the team is undertaking. For example, a team looking at the introduction of new products is likely to be led by someone from the marketing function, even though there will almost certainly be someone more 'senior' from another function within the business team.

Matrix structure at Siemens

The following are some of the features and benefits of a matrix organisational structure that have been identified in the literature. However, for a full review of matrix organisation and project management see Ford and Randolph (1992).

- *Provision of additional channels of communication.* The combination of a matrix structure and business teams ensures that there is extensive lateral communication between functions. The diagram in Figure 16.9 shows how marketing personnel involved in business teams 1, 2 and 3 bring back to the marketing function knowledge of activities of the other functions. Communication skills are also developed as individual business team members learn the 'languages' of the other functions (Allen, 1984).

- *Increase in informal communication channels*. In addition to the increase in formal linkages, there is also an increase in informal networks between personnel from different functions. These develop from friendships and cooperation formed as a product of formal linkages.
- *Increase in information loads*. The increase in formal and informal channels of communication means that individuals collect more information. This information is brought back into the function and disseminated among colleagues in the group. There is support for this view in Joyce (1986).
- *Increase in diversity for individuals*. Some individuals may be involved in two or three business teams. Their role may be part time or full time. This enables them to work with a variety of people from different backgrounds and disciplines across the organisation. This type of working environment enlarges an individual's experience and outlook and provides them with an improved understanding of the organisation's entire activities (Kolodny, 1979).

Corporate venturing

The idea behind corporate venturing is that fledgling businesses should be given the freedom to grow outside the constraints of an existing large, established organisation. Conventional management thinking argues that new ventures should be sheltered from the normal planning and control systems, otherwise they will be strangled. Ideally, they should be given high-level sponsorship from senior management, but must be able to manage their own relationships with other companies. Many large organisations such as Nokia, IBM and General Electric have a long experience of corporate venturing stretching back to the 1960s. However, following some high-profile failures, most notably by Shell in the mid-1980s, corporate venturing fell out of favour. More recent research suggests that the record of corporate venturing compared to external venture capitalists shows that the latter do no better than the corporations (Lorenz, 1993).

An internal corporate venture is a separate organisation or system designed to facilitate the needs of a new business. Companies usually adopt an internal corporate venture when the product involved is outside their existing activities. The case study at the end of this chapter shows how 3M use internal corporate venturing to help transform business ideas into genuine businesses.

Project management

Whichever organisation structure is adopted, the project itself has to be well planned, managed and controlled. It is the setting of achievable targets and realistic objectives that helps to ensure a successful project. In addition, ensuring that resources are available at the appropriate time contributes to good project management.

Many organisations have tried and tested project management programmes and organisational systems to help ensure that projects are well managed. But even in these well-run organisations there will often be individual project managers who build a reputation for delivering on time and for being able to turn a doubtful project into a successful project. This introduces the subject of managing people within organisations. This is not the place to explore these issues which are at the heart of theories of organisational behaviour. They are comprehensively examined by others such as Mullins (2003).

Reducing product development times through computer-aided design

When concurrent engineering is used in conjunction with other management tools the results can be very impressive. For example, the aerospace and automobile industries have been using computer-aided design (CAD) for more than 20 years. In both these industries product development times are relatively long, sometimes lasting 10 years. The ability to use CAD lies at the heart of broader efforts to compress product development times and share information across an organisation. This is even more important when there are several companies involved in the manufacture of a single product. The Airbus consortium of companies which manufactures aircraft has been using CAD to help with its very complicated product data management (PDM). This is particularly useful in helping speed up engineering and manufacturing processes. In addition, the Airbus Concurrent Engineering (ACE) project is helping to develop common product development processes across the consortium (Baxter, 1997).

The marketing/R&D interface

There are many difficulties in managing cross-functional teams in technology-intensive industries where the technology being used is complex and difficult to understand for those without scientific training. In such industries, scientists and engineers are often heard berating their commercial colleagues for failing to comprehend the technical aspects of the project. This introduces a common difficulty: the need to manage communication flows across the marketing and R&D boundaries. This problem was first recognised as important in the 1970s (Rubenstein *et al.*, 1976) and remains a critical issue in new product development (Souder and Sherman, 1993).

The main barriers to an effective R&D/marketing interface have been found to be related to perceptual, cultural, organisational and language factors (Wang, 1997). Marketing managers tend to focus on shorter time-spans than R&D managers, who adopt much longer time-frames for projects. In addition, the cultural difference results from the different training and backgrounds of the two groups. For example, scientists seek recognition from their peers in the form of published papers and ultimately Nobel prizes, as well as recognition from the company that employs them. Marketing managers, on the other hand, are able only to seek recognition from their employer, usually in the form of bonuses, promotions, etc. The organisational boundaries arise out of departmental structures and the different activities of the two groups. Finally, the language barrier is soon identified in discussions with the two groups, because while marketers talk about product benefits and market position, R&D managers talk the quantitative language of performance and specifications.

Table 16.2 How marketing and R&D perceive each other

Marketing people about technical people	Technical people about marketing people
Have a very narrow view of the world	Want everything now
Never finish developing a product	Are focusing on customers who do not know what they want
Have no sense of time	Quick to make promises they cannot keep
Are interested only in technology	Cannot make up their minds
Do not care about costs	Cannot possibly understand technology
Have no idea of the real world	Are superficial
Are in a different world	Too quick in introducing new products
Always looking for standardisation	Want to ship products before they are ready
Should be kept away from customers	Are not interested in the scientist's problems

The extent of the integration required between marketing and R&D depends on the environment within which product development occurs. In many technology-intensive industries where the customer's level of sophistication is low, the extent of integration required may be less than that needed where the customer's level of sophistication is high and the technology intensity of the industry low. For example, in the pharmaceutical industry (high level of technological intensity) customers' sophistication is low because they are unable to communicate their needs. They may want a cure for cancer but have no idea how this can be achieved. On the other hand, in the food industry (low level of technological intensity) customers are able to articulate their needs. For example, they can explain that a particular food might taste better or look better if it contained certain ingredients. (For a more detailed discussion on the difficulties of managing the relations between R&D and marketing, *see* Bruce and Cooper, 1997.) Table 16.2 illustrates some commonly held beliefs by marketing colleagues and R&D colleagues about one another.

Pause for thought 

It seems hybrid managers are necessary to bridge the communication gap between scientists and marketing! What does this mean?

High attrition rate of new products

As new product projects evolve and progress through each stage of development, many will be rightly cancelled or stopped for a wide variety of reasons. The failure of a product idea to be developed into a product is not necessarily a bad thing. Indeed, it may save the company enormous sums of money. This is explored more fully in Chapter 8. More serious problems arise when, as often happens, new products are launched in the expectation of success, but then ultimately fail, leaving high costs to be met by the company. Sometimes a product can cause harm and suffering, but these are rare; the example of the Thalidomide drug is a chilling reminder of a product failure.

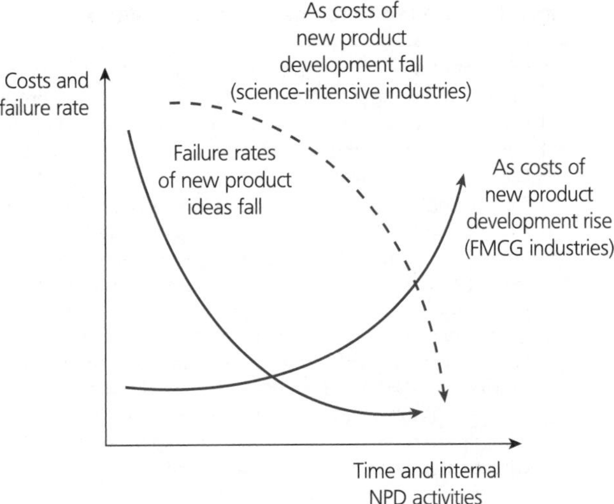

Figure 16.10 Product failures

Clearly, product ideas are rejected throughout the new product development process. Figure 16.10 shows the traditional view of the rising cost of new product development as it moves closer to launch. This is based on FMCG industries which involves high-cost promotional campaigns. Arguably, the cost curve for science-intensive industries is inverse, with high costs being associated with R&D activities and relatively low-cost promotional activities towards the end of the development.

Studies of why new products fail are difficult to undertake. This is partly due to an unwillingness by companies to let outsiders know that they have been unsuccessful. Also, it is difficult to untangle what happened and identify the cause of failure. With hindsight things often do not look the same. People are, in many cases, very defensive about their role in the development of a new product. There is always a reluctance to be associated with failure. Studies by Cooper (1988a), Urban *et al.* (1987) and Crawford and Di Benedetto (2008) have identified many of the often cited reasons for failure. These are listed in Table 16.3.

There is much debate about the failure rates of new products, which vary widely. The collection of data on this issue is problematic, with a wide range of different definitions being used across industries and countries. Some companies now claim a maximum failure rate of 10 per cent. This is a long way from the failure rate often quoted in the popular business press of 90 per cent. Products rarely fail in the marketplace: weak products are usually eliminated prior to entry to the market. Consequently any such failures command huge publicity, as Illustration 16.3 shows.

The article from the *Financial Times* shows that even multinational companies with an impressive heritage of developing brands and managing products can make mistakes. For Coca-Cola the difficulties encountered with its Dasani brand potentially highlight a poor match with its perception in Europe and the new product. Dasani has been very successful in the United States. Indeed, sales in 2003 place it second in terms of market share of bottled water. It could simply be a combination of poor marketing communications and public relations and maybe some misfortune. But, it could also signify a more serious concern. That is, the reluctance on the part of the European consumer to separate Dasani from its parent brand

Table 16.3 Reasons for new product failure

1	Product offers nothing new or no improved performance
2	Inadequate budget to develop ideas or market the product
3	Poor market research, positioning, misunderstanding consumer needs
4	Lack of top management support
5	Did not involve customer
6	Exceptional factors such as government decision (e.g. new law on handgun control may seriously affect the manufacturer of a new handgun)
7	Market too small, either forecasting error with sales or insufficient demand
8	Poor match with company's capabilities, company has insufficient experience of the technology or market
9	Inadequate support from channel (a problem experienced by Dyson)
10	Competitive response was strong and competitors were able to move quickly to face the challenge of the new product (P&G highlighted weaknesses with Unilever's Persil Power)
11	Internal organisational problems, often associated with poor communication
12	Poor return on investment forcing company to abandon project
13	Unexpected changes in consumer tastes/fashion

Source: Cooper, R.G. (1988a) The dimensions of industrial new product success and failure, *Journal of Marketing*, Vol. 43, No. 3, 93–103. Crawford, M. and Di Benedetto, A. (2008) *New Products Management*, 9th (International) edn, McGrawHill, USA. Urban, G.L., Hauser, J.R. and Dholaka, N. (1987) *Essentials of New Product Management*, Prentice-Hall, Englewood Cliffs, NJ.

Illustration 16.3

Coke cans plans for Dasani in France

Coca-Cola has shelved plans for a spring launch of its Dasani bottled mineral water in France – regarded by the company as its most important product debut there since Diet Coke – and Germany.

The US drinks company's decision followed the recall of the brand in the UK after a health scare. Plans for a relaunch there have been dropped.

It said: 'Although this is an isolated and resolved incident in Great Britain, Coca-Cola has also decided to postpone the introduction of the Dasani brand in France and Germany, as the timing is no longer considered optimal.' It added, however, that it would launch in France and Germany later and claimed the brand might yet have some future in the UK.

Coke withdrew Dasani after discovering in it illegal levels of bromate, a chemical that could increase the risk of cancer. It followed ridicule in the media after it became known the product was processed tap water from Sidcup, south-east London.

The Dasani for continental Europe, however, would have been sourced from a spring in Belgium. However, few analysts believed the brand could have competed against Perrier, Evian and Vittel in France after its UK difficulties. The company said it had spent about £1.75 million on marketing Dasani in the UK before withdrawal. It would not give an estimate of the cost of the UK recall.

Source: Pearson Education Ltd/81A Productions/Photolibrary

Source: J. Johnson and A. Jones (2004) Coke cans plans for Dasani in France, *Financial Times*, 25 March. Reprinted with permission.

Coca-Cola. In the bottled-water market the association with all things pure may be particularly necessary, hence Evian's association with the Alps and Buxton's association with the hills in the peak district in Britain. In Europe it may be that Coca-Cola may have to work particularly hard to distance itself from Dasani. This may lead some to question the financial benefits of entering the very competitive European bottled-water market.

Case study

An analysis of 3M, the innovation company

Introduction

Any review of the literature on new product development and innovation management will uncover numerous references to 3M. The organisation is synonymous with innovation and has been described as 'a smooth running innovation machine' (Mitchell, 1989). Year after year 3M is celebrated in the *Fortune* 500 rankings as the 'most respected company' and the 'most innovative company'. Management gurus from Peter Drucker to Tom Peters continually refer to the company as a shining example of an innovative company. This case study takes a look at the company behind some of the most famous brands in the marketplace, including Post-it® Notes. It examines the company's heritage and shows how it has arrived at this enviable position. Furthermore, the case study attempts to clarify what it is that makes 3M stand out from other organisations.

Background

Originally known as the Minnesota Mining and Manufacturing Company, with its headquarters in St Paul, Minnesota, 3M was established in 1902 to mine abrasive minerals for the production of a single product, sandpaper. From these inauspicious beginnings, the company has grown organically, concentrating on the internal development of new products in a variety of different industries. The latest review of the company's position reveals that it manufactures over 60,000 products, has operations in 61 countries, employs 75,000 people and has achieved an average year-on-year growth in sales of 10 per cent (see Figure 16.11). Its products include Scotch adhesive tapes, fibre-optic connectors, abrasives, adhesives, floppy disks, aerosol inhalers, medical diagnostic products and Post-it Notes.

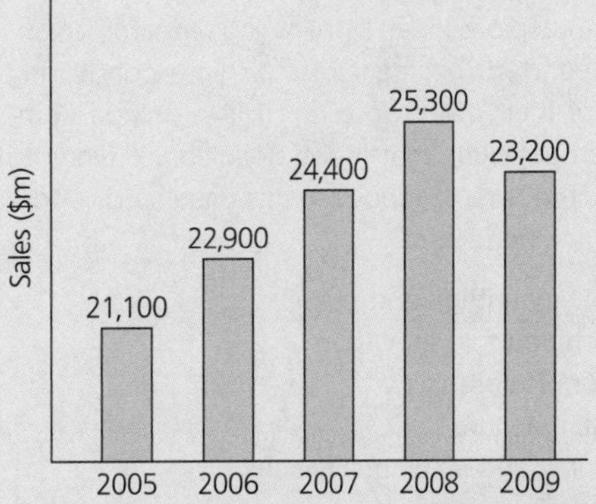

Figure 16.11 3M sales over the past five years

Source: Compiled from data from 3M international web page: www.3m.com.

3M gave the world 'wet or dry' abrasives, which did so much to reduce the incidence of respiratory disease in the 1920s. It invented self-adhesive tape in 1925, light-reflective materials in the 1940s and pioneered magnetic recording and photocopying. This heritage established the technology from which many of its products are still derived. To reinforce this impressive performance, 3M is consistently ranked among the top 10 of America's most admired companies in the US journal *Fortune*, in its annual review

Source: A. Harrison/Pearson Education Ltd

→

of the top 500 companies in the United States. 3M is a large and unusually diverse company.

The 3M approach to innovation

Many writers, academics and business leaders have argued that the key to successful innovation is good management (Henderson, 1994). Arguably, this is precisely what 3M has mastered. A closer inspection, however, will reveal that the company has combined a variety of management techniques, such as good communications and the setting of clear objectives with a company culture built on more than 90 years of nurturing ideas and fostering creativity. It uses a combination of structured research and individual freedom to explore ideas by allowing research scientists to spend 15 per cent of their time conducting projects of their own choosing. It is a unique combination of activities that is, by definition, difficult to replicate. They are described in this case study under the following headings:

1. Company heritage and culture
2. The demand for innovation
3. Freedom for creativity
4. Tolerating failure
5. Autonomy and small businesses
6. High profile for science and technology
7. Communication and technology transfer

Company heritage and culture

Through a combination of formal and informal processes, the company has developed a culture devoted to creating new products and building new businesses. This is partly based on the simple idea of hiring good people and trusting them. Indeed, this is the first goal that is stated in 3M's formal principles of management: 'the promotion of entrepreneurship and the insistence upon freedom in the workplace to pursue innovative ideas' (Osborn, 1988: 18).

The demand for innovation

While the sales performance in Figure 16.11 is impressive, it conceals an important statistic; that is, 30 per cent of the company's sales come from products that are less than four years old. Indeed, this is a business objective that every 3M business manager has to try to achieve. What this means is that these business managers are under pressure to ensure that not only do they develop new products but that these new products will eventually represent 30 per cent of the business's sales. This objective has been effectively communicated throughout the organisation and is now ingrained within the management style and part of the culture of the company. Hence, the search for new ideas is part of daily activities.

Senior managers from other large manufacturing companies would rightly argue that a similar percentage of sales within their own companies comes from products less than four years old. However, the difference between 3M and other organisations is that 3M has developed this approach over many years and has worked hard to ensure that developing new products is much higher on the agenda in management meetings than at other companies. Moreover, the success of the approach is due to the continual reinforcement of the objective. Indeed, the performance of individual business managers is partly judged on whether they are able to achieve the objective.

The 30 per cent objective was first introduced in the 1980s when 25 per cent of sales had to come from products less than four years old. This was altered in 1992 to 30 per cent. 3M has recently added another goal, which is to ensure that 10 per cent of sales come from products that have been in the market for only one year.

Freedom for creativity

Scientists and engineers are given time to work on projects and ideas that they consider to be of potential interest to the company and 15 per cent of an individual's work week time may be dedicated to such activities. This is not exclusive to 3M and is common practice in most large R&D laboratories. None the less, it is an effective method of providing room for creativity and another way of showing that the organisation encourages innovative effort. Indeed, it is a method of providing resources to entrepreneurs, allowing them to work on ideas without having to seek out approval from the organisation. Another way of allocating resources is the use of grants. Known as 'genesis grants', these give researchers up to $75,000 to develop their ideas into potential product opportunities.

One of 3M's most famous new products was the result of this practice, the Post-it Note. Spencer Silver and Arthur Fry both invoked the 15 per cent rule to allow them to work on the project that eventually led to its development.

Spencer Silver was a 3M research chemist working on adhesive technology. His brief was to produce the strongest adhesive on the market. By some extraordinary mischance he developed an adhesive that had none of the properties he was looking for, but which did have two interesting properties which he had never previously encountered: it could be reused and it left no residue on the material to which it was applied. Yet no one could find a use for it and the idea was shelved.

Art Fry, one of Spencer Silver's colleagues, sang in a choir. Every Sunday he would carefully mark his hymnbook with slips of paper and every Sunday the slips fell out. Then he remembered Spencer Silver's useless adhesive. Applied to paper strips, Art Fry found that they made fine book markers that did not fall out when he opened the book. Post-it brand technology had been developed ten years before Art Fry discovered what to do with it!

In a lecture on the subject of innovation, the 3M vice-president for research and development (Coyne, 1996) reported that:

> *The 15 per cent rule is meaningless. Some of our technical people use more than 15 per cent of their time on projects of their own choosing. Some use less than that; some none at all. The figure is not so important as the message, which is this: the system has some slack in it. If you have a good idea, and the commitment to squirrel away time to work on it, and the raw nerve to skirt your manager's expressed desires, then fine.*

Tolerating failure

'It's easier to be critical than creative' is an adaptation of a famous quote from Benjamin Disraeli. It captures the essence of 3M's approach to tolerating failure. Most large companies with large R&D departments will have many ongoing new product research projects. Many will consume large amounts of resources and will not result in a new product. This fact is part of the new product game. Those close to the game are aware of this; at 3M it is argued that everyone is aware of the need to try new ideas. Its founder and early chief executive, W.L. Knight, stated over 60 years ago that:

> *A management that is destructively critical when mistakes are made, kills initiative, and it is essential that we have people with initiative if we are to continue to grow.*

Vasilash (1995) suggests that many of the senior managers within 3M are known to have made at least one mistake in their career while they tried to be innovative, thereby suggesting that W.L. Knight's philosophy continues.

3M has had its share of colossal failures. In the 1920s one of the company's top inventors had an incredible flash of brilliance: maybe people could use sandpaper as a replacement for razor blades. Instead of shaving your face or legs, you could just sand off the whiskers. Every man and woman would need it. The company would sell the product by the ton! Not surprisingly the idea was not realised in practice – but the inventor was not punished for following his idea. For every 1,000 ideas only 100 are written up as formal proposals. Only a fraction of these become new product ventures and over half of the company's new product ventures fail (Coyne, 1996).

Autonomy and small businesses

Like many companies 3M realises that large organisations, with their inevitable corresponding structures and systems, can sometimes inhibit the creative dynamism often required to foster innovative effort. Hence, it has adopted an approach that enables individuals and groups within the organisation to establish small internal venture groups, with managers free to make their own decisions, develop their own product lines and take responsibility for the results, without continuous coordination across the company (Stewart, 1996). This approach attempts to offer an entrepreneurial environment under a corporate umbrella.

Provided that certain financial measures are met, such start-up venture groups follow a well-trodden path: a new business operation starts out as a project, if sales reach $1 million it becomes a fully fledged product. At $20 million, it becomes an independent product department separate from its parent department. If it continues to grow it will be spun off as a separate autonomous division. Currently, divisions characteristically have $200 million in sales. Experience has taught the company that in the early days of a business's life, many decisions are taken through informal discussions among the individuals involved. There are usually insufficient resources to allow for lengthy and detailed analysis, which is more common in more established businesses.

→

High profile for science and technology

Although the company was formed around a single technology, sandpaper, today 3M makes use of more than 100 technologies such as membranes, biotechnology, artificial intelligence, high-vacuum thin films and superconductivity. These technologies underpin the products that the company develops and manufactures. To support these activities the company invests 6.5 per cent of its annual sales turnover in research and development. This is about twice that of the top 50 industrial companies in the United States. The money is used to employ over 7,500 scientists and technologists in developing new and interesting technology. It is this technological intensity that provides the company with the competitive advantage to compete with its rivals.

It is important to note that while the company is technology-intensive, this does not imply a single-minded, technology-push approach to innovation.The role of the marketplace and users plays an important part in product development. For example, 3M's famous Scotch tape was once manufactured strictly as an industrial product, until a salesman got the idea of packaging it in clear plastic dispensers for home and office use.

Communication and technology transfer

The communication of ideas helps to ensure that a company can maximise the return on its substantial investments in the technology. Very often it is the combination of apparently diverse technologies through technology transfer that has led to major product innovations. For example, microreplication technology is the creation of precise microscopic, three-dimensional patterns on a variety of surfaces, including plastic film. When the surface is changed numerous product possibilities emerge. It was first developed for overhead projectors, its innovative feature being a lens made of a thin piece of plastic with thousands of tiny grooves on its surface. Microreplication helped the plastic lens to perform better than the conventional lens made of heavy glass. 3M became the world's leading producer of overhead projectors. It is this technology, which can be traced back to the 1960s, that has spread throughout 3M and led to a wide range of products, including better and brighter reflective material for traffic signs; 'floptical' disks for data storage; laptop computer screens; and films.

Struggling with the innovation dilemma: efficiency vs creativity

In December 2000, James McNerney, a former General Electric executive was selected as 3M's next CEO. McNerney was the first 3M CEO to come from outside the company and brought with him the GE playbook for achieving operational efficiency. One of his key initiatives was introducing the total quality management Six Sigma programme, a series of management techniques designed to increase efficiency. For the most part the implementation of the Six Sigma programme was successful as it focused on the operations (manufacturing/logistics) side of the business. However, when 3M's R&D personnel were asked to adopt Six Sigma processes, the results were less favourable. While established operational processes like manufacturing require strict monitoring, measuring, and a regimented set of procedures, the innovation process requires a different approach.

3M felt stifled by the new structure and pressured to produce more new products faster. The result was a greater number of incremental product-line extensions than true new product innovations. Traditionally, 3M drew at least one-third of sales from products released in the past five years, but in 2006 that fraction has fallen to one-quarter of sales. In 2004, 3M was ranked No. 1 on the *Business Week*/BCG list of Most Innovative Companies. In 2007 the company dropped to number seven.

After four and a half years at 3M, McNerney left to take the CEO position at Boeing. Now his successor, George Buckley, seems to recognise the negative impact the process-focused programme had on the company's creativity. Many of the workers say they feel reinvigorated now that the corporate emphasis has shifted back to growth and innovation from McNerney's focus on process and short-term profits (see Chapter 3 for more on the innovation dilemma).

2010

3M is everywhere, says George Buckley, the chairman and CEO of 3M. (He is British, with a PhD in electrical engineering.) In 2009, he said, 'even in the worst economic times in memory, we released over 1,000 new products'. Apple and many others could not do what they do without 3M. Most people do not realise that 3M products are embedded in other products and places: cars, factories, hospitals, homes and offices (Feldman and Feldman, 2010).

3M continues to inspire and encourage innovation and creativity to accelerate growth and deliver excellent financial results. Buckley told stockholders at the company's annual meeting in St. Paul:

> *The people of 3M are once again driving innovation through their energy and imagination . . . At its core, 3M remains an idea company that prospers best when we commit ourselves to invest in ideas, technology development and new products.*

Buckley cited increased investments in research and development – up more than 11 per cent – and the steady increase in the introduction of new products – up by about 4 per cent in the past two years – as examples of 3M's commitment to innovation.

Why is that important? Because as 3M's older products grow outmoded or become commodities, it must replace them. 'Our business model is literally new-product innovation', says Larry Wendling, who oversees 3M's corporate research. The company, as a result, had in place a goal to generate 30 per cent of revenue from new products introduced in the past five years. By 2005, when McNerney left to run Boeing, the percentage was down to 21 per cent, and much of the new-product revenue had come from a single category, optical films. (3M also has a history of acquisitions and has announced deals recently.)

It is safe to say that no 3M product will generate the buzz of, say, the next iPhone. But 3M has never been about inventing the Next Big Thing. It's about inventing hundreds and hundreds of Next Small Things, year after year. Things like Cubitron II. Buckley explains that Cubitron II is an industrial abrasive that cuts faster, lasts longer, sharpens itself, and requires less elbow grease than any other abrasive on the market. Introduced last year, it's selling like crazy, to the CEO's delight. 'How the heck do [you] innovate in abrasives?', he asks. 'A 106-year-old business for us! For goodness' sake – it's sandpaper!' Catching himself a moment later, he jokes, 'I probably need to get out more.' Maybe so, but you can understand what he is excited about: little things like grains of sand that add up to the big business that is 3M (Feldman and Feldman, 2010).

Discussion

While few would argue with 3M's successful record on innovation, there may be some who would argue that, compared to companies such as Microsoft, IBM and GlaxoSmithKline, its achievements in terms of growth have not been as spectacular. However, the point here is not that 3M is the most successful company or even that it is the most innovative, although one could surely construct a strong case, merely that the company has a long and impressive performance when it comes to developing new products.

This case study has highlighted some of the key activities and principles that contribute to 3M's performance. Many of these are not new and are indeed used by other companies. In 3M's case they may be summarised as an effective company culture that nurtures innovation and a range of management techniques and strategies that together have delivered long-term success. Many companies pay lip service to the management principles and practice set out in this case study. There is evidence that 3M supports these fine words with actions.

The struggle between efficiency and creativity is one many public companies face. The market values of company stocks are impacted more by short-term results rather than long-term prospects; and executives have an incentive to drive those results.

There are no easy answers and the best solution most likely lies somewhere between the two extremes of either process control or open-ended innovation.

Source: Coyne, W.E. (1996) Innovation lecture given at the Royal Society, 5 March; Henderson, R. (1994) Managing innovation in the information age, *Harvard Business Review*, January–February, 100–105; Mitchell, R. (1989) Masters of innovation: how 3M keeps its new products coming, *Business Week*, April, 58–63; Osborn, T. (1988) How 3M manages innovation, *Marketing Communications*, November/December, 17–22; Stewart, T. (1996) 3M fights back, *Fortune*, Vol. 133, No. 2, 5 February, 42–7; Vasilash, G.S. (1995) Heart and soul of 3M, *Production*, Vol. 107, No. 6, 38–9; Feldman, A. and Feldman, B. (2010) 3M's Innovation revival, Fortune500.com, 24 February. For further information about 3M and its business activities, visit the 3M international web page at www.3m.com.

Questions

1 There are many examples of successful companies. To what extent is 3M justifiably highlighted as the 'innovating machine'?

2 In the 3M case study, what is meant by the statement: 'the message is more important than the figures'?

→

3 Discuss the merits and problems with the so-called '15 per cent rule'. Consider cost implications and a busy environment with deadlines to meet. To what extent is this realistic or mere rhetoric?

4 Encouraging product and brand managers to achieve 25 per cent of sales from recently introduced products would be welcomed by shareholders, but what happens if a successful business delivers profits without 25 per cent of sales from recently introduced products?

5 Some people may argue that 3M's success is largely due to the significance given to science and technology and this is the main lesson for other firms. Discuss the merits of such a view and the extent to which this is the case.

6 Explain how the innovation dilemma affected 3M.

Note: This case has been written as a basis for class discussion rather than to illustrate effective or ineffective managerial or administrative behaviour. It has been prepared from a variety of published sources, as indicated, and from observations.

Chapter summary

The main focus of this chapter has been an examination of the activities of the NPD process. Adopting a practitioner standpoint, the new product development process is viewed as a series of linked activities. Emphasis is placed on the iterative nature of the process and many of the activities occur concurrently. A new product needs to be viewed as a project that acquires knowledge gradually over time as an idea is transformed into a physical product. The knowledge base of the organisation will provide for a diverse range of contributions to a project. Furthermore, during this process there is continual evaluation of the project.

This chapter also offered a view of NPD across a variety of industries. The key point here is that the balance of technical and commercial activities will clearly vary depending on the nature of the industry and the product being developed.

Discussion questions

1 Explain why there is not one best organisational structure for new product development.

2 Explain how sales representatives especially with technology intensive products play a crucial role in the success or not of a new product and illustrate how their image as 'second-hand car dealers' is pejorative and incorrect.

3 Examine whether the virtual world (such as Second Life) may be able to help firms trial new products.

4 Explain why the 'Valley of Death' presents a genuine challenge to product champions or project leaders.

5 'New products are a necessary evil.' From whose viewpoint are they necessary and from whose viewpoint are they evil?

6 Discuss the many reasons why so many new products fail? Are there additional reasons?

Key words and phrases

Business opportunity *556*

Product concept *556*

Screening *556*

Prototype *556*

Cross-functional teams *572*

Matrix structure *574*

Corporate venturing *576*

Marketing/R&D interface *577*

References

Allen, T. (1984) *Managing the Flow of Technology*, MIT Press, MA.

Baxter, A. (1997) Designs for survival, *Financial Times*, 20 November, 16.

Brassington, F. and Pettitt, S. (2003) *Principles of Marketing*, 3rd edn, Financial Times Pitman Publishing, London.

Bruce, M. and Cooper, R.C. (1997) *Marketing and Design Management*, Thomson Business Press, London.

Bunduchi, R. (2009) Implementing best practices to support creativity in NPD cross-functional teams, *International Journal of Innovation Management*, Vol. 13, No. 4, 537–54.

Buxton, P. (2000) Time to market is NPD's top priority, *Marketing*, 30 March, 35–6.

Christensen, C.M. and Bower, J.L. (1995) Customer power, strategic investment, and the failure of leading firms, *Strategic Management Journal*, Vol. 17, 197–218.

Cooper, R.G. (1979) The dimensions of industrial new product success and failure, *Journal of Marketing*, Vol. 43, 93–103.

Cooper, R.G. (1988a) The dimensions of industrial new product success and failure, *Journal of Marketing*, Vol. 43, No. 3, 93–103.

Cooper, R.G. (1988b) Predevelopment activities determine new product success, *Industrial Marketing Management*, Vol. 17, No. 3, 237–47.

Craig, A. and Hart, S. (1992) Where to now in new product development?, *European Journal of Marketing*, Vol. 26, 11.

Crawford, M. and Di Benedetto, A. (2008) *New Product Management*, 9th (International) edn, McGraw-Hill, New York.

Daily, C. (1996) Is the customer always right? (Effects of customers' influence on product development strategies), *Academy of Management Executive*, Vol. 10, No. 4, 105.

Droge, C., Stanko, M.A. and Pollitte, W.A. (2010) Lead Users and Early Adopters on the Web: The Role of New Technology Product Blogs, *Journal of Product Innovation Management*, Vol. 27, 66–82.

Ford, R.C. and Randolph, W.A. (1992) Cross functional structures: a review and integration of matrix organisations and project management, *Project Management Journal*, Vol. 18, No. 2, 269–94.

Gordon, W.J. (1962) 'Defining a creativeness in people', in Parnes, S.J. and Harding, H.F. (eds) *Source Book for Creative Thinking*, Scribners, New York.

Jones, T. (1997) *New Product Development: An Introduction to a Multifunctional Process*, Butterworth-Heinemann, Oxford.

Joyce, W.F. (1986) Matrix organisation: a social experiment, *Academy of Management Journal*, Vol. 29, No. 3, 536–61.

Kohler, T., Matzler, K. and Füller, J. (2009) Avatar-based innovation: Using virtual worlds for real-world innovation, *Technovation*, Vol. 29, Nos. 6–7, 395–407.

Kolodny, H.F. (1979) Evolution to a matrix organisation, *Academy of Management Review*, Vol. 4, No. 4, 543–53.

Kotler, P. (2003) *Marketing Management*, 11th edn, Prentice-Hall, Englewood Cliffs, NJ.

Lawrence, P.R., Kolodny, F.H. and Davis, S.M. (1982) 'The human side of the matrix', in Tushman, M.L. and Moore, W.L. (eds) *Readings in the Management of Innovation*, HarperCollins, New York.

Lorenz, C. (1993) The best way to rear corporate babies, *Financial Times*, 8 October, 23.

Mahajan, V. and Wind, Y. (1988) New product forecasting models: directions for research and implementation, *International Journal of Forecasting*, Vol. 14, 341–58.

Management Today (1995) Why new products are bypassing the market test, 12 October.

Markham, S.K., Ward, S.J., Aiman-Smith, L. and Kingon, A.I. (2010) The Valley of Death as Context for Role Theory in Product Innovation, *Journal of Product Innovation Management*, Vol. 27, 402–17.

Mullins, L.J. (2003) *Management and Organisational Behaviour*, 6th edn, Financial Times Pitman Publishing, London.

Nijssen, E.J. and Lieshout, K.F. (1995) Awareness, use and effectiveness of models for new product development, *European Journal of Marketing*, Vol. 29, No. 10, 27–39.

Olson, E.M., Orville, C.W. and Ruekert, R.W. (1995) Organising for effective new product development: the moderating role of product innovativeness, *Journal of Marketing*, Vol. 59, 48–62.

Ozer, M. (2009) The roles of product lead-users and product experts in new product evaluation, *Research Policy*, Vol. 38, No. 8, 1340–9.

Rubenstein, A.H., Chakrabarti, A.K., O'Keefe, R.D., Souder, W.E. and Young, H.C. (1976) Factors influencing innovation success at the project level, *Research Management*, Vol. 19, No. 3, 15–20.

Salomo, S., Keinschmidt, E.J. and De Brentani, U. (2010) Managing New Product Development Teams in a Globally Dispersed NPD Program, *Journal of Product Innovation Management*, Vol. 27, 955–71.

Sanchez, A.M. and Elola, L.N. (1991) Product innovation in Spain, *Journal of Product Innovation Management*, Vol. 11, No. 2, 105–18.

Schmidt, J.B. (1995) New product myopia, *Journal of Business and Industrial Marketing*, Vol. 10, No. 1, 23.

Souder, W.E. and Sherman, J.D. (1993) Organisational design and organisational development solutions to the problem of R&D marketing integration, *Research in Organisational Change and Development*, Vol. 7, 181–215.

Tidd, J., Bessant, J. and Pavitt, K. (2005) *Managing Innovation*, 3rd edn, Wiley, Chichester.

Tushman, M.L. and Nadler, D. (1978) An information processing approach to organisational design, *Academy of Management Review*, Vol. 3, 613–24.

Urban, G.L., Hauser, J.R. and Dholaka, N. (1987) *Essentials of New Product Management*, Prentice-Hall, Englewood Cliffs, NJ.

von Hippel, E. (1988) *The Sources of Innovation*, Oxford University Press, New York.

Wang, Q. (1997) R&D/marketing interface in a firm's capability-building process: evidence from pharmaceutical firms, *International Journal of Innovation Management*, Vol. 1, No. 1, 23–52.

Further reading

For a more detailed review of the new product development literature, the following develop many of the issues raised in this chapter:

Barczak, G., Griffin, A. and Kahn, K.B. (2009) PERSPECTIVE: Trends and Drivers of Success in NPD Practices: Results of the 2003 PDMA Best Practices Study, *Journal of Product Innovation Management*, Vol. 26, No. 1, 3–23.

Belliveau, P., Griffin, A. and Somermeyer, S. (eds) (2002) *The PDMA ToolBook for New Product Development*, John Wiley & Sons, New York.

Biemans, W.G., Griffin, A. and Moenaert, R.K. (2007) Twenty Years of the Journal of Product Innovation Management: History, Participants, and Knowledge Stocks and Flows, *Journal of Product Innovation Management*, Vol. 24, 193–213.

Biemans, W., Griffin, A. and Moenaert, R. (2010) In Search of the Classics: A Study of the Impact of *JPIM* Papers from 1984 to 2003, *Journal of Product Innovation Management*, Vol. 27, 461–84.

Christensen, C.M. (2003) *The Innovator's Dilemma: When New Technologies Cause Great Firms to Fail*, 3rd edn, Harvard Business School Press, Boston, MA.

HSBC (2010) 100 Thoughts, HSBC, London.

Salomo, S., Keinschmidt, E.J. and De Brentani, U. (2010) Managing New Product Development Teams in a Globally Dispersed NPD Program, *Journal of Product Innovation Management*, Vol. 27, 955–71.

Appendix
Guinness patent

(12) **UK Patent Application** (19) **GB** (11) **2 183 592** (13) A
(43) Application published **10 Jun 1987**
(21) Application No **8529441**
(22) Date of filing **29 Nov 1985**
(71) Applicant
Arthur Guinness Son & Company (Dublin) Limited,
(Incorporated in Irish Republic),
St. James's Gate, Dublin 8, Republic of Ireland
(72) Inventors
Alan James Forage,
William John Byrne
(74) Agent and/or Address for Service
Urquhart-Dykes & Lord, 47 Marylebone Lane,
London W1M 6DL
(51) INTCL
B65D 25/00 5/40
(52) Domestic classification (Edition I)
B8D 12 13 19 7C 7G 7M 7P1 7PY SC1
B8P AX
U1S 1106 1110 1111 B8D B8P
(56) Documents cited
GB 1266351
(58) Field of search
B8D
B8P
Selected US specifications from IPC sub-class B65D
(54) **Carbonated beverage container**
(57) A container for a beverage having gas (preferably at least one of carbon dioxide and inert (nitrogen) gases) in solution consists of a non-resealable container 1 within which is located a hollow secondary chamber 4, eg a polypropylene envelope, having a restricted aperture 7 in a side wall. The container is charged with the beverage 8 and sealed. Beverage from the main chamber of the container enters the chamber 4 (shown at 8*a*) by way of the aperture 7 to provide headspaces 1*a* in the container and 4*a* in the pod 4. Gas within the headspaces 1*a* and 4*a* is at greater than atmospheric pressure. Preferably the beverage is drawn into the chamber 4 by subjecting the package to a heating and cooling cycle. Upon opening the container 1, eg by draw ring/region 13, the headspace 1*a* is vented to atmosphere and the pressure differential

(12) UK Patent Application (19) GB (11) 2 183 592 (13) A

(43) Application published **10 Jun 1987**

(21) Application No **8529441**

(22) Date of filing **29 Nov 1985**

(71) Applicant
Arthur Guinness Son & Company (Dublin) Limited,

(Incorporated in Irish Republic),

St. James's Gate, Dublin 8, Republic of Ireland

(72) Inventors
Alan James Forage,
William John Byrne

(74) Agent and/or Address for Service
Urquhart-Dykes & Lord, 47 Marylebone Lane, London W1M 6DL

(51) INT CL[4]
B65D 25/00 5/40

(52) Domestic classification (Edition I)
B8D 12 13 19 7C 7G 7M 7P1 7PY SC1
B8P AX
U1S 1106 1110 1111 B8D B8P

(56) Documents cited
GB 1266351

(58) Field of search
B8D
B8P
Selected US specifications from IPC sub-class B65D

(54) **Carbonated beverage container**

(57) A container for a beverage having gas (preferably at least one of carbon dioxide and inert (nitrogen) gases) in solution consists of a non-resealable container 1 within which is located a hollow secondary chamber 4, eg a polypropylene envelope, having a restricted aperture 7 in a side wall. The container is charged with the beverage 8 and sealed. Beverage from the main chamber of the container enters the chamber 4 (shown at 8*a*) by way of the aperture 7 to provide headspaces 1*a* in the container and 4*a* in the pod 4. Gas within the headspaces 1*a* and 4*a* is at greater than atmospheric pressure. Preferably the beverage is drawn into the chamber 4 by subjecting the package to a heating and cooling cycle. Upon opening the container 1, eg by draw ring/region 13, the headspace 1*a* is vented to atmosphere and the pressure differential resulting from the pressure in the chamber headspace 4*a* causes gas/beverage to be ejected from the chamber 4 (by way of the aperture 7) into the beverage 8. Said ejection causes gas to be evolved from solution in the beverage in the main container chamber to form a head of froth on the beverage. The chamber 4 is preferably formed by blow moulding and located below beverage level by weighting it or as a press fit within the container 1 by lugs 6 engaging the container walls, the container being preferably a can, carton or bottle. The chamber 4 may initially be filled with gas, eg nitrogen, at or slightly above atmospheric pressure, the orifice being formed by laser boring, drilling or punching immediately prior to locating the chamber 4 in the container 1.

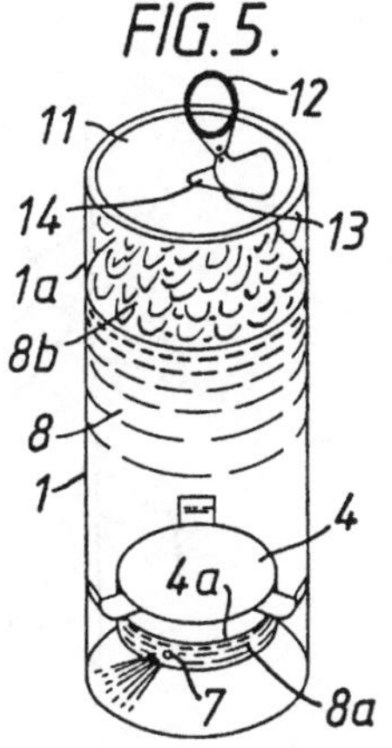

The drawings originally filed were informal and the print here reproduced is taken from a later filed formal copy.

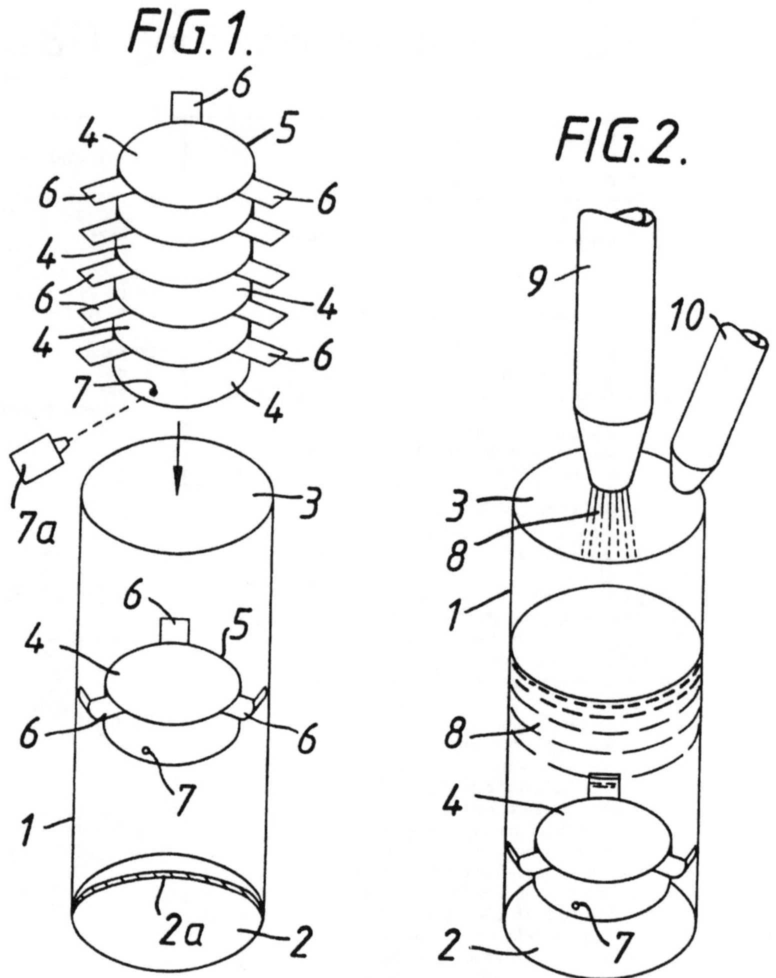

resulting from the pressure in the chamber headspace 4*a* causes gas/beverage to be ejected from the chamber 4 (by way of the aperture 7) into the beverage 8. Said ejection causes gas to be evolved from solution in the beverage in the main container chamber to form a head of froth on the beverage. The chamber 4 is preferably formed by blow moulding and located below beverage level by weighting it or as a press fit within the container 1 by lugs 6 engaging the container walls, the container being preferably a can, carton or bottle. The chamber 4 may initially be filled with gas, eg nitrogen, at or slightly above atmospheric pressure, the orifice being formed by laser boring, drilling or punching immediately prior to locating the chamber 4 in the container 1.

The drawings originally filed were informal and the print here reproduced is taken from a later filed formal copy.

Reference to UK Patent Application 2,183,592A is made with kind permission of Guinness Brewing Worldwide Limited and their Patent Attorneys, Urquhart-Dykes & Lord.

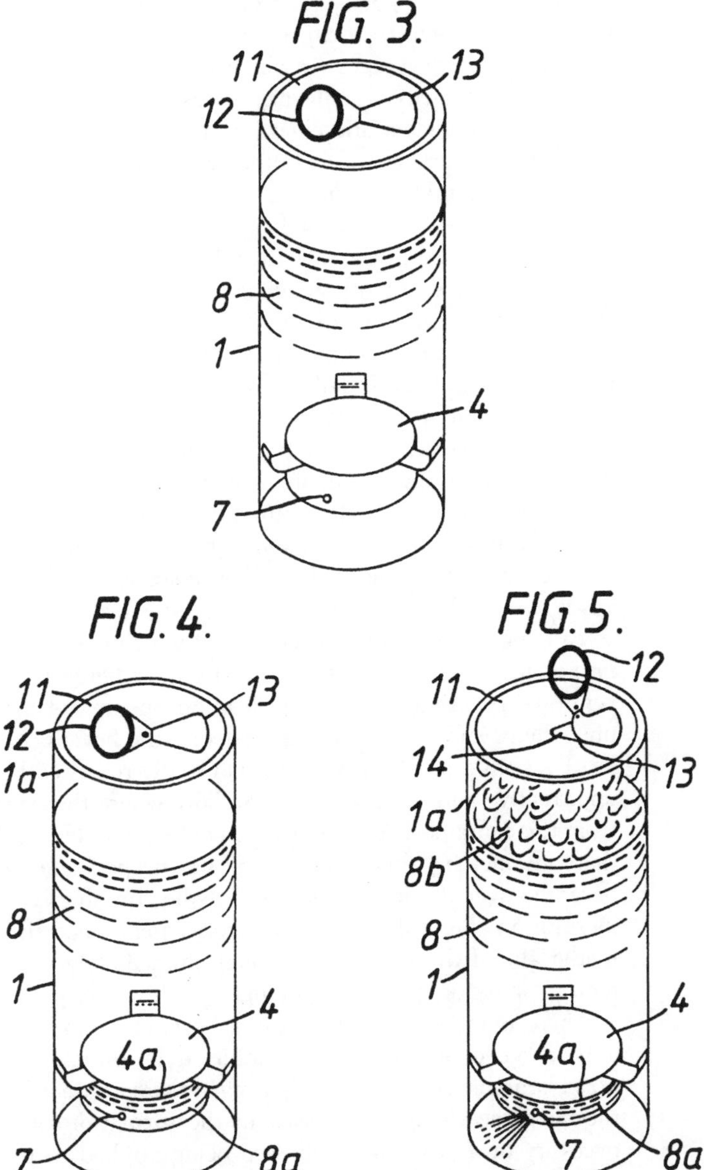

SPECIFICATION A beverage package and a method of packaging a beverage containing gas in solution

Technical field and background art

This invention relates to a beverage package and a method of packaging a beverage containing gas in solution. The invention more particularly concerns beverages containing gas in solution and packaged in a sealed, non-resealable, container which, when opened for dispensing or consumption, permits gas to be evolved or liberated from the beverage to form, or assist in the formation of, a head or froth on the beverage. The beverages to which the invention relates may be alcoholic or non-alcoholic; primarily the invention was developed for fermented beverages such as beer, stout, ale, lager and cider but may be applied with advantage to so-called soft drinks and beverages (for example fruit juices, squashes, colas, lemonades, milk and milk based drinks and similar type drinks) and to alcoholic drinks (for example spirits, liquers, wine or wine based drinks and similar).

It is recognised in the beverage dispensing and packaging art that the characteristics of the head of froth which is provided on the beverage by the liberation of gas from the beverage immediately prior to consumption are an important consideration to the consumer's enjoyment of the product and are therefore of commercial importance. Conventionally beverages of the type discussed above containing gas in solution and packaged in a non-resealable container (such as a can, bottle or carton) provide a headspace in the container within which gas is maintained under pressure. Upon opening of the package, the headspace gas is vented to atmosphere and the beverage is usually poured into a drinking vessel. During such dispensing of the beverage it is usual for gas in solution to be liberated to create the froth or head. It is generally recognised that when dispensing a beverage as aforementioned, the gas is liberated as a result of the movement of the beverage over a surface having so-called gas nucleation or active sites which may be the wall of the drinking vessel into which the beverage is poured. There is therefore a distinct possibility with conventional beverage packages that upon opening of the container after storage and until the beverage is poured there-from, the beverage will have little or no froth or head – such a headless beverage is usually regarded by the consumer as somewhat unattractive and unappealing especially where the beverage is to be drunk directly from the container. Admittedly it may be possible to develop a head or froth within the container by agitating or shaking the package (so that the movement of the beverage over the interior surface of the container causes the liberation of the gas in solution) but this is clearly inconvenient once the container is opened and is inadvisable if the package is shaken immediately prior to opening as the contents tend to spray or spurt on opening.

There is therefore a need for a beverage package and a method of packaging a beverage containing gas in solution by which the beverage is packaged in a non-resealable container so that when the container is opened gas is liberated from the beverage to form or assist in the formation of a head or froth without the necessity of an external influence being applied to the package; it is an object of the present invention to satisfy this need in a simple, economic and commercially viable manner.

Statements of invention and advantages

According to the present invention there is provided a beverage package comprising a sealed, non-resealable, container having a primary chamber containing beverage having gas in solution therewith and forming a primary headspace comprising gas at a pressure greater than atmospheric; a secondary chamber having a volume less than said primary chamber and which communicates with the beverage in said primary chamber through a restricted orifice, said secondary chamber containing beverage derived from the primary chamber and having a secondary headspace therein comprising gas at a pressure greater than atmospheric so that the pressures within the primary and secondary chambers are substantially at equilibrium, and wherein said package is openable, to open the primary headspace to atmospheric pressure and the secondary chamber is arranged so that on said opening the pressure differential caused by the decrease in pressure at the primary headspace causes at least one of the beverage and gas in the secondary chamber to be ejected by way of the restricted orifice into the beverage of the primary chamber and said ejection causes gas in the solution to be evolved and form, or assist in the formation of, a head of froth on the beverage.

Further according to the present invention there is provided a method of packaging a beverage having gas in solution therewith which comprises providing a container with a primary chamber and a secondary chamber of which the volume of the secondary chamber is less than that of the primary chamber and with a restricted orifice through which the secondary chamber communicates with the primary chamber, and charging and sealing the primary chamber with the beverage to contain the gas in solution and to form a primary headspace in the primary chamber, and charging the secondary chamber with beverage derived from the primary chamber by way of said restricted orifice to form a secondary headspace in the secondary chamber whereby the pressures in both the primary and secondary chambers are at equilibrium and gaseous pressures in both the primary and secondary headspaces are at a pressure greater than atmospheric so that, when the container is broached to open the primary headspace to atmospheric pressure, the pressure differential caused by the decrease in pressure at the primary headspace causes at least one of the beverage and gas in the secondary chamber to be ejected into the beverage of the primary chamber by way of said restricted orifice and the said ejection causes gas to be evolved from solution in the beverage in the primary chamber to form, or assist in the formation of, a head of froth on the beverage.

The present invention is applicable to a wide range of beverages of the type as previously discussed and where those beverages contain gas in solution which gas is intended to be liberated to form or assist in the formation of the head or froth on the beverage. Understandably the gas in solution must not detract from, and should preferably enhance the characteristics required of the beverage and be acceptable for use with food products; preferably therefore the gas is at least one of carbon dioxide and inert gases (by which latter term is included nitrogen) although it is to be realised that other gases may be appropriate.

The present invention was primarily developed for the packaging of fermented beverages such as beer, ale, stout, lager and cider where among the desirable qualities sought in a head are a consistent and regular, relatively fine, bubble size; a bubble structure which is substantially homogeneous so that the head is not formed with large irregularly shaped and random gaps; the ability for the head or bubble structure to endure during a reasonable period over which it is likely to be consumed, and a so-called 'mouth-feel' and flavour which may improve the enjoyment of the beverage during consumption and not detract from the desirable flavour characteristics required of the beverage. These desirable qualities are of course equally applicable to non-fermented beverages, for example with so-called soft drinks. Conventionally, beverages of the type to which the invention relates are packaged in a non-resealable container which when opened totally vents the headspace to atmosphere, contain carbon dioxide in solution and it is the liberation of the carbon dioxide on opening of the package and dispensing of the beverage into a drinking vessel which creates the froth or head; however, the head so formed has very few of the aforementioned desirable qualities – in particular it is usually irregular, lacks homogeneity and has very little endurance so that there is a tendency for it to collapse after a short period. It has been known for approximately 25 years and as discussed in our G.B. Patent No. 876,628, that beverages having in solution a mixture of carbon dioxide gas and inert gas (such as nitrogen or argon) will, when dispensed in a manner whereby the mixed gases are caused to evolve to develop the head or foam from small bubbles containing the mixture of carbon dioxide and, say, nitrogen gases, provide the desirable qualities for the head as previously discussed. Commercially the formation of the head by the use of mixed gases as aforementioned has been widely employed in the dispensing of beverage in a draught system and on demand from a bulk container (such as a keg or barrel) where the gases are caused to evolve by subjecting the beverage to intense shear forces in passing it under pressure through a set of small holes. Beverages, particularly stout, having a mixture of carbon dioxide and nitrogen gases in solution and dispensed in draught using the aforementioned technique have met with considerable commercial success and it was soon realized that there was a need to make available for consumption a similar beverage derived from a small non-resealable container suitable for shelf storage and retail purposes.

Research has indicated that to achieve the initiation of a head on a beverage containing carbon dioxide and inert gas such as nitrogen in solution it is necessary to provide so-called 'active sites' which are regions where the beverage is subjected to a high local strain (such a strain being higher than the cohesive force of the beverage). In these conditions the beverage prefers to generate a bubble of mixed gases instead of 'bending around' the active site. It was found that an active site could be solid, liquid or gas such as granules, restrictor holes, rapid streams of liquid or bubbles and the like. It was also found that ultrasonics could produce a 'ghost' active site by the formation of extreme pressure gradients. There has however been a problem in providing an 'active site' in a beverage packaged in a non-resealable small container in a manner whichis commercially and economically acceptable. During the past 25 years considerable expenditure has been devoted to research and development in an attempt to overcome the aforementioned problem. For example, our G.B. Patent No. 1,588,624 proposes initiating the evolution of mixed carbon dioxide and nitrogen gases from a beverage by subjecting the beverage to ultrasonic excitement, by injecting a gas, liquid and/or foam into the beverage by use of a syringe-type device, or by pouring the beverage over an excitation surface such as polystyrene granules. Although these latter proposals were successful in achieving the desired head formation, the necessity to use ancilliary apparatus had commercial disadvantages (for example, it is unreasonable to expect a retail customer to have available an ultrasonic signal generator; also the steps required to effect initiation of the head following opening of the beverage package involved an inconvenient discipline and time factor). In a further example our G.B. Patent No. 1,266,351 relates to a non-resealable package containing beverage having mixed carbon dioxide and inert gases in solution; in this disclosure a can or bottle has two chambers of which a larger chamber contains the beverage while the smaller chamber is charged under pressure with the mixed gases. On opening of the can or bottle to expose the larger chamber to atmosphere, its internal pressure falls to atmospheric permitting the pressurized gas in the small chamber to jet into the beverage by way of a small orifice between the two chambers. This jet of gas provides sufficient energy to initiate the formation of minute bubbles and thereby the head from the evolution of the mixed gases in the beverage coming out of solution. By this proposal the small gas chamber is initially pressurized with the mixed gases to a pressure greater than atmospheric and from a source remote from the beverage; as a consequence it was found necessary, particularly in the case of cans, to provide a special design of two chambered container and an appropriate means for sealing the smaller chamber following the charging of that chamber with the mixed gases (such charging usually being effected, in the case of cans, by injecting the mixed gases into the small chamber through a wall of the can which then had to be sealed). Because of the inconvenience and high costs involved in the development of an appropriate two chambered container and the special facilities required for charging the mixed gases and sealing the container, the proposal proved commercially unacceptable.

The container employed in the present invention will usually be in the form of a can, bottle or carton capable of withstanding the internal pressures of the primary and secondary chambers and of a size suitable for conventional shelf storage by the retail trade so that, the overall volume of the container may be, typically, 0.5 litres but is unlikely to be greater than 3 litres.

By the present invention a two chambered container is employed as broadly proposed in G.B. Patent No. 1,266,351; however, unlike the prior proposal the secondary chamber is partly filled with beverage containing gases in solution and the beverage in the secondary chamber is derived wholly from the beverage in the primary chamber so that when the contents of the primary and secondary chambers are in equilibrium (and the primary and secondary headspaces are at a pressure greater than atmospheric) immediately prior to broaching the container to open the primary headspace to atmosphere, the pressure differential between that in the secondary headspace and atmospheric pressure causes at least one of the beverage and the headspace gas in the secondary chamber to be ejected by way of the restricted orifice into the beverage in the primary chamber to promote the formation of the head of froth without the necessity of any external influence being applied to the package. The pressurisation of the headspace gas in the secondary chamber is intended to result from the evolution of gas in the sealed container as the contents of the container come into equilibrium at ambient or dispensing temperature (which should be greater than the temperature at which the container is charged and sealed). Consequently the present invention alleviates the necessity for pressurizing the secondary chamber from a source externally of the container so that the secondary chamber can be formed as a simple envelope or hollow pod of any convenient shape (such as cylindrical or spherical) which is located as a discrete insert within a conventional form of can, bottle or carton (thereby alleviating the requirement for a special structure of can or bottle as envisaged in G.B. Patent No. 1,266,351).

Although the head or froth formed by pouring wholly carbonated beverages tends to lack many of the desirable qualities required of a head as previously discussed; our tests have indicated that by use of the present invention with wholly carbonated beverages (where the head is formed by injection of gas or beverage from the secondary chamber into the primary chamber) the resultant head is considerably tighter or denser than that achieved solely by pouring and as such will normally have a greater life expectancy.

The beverage is preferably saturated or supersaturated with the gas (especially if mixed carbon dioxide and insert gases are employed) and the primary chamber charged with the beverage under a counterpressure and at a low temperature (to alleviate gas losses and, say, at a slightly higher temperature than that at which the beverage freezes) so that when the container is sealed (which may be achieved under atmospheric pressure using conventional systems such as a canning or bottling line), the pressurisation of the primary and secondary headspaces is achieved by the evolution of gas from the beverage within the primary and secondary chambers as the package is handled or stored at an ambient or dispensing temperature (greater than the charging temperature) and the contents of the container adopt a state of equilibrium. As an optional but preferred feature of the present invention, following the sealing of the container, the package may be subjected to a heating and cooling cycle, conveniently during pasteurisation of the beverage. During such a cycle the gas within the secondary chamber is caused to expand and eject into the primary chamber; during subsequent cooling of the package, the gas in the secondary chamber contracts and creates a low pressure or vacuum effect relative to the pressure in the primary chamber so that beverage from the primary chamber is drawn into the secondary chamber by way of the restricted orifice. By use of this preferred technique it is possible to ensure that the secondary chamber is efficiently and adequately charged with beverage and has the desired secondary headspace.

The restricted orifice through which the primary and secondary chambers communicate is conveniently formed by a single aperture in a side wall of the secondary chamber and such an aperture should have a size which is sufficiently great to alleviate 'clogging' or its obturation by particles which may normally be expected to occur within the beverage and yet be restricted in its dimensions to ensure that there is an adequate jetting effect in the ejection of the gas and/or beverage therethrough from the secondary chamber into the primary chamber to promote the head formation upon opening of the container. The restricted orifice may be of any profile (such as a slit or a star shape) but will usually be circular; experiments have indicated that a restricted orifice having a diameter in the range of 0.02 to 0.25 centimetres is likely to be appropriate for fermented beverages (the preferred diameter being 0.061 centi-metres). It is also preferred that when the package is positioned in an upstanding condition in which it is likely to be transported, shelf stored or opened, the restricted orifice is located in an upwardly extending side wall or in a bottom wall of the secondary chamber and preferably at a position slightly spaced from the bottom of the primary chamber. It is also preferred, particularly for fermented beverages, that when the contents of the sealed package are in equilibrium and the package is in an upstanding condition as aforementioned, the restricted orifice is located below the depth of the beverage in the secondary chamber so that on opening of the container the pressure of gas in the secondary headspace initially ejects beverage from that chamber into the beverage in the primary chamber to promote the head formation. It is believed that such ejection of beverage through the restricted orifice is likely to provide a greater efficiency in the development of the head in a liquid supersaturated with gas than will the ejection of gas alone through the restricted orifice; the reason for this is that the restricted orifice provides a very active site which causes the beverage to 'rip itself apart' generating extremely minute bubbles which themselves act as active sites for the beverage in the primary chamber, these extremely minute bubbles leave 'vapour trails' of larger initiated bubbles which in turn produce the head. Since the extremely minute bubbles are travelling at relatively high speed during their injection into the beverage in the primary chamber, they not only generate shear forces on the beverage in that chamber but the effect of each such bubble is distributed over a volume of beverage much larger than the immediate surroundings of an otherwise stationary bubble.

A particular advantage of the present invention is that prior to the container being charged with beverage both the primary and secondary chambers can be at atmospheric pressure and indeed may contain air. However, it is recognised that for many beverages, particularly a fermented beverage, prolonged storage of the beverage in contact with air, especially oxygen, is undesirable as adversely affecting the characteristics of the beverage. To alleviate this possibility the secondary chamber may initially be filled with a 'non-contaminant' gas such as nitrogen (or other inert gas or carbon dioxide) which does not adversely affect the characteristics of the beverage during prolonged contact therewith. The secondary chamber may be filled with the non-contaminant gas at atmospheric pressure or slightly greater (to alleviate the inadvertent intake of air) so that when the container is charged with the beverage, the non-contaminant gas will form part of the pressurised headspace in the secondary chamber. As previously mentioned, the secondary chamber may be formed by an envelope or hollow pod which is located as a discrete insert within a conventional form of can, bottle or carton and such a discrete insert permits the secondary chamber to be filled with the non-contaminant gas prior to the envelope or pod being located within the can, bottle or carton. A convenient means of achieving this latter effect is by blow moulding the envelope or pod in a food grade plastics material using the non-contaminant gas as the blowing medium and thereafter sealing the envelope or pod to retain the non-contaminant gas therein; immediately prior to the pod or envelope being inserted into the can, bottle or carton, the restricted orifice can be formed in a side wall of the pod or envelope (for example, by laser boring). Immediately prior to the container being sealed it is also preferable to remove air from the primary headspace and this may be achieved using conventional techniques such as filling the headspace with froth or fob developed from a source remote from the container and having characteristics similar to those of the head which is to be formed from the beverage in the container; charging the primary chamber with the beverage in a nitrogen or other inert gas atmosphere so that the headspace is filled with that inert gas or nitrogen; dosing the headspace with liquid nitrogen so that the gas evolved therefrom expels the air from the headspace, or by use of undercover gassing or water jetting techniques to exclude air.

Although the secondary chamber may be constructed as an integral part of the container, for the reasons discussed above and also convenience of manufacture, it is preferred that the secondary chamber is formed as a discrete insert which is simply deposited or pushed into a conventional form of can, bottle or carton. With cans or cartons such an insert will not be visible to the end user and many bottled beverages are traditionally marketed in dark coloured glass or plastics so that the insert is unlikely to adversely affect the aesthetics of the package. The discrete insert may be suspended or float in the beverage in the primary chamber provided that the restricted orifice is maintained below the surface of the beverage in the primary chamber on opening of the container; for example the insert may be loaded or weighted to appropriately orientate the position of the restricted orifice. Desirably however the insert is restrained from displacement within the outer container of the package and may be retained in position, for example at the bottom of the outer container, by an appropriate adhesive or by mechanical means such as projections on the package which may flex to abut and grip a side wall of the outer container or which may engage beneath an internal abutment on the side wall of the outer container.

Drawings

One embodiment of the present invention as applied to the packaging of a fermented beverage such as stout in a can will now be described, by way of example only, with reference to the accompanying illustrative drawings, in which:

Figures 1 to *4* diagrammatically illustrate the progressive stages in the formation of the beverage package in a canning line, and

Figure 5 diagrammatically illustrates the effect on opening the beverage package prior to consumption of the beverage and the development of the head of froth on the beverage.

Detailed description of drawings

The present embodiment will be considered in relation to the preparation of a sealed can containing stout having in solution a mixture of nitrogen and carbon dioxide gases, the former preferably being present to the extent of at least 1.5% vols/vol and typically in the range 1.5% to 3.5% vols/vol and the carbon dioxide being present at a considerably lower level than the amount of carbon dioxide which would normally be present in conventional, wholly carbonated, bottled or canned stout and typically in the range 0.8 to 1.8 vols/vol (1.46 to 3.29 grams/litre). For the avoidance of doubt, a definition of the term 'vols/vol' is to be found in our G.B. Patent No. 1,588,624.

The stout is to be packaged in a conventional form of cylindrical can (typically of aluminium alloy) which, in the present example, will be regarded as having a capacity of 500 millilitres and by use of a conventional form of filling and canning line appropriately modified as will hereinafter be described. A cylindrical shell for the can 1 having a sealed base 2 and an open top 3 is passed in an upstanding condition along the line to a station shown in Figure 1 to present its open top beneath a stack of hollow pods 4. Each pod 4 is moulded in a food grade plastics material such as polypropylene to have a short (say 5 millimetres) hollow cylindrical housing part 5 and a circumferentially spaced array of radially outwardly extending flexible tabs or lugs 6. The pods 4 are placed in the stack with the chamber formed by the housing part 5 sealed and containing nitrogen gas at atmospheric pressure (or at pressure slightly above atmospheric); conveniently this is achieved by blow moulding the housing part 5 using nitrogen gas. The volume within the housing part 5 is approximately 15 millilitres. At the station shown in Figure 1 the bottom pod 4 of the stack is displaced by suitable means (not shown) into the open topped can 1 as shown. However, immediately prior to the pod 4 being moved into the can 1 a small (restricted) hole 7 is bored in the cylindrical side wall of the housing part 5. In the present example, the hole 7 has a diameter in the order of 0.61 millimetres and is conveniently bored by a laser beam generated by device *7a* (although the hole could be formed by punching or drilling). The hole 7 is located towards the bottom of the cylindrical chamber within the housing part 5. Since the hollow pod 4 contains nitrogen gas at atmospheric pressure (or slightly higher) it is unlikely that air will enter the hollow pod through the hole 7 during the period between boring the hole 7 and charging of the can 1 with stout (thereby alleviating contamination of the stout by an oxygen content within the hollow pod 4).

The hollow pod 4 is pressed into the can 1 to be seated on the base 2. Conventional cans 1 have a domed base 2 (shown by the section 2a) which presents a convex internal face so that when the pod 4 abuts this face a clearance is provided between the hole 7 and the underlying bottom of the chamber within the can 1. It will be seen from Figure 1 that the diameter of the housing part 5 of the pod 4 is less than the internal diameter of the can 1 while the diameter of the outermost edges of the lugs 6 is greater than the diameter of the can 1 so that as the pod 4 is pressed downwardly into the can, the lugs 6 abut the side wall of the can and flex upwardly as shown to grip the can side wall and thereby restrain the hollow pod from displacement away from the base 2.

The open topped can with its pod 4 is now displaced along the canning line to the station shown in Figure 2 where the can is charged with approximately 440 millilitres of stout 8 from an appropriate source 9. The stout 8 is supersaturated with the mixed carbon dioxide and nitrogen gases, typically the carbon dioxide gas being present at 1.5 vols/vol (2.74 grams/litre) and the nitrogen gas being present at 2% vols/vol. The charging of the can 1 with the stout may be achieved in conventional manner, that is under a counterpressure and at a temperature of approximately 0°C. When the can 1 is charged with the appropriate quantity of stout 8, the headspace above the stout is purged of air, for example by use of liquid nitrogen dosing or with nitrogen gas delivered by means indicated at 10 to alleviate contamination of the stout from oxygen in the headspace.

Following charging of the can 1 with stout and purging of the headspace, the can moves to the station shown in Figure 3 where it is closed and sealed under atmospheric pressure and in conventional manner by a lid 11 seamed to the cylindrical side wall of the can. The lid 11 has a pull-ring 12 attached to a weakened tear-out region 13 by which the can is intended to be broached in conventional manner for dispensing of the contents.

Following sealing, the packaged stout is subjected to a pasteurization process whereby the package is heated to approximately 60°C for 15–20 minutes and is thereafter cooled to ambient temperature. During this process the nitrogen gas in the hollow pod 4*a* initially expands and a proportion of that gas passes by way of the hole 7 into the stout 8 in the main chamber of the can. During cooling of the package in the pasteurisation cycle, the nitrogen gas in the hollow pod 4 contracts to create a vacuum effect within the hollow pod causing stout 8 to be drawn, by way of the hole 7, from the chamber of the can into the chamber of the pod so that when the package is at ambient temperature the hole 7 is located below the depth of stout 8*a* within the hollow pod 4.

Following the pasteurisation process the contents of the can 1 will stabilise in a condition of equilibrium with a headspace 1*a* over the stout 8 in the primary chamber of the can and a headspace 4*a* over the stout 8*a* in the secondary chamber formed by the hollow pod 4 and in the equilibrium condition. With the sealed can at ambient temperature (or a typical storage or dispensing temperature which may be, say, 8°C) the pressure of mixed gases carbon dioxide and nitrogen (which largely results from the evolution of such gases from the stout) is substantially the same in the headspaces 1*a* and 4*a* and this pressure will be greater than atmospheric pressure, typically in the order of 25lbs per square inch (1.72 bars).

The package in the condition shown in Figure 4 is typically that which would be made available for storage and retail purposes. During handling it is realised that the package may be tipped from its upright condition; in practice however this is unlikely to adversely affect the contents of the hollow pod 4 because of the condition of equilibrium within the can.

When the stout is to be made available for consumption, the can 1 is opened by ripping out the region 13 with the pull-ring 12. On broaching the lid 11 as indicated at 14 the headspace 1*a* rapidly depressurises to atmospheric pressure. As a consequence the pressure within the headspace 4*a* of the secondary chamber in the pod 4 exceeds that in the headspace 1*a* and causes stout 8*a* in the hollow pod to be ejected by way of the hole 7 into the stout 8 in the primary chamber of the can. The restrictor hole 7 acts as a very 'active site' to the supersaturated stout 8*a* which passes therethrough to be injected into the stout 8 and that stout is effectively 'ripped apart' to generate extremely minute bubbles which themselves act as active sites for the stout 8 into which they are injected. These minute bubbles leave 'vapour trails' of larger initiated bubbles which develop within the headspace 1*a* a head 8*b* having the previously discussed desirable characteristics.

It is appreciated that the headspace 1*a* occupies a larger proportion of the volume of the can 1 than that which would normally be expected in a 500 millilitre capacity can; the reason for this is to ensure that there is adequate volume in the headspace 1*a* for the head of froth 8*b* to develop efficiently in the event, for example, that the stout is to be consumed directly from the can when the tear-out region 13 is removed. Normally however the stout 8 will first be poured from the can into an open topped drinking vessel prior to consumption but this pouring should not adversely affect the desirable characteristics of the head of froth which will eventually be presented in the drinking vessel.

In the aforegoing embodiment the can 1 is charged with stout 8 (from the source 9) having in solution the required respective volumes of the carbon dioxide and the nitrogen gases. In a modification the can 1 is charged with stout (from source 9) having the carbon dioxide gas only in solution to the required volume; the 2% vols/vol nitrogen gas necessary to achieve the required solution of mixed gas in the packaged stout is derived from the liquid nitrogen dosing of the headspace in the can.

CLAIMS

1 A beverage package comprising a sealed, non-resealable, container having a primary chamber containing beverage having gas in solution therewith and forming a primary headspace comprising gas at a pressure greater than atmospheric; a secondary chamber having a volume less than said primary chamber and which communicates with the beverage in said primary chamber through a restricted orifice, said secondary chamber containing beverage derived from the primary chamber and having a secondary headspace therein comprising gas at a pressure greater than atmospheric so that the pressure within the primary and secondary chambers are substantially at equilibrium, and wherein said package is openable, to open the primary headspace to atmospheric pressure and the secondary chamber is arranged so that on said opening the pressure differential

caused by the decrease in pressure at the primary headspace causes at least one of the beverage and gas in the secondary chamber to be ejected by way of the restricted orifice into the beverage of the primary chamber and said ejection causes gas in the solution to be evolved and form, or assist in the formation of, a head of froth on the beverage.

2 A package as claimed in claim 1 in which the container has a normal upstanding condition with an openable top and said secondary chamber has an upwardly extending side wall or a bottom wall within which said restricted orifice is located.

3 A package as claimed in either claim 1 or claim 2 in which with the pressures within the primary and secondary chambers substantially at equilibrium the restricted orifice is located below the depth of the beverage within the secondary chamber.

4 A package as claimed in any one of the preceding claims wherein the secondary chamber comprises a hollow and discrete insert within the container.

5 A package as claimed in claim 4 in which the insert floats or is suspended in the beverage in the primary chamber and means is provided for locating the restricted orifice below the surface of the beverage in the primary chamber.

6 A package as claimed in claim 5 in which the insert is weighted or loaded to locate the restricted orifice below the surface of the beverage in the primary chamber.

7 A package as claimed in claim 4 wherein means is provided for retaining the insert at a predetermined position within the container.

8 A package as claimed in claim 7 wherein the container has a normal upstanding condition with an openable top and said insert is located at or towards the bottom of said container.

9 A package as claimed in either claim 7 or claim 8 wherein the insert comprises a hollow pod or envelope having means thereon for retaining it in position within the container.

10 A package as claimed in claim 9 wherein the retaining means comprise flexible tab means which engage a side wall of the container to retain the insert.

11 A package as claimed in any one of claims 4 to 10 wherein the insert comprises a hollow moulding.

12 A package as claimed in claim 11 when appendant to claim 10 in which the container has a side wall and the moulding is substantially cylindrical with radially extending tabs engaging the wall of the container.

13 A package as claimed in any one of claims 4 to 12 in which the container has a base on which the insert is located and said restricted orifice is located in an upwardly extending side wall of the insert spaced from said base.

14 A package as claimed in any one of the preceding claims in which the beverage has in solution therewith at least one of carbon dioxide gas and inert gas (which latter term includes nitrogen).

15 A package as claimed in claim 14 in which the beverage is saturated or supersaturated with said gas or gases.

16 A package as claimed in any one of the preceding claims in which the container is in the form of a can, bottle or carton.

17 A package as claimed in any one of the preceding claims in which the restricted orifice comprises a circular aperture having a diameter in the range of 0.02 to 0.25 centimetres.

18 A package as claimed in any one of the preceding claims and comprising a fermented beverage having in solution therewith carbon dioxide in the range 0.8 to 1.8 vols/vol (1.46 to 3.29 grams/litre) and nitrogen in the range 1.5% to 3.5% vols/vol.

19 A beverage package substantially as herein described with reference to the accompanying illustrative drawings.

20 A method of packaging a beverage having gas in solution therewith which comprises providing a container with a primary chamber and a secondary chamber of which the volume of the secondary chamber is less than that of the primary chamber and with a restricted orifice through which the secondary chamber communicates with the primary chamber, and charging and sealing the primary chamber with the beverage to contain the gas in solution and to form a primary headspace in the primary chamber, and charging the secondary chamber with beverage derived from the primary chamber by way of said restricted orifice to form a secondary headspace in the secondary chamber whereby the pressures in both the primary and secondary chambers are at equilibrium and gaseous pressures in both the primary and secondary headspaces are at a pressure greater than atmospheric so that, when the container is broached to open the primary headspace to atmospheric pressure, the pressure differential caused by the decrease in pressure at the primary headspace causes at least one of the beverage and gas in the secondary chamber to be ejected into the beverage of the primary chamber by way of said restricted orifice and the said ejection causes gas to be evolved from solution in the beverage in the primary chamber to form, or assist in the formation of, a head of froth on the beverage.

21 A method as claimed in claim 20 which comprises subjecting the sealed container to a heating and cooling cycle whereby gas within the secondary chamber is caused to expand and eject by way of the restricted orifice into the primary chamber and subsequently to contract and create a low pressure effect in the secondary chamber relative to the primary chamber to draw beverage from the primary chamber into the secondary chamber by way of said restricted orifice.

22 A method as claimed in claim 21 in which the heating and cooling cycle comprises pasteurisation of the beverage.

23 A method as claimed in any one of claims 20 to 22 in which the container has an upstanding condition with an openable top and which comprises locating the restricted orifice within an upwardly extending side wall or bottom wall of the secondary chamber.

24 A method as claimed in any one of claims 20 to 23 which comprises charging the secondary chamber with beverage from the primary chamber to the extent that the restricted orifice is located below the depth of beverage in the secondary chamber.

25 A method as claimed in any one of claims 20 to 23 which comprises forming the secondary chamber by a discrete hollow insert located within the primary chamber of the container.

26 A method as claimed in claim 25 in which the hollow insert is to float or be suspended in the beverage in the primary chamber and which comprises loading or weighting the insert to locate the restricted orifice below the surface of the beverage in the primary chamber.

27 A method as claimed in claim 25 which comprises retaining the insert at a predetermined position within the container.

28 A method as claimed in any one of claims 25 to 27 which comprises forming the hollow insert having the restricted orifice in a wall thereof and locating the insert within the primary chamber prior to the charging and sealing of the primary chamber.

29 A method as claimed in any one of claims 25 to 28 which comprises forming the hollow insert by blow moulding.

30 A method as claimed in claim 29 which comprises blow moulding the hollow insert with gas for dissolution in the beverage so that said gas is sealed within the secondary chamber, and forming said restricted orifice in the wall of the insert immediately prior to locating the insert in the primary chamber.

31 A method as claimed in claim 30 which comprises sealing said gas in the secondary chamber at atmospheric pressure or at a pressure slightly greater than atmospheric.

32 A method as claimed in any one of claims 25 to 31 which comprises forming the restricted orifice in the hollow insert by laser boring, drilling or punching.

33 A method as claimed in any one of claims 25 to 32 in which, prior to it being sealed, the container has an upstanding condition with an open top through which the primary chamber is charged with beverage and which comprises locating the insert through said open top to provide the secondary chamber within the container.

34 A method as claimed in claim 33 when appendant to claim 27 which comprises press fitting the insert within the container so that during its location the insert engages with a side wall of the container to be retained in position.

35 A method as claimed in any one of claims 20 to 34 which comprises, prior to sealing the primary chamber, purging the primary head space to exclude air.

36 A method as claimed in any one of claims 20 to 35 in which the gas comprises at least one of carbon dioxide gas and inert gas (which latter term includes nitrogen).

37 A method as claimed in claim 36 in which the beverage is fermented and has in solution carbon dioxide in the range 0.8 to 1.8 vols/vol (1.46 to 3.29 grams/litre) and nitrogen in the range 1.5% to 3.5% vols/vol.

38 A method of packaging a beverage as claimed in claim 20 and substantially as herein described.

39 A beverage when packaged by the method as claimed in any one of claims 20 to 38.

Printed for Her Majesty's Stationery Office by
Croydon Printing Company (UK) Ltd, 4/87, D8991685.
Published by The Patent Office, 25 Southampton Buildings, London,
WC2A 1AY, from which copies may be obtained.

Index